Wars of Position?

Historical Materialism Book Series

Editorial Board

Loren Balhorn (*Berlin*)
David Broder (*Rome*)
Sebastian Budgen (*Paris*)
Steve Edwards (*London*)
Juan Grigera (*London*)
Marcel van der Linden (*Amsterdam*)
Peter Thomas (*London*)

VOLUME 248

The titles published in this series are listed at *brill.com/hm*

Wars of Position?

Marxism Today, *Cultural Politics and the Remaking of the Left Press, 1979-90*

By

H.F. Pimlott

BRILL

LEIDEN | BOSTON

The Library of Congress Cataloging-in-Publication Data is available online at https://catalog.loc.gov
LC record available at https://lccn.loc.gov/2021050632

Typeface for the Latin, Greek, and Cyrillic scripts: "Brill". See and download: brill.com/brill-typeface.

ISSN 1570-1522
ISBN 978-90-04-23189-4 (hardback)
ISBN 978-90-04-50343-4 (e-book)

Copyright 2022 by Koninklijke Brill NV, Leiden, The Netherlands.
Koninklijke Brill NV incorporates the imprints Brill, Brill Nijhoff, Brill Hotei, Brill Schöningh, Brill Fink, Brill mentis, Vandenhoeck & Ruprecht, Böhlau Verlag and V&R Unipress.
All rights reserved. No part of this publication may be reproduced, translated, stored in a retrieval system, or transmitted in any form or by any means, electronic, mechanical, photocopying, recording or otherwise, without prior written permission from the publisher. Requests for re-use and/or translations must be addressed to Koninklijke Brill NV via brill.com or copyright.com.
Brill has made all reasonable efforts to trace all rights holders to any copyrighted material used in this work. In cases where these efforts have not been successful the publisher welcomes communications from copyrights holders, so that the appropriate acknowledgements can be made in future editions, and to settle other permission matters.

This book is printed on acid-free paper and produced in a sustainable manner.

I dedicate this book to the memory of my father, J.F. Pimlott: master mariner, working-class autodidact, union organiser and dissident, iconoclast, general malcontent and consummate storyteller.

Contents

Acknowledgements XI
Preface XIII
List of Tables and Illustrations XVI
Abbreviations XVIII

Introduction: The Left, Cultural Form and Political Practice 1
1. Sign(ifier) of the Times? 2
2. The Production of the 'Marketplace of the Ideas' 5
3. Overview of the Book 7

1 *Marxism Today*'s Story: An Historical Narrative of a Cultural Form 15
1. The Left, Cultural Form and Political Practice 15
2. The Party and the Party Paper: Leninist Communication Practices 17
3. Leninist Communication Practices: The Party as a Medium of Communication 20
4. The CPGB's Practice of 'Democratic Centralism' 21
5. Leninist Communication Practices: Agitation and Propaganda 22
6. Leninist Communication Practices: The Party Paper 24
7. A Basic Typology of Communist Party Publications 25
8. The Beginnings of Postwar Reconstruction and Periodical Developments 33
9. Precursors: The Commission on Party Journals 1953 34
10. Precursors: *Marxist Quarterly* (1954–57) 39
11. Precursors: The Commission on Inner Party Democracy 1957 40
12. *Marxism Today*: 'The First Generation': 1957–77 44
13. A Party of Two Wings 57
14. The Brief Rise of 'Eurocommunism' 61
15. *Marxism Today*'s Transformation: 'Caution & Compromise', 1977–83 65
16. 'Reaction & Realignment' 1983–87 78
17. 'The Tail Wags the Dog': 1987–89 88
18. 'New Times', 1989–91 96
19. Conclusion 101

2 From 'New Left' to 'New Labour': *Marxism Today*'s 'Political Project' and the 'Retreat from Class'   103
  1   'Forward March of Labour Halted?'   104
  2   'Thatcherism'   115
  3   Thatcherism: Critiques   123
  4   Separation of 'The Economic'   123
  5   Alternate Political Explanations   126
  6   Elections, Polling and Public Opinion   131
  7   'Common Sense'   134
  8   Thatcherism's Theoretical Underpinnings: The 'Wrong' Gramsci?   140
  9   'Ideology' vs. 'Discourse'   144
  10 'Hegemony'   146
  11 Social Production of Ideologies   149
  12 The Hegemonic Apparatus   153
  13 'New Times': From New Left to New Labour?   165
  14 Part II: 'From Wars of Position to Cultural Politics'   176
  15 'Popular Politics'   177
  16 Feminism and the New Social Movements   183
  17 'Municipal Socialism'   186
  18 The Communist Party, Popular Culture and *Marxism Today*   188
  19 From 'Rock Against Racism' to 'Designer Socialism'   192
  20 Conclusion   197

3 'The Party Line versus the Bottom Line'? The Political Economy of Left Magazine Production   199
  1   'Passive' and 'Active' Editorships, 1957–91   199
  2   'Editorial Control' or 'Cultural Circle'?   210
  3   'Who Pays the Piper, Calls the Tune?' Financing *Marxism Today*   217
  4   Advertising   230
  5   'Private Enterprise or Political Commitment?' Printing and Subscriptions   233
  6   'A Little Help From My Friends': The Process of Magazine Production   241
  7   The Production Process   248
  8   Conclusion   252

4 'From the Party Line to the Politics of Design': *Marxism Today*'s Cultural Transformation   255
  1   The Theory of the Periodical and Magazine Design in the 1980s   256
  2   Format: 'From a Journal into a Magazine'   260

3 The First Format: 1957–79   261
   4 The Second Format: 1979–86   266
   5 The Third Format: 1986–91   269
   6 Front covers   271
   7 Visual Communication, Advertising and Design   278
   8 Editorial Sections: Features   284
   9 Features: Alternative Modes of Presentation   293
  10 Modes of/for Discussion   296
  11 Other Editorial Sections   299
  12 Cultural Coverage: From 'Reviews' to 'Channel Five'   301
  13 The Politics of Form and the Form of Politics   305
  14 Conclusion   310

5 'From the Margins into the Mainstream': Publicity, Promotion and Distribution in the Marketplace of Ideas   312
   1 Party Distribution   313
   2 'Out-of-Party' Distribution   316
   3 In the Marketplace of Left Periodicals   319
   4 'Cadres to Consumers': Changes in Readership, 1957–91   323
   5 Contributors   331
   6 Book Publishing   335
   7 'The Art of Talking': Discussion Groups, Talks, Events, Conferences   337
   8 Promotion   343
   9 Publicity   347
  10 National Press Coverage   348
  11 'Thinking the Unthinkable'   360
  12 Conclusion   362

6 'Write Out of the Margins': Communist Ideology and Accessibility, Rhetoric and Writing Style   364
   1 Twentieth-Century Communist Rhetoric   366
   2 Accessibility   368
   3 *Marxism Today*'s Defensive Rhetorical Strategy 1957–77   372
   4 'Solidification'   376
   5 Principles of Good Style   378
   6 Language   386
   7 Plain Style   391
   8 *Marxism Today*'s Top Two Contributors: Eric Hobsbawm and Stuart Hall   402

	9	Eric Hobsbawm and the Rhetorical Style of 'Realistic Marxism' 403
	10	Rhetorical Strategy and Writing Style 411
	11	Stuart Hall: Socialist Public Intellectual and Polemical Rhetorician 416
	12	Stuart Hall's Rhetorical Techniques and Writing Style 422
	13	Qualification and Conditionality 424
	14	Unity and Division on the Left: From 'Common Sense' to Caricature? 430
	15	Tropes and Metaphors 431
	16	Stuart Hall's 'Realism' 436
	17	Conclusion 438
7		'W(h)ither the Party Paper'? What Lessons for the Left Press 442
	1	A Perennial Question 454
	2	Epilogue 457

Illustrations: *Marxism Today* 1957–1991   461
References   475
Index   518

Preface

In August of 1998, I received a telephone call asking me if I wanted to participate in a *Marxism Today* weekend seminar. The caller, Martin Jacques, said, 'It's like studying history and your subject comes back from the dead'. I could not resist the opportunity to invesitage and see for myself what a *Marxism Today* weekend event would be like in terms of studying the social-cultural processes and practices through which the periodical had been produced during the 1980s and early 1990s, and of which I had heard so much from interviewees and past participants. I, myself, had briefly participated in some MT discussion groups in north London in the late 1980s in which I had enjoyed particularly refreshing approaches to the politics of all sorts of issues, from gender, sexuality, fashion and other issues. My own politics had been borne of a steadfast commitment to the working class, in terms of my origins and experience in life, and to a class analysis, which has yet to be surpassed in understanding our very real, material lives, but they were also borne of a need to be pragmatic in working with others to defeat those who would exploit the labour of ordinary people. Otherwise, would there be no end to Thatcherism's long reign?

Yet, my pragmatism had shifted under the seeming perennial domination of neoliberal or 'free-market' capitalist thinking that led to my own symbolic gesture (of despair or hope, I was never really certain) in joining the Labour Party after Tony Blair became leader. I had known the welfare state in both Canada and the UK, and in both countries, it was being dismantled or eviscerated. Was there no alternative to following in the footsteps of those who exploit the poor and the working class?

In some ways, it was quite surprising in the one-off, 'comeback' issue of *Marxism Today* in October 1998, only 18 months after Labour's landslide on 1 May 1997, and around six months after criticisms from several 'Brit Pop' bands against the New Labour's legislative changes for youth in the 14 March 1998 cover story in NME (NME had once been my own 'bible' of sorts, during my years of politics and punk). Although *Marxism Today* had helped to pave the way for 'New Labour' and Tony Blair, the establishment media were quick to launch their attacks on MT after its 'comeback' issue was launched in the West End. There had been an intense discussion about whether the front cover with its closeup of Tony Blair and the word 'wrong' across the top should have had a question mark or not. There were a couple of contributions supporting Blair, but most were critical takes on New Labour, which caused consternation amongst the commentariat, especially the progressive ones.

Yet, what I have found in my research and attempts to find a publisher is that there tends to be one of two reactions to *Marxism Today*: one was to be completely in awe and supportive of the periodical and its politics, with little questioning of anything; the other was to be extremely dismissive of what it was and of any possible lessons from its history. While both reactions tended to be based around the political and philosophical differences expressed by the individuals and their perception of MT, both overlook some important and significant understandings of how just such a periodical does operate and how it might change or adapt to differences in the 'marketplace of ideas'. These include a failure to recognise what Raymond Williams saw as critical to any cultural materialist approach to understanding our present conjuncture and the 'resources for a journey of hope'. I believe that the narrative of the story of MT and its production, distribution and promotion offers us a basis for better understanding what might become part of a (counter-)hegemonic apparatus to bridge our silos and divisions in support of a new democratic socialist project at a time when climate catastrophe and horrendous inequalities threaten the very existence of humanity, the choice between socialism or barbarism remains our only choice.

Waterloo, Canada, 2019

Acknowledgements

Many things have happened since I began my investigation of *Marxism Today* nearly three decades ago when it was initially just one part of my original PhD dissertation proposal. There are too many people for me to thank personally and some I am sorry to say that I have forgotten. For that, I apologise. Many of my PhD student colleagues contributed in their own way as did many of my activist (lapsed and as ever) friends. I also wish to acknowledge the opportunity to publish some of the ideas and analysis from my PhD dissertation and precursors to this book in such journals as *Labour/Le Travail, Socialist Studies, Journalism Studies* and *Journalism*. My experiences with editors and anonymous reviewers were most helpful and contributed in many ways to the evolution of the ideas contained herein. Yet, no book chapter is in any substantial way a reproduction of previously published articles, except for the section on Eric Hobsbawm in Chapter 6 that was first published in *Labour/Le Travail*, with the kind permission of the publisher.

However, there are two previously published academic articles that were integrated after substantial revision, editing and rewriting into Chapters 5 and 6. I wish to thank SAGE publishing for their kind permission to integrate Tables 1–5 and several excerpts from my previously published 2004 article, "'From the Margins into the Mainstream': The Promotion and Distribution of Marxism Today", *Journalism*, 5, 2: 203–26, into Chapter 5. I also wish to thank Taylor & Francis for their kind permission to reproduce substantial parts of my previously published 2006 article, "'Write Out of the Margins': Accessibility, Editorship and House Style in Marxism Today, 1957–91," *Journalism Studies*, 7, 5: 782–806, in Chapter 6.

I owe a deep debt of gratitude to those former members of the Communist Party of Great Britain and the *Marxism Today* Editorial Board, staff and volunteers, who generously answered questions and shared their thoughts in their interviews with me when I was doing my research for my PhD dissertation between 1993 and 2000. Most of all, I want to thank Martin Jacques, especially, for most generously granting me four interviews and access to all the *Marxism Today* files, memos, etc., that he had at home at the time (1996), and for inviting me to participate in the magazine's one-off 'comeback issue' in the autumn of 1998. I know that we differ in our assessment of the magazine and in our respective political positions, but I believe there is much to recognise as valuable in his accomplishments as editor regardless of one's politics. I also owe special thanks to Mark Perryman and Geoff Andrews for their friendship during this time and for their help in obtaining a more general understanding of how the CPGB as a party worked. Their help and friendship during the 1990s were invaluable. I suspect that we will also differ in our respective analyses of the magazine. In addition, Sally Townsend, Jan Brown, Jane Taylor and Julian Turner were all very helpful in their explanations that provided me with a much better understanding of how MT worked even if some of my questions must have seemed obvious at times. As someone who is usually focussed on verbal rhetoric and language, Peter Hammarling and John Minnion were incredibly helpful in explaining visual aspects of periodicals, their production and images more generally.

I also owe a great debt of gratitude for the late Stuart Hall's invaluable interview back in January 1997, even if I think he would be critical but courteous over our differing interpretations, including of his Thatcherism thesis. There are others who have sinced passed away, such as Monty Johnstone, Irene Brennan, Gordon MacLennan, and Betty and George Matthews, who provided insights into MT and the party from different political positions.

Of course, it goes without saying that no-one bears any responsibility for my views and analysis as I lay it out in this book, and I know that many, perhaps all, will dispute or challenge what I have written. I do hope that they will accept my genuine thanks and respect (as a former reader of MT and as someone who was never a member or 'fellow-traveller' of the CPGB) for the dedication that they have shown in their involvement in MT or the CPGB.

I especially want to thank James Curran, the supervisor of my PhD dissertation, in which this book had its beginnings, for his encouragement, questions and conversations during the course of my part-time graduate studies. Even though they may not think it, the commentary and criticisms offered by my dissertation examiners, Dave Morley and Tony Bennett, contributed to my own rethinking of this subject over the years. Of the Goldsmiths' College faculty that also contributed to my journey in different ways, I especially want to thank Christine Geraghty and Valerie Walkerdine. The other PhD students, who made for such a great environment and contributed in their own ways to my journey: Garth, Maria, Aeron, Dave, Milly, Alessio, Jane, Alida, Joanne et al. (and I apologise for not remembering everyone's name!) and my co-workers at UEL, UNL (now part of LondonMet) and Middlesex, Tom, Kathy, Glen, Ash, Jeremy, Sandi, Juliet, Miriam, Anita et al. My colleagues and comrades in Ontario, Canada: Penelope, Garry, Alex, Ash, Ian, Kimberly, David, Gregory, Dee, Helen, Gord, Pat, Kathryn, Kari et al. There is, of course, so many from a London of a much earlier time and different milieux, but who remain true friends: Raymond and Shanti, Martin, Sam and Anna, Lucy, Maggie, Pete, Colette, Myk, Kyri, Barry, Laura, Ian, Sheridan, Alex and Angie. I regret that my mate Rob is no longer here to see the book completed.

Finally, I dedicate this also to my soulmate and partner, A.M., who has had to live with this project – on and off – for far too long.

H.F. Pimlott

Tables and Illustrations

Tables

1	Annual Income and Expenditure, 1977–91	220
2	Finances (%), 1979–89	221
3	Monthly Averages of Income and Expenditure: Selected Years	223
4	Breakdown of Feature Articles by Topic in Selected Years, 1958–88	288
5	Breakdown of Editorial Contents, 1958–88	292
6	[and former Table 5.2] Comparison of Selected Modes of Presentation, 1958–88	293
7	Distribution, Selected Issues (% of total)	314
8	Periodical Circulations in Averages for Selected Years, 1977–89	322
9A	Age and Gender (% of total)	327
9B	Education (% of total)	327
9C	Occupation (% of total)	328
9D	Full-Time Employees (% of total)	328
9E	Newspapers (%)	328
9F	Periodicals (%)	329
9G	Party Members (% of total)	329
10	Breakdown of Contributors by Occupation in Sample Years (% of total)	332
11A	Print Media Coverage of *Marxism Today*, 1978–91	350
11B	National Broadsheet Coverage of *Marxism Today*, 1978–91 (number of articles)	351
12	National Broadsheet Press Coverage by Subject, 1978–91	353
13	National Press Coverage by Article Type and/or Use, 1978–91	354
14	FOG Index Rating for Features, 1958–88	370
15	FOG Index Rating for Non-Feature Contributions, 1958–88	370
16	*Marxism Today*: Three Formats, Two Periodical Types, 1957–91	448

Illustrations

All illustrations can be found in the separate Illustrations section following the Bibliography.

1	*Marxism Today* October 1957: The very first issue and first format. Cover Design: Farleigh Press – *Marxism Today*	461
2	*Marxism Today* February 1975. Cover Design: Pat Cook and George Grosz; Photograph Courtesy of Studio Vista – *Marxism Today*	462

TABLES AND ILLUSTRATIONS XVII

3 *Marxism Today* March 1976. Cover Design: Pat Cook – *Marxism Today* 463
4 *Marxism Today* October 1979: Launch issue for the second format. Cover Design: Anna Aubrey and Peter Hammarling – *Marxism Today* 464
5 *Marxism Today* October 1979: 'Focus' section in layout in second format. Design: Anna Aubrey and Peter Hammarling – *Marxism Today* 465
6 *Marxism Today* October 1983: Neil Kinnock as Superman. Cover Design: Peter Hammarling, Kathryn Tattersall and Lee Robinson; Cover Illustration: Brett Ewins – *Marxism Today* 466
7 *Marxism Today* October 1983: 'Channel Five' in layout in second format. Design: Lee Robinson and Katherine Gutkind – *Marxism Today* 467
8 *Marxism Today* October 1986: Launch issue for the third format. Cover Concept: Keith Ablitt; Cover Illustration: Tony McSweeney – *Marxism Today* 468
9 *Marxism Today* January 1987: 'aids'. Cover Design: Keith Ablitt – *Marxism Today* 469
10 *Marxism Today* April 1988: 'men'. Cover Design: Jan Brown; Photograph: Abel Lagos – *Marxism Today* 470
11 *Marxism Today* April 1988 'Feature' article in layout. Design: Jan Brown; Illustration: Clifford Harper – *Marxism Today* 471
12 *Marxism Today* October 1988: 'New Times' launch issue. Cover Design: Jan Brown; Collage: Jan Brown – *Marxism Today* 472
13 *Marxism Today* October 1988: 'Feature' article in layout. Design: Jan Brown; Photograph: National Motor Museum, Beaulieu – *Marxism Today* 473
14 *Marxism Today* December 1991-January 1992: 'The End' final issue. Cover Design: Pearce Marchbank – *Marxism Today* 474

Abbreviations

AES	Alternative Economic Strategy
AMA	Anti-Monopoly Alliance
ANL	Anti-Nazi League, SWP
ALC	Arts and Leisure Committee, CPGB
BSA	British Survey of Attitudes
BDA	Broad Democratic Alliance
BPA	Broad Popular Alliance
CARM	Campaign Against Racism in Media
CCCS	Centre for Contemporary Cultural Studies, Birmingham University
CIPD	Commission on Inner Party Democracy, CPGB
CPJ	Commission on Party Journals, CPGB
CP	Communist Party
CPHG	Communist Party Historians' Group, CPGB
CPB	Communist Party of Britain (*The Morning Star* Group)
PCF	Communist Party of France (*Parti communiste français*)
CPGB	Communist Party of Great Britain
PCI	Communist Party of Italy (*Partito Comunista Italiano*)
CPSU	Communist Party of the Soviet Union
CR	*Communist Review*, CPGB
DW	*Daily Worker, The*, CPGB
EC	Executive Committee, CPGB
ECSub	Executive Committee, Sub-Committee, CPGB
FUTTF	*Facing Up To The Future*, CPGB
FPTP	'First-Past-The-Post', Westminster parliamentary system
FMLH	'Forward March of Labour Halted?' Eric Hobsbawm
GUMG	Glasgow University Media Group
ISA	Ideological State Apparatus
IMF	International Monetary Fund
IPPR	Institute for Public Policy Research
ISJ	*International Socialism*, SWP
LDCP	London District Communist Party, CPGB
MNT	*Manifesto for New Times, The*, CPGB
MT	*Marxism Today*, CPGB
MTEC	*Marxism Today* Editorial Collective
MQ	*Marxist Quarterly*, CPGB
ModQ	*Modern Quarterly*, CPGB
MPS	Mont Pelerin Society

The Star	*The Morning Star*, CPGB
MLS	'Moving Left Show', *Marxism Today*
NCC	National Cultural Committee, CPGB
NHS	National Health Service
NPC	National Party Congress, CPGB
NSO	National Student Organiser, CPGB
NCP	New Communist Party
NI	*New Internationalist*
NLR	*New Left Review*
NS	*New Socialist*, Labour Party
NSS	*New Statesman*
OU	Open University
PMJ	People's March for Jobs
PPPS	People's Press Printing Society (*The Morning Star*)
PTC	*Policing the Crisis* (Hall et al., 1978)
PC	Political Committee, CPGB
PCSub	Political Sub-Committee, CPGB
PMC	Professional-Managerial Class
RSA	Repressive State Apparatus
RAR	Rock Against Racism
SDP	Social Democratic Party
SPC	Special Party Congress, CPGB
SR	*Socialist Review*, SWP
SW	*Socialist Worker*, SWP
SWP	Socialist Workers' Party
SL	*Straight Left*, Straight Left
TIC	Theory and Ideology Committee, CPGB
TINA	'There is no alternative', Margaret Thatcher
TUC	Trades Union Congress
WNV	*World News and Views*
ULR	*Universities and Left Review*
YCL	Young Communist League, CPGB

INTRODUCTION

The Left, Cultural Form and Political Practice

At the start of December 2011, the Institute for Public Policy Research, a centre-left think tank, published a special anniversary issue to mark the twentieth anniversary of the closure of *Marxism Today*. Perhaps the first reaction might be surprise at the IPPR's lament for any publication with 'Marxism' in the title and, indeed, perhaps an even greater surprise given its subtitle: 'the theoretical and discussion journal of the Communist Party of Great Britain' (which also ceased to exist around the same time that MT closed down). More importantly, however, is that at the core of this lament of the IPPR's journal's special issue is the loss of a 'means of communication', that reached beyond an immediate audience of like-minded individuals, identified trends and analyses, and influenced many on the left well beyond *Marxism Today*'s small circulation. This lament offers little in the way of understanding *how* it was that MT was able to achieve its position of influence, particularly as it had done so under the rise of the New Right or 'Thatcherism', so named in the pages of the same periodical four months prior to Margaret Thatcher's first general election victory as leader of the Conservative Party. Second, it is also a lament for an approach and an attitude that was seen as critical, even flippant, at times: at least in its behaviour towards the 'Old Left'.

Whether revered or reviled, *Marxism Today*'s influence on the left between 1978 and 1991 is irrefutable. It was responsible for promoting debates about Eric Hobsbawm's 'Forward March of Labour Halted?' and Stuart Hall's 'Thatcherism' thesis from the end of the 1970s through to the analysis of 'New Times' a decade later. It was also responsible for identifying some of the future shapers of Labour, including John Smith, Tony Blair and Peter Mandelson, and in promoting themes that would help shape the trajectory that led to New Labour, including some regular contributors, such as Geoff Mulgan and Charlie Leadbeater, who would become public intellectuals closely aligned with New Labour at the end of the 1990s, although this influence has only come to be acknowledged with hindsight.[1]

Yet, a key aspect of this periodical's success is missing in this lament: how was MT able to produce, circulate and promote its ideas and gain the public posi-

---

1 E.g. Blair 1990, 1991; Mandelson 1987, 1989; Leadbeater 1989, 1990; Mulgan 1989, 1990; Smith 1986.

tion and influence that it had despite its inauspicious beginnings and history. It was not just the ideas with which MT was associated that were responsible for its relative success, compared to other publications on the left, but its adoption of and adaptation to marketplace mechanisms, paving one possible path for alternative and radical media out of – and beyond – the 'radical ghetto'. The degree to which such mechanisms helped or hindered MT is part of the analysis presented in this book that connects to MT's role in the 'battle of ideas' in the 1980s via its 'political' and 'journalistic' project.[2] This book is not a conventional political-historical narrative of a periodical and its influence on the Left, whether Communist or Labour, although the first chapter will tell MT's story in terms of its relationship with the CPGB as one type of three basic publications closely associated with Communist parties in the twentieth century. Others have provided the analytical narratives of the Labour Left's defeat or the domination of the Thatcherite Conservative Party in the 1980s.[3] This book is, however, an in-depth examination of that absence in the IPPR's lament, the 'how' of periodical production, distribution and promotion: the cultural forms, social processes, and political practices by which *Marxism Today* was produced, distributed and promoted, and how these practices combined to make the impacts that they did, and how such practices were undertaken during a time of right-wing ideological hegemony and of considerable intellectual, political and social unrest, especially on the left.

1   Sign(ifier) of the Times?

During Thatcherism's heyday in the 1980s, *Marxism Today* became one of the left's few 'success' stories, popularising critiques of Thatcherism and the left as it moved from the margins into the mainstream of national debate. MT became a signifier of both a political stance and a cultural disposition on the left, and its influence on the production and distribution of radical and alternative media was significant during the 1980s, if not beyond. Yet, it began life as a marginal publication of a marginal political organisation, 'the theoretical and discussion journal of the Communist Party of Great Britain', as its subtitle put it, which gained access to the national public sphere and set the agenda for debate on the left from the late 1970s until its closure in 1991, paving the way for 'New

---

[2] Jacques 1996a.
[3] E.g. Jackson and Saunders 2012; Panitch and Leys 1997; Pearmain 2011; Thompson 1992; Wright 1996.

Labour': its influence was much greater than its best monthly sales figures for an individual issue (around 20,000) could ever suggest.⁴

The Labour Party backed the launching of its first – and only – 'theoretical' journal, *New Socialist*, in September 1981 in response to *Marxism Today*'s growing influence on the left, as MT reached out beyond the CPGB with its interventions in national public debates over the direction of the Labour Party. In some ways, the success of the CPGB's 'theoretical and discussion' journal was what the party had aimed for historically in terms of its attempts to affiliate to the Labour Party with the hopes of wielding influence over the LP's political direction.⁵

The publications of political parties are differentiated from those of commercial newspapers and periodicals not because the former are ideological and the latter are not,⁶ but because political publications are expected to express the viewpoint of their parent or affiliated organisations (just as commercial publications reflect their publishers' and financiers' ideologies). In Leninist theory, socialist newspapers have an absolutely integral role to play in educating, organising and agitating amongst the working class and they are *the* vehicle around which the party itself is supposed to be built. The role of a theoretical journal is primarily to establish 'the political-ideological line' for the party (and publisher) by discussing issues and developing an analysis of the political conjuncture that helps to guide the party's strategies. Parties adapt their publications to changing political and economic circumstances within different socio-historical contexts: a party's strength would help determine not only the number of publications it could support but also their format, production and distribution. Nevertheless, as with the so-called 'free press', editors and editorial board members of political publications are often chosen for their ideological commitment to the publishers (i.e. the party). *Marxism Today*, however, represents a very special case in the history of left periodicals: typical in some respects, but unique or anomalous in others.

During the course of the 1980s, as MT published critiques of the labour movement and left shibboleths, it became increasingly singled out, by critics and supporters alike, for an apparent contradiction between its title and its lack of 'Marxist' content. MT's critics in the party also pointed to a contradiction between its role, as the CPGB's 'theoretical and discussion journal', and the lack of reference to, or contributions from, the party. Thus, MT came to be seen

---
4 Perryman 1998.
5 Callaghan 2005.
6 Some former editors of establishment newspapers have provided anecdotal evidence of ideological interventions or expectations of their newspapers' owners (e.g. Neil 1997).

as a paradox: as a party journal it gradually moved away from its marginal status as a minor Communist publication, printed and distributed by CPGB enterprises, such as Farleigh Press, and read primarily by party members, to a semi-autonomous magazine, printed and distributed commercially by non-party businesses, and sold in newsagents to a non-party centre-left readership, even though it was still subsidised by the very party from which it was securing greater autonomy. Its increasing autonomy in production and distribution followed its gradual intellectual and political autonomy from the CPGB, perhaps a necessary part of reaching a broader audience. However, MT became *more* (not less!) financially dependent upon the party despite increasing amounts of revenue from advertising and sales during the 1980s; by 1991, the limitations of MT's name and its reliance on CPGB subsidies meant that in the short term, it was unsustainable, financially *and* ideologically.

What is curious, though, is the willingness of the party to continue to fund *Marxism Today* even as it apparently deconstructed nearly every shibboleth held by Communists and thus shifted, ideologically speaking, away from the CPGB: indeed, the apparent divergence between periodical and party was permitted even as the costs of subsidies to MT increased dramatically after 1986. However, in 1988–89 the party leadership and MT moved closer together with the discussions around 'New Times'. What was the relationship between MT and the CPGB, such that the former was able to achieve a degree of operational autonomy from the latter, which was far greater than most private, for-profit or commercial publications ever achieve from their owner-publishers?[7] Its ability to operate relatively autonomously did not stop the party from providing financial support, even when the latter had difficulty meeting its own financial requirements. Nonetheless, MT's move towards greater independence was neither smooth nor peaceful because of the tensions in the relationship between party, editor and periodical, which had consequences for and during its transformation, affecting all aspects of its production and circulation.

---

7 Ironically, Jacques's autonomy superceded that of editors of the so-called 'free press' (e.g. Chippindale and Horrie 1992; Neil 1997).

2   The Production of the 'Marketplace of the Ideas'

> *Ideas and opinions are not spontaneously 'born' in each individual brain: they have had a centre of formation, or irradiation, of dissemination, of persuasion – a group of men, or a single individual even, which has developed them and presented them in the political form of current reality.*
>
> ANTONIO GRAMSCI[8]

∴

Contrary to what many people believe, ideas are not born fully formed nor do they circulate in a marketplace where the best ideas – or the most 'truthful' – win out over false ideas.[9] We have seen how the rise of neoliberalism has been based upon the systematic funding, cultivation and dissemination of free market ideology via the establishment and promotion of think tanks, public intellectuals and academics, and media (including their own in-house media and corporate media):[10] part of what Antonio Gramsci called the 'hegemonic apparatus'.[11] Without the means of communication, there would not be the ideas, analyses and perspectives that make up what is ostensibly the left's (counter) public sphere. It is not just that ideas have a point of origin, but that they also have to be produced and distributed before they can be received and read, and maybe even discussed. While this might seem to be so obvious that it should not need stating, it is precisely because such processes are most frequently overlooked, despite the ubiquitousness of the requisite practices with old and new communication technologies to produce and distribute ideas, that attention needs to be drawn to this process to better understand how it functions and how it might impede, enable or be bettered. (The focus has always tended to be on the substance or content rather than the form of communication, and the mode of address and style.) And without the means to fund, produce and distribute such ideas, such views and thinking are lost to the public, while still other ideas, with only limited means of production and distribution, are marginalised, ignored or neglected.

---

8   Gramsci 1971, p. 192.
9   Peters 2004.
10 E.g. Harvey 2005, Chapter 2; Gutstein 2009.
11 Bollinger and Koivisto 2009.

In spite of extensive scholarly and activist literatures on the problems and potential, and successes and failures of Marxist philosophy, ideology, politics and parties during the twentieth century, one area central to Marxist organisation and political strategy that has been largely overlooked by scholars, including historical materialists, is communication.[12] Although Marxists did consider the ideological nature of the media and messages, they have usually failed to take into account a core aspect of how 'mass communication' operates, which is to deliver audiences to advertisers via media.[13] However, another approach was to consider the nature of how socialist or Communist organisations communicated with their prospective audiences, which highlights another weakness: Marxism's 'communicative crisis'.[14] Ironically, historical materialists themselves have tended to ignore or neglect the actual material aspects involved in the production and distribution of ideas: most discussions of the 'battle of ideas' focus on either egos and personalities or the ideas themselves, without taking into consideration the necessary 'means of communication' required to actually produce and distribute those ideas.[15] Such a 'blank-

---

12 For some exceptions, see: Aune 1994; Lih 2005; Pimlott 2006b; Swartz 1999; Williamson 2002.

13 Smythe 1977 contributed to rethinking media systems as a means for exploiting the free labour of audiences who undertook watching and listening to ads in-between songs or news.

14 Pimlott 2006b.

15 There was a flurry of popular and scholarly studies of the radical, alternative and left press between the late 1970s and 1980s, primarily highlighting 1960s underground papers or the Marxist and radical left press: e.g. Downing 1984; Fountain 1988; Gardner 1979; Mattelart and Siegelaub 1979, 1983; Shore 1988. Developments since the early 1990s have tended to focus primarily on 'alternative' weeklies, 'zines and other media or the alternative journalism of anarchists, environmentalists and 'post-political' groups (e.g. 'Stop the City' demonstrations; *Schnews*): e.g. Atton 2002; Dickinson 1997; Downing 2001; Duncombe 1997; Ostertag 2006; Waltz 2005. There has been some attention paid to Labour, socialist, social-democratic, New Left and progressive publishers, newspapers and journals: e.g. Chippindale and Horrie 1988; Richards 1997; Ruff 1997; Smith 1996; Stoltzfus 2007. The left press since the 1960s has generally been ignored and most accounts that have been written have tended towards more traditional, intellectual-historical accounts of these papers, including political differences between editors and boards or parent organisations, though some do include attention to marketplace mechanisms and issues of production and circulation. Even when the materiality of ideas and the mechanisms of their production and distribution are recognised or not completely overlooked, the tendency is one in which many accounts still resemble more conventional political and biographical histories of intellectual journals: e.g. Blackledge 2004; Ffrench 1995; Kauppi 1994; Marx-Scouras 1996; Mulhern 1979. Thompson 2007 and Pearmain 2011 address the contribution of left media to the developments of the UK left, even if their focus is again more on the political-ideological dimensions.

spot' on the part of Marxist approaches, 'inspired' Raymond Williams to work out his ideas in terms of this relationship, including the development of various strands of Marxist cultural analysis into 'cultural materialism'.[16] Williams's approach emphasises the importance of the material basis upon which ideas are produced and circulated, including the writing (and editing) processes, and these emphases on the processual and practices is what is neglected in other approaches.[17]

Whereas most accounts of intellectual, literary or political periodicals tend to focus almost solely on the ideas and/or leading personalities, *Wars of Position* demonstrates the importance of the *material* production of political ideas, highlighting how the social-cultural processes of production and distribution were central to *Marxism Today*'s 'success', albeit while still recognising the agency of individual editors and party leaders et al. *Wars of Position* is a unique investigation into that material relationship between cultural form and political practice, as exemplified by MT's transformation from an internal party 'journal' into a 'magazine' of opinion addressing a broader left beyond the party, and in its relationship with the party, labour movement and national media. It examines its production and distribution processes, press coverage, institutional relationships and social networks, editorships, staffing, accessibility, rhetorical strategies and writing style, publicity and promotion, format, visuals, and design and layout, situated within the post-war context of the Communist and Labour parties. *Marxism Today* began to set the standards that other left publications sought to meet or borrow, such as *New Socialist* or *Living Marxism*.[18]

3   Overview of the Book

The title acknowledges the influence of a key concept of Antonio Gramsci, 'war of position', across the left since the 1970s (including some New Labour luminaries!),[19] which was his strategy for establishing 'moral-intellectual' lead-

---

16   Williams 1977a, 1981a, 1983c. Jones 2004 argues that Williams's 'cultural materialism' should be renamed 'sociology of culture' because of the latter's transition away from the emphasis on the production paradigm, in line with the title of the US edition of Williams's 1981 book, *Culture*. Milner 2002, however, stresses Williams's approach as 'cultural materialism', which I prefer given the need to develop a historical materialist approach to communication, media and culture.
17   Williams 1977a; Jones 2004, pp. 95–105.
18   The latter magazine rebranded itself as 'LM' in 'borrowing' from MT's presentational style.
19   E.g. Steele 1999, pp. 26–7.

ership (i.e. hegemony) in western capitalist democracies. The 'war of position' (and other concepts) from his theory of hegemony could not realistically be applied to the CPGB (let alone to *Marxism Today*) since it was not of sufficient 'mass' to be able to act as a means to establish a (counter-)hegemonic ruling bloc on its own. The application of Gramsci's ideas became attenuated from their original meanings as they were employed especially from the early 1980s onwards. Gramsci became more than an influential Communist journalist, Marxist theoretician and revolutionary leader. He also became an icon and signifier of all that is understood as political or is used, as Lenin and Marx before him, to justify a particular political-cultural project, regardless of one's connections, or lack thereof, to a 'modern prince', i.e. the revolutionary mass working-class party.

Since the beginnings of socialism, print media have been integral to sustaining the movement via its role as 'agitator, propagandist and organiser'.[20] Despite this emphasis on and connection to print media (and journalism), still little exists in the way of scholarship that examines the actual processes of production and distribution of the ideas of the organised left. Most accounts of alternative and radical media focus on 'heroic' individuals and/or ideological developments and positions, all of which are valuable but, rather ironically, ignore the actual *material* basis for understanding the circulation and success or failure of different ideas, via the periodicals that produce them for the 'marketplace of ideas'.

The approach of cultural materialism is neither about economic reductionism or vulgar Marxism reducing everything to the differences between the divisions of the social relations of the capitalist mode of production, nor does it see everything through an explanation of ideology or culture in the abstract or ideal, as a means to explain everything. Cultural materialism seeks to reduce neither the superstructure to the base nor *vice versa*, but to make the connections between culture and materialism, between ideas and their production and distribution while recognising that language as practical consciousness cannot be separated from labour.[21] Cultural materialism, in the words of Raymond Williams, 'is the analysis of all forms of signification, including quite centrally writing, within the actual means and conditions of their production'.[22]

---

20   Lenin 1902. See Debray 2007, *Historical Materialism* 18(3), Lih 2005 and Pimlott 2006b.
21   Williams 1977a, pp. 21–44; Jones 2004, pp. 95–105. Both refer to the discussion of language in Marx and Engels 1970 [1845–46].
22   Williams 1983c [1981], p. 210.

Cultural materialism's strength lies in redressing the limitations of conventional approaches to the history of ideas and publications that over-emphasise ideas, simply based upon their supposed veracity or popular appeal, as if ideas somehow circulate without a centre of production and distribution. As in Gramsci's quote above, where he wrote about how 'ideas and opinions' have 'a centre of formation, or irradiation, of dissemination, of persuasion', which usually requires groups (or occasionally an individual) working at those centres to produce and distribute those ideas.[23] Gramsci's quote was not a one-off comment but part of his recogniton of the importance of studying the bourgeois press as if they were political parties because of their influence, and his focus on the importance of intellectuals, culture, language, education and popular religion amongst other aspects of the 'hegemonic apparatus'. This quote is an example of his identification of problems and possibilities along the revolutionary route towards developing a (counter-)hegemonic project, and yet it continues arguably to be a weakness on the part of socialist and communist movements to date. Williams argues that Marxists had been less capable in analysing cultural forms in historical shifts rather than at the epochal level[24] and that their approach was '... not so much an excess, but ... a deficit of materialism'.[25] Perhaps, only by looking at epochal shifts in the mode of production from feudalism to mercantile capitalism, say, can you make some kind of broad equivalence as Karl Marx did in 1845 in *The German Ideology*:

> The ideas of the ruling class are in every epoch the ruling ideas, i.e. the class which is the ruling material force of society, is at the same time its ruling intellectual force. The class which has the means of material production at its disposal, has control at the same time over the means of mental production, so that thereby, generally speaking, the ideas of those who lack the means of mental production are subject to it.

I should make it perfectly clear that I am *not* arguing against ideological critique nor am I opposed to understanding the ideologies that are part of the battle of ideas, since these are integral to any cultural materialist account of any particular periodical or cultural form.

However, the emphasis on biographical and journalistic accounts, or historical narratives of periodicals and journals, have a tendency to reinforce the 'great men' or idealist approaches to understanding the influence, success or

---

23 Gramsci 1971, p. 192.
24 Williams 1977a.
25 Williams 1979, p. 350.

failure of any publication. And yet there has to be a role for human agency, which remains of perhaps greater importance within small publications where one person, an editor or publisher, can have a much greater impact than in a larger publication subject to outside investors and shareholders or other stakeholders. This is why experience remains an important part of the approach of cultural materialism. Thus, any cultural materialist analysis will clearly include an analysis of the role of the two primary editors of *Marxism Today*, whose agency played important roles in shaping its trajectory and influence even as the periodical was itself a product of the structures of the party that are affected in turn by human agency as engaged in through the social-cultural practices and processes by which the party and the periodical operate. By drawing upon Williams's cultural materialism, however, I hope to demonstrate how important it is to look beyond the over-emphasis on 'heroic' individuals or 'ideas' by demonstrating how the analysis of cultural production enables a better understanding of *how* the 'battle of ideas' actually work in practice and in history.

In the first part of the next chapter, I provide an overview of the historical relationship between communist political practices and cultural forms, particularly the Leninist model of the party paper and particular Communist communication practices as well as the CPGB's relationship with its publications. This sets the background to help situate *Marxism Today* within the historical context of its parent political organisation and its *modus operandi* as a specific example of this relationship between radical political practice and cultural form. The first chapter then provides the 'story' of MT from its origins in the CPGB's crisis during the early years of the Cold War prior to its launch in 1957 until its closure in 1991 around the same time as its 'publisher' also dissolved itself. The story of MT cannot be told without telling something of the CPGB's story as their stories are closely connected and provide a sense of the shift in the political conjuncture amidst economic restructuring in the 1980s that is necessary to understand the overall narrative of the periodical's history, especially from the start of Martin Jacques's editorship in 1977.

Chapter 2 offers a more conventional history of the ideas and themes most closely associated with *Marxism Today* during the 'Thatcher decade', 1979–90. The chapter's first part examines three key themes of MT's political project around which the periodical organised and for which it became internationally known between 1978 and 1991: the 'crisis of the Left'; the 'rise of the Right'; and 'New Times'. While these themes were integral to both the periodical's identity and its role in helping to pave the way for New Labour's 'Third Way', MT's version of Gramsci's idea of the 'war of position' was taken up with a focus on two areas that can be defined as 'popular politics' and 'popular culture'. These two subjects provided some hope of overcoming Thatcherism for readers as the

1980s wore on and MT sought a vehicle for bringing together a 'popular alliance' to defeat Thatcherism at the ballot box. These themes provide the political-ideological content that Jacques and his staff oversaw in MT's production and distribution, and which defined its relationship with the party and the labour movement in the UK under Thatcher(ism), 1979–90.

It is the political economy of the production and distribution of *Marxism Today*, which we must engage with next to identify those elements that are an integral part of the material 'base'. This is Chapter 3's focus, which includes an emphasis on the impact and implications of its transformation from a 'journal' into a 'magazine', the role of subsidies, and its relationship *with* the party and *to* the 'marketplace of ideas'. Can a radical political organisation or party produce a periodical that can succeed in the commercial marketplace? Or does it have to make use of party or other organisational subsidies?[26] What impact, if any, might the marketplace have on the publication and its relationship with its party-publisher? This chapter raises the challenge of thinking about the three primary models of alternative or radical media, which emphasise differences in their organisation and production: Leninist (or Bolshevik); self-managed; and Comedia.[27] The Leninist, or vanguard, model was dominant until the 1980s, with an emphasis on the relationship between the political organisation or party and the paper, and the understanding that the paper would need to be subsidised because it would not attract the advertising that commercial media do.[28] The self-managed model is one that emphasises the importance of prefigurative politics in the structuring of alternative media, where the collaborative ways in which such media work are part of the objectives for society and this approach is closely aligned with the alternative media of a number of anarchist, and direct-action oriented environmental and single-issue movements. The Comedia model emphasises the usefulness of marketplace mechanisms, such as wholesale distributors and newsagents, to reach a broader audience and to become, thereby, more financially sustainable over the long term, since most alternative and radical media have usually only lasted for a short time.

---

26 Even the so-called 'free market' or neoliberal right has to subsidise their output to the media and the public (e.g. Lorimer 1993; Gutstein 2009; Brownlee 2005; Williams 1978). Historically, the market has also worked to censor the radical working-class press (e.g. Curran and Seaton 1991).

27 The Comedia model is named after the consultancy and research organisation that developed out of the Minority Press Group in 1980–81 and which promoted alternative and radical cultural production.

28 Although most far left political organisations could not be characterised as a 'party' in terms of their membership numbers, the term provides a shorthand to speak about all organisations that have adopted the Leninist or vanguard model in their approach to agitation and propaganda.

The production history of *Marxism Today* in Chapter 3, therefore, raises new questions on the relationship between a political party and its publications, or more accurately between the means of the production of political ideas and the ideas themselves. It lays out the ways in which the editors and staff prepared strategies for producing and engaging in the marketplace (of ideas), the interplay between commercial and political decisions, and the transformation of internal power struggles into disputes over such things as typesetting, subscriptions, printing and staffing issues. The organisation of staff and volunteers into a 'collective' and then into 'mini-collectives' within the larger MT editorial 'collective' meant that staff, at least, acted as an extension of the editor in overseeing the periodical. This is an example of agency within structure as political and commercial decisions had to be balanced when confronting problems of market demands that have to be taken into account when radical media operate on the margins of the mainstream media marketplace.

The continuation of this book's focus on *Marxism Today*'s production history in Chapter 4 offers a unique view of the relationship between political practice and cultural form by examining changes in format, imagery, design and layout in *Marxism Today*'s transformation from a 'journal' into a 'magazine'. An important understanding of the material transformation of the periodical from the journal form into a magazine is recognising how its physical and material changes enabled certain developments and changes in imagery, layout and design to take place in order to reach out to a potential new, broader audience beyond the party's networks. It is in this transformation of the intended or target audience that made MT's transformation a necessity to draw the attention of a new potential readership to the magazine.

As *Marxism Today* was picked up by a new(er) readership in the newsagent, changes had to be made in distribution and circulation, which are addressed in Chapter 5. How did the changes in distribution and publicity processes contribute to making MT the 'voice of the left' on the national stage during the 1980s? A key part in ensuring success in the marketplace means a periodical has to adopt the appropriate means of promotion and distribution to link the periodical to mainstream distribution and retail outlets, such as high street newsagents. This chapter provides detailed analysis of the publicity and national press coverage by which MT was able to gain access to the national public sphere. The detailed quantitative and qualitative analyses of press coverage, distribution, contributors, readership, weekend events and discussion groups, market research and publicity help to explain how and why MT succeeded in gaining access to a broader public where most other left magazines have failed or had limited success.

Marxism Today's publicity, promotion and distribution were integral to its influence on the left, although the analysis of its relationship with the national press raises questions for radical media about the desire for access to the national public sphere as mediated by the national media. This remains a key question for contemporary media activists of all alternative and radical traditions. Chapters 3 and 5 together also challenge the orthodoxy amongst alternative media scholars and activists by highlighting the benefits and disadvantages of the marketplace for radical media, which was central to the Comedia model.

Whereas Chapters 3, 4 and 5 examine *Marxism Today*'s production, changes in format and design, and promotion and distribution, Chapter 6 focuses on the writing itself, the core of cultural materialism: 'the analysis of all forms of signification, including quite centrally writing, within the actual means and conditions of their production'.[29] Since the start of the twentieth century, socialists, communists and other radicals, including many leading Marxists, such as Lenin and Trotsky, have been urging their comrades to write in an accessible manner and avoid jargon.[30] Yet, despite these exhortations, the common perception of 'Communist writing' or 'journalism' is as an oxymoron. Is it impossible for the Marxist left, or even socialists more generally, to communicate in an accessible manner? Through an examination of the language, writing styles and accessibility, this chapter identifies the transformation of texts that follow developments in all three formats, albeit the transformations are not straightforward or simple. Did MT transform its writing in the ways that its publicity and promotional material claimed? Chapter 6 also identifies changes in rhetorical strategies and how they helped in appealing beyond the 'radical ghetto' to non-party readers. A key part of this chapter's focus is an analysis of two of MT's most important contributors, Eric Hobsbawm and Stuart Hall, and their rhetorical strategies and techniques. This examination helps to demonstrate how and why their political interventions were persuasive with, and beyond, the left and, ultimately, helped to prepare the ground for New Labour. It demonstrates the power of Hobsbawm's 'realistic Marxism' and Hall's polemical appeals that combined to help create MT's 'persona', while demonising opponents on the left through the power of metaphor.

The final chapter draws together the different strands of analysis of *Marxism Today*'s production and distribution to try and draw the connections between the different aspects of political practice and cultural form. This process is to try and explain the links between the core ideas, their presentation and pro-

---

29   Williams 1983c, p. 210.
30   Pimlott 2006b.

motion against the other forms of structure and agency and within the cycle of production and distribution. This approach allows us in turn to rethink the 'party paper', and the Leninist and Comedia models in terms of what advantages and disadvantages of adaptations to the commercial 'marketplace of ideas' hold in store for future radical left or revolutionary socialist 'means of communication'.

CHAPTER 1

Marxism Today's Story: An Historical Narrative of a Cultural Form

While it might be a truism to state that there is no 'story' about *Marxism Today* that is not also a 'story' about the Communist Party of Great Britain, it is equally a truism to state that there is no party without (print) media. It is through those practices which the party and its ideology are constituted, and which provide the editorial material around which members and supporters organise, agitate, educate, mobilise and identify. Indeed, it is what the print media leave behind after a political organisation or party has ceased to exist that provides us with that organisation's 'story' or 'history'. Without these media, political organisations would not 'exist'. And they definitely would not exist without the media that also 'record' them or provide a record *of* them: they provide historians and others with a record of the mundane and the significant for others who succeed them in time and history. This is why cultural materialism places 'the analysis of all forms of signification, including quite centrally writing, within the actual means and conditions of their production'.[1] This chapter, therefore, provides a general overview of the cultural forms, such as the three key publications produced by Leninist parties, two principles of communication, and the CP's practice of democratic centralism, all of which are key to understanding the ways in which the CP operates and how it engages in politics. After this overview, the story of *Marxism Today* will be told from its precursors in postwar developments with different periodicals through James Klugmann's conventional editorship to a more concentrated focus on Martin Jacques's more tumultuous editorship, in which the journal was transformed into a magazine.

1   The Left, Cultural Form and Political Practice

The radical left political movements of the working class during the nineteenth and twentieth centuries in Europe, Canada and the United States of America were always intimately connected to print media and radical journalists and pamphleteers, even as these latter forms of print media (periodicals, pamph-

---

1 Williams 1983c, p. 210.

lets) ceased to be the dominant or pre-eminent cultural forms as new media technologies revolutionised the availability, accessibility and range of editorial material by the second half of the twentieth century. Whether or not there was a paper published on a serial basis, the printing press in some form was integral to the survival of all socialist and radical left organisations, if not their success. Where they lacked a regular, serial publication to distribute to the public, irregular one-off publications, most notably the pamphlet, was the most common medium or cultural form.[2]

By the start of the twentieth century, the dominant communicative practice for most, if not all, parties of the left, from socialists to communists to anarchists, revolved around the 'party paper' in some form, that was the focus of developing and distributing ideas to the broader public, the single most accessible medium (in terms of skills that could be learned, production costs and the means of distribution) for agitation and propaganda while acting as a means of organising a party or other political organisation.[3] Even where radical organisations adopted new(er) communication and media technologies, print remained the primary means of communication for the left, from social democrats to Communists to revolutionary syndicalists, socialists and anarchists.

Régis Debray identifies three pillars of socialism since its birth in the French Revolution more than 200 years ago, which significantly included an occupation intimately linked to the printing press and the production of newspapers, books and pamphlets:

> Typographers, intellectuals and teachers were the three supports of the socialist movement, each corresponding to one leg of the mediological tripod. What was on offer at any workers' lodge or *maison du peuple*? A library, newspapers, evening classes and lectures. Today, there are still platforms, books and newspapers. But the central axis of transmission has moved elsewhere, taking with it the apparatus of celebration, prestige and values that formerly conferred such an aura upon the books, teachers or peripatetic lecturers at workers' educational associations and *universités populaires*.[4]

---

2 Pimlott 2011.
3 Although anarchist, anarchist-syndicalist and libertarian communist movements usually reject the idea of 'the party', vanguard or not, many still operate via organised, structured entities contrary to popular mythology of these kinds of worldviews.
4 Debray 2007, p. 7.

Debray's identification of the three 'ages of communication', with the 'graphosphere' referencing the close, interdependent relationship between print media and socialism is useful for thinking about the left's crisis in the 1970s and 1980s. During this period of crises in the economy and the welfare state, with massive unemployment and inflation, de-industrialisation and public-sector spending cuts, there was also a crisis of organisation and communication as well as changes in moving towards desktop publishing and digital production, which would transform the print marketplace of ideas, particularly by the late 1980s and early 1990s.

The connection between the crisis of the left and its primary means of communication, print media, was closely connected to its political practice, which involved the 'selling' of ideas and membership via the paper on the streets, at demonstrations or door-to-door in neighbourhoods. Part of this crisis is related to the process of communication and how it has been an integral part of any kind of radical political practice but yet has largely gone un-recognised. As the last editor of *Marxism Today*, who had taken over the editorship at a time when the Eurocommunist and reformist wing of the Communist Party of Great Britain was gaining ground, Martin Jacques proclaimed that MT's transformation into its second format was both a 'political' *and* a 'journalistic' project, linking the crisis in the CPGB with its ability to reach out beyond the party to the broader left via its means of communication, and especially MT.[5]

2   The Party and the Party Paper: Leninist Communication Practices

Despite the central role of the party paper in Leninist practice as a collective 'agitator, propagandist and organiser' in both 'building the party' and mobilising the working class, most Leninists have overlooked or neglected the centrality of communication in class struggles and counter-hegemonic strategies, even when V.I. Lenin, Leon Trotsky and others have urged militants to pay attention to how they communicate.[6] The metaphor of the paper as 'scaffolding' for the party is Lenin's trope and it becomes a principal factor for thinking about the role of the party paper that distinguishes it from early radical papers as well as from the mainstream or bourgeois press. However, it should be noted that Lenin never did develop a systematic theory of the press,[7] although *What is*

---

5   E.g. Jacques 1977, 1978b, 1978e, 1979b.
6   Pimlott 2006b.
7   Sparks 1995.

to be Done? was as much about the need for a party paper as it was about the political debates in the Russian Social Democratic Party in 1902.[8]

The party paper was an integral concern in the 'communicative crisis' that was addressed, debated and negotiated over by Marxist party leaders, intellectuals and activists throughout the twentieth century, albeit not one in which the debates were made central, for the most part, in the disputes over leadership or direction for the various parties concerned. As early as 1921, there was a prescription or codification of the 'Party Press' in the Communist International's *Thesis on the Organisation and Structure of Communist Parties*,[9] and Adalbert Fogarasi, an Austrian Marxist, penned one of the earliest statements on a 'Theory of the Communist Press'.[10] The statement reiterates the need to constantly work 'to develop and improve' the paper, while recognising the need to maintain its complete autonomy from capitalist institutions, such as advertisers, which would otherwise determine its editorial (i.e. ideological) views.[11] And yet, the question over 'for whom to write' was never really resolved.

Despite the scholarly neglect, however, the importance of communication in various guises, as noted by leading Marxists, explicitly affected Communist parties throughout the twentieth century and these debates, whether implicitly or explicitly, were addressed by party leaders, intellectuals and activists.[12] These debates revolved around the 'correct' approach in three areas: first, the primary means of communication, the party paper; second, whether professional journalists, who were also Communists, should write for the paper, or whether Communist proletarians should (learn to) write; and third, language and writing style.[13] Debates over language and writing style were based upon differences in the understanding of which target audience to appeal to: either the most militant or politicised sections of the working class or a broader general public of the (lower) middle and working classes. These debates over Leninist print-media practices, therefore, remain critical to thinking through the means of disseminating radical ideas to the public and determining what role the party paper can play today, if there is still a role for it. The fate

---

8   For a challenge to conventional understandings of Lenin's classic text, see Lih 2005 and *Historical Materialism*, 18(3). For a recent perspective from the former USSR, see Baluyev 1983.
9   Communist International 1979 [1921].
10   Fogarasi 1979 [1921].
11   Pimlott 2006b, p. 60; Communist International 1979 [1921], pp. 251, 252.
12   I have referred to this situation as Marxism's 'communicative crisis' (Pimlott 2006b).
13   For an overview, see Pimlott 2006b. For aspects of these debates, see Aune 1994; Pimlott 2000b, 2005; Williamson 2002.

of the Leninist party is tied to that of the paper: a question of organisation is also inextricably a question of communication.

Although Communists and socialists have attempted to make use of the latest communication technologies since at least the Bolshevik revolution (e.g. when Bolsheviks used film, posters and wall newspapers to reach workers and peasants in the 1920s), print communication practices remain fundamental to a radical transformation of society for at least three important reasons. First, the characteristics of print media, especially books, newspapers, pamphlets and periodicals, are superior to oral and broadcast media in developing sustained arguments over time, and it is time and space that are needed to challenge and unravel ruling myths, common-sense ideas and systemic realities as well as to promote a new worldview and political praxis. Second, print media have historically been more accessible to those with limited financial means and professional expertise than other media; print has traditionally had greater portability and flexibility than broadcast and digital technologies and print can be referred to, re-examined and studied at one's leisure more readily than broadcast and electronic media, although that has changed considerably in the last ten years.[14] Nevertheless, electronic media still face obstacles, such as requiring some kind of outreach or 'push' campaign to let potential readers, viewers, listeners or subscribers know about their existence. It is not just the costs but the materiality of print media that make it a particularly useful means to engage in various agitational activities.[15] Third, print media are not just an integral part of Marxist political organisations, but are also constitutive of such parties (from far left to far right to everything in-between), because publications disseminate ideas and publicise programmes and actions: without print media, it would be virtually impossible to sustain any political organisation and still compete over ideas and for members.[16]

---

14 Technological developments in the twenty-first century have made it easier to reference and archive both broadcast and digital media.
15 Pimlott 2011.
16 Pimlott 2006b, p. 59. For the rhetorical perspective on the strategic employment of language as constitutive, see especially Charland 1987. The importance of language as constitutive works well with Raymond Williams's idea of language as 'practical consciousness', which he draws from Marx (Williams 1977a, pp. 21–44). Yet, without the means to circulate the rhetorical appeals means limited influence and impact, which is why the necessary attention to means of communication that extend beyond the human voice and person-to-person communication to what Williams calls non-human communication (e.g. Williams 1981).

3 Leninist Communication Practices: The Party as a Medium of Communication

Before discussing the different types of print media, it is necessary to understand some of the other key communicative practices of the Leninist or vanguard party. Although it might not be readily understood, communication was and is integral to the Leninist party organisation. Indeed, following Michael McGerr's analysis of US political campaigns in the nineteenth century, one could easily make the argument for understanding any political organisation or party, including the Communist Party, as a 'medium of communication'.[17] Since all political parties are organisations that are built around structures that enable communication between various office-holders or officers, the structure of hierarchies are 'chains of command' that enable orders to be sent, received and carried out, i.e. the lines of communication, which in turn provide the scaffolding (or skeleton) around which the party (or body politic) takes form.

Just as with other political parties, the vanguard party, in theory, seeks to politicise, mobilise and lead the working class to overthrow bourgeois society and the capitalist mode of production upon which it is based. While an underground party, the Bolsheviks operated under a very strict discipline with the organisation separated into a cell-like network to avoid detection and, if and when that failed, at least to avoid losing whole sections or branches to arrests and other acts of state repression. The party network was the means for communicating between the leadership and activists in their various cells, who would, in turn, communicate with the workers. The basic structure was subsumed to surviving state repression by the Tsarist regime and it ensured a 'transmission belt' model of 'top-down' communication. Strict discipline and tight organisation were also necessary during 'War Communism' to fight the 'Whites' and foreign military intervention in the Russian Civil War, 1917–21.

The theory and practice of 'democratic centralism', bequeathed to the worldwide Communist movement, was instituted in the years preceding the 1917 Revolution as a means to ensure that the rank-and-file members would have ultimate control over the general policies and political direction of the party. This was done through the decisions taken by delegates at party congresses, after which the leadership was meant to implement congress decisions and exercise the day-to-day running of the party in the months or years in-between national party congresses. The nature of authority and control of the CP and its lines of communication is based upon the practice of democratic central-

---

17   McGerr 1986.

ism, a core concept of the Leninist party that tried to balance the differences between a small group of officers and staff operating a complex organisation with a mass membership on a day-to-day basis and the rank-and-file being able to exert democratic control over the organisation via policies and practices on a regular, albeit longer term, basis.

4 The CPGB's Practice of 'Democratic Centralism'

It is important to remember that a key part of the CPGB's organisational practice that enabled the leadership to maintain control was its practice of 'democratic centralism' (rather than its theory). Democratic centralism enabled the leadership to maintain control through the party apparatus by ensuring that a majority of its supporters were on the recommended list, while including a few representatives of some dissenting views, as with the inclusion of members of the traditionalist and reformist tendencies to balance each other out during the 1970s.[18] Since 'the principle of unity ... was indissolubly linked to that of authority' in the CPGB, democratic centralism was the political practice through which this was expressed.[19] It was supposed to ensure that members would determine the party's general direction and policies at congress every two years, while the leadership directed the party and oversaw the implementation of congress decisions during the interval. It was important for all party bodies to follow the 'party line' as determined by the National Party Congress. Though there was a range of opinions tolerated inside the CPGB, it was limited; any questioning of the party line was permitted only in the pre-congress discussion period. Those who failed to observe these guidelines could be disciplined or expelled. The 1957 Commission on Inner-Party Democracy report, as explored below, had recommended that the party should permit some openness and discussion in the run-up to its biennial NPC.

It is in trying to maintain a balance between the party line and open discussion that the CPGB's use of democratic centralism, which was meant to ensure that members have ultimate control over the party in theory, ensured the leadership's control over the party in practice, as the experience of other CPs confirm.[20] Under democratic centralism, the leadership was elected to the Executive Committee by a 'recommended list', approved and submitted by the EC to the NPC delegates. The expectation was that the delegates would vote for

---

18 These are defined below.
19 Samuel 1986a, p. 65.
20 E.g. Shore 1990, pp. 165–70.

everyone on the list and the list would thereby fill all the positions on the EC. The leadership was able to ensure its continuity by handpicking its successors, even including some representatives of different viewpoints on the EC.[21]

All full-time party posts were elected by the EC only and PC members were selected from within the newly elected EC, to handle party affairs between meetings of the larger EC. Yet, even from within the membership of the PC, an even smaller group would sometimes be formed, called the Political Sub-Committee, to ensure the day-to-day running of the party. This move inevitably meant that the running of the CPGB was handled by a small inner circle, composed almost entirely of full-time party workers and elected full-time (paid) officers, such as the general and assistant general secretaries. The EC usually met every second month and was an important body for discussing general policies and strategy, but it was the PC or PCSub which usually set the agenda and parameters of discussion: the EC often agreed to the decisions made by the PC or PCSub *post-hoc*. Thus, the election of members of factions to the EC would not necessarily ensure that their views would prevail, unless they could secure a majority on the EC, which in turn would enable them to secure positions on the PC.

5   Leninist Communication Practices: Agitation and Propaganda

After acknowledging the party as a medium of communication and the integral role of democratic centralism to the party's operations, agitation and propaganda are the two key communicative practices of Communist parties, albeit by no means limited only to those organisations. From the French Revolution onwards, we see the development of techniques and practices used to agitate and mobilise crowds that can be labelled as 'agitation' and 'propaganda'. Of course, the latter term stems from the Catholic Church's ideological war against Protestantism in the 1600s.[22] It should be noted here that the differences between agitation and propaganda emphasise different audiences and their respective demands, and therefore, the need for different communicative practices. At a more basic level, there is the mode of communication known

---

21   This is not that different in practice with most, perhaps all, parties across the political spectrum.
22   Edward Bernays, Sigmund Freud's nephew and one of the 'godfathers' of 'public relations', preferred the word 'propaganda' but because of the negative connotations, he came up with an alternative, 'counsel of public relations' from which 'PR' originates (e.g. Bernays 1928; Ewen 1995).

as 'agitation'. This can be defined simply as the attempt to distribute or circulate 'a few ideas to lots of people' and was seen as 'short term information tactics to bring immediate abuses and problems to public notice'.[23] Agitators, for example, would work the crowds on the street, at demonstrations and in factories orally and, with increasing frequency (as accessibility in costs and skills of new technologies grew), via the distribution of leaflets to support their actions around immediate or short-term issues (e.g. strikes, demonstrations).[24] The party paper provides agitators with background material (information, news, commentary, analysis) that they deliver orally at workplaces, in neighbourhoods and on the streets.[25]

Propaganda, on the other hand, is the long-term process of educating the more political and militant workers, and relies on the party paper informing and sustaining them by providing the 'correct' interpretations of events, and drawing the links between seemingly discrete subjects, such as the fine arts and the economy. The paper provides the 'ideological glue that will join up the disparate struggles of workers', which is meant ultimately to win them over to the party.[26] 'Propaganda' was the practice by which 'longer-term political communication strategies' were put into place to get 'lots of ideas to a few people'.[27] Propagandists, for example, would work with the printed word, such as the Bolshevik papers, *Iskra* or *Pravda*, to politicise the more militant workers in trade unions and factories, and to thereby help to organise them into the revolutionary vanguard. To support the activities of both agitators and propagandists, Lenin developed the concept of the 'party paper'.[28]

---

23   Downing 2001, p. 68.
24   Research on contemporary trade unions demonstrates that leaflets are more effective than glossy magazines in reaching the rank-and-file (e.g. Witt 2005). 'Disposable literature' (flyposters, leaflets, pamphlets) are an integral part of the practices of agitation, education and organising (Pimlott 2011).
25   Downing 2001, p. 68.
26   Protz 1979, p. 91; Downing 2001, p. 68.
27   Downing 2001, p. 68.
28   The term 'agitprop' should be mentioned since it replaces both agitation and propaganda as a generic term. It has been used since at least the 1920s as a description for attempts to raise consciousness or mobilise people quickly, and it is associated with some of the more 'shocking' forms of visual communication used since the 1960s. Early on, Communist movements did engage in innovative experiments with print, film and radio, of which the most notable were John Heartfield's photomontages that were used as covers for *Die Arbeiter-Illustrierte-Zeitung* (Zervigón 2010; Cuevas-Wolf 2009).

6   Leninist Communication Practices: The Party Paper

The Bolshevik or Leninist model of the press draws upon Lenin's ideas of (clandestine) political organisation and strategy, and the experience of the party papers, *Iskra* and *Pravda*. From Bolshevism's beginnings in 1902, the party paper was seen as integral to Marxist political organisation and strategy: Lenin's most famous pamphlet, *What is to be Done?*, is as much an argument for a 'revolutionary paper' as it is about anything else.[29] The party paper is central to the conception of the vanguard political party as a 'collective organiser'.

> *A newspaper is not only a collective propagandist and a collective agitator, it is also a collective organiser. In this respect it may be compared to the scaffolding erected round a building under construction ... The organisation which forms [a]round this newspaper will be ready for everything, from upholding the banner, the prestige and the continuity of the party in periods of acute revolutionary depression to preparing for the nationwide armed insurrection.*[30]

It puts the paper at the core of its political strategy, where the paper's roles as *collective* agitator, propagandist and organiser are at the centre of party efforts to disseminate its ideas, build the party and, ultimately, organise the working class into a revolutionary movement with the vanguard party at its head.[31] This conception of the role of 'collective organiser' is equally that of 'collective communicator'; as it reaches out to internal and external audiences, the paper's primary function is not 'as adjunct to the building of an organisation per se, but as an integral part in the constitution of that organisation'.[32] Party and paper are inseparable.[33]

As a principle of democratic centralism, it is accepted that dissent is permitted in the run-up to the party congress but, once delegates make their decisions, members are to avoid engaging in expressing dissent from the party line to prevent factionalism. This principle of democratic centralism arose because of the

---

29   Harman 1984, p. 5.
30   Lenin, cited in Harman 1984, p. 5.
31   Bambery 1996; Socialist Workers Party 2002.
32   Sparks 1985, pp. 142–3.
33   It is not just the Communist party, but all political organisations: e.g. Gramsci argued for studying bourgeois newspapers as political parties as they often acted as such (1985, pp. 390–9). Although Gramsci was writing about Italy in the early twentieth century, his argument remains pertinent to studying the establishment media (and not just newspapers or news media) in the twenty-first century.

repressive conditions under which the Bolshevik Party operated in Tsarist Russia. The CPGB's policy to oppose internal factions was not always the policy with Communist parties elsewhere.[34] With the spread of digital media and the internet by the late 1990s, substantial changes began to take place in the nature of communication processes which have had an enormous impact on top-down chains-of-command within many organisations, including Leninist and bourgeois parties. Yet, it still has not changed that fundamental relationship between communication and organisation.

The Leninist or Bolshevik model became the model for all CPs, though the degree to which it was followed varied considerably as different national parties situated within different political cultures faced their own specific historical contexts. Despite its negative representation, this model does have advantages. First of all, there are clear power structures and a division of labour, just as with commercial media and the capitalist press, which ensure that the paper can be produced efficiently to tight deadlines. Second, at least according to the principles of democratic centralism (in theory), the paper must reflect the party as directed by the resolutions passed by a majority of delegates at congresses, which should determine the form and content of the paper. Third, it provides the primary 'scaffolding' or means of communication around which to build the party by engaging supporters and sympathisers with activities through which identification, organisation and mobilisation with the party is enacted.

7   A Basic Typology of Communist Party Publications

Print media are usually an integral part of any left political group because publications are used to promote both their ideas and organisations. Depending upon the party's size, resources and membership base, the number of publications may be considerable, ranging from neighbourhood news-sheets to highly specialised theoretical journals covering Marxist approaches to science and literature, and so on. Although the CPGB, like its sister parties in western Europe, published a range of newsletters, periodicals, pamphlets and books catering to both internal and external audiences, and for both specialists and the general public, there were three primary types of publications that were most important to its operations.[35] These were: the 'party paper', which was similar to a

---

34   For an historical perspective on factions and factionalism in Communist parties, see Riddell 2013.
35   See Pimlott 2000a, pp. 22–31.

newspaper in style, design and format; the 'party review', the formats of which varied, from newsletter to magazine, but primarily addressed to party members and offering more in-depth coverage of subjects promoted in the party paper, which included coverage of internal organisational matters; and the 'theoretical journal', most frequently similar to an academic journal in terms of mode of address, writing style and format, but which might also address sympathetic intellectuals outside the party. A good example of this typology since the 1980s is the Trotskyist Socialist Workers Party, which publishes three key publications: the weekly 'party paper', *Socialist Worker*; the monthly 'party review', *Socialist Review*; and the quarterly 'theoretical journal', *International Socialism*.

The first type of publication, the 'party paper', is *the* primary vehicle for the dissemination of Communist news and views. Generally, this publication is the one that is produced in the greatest frequency and targetted at the broadest audience; it is the public face of the party and, according to Marxist-Leninist theory, it usually plays the role of 'agitator' in providing a few ideas to lots of people. This might be daily, weekly, fortnightly, monthly or even less frequently, depending upon an organisation's resources and membership (the paper may also have to play a 'propagandist' role in providing in-depth articles on lots of ideas for a few of the most politicised or militant workers). The question facing the CPGB from its founding was whether its paper should address the most politicised workers (i.e. the vanguard) or a broader, but less politicised, general public. This dichotomy was never fully resolved, despite the implications for editorial content, writing style, and whether 'professionals or proletarians' should write for the party's publications (i.e. professional journalists who were Communists or Communist workers who could write).[36]

These questions became particularly acute during periods of social and industrial unrest. *Workers' Weekly*, which had replaced *The Communist* (1920–22) as the CPGB's paper, experienced rapid growth in circulation after Rajani Palme Dutt, a leading theoretician with close ties to the Comintern, took over as editor in 1923: increasing from 19,000 to 51,000 copies sold per issue in just eight weeks.[37] This growth reflected something of the views that *Workers' Weekly* voiced that was felt and understood by the readers whose other newspaper choices did not offer views in support of their interests. Equally, unlike a daily or monthly, the weekly met a need that capitalist media failed to provide at that time. This growth in the circulation was a reflection of the CPGB's growing support amongst the working class amidst increasing industrial strife in the

---

36   Pimlott 2006b.
37   Macfarlane 1966, p. 83.

lead-up to the 1926 General Strike. The *Workers' Weekly* reached 80,000 copies by August 1926, *despite* wholesalers' and distributors' boycotts of CPGB publications. Given this growth during an upturn in class struggle, it should be no surprise that, in the 18 months after the defeat of the General Strike, its successor's, *Workers' Life*'s,[38] circulation dropped by 25 percent to 60,000, as did the number of individual factory, pit and workplace papers (from 74 to 54).[39] The CPGB's fortunes were clearly tied to those of the paper and historical circumstances of the political conjuncture of the mid-1920s.[40]

However, it was not only a case of whether industrial struggles were growing or shrinking, but whether the Communist Party's political line appealed to the workers. The adoption of a 'hard line', as when the CPGB turned against former allies, meant its publications became similarly isolated and unappealing. The worsening economic conditions in the West, for example, did not improve the paper's chances of reaching a general audience of the working class or of activists because the 'Class-against-Class' policy (i.e. the Communist International's 'Third Period', 1928–34), meant their obvious allies, socialists and social democrats, were labelled 'class enemies' and 'social fascists': sales of party literature declined further still. By July 1929, for example, only months before the Wall Street stock market crash and the start of the Great Depression, *Workers' Life*'s weekly circulation had dropped to 27,500, barely one-third of its peak circulation of 80,000 just three years earlier.[41]

Despite the inauspicious situation of a deepening depression, mass unemployment and the CPGB's isolation from the left, as well as the Trades Union Congress' loss of control of *The Daily Herald* (the labour movement's only daily paper), the 'party pessimists' lost the argument against launching the CPGB's first daily newspaper.[42] It is clear that it was difficult to find the resources necessary to continue the production and distribution of the party paper, but this became especially so once *The Daily Worker* was launched; the central focus of the CPGB was on *The Daily Worker* which drew resources away from other struggles into the organisation, infrastructure and fundraising needed to sustain such an endeavour (even as the USSR provided funding for the CPGB's daily newspaper).[43] The paper became a central focus of party activity for members who were expected to try and sell it in their workplaces and neighbourhoods,

---

38   *Workers' Weekly* had been forced to close because of a lawsuit (Macfarlane 1966, p. 178).
39   Macfarlane 1966, p. 178.
40   Pimlott 2006b, p. 61.
41   Macfarlane 1966, p. 234.
42   Richards 1997, pp. 2, 136–9; Rust 1949, p. 10.
43   Anderson and Davey 1995; Andrews 2004; Beckett 1995.

even after it made it into newsagents. These efforts were about trying to situate *The Daily Worker* within the working class and have it speak with their voices, even as the party leadership retained control of it.[44]

Yet, *The Daily Worker*'s role remained subject to dispute: debates raged over which events, issues and ideas to cover *and* how. There was a constant struggle over whether the party paper should focus on a narrow area of political and industrial struggles, forming a communications link for party members and sympathetic trade unionists? Or whether the party paper should aim at reaching a broader audience and, therefore, provide a variety of news besides political issues, strikes and party debates? The debates sparked by these types of questions increased in intensity during periods of political crisis, which was exacerbated by and contributed to the decline in circulation and party membership.[45] In part, this was also due to the adoption of precise language or jargon whereby words and phrases acquired very specific meanings within discussions within the party press, which limited the latter's appeal to non-members. For example, *The Daily Worker*'s circulation rose as it began adopting a more popular approach by the mid-1930s, with the shift to the Communist International's promotion of the 'Popular Front' policy. While both party and paper suffered as a result of the Nazi-Soviet, Non-Aggression Pact of 1939, their fortunes changed considerably after the German invasion of the USSR in 1941: *The Daily Worker* relaunched in 1942, after having been proscribed for two years and its circulation increased to over 100,000 in the latter years of World War II, eventually peaking at 120,000 in 1949, shortly after the Cold War had begun in earnest.[46]

Disputes at *The Daily Worker* recurred over whether its direction should be more openly agitational or propagandist, which would help determine whether to include such subjects covered by the capitalist press that appealed to the working class, such as sports and betting. In the aftermath of 1956 and the loss of between 25 and 33 percent of the party's membership, debates were quite intense about the way forward. The debate was between a 'more pronouncedly party paper', reflecting the party's actions more and containing 'more fundamental theoretical articles', and a majority who wanted the paper remade along the lines of the popular press, using the 'most exciting and attractive items of news' and in an attractive layout to reach a broader audience; also, space for political items would be reduced, while retaining a 'sound core of Communist

---

44   Young 2016.
45   E.g. Allen 1985; Macfarlane 1966; Morgan 1995; Sparks 1985.
46   Morgan 1995, pp. 151, 152.

politics'.⁴⁷ Such discussions were never fully resolved and continued to exercise editorial staff, party leaders and the rank-and-file and can be seen, for example, in the heated dispute in April 1966 over renaming *The Daily Worker* as *The Morning Star*.⁴⁸

The SWP's weekly, *Socialist Worker*, is another example of divisions over the editorial and political direction of a socialist newspaper during shifts in industrial militancy and social unrest between 1968 and 1974. The SWP, which had begun to rival the CPGB's dominant position on the far left by the 1970s, was subject to two intense debates over the paper's focus and audience, which led to internal splits and resignations of editorial staff. Differences over who the target audience should be was a fundamental part of the dispute during 1973–74, between those who argued for writing for a broader, but less politicised, audience and those who argued for writing for a narrower, but more class-conscious, politically engaged readership. This latter audience demanded longer, more in-depth articles, critical analysis and good writing, whereas writing to reach a more general audience would mean producing shorter, less complex and more accessible, albeit also well-written, articles. This dispute over the paper's direction is a result of changes in social-political conditions while attempting to reach out to different audiences during the last year of a six-year surge in industrial unrest, when far left organisations were experiencing growth.⁴⁹

The editor played an extremely important role in party activities and, therefore, the person selected was usually, if not always, someone who would have been selected more for party-political *nous* and loyalties than journalistic skill, and was invariably closely allied to the party leadership. This became a problem for the leadership when divisions within the CPGB became subject to increasingly hardened lines that were to split the party and divide various party public-

---

47   Quoted in Pimlott 2006b, p. 62; Hutt 1956, p. 1.
48   It was a bitter affair for G. Allen Hutt, the architect of the professionalism and design of *The Daily Worker* (including four national newspaper awards), who had forsaken a more lucrative, high-profile career with established, left-leaning papers (e.g. *Reynolds' News*) to work on the party daily. Despite attempts to expel him from the National Union of Journalists for his CPGB membership, Hutt edited the NUJ's monthly journal for 24 years (the longest tenure to date), and accrued enormous influence as an internationally renowned newspaper designer and typographer, who was consulted by more than 250 newspapers and periodicals from around the world. While this competition between party-political reasoning and professional expertise was never resolved, Hutt was adamant that it was his Marxism that made him such a good professional journalist and newspaper designer and typographer (Pimlott 2013).
49   Another dispute over whether the paper should adopt a more 'punk' style to appeal to youth arose just a couple of years later (Allen 1985).

ations in the early 1980s, although many of the specialist journals were already aligned with one or the other of the party's two major tendencies when they were founded.

The second publication is often the 'party review': a newsletter, journal or magazine produced weekly, fortnightly, monthly or less frequently for party members, which will highlight party priorities, including events, speeches and policies, and provide a forum for internal party discussion and debate. During the course of its lifetime, the CPGB published a succession of party reviews, with different formats and frequencies of publication, the most important of which was the weekly-cum-fortnightly *Comment* 1963–82, especially during the late 1970s.

An important parallel to the 'party review' was the CPGB's Young Communist League which produced its own publications to directly target a specific audience of youth, which was an important development in training future writers and editors for other party publications and reaching out via its magazine, *Challenge*, which was revamped using the latest techniques in design and layout, including using the Beatles on a cover to appeal to a broad non-party audience of youth (membership did increase to 5,000 by 1965), although these kinds of changes provoked a backlash from some older party members.[50] The YCL even produced a theoretical journal, *Cogito*, in the late 1960s and these two publications appealed to a younger generation of Communists who were willing to challenge the authority of their parents and the party, and many of these participants would later become organisers and activists of the reformist wing in the 1970s and 1980s as well as readers of and writers for MT.

In 1978, a young, Eurocommunist feminist, Sarah Benton, was chosen as editor, who turned *Comment* into a lively forum of debate and discussion over party policies and other important issues, including a critical examination of Stalin's legacy, and who tried to make it more publicly accessible. She also helped to re-establish a Communist Design Group to help with improving the look and appeal of party materials generally. In her attempt to appeal to a broader audience, Benton started publishing a regular column on television shared by three leading cultural studies scholars, an innovation that preceded *Marxism Today*'s own cultural coverage. Benton, however, was forced to resign in 1980 as a result of her attempt to make changes and to appeal to a broader left public. Her example demonstrates the limitations that editors face when they lack support in the party hierarchy.[51]

---

50 Waite 1995, pp. 218–20; Thompson 1992, pp. 153–4.
51 This was something of which Jacques was keenly aware, especially after her resignation (Jacques 1996a).

The third publication type is the 'theoretical journal', a monthly, bi-monthly or quarterly publication, elaborating on theoretical and political-ideological issues and produced for party intellectuals, albeit not exclusively. An early, important development of the Communist Party's publishing efforts was a journal called *Discussion*, published between 1936 and 1938, during the height of the Popular Front. Its stated aim was 'to clarify and examine the policy of the Communist Party' and in so doing its aim was 'to raise the general political level of the Party membership and that of the more advanced sections of the working class'.[52] The journal had 'an educational, not an agitational, function' the policy of which was not 'to re-state the Party line, but to help develop the effective application of that line'; its purpose was 'not only to reflect but also to direct discussions'.[53] *Discussion*'s role was to see that opposition arguments were 'stated, analysed and demolished' so that members would be able to deal 'effectively with plausible counter-argument'.[54] Thus, we can see that 'discussion' plays an important role in helping to prepare supporters and activists rhetorically for arguments against the party's position or line. In the subsequent two decades leading up to the launch of MT, the 'discussion' section became an integral part of this third type of party publication.

Marxism Today became the party's last 'theoretical and discussion journal' and, although intended for intellectuals and ignored by the leadership in favour of both the daily newspaper and the party review until the early 1980s, MT's marginal situation changed dramatically after its relaunch in a new format in October 1979. By 1983, the CPGB's theoretical journal had eclipsed both *The Morning Star* and *Comment* in terms of influence and even as the Communist Party's public 'face' and 'voice'. By 1985, the party leadership had permanently lost control of *The Star*, and was forced to rely on *Comment* and advertising in MT as its public 'face', since it no longer had its daily 'voice' on the national stage.[55] The transformation of MT from a journal into a magazine was integral to its changing role for, and its autonomy from, the Communist Party. The tail had begun to wag the dog.

The history of the Communist Party's idea of the 'party paper' is meant to highlight ongoing disputes over its role and target audience, its language and writing style, and who should write for it (professionals or proletarians). It reit-

---

52 *Discussion* Editorial Board 1937, p. 1.
53 Ibid.
54 *Discussion* Editorial Board 1937, p. 2.
55 It is important to recognise the difference between advertising and a newspaper, since the former can represent a party or policy but it cannot 'speak' in the same way as the latter, hence my use of the terms of public 'face' versus public 'voice' to represent this difference.

erated the importance of print-media practices in their constitutive role in the Leninist's conceptualisation of the party paper as the 'collective organiser' of the working class. It is difficult to offer any direct assessment of the impact of print practices on the political effectiveness, success or failure of Communist parties. However, it does suggest the need to pay closer attention to the central role of communication in the organisation of Communist parties, especially since communication is constitutive of the organisation itself and the party acts as a medium of communication as it engages in any form of politics, in addition to the debates around the party press. With the changes to electronic communication, the ability to sustain a party shifts and organisational practices, such as branch activities and face-to-face meetings, remain integral to any party that wishes to act as a political instrument.

Marxism Today's history of cultural and material changes identifies both key concerns and attempts to overcome both the limitations of a Communist or other left periodical and its small audience. The question becomes what were the particular conditions under which MT was able to overcome its limitations and reach a broader audience on the left? Part of the answer will be addressed in later chapters on funding and production, distribution and promotion, design and layout, and writing style. However, most crucial is the conjuncture within which MT was launched in its second format that made its intervention in the left public sphere significant, and before we can understand that particular conjuncture, we need to examine MT's story from its origins in the aftermath of 1956 until its closure in 1991 as the USSR ceased to exist.

Out of the three primary types of publications, in *Wars of Position* we focus on the CP's third type, *Marxism Today*, 'the theoretical and discussion journal of the Communist Party of Great Britain'. Looking back at the history of *Marxism Today*, it is all too easy to criticise the periodical for its first 22 years, 1957–79, the period of its first format, as a jargon-riddled, unattractive and densely written 'journal', and one in which the party leadership directed it in a form of strict obeisance to party ideology and programme by which the intellectuals justified or legitimised the party line, especially in contrast to MT in its later two formats, 1979–91. Yet, such a critique does not take its subject of study as it was situated within the particular time, political context and historical conjuncture. It is necessary to begin MT's story by locating its origins, not only in the historical context preceding its launch, but also in its precursors and the party's thinking behind the role of a theoretical and discussion journal. In the discussion of the precursors to MT and the debates over the attempts to balance openness with discussion and promoting the party line, it is necessary to keep in mind that the thinking behind the singular most important political practice in Communist organisational process was that of 'democratic centralism'.

8 The Beginnings of Postwar Reconstruction and Periodical Developments

In the immediate aftermath of the Second World War, the Communist Party of Great Britain had benefitted from the USSR's popularity as a result of the latter's contribution to the Allied triumph over Naziism in the Second World War, as party membership reached a post-war high of more than 50,000 and the *Daily Worker*'s circulation surpassed 100,000.[56] Similarly, a number of monthly and quarterly journals, either linked directly to the CPGB or sympathetic to it, also achieved (relatively) high circulations in the immediate postwar period (until early 1948), the most important of which were *World News and Views*, *Arena*, *Communist Review*, *Labour Monthly*, *Daylight* and *Modern Quarterly*.

As the post-war peace turned into the Cold War, and the euphoria of the initial Labour Party landslide in 1945 dampened down as post-war difficulties and rationing continued, the CPGB began to find itself increasingly isolated politically and facing a concomitant and rapid decline in demand for its journals. Through this period of the late 1940s and early 1950s, these periodicals suffered substantial decreases in circulation, which in turn contributed to the financial burdens on the Communist Party due to a combination of limited advertising and a rapid loss of subscribers, as both party membership and *Daily Worker* circulation also declined: 'Party Centre'[57] was forced to rationalise its publishing output.

The genesis of *Marxism Today* as the 'theoretical and discussion journal of the Communist Party of Great Britain' was the result of at least three strands: the crisis of Communism in the aftermath of 1956; a prior decade of attempting to develop a vehicle for reaching out to non-party intellectuals; and attempts to popularise the CPGB's 'Marxism' amidst the Cold War. The Communist Party had a legacy of attempting to establish forums to include both party and non-party intellectuals (in part to recruit the latter), the publication of controversial debates over left ideas, and discussions over the role of party press, all of which can be traced to MT's origins in a number of political and cultural journals of the 1940s and 1950s. Three of its most important precursors were a cultural journal, *Arena*, a theoretical monthly, *Communist Review* (1946–53), and *Modern Quarterly* (1936–38; 1945–53), a 'popular front' (Communist and non-Communist) discussion journal on the arts and sciences. Another critical factor in MT's founding included the issues of carrying a large burden of

---

56 During the war, membership hit its highest number ever: 60,000 (Thompson 1992).
57 'Party Centre' refers to the CPGB's leading bodies responsible for directing its activities, which usually worked out of party headquarters, hence the name.

expectations of what MT's predecessor, *Marxist Quarterly* was supposed to have accomplished, which in turn had been published to address the shortcomings of its predecessor, *Modern Quarterly*. The party's failures to meet various aims and objectives were frequently laid at the feet of the periodicals themselves. The changes were initially identified with the analysis of the crisis affecting the CPGB's periodicals and the crisis of the party's internal democracy. The party leadership scaled 'back on the Battle of Ideas' to justify the 'reallocation of party resources into political and industrial channels, priorities which quickly closed down the spaces where the necessary debates were beginning to ferment'.[58]

9 Precursors: The Commission on Party Journals 1953

Continuing difficulties with party periodicals led to the establishment of the Commission on Party Journals in 1953, the year of Stalin's death, the last year of the Korean War (1950–53) and the year of the workers' uprising in East Berlin, to discuss the problems and put forward proposals for 'the future development of Party and Marxist journals' for the Political Committee's consideration. The CPJ, which was established at the end of February 1953, consisted of six leading CPGB intellectuals and officials: R.P. Dutt (owner/publisher, *Labour Monthly*), John Gollan (General Secretary), Emile Burns ('Marxist writer' and party official, who was also known as the party's 'cultural commissar'),[59] Mick Bennett (party official), Margot Heinemann (lecturer and writer) and James Klugmann (party intellectual) as the CPJ Chair. This membership testifies to the CPJ's importance in developing a proposal for a new periodical to address political and ideological issues: i.e. one which could be trusted to develop an intellectual journal, which would still promote the 'party line'. It met four times in rapid succession, including one session with the *Modern Quarterly*'s editorial board, before submitting its final report in September 1953. The report sought to rationalise the CPGB's production of journals and concentrated on five periodicals: *World News and Views*, LM,[60] *Communist Review*, ModQ and *Daylight*.

Attempts by *Modern Quarterly*'s editorial board to establish clear functions for the journal had been unsuccessful in solving the problems facing it. Subsequently, the 'Publisher's Note' in its last issue in the autumn of 1953 stated that the new journal, *Marxist Quarterly* (1954–57), will 'deal with current political and cultural issues from the standpoint of Marxism' and asked that ModQ's

---

58   Harker n.d. [2019], Chapter 3, p. 69.
59   Croft 1995, p. 97.
60   *Labour Monthly* was not technically a CPGB publication.

readers 'transfer their support' to the new journal.[61] There was no longer any room for a journal to attract progressive intellectuals to try and win them over. And the CPGB had neither the political nor the financial[62] will to continue to support such a 'popular front' type journal as ModQ. Instead, in the increasingly hostile environment of the Cold War, the party leadership wanted a journal to promote 'Marxism' to intellectuals, even though there was little likelihood of drawing in non-Marxists given the demonisation of the CPGB by its association with Stalin and the threat of international Communism.

Concerns over presentation, including accessibility, writing style, design and layout, were a major issue for party publications well before the debates over 'designer socialism' in the mid-1980s. The CPJ urged all publications to try and win broader audiences by improving presentation and content, a move made all the more urgent since the CPGB's financial crisis forced the closure of several publications. The CPJ criticised *Modern Quarterly* for its 'remote and erudite presentation' of issues, which it claimed was more appropriate for specialist journals, and for problems with its theoretical treatment of political, economic and cultural issues, which was due to a 'confusion' between its two roles: as a theoretical organ articulating a 'Marxist' (i.e. CPGB)[63] viewpoint and as a 'popular front' vehicle for discussion between party and non-party scholars; it would take a lot more than revamping the design and presentation of the content given the Cold War context of 1953 (i.e. the Korean War).[64] In the CPJ's view, ModQ was neither seen as the 'authoritative theoretical expression of the Marxist standpoint' nor was it broad enough to serve as 'a forum of progressive intellectuals'.[65] Although ModQ's rapid 40 percent drop in circulation in six years, from 7,500 in 1947 to 4,500 in 1953, was read as a failure to fulfil either

---

61 Lawrence and Wishart 1953, p. 197. The name for the new journal had been arrived at during the writing of the Commission's report whereby references to a 'Marxist Quarterly' is preceded by the use of both definite and indefinite articles throughout the document, although the use of upper-case letters does not necessarily indicate in and of itself that the name had been agreed. Regardless, the title gave a clear indication of the perspective that was being put forward, since 'Marxism' was the CPGB's 'monopoly', as the party saw it. The Commission reported that it was a necessity to have an unequivocal Marxist view being promoted: i.e. a viewpoint that supported the USSR's initiatives in international affairs (e.g. peace, nuclear weaponry, decolonisation) (CPJ 1953).
62 CPJ 1953.
63 In the CPGB, 'Marxist' meant an interpretation that was generally in accord with the 'party line', but this did not mean that there were no disputes over particular issues, meanings or stances amongst those who called themselves 'Marxists' or 'Communists' (Matthews and Matthews 1996; McLennan 1996).
64 CPJ 1953, p. 2.
65 Ibid.

role, it was the impact of the Cold War after 1948 that was particularly critical because in the immediate postwar period, there had been a considerable expansion of CPGB and allied publications' circulations.⁶⁶

The Commission's solution was to establish the *Marxist Quarterly*, which would incorporate the functions of the monthly theoretical journal, *Communist Review*, with those that ModQ was supposed to have been carrying out. The CPGB felt it necessary to produce a journal which would represent the 'Marxist' perspective on different theoretical and ideological matters, and which would be understood as the party's 'voice' in debates over more complex issues. It would provide the intellectual backing for the leadership's decisions and policies, such as fighting for the acceptance of 'Zhdanovism' and 'Socialist Realism', something that the ModQ had failed to do in the eyes of the leadership. *Marxist Quarterly* was to be produced in its stead:

> ... on the direct responsibility of the Party, a Marxist theoretical quarterly treating both [sic] political, economic and general ideological and cultural subjects from a Marxist standpoint.⁶⁷

The appointment of Emile Burns as editor was a move to help ensure the journal's promotion of party perspectives. The close working relationship between the editor, editorial board and party leadership, meant that MQ would be able to declare itself on topics and be seen as the party's voice. Thus, it was to have a corresponding role to promote Marxism with the 'whole field of the theoretical and cultural work of the Party'.⁶⁸

The CPJ report also recommended that the weekly party review, *World News and Views*, the second Communist publication type and the second most important publication after *The Daily Worker*, should be expanded and improved in terms of both content and presentation to reach a broader audience beyond its party readership. WNV published PC and EC decisions, political news, commentary and analysis, statements from various Communist parties from around the world, information for speakers engaging in propaganda work, and theoretical and polemical work (albeit not with the same depth provided by the theoretical journal, *Communist Review*). The report recommended that the party review should increase its focus on the labour movement by 'improved industrial coverage', including firsthand reports, and articles on cultural issues and reviews. In addition, *Daylight*, which had been a journal of working-class

---

66   Ibid.
67   Ibid.
68   CPJ 1953, p. 3.

literary expression (i.e. creative writing but not literary criticism), was to continue as an occasional supplement published in WNV.[69] Thus, the weekly party review had quite a full job covering functions of all three types of Communist papers: an expectation that was maintained about every successive journal about party affairs right until the CPGB's transformation into the Democratic Left.[70]

Labour Monthly was urged to try and extend its role to reach a wider labour movement audience, to promote unity around progressive policies and to approach problems from a Marxist point-of-view. The CPJ could only make suggestions since the CPGB did not control the periodical; its owner was Rajani Palme Dutt, a leading Soviet loyalist and Stalinist, with close links to the Soviet Communist Party, and a member of the CPJ.[71]

It was felt that MQ being a quarterly, rather than a monthly (as CR had been), it would enable PC and EC members, and other leading party members and intellectuals, who were authorities in their respective fields, the time and opportunity to contribute 'well-prepared and well-considered articles': i.e. articles that had been vetted to ensure they matched the 'party line'.[72] It would also cost less to produce four rather than 12 issues per year, which was a pressing consideration given the Cold War and poor sales. The authors were expected to take into consideration the CPGB's positions when preparing analyses on topical issues such as social democracy, the state, the history of the labour movement and democracy.[73] Other areas of MQ's contents were to be more in-depth, long-term or theoretical in their consideration and focus on issues such as philosophy, politics, economics, and on Marxism's relationship with culture and science. These changes were being made because of the redirection of (decreasing) party resources into industrial and political work.

In addition to theoretical issues, the Commission on Party Journals stated that the new periodical should also publish discussion articles on 'problems arising'. Non-Marxists, the CPJ claimed, would be interested in the *Marxist Quarterly* because 'they want, not some sort of diluted Marxism, bowdlerised

---

69 CPJ 1953, pp. 3–5.
70 For example, the correspondence to the EC and PC about *Comment*'s termination in 1982 carried in *Comment* in July and August 1982; minutes of EC and PC Meetings between May and September 1982 (EC 1982a, 1982b). See also the proposals to launch the successor journal, *Communist Focus*, and its successor, *News and Views* (EC 1990; PC 1984; PCSub 1984a, 1984b).
71 Callaghan 1993b.
72 CPJ 1953, pp. 5–6.
73 Ibid.

for respectability, but to know what Marxism teaches on particular problems'.[74] The language used here reflects the increasing isolation from the rest of the left and having to fight for its own position in support of the USSR. 'Marxism' was clearly a singular ideology of which there was only one and, therefore, 'correct' interpretation: this was the CPGB's Marxism-Leninism.[75] The CPGB was still the only sizeable organised force to the Labour Party's left and could, therefore, claim to be the only 'Marxist' voice in the public sphere.

These changes were being proposed just two years after the CPGB's adoption of a new manifesto, *The British Road to Socialism*, in 1951, which represented the party's first break, at least nominally, with Leninism and committed the CPGB to a parliamentary strategy to establish socialism in one country.[76] One could point to the irony of adopting this manifesto in the same year that the party lost its only two elected MPs in the general election or that the CPGB's 'peak performance' in elections was in 1945.[77] Tensions between East and West had been heightened by the Korean War at a time when there was a gradual, growing improvement in the standard of living for most people. The Conservative Party was invested in the postwar consensus as much as the Labour Party, including the establishment of the welfare state, the National Health Service and the nationalisation of certain industries.

At a time when the CPGB faced even further political isolation, it became concerned to put forward a consistent party line on ideological, political and theoretical issues in its journals. Therefore, the new journal's editorial board would be smaller and composed of full-time party workers and leading party intellectuals in their respective fields of specialisation. Thus, in addition to the editor, Emile Burns, and future General Secretary, John Gollan, *Marxist Quarterly*'s editorial board consisted of loyal intellectuals: James Klugmann, Jack Lindsay, John Lewis, Arnold Kettle, Maurice Cornforth and Dona Torr. MQ sought to put forward the 'materialist, scientific approach' on subjects that 'are of interest to all progressively minded people' and to present such work in a way that 'can be understood and appreciated by all readers, and not only by experts'.[78] The EC wanted the journal to appeal to a non-specialist

---

74 CPJ 1953, p. 6.
75 Although there were some tiny groups opposed to the CPGB, they largely remained beyond the knowledge of the general public. This precedes the growth in different Marxisms in the 1960s and 1970s in academia, such as structuralist and Althusserian, and the expansion of far left groups offering different political Marxisms, such as Trotskyism and Maoism (Smith and Worley 2014, 2017).
76 E.g. Andrews 2004, p. 74; Beckett 1995; Thompson 1992.
77 Callaghan 2005, p. 709.
78 CPGB 1957a.

readership and a wider audience amongst members and the working class to increase party influence and recruit more members, which would, in turn, help to increase revenue to establish a more stable base to fund its production.

10   Precursors: *Marxist Quarterly* (1954–57)

Launched in 1954 to replace both *Modern Quarterly* and *Communist Review* as 'a fundamental theoretical organ',[79] *Marxist Quarterly*'s name made explicit its perspective as the only Marxism there was: that of the CPSU and affiliated parties.[80] Despite closely following the party line, MQ proved to be even less successful than its predecessor, ModQ, since this was a particularly difficult time for the CPGB, with political developments and organisational decline.

The composition of its editorial board, therefore, was a conscious attempt to reach out to a new generation of non-party intellectuals while reassuring the CPGB's leadership and the party's more conservative wing that it was loyal, since many journalists and editorial staff had resigned from the *Daily Worker* because of 1956, including those reporting on the Soviet invasion of Hungary.[81]

In the last issue, published in January 1957, the 'publisher', the CPGB, promised that a 'new monthly journal of Marxist discussion' would be published after Easter, 'which will regularly include longer theoretical articles as well as shorter contributions to current discussion'.[82] The MQ editorial board felt that it should discontinue publication in light of the party's plan for this new publication. Although *Marxism Today* would continue the work of *Marxist Quarterly*, it was not simply the latter's successor, but it was also meant to incorporate aspects of the role of the CPGB's theoretical and discussion journal, *Communist Review*.[83]

To try and address the crisis of Communism in the aftermath of 1956, the Executive Committee initiated a series of discussions on the BRS and working-class unity through the party review, *World News and Views*, and other party journals. The EC took the decision to also publish a regular 'theoretical and discussion journal', that would print articles that would not necessarily conform

---

79   CPJ 1953, pp. 3–5.
80   Matthews and Matthews 1996; McLennan 1996.
81   MacEwen 1991; Morgan 1995; Thompson 1992.
82   CPGB 1957a, p. 1.
83   Cope 2016, p. 157. The CPGB's earliest theoretical journal had the same name and was also a monthly, 1921–27. CR was the third such theoretical journal of that name when it was launched in 1946.

to the editorial board's views, encouraging opposing points-of-view to be published. The failure of MQ and other party publications was not just the failure of periodicals to sustain themselves with sales to large enough audiences, but also the failure to meet the internal demands for those views and opinions that differed from the leadership's and authorised 'perspectives' that were not being offered space in party publications. The question of organisational, financial and periodical consolidation was also a question of 'inner party democracy'.

11 Precursors: The Commission on Inner Party Democracy 1957

The response in the 1957 Commission on Inner Party Democracy report can be read in light of the failure of *Marxist Quarterly* and *Communist Review* to play an adequate role in encouraging internal party debate *and* in making the party line more widely accepted, which were expected to have prevented some of the more effective dissent from surfacing or to have brought it to the leadership's attention before it was too late; yet, these two roles could and did contradict each other. This failure was highlighted by the publication of *The Reasoner* by John Saville, E.P. Thompson and Peter Worsley (and their justifications),[84] and their subsequent decision to leave (or expulsion from) the party and continue with their journal's successor, *The New Reasoner*, the existence of which continued to provoke the leadership's ire before it merged with *Universities and Left Review* to become the *New Left Review*.

The CIPD report tried to resolve these contradictory demands: that a journal should promote the party line on topical issues *and* still publish opposing viewpoints. Whereas editorial control 'must be exercised flexibly with appreciation of the need for different views to find expression and for the fullest provision of information', it was important to promote the party line within the publication.[85] The freedom of editors and editorial boards to edit, which clearly involves the exercise of political judgement, had to be balanced against the leadership's control over all sections of the party press.[86] This balance was determined ultimately either by the editor or the editorial board rather than by the party leadership or membership, though the leadership could exercise its power by simply cutting off funding or by refusing the editor's requests and exercising active control over appointments to editorial boards via the PC and EC.

---

84   Thompson 1992, pp. 102–3.
85   CIPD 1957, p. 13.
86   Ibid.

To counter the criticisms of dissidents, who had attempted to establish a forum for internal debate that was not censored by the leadership (e.g. *The Reasoner*), the CIPD report argued that the main function of the party press was 'to advocate the policy of the Party' and, therefore, there could not be an 'unrestricted right of publication of individuals and branches'; and yet, the report advocated that the EC should 'take steps to promote the greatest discussion in the Party press' and that meant there had to be 'the maximum publication of individual views and particularly of the collective views of branches and elected leading committees'.[87] The EC was also criticised for not taking a more active role in expressing its views and guiding discussion: although discussion was not meant to be 'left to take its own course without guidance', the report also suggested that guiding discussion did 'not mean limiting it'.[88]

The CIPD Report attempted to balance out the two views but it was not really successful. Each statement it made justifying the role of 'leading' bodies or officers was usually qualified immediately afterwards in an awkward attempt to balance editorial freedom with party control, but ultimately deferring to the leadership. In its monthly *Political Letter*, in May 1957 before the CIPD had finished its report, the Political Committee reasserted the decisions of the 25th National Party Congress and called for party members to guard against efforts 'to disrupt the Party'.[89] New forms of disruption were being organised by including ex-members 'in "independent" journals, or "discussion forums"', which in effect were seeking to attack 'Marxism-Leninism, the international Communist movement and the Communist Party'.[90] The leadership's view was made clear that a journal's role in promoting the party line would prevail over that of encouraging internal party discussion.

The tension in the CIPD report between permitting discussion of issues and promoting party policy was exacerbated by then recent events of suppressing internal dissent expressed as continuing concerns over 'factional activity'.[91] At what point though does discussion become 'factional activity'?[92] The tensions between permitting debate and promoting policy were exacerbated by con-

---

87   CIPD 1957, p. 14.
88   Ibid.
89   PC 1957, p. 3.
90   Ibid.
91   Factions and factional activity had not always been proscribed, at least not during the Comintern's first years, as different factions were represented within delegations and the leaderships of various communist parties, though this practice had ceased long before the 1950s (Riddell 2013).
92   Riddell 2013.

cerns over 'factional activity' as exemplified (in the eyes of the faithful), by Saville, Thompson et al., though they had only sought to further internal debate when party journals refused to publish dissenting views.[93] Though members could express their own views in committees, according to the leadership's view, it did not necessarily give leading members the right to express those views to other bodies lower down in the party hierarchy, thereby limiting discussion of some topics to verbal discussion only in small bodies rather than in any kind of larger venue or in print where it would have reached other members well beyond committee or branch boundaries.[94]

Authors were given the right to appeal any decision to reject their work and the journal was expected to indicate the reason(s) for rejection when informing the author of its decision. Thereby, the author was supposed to be able to 'raise the matter with the appropriate committee of the Party' and this is exactly what one dissident party intellectual, Monty Johnstone, sought to do.[95] Johnstone, an anti-Stalinist intellectual who chose to remain inside the CPGB after 1956 and continue to seek to reform the party from the inside, was constantly rebuffed every time he attempted to get his articles published. His appeals through the appropriate channels were to no avail, even though this process had been instituted as a result of the 1957 CIPD to avoid provoking dissidents into publishing their own journals (e.g. *The Reasoner*).[96] By 1967, when Johnstone was sufficiently 'rehabilitated', he was given somewhat more freedom in his expository prose than the occasional 500-word contribution to pre-congress discussions,[97] which was all he had been permitted when his letters were not denied publication outright as with other critics.[98] Obviously, it is difficult to sustain an argument with only 500 words, especially when you are arguing against commonly accepted assumptions, beliefs and practices.[99]

The CIPD Report urged members to try and open internal channels of communication if these had been 'wrongfully closed' by pressurising branches and committees to re-open them, but this would not have beeen the case

---

[93] Thompson 1992, pp. 102–3.
[94] CIPD 1957, pp. 28–30.
[95] CIPD 1957, p. 14; Johnstone 1995.
[96] Johnstone 1995.
[97] Over a period of months preceding the biennial party congress, all members were, in theory at least, permitted to express their views on any topic for discussion within designated party publications.
[98] Johnstone 1995. See also the dispute between the MTEB and readers over the leadership's position on the Warsaw Pact invasion of Czechoslovakia (e.g. Laithwaite 1968; Klugmann 1968; Carritt 1970b).
[99] Johnstone 1995.

where dissidents did not have the support of their party branch or committee, and even that pressure would not necessarily guarantee opening up space for the dissenting views that were initially refused publication. Without mentioning *The Reasoner*, the Report argues that such journals were not the solution because they not only 'siphoned off energies', but also 'encouraged factional activity'.[100] In an unintentionally prophetic statement, the report pointed out:

> Once such a journal is established it has to have people to write for it, finance it, circulate it and read it – that is, to establish an organisation apart from that of the Party. It thereby inevitably becomes the focus of factional activity, whether its originator had that intention or not.[101]

As we will see with *Marxist Quarterly*'s successor, *Marxism Today*, it would eventually come to be virtually a separate organisation at least vis-à-vis the CPGB in terms of party decisions and membership demands. Since Communist Party officers and intellectuals never developed a theorised understanding of the connection between the media of communication and the party's organisational structure, their search for answers to the questions of balancing the roles of editor, editorial board and party leadership had no way of figuring out how it might work in practice. Essentially, it functioned on an ad-hoc basis and the reports of the 1953 Commission on Party Journals and the 1957 Commission on Inner Party Democracy, regardless of one's cynicism towards Stalinist leanings of key party officers, reflect this inability to do more than constantly qualify answers in weighing up the different roles and the degree of freedom to be granted.

As we can see from the events, demands and hopes that were unfolding in this period from the end of the war to 1957, *Marxism Today*'s launch was made at a time of the considerable consolidation of the CPGB at both organisational and ideological levels in the aftermath of the loss of a substantial part of the party and its influence and prestige. This consolidation also meant the consolidation of the party's means of communication, by which it made its interventions and solidified its membership at a time of considerable loss and disorganisation. The consolidation of journals and other publications into the new party 'theoretical and discussion journal', *Marxism Today*, was a recognition of the situation into which the party had been put and it became a particular means

---

100   CIPD 1957, p. 29.
101   Ibid.

of communication that was meant to work on a number of fronts highlighted prior to the launch of the *Marxist Quarterly* with the CPJ Report in 1953 and after MQ's closure prior to the 1957 CIPD Report.

12   *Marxism Today*: 'The First Generation': 1957–77

Anticipating the 1957 report of the Commission on Inner Party Democracy, the last issue of *Marxist Quarterly*, in January 1957, promised that a 'new monthly journal of Marxist discussion' would be published after Easter, with longer articles on theory and shorter discussion contributions.[102] The replacement was only launched in late September 1957, when *Marxism Today*'s declared aim was 'to promote Marxist thought over a wide-ranging field of interest and to encourage as much discussion as possible with this object in view'; it was to be a vehicle for a broader range of opinions from within the party and as a forum for opinions from progressive, but non-party, intellectuals in the discussion section.[103] MT's launch was meant to be also an answer to issues around factional activity and the publishing of criticisms on the party's periphery, and yet it was supposed to win over progressive and win back wayward Communist intellectuals to the party.

The editorial board, which was appointed by the Political Committee and ratified by the Executive Committee, was meant to ensure, at least nominally, the representation of different perspectives and expertise while providing the leadership with the means to exert control over a publication, even though congress had the nominal power over all party periodicals.

The leadership also realised that they would have to be more cautious in treating dissent because they faced competition for a younger generation of progressive intellectuals attracted to the New Left journals, such as ULR and TNR, which were produced independently of both the Labour and Communist parties.[104] These journals were the New Left's threat to the CPGB's monopoly as the preeminent force to Labour's left. Some party intellectuals, including Johnstone and Hobsbawm, also sought to persuade party leaders to engage with the New Left.

The threat of the New Left meant that the new journal's editorial board had to have a credible intellectual presence to be taken seriously outside the party and yet still satisfy the leadership's desire for it to be 'very strong politically':

---

102   CPGB 1957a.
103   CPGB 1957c, p. 1.
104   Klugmann 1957.

i.e. a board with a majority of party intellectuals with a demonstrated loyalty to the leadership and the party line.[105] This was felt to be necessary by both the leadership and rank-and-file, who had remained in the party in the aftermath of 1956 and, therefore, expressed a distrust of 'intellectuals'. The leadership's claim for the journal's 'political direction' meant that they would appoint prominent party workers and officials to make up half of the board: the General Secretary was 'the Editor' on paper, but in reality Gollan was just a figurehead; officially, James Klugmann was his 'Assistant Editor' but he was in fact the *de facto* editor, and since he was deferential to the leadership, he was an intellectual who could be 'trusted'.[106] Yet, it attests to the relative importance ascribed to the CPGB leader that he be seen as both an intellectual and an organisational leader, which also demonstrated MT's importance to the party. Nonetheless, MT's first decade saw only a gradual opening up of space for critical discussion. Thus, after 1956, with space still restricted within the CPGB, those members interested in the ideas of the New Left could only flourish outside it, even though MT was meant to win over progressive intellectuals to the party line.[107] Such a role required the editorial line being open to a considerable degree to encourage discussion, since the latter is clearly a two-way form of communication and cannot work as a monologue or simulated dialogue.

The new theoretical and discussion journal was charged with being both the authoritative 'voice' of the CPGB, providing the pro-Soviet 'Marxist' perspective on issues of the day, and a forum where viewpoints sympathetic to 'Marxism', but not necessarily 'correct', could be put forward and debated. The initiator of each debate was given the opportunity to reply after all contributions had been published and the debate was brought to an end, which ensured that the party had the final say.

Thus, in theory *Marxism Today* was to be both the party's theoretical journal, the role that both the *Marxist Quarterly* and *Communist Review* had been expected to perform, *and* the 'united front organ', which had been the function

---

105   Ibid., p. 2.
106   Johnstone 1995; King 1994. Klugmann's trustworthiness in the eyes of the leadership (and Moscow) were due to his willingness to write the hatchet job on Yugoslavia, *From Trotsky to Tito*, after the relations between the USSR and Yugoslavia had soured at the end of the 1940s. Klugmann wrote this even though he had worked with Yugoslav Communists through his involvement with the international student movement when he was based in Paris in the 1930s and when he was commissioned by the Special Operations Executive in 1942 to work on Yugoslavia and helped to swing Allied support to Tito's Partisans (Andrews 2015).
107   Pitcairn 1985, pp. 108–9; Johnstone 1995; Hobsbawm 1958.

that *Modern Quarterly* was meant to fulfill.[108] This formulation appears 'ironic' given the CPJ's argument that ModQ's attempt at being a journal for discussion between progressive and party intellectuals had contributed to its loss in circulation and appeal.[109] It highlights the difficulty of publishing periodicals that promoted a strict adherence to the party line, the role of a 'fundamental' party organ, but were still expected to reach out to non-party intellectuals.

Although MT was to continue the work of its predecessor, *Marxist Quarterly*, and support the CPGB at a time of organisational and ideological consolidation in the aftermath of 1956, the EC decided that as a theoretical and discussion journal, MT should also publish articles that did not conform to the MTEB's opinions, including opposing viewpoints.[110] Most of the functions and roles of other cultural journals, such as *Arena*, *Time Out*[111] and *Daylight*, with their specialist focus on the arts, culture, literature and science, were to be MT's responsibility. MT was seen as a 'safer' outlet for ideas outside the party line because it was not dealing with organisational matters or even party policies per se. It operated as a potential 'safety valve' even though the pressure was never allowed to build up because James Klugmann exercised a fair degree of control over how far beyond the party line opinions could roam before he would refuse to publish them. In conception and practice, MT remained closely linked to the leadership via the editor and editorial board.

James Klugmann was responsible for putting forward proposals for the new theoretical journal to the Executive Committee. He expressed doubts that the leadership should appoint people to the new editorial board, 'whose attitude is at present vacillating in order to win them over' and called for certain members of *Marxist Quarterly*'s editorial board to be excluded from MT's editorial board: Jack Lindsay, J.D. Bernal, Christopher Hill, Henry Collins and John Horner.[112] Oddly, Professor Bernal, the only one of the five who was no longer officially a party member, was the only one appointed to MT's first editorial board.[113] He was joined by Maurice Cornforth, philosopher, Maurice Dobb, economics lecturer at Cambridge, Dr John Lewis, ex-Unitarian minister and former editor of *Modern Quarterly*, Arnold Kettle, English lecturer at Leeds University, and

---

108   CPJ 1953, p. 2.
109   Ibid.
110   Matthews and Matthews 1996; McLennan 1996.
111   Not to be confused with the London listings magazine of the same name that was launched in 1968.
112   Klugmann 1957, p. 2.
113   CPGB 1957c, p. 1. Bernal had resigned from the party in 1933 but subsequently became a 'fellow traveller' (McIlroy 2006, p. 226).

George Thomson, Professor of Greek poetry at the University of Birmingham.[114] Cornforth, Lewis and Kettle had all been members of *Marxist Quarterly*'s editorial board. This gathering of some of the party's most renowned and loyal intellectuals demonstrates the importance of winning intellectual credibility for the new theoretical journal that the party leadership attached to these appointments.

Nevertheless, the Stalinist legacy of bureaucratic control of party organisations and a 'workerist' distrust of 'intellectuals' meant that the board had 'need' to include prominent party leaders and trade unionists. Thus, party workers and officials made up half the board: John Mahon, Secretary of the London District CP; Les Burt, a shop steward in the electrical industry; Frank Stanley, secretary of a CPGB factory branch and an engineering shop steward; and John Wood, Secretary of the Scottish Miners' Union.[115] The appointment of the party's General Secretary, John Gollan, as the first editor was also significant.[116] The concerns when MT was first established was that it should be a party 'voice' and there was no better way to demonstrate this than to have the General Secretary as 'the Editor', which was especially important in light of the loss of thousands of members and the feeling of 'distrust' exhibited towards the remaining intellectuals amongst 'workerist' leaders and activists (even though many industrial workers also left the party).

The PC decision that any participation by CPGB members in public meetings meant that they should fight for the line as decided by the party at its biennial congresses was reiterated at the May 1958 EC meeting in light of the increasing importance of the New Left's journals and discussion groups.[117] Although opposed to the CPGB's support for the USSR's attack on Hungary,[118] Eric Hobsbawm, who had remained a party member, delivered a report on *Universities and Left Review* to the EC.[119] Hobsbawm had contributed to the first issue of ULR, and so could speak with some authority on the subject, as most CPGB

---

114   CPGB 1957c, p. 1.
115   Ibid.
116   Johnstone 1995; King 1994. No announcement was made in MT, however, when Gollan stepped down from the position after December 1962.
117   PC 1957; EC 1958.
118   Monty Johnstone also opposed the CPGB's line on Hungary and its Stalinist practices; he remained committed to fighting for change within the party. Unlike Hobsbawm, who could remain as a kind 'free-floating' party intellectual, Johnstone, a writer and further education lecturer, was one of the few anti-Stalininsts who remained involved in branch life (Johnstone 1995).
119   Hobsbawm 1958.

members were unlikely to have participated at the time.[120] In addition, Hobsbawm is also critical of the EC's attitude to the 'ULR movement', which was not a result of the crisis in the CPGB, such as 'the Peter Fryer Newsletter, defunct Socialist Forums and the *New Reasoner*', but came about through the 'repoliticisation of middle class and intellectual youth … evident since Suez'.[121] Hobsbawm argued that the EC's attitude to the 'ULR movement' could be explained by the 'defective' information that the party had received; he had seen no party officials or members attending, let alone CPGB student or youth organisers who should have been keeping the party informed about these kinds of activities.

Hobsbawm casts doubt on the ULR's self-proclaimed circulation of 8,000 for its first issue, and no figures were published in subsequent issues; yet he did point out that ULR received 'consistent and wide publicity'.[122] ULR sponsored meetings in London and the provinces as well as a 'coffee house'. Eventually, MT published a discussion on the New Left initiated by Arnold Kettle,[123] who spoke for the majority of the leadership when he dismissed its importance because of the 'petty bourgeois' background of most of its activists and supporters. Nevertheless, ULR's activities and its subsequent joint project with TNR, *New Left Review*, had an impact because MT also began sponsoring forums, discussions, meetings and weeklong events between 1962 and 1964, in London and some smaller cities, such as Leeds, to compete against the NLR and New Left clubs, events and so on.

Marxism Today's relatively uncontroversial albeit marginal role, however, is evident in the leadership's lack of attention to it: in its first 20 years, James Klugmann submitted only three reports on MT to the Executive Committee. In the first report to the EC, Klugmann argued that, despite doing a 'good job', MT's weaknesses were due to its still 'insufficient development of theoretical treatment and theoretical work' and that its analysis of current problems was 'still … a somewhat deeper treatment … rather than a more theoretical examination of things'.[124] As part of the proposed improvement, the report suggested that the party's theoretical purpose needed to be made explicit to MT contributors and the participation of leading party members would help in this matter; for example, the successful 'Marxist' (i.e. CPGB) treatment of economic issues in MT during the first two years could be ascribed to the contribution

---

120 Hobsbawm 1957. His article is followed by 'Socialism and the Intellectuals' by Thompson (1957).
121 Hobsbawm 1958, p. 2.
122 Hobsbawm 1958, p. 1.
123 Kettle 1960.
124 Klugmann 1960, p. 1.

of members of the Economic Sub-Committee, who were responsible for carrying out discussions and educational work on economic issues on behalf of the party. Organisational matters, on the other hand, did not appear to be a concern at the time, since MT published only three items on the party out of 188 articles in the first 27 months. However, there was interest in debates over the future of the labour movement in the late 1950s as a result of both 'the *embourgeoisiement* thesis' (affluent workers)[125] and the 'revisionist' attacks on Labour's Clause IV.[126] Therefore, the successful development of MT and the improvement in the theoretical treatment of different topics would require the participation of EC members in a number of selected areas, providing that the EC agreed to them: Britain's economic future; crisis in the labour movement and the future of socialism; problems of peaceful co-existence; freedom and democracy; problems of party development; and other areas such as philosophy, history, the British state, culture and science. These suggestions were endorsed by the EC.[127]

The time lag between contemporary events and issues, and feature article treatment of those same events in *Marxism Today* was considerable. Significantly, the report, therefore, suggested that MT's contributors would have to be 'quicker off the mark in taking up the challenge in all fields by bourgeois writers and thinkers, even if the results are not as good as they would be if we waited. Important problems must be dealt with as they come along'.[128] Klugmann therefore suggested that MT should publish some form of editorial, but not the same kind of 'monthly analysis of the political situation' as provided by *Labour Monthly*.[129] This new section, 'Editorial Comments', would enable brief statements about political developments, new ideas and recent publications to be published, without waiting for a polished feature of 2,500-plus words; editorial board members were also expected to contribute. Thus, early in MT's history it was recognised that the periodical needed to respond to current events as they arose, which foreshadowed later pressures, albeit of greater intensity when MT was distributed to newsagents nationwide.[130]

Circulation had remained relatively stable in this period, from initial sales of the first issue of *Marxism Today* (October 1957) of 4,307, to around 4,341 sales of the January 1960 MT (the loss of several hundred copies normally sent to

---

125   There was also a debate in the 1960s about 'productive' versus 'unproductive' workers.
126   These debates foreshadowed New Labour's rise decades later and the removal of Clause IV.
127   EC 1960.
128   Klugmann 1960, p. 2.
129   Ibid.
130   Ibid.

China had only a minor impact on circulation after the Sino-Soviet break in 1959–60).[131] During this period, the subjects covered were varied: out of 143 articles and 45 discussion items published in the first 27 issues, from October 1957 to December 1959 inclusive, 18 had dealt with economic issues, three each with the CPGB and with industrial issues, four with trade unions, and 10 with the labour movement compared to nine reviews and 26 articles dealing with social and cultural issues.[132] Out of the 45 discussion items, nine resulted from the 26 social and cultural articles while the four trade union articles provoked 10 discussion contributions while one article dealing with the (problematically named) 'Jewish Problem' brought out eight items. Of the rest of the issues, eight were historical, five dealt with Africa (plus five response items) and five dealt either with imperialism or colonial liberation struggles, and another four dealt with other non-Western countries; in addition, there were two articles on Poland, the only other Communist country besides China discussed in addition to the eight articles on the USSR. The articles on these issues provoked no published responses. There were only eight articles classified as historical with three discussion contributions.[133] Interestingly, there was a minimal focus on the CPGB itself, even in the aftermath of 1956, or perhaps because of it. This contrasts with the calls for the later MT under Martin Jacques's editorship to provide more coverage of the party.

While the CPGB's revision of the BRS in 1958, just prior to the Sino-Soviet dispute of 1959–61, had led to some dissension within the party, only a handful of members left the CPGB to form pro-Chinese organisations. Nevertheless, a group of pro-Soviet traditionalists emerged to criticise the leadership's attempts to maintain relations with both parties, which marked the origins of postwar factional activity.[134] From the late 1950s, the traditionalists, backed by leading members, including the former general secretary, Harry Pollitt, became increasingly trenchant in their criticisms of party liberalisation. The CPGB was criticised for 'moving away from the working class': changing the party newspaper's name from *The Daily Worker* to *The Morning Star* and the EC's stand over the trial of Iu. Daniel and A.D. Sinyavsky in 1966. These divisions were further deepened with the 1967 EC 'Statement on Ideology and Culture'.

The early 1960s was also a time when the CPGB's growth in membership gave it the confidence 'to seek out a new mass base',[135] a shift that was marked by

---

131 Klugmann 1960, Appendix C.
132 Klugmann 1960.
133 Ibid.
134 Parker 2014.
135 Andrews 2004, pp. 74–5.

the 1965 National Party Congress, where there was a major changeover in the leadership, as many of the first wave of party leaders from the 1920s, such as J.R. Campbell, Peter Kerrigan and R.P. Dutt, were replaced by a new caste which included Gordon McLennan and Bert Ramelson.[136] This was a time of renewal of industrial struggles in which Ramelson, the Industrial Organiser, had to work assiduously to make up for the Electrical Trades Union 'vote-rigging' scandal of the early 1960s, when the CPGB was brought into some disrepute for its role, and he strengthened the party's contacts and influence within the trade unions, so that by the late 1960s, two prominent, left-wing union leaders, Jack Jones and Hugh Scanlon, were seen as examples of how 'strong broad left and party presences were established in large sections of the trade union movement'.[137] Despite 'relying on tightly-knit and centralised forms of control', Ramelson's contributions 'had the effect of consolidating and extending the party's break with Leninism' while 'strengthening its links with mainstream trade union movement'.[138] As John Callaghan has argued, the CPGB's strategy 'was remarkably attuned to British institutions' and developed its 'influence within the trade unions at both the grassroots level and within leadership structures' with 'wage militancy' as the 'principal tactic' promoted by 'both elected CP trade union leader and shop steward', as Communists came to dominate the labour movement.[139] The result of the practical work of Ramelson and other party activists involved in union struggles helped to develop 'militant labourism'.[140]

Many of those identified with 'militant labourism' also attacked the leadership's attempt to attract a younger generation of intellectuals and artists with the adoption of the March 1967 EC statement on 'Questions of Ideology and Culture'.[141] This statement could be seen as representing shades of interest in Gramsci and the 'battle of ideas' at a time of considerable growth to the CPGB's left that was challenging its position as *the* vanguard party of Marxism-Leninism. The statement signified a shift from a party line to an open line on scientific, religious, artistic, cultural and even ideological matters, justified as the application of the BRS.[142] Yet, it also appeared to validate traditionalists' criticisms of it as 'a withdrawal from real ideological struggle' that would lead to the abandonment of class struggle and the adoption of 'class collaboration'.[143]

---

136 Andrews 2004, p. 75.
137 Andrews 2004, pp. 75–6, 75.
138 Ibid.
139 Callaghan 2005, p. 709.
140 Andrews 2004.
141 EC 1967: it was published in MT and as a separate pamphlet.
142 Simon 1968; Andrews 1995a, p. 227.
143 Lewis 1967a, p. 222; Simon 1968, p. 156.

The EC statement was further confirmation for traditionalists that the leadership was moving in the wrong direction; a year earlier, they had criticised *The Daily Worker*'s change of name to *The Morning Star*.[144]

In 1968, which is considered a year of revolutions across the globe, the 'Prague Spring' had offered a renewed sense of hope in reforming Soviet-style Communism in Eastern Europe, but this sense of hope did not last long. In August, a Warsaw Pact collection of allied armies led by the USSR invaded Czechoslovakia. This led to a crisis within the CPGB over the appropriate stance, including those who supported the USSR-led 'intervention' (who were nicknamed 'tankies', a common slur used against Stalinists and many traditionalists over the next two decades) and those who wanted the CPGB to condemn the invasion more forcefully than the leadership did. This was a period of growing differences between those who are labelled 'traditionalist' and those labelled 'reformist'. In addition, 1968 was also the year of a new revised edition of the *British Road to Socialism*.[145]

The second half of the 1960s also marked a shift in target demographics for recruitment as the party appealed to intellectuals, university students and white-collar workers as part of an attempt to renew itself, while its main source of recruits from the skilled working class, the Young Communist League, went into rapid decline after 1965.[146] The growth in white-collar workers joining the party helped to offset the loss of working-class recruits. In its first decade, MT's circulation began to decline from about 4,300 to less than 2,500, except for special issues (e.g. centenary of Lenin's birth).

Nevertheless, *Marxism Today*'s position was gradually gaining in importance despite declining circulation because of the leadership's '*rapprochement* with intellectuals who had taken a critical line in 1956 but had chosen to remain in the party',[147] the membership's changing profile and the adoption of the Executive Committee's statement on 'Questions of Ideology and Culture' in 1967, which acknowledged the party's new commitment to 'pluralism' in scientific, religious and cultural matters. Political, ideological and theoret-

---

144　Allen Hutt, who had served on many CPGB and Labour publications since the 1920s, had been with *The Daily Worker* almost continuously since its start in 1930 and argued strongly against the change of name. He brought forward his retirement to leave before the new name took effect (Pimlott 2013, p. 88).

145　Thompson 1992, p. 154. Johnstone, a dissident, anti-Stalinist intellectual, spoke to the BBC about the Daniel and Sinyavsky trial with the leadership's backing; this was his 'rehabilitation' that enabled him to participate again in the party beyond his branch (Johnstone 1995; McLennan 1996).

146　Fishman 1994; Samuel 1987, pp. 74–5; Waite 1995.

147　Andrews 1995a, p. 228.

ical issues became ever more important, especially as the formerly 'monolithic' ideology of 'Marxism-Leninism' could no longer be equated with the CPGB or the USSR, especially as the former expressed criticisms of the latter's actions on occasion (e.g. 'Prague Spring'). Other events such as May '68, Vietnam, industrial unrest and the counter-culture, contributed to the new importance of politics and renewed debates over Marxism. Despite the CPGB's international connections, the party was often outflanked on the left by a number of radical groups, such as the International Marxist Group and International Socialists/Socialist Workers' Party, which made the CPGB appear as a more conservative force; it was even outflanked by the Vietnam Solidarity Campaign's mobilisations against the US war.

These social, political and ideological challenges, and the decline in circulation, despite an upturn in industrial and social unrest, helped to instigate the second report to the EC 13 years after the first one. James Klugmann's 1973 report reiterated MT's role as the party's 'theoretical and discussion journal', which was to contribute to the development of the party's ideology, analyse its 'key problems', which were of a political and economic nature, help develop 'the socialist consciousness of the working class and progressive movement, and lift the level of understanding' of party activists; despite the liberalisation on issues of culture and ideology six years earlier, MT still needed 'to develop a Marxist approach' to these very topics.[148] Klugmann drew upon the example of the French CP that, as a mass party, it could produce several journals specialising in different subjects. MT, however, was expected to cover all possible subjects, which made it difficult to build and retain a sizeable readership since diverse topics usually only appealed to some, but not all, readers.[149]

Klugmann's editorship was not controversial, for the most part, because it followed the parameters set by the party; though as the CPGB opened up ideologically, he did help initiate the Christian-Marxist dialogue in 1966. He also encouraged others to engage in critical debate with orthodox Marxist ideas, though he was unwilling to do so himself.[150] However, Klugmann did consult with the leadership over controversial articles about political and economic issues: this policy meant that both pro-Soviet advocates and radical Eurocommunists often found themselves refused publication. Criticisms of the leadership's condemnation of the USSR's suppression of the 'Prague Spring'[151] ('inter-

---

148 Klugmann 1973, p. 2.
149 Ibid. See Andrews 2015, Chapter 19; Jacques 1996a.
150 Jacques 1996b; Johnstone 1995.
151 'Prague Spring' was the name for 'socialism with a human face' in Czechoslovakia in 1968, where the Communist Party government of Alexander Dubček was reforming the system.

vention' or 'invasion'?) did not break the 'consensus': articles and discussion contributions reflected different viewpoints within 'acceptable' limits. Thus, as some dissident Marxists were rehabilitated and published by the late 1960s, other, uncritically pro-Soviet contributions were not always deemed suitable for publication.[152]

By the mid-1970s, circulation had begun to pick up despite the overall decline in party membership, with some attempts at improvements in presentation and increased advertising: the annual Communist University of London (July) MT issues attracted advertising from some commercial academic publishers, which saw the potential of reaching an audience interested in books either about Marxism or treating various subjects from a Marxist perspective. MT's March 1977 issue, which included a feature on Antonio Gramsci by Roger Simon, sold 115 copies at a conference on Gramsci (proving that coordinating editorial content with public events can be a means to market and sell more copies).[153] However, Klugmann had difficulties meeting these additional demands with minimal personnel: three days a week secretarial help for administrative tasks; Jack Cohen, a party education officer, helped with editorial and production work; and some MTEB members provided occasional editorial help.[154]

During the political ferment of the mid-1970s, General Secretary John Gollan initiated a rancorous internal debate with his reassessment of Khrushchev's 'secret speech' on its twentieth anniversary.[155] It sparked off an intense debate over the legacy of Stalinism and 1956 that pointed to party divisions coming to the surface. Conservative and traditionalist members felt that there was no purpose in dredging up old events, which only deflected the party from fighting 'monopoly capital', and that too much time was being wasted on 'old events'; whereas party reformists were angered that Gollan's article showed little progress in the leadership's thinking about internal democracy since 1956: only the leadership and its supporters, party loyalists, welcomed it because they saw it as a significant step forward.[156] The response was overwhelming and revealed an enormous range of opinion within the party over a number of critical issues, such as the USSR, Leninism and Stalin's record, highlighting the

---

152   Johnstone 1995. See Laithwaite 1968; Klugmann 1968; Carritt 1970b.
153   MTEB 1977a, p. 1.
154   Cohen also took over Klugmann's editorial duties when he was ill (Andrews 2015, Chapter 19).
155   Gollan 1976.
156   Andrews 1995a, p. 238; Thompson 1992, p. 172. Two decades later, McLennan compared his predecessor's speech to Mikhail Gorbachev's advocacy of *glasnost* and *perestroika* (McLennan 1996).

difficulty of characterising these two broad internal factions beyond 'tendencies', even though there were 'core' groupings committed to one line or the other.[157] Yet, many of the exchanges were characterised by '[b]itter rancour and intransigent hostility' between the rival tendencies (a foretaste of the intensity of internal strife in the 1980s).[158]

On behalf of the Executive Committee, Reuben Falber responded to complaints, from party members claiming that the leadership was 'scared' of open discussion and questioning the degree of 'inner democracy', by pointing to the 'ongoing discussions' in MT that allowed different positions to be examined.[159] In the same meeting, it was noted that the EC rarely discusses MT: the journal was largely neglected because the intellectuals were not seen by most members, including the leadership, as important to the party's role in industrial and political struggles. Nevertheless, it is important to recognise that another legacy of 1956 was that some of the successors of John Gollan's generation of leading Communists, became somewhat more willing during the 1970s to refrain from interfering with the rights of editors and editorial boards to decide what to publish, which would later work to Jacques's advantage.[160]

It was not only in the party press that discussions occurred over differences between promoting the party line and enabling open discussions, but also with some district and branch CPs over their public meetings. The South Essex District Communist Party (Ilford), for example, had been holding public meetings since the autumn of 1976 and had begun the new year with a series of public talks by leading party intellectuals and officers, including Martin Jacques, where the discussion of the BRS was opened up for public participation. Margaret Woddis, SEDCP Secretary, pointed out to the EC that her branch produced a bulletin,[161] and were planning talks which would include the speakers from both the Labour Party and the CPGB, which she pointed out were part of the processes by which the SEDCP took the EC at its word to engage in the fullest discussion with public and party.

A series of letters between Woddis and members of the EC, and the discussions of which at the January 1977 EC meeting, point to the same kinds of tensions that preceded MT's foundation. On the one hand, Woddis argues that

---

157   Callaghan 1988, p. 234. MT received 93 contributions alone by the closing date of 30 September 1976, but only 27 had been printed in MT by December 1976; another 15 were published in a separate pamphlet (MTEB 1976b).
158   Thompson 1992, p. 172.
159   Thorneycroft 1976; Street 1976; EC 1976.
160   McLennan 1996. This principle was reiterated by the 1979 CIPD report (CIPD 1979).
161   SEDCP 1977. Introduced by Alan Booth, CPGB's Education Officer, this issue included articles by Jacques and Alan Hunt based upon their public talks for the series.

the SEDCP is not enabling factional activists to promote their interests contrary to the party, since factional activists 'will find the way to propagate their ideas outside their own branch or district in any case'.[162] McLennan expresses his frustration at persuading the 'South Essex comrades' that what they are doing is not what the Political Committee had in mind, even though Woddis insists that it is in the spirit of McLennan's letter of 11 January 1977. McLennan and Falber, for the EC, use two key arguments against Woddis: they argue that, since District CPs vary in size, it would be unfair for the larger ones to ensure that everyone gets published, and that bulletins, such as the SEDCP's, might promote 'differences between districts' and make the CPGB appear divided.[163] The EC, via the PC and Falber, urged Woddis and her District CP to 'instead make the fullest use of the available facilities': i.e. the party press.[164]

The EC decided that it would have the PC prepare 'some guidance for Party organisations on the production of bulletins and journals, particularly in relation to the discussion on the *British Road to Socialism*'.[165] As identified here, similar tensions arose between enabling open discussion on matters of party interest and the leadership's fear that they will not be able to control the discussion, and since, after leading Eurocommunist party members spoke at its meetings, the SEDCP had their speeches published as pamphlets for further distribution and discussion, these autonomous actions of the SEDCP were seen as akin to 'factional activity'.

The Executive Committee Meeting of 12–13 March 1977 discussed the proposal to appoint Martin Jacques as MT editor on James Klugmann's retirement in September. Jacques proposed that the Political Committee consider 'for the future how not only the report but the discussion in the EC could be conveyed to the Party'.[166] A number of items at the EC meeting dealt with complaints from both wings about problems with getting published or with the leadership's stance in criticising 'a brother party' for its repression of the Charter 77 group in Czechoslovakia. Monty Johnstone complained about being refused publication by *The Morning Star*'s editor, Tony Chater, and pointed out that his action involved 'a question of political policy'.[167]

---

162 Woddis 1977.
163 Falber 1977.
164 Ibid.
165 EC 1977a, p. 3.
166 EC 1977a, p. 1.
167 Johnstone 1977.

13 A Party of Two Wings

The leadership's 'managerialism', in attempting to maintain control of the party by placating each wing at different times or even playing them off against one another, can be seen in its attempt to accommodate the pressures for reform during the 1970s, by supporting changes to the party manifesto, the BRS, at the 1977 congress, but then minimising any reform to party structures, which were necessary to make the initial reforms meaningful, at the subsequent 1979 congress: to accommodate the conservative reaction *and* to maintain its own control. The BRS was, therefore, constructed as a 'pragmatic' document intended to balance competing methods and aims, the implications of which were never worked out nor theorised beyond claiming it as a 'revolutionary', 'socialist' manifesto.[168] It committed the CPGB, in the reformists' vision, to demonstrating 'moral and intellectual leadership' via a 'war of position' for socialist hegemony based upon 'the broadest possible alliance of all those groups and classes objectively at odds with monopoly capital'.[169] The more radical traditionalists and reformists became frustrated with the leadership's compromises with each other's opponents, though it is thought that this leadership style actually succeeded in keeping both wings in the party for far longer than might otherwise have been possible.[170]

These early expressions of dissatisfaction were often from loosely organised groups of 'hard-liners', since factions were officially proscribed, although by 1971 the first organised faction had formed, the Party Group, which had evolved out of an informal discussion group of party and non-party members. It included people who later joined opposing tendencies, such as Beatrix Campbell, Mike Prior, Ken Gill and Mary Davis.[171] It took positions on party issues, held meetings, circulated discussion papers and sought changes on policy at the 1971 Congress, but which declined into a degree of inactivity and many drifted away until wrapping up in 1975.[172] Despite attacks on 'revisionism', the Smith/Party Group and its leading intellectual and organiser, Bill Warren, more closely foreshadowed the Eurocommunists with their criticisms of the CPGB's 'lack of theoretical rigour' in the 1968 BRS, lack of clarity in its talk about democracy, inability to go beyond 'economism' and the defence of unions, and its unwillingness to confront its own sexism and 'lack of commitment to femin-

---

168 Callaghan 1988, p. 227.
169 Callaghan 1988, pp. 226, 227.
170 Callaghan 1988, pp. 234–5.
171 Andrews 1995a, pp. 230, 246; Andrews 2004, p. 63.
172 Pearmain 2014.

ism'.[173] The Smith/Party Group's significance was not in terms of its size or even influence on the CPGB *per se*, but in terms of its articulation of a left democratic communist position within the CPGB.[174]

Gradually, during the 1970s, the two opposing tendencies, 'traditionalist' and 'reformist', took shape. While such terms only characterise the differences between tendencies, they have been chosen in order to avoid too pejorative or sympathetic terminology (e.g. 'Stalinist', 'moderniser'). Both tendencies encompassed smaller, factional groups which became better organised and entrenched within the apparatus. There were many who were in favour of democratic internal reforms but unconditional in their support for the USSR or opposed to both. The traditionalist tendency, composed of Stalinists, hardliners and conservatives, were well ensconced within the Industrial Department, as befitted their emphasis on 'class politics' and their base within the labour movement, which also explains the political and tactical closeness between them and some groups within the Labour Party. The reformist tendency, composed of Eurocommunists, Gramscians, anti-Stalinists and dissident Marxists, dominated ideological-political work in several specialist committees and journals, such as the Theory and Ideology Committee and *Euro-Red*, providing the reformists with an influential intellectual base. Other party agencies were more evenly mixed between these two broad tendencies, such as the *Morning Star* and the Education Department.

The two, increasingly irreconcilable, wings began to emerge almost as separate 'parties', contributing to the CPGB's split 'personality'. For example, two versions of Marxist theory were taught: the reformist-dominated Communist University of London in the mid- to late 1970s engaged in rethinking Marxist theory with the influx of the ideas of Gramsci, Althusser and others, while the theory taught in traditionalist-run summer schools and branch meetings had not moved on from Lenin's *State and Revolution*.[175] The leadership, however, could retain control as long as they could rely on a majority of members, the 'centrists', to follow their recommendations and as long as the two tendencies lacked internal cohesion: the EC alternated its support between the two to retain both wings in the party. For either tendency to have any hope of influencing, let alone winning control of, the party, they had to make concessions to the leadership to secure positions on the EC and elsewhere. This division eventually undermined the leadership's managerialism, the tactics of which could

---

173 Andrews 1995a, p. 229; Andrews 2004, p. 63; Pearmain 2014.
174 Harker n.d. [2019]; Pearmain 2014.
175 Andrews 1995a, p. 234.

not have sustained the party indefinitely, as frustration and resentment built-up which led to major losses of members from both wings at critical junctures (e.g. 1979, 1985, 1989).

Many CPGB activists turned their attention to industrial struggles as election results proved disappointing from 1950 onwards. These activists were especially encouraged by the upturn in industrial militancy in 1968–74.[176] The industrial activists supported rank-and-file militancy wherever it arose. However, Eurocommunists criticised the Industrial Department and the party for their support of 'wage-militancy' and defending 'sectional interests' against the interests of the working class as a whole and they cited Lenin on the inability of 'economic' (trade union) struggles to instill a 'political class consciousness'. Under James Klugmann's editorship, debates took place in *Marxism Today* in the 1970s, with Eurocommunist members of the Economic Committee (including a few members of the Smith/Party Group) arguing for an incomes policy, contrary to the party line.[177] Criticisms of economism, which became stronger after Thatcher came to power in 1979, developed into criticisms of corporatism, focusing on 'the whole range of newly institutionalised union powers'.[178] There was also a general dislike and criticism of bureaucracy, which fed into the criticisms of unions.

The CPGB's longstanding commitment to workplace politics did pay off eventually as many party activists in the labour movement entered the middle ranks of union officialdom and into the leadership of the Trades Union Congress. The strategy of alliances was advocated by party activists in organising 'broad left' fronts within trade unions to try and oust right-wing leaders, which enabled the party to have a greater impact than its numbers would otherwise suggest; although the CPGB was on Labour's list of proscribed organisations, it was able to wield influence inside Labour via the unions.[179] Paradoxically, many of these industrial activists opposed similar approaches on the political front advocated by reformists and MT.

With the rise in industrial militancy in 1968–74, most far left groups became 'workerist', redirecting their energies into trying to recruit industrial workers and focusing their propaganda work into reasserting the primacy of 'class politics'. The CPGB, however, found itself facing a contradiction between support for rank-and-file militancy and support for its members among various union leaderships. The Industrial Department, a veritable 'party-within-a-party', wielded

---

176   Nicolson 1986, p. 11. See also Callaghan 2005.
177   E.g. Devine 1974; Purdy 1974.
178   Samuel 1987, p. 90.
179   Thompson 1992, p. 134; Callaghan 2005.

considerable influence since it could lay claim to labour's radical traditions, a heritage of which Communists could be proud. The Industrial Department subsequently became the natural rallying point for those unhappy with the demands of reformists, Gramscians and Eurocommunists.

Between 1970 and 1974, when the Labour Party was in opposition, the 'Labour new left' managed to shift:

> the discourse of the party, including that of its leadership, to a more radical plane then at any time since the 1930s. But, it had achieved very little in terms of democratising the party or changing its structure so that socialist mobilisation would replace 'parliamentary paternalism'.[180]

Thus, Labour's victory in both 1974 elections were hollow victories for the left because the Labour government did not implement its own election manifesto, which was based upon the Alternative Economic Strategy, supported by both the Labour Left and the CPGB. Instead, the government sought to implement the 'social contract' to reign in inflation by keeping wages and prices down, which the CPGB attacked as a 'social con-trick'.[181] Increasing dissatisfaction amongst the rank-and-file led to an explosion of wildcat strikes and the 'Winter of Discontent', 1978–79.[182]

During this period, the CPGB's internal divisions began to deepen. A minority opposed the party's 'knee-jerk' support for all wage struggles, official or not. This group argued that these actions were limited at best, promoting 'economism' and 'sectionalism'.[183] A number of party economists, including Dave Purdy, Pat Devine and Bob Rowthorn, argued that the wave of strikes in the early 1970s were a 'defensive response to the worsening economic situation and one that added to the inflationary problem' and that the left had no 'credible solution' to put forward: they accused the AES 'of being irredeemably statist, inflationary and politically naïve'.[184] The Gramscian minority also criticised the party for being unrealistic: the CPGB not only opposed all wage restraints but demanded at the same time increased public spending on healthcare, pensions etc. But to become a leading political force, it would have had to offer 'specific socialist

---

180   Panitch and Leys 1997, p. 85.
181   The pun was Bert Ramelson's.
182   E.g. Hay 1996, 2010; Thomas 2007.
183   'Economism' refers to the 'limited vision' of trade unions in their (wage) struggles for a bigger slice of the capitalist pie. 'Sectionalism' refers to groups of workers fighting for their own particular interests to the exclusion of the general interests of all workers, including the general public.
184   Callaghan 1988, p. 231. See also Callaghan 2005.

solutions to specific economic problems'.[185] These Gramscians were 'increasingly ready to question the traditional political and social verities within which [the party] operated and to point to the inadequacies of its theoretical analysis'.[186]

14   The Brief Rise of 'Eurocommunism'

During the 1970s, the Eurocommunists became the single most important group of the reformist wing, as they rode a wave of popularity generated by the electoral advances of western European Communist parties, especially after the *Partito Comunista Italiano* made the 'historic compromise' with the Christian Democratic Party in 1976 in preparation for entering government for the first time since 1947. The PCI's electoral success fuelled interest in its tactics and strategy, which enhanced the reformists' call for alliances. However, it was Gramsci's ideas which spread rapidly across the left, aided by committees, CUL seminars and specialist journals, and which achieved deeper roots than the rather short-lived example of Eurocommunist politics, which had blossomed briefly.[187] The Gramscian emphasis was on the ideological struggle for moral and intellectual leadership via language, 'common sense' and 'folklore' or 'popular culture', including mass media.

Eurocommunists were critical of demands for planning and nationalisation, not just because they saw these approaches as unpopular, but also because these 'policies were increasingly seen as incompatible with democracy and prefigurative politics favoured by the new social movements'.[188] Only after the Conservatives won the 1979 election did 'these heretical doubts' spread from a minority of party intellectuals to a wider audience across the left.[189]

Eurocommunist influence spread as some adherents acquired important positions within the party apparatus. Four important examples demonstrating the growing importance of reformists in key positions, started with Dave Cook's appoinment as National Organiser in 1975, Jon Bloomfield's succession as Secretary of the Birmingham Communist Party in 1976, Martin Jacques's appointment to the *Marxism Today* Editorial Board in April 1977 prior to succeeding James Klugmann as editor in September of the same year, and Sarah

---

185   Callaghan 1988, p. 232.
186   Thompson 1992, p. 164.
187   Andrews 1995a, p. 237. See also Pearmain 2011.
188   Callaghan 1988, p. 232; Purdy 1976.
189   Callaghan 1988, p. 231.

Benton's appointment as editor of the party review, *Comment*, in 1978. Tensions in a key advisory committee, the Economic Committee, attested to their growing influence, where they formulated 'some of the most advanced criticisms of the party's industrial strategy which went to the heart of the party's overall political position'.[190] Several younger committee members, including Bob Rowthorn, Dave Purdy, Pat Devine, David Currie and John Grahl, went on to contribute to MT under Jacques's editorship. Disputes over the causes of inflation found Eurocommunist economists arguing for the controversial 'incomes policy', which targetted wage demands as inflationary, and against freezing prices and import controls as demanded by the Communist Party.

After intense debates throughout the CPGB, the fourth edition of the *British Road to Socialism* in 1977, primarily drafted by Jacques and George Matthews, represented a partial victory for the reformists, socialist humanists, Eurocommunists and Gramscians: it was, in keeping with the leadership's balancing act, a compromise document.[191] It just about 'managed to accommodate all shades of party opinion': the earlier concept of the 'anti-monopoly alliance', in which the organised working class held the leading position (aka vanguard) in the alliance, shifted to the Gramscian 'broad democratic alliance', which meant that 'all the old arguments were now illustrated by reference to the "new social movements"'; yet, the BRS also included references to 'the superiority of actually existing socialism' and Marxist-Leninism, the 'leading role of the party' and its 'commitment to democratic centralism'.[192] The BRS also showed Gramsci's influence in its notion of 'revolution as a process', although it offered 'little insight into the nature of ruling-class hegemony', and while the 'broad' definition of the working class was accepted, its 'leading role' left the nature of its relationship to the NSMs ill-defined.[193]

Dissatisfaction with the reformist trend led to the defection of 700 members and three districts to establish the New Communist Party in the summer prior to the 1977 National Party Congress. This move dashed traditionalists' hopes of stopping the reformist draft manifesto. While the Eurocommunists won their victory over the wording of the new BRS, the NPC passed Resolution 72, with virtually unanimous support, which acknowledged the debt to the CPSU as a 'great example and inspiration' on the 60th anniversary of the October Revolution.[194] The more experienced reformists, including Cook and Jacques, were willing

---

190 Andrews 1995a, p. 235.
191 Andrews 1995a, p. 239.
192 Callaghan 1988, p. 235.
193 Andrews 1995a, p. 240.
194 Andrews 1995a, p. 241.

to make tactical compromises and support such resolutions, whether or not they believed in the substance of such texts, in their more cautious approach to change. However, a few radical Eurocommunists wanted an open confrontation over the USSR with the traditionalists but failed to force the issue.[195] This resolution's overwhelming support is evidence of a complex duality amongst reformists, many of whom favoured reforms but still retained strong sympathies for the USSR.

Traditionalists were unwilling to tolerate any criticism of the USSR or the party's relationship with it, whereas reformists often felt that this relationship jeopardised the building of the BDA. Nevertheless, it was this relationship and the connections with national liberation movements which had made the CPGB's internationalism attractive to many, especially in the growth of the anti-Vietnam War movement and the USSR's support for national liberation movements struggles in the global South.[196] The reformists' support grew in tandem with the increase in feminist and student members during the 1970s, while traditionalist support fell as recruitment through the workplace waned.[197] Many reformists, feminists and students came from the same class background as did industrial recruits, although many of the former were part of the socially mobile working class that were taking up white-collar, (para) professional and public sector jobs as these sectors expanded, while traditional industries stagnated.

However, after the 1977 Congress, a minority grouping within the traditionalist tendency remained opposed to the new BRS, as traditionalists and reformists struggled against each other to gain control of branches and district committees, all of which contributed to deepening the internal rift. Jacques was closely involved in the reformists' move to win the membership over to a new leadership that would renew the party ideologically and politically.[198] They were hopeful because of social and political developments taking place domestically and internationally, particularly the PCI's electoral popularity, which helped to fuel the popularity of Eurocommunism and Gramsci's ideas. For many members, orthodox Marxism could not satisfactorily explain youth cultures, femin-

---

195   Andrews 1995a, p. 237. The CPSU's highest ranking member to visit the CPGB attended the 1977 NPC and this was seen as tacit support for the 'hardliners'.
196   Irene Brennan cites the CPGB's international connections as a primary reason for her decision to join the CPGB in 1970 (Brennan 1996).
197   Andrews 1995a; Callaghan 1988.
198   This was a large grouping, but it did not include all reformists. Jacques and Johnstone, for example, did not identify with the term, Eurocommunist, despite being closely identified with the objectives of the party's reformist wing (Andrews 1995a, pp. 237, 248; Jacques 1996b; Johnstone 1995).

ism, racism etc., and the annual CUL (1969–81) came to provide a stimulating environment by the mid-1970s in which debates on Marxism and other contemporary issues flourished. Out of this intellectual ferment, grew the specialist committees, such as the Theory and Ideology, and Arts and Leisure committees, and specialist journals, such as *Red Letters* and *Euro-Red*.[199] Their emphasis on theoretical and ideological issues was also a source of dissatisfaction with the EC's managerialism and the party's pro-Soviet Marxism. MT's success in the 1970s can be measured by the increased attention it received in EC reports (and not just in MT's reports to the EC). These reformists hoped to change party structures and practices after the revised BRS was adopted in 1977, since their strength lay in many of these specialist committees and with party intellectuals, whose expertise would be needed if theory was made more central to the party's work.

The 1977 National Party Congress agreed to set up the Commission on Inner Party Democracy, the second in two decades, to investigate and report back to the next NPC. However, the CIPD brought divisions amongst reformists to the surface: older reformists, such as Dave Priscott and Bert Pearce, were unwilling to support the wishes of younger reformists, like Jacques and Cook, who wanted a radical overhaul of party organisation. Priscott, for example, while supportive of the new BRS, feared that organisational changes would neutralise the party as 'an effective revolutionary force'.[200] The six Eurocommunists on the CIPD (out of 16 members) submitted 'alternative proposals', in addition to signing the majority report: they proposed a radical re-organisation that 'challenged the leadership's grip over the party'.[201] The leadership realigned itself with traditionalists to defeat the alternative proposals at the 1979 NPC, which received one-third of the vote, a gauge of the reformists' strength, and the latter's influence was effectively stymied. This defeat forced reformists to recognise the limitations of working inside the party.

This breakdown gives some sense of the strengths of the opposing wings since the leadership's loyal supporters probably numbered about 40 percent of the membership. This means that neither traditionalists nor reformists had enough support to gain control of the EC. Each side had to seek the leadership's support to try and block the other, since both tendencies were shifting aggregations of groups of dissenters rather than single cohesive factions. However, it meant that the leadership was stuck in a 'holding pattern' in trying to maintain control while playing both sides against each other.

---

199   E.g. EC 1971, 1977.
200   Andrews 1995a, p. 242.
201   Ibid.

15 *Marxism Today*'s Transformation: 'Caution & Compromise', 1977–83

The transformation of *Marxism Today* under Martin Jacques's editorship, 1977–91, is an important story to tell because of the central role the periodical played, not only in the political trajectory of the Communist Party, but also in Labour's shift towards 'New Labour'. In this story, both the trajectory and fates of both editor and periodical are closely intertwined from 1977 until its closure in 1991. The first six years were perhaps most important and demonstrated an attempt to move the party and its members into a position of working on and across the left beyond its own limitations.

Jacques's selection for the recommended list for election to the Executive Committee in 1967 at 22 years of age made him one of its youngest ever candidates: according to Jacques, the leadership picked him for his intelligence, capabilities as an organiser and (then) orthodox views.[202] However, Jacques claims that his views began to change as a direct result of that revolutionary year, '1968', and its aftermath; he became part of the reformist tendency with hopes of renewing the Communist Party intellectually and politically.[203] As part of his ambition to become part of a new leadership, if not to actually take the top position as General Secretary, Jacques gave up his academic career to become editor in September 1977. As with other full-time party officers, Jacques had to take on additional responsibilities, such as chairing committees, preparing reports etc., which would later prove critical to support his position as MT's editor when challenged by internal opponents. It was also desirable because the position offered the possibility of bringing about changes in the party by working with other reformers in various positions in the party's hierarchy.

From his very first memorandum on *Marxism Today*, Jacques identified his ambitions for the periodical:

> To develop a journal which seeks to develop the political culture of the party and the left. It must create a new relationship between theory and practice (thereby seeking to overcome the elements of elitism, liberalism, etc., which stem from the Stalinist tradition).[204]

He makes it clear that, for MT to meet this objective, it would have to 'broaden the readership', which meant trying to 'de-ghettoise' the journal by includ-

---

202 Jacques 1996b.
203 Ibid.
204 Jacques 1977, p. 1.

ing 'significant [numbers of] non-party as well as party' readers.[205] The new editor asked why MT could not 'begin to play the role *Labour Monthly* used to'?[206] What was 'most striking about this readership is its *diversity*', and Jacques quotes a *Times* leader on the BRS, the politics of which has to hold together 'the Merseyside docker and the London women's libber', a left that is nonetheless fragmented, even within the party with its differing tendencies.[207] Confronted by this diversity of audiences, Jacques argues that MT 'must seek to cohere, unify and not simply reflect' each audience, even as he admits that they 'must try and cater for' each, which means making the journal 'available through a more diverse range of outlets'.[208]

From the beginning, Jacques wanted to reach both a non-party readership in addition to (more) CPGB readers and to work at developing a cohesive formation that would bridge the divide between different orientations and occupations: he saw this process as part of an objective of changing the party's culture as well. Even so, Jacques moved cautiously, using reports for the EC to try to persuade the leadership of the necessity of making changes to MT, such as permitting a theoretical journal the space to explore topical and strategic issues. Jacques's first report called for the leadership to move into a closer working relationship with MT and it identified different roles for the MT Editorial Board and the MT 'editorial collective' or 'editorial committee'.[209] The MTEB was to meet more often than it had done in the recent past to provide strategic thinking about the content, issues and direction while fulfilling a representative function for the regions, industry, intellectuals and cadres. The MTEC was to have responsibility for production, promotion and distribution.[210] Yet, Jacques was aware of how the MTEC might look to the leadership and wanted to head off any potential criticisms (and possible consequences), so he claimed that the MTEC did not control the journal because MT was the CPGB's 'theoretical journal'.[211]

---

205 Jacques 1977, p. 2.
206 Jacques 1977, p. 1. Dutt's LM could play its role because it did publish official CPGB policy but increasingly it offered a place for left-wing trade unionists to write in the 1970s. LM was published until 1981, seven years after Dutt's death.
207 Jacques 1977, p. 2 (original emphasis).
208 Jacques 1977, pp. 1, 2.
209 Jacques 1978c, p. 5. It appears that while it was not a 'collective' in the vision of equal input in decision-making and power sharing, it was referred to as both a 'collective' and, later, as a 'committee'. In either case, Jacques retained control over decisions in MT's production and distribution.
210 Jacques 1978c, pp. 4–5.
211 Jacques 1979e, p. 151. Jacques was responding at a time when some traditionalists raised concerns about MT's discussion groups that had been advertised in the periodical.

One of MT's key objectives, Jacques claimed, was to develop the party's political culture by establishing a closer, more concrete relationship between theoretical and practical work: raising the 'political level of our practical work while making our theoretical work more relevant to the needs, concerns and interests of our activists'.[212] MT also needed a broad remit to cover a wide range of issues, be interesting and carry out its role as the CPGB's 'theoretical and discussion journal' more effectively. Initially, Jacques and MTEC developed 'The Grid' to try and establish a means of covering the range of issues and developments across an annual cycle as well as monthly articles on 'strategic topical' and 'political topical' events and issues.[213] 'The Grid' appears to have disappeared during the development of the new second format, which was a concerted move to solve the weaknesses in presentation identified under Klugmann's editorship, and to expand the space available for articles and hence increase the diversity of topics, advertising etc.[214]

Marxism Today's first relaunch with the October 1979 issue, the first in the second format, was an important first step in trying to reach a broader audience of both workers and intellectuals on the left. Jacques's argument for MT's transformation was about making that relationship between theory and practice 'concrete'. MT could not be 'an academic journal aimed narrowly at professional intellectuals' because that would prevent it from establishing a 'closer relationship between theory and practice': it had to 'confront theoretical issues which have a concrete bearing on the practice and perspectives of the left', issues which feminism and the 'new social movements' sought to address.[215] His appeal to the leadership became an appeal to the membership via the party review, *Comment*, about four months before its relaunch, where Jacques emphasised that MT's links with the party gave it the potential to reach out to the labour movement, because of the CPGB's 'special relationship', as well as to NSMs;[216] the party provided the political 'anchorage' to a section of the left and the labour movement, which unaligned left journals lacked (something from which MT would choose to 'slip anchor' later in the 1980s).

Key to rethinking the role of a 'theoretical and discussion journal', as Jacques put it to the membership, was to link theory and practice while paying attention to contemporary developments, that MT had to address a combination of 'stra-

---

212   Jacques 1978c, p. 1.
213   Jacques 1978d.
214   Jacques 1978c, p. 2.
215   Jacques 1979e, p. 151.
216   The acronym 'NSM' always includes feminism and the women's movement, even though it is one of the oldest of social movements, except where its added for emphasis.

tegic questions' and 'topical political issues' (i.e. issues that were not sanctioned by the CPGB leadership or the party line), which meant internal party discussion and debates across the left: this is what theoretical debate was about in 'a revolutionary party'.[217] As a theoretical journal, therefore, MT needed greater latitude to 'explore the wider context, the deeper meanings of particular problems' rather than being used to promote the party line.[218] Even its writing style had been marked by 'mistaken ideas' as to what a theoretical journal was: theory was thought of 'as either the legitimation (or presentation) of the line in flowery marxist jargon, or the discussion of relatively abstruse issues with no obvious bearing on the practical tasks of the party', though in a more placatory manner, Jacques suggested that the CPGB had recently managed to break with this 'damaging conception'.[219]

This greater latitude meant, paradoxically, as Jacques himself called for a closer working relationship with the party leadership, that MT had to be an 'open' journal with both party and non-party contributors, because the CPGB was 'not the fount of all wisdom' and needed 'to draw together the ideas, learning and experiences of a wide range of people'; although Jacques claimed that there was even 'a substantial proportion of the readership' who were not members, this was probably more true of those issues that were sold at public events, such as the July issue at the CULs, where extra sales were noticeable, and it was to reach out to a broader, non-party left audience, many of whom were attending the CULs in substantial numbers, that Jacques's justified his argument.[220] This potential audience became increasingly important, not only as membership declined, but also if the CPGB was to be transformed into something more like a Eurocommunist-type organisation in the eyes of the reformists and if MT was going to have a role to play in the 'broad democratic alliance' and the Gramscian 'war of position'.

Even as Martin Jacques made his pitch, he reassured the leadership that the bulk of discussion would still take place within the context of the CPGB's strategy and orientation, where there was still much to be 'argued over'. It was this underlying tension between permitting open discussion and promoting the party line that Jacques was negotiating over, which the 1957 CIPD report had recognised but never resolved and which Jacques would have been well aware of since he was also a member of the 1977 CIPD (which reported in 1979). However, there were important differences between 1957 and 1979 in the polit-

217   Jacques 1979e, p. 151.
218   Ibid.
219   Ibid.
220   Ibid.

ical strategies and historical contexts. In the wake of 1956, politically isolated and on the defensive, the CPGB needed to consolidate its organisation. In 1977–79, Eurocommunist influence reached its peak within the party, Labour was in government and the left retained an air of confidence. Jacques made very clear links in his argument for this rethinking of MT's role with its presentation and desire to reach a broader public beyond the party. This 'creative tension' lay at the heart of MT, 'in its pages and in its production', as a 'major political challenge' because the periodical had 'to speak to and communicate with and between *different* audiences'.[221] Jacques's ambitions both to be party leader and to reform the party meant that he saw MT, at least in part, as the vehicle to make changes.

Worried by the growing support for reformists and fearing a backlash from conservative elements, the leadership backed moves to restrict reformist influence in the leadup to the 1979 Congress.[222] Despite the leadership's attempts to balance the rival tendencies, battles broke out for control of branches, districts and advisory committees. The London District Communist Party, for example, became a centre of the traditionalist opposition, though different factions controlled different branches within the LDCP: e.g. reformists dominated the Hackney and Lewisham branches. The leadership refused to intervene against the traditionalists despite urging from reformists, while reformists also used the apparatus against their opponents where they had control, and this, in turn, generated complaints to the leadership against reformists abusing their positions.[223] The Executive Committee, for example, resisted calls to intervene against the LDCP leadership because of allegations of abusing its power; the London Student Advisory warned that the leadership's failure to deal with the LDCP leadership and 'opponents of the BRS' would cause problems in the future.[224] MT's attempt to set up readers' groups was stopped by the EC because they said it could lead to 'factional activity': critics accused Jacques of trying to establish a dual power structure outside of party control.[225]

Established by the 1977 Congress, the second CIPD submitted a majority report signed by all Commissioners, while its six Eurocommunist members, including Jacques, also submitted a set of alternative proposals, prior to the 1979 NPC. The EC agreed to keep discussion on the report confined to the party

---

221 Ibid. (original emphasis).
222 Andrews 1995a, pp. 239–43.
223 E.g. Mullen 1978; EC 1979a.
224 Barron 1978; EC 1978; EC 1979a.
225 The EC only acted nine months after MT first announced the groups (EC 1979c, p. 1).

review, *Comment*, and the CPGB Women's Group's journal, *Link*.[226] MT's exclusion from acting as a vehicle for internal debate was what Jacques had wanted so that the journal would not be seen as tied to the party in case it conveyed the idea that the leadership sanctioned its articles, which was put into effect when the 'Editorial Comments' section was removed from the October 1979, second-format launch issue. However, despite the leadership's support for the party's revised 1977 programme, they were unwilling to contemplate the necessary organisational changes to make the party more democratic and accountable to the membership, which the reformists had argued were necessary to the spirit and line of the new BRS. Approximately two-thirds of the delegates rejected the alternative proposals, which not only disheartened many reformists, but also left the party with a political strategy that was, on the one hand, more attuned to the shifting social and political currents of the time, and, on the other hand, wedded to an older, inflexible, hierarchical structure; combined with the leadership's 'managerialism', this situation only furthered the party's inability to act decisively.[227]

Subsequently, prominent reformists found themselves voted off committees or had their positions 'neutralised' months after Thatcher's Tories defeated the Labour government: Jacques was 'thrown off' the Political Committee after the 1979 Congress; Dave Cook, National Organiser, had his job description rewritten in 1979 and many of his initiatives blocked; Sarah Benton resigned as *Comment* editor in 1980 because of the hostility of leading members.[228] This downturn in the fortunes of the leading reformists, paralleled and was affected by political setbacks of western Eurocommunist parties, which contributed to the loss of more than 27 percent of CPGB members (6,853 out of 25,293) between 1977 and 1981, including many Gramscian intellectuals: a loss that rivalled that of 1956.[229] However, the failure of the reformists to gain control of the party had been preceded by the loss of some of the ultra-orthodox and Stalinist groupings, including the Surrey branch that formed the NCP just weeks before the 1977 NPC, to the chagrin of the remaining traditionalists.

Nevertheless, there was support for MT from party loyalists and leading members, such as Dave Priscott, George Matthews and Bert Pearce, who did support the new 1977 draft of the BRS but opposed organisational reform.

---

226 EC 1979b.
227 Andrews 1995a, p. 242.
228 Benton 1980; EC 1981a; Jacques 1996b.
229 Andrews 1995a, pp. 242–4; Callaghan 1988, p. 242. However, it was not only reformists that left the party; many traditionalists, like Irene Brennan, also chose to leave because of the strife (Brennan 1996).

Responding to complaints about MT, Priscott argued that it had a role in developing a British Marxist tradition, 'as per the BRS', and that the leadership should encourage those, like Jacques, attempting to do so.[230] Since MT was 'trying to bring our theory closer to contemporary political problems', this was a 'contentious area', and while Priscott did not 'agree with everything' in the periodical, he argued that it was necessary to 'make more of a deep analysis of the Tory Party' etc.[231] Priscott reminded the EC of resolutions passed at the 1979 Congress, which called for focusing on the rise of radical right-wing ideologies and their popular appeal, and on the 'failure of the labour and progressive movements' to take the initiative away from the ruling class.[232] Priscott, Matthews, Pearce and other party loyalists demonstrate that MT was able to garner support amongst both leading and ordinary members, who were not necessarily interested in internal reforms, or did not wholly support leading reformists, like Jacques, Cook and Benton. Their support, however, would prove crucial in the 1980s as these divisions turned into a virtual 'civil war'.

Between 1979 and 1981, when Jacques was no longer a member of the PC and, therefore, had much less influence on the day-to-day operations of the party, he had more time to concentrate on making MT a success by extending the range of contributors, advertising and distribution outlets as well as working on design, layout and editorial style. This focus was serendipitous for Jacques as prospects for the left in the Labour Party increased, MT's promotion of the timely analyses of Labour's decline ('Forward March of Labour Halted?') and the rise of the right ('Thatcherism') ensured the periodical a prominence on the left which was enhanced by *The Guardian*'s inclusion and promotion of MT's key contributions during the 1980s.[233] MT's orientation towards the Labour Left was part of Jacques's promotion of MT at the TUC and Labour Party conferences that included interviews with union and Labour Left leaders,[234] although this would change after 1983, as MT became increasingly polemical in its ideological struggles against the Labour Left and left-wing 'shibboleths' and in favour of centre-left and social-democratic approaches to Labour politics.[235]

Marxism Today's success, however, also cultivated resentment amongst some party members, not least Tony Chater and traditionalists at *The Morn-*

---

230   Priscott 1980.
231   Ibid.
232   Ibid.
233   Chapter 5.
234   E.g. Wright 1978; Benn 1980.
235   See Chapter 2 for the ideological 'war of position' and Chapter 5 for how this played out in terms of media coverage.

ing Star.²³⁶ At the 1977 Congress, an amendment critical of Chater's editorship of *The Star* was passed despite the leadership's opposition to it.²³⁷ This was 'a highly remarkable if not unique outcome' at a NPC and 'indicative of the degree of grassroots dissatisfaction with the party's daily organ', though the subsequent report on *The Star* 'was a rather bland and anodyne document' which just encouraged everyone 'to do better'.²³⁸ Chater, resentful of any criticisms, refused to take notice of the Congress decision and circulation continued to decline as *The Star* showed no improvements in presentation or content. The outcome of the report was thus to increase the hostility felt between Chater and his critics, and to fuel his antipathy towards the leadership for not preventing NPC from passing the motion.

With no let-up in *The Star*'s decline, strong criticisms of its editorship were made in motions submitted for the 1981 NPC. MT, by contrast, went from strength to strength in its presentation, design, circulation, advertising and distribution. Just prior to the 1981 Congress, MT announced that it was going to be distributed nationwide through W.H. Smith's newsagents beginning with the October 1981 issue. As MT succeeded where *The Star* failed, MT received kudos from leading officials and rank-and-file members alike: indeed, as party membership and public presence declined, MT was fast becoming the CPGB's only 'success story' and its success was inextricably intertwined with the editor's, as the party's 'public face', and Jacques was duly elected back onto the PC at Congress. Against Chater's expectations, especially since he was still a member of the PC, the EC swung its support behind the criticisms of *The Star* during the debate on the motion: Chater felt betrayed and the traditionalist opposition secured a useful ally.

That the traditionalists nearly succeeded in defeating the EC's stand against the USSR's invasion of Afghanistan indicates the continuing strength of feeling for the birthplace of the Bolshevik Revolution amongst many party members, including many who could not be labelled as orthodox, conservative, Stalinist or traditionalist.²³⁹ It was not always clear where all the delegates would line up on voting because of a certain amount of fluidity on different issues amongst party members of all sides, as in the case of Chater himself. The

---

236 *The Star*'s staff reflected the internal party divisions between traditionalists, loyalists and reformists.
237 Chater was part of the leadership and not yet allied to the traditionalist opposition.
238 Thompson 1992, p. 174.
239 The traditionalists received 47 percent of the votes against the EC's 53 percent: the closest the leadership had come to being defeated at any congress. The experience would be repeated once more, in the vote on the 'New Times' manifesto at the 1989 NPC.

attacks on MT, therefore, cannot be seen as just lining up pro-Soviet Stalinists versus pro-reform Eurocommunists because, as Geoff Andrews argues, the real fight was developing over the Tony Lane article and other criticisms of the labour movement which highlighted the increasing divisions between 'militant labourism' and 'socialist humanism' as the two dominant, broad tendencies within the party, which I have labelled 'traditionalist' and 'reformist' respectively.[240] Internal divisions sharpened and MT became increasingly the focus of traditionalists' attacks on the party's 'revisionism'. Jacques's re-election back onto the PC came with the leadership's support and each would prove to be a valuable ally to the other during the next four years of internal strife.

The 'traditionalist' opposition was an amalgam of several groupings, of which two of the most cohesive were those fronted by the journals, *Straight Left* and *The Leninist*. *Straight Left* was the first traditionalist faction formed in the CPGB in the aftermath of Labour's defeat in 1979 and it promoted its paper as a 'broad labour movement journal'.[241] *The Leninist* faction was a 'shadowy' group formed by a splinter from the NCP's youth wing in 1981 that re-entered the CPGB.[242] *The Leninist* was turned from a quarterly into a monthly in May 1984 in an attempt to intervene more actively in the party as the 'civil war' heated up. Attempts by the leadership to stop members from contributing to these journals were not always successful; the CPGB leadership reversed an earlier decision not to allow members to write for *Straight Left* because the faction observed restrictions in its criticisms and because of its connections with 'labour movement figures'.[243] *The Leninist* was, however, proscribed: it promoted 'ultra-bolshevism' and denounced all versions of the BRS.[244] Although these groups opposed many of the same things, they did not necessarily approve of each other nor agree to the same objectives beyond defeating the reformists and the leadership. Their differences proved to be greater obstacles than the need for unity to overcome their 'common enemy'.

The first serious challenge to Jacques's editorship, nevertheless, came in August 1982 from Chater and the party's Industrial Organiser, Mick Costello, when they launched a public attack over that issue's feature article on trade unions. The author, Tony Lane, a sociologist and party member, criticised some

---

240   Andrews 2004.
241   Thompson 1992, pp. 181–3.
242   Ibid. They operated out of a post office box number in London (Mitchell 1984, p. 5).
243   Thompson 1992, p. 182; EC 1981b. This is an interesting contrast to *The Reasoner*'s history in the 1950s or *Red Rag*'s in the early 1970s or of other papers seen as 'factional' by the leadership.
244   Thompson 1992, p. 182; EC 1981b.

union officials 'sharing in the expense account syndrome: the franchise of perks and fiddles', which he saw as part of a 'crisis of legitimacy' affecting the labour movement.[245] One critic even agreed that Lane's article was 'simply nondescript'; however, it was the final sections that were deemed 'gravely offensive'.[246] Critics argued for solidarity with shop stewards and unions because of Thatcher's attacks, rhetorical and legislative, on unions. Two MTEB members argued for closer liaison between the party, Industrial Organiser and MT on articles relevant to the TUC but they directed their criticisms to McLennan, as party leader, and to the PC.[247] However, others, including some union officials who harboured reservations about the article, argued for 'our right to be self-critical' and that Thatcherism's existence did not 'suspend this right'.[248]

Costello's attack appeared on the front page of *The Morning Star* and it was written as if it had the Executive Committee's backing.[249] Costello used his press contacts to get the *Daily Mirror* and *The Telegraph* to pick up Lane's comments to help press home his attack on *Marxism Today* by pointing to the 'anti-left *Mirror*' picking up Lane's article (and MT by implication) as 'anti-working class'.[250] Jacques only learned of the attack upon his return home from holiday and he assumed that the EC had taken a decision in his absence; otherwise, such public criticism of one party publication in another party paper was inexplicable without the leadership's agreement, which was why he thought his position looked 'untenable'.[251] He was also worried that he would lose MT just as it was taking off. Yet, he refused to accept that he had done anything wrong and told McLennan that he would resign if the EC allowed these criticisms to stand.[252] As events unfolded, it became clear that not only had Costello blown Lane's comments way out of proportion, but he also had acted without the EC's approval.[253] The EC also recognised that Chater's and Costello's actions

---

245 Lane 1982, pp. 13, 11–13.
246 Foster 1982b.
247 Foster 1982a; Seifert 1982.
248 Lanning 1982; Gardiner 1982; Betty Matthews 1982.
249 Well aware of Benton's predicament as *Comment* editor and of the pushback against the reformists at the 1979 Congress, Jacques thought he was being cautious about what he published, which is why he was shocked that Lane's article had caused 'offence' (Jacques 1996b).
250 Thompson 1992, p. 187.
251 Jacques 1996b.
252 Jacques had established a personal relationship with McLennan having taught his son at Bristol; McLennan, in turn, was supportive of Jacques and MT. Jacques made his threat only known to McLennan, although McLennan did not view it as a 'threat' (Jacques 1996b; McLennan 1996).
253 Jacques 1996b.

threatened to undermine its own authority and so it backed Jacques fully, although he was mildly reproached for not having 'consulted more widely' before publishing the article, the EC defended the editor's right 'to explore issues'.[254] Here we have differences in both expectations amongst party officials and readers that party publications act as 'voices' for the party and its line, even when such expectations are used opportunistically in organisational (i.e. internal) politics, which also highlights the ongoing tensions between party and periodical, and leaders and editors, first properly recognised in the 1957 CIPD Report.

The Chaterites were nonetheless fairly successful at promoting *Marxism Today* as 'anti-working class' and 'anti-trade union' because it was unusual for a Communist publication to be openly critical of the labour movement, especially as Thatcher's government increased attacks on it: the reaction to Lane's criticisms, despite their mildness, are an indication of how unusual it was at the time. Such criticisms would have also been seen, implicitly or not, as a criticism of the party's 'militant labourism' tendency. This incident demonstrates how minor criticisms of union staff could provoke the 'militant labourist' section of the traditionalist wing, since many party union activists were worried that their influence within the labour movement was being undermined. It also demonstrates that MT, especially as its success grew, had become the primary focus of internal attacks against reformists. Of course, MT's popularity with many Labour Left supporters at the time, which was a period of at least nominal unity across the left, gave it a certain prominence within the Labour Party even as it was in competition with Labour's first (and only) theoretical and discussion journal, *New Socialist*.[255]

The EC was inundated with motions from party branches over the Lane affair as well as others dealing with subsidiary issues, such as *The Star*'s refusal to publish letters critical of the actions of Chater and Costello.[256] Even with the backing of one hundred delegates to the TUC annual conference, Chater and Costello were unsuccessful in trying to turn the party leadership against MT. Instead, they helped bring the internal divisions into the open in the run-up to the 1983 Congress. MT's critics focused on the Lane article and on Roy Medvedev's article on the USSR (some suspected it was actually the Medvedev article that was the primary motivation behind the Chater-Costello attack, but criticism of the USSR would not have mobilised as much support as playing the

---

254   EC 1982b.
255   See Chapter 5.
256   EC 1982a, p. 4; EC 1982c; G. Matthews 1982.

'workerist' card did).[257] A third article by Bob Rowthorn, a CPGB academic, published in MT's May 1982 issue, on western Europe and the 'common market' also raised concerns among some orthodox members because they claimed it supported Britain's membership in the European Economic Community contrary to party policy, even though Rowthorn actually refuted such claims.[258]

In one small, albeit important, matter, however, these attacks did bring about change. The MTEB eventually agreed to the publication of a 'disclaimer', similar to those published in other non-party periodicals in the marketplace: 'The views expressed by authors are personal and not necessarily those of the editor or editorial board'.[259] Introduced in the February 1983 issue, almost one year after the introduction of a letters-to-the-editor page, the disclaimer provided further support for Jacques's claim that articles published in MT were individuals' views rather than statements of MT's editorial line. It was also part of MT's ongoing transformation from a party journal into a magazine, where the editorial content is not necessarily that determined by the party-publisher but by the editor's solicitation and acceptance of party and non-party contributions.

For those who supported the magazine's editorial line and political direction, or to whom its changes in presentation appealed, or who at least appreciated broader debates about contemporary political and cultural issues, it appeared that *Marxism Today* was under attack because it represented 'the threat of a good example'. It must have been infuriating for those who opposed Jacques and MT because it was succeeding where *The Morning Star* was failing, by increasing circulation as *The Star*'s was decreasing, and it was happening for all the 'wrong reasons', according to its critics. Where traditionalists continued to argue for the centrality of the working class to 'socialist advance', MT talked about building a counter-hegemonic force by bringing together a cross-class, 'popular alliance', which would not only include labour, but also appeal across the left and to new social movements. MT could point to its strategy as part of the 'broad democratic alliance', which complemented the CPGB's increasing openness towards women's, peace, ethnic, gay and lesbian, and student movements: i.e. the NSMs. Between 1981 and 1983, MT and the CPGB initiated or became involved in a number of broad campaigns, the most important of

---

257 Jacques 1996b. The CPSU's International Bureau got Roy Medvedev, who was living in England, mixed up with his brother, Zhores Medvedev, who at that time was a dissident living in Moscow, and criticised the CPGB leadership for publishing an article by the latter (Johnstone 1995).
258 Rowthorn 1982a, 1982b; Jacques 1982a.
259 MT 1983c; Jacques 1982c; MTEB 1982b.

which was the national People's March for Jobs, because it was the closest manifestation of the BDA, according to Jacques.²⁶⁰

The beginnings of MT's media coverage enhanced its position *vis-à-vis* the party leadership and many ordinary members, and this coverage was reinforced by public conferences and weekend events that it began organising in 1982. This year also marked an attempt to bring together socialist intellectuals from the Labour Left, the CPGB (including Jacques), the Socialist Workers' Party and other left organisations and unaffiliated individuals together under the banner of the Socialist Society. However, this attempt at a broad unity did not last as it became fragmented over such issues as how to counter Thatcherism, which remained a contentious issue on the left at that time. Later that same year, however, MT launched its first weekend event, which replaced the annual Communist University of London, as part of its promotion of 'left unity', which was held in October 1982: the 'Moving Left Show',²⁶¹ which attracted over 1,200 people from across the left. The key debate took place between a leading member of the PCI, Giorgio Napolitano, and Tony Benn, the leader of the Labour Left, which signalled the beginnings of a shift in MT's position. The MLS helped to establish MT as an increasingly independent player on the left political stage beyond the 'party ghetto' and highlighted its increasing focus on various leading and up-and-coming Labour personalities, which provoked yet more criticisms from traditionalists: they pointed to the first favourable press reports²⁶² of MT as proof of its 'questionable' politics.

Three subsequent MT weekend events, 'Left Alive' (1984), 'Left Unlimited' (1986) and 'New Times' (1989), attracted larger crowds and more media coverage than MLS; equally important, however, were the numerous smaller, local events, meetings and festivals that were spun off from these national (i.e. London) events, such as 'Women Alive' (1986) and Gramsci anniversary (1987) events in Cardiff and Birmingham.²⁶³ These events all helped to increase MT's public profile and spread its ideas, and when high profile contributors, such as Beatrix Campbell and Stuart Hall, spoke at events that, in turn, helped to generate local media coverage.

---

260   Jacques 1981.
261   This title had first been used in 1976 by the CPGB for a very popular conference with attendees of around 500 for each of two sessions. See Jacques 1976.
262   E.g. Rutherford 1982.
263   Feminism was never integral to MT; it was always an 'add on'. Some of the most important feminist contributors were: Beatrix Campbell, Cynthia Cockburn, Tricia Davis and Suzanne Moore.

The fight over interpretations of representations (e.g. Lane affair) points to the importance and significance of the periodical's or paper's constitutive function in depiction and representation of a political organisation and its politics. In this struggle, MT's position became clearly identified with that of the reformists within the party while being viewed as a threat to the traditionalists's understanding of Communism and the role of the Communist Party. Similarly, *The Star* was increasingly relegated to the limitations of its ability to act in a journalistic manner as the CPGB's voice in the national public sphere.

It is equally important to note that MT's ability to operate as an 'independent player' on the political stage was dependent on three key factors: (1) it was successful enough in securing more sales and media coverage, which generated public interest; (2) it continued to invest (and use) financial (and even readership) support to enable the development and expansion of production and distribution, including continued party funding; and (3) the 'third-party' endorsements which enabled MT to use as arguments for point (2) against traditionalists and other internal critics, and to highlight point (1) for securing more sales. All three of these factors were enhanced through media coverage, the central link between them all and which MT leveraged as part of its move against internal critics.[264]

16 'Reaction & Realignment' 1983–87

As internal divisions became more openly expressed after the Lane affair (and to a lesser extent around Medvedev on the USSR and Rowthorn on the EEC),[265] it became crucial for Martin Jacques to counter the ongoing criticisms of *Marxism Today* by operating at two levels to persuade both the leadership and the Communist Party that nothing was amiss. MT was gaining support for its ideas by sending contributors to speak at party meetings and by producing articles for internal bulletins;[266] special conferences were introduced in 1983 and 1984 to help explain MT's (changing) role to party members.[267] In his March 1983 Report to the Executive Committee, part of his regular duties as a party officer, Jacques justified MT to the leadership and defended it against its traditionalist critics, by reiterating the party's original rationale for publishing it: 'to promote Marxist thought over a wide-ranging field of interest and to encourage as much

---

264 Chapters 3 and 5.
265 Medvedev 1982; Rowthorn 1982a.
266 Webster 1980, 1983.
267 Farrington 1984; Jacques 1984a.

discussion as possible with this object in view'.²⁶⁸ In contrast to the party's declining membership, MT's success spoke for itself: it had reached its largest audience to date with sales more than double its 1977 level at 11,500 by March 1983,²⁶⁹ part of its continued growth since October 1981 with the nationwide newsagent launch. Party readership had held steady, if not increased, and MT could even claim to be the party's best source of recruits.²⁷⁰ The conflict for party leaders was that while MT was getting more coverage or mentions of the CPGB in the national press, these were largely criticisms of the party or ideas that were not promoting the party's fortunes. Contrary to the old adage, not all publicity is good publicity.²⁷¹

Whereas the MT editor's reports were infrequent and of minor interest to the EC prior to 1979, the changes Jacques initiated brought about greater interest and scrutiny. In the aftermath of the Lane Affair, and critics' charges of producing articles contrary to the party line, Jacques used his reports to the EC, party committees and congress to justify and legitimise the changes to MT, including an emphasis that changes had been taken in conjunction with the party, via the MTEB and the EC. Jacques defended MT's changes, agreed to by the leadership and MTEB, on the basis that it was bringing together the theoretical and practical in its approach, and MT's success demonstrated the need for a 'flexible and open Marxist analysis' which was neither dogmatic nor ladened down with jargon.²⁷²

Jacques claimed that MT was not only an expression of the 1977 BRS but also part of the 'creative development of the British Marxist tradition': a party phrase that he invoked to justify MT's record, sales success and even the internal party controversy that encircled the periodical. This tradition could only be built upon by engaging with 'a broad range of experiences, traditions and ideas', justifying MT's need to reach beyond the party.²⁷³ Countering criticisms that MT had 'consistently sought to be topical', Jacques argued that the most important change since 1977 was the shift to the major political issues of the day, which

---

268 CPGB 1957c cited in Jacques 1983, p. 1.
269 Before 1979, only sales of special issues reached 5,000 or more. For example, Gollan's assessment of 'Socialist Democracy', in the January 1976 MT, nearly sold out the 7,500 print run.
270 Jacques 1983, pp. 6–7, 13. CPGB ads in MT attracted 83 membership applications and enquiries between October 1981 and March 1982 (McKay 1982), surpassing *The Star* in recruitment, though it is an especially low number for a party that was meant to represent a political alternative to Labour.
271 This is taken up in more detail in Chapter 5.
272 Jacques 1983, p. 2.
273 Ibid.

meant addressing 'the concrete problems facing the Left' (e.g. SDP, unemployment, Falklands): MT's success could be seen in the debates taking place across the left on 'The Forward March of Labour Halted?' and 'Thatcherism'.[274]

Through a series of political interventions, Jacques argued for '*Marxism Today*'s approach' to the subjects covered by justifying it as fulfilling the broad democratic alliance in substance and as endorsed in the revised 1977 party programme. MT's transformation was justified to both the leadership and the membership on the basis that it ensured that the party would be better prepared to engage with new constituencies, which made it necessary to expand the range of contributors to include non-party authors, to broaden its appeal and enhance its quality. The breadth of articles drew 'more people both closer to the Party and involved them in helping to develop the strategic perspectives, analysis and understanding of our Party and the wider Left'.[275] This appeal to a broader range of contributors and audiences, of engaging in a BDA through publishing, meant 'a dialogue with forces in the first instance outside the Party on the Left, but beyond that also outside the organised Left'.[276] Here, Jacques identifies the need to go beyond even Labour (i.e. 'the organised Left') to the NSMs and grassroot community activists. Since theory was 'intimately linked to action', MT had to include activists as contributors and address them as readers to try and break down the division between theorists and activists, and such ambitions meant making its language, design and coverage more accessible.[277]

Jacques conceded that MT needed to publish more articles 'of a strictly theoretical character – on Marxism, the State, the economic crisis and so forth', but he stressed that MT published a wide range of viewpoints and not only views which were against CPGB policy, as his critics claimed.[278] It was not MT's duty to present congress resolutions and the position of the party *per se*, 'but rather in the totality of what it publishes to make clear the stance of our Party on the major issues of British and international politics'.[279] Assumptions about a communist theoretical journal included the idea that it should promote the party line. In some ways, MT was doing just that: the CPGB finally adopted the analyses of Thatcherism and the labour movement's crisis at the 37th (1981) National Party Congress, two to three years after MT had introduced them to readers. Such CPGB resolutions that were adopted at the NPC helped to jus-

---

274 Jacques 1983, p. 3. See Chapter 2.
275 Ibid.
276 Jacques 1983, p. 4.
277 Ibid.
278 Jacques 1983, p. 5.
279 Jacques 1983, p. 6.

tify Jacques's claim to be representing (or *re*-presenting) policies and positions adopted by the party, even if that was not necessarily the function or role of a communist 'theoretical and discussion journal'.

Marxism Today was reaching a watershed, however, as it began distancing itself from the Bennite Left, a process which quickened in the disputes over the interpretation of Thatcher's second general election victory of June 1983. The consolidation of changes in design, layout, contributors and production had brought about a much heralded triumph in increased circulation and distribution, which continued to help ward off criticisms, although sales' success was not sufficient protection from criticism in the long run. As MT's prestige grew with the increasingly favourable media coverage, its critics also responded to what they saw as a move away from core subjects of Communist ideology for analysis and discussion, such as the USSR, the industrial working class and trade unions, as it focussed on issues, events and personalities more closely attuned to the Labour Party as part of its attempts to increase its readership and broaden its newsagent audiences and, in turn, help to influence the left.

The critiques that MT fostered might have encountered greater resistance in their reception within the party except for the fact that Chater and his allies refused to accept the disciplinary actions imposed by the leadership and the latter's attempts at reconciliation.[280] Despite the uneasy relations between party leaders and *The Morning Star*, the EC initiated a campaign to increase the party newspaper's sales in January 1983. However, Chater and Costello remained committed to carrying on their campaign against MT, Jacques and the leadership. Not only did Chater ignore attempts by the EC and the PC to meet with him, but he also fanned the flames of animosity by appointing Costello as *The Star*'s Industrial Correspondent less than two months after his resignation from the post of Industrial Organiser and without consulting the EC. The EC was compelled to take action against this breach of party discipline: Chater, Costello and deputy editor, David Whitfield, were censured.[281] The Chater group succeeded in defeating the leadership's candidates at the annual general meeting of *The Star*'s shareholders in June 1983; this 'hi-jacking' of the paper definitively soured relations between the EC and the Management Committee of the People's Press Printing Society:[282] the CPGB had been described

---

280   Thompson 1992, pp. 185–6.
281   EC 1983, p. 3.
282   In 1946, the PPPS was set up so that the paper would survive if the CPGB was made illegal, as had happened in the opening years of the Second World War; the EC exercised control through the election of its nominees to the PPPS Management Committee.

as an 'outside body' trying to 'interfere' in *The Star*'s affairs.²⁸³ This was contrary to the party's normal relationship with its daily newspaper. This victory gave the Chater group confidence that they would be able to win elections to the EC at the 38th Congress.

Despite the depths of their negative feelings towards MT and the leadership, the traditionalists were not united. The Chaterites promoted their version of 'class politics' based around a defence of trade unions and adopted a more sympathetic line on the Soviet bloc to attract more orthodox members, especially *Straight Left* supporters. However, *Straight Left* was critical of the Chaterites for their 'opportunism': as part of the EC, Chater and Costello had supported the EC's line on Czechoslovakia and Afghanistan.²⁸⁴ *The Star* group and *Straight Left* did, however, realise that they needed to work together if they were to have a chance to succeed: they agreed on an alternative electoral list of 42 names for the EC.²⁸⁵ However, this co-operation did not even last for the duration of 38th NPC, once the leadership denounced the alternative electoral list and *Congress Truth* (the *Straight Left*'s daily bulletin during Congress).

> *Congress Truth* offended the Chaterites, who regarded it as excessive and adventurist – apart from the fact that it did not spare them either – and piously disowned as a serious breach of discipline the alternative list they had collaborated in producing, thus destroying all possibility of combining the two oppositions.²⁸⁶

Regardless of the respective positions held by these two groups, their inability to work together is a classic example of how far left groups can descend into sectarianism, which is often expressed as one-time allies are suddenly worse than the original opponents against whom they were organising collectively.

As with many in the party leadership, Jacques was well aware of the dangers that the opposition represented. In an effort to try and deflect or pre-empt criticisms, *Marxism Today* published a roundtable discussion between four party members representing views of the different tendencies, including traditional-

---

283   This comment infuriated many ordinary members when they realised that 'their' paper was referring to their party as an 'outside body' (Thompson 1992, p. 186; see Mitchell 1984, pp. 18–27).
284   Teachers on the 1979 Anglo-East German exchange refused to send proceeds from fundraising to *The Star* because of Chater's 'Eurocommunist' and 'anti-Soviet' policies (Taylor 1987, p. 4).
285   Mitchell 1984, pp. 52–7; Thompson 1992, pp. 183, 186–7, 189.
286   Thompson 1992, p. 190.

ist, in the November 1983 issue, just in time for the NPC.[287] At congress, Jacques admitted to a subsidy of £567 per issue, which opponents attempted to use to discredit MT despite the relatively small amount that that figure represented when counted against monthly income and expenditures of around £6,500 and £7,900 respectively (Table 3). Such criticism ignores the fact that all parties subsidise their publications to a greater or lesser degree, and not just the CPGB. Although MT's subsidies were still small at this point (at least those which were admitted to publicly), and especially when compared to other party papers and agencies, they were well spent in terms of production values, distribution and public profile.

However, it was the use of non-party writers and critiques of left 'shibboleths' that were much more controversial and led to a composite resolution on MT.[288] The motion praised MT for its design and appearance, recruitment of new members, doubling of circulation and 'its growing influence and respect on the left, in the trade union movement and amongst progressive and democratic forces' and its 'striking analyses of the current political situation', and its success was 'a demonstration of the possibilities opened to the party by a bold presentation of the ideas and approach' of the BRS.[289] Nevertheless, the motion pointed to six areas for improvement: the party's contribution should 'be featured more consistently and in a more lively way' (the authors of the motion were clearly concerned with how the party's views might be presented if MT were compelled to do so); more party contributors, including 'members at all levels and across a spectrum of views'; more women writers; greater coverage of feminism and black people; to maintain and develop the involvement of trade unionists; and to increase space for letters and discussion.[290] Letters-to-the-editor is one type of contribution that has traditionally been of great interest to readers. More importantly, it was a means by which MT could at least claim to host a range of other views without having to expend a lot of space. The motion reflected criticisms that MT was not permitting all views equal access and that it marginalised the CPGB's involvement in the periodical. As long as he could have retained his autonomy from the leadership as well as his opponents, Jacques would not have implemented those recommendations except as a 'token' change in some way.

The 1983 Congress enabled the leadership, allied with reformists and supported by 'rank-and-file loyalists who ... resented the "hi-jack" of their newspaper',

---

287 Jacques 1996c.
288 NPC 1983.
289 Ibid.
290 Ibid.

to gain the upper hand, which ensured that most traditionalist opponents, including Chater and Costello, were voted off of the EC.[291] The leadership and reformists combined to suspend or remove many of their opponents from the party apparatus. However, though the leadership had gained the upper hand at congress, the oppositionists, representing around two-fifths of delegates, remained a potent threat to both the leadership and MT. Low-level 'civil wars' in branches heated up, except this time the EC was prepared to intervene against the traditionalists, when and where possible: it removed them from staff positions, and closed down districts and branches to prevent them from sending oppositionist delegates to congress.

When the London District Communist Party Secretary died, the PC appointed Ian McKay, a loyal party worker, to the post; against traditionalist opposition, the leadership closed down the LDCP's own congress in November 1984, expelling those who refused to comply: *Straight Left* followers walked out with party loyalists leaving their erstwhile allies behind to face disciplinary action.[292] Other factional groups, such as *The Leninist*, were banned because their objectives were 'to conduct a factional battle within the Communist Party to reverse Congress policy and to oppose the elected leadership'.[293] Feelings were intense on both sides; at one point, when rumours of an impending compromise between the leadership and the Chaterites began circulating in some of the mainstream media coverage, one party member argued against any compromise to get rid of 'Stalinist hangovers'.[294] In effect, the survival of the leadership and its supporters, alongside the reformists in their alliance, meant amputating parts of the party to save the party.

The CPGB's crisis and loss of control over *The Star* left the leadership without its daily paper for only the second time since it was launched on 1 January 1930.[295] It forced the party to rely on its internal monthly party review, *Focus*, as its primary means of communicating with members, while MT became the CPGB's only public face that further strengthened its hand *vis-à-vis* the leadership. Though MT continued to intervene in the debates over the significance of Labour's 1983 electoral defeat, it did provide some space for internal debates, particularly in the run-up to the 1985 Congress.[296] However, this attention to

---

291 Thompson 1992, p. 186.
292 EC 1984d, 1984e. Only five out of 31 EC members opposed McKay's appointment, but there were more letters protesting than supporting the EC's actions in the archive file.
293 EC 1984a.
294 Thompson 1984; EC 1984b.
295 The first time was from January 1941 to September 1942.
296 E.g. Cook 1985; Priscott 1983.

internal debate was justified by claiming that these were similar issues facing the rest of the left in the 'realignment of the left' via the struggle between 'hard' and 'soft' lefts to decide Labour's political direction.

Despite their own criticisms of the practice of democratic centralism, it worked to the reformists' advantage in their battles with their traditionalist opponents in 1983–85, as the leadership found itself trying to manoeuvre against those traditionalists and conservatives who took control of the party's daily newspaper, *The Morning Star*. Nevertheless, democratic centralism in practice failed to stop the emergence of factions because each one sought to promote their own interpretations of the BRS as the only correct understanding and organised to try and win support for their positions.

The importance of *Marxism Today*'s public profile and strategic interventions in left debates positioned it within the CPGB's public work, enhanced by continuing increases in circulation and national media coverage. The party also recognised that MT brought it 'a great deal of credit' through its interventions in, and initiation of, political debates, and because it attracted people who would not normally come to its public meetings.[297] If MT appealed to a majority of members, not necessarily because they agreed with its analyses, but because MT represented a successful Communist enterprise,[298] then many loyalists believed that they were moving into the mainstream of public debate because of MT's 'public relations success'.[299]

The pressing issue facing the EC was *The Morning Star*'s break from the party and its refusal to abide by party decisions. The EC brought the 39th Congress forward to May 1985 to mobilise the rank-and-file to win back control of the PPPS at its AGM in June. In the run-up to congress, MT published a number of articles that were critical of the traditionalists' positions and sought to win over other party members. Both camps had sought to out-do each other in their support for the National Union of Mineworkers during the 1984–85 miners' strike, as the demonstration of solidarity with the labour movement was crucial to winning over the majority of members (or at least their delegates). Although a number of leading NUM officials, who were also CPGB members, including Mick McGahey, President of the Scottish NUM, supported MT, the latter still

---

297 Temple 1984, p. 4.
298 Andrews 1998. Andrews points out that there was a tradition of loyalty between members of the same branch, even when they disagreed with each other's views; so your branch comrades might cheer you on when giving a speech at congress but still vote against your motion for political reasons.
299 Samuel 1985, pp. 18–19.

expressed reservations about the failure of NUM leaders to call for a ballot on the strike and to do more to win public opinion.[300]

As its continuing high media profile and the CPGB's adoption of the themes promoted through its pages angered traditionalists, MTEC prepared an eight-page pamphlet for the Special Congress delegates which addressed criticisms and highlighted the periodical's achievements.[301] MT had to win over those who were uncertain about it and its ideas, and as the majority still looked to the leadership for direction, the support of McLennan, McGahey, Betty and George Matthews, and others amongst this older generation, was crucial.[302]

The oppositionists ranged from those who were 'hard-liners', who opposed the BRS and anything but unswerving loyalty to the USSR, as with *The Leninist*, to the *Straight Left* Stalinists, who would abide by party discipline, but otherwise maintained a faith in the USSR as the home of 'socialist revolution',[303] to *The Star* group, who portrayed themselves as the true inheritors of the CPGB's traditions and promoted working-class struggles and union militancy. A number of prominent intellectuals joined with *The Star* oppositionists: Elizabeth Wilson, Angela Weir, Ben Fine, Laurence Harris and Marjorie Mayo, who jointly authored *Class Politics: An Answer to Its Critics*.[304] The CPGB's crisis had caught the attention of former comrades, like Irene Brennan and Raphael Samuel, other left groups, like the Workers' Revolutionary Party and the SWP,[305] and capitalist media: different factions fed information to different media, a tactic which Costello had initiated during the Lane Affair.[306]

---

300   E.g. Francis 1985.
301   MTEC 1985.
302   Betty Matthews was chosen as the MT delegate to the 39th Congress. The support for MT and Jacques from leading party members like the Matthews, McLennan and Hobsbawm, was enthusiastic and virtually unconditional (Hobsbawm 1997; Matthews and Matthews 1996; McLennan 1996). Yet, at least in the first two or three years of Jacques's editorship, McLennan expressed concerns over some articles: e.g. in McLennan n.d. [1979a], he tells Jacques that he phoned Priscott about the shortcomings in his article on the contribution of the party leadership; in McLennan n.d. [1979c] he wants to ask Corrigan (1979b) for the 'scientific evidence' for the 'mass swing to the Right which put Thatcher in' because he says the author should not be making claims about the 'mass depoliticisation of the working class' without it. See also McLennan n.d. [1979b] on Corrigan 1979a.
303   John Foster, a MTEB member and labour historian, was a supporter of this group.
304   This pamphlet was treated by reformists as *The Star*'s 'theoretical statement' (Davis 1985, p. 36).
305   E.g. Birchall 1985; Callinicos 1985; Mitchell 1984. There was a 'spy' who volunteered at MT to feed information to the WRP's paper, *News Line* (Jacques 1996c).
306   Brennan says that she became active again in the CPGB to help her former comrades against the reformists (Brennan 1996). While NLR usually paid little attention to domestic

Gordon McLennan's speech to the 39th Special Party Congress reiterated the Executive Committee's critique of *The Star* and equated criticisms of *Marxism Today* with 'attacking the Party itself'.[307] Old friendships broke down as McLennan braved a lot of ill-will at meetings around the UK in the months leading up to Congress.[308] At the 1985 Congress, Jacques apparently came to an understanding with McLennan not to run for the position of General Secretary as long as McLennan continued to support MT against its critics.[309] McLennan denies that any 'deal' was struck; he claims that his and Jacques's political views came together and, therefore, they found themselves in favour of the same things.[310] Jacques could not have carried a majority of the membership to defeat the oppositionists; it was only with McLennan's and the leadership's backing that they blocked a takeover of the CPGB by the traditionalists. MT's success in building up a large readership and media coverage, which contributed to the CPGB's public profile, helped to justify the party's ongoing financial support for MT.[311] For their own reasons, if not for sheer necessity, McLennan and Jacques had to support each other against this opposition. For loyalists to support the opposition, they would have had, not only to renounce the 1977 BRS and their most successful publication, but also to reverse a tradition of loyalty to the leadership, especially when the party's very survival was, or appeared to be, at stake.

Jacques and MT supporters must have been worried by the number of amendments being put forward at the 39th Congress which represented a serious critique of, and an attempt to intervene in, the editorial direction of MT. Composite 19, based on nine amendments, sought to amend the principal EC resolution before Congress; it suggested that MT had moved away from James Klugmann's policy of opening MT's pages 'to all trends within the party so as to encourage genuine debate, dialogue and discussion', and Jacques was accused of only permitting a 'relatively narrow political spectrum' of contributors to the features, with the rest 'relegated to the letter[s'] page or to an occasional

---

left politics, it did publish articles on the 'civil war', including Raphael Samuel, a CPGB member who left in 1956, who wrote three articles on the CPGB (e.g. Miliband 1985; Pitcairn 1985; Samuel 1985, 1986a, 1987).

307 McLennan 1985, p. 6.
308 Beckett 1995, p. 214; Mitchell 1984, pp. 31, 46, *passim*.
309 Andrews 1995b. Nina Temple suggests that Jacques's motivation was to ensure the continuation of the CPGB's annual subsidies for MT (Temple 1994).
310 McLennan says that he did not want to retire until he had reached sixty (McLennan 1996).
311 It was not until Christmas 1987 that MT's debts, which had increased dramatically during 1986, were revealed.

discussion column'.³¹² But, the motion ignored how Klugmann had tacked to the changes in the party line in the 1960s and 1970s. The motion was carried because it was acknowledged as 'legitimate criticism'. However, Jacques's position was strengthened in the aftermath of expulsions of oppositionists at the Special Congress³¹³ and the confirmation of the CPGB's loss of its daily paper at the PPPS AGM in June 1985³¹⁴ (and the subsequent loss of members): MT became vital to the party if it was to avoid a complete slide into obscurity.

Indeed, it had been clear from the autumn of 1983 that 'the boot was on the other foot'³¹⁵ because MT's readership was already greater than the CPGB's membership. The subsequent confirmation of the leadership's loss of control over *The Star* (*de facto* since the summer of 1982) only made the party more dependent upon MT. The leadership's support for the magazine makes sense because of its potential reach and influence, as well as its high public profile. Whether or not the kind of readers drawn to MT were interested in the party or membership is a separate issue.

17   'The Tail Wags the Dog': 1987–89

By January 1987, *Marxism Today*'s position *vis-à-vis* the Communist Party was strengthened considerably by the loss of *The Morning Star*, the defeat of traditionalist opponents, its public profile and intervention in left debates, and its continued growth in circulation. With the traditionalists out of the way and the reformists ascendant, many of the latter began to argue for the magazine to involve itself more closely with the party: both the 1983 and 1985 congresses had passed motions which, while acknowledging the gains that MT had made during the 1980s, also criticised MT for its failure to include more leading members, a wider range of contributors, more women and ethnic minority writers and a broader coverage of issues. Martin Jacques had to retain the support of the leadership to help prevent 'interference' from congress and to maintain MT's editorial and organisational autonomy to continue into its next phase as its project shifted from 'critique' to 'modernisation' of the left.

---

312   Special Party Congress 1985.
313   The 1985 Congress confirmed the expulsions of the oppositionists: e.g. Chater, Whitfield, and Ken Gill (who became chairman of the TUC later in the same year).
314   The CPGB leadership resolved not to take legal action against Chater et al. despite having 'a strong case' because they did not want a judge, who was part of the legal establishment, deciding the fate of a Communist paper (McLennan 1996).
315   Hall 1997.

Since the traditionalists were no longer a threat, Jacques had to work to keep his reformist allies at arm's length to maintain *Marxism Today*'s autonomy, evident in his report to the EC in June 1987, just months before the 40th Congress. Jacques claimed that MT's critiques had become 'common-sense', but socialism had lost 'its sense of direction' and the left had become isolated, even 'estranged from modern society' (hyperbole that appears to set MT apart from both the party and the left, as if an 'oracle' perhaps?).[316] If MT's project to modernise the left meant examining it as a complete entity, the magazine had to be 'accessible to and the property of the whole of the left', and because it was not a magazine with a 'line' but one 'of approach, of orientation ... a trajectory rather than a set "position"', the party should maintain its distance.[317] Moving away from its traditional priorities, MT would instead seek 'to occupy the political high-ground' by trying 'to set the terms of political debate', since it had recruited the 'best writers around'; it went against the left's dominant tradition, which worked backwards from the party line.[318] He was making the case for MT's move away from both its original role as a 'theoretical and discussion' journal, and from the BRS, by stressing political analysis over theoretical debate. In a subtle way, he also sought to justify the continuation of subsidies for its production, distribution, publicity, promotion and public events.

In identifying the key problems facing the left, Jacques nevertheless claimed that MT did so within the Gramscian tradition, though not all MT contributors thought along the same lines. Essential to MT's appeal were the tensions and conflicts between 'identity and pluralism': between its identity in its 'central tradition' and 'defining characteristic', Marxism, and the plurality of 'contrasting views and approaches', expressed 'politically and journalistically'.[319] The sub-title no longer described what it had become, and though the 'discussion of theoretical issues as such' was limited, the Marxist tradition was responsible for MT's origins and its coherence and influence. Its identity and politics were based on the oft-cited 'creative development of Marxism': 'But the object of the analysis is the political situation or conjuncture', not about some 'relatively removed zone of "ideology"'.[320] This marked MT out from the others, Jacques claimed, because it 'operated at the interface of politics and theory', which enabled it to be 'a political intervention in the Left, in the Labour Party,

---

316   Jacques 1987b, p. 1.
317   Jacques 1987b, p. 2.
318   Jacques 1987b, pp. 2–3.
319   Jacques 1987b, p. 3.
320   Jacques 1987b, p. 4.

in and of the CP, in the peace movement, in British politics more generally'; its approach made it 'both stimulating and disturbing, even painful, to its readership'.[321]

After reassuring his audience about *Marxism Today*'s political position, Jacques acknowledged that he should have been clearer earlier about spelling out its project and the lessons it had for the CPGB, despite the differences between a party and a magazine.[322] However, it was MT which gave the CPGB 'a quite new political and ideological credibility', which opened up new spheres for the party to operate in and changed the form of public events from the 'meeting with a Party speaker or two' to events with 'a range of speakers, [and] a new type of political discussion', such as 'Left Unlimited'.[323] Jacques even suggested that the party had 'pioneered a new conception' of the party-press relationship: the CPGB was the 'sponsor and publisher' of its 'theoretical and discussion journal' but that did not mean that MT was the party's public organ.[324] For Jacques, there are two elements to this: one is MT as 'a dimension of the CP's own work, a form to use and develop'; the other is:

> MT as a form of politics, as an intervention which does not belong *organisationally* or *instrumentally* to the CP, but can have a presence in CND or the Labour Party or whatever.[325]

This was why Jacques argued for MT's autonomy so that it could be used by the Labour Party, CND, etc., as a basis for their meetings. However, Jacques provocatively suggested that:

> MT is a political challenge to the Communist Party, a challenge which remains largely unmet, in my opinion for political reasons. So far we have failed to explore and use the potential of MT for the CP. At the same time the CP has largely failed to learn from MT, to develop a hegemonic role rather than a somewhat sectarian and isolated one.[326]

The CPGB, however, still had to work out what its relationship with MT was.

---

321   Ibid.
322   Jacques 1987b, p. 7.
323   Jacques 1987b, pp. 5, 6.
324   Jacques 1987b, p. 6.
325   Ibid. (original emphasis).
326   Jacques 1987b, p. 9.

With the prospect of a third Conservative election victory looming, the May 1987 issue carried an article by Eric Hobsbawm in favour of 'tactical voting': voting for the best placed candidates to maximise anti-Thatcher votes to oust the government.[327] There was no better placed person to have authored this article than Hobsbawm, given his particular position within the CPGB as a(n) (independent-minded) Marxist historian and the *ethos* around which his personal intervention would have been deemed more acceptable for many than most other contributors to MT, such as Jacques or even Stuart Hall (who was never a party member). A special EC meeting was called to discuss MT's role because 'tactical voting' contradicted party policy and MT was accused of 'hoisting policies' onto the party, according to Nina Temple.[328] Reformists, such as Temple, whose commitment to the CPGB was greater than to MT, were not against the publication of Hobsbawm's article, but felt that a contrary position should have been published alongside it: thus, the EC defeated overwhelmingly a motion that it was 'an error of judgement' to have published Hobsbawm's article (4 to 24), but agreed (19 to 9) that, although the move was 'quite legitimate', there was 'imbalance in the presentation'.[329]

It is also testimony to the way in which MT could still generate controversy within the party even after the purge of leading traditionalists and indicates the uneasiness with which MT was viewed by many reformist allies. Temple, a former MT supporter, wanted to see the magazine brought back within the party's fold because she saw that it could play an important role in promoting the ideas and approaches of a new, reformist leadership: a view echoed by other reformists like Monty Johnstone.[330]

This uneasiness was also felt by many *Marxism Today* supporters as expressed in resolutions put forward for the 40th Congress. Some opposition to MT arose amongst CPGB members who objected to the way in which MT lumped together groups as diverse as Tony Benn's followers, militant trade unionists, *The Star* group, Militant Tendency etc., as the 'hard left'.[331] These tactics were seen as divisive and counter-productive to calls for 'left unity' by both reformists and traditionalists, although the substance of their criticisms

---

327 Hobsbawm 1987a.
328 EC 1987a.
329 EC 1987b. Jacques's illness saved him from more serious criticisms. ME, the so-called 'yuppie flu', had a debilitating effect on him for several months and he changed his approach to work and lifestyle, as he was unable to oversee the production process and supervise new staff (Jacques 1996d). Jane Taylor became acting editor while Jacques was ill (Taylor 1995).
330 Johnstone 1990.
331 Ramelson 1987.

diverged.[332] Bert Ramelson, a former Industrial Organiser and traditionalist, argued that MT had 'not been a *discussion* but a *campaigning* journal for a particular tendency', restricting 'discussion' to its supporters, whereas some reformists endorsed MT's 'general line and sentiment' but criticised it for its advertising (e.g. personal ads, expensive consumer items).[333]

The principal EC resolution introduced for discussion in the run-up to the 40th Congress included a critique of the magazine. It acknowledged MT's gains in circulation and influence, its success in playing 'an important role in political debate on the left' and in projecting an image of the CPGB as a 'powerful political and ideological influence'; the resolution also recognised MT as the principal source of new recruits to the party and its events as among the 'most successful' of the party's public activities. The EC suggested, however, that during the next two years, 'the magazine will need to shift its ground towards the reconstruction of the left and its perspective', because though MT's strength had been in its critiques of the problems facing the left, 'its weakness, like the rest of the left, has been what to do about them'.[334] Therefore, the EC, Jacques and the MTEB needed to discuss how to implement the decisions of the two previous congresses, 'to have more articles by leading Communists' while carrying out its task of 'modernisation'; the resolution also suggested that in discussions over a new draft of the *British Road to Socialism* it would 'be valuable ... if such articles span a wide spectrum of views' within the CPGB.[335]

A composite motion on *Marxism Today*, carried at the 40th Congress, expressed reservations about its development from reformists and loyalists, who wanted MT, as the CPGB's only successful publication, to work more closely with the party. The motion acknowledged that there were 'misunderstandings and misgivings' about its role and the areas for redress were similar to earlier resolutions: to improve coverage of labour and black politics; to redress the imbalance of MT's Metropolitan bias by providing more space for Scotland, Wales and the regions, and 'an even broader range of contributors'. However, the motion also recognised that because MT had 'changed considerably' during the 1980s it could 'no longer be considered simply as a theoretical journal', but it was clear to the majority of delegates that it was the party's responsibility, through the EC and MTEB, to 'consider the precise definition of the journal': this

---

332 Ibid.; Priscott 1986, 1988.
333 Ramelson 1987 (original emphasis). There was disapproval of some personal ads from some MTEB members and from younger party members (e.g. John and Field 1987, p. 2).
334 EC 1987c, p. 7.
335 Ibid.

was part of the membership's attempt to reassert its authority over MT.[336] The motion also called for 'close consultation' and 'better communication' between the leadership and MT to 'enhance mutual understanding', but it also stated that this process 'should in no way curb initiative'. This motion is an attempt to balance the party requirement to have a closer relationship with MT in reaching out to the public, while helping to articulate the party's position more publicly, especially because of MT's apparent connections with particular national media outlets, while at the same time permitting the editor and magazine to take the initiative to experiment and innovate, and to act to expand its circulation and public profile.

The 40th Congress also re-confirmed the 1985 purge of leading traditionalists and the use of the Stalinist practice of democratic centralism. It enabled Gordon McLennan's and *Marxism Today*'s supporters amongst the leadership to maintain its autonomy. Whereas Jacques and the reformists had complained in the past about Stalinist practices, from 1983 onwards they benefited from its use in seeing off the opposition. Democratic centralism enabled MT and the reformists, with the Executive Committee's backing, to control the committees that prepared composite motions, lists of speakers and 'recommended' electoral lists. Though the use of democratic centralism against traditionalists may have been ignored by reformists, the conduct of the 40th Congress brought criticisms against MT's supporters from other reformists: those allowed to speak to the motion on MT either represented views strongly sympathetic to MT or 'spoke from a stance of political opposition which was, in our view, rightly marginalised by the Congress'.[337] These speakers did not represent the range of views which expressed 'concerns about the content and direction of MT' and its relationship with the EC: by polarising the debate, 'intermediate views' could be excluded and MT's autonomy maintained.[338] That is, criticisms and concerns raised by those excluded from the debate might have been harder to avoid, if they had been permitted a hearing at the 1987 Congress.

The reformists were divided basically between MT's supporters and those who wanted the magazine to play a closer role in rebuilding the party, which included former Eurocommunists and dissident Marxists. Continuing internal divisions provoked further membership losses. Although years of internecine struggle in fighting off traditionalists had left many reformists frustrated and

---

336 NPC 1987.
337 Rodriguez 1988. The sympathetic speakers were: Doug Chalmers, Paul Hassan, Mark Perryman, Beatrix Campbell and Steve Hart; the 'critic', speaking from a position of the traditionalist opposition, was Will Gee.
338 Rodriguez 1988. See Thompson 1987.

exhausted, they looked to MT as the basis for party renewal.[339] However, MT refused to work more closely with the CPGB because it had 'failed to learn' from the magazine. Jacques and staff sought to keep their 'friends' at a distance because they saw MT's success at the newsagents as dependent upon maintaining its distinction from the party.

Despite these differences, MT and the CPGB began moving closer together ideologically at least towards the end of the 1980s, which was enhanced by growing enthusiasm for the USSR's new reformer, Mikhail Gorbachev.[340] This was a particularly important change after the USSR had invaded Afghanistan in December 1978 and backed the military *coup d'etat* in Poland in 1981. After the death of CPSU leader, Konstantin Chernenko, in 1985, Gorbachev had taken over, a reformer intent on changing and adapting the USSR, introducing market reforms (*perestroika*: 'restructuring'), opening up public debate (*glasnost*: 'speaking out'), introducing democracy (*demokratizatsiya*: 'democratisation'), establishing peace and reducing the arms race.[341] By 1987 (and despite the disaster of Chernobyl the previous year), 'Gorbymania' had taken over the CPGB and once again one could find articles on the USSR in MT.[342] Gorbachev represented the hope that the USSR might be reformable, even though initial predictions had been less optimistic.[343] Yet by 1989, CPGB members faced disappointment with the problems that beset Gorbachev's reform programme, compounded by the Chinese People's Liberation Army's massacre of unarmed pro-democracy protestors in Tiananmen Square and the civic revolutions in Eastern Europe. For Jacques, this was the Communist system's 'terminal crisis' which signalled the end of not only Stalinism, but also Leninism, with which the Soviet Bloc regimes were equated.[344]

Social and economic changes taking place in Britain and globally began to have an impact, especially as Labour seemed unable to stop Thatcherism despite mass unemployment, de-industrialisation and authoritarian state responses to labour and civil unrest. Both Britain and the world seemed to be changing irrevocably under the neoliberal agenda and 'globalisation'; the left

---

339 Rodriguez 1988.
340 Callaghan 1993a.
341 Galeotti 1997.
342 However, MT contributors on Soviet and Eastern European affairs had shifted from dissident CPGB intellectuals to academic experts and broadsheet journalists. In 1987, MT organised a satellite hook-up at Riverside Studios, London, to watch the parade marking the 70th anniversary of the October Revolution in Moscow.
343 Johnstone 1985a, 1985b.
344 Jacques 1989b. However, there had been Marxist critiques of the USSR since at least the 1920s.

seemed tired and bereft of strategies to counter it. It was this awareness, charted through *Marxism Today* in the preceding decade, which was influencing discussions across the left. The 'world' as captured in the 1977 *British Road to Socialism* no longer existed: wholesale rethinking was needed. Under pressure from the reformists, the 40th Congress called for a commission to develop a new manifesto. Crucially, it included key MT contributors such as Jacques, Beatrix Campbell and Charlie Leadbeater. The commission launched a discussion document, *Facing Up to the Future*, which pointed to significant changes in the economy, society, politics and culture: it renewed MT supporters' interest in the party.[345]

In the meantime, however, finances had become a serious threat to MT's existence. Though finances were always a matter of 'sharp exchanges' between McLennan and Jacques, McLennan argued that the party always put politics before finances: 'we could always find the money, and not from Moscow either, for a political purpose, whether conducting a campaign or a daily paper'.[346] Nevertheless, the subsequent revelation of a massive deficit of more than £43,000 at Christmas 1987, only one month after the 40th Congress, caused serious difficulties for MT: it was forced to deal with the consequent criticisms and decisions. Though complaints had been made before about subsidies, they had usually been ignored, because it was usually oppositionists making the complaints or the debts were initially comparable to those of the party's Press and Publicity Department. The 1987 deficit figure, however, was much greater than anything before: more than twice the previous year's loss of approximately £19,000 and nearly four times the 1985 debt.[347]

This new level of debt meant that MT could no longer ignore resentment at its disregard for previous congress decisions, although because the revelation of the 1987 deficit only came after the 40th Congress, it meant that the membership could do little until the next biennial congress in 1989, except pass motions at branch and district levels, and send letters appealing to the Executive Committee. The EC was concerned because the deficit hampered MT's cash flow: from May 1988, MT was required to report to and consult with the Political

---

345   Fishman 1994, pp. 160–1.
346   McLennan 1996. 'Moscow gold' ended in 1979 after being reduced substantially in 1971 (Anderson and Davey 1995; Beckett 1995).
347   This amount was not large by the standards of most commercial magazines. Political magazines of both left and right had financial difficulties during the 1980s: e.g. *New Statesman*, *The Spectator*. The debt for MT's twelve months of 1985, c.£12,000, was considerably larger than for the first 12 months of its first year of financial autonomy (e.g. October 1984-September 1985), at just under £5,000 (see Table 1). As of May 1988, MT's deficit was £43,461.00 (EC 1988b). See Chapter 3.

Committee over financial issues every month in return for further subsidies. A new staff member, Julian Turner, had proved himself adept with financial matters and became the business manager, freeing Jacques from this more onerous side of publishing so he could focus more on the editorial side.[348]

Gordon McLennan addressed the MT Editorial Board in July 1988 to help MT demonstrate to the EC its progress on 'specific deficiencies referred to in the resolution'.[349] McLennan also urged other EC members to support MT: at a May 1988 meeting, he argued before the PC that MT 'must not be allowed to close'.[350] Jacques used the meeting to redefine MT's role (one of the resolution's demands), pointing out the differences between the party and a periodical and the need to be able to explore issues without having to promote a party line; this was also to try and pre-empt criticisms of MT's independence and demands for party involvement. The EC seemed 'generally positive' towards MT, though Ros Brunt, a MTEB member, suggested that the board had to educate the CPGB about the 'reality of running a successful magazine': the differences between running a party and running a magazine, and between a journal and a magazine were possible reasons for the continuing problems between the party and MT.[351] There was:

> still a depressing lack of consensus on the role of MT within the Party: as a platform for diversity, or as the expression of a broad political-theoretical trajectory that would challenge prevailing orthodoxy.[352]

18   'New Times', 1989–91

Until 1987, Martin Jacques had been able to sustain some disregard for congress decisions because of *Marxism Today*'s success *and* internal party conflict, the latter of which actually worked to compel closer cooperation between MT and the leadership which otherwise might have developed differently. Nevertheless, with the financial crisis, MT's future became more difficult to envision, let alone ensure, especially as the continued decline in party membership and income forced a rethinking of MT's relationship with the party, despite MT's autonomous public activities (and occasional joint effort with the

---

348   Finances had put considerable strain on his health (Jacques 1996d).
349   MTEB 1988a.
350   PC 1988.
351   PC 1988.
352   Ibid.

party). At least three factors had to be taken into account: its name posed obstacles for potential advertisers and readers; the CPGB's decline meant it was becoming a less reliable source of funding; and the historic events of 1989 would make the Communist connection even more of a liability. A majority on the MTEB agreed with Jacques and staff that MT's organisational independence, therefore, would be absolutely necessary to try and secure its financial future.[353]

With internal resentment growing and former allies calling on the magazine to work more closely with the party since the defeat and expulsion of many traditionalists, Jacques had to make the case for *Marxism Today*'s autonomy by more clearly redefining its role, even though he had been making the case since 1978.[354] He pointed to MT's transformation as a clear indication that the critics were wrong because their criticisms were based on the old definition, when MT was read and sold mostly within the party, compared to 1988 when more than 80 percent of readers were not members and it was being sold in the marketplace.[355] Thus, Jacques asked if its sub-title was any longer 'adequate' to what it had become, pointing out that MT was 'no longer a journal but a magazine', which was 'not a semantic question', although he did not elaborate.[356] The publication of *Facing Up To The Future* indicated how 'perfectly compatible' MT's new role was with the CPGB, perhaps trying to assuage the concerns of some of his former allies that wanted the closer relationship between MT and the party. Jacques used MT's relationship with the national media as a selling point for its autonomy and for the CPGB's (continued) financial support. The FUTTF 'made a very positive contribution to the magazine's editorial dynamics', and because MT helped to promote the document, Jacques claimed, it reached many on the left who would not normally have seen it. Due to MT's reputation, FUTTF 'had an immediate and greatly enhanced credibility with the media', which in turn meant it entered 'the bloodstream of political debate in a new way for a party document'; therefore, Jacques argued, the CPGB and MT had to be 'more creative' about their relationship because of 'the new terrain' that MT 'actually occupies'.[357]

Most of the ideas in FUTTF were adopted and promoted in the launch of *The Manifesto for New Times*, published as a supplement with the June 1989 MT, and which was put before the 41st National Party Congress in November

---

353   MTEB 1990.
354   Jacques 1988a.
355   Jacques 1988a, p. 9.
356   Ibid.
357   Ibid.

1989. The NPC broke with old traditions in at least two respects: Jacques made the opening address instead of the General Secretary; and the delegates were given no guidance from the EC on which way they should vote. This break with tradition made it harder for Jacques and the others to win over the party membership to the MNT since there was a lot of disagreement over its ideas and concepts. McLennan's intervention helped to rally loyalists who wanted to retain some of the CPGB's traditions, such as class and the role of the party: 'Marxism-Leninism' was even retained for a short time, as a key, albeit nominal, political-ideological marker.[358] The vote on the MNT was only the second time that NPC came close to defeating the EC: there was even an attempt to have the MNT accepted only as a 'discussion document'.[359]

Resentment of *Marxism Today*'s autonomy ensured the passage of two critical motions at the 41st Congress. One called for MT's sub-title to be:

> restored to a more prominent display in the magazine even if this implies that the welcome innovation of an editorial/leader should be expanded and developed to present the Party's view of current politics.[360]

The other, while congratulating MT on its sales and role in politics, disputed the assertion that the inclusion of two CPGB documents in separate issues could 'be said to have "vastly improved"' the party's profile since the last NPC, and it pointed out that even when party members participate in MT they are not identified as such.[361] The NPC noted its concern at the party's large ongoing subsidies and called upon the EC to investigate and monitor MT's financial situation and that both parties should agree a survival plan to 'rectify the situation'.[362]

Four significant groups remained in the party: oppositionists; loyalists; MT supporters; and reformists committed to a political organisation. Each had their own candidates to replace McLennan, but both Ian McKay, the loyalists' favourite, and Jacques, declined to stand. McLennan had tried to convince first Jacques and then McKay to run; however, Jacques did not want to, and McKay chose not to run when Nina Temple decided to seek the position of General Secretary.[363] Only three months after Temple's election as

---

358 Fishman 1994, p. 168; Thompson 1992, p. 203.
359 NPC 1989, p. 1.
360 Ibid.
361 NPC 1989, p. 2.
362 Ibid.
363 Fishman 1994, p. 166; Thompson 1992, pp. 202–3.

the new 'Secretary'.[364] Jacques withdrew 'abruptly' from party affairs, leaving MT supporters within the party 'leaderless'.[365]

Differences over the party's future were becoming critical to its survival; with the exception of the *Straight Left* faction, which demanded 'the retention of the essential CP', most accepted that the party could not remain as it was.[366] After the 1983 Congress, SL had 'maintained a low profile, avoided confrontation with the leadership and worked patiently', assuming responsibilities in order to gain some influence within the party: SL was thought to have a majority in the London district and sizeable groupings elsewhere.[367] Nevertheless, traditionalists had little choice but to support the one option of 'transformation' of the party to oppose those who favoured a 'network'.

Despite MT's prominence and growth, its circulation was declining during 1988 until the 'New Times' issues, October 1988 to January 1989, which gave it a tremendous, albeit temporary, lift; however, circulation continued its decline during 1989 and remained 'far below what might be expected'.[368] The magazine had to find new, outside sources of funding as the CPGB disintegrated. In October 1989, 'in consultation with the leadership', Jacques engaged an outside financial consultant to research MT's feasibility[369] and it still continued to pursue possible outside investors, even as the decision was reached by September 1990 that MT would have to close. The CPGB's decline accelerated after the 41st Congress, which meant that MT's funding would dry up more quickly than expected.

Internal political changes, especially the retirement of McLennan and the old EC and their replacement by Temple and other reformists, was not favourable for MT; it indicated a waning of Jacques's influence: he failed to get elected to the inner circle of power within the leadership, the PC in July 1990. Of 13 positions and 31 EC members present, Jacques received 13 votes, the second lowest.[370] Two PC members were appointed as EC representatives to replace Jackie Heywood and Vishnu Sharma on the MTEB as part of the ongoing consultation over financial matters.[371] The new EC had to sort out the party's future before there was no one left. In a classic 'managerial' move to keep both sides on board, Temple proposed a third way between the two options of party or

---

364 Temple disliked the term 'General Secretary'.
365 Fishman 1994, pp. 168–9.
366 Thompson 1992, p. 205.
367 Thompson 1992, pp. 205–6.
368 Steward 1990. Other MTEB members raised this question (MTEB 1990).
369 MT 1990b.
370 EC 1990.
371 Ibid.

network.³⁷² Although it had been planned for the spring of 1991, the Special Congress was moved forward to December 1990 as membership was declining faster than expected: from 10,350 in July 1987 to 7,615 in June 1989 to 4,742 in June 1991.³⁷³

Martin Jacques and Julian Turner put to the EC three possible options for *Marxism Today*: close it down, which would incur substantial costs (suppliers, subscribers, etc.); reduce it to an old-style 'journal' (without colour, design, etc.); or find alternative investors.³⁷⁴ These options also included keeping both an investment in, and a political association with, MT. In September 1990, the EC agreed that MT would be set up as an independent, limited company with five shareholders,³⁷⁵ to take effect on 1 April 1991 and the CPGB would continue financing it until September 1991. It was only in September 1991 that the decision to close MT in December 1991 was taken, although preparations for a replacement continued for a year afterwards, until Jacques called it off.³⁷⁶ Without financing from the CPGB, MT was clearly not viable despite the national newsagent distribution, range of advertising, the high production values, rigorous and frequent publicity and promotion, national press attention, and the use of images and more accessible prose.

The majority of the remaining members wanted to keep the party, though Temple's 'twin track' proposal won out at the 42nd Special Congress. Though the delegates had voted to transform the party and Marxism-Leninism was 'finally rejected', the exact form it would take was left undecided.³⁷⁷ Of all the European Communist parties, it was the PCI, renamed 'Party of the Democratic Left', which once again provided inspiration, at least in name, as the final congress adopted the title 'Democratic Left' and a federal network structure.³⁷⁸ Jacques and others ripped up their membership cards when the USSR's funding of the CPGB was revealed in November 1991, shortly before MT's final issue was published: the break with the past was complete.

---

372 Fishman 1994, pp. 169–71. Opponents accused each other of staying on only to secure some £3 million in assets (Thompson 1992, p. 206).
373 Fishman 1994, pp. 150–1.
374 MT 1990b. The documents included a MORI study (MORI 1990; MT 1991).
375 The five were: Jacques, McKay, Turner, Charlie Leadbeater and Paul Webster (MT 1990a).
376 During the last year, Jacques and Turner sought investors to match *Guardian* funding for a new centre-left political magazine, *Agenda*. However, after Labour's general election defeat in April 1992, the focus and emphasis changed, and the idea of a more European-based, political monthly, *Politics*, took up their remaining energies until Jacques decided he was exhausted (Jacques 1996d; Turner 1998).
377 Thompson 1992, p. 208; Fishman 1994, p. 170.
378 By June 1993, membership was a mere 1,234.

19 Conclusion

Marxism Today's autonomy from its publisher, the party, was obtained over time through a process which utilised political and personal relationships and, in which as MT's editor, Martin Jacques's organisational skills and political acumen were absolutely crucial to the success of this process. Though Jacques's high profile drew the attention of critics, his years on the Executive Committee and in party work meant that he had a network of personal and political relationships within the party leadership and hierarchy to draw upon that ensured party support. Jacques kept the leadership informed and justified MT's changes; the leadership for its part, was happy with MT's 'success' and its public profile, which was in keeping with the desire that it would reach non-party readers. Once the traditionalists were defeated, however, MT's position became almost unassailable: Jacques became more confident in redefining its role and relationship to the CPGB.

One of MT's two official roles, however, was to ensure internal party debate to prevent a repeat of 1956. Yet the party itself was not sure how to balance out the contradictory demands of editorial independence and promoting the party line, between reaching a large general public (even on the left) and engendering internal debate and identity: there was some sense, though, that the party should be able to participate and help determine a periodical's direction as the 'owner-publisher'. While the 1957 CIPD Report reiterated this confusion, Gordon McLennan as General Secretary was uneasy about interfering in the editorial process, as part of the new generation of party leaders who entered their positions from the 1960s.[379] As defined by the 1957 CIPD Report, MT had become a 'factional journal', whether intentional or not: 'it has to have people to write for it, finance it, circulate it and read it: that is, to establish an organisation apart from that of the Party'.[380]

Marxism Today's major successes in presentation, national press coverage and distribution and circulation, 1979–89, ensured support from the majority of party members, providing it with room to manoeuvre, politically and financially. Even as the costs increased significantly after 1987, there was a reluctance to close MT; there was also no question of removing Jacques because he was intimately tied up with its success (and had the support of McLennan). The Communist tradition of supporting party bodies, politically and financially, even if not in agreement with them, worked in MT's favour: as it had done with

---

379 McLennan 1996.
380 CIPD 1957, p. 29.

The Star (despite the latter's lack of editorial flair and sales). *The Star* group's attack forced the EC and loyalists into an alliance with MT and reformists, which put MT in a much stronger position *vis-à-vis* the leadership. It was part of MT's success that Jacques maintained its autonomy from not only its enemies and the leadership but also from its friends, the same reformist tendency of which Jacques had been a leading member, ensuring that MT's content did not reflect internal struggles or a (changing) party line, even when the party took up MT's ideas. It was MT, despite attacking left shibboleths in the 1980s, which ironically benefited from the Stalinist practice of democratic centralism in defeating opponents and shutting down sections of the party, thereby shrinking the force with which MT had been associated since its launch in 1957.

Despite the negative drain on energies that *Marxism Today*'s relationship with the Communist Party entailed during its process of transformation, the party provided a useful institutional nexus for the periodical. It supplied human, financial and material resources as well as a political-cultural milieu that helped to incubate and promote its ideas; the network of district and branch organisations hosted events, which helped to circulate its ideas at local levels in addition to the national stage. The CPGB's position within the labour movement ensured that MT's analyses would be picked up by the media, especially for the 'newsworthy' contradiction between its title and its willingness to question left 'shibboleths' (as understood by mainstream media). Yet, MT's struggle for political autonomy from the party was only part of its transformation; equally important were the battles to transform the production and distribution process to reinforce that very political autonomy which enabled it to make independent ideological interventions into the left public sphere. While later chapters examine MT's transformation from a journal into a magazine, the next chapter engages in examining the three primary ideas or theses of MT's political project, and two particular themes with which the periodical was associated, all of which would be part of MT's influence on the left during the 1980s and beyond.

CHAPTER 2

From 'New Left' to 'New Labour': *Marxism Today*'s 'Political Project' and the 'Retreat from Class'

A key part of *Marxism Today*'s trajectory and public profile under Martin Jacques's editorship, 1977–91, was tied to the ideas that it popularised across the left and promoted to the mainstream media. These ideas were tied to what Jacques's referred to as MT's political project, which shifted during the course of the 1980s. Alongside the political project were two abiding interests in both 'popular politics' and 'popular culture', which were both linked to the political project but not always clearly integrated into the political thinking or clearly articulated as a key component, and yet they were part of what MT either implicitly or explicitly identified as part of the Gramscian 'war of position' in 'civil society'. That the thinking around MT's understanding of Gramsci's ideas was flawed will be examined in the first part, but this misunderstanding also had an impact upon the 'war of position' that MT thought it was engaged in. This chapter is divided into two parts, with the second part taking up MT's understanding and interest in popular politics and popular culture, and the first part focusing upon the three key theses at the core of *Marxism Today*'s political project.

One can see the enduring legacy of Stuart Hall's Thatcherism thesis, for example, as attempts to employ it as a model for analysing more recent changes as well as more recent critiques of it.[1] Two of these three core theses, the 'Forward March of Labour Halted?' and 'Thatcherism', which helped to establish the periodical as the preeminent space for left debate, were actually published during Jacques's first eighteen months as editor and in the first or 'journal' format, although the debates around Thatcherism would only pick up in earnest from 1983 onwards. The third thesis, 'New Times', was an attempt to rethink the late 1980s as neoliberalism continued to restructure domestic and international economies; it was influential for a limited time, particularly amongst postmodernist academic and left circles in cultural studies and sociology.[2]

---

1 E.g. Bruff 2014; Fuchs 2016; Gallas 2015; Hall and O'Shea 2013; Lehtonen 2015.
2 Although the 'New Times' project sought to make sense of neoliberalism, Raymond Williams had already presented it as 'Plan X' in 1983 in *Towards 2000* (McGuigan 2015).

1   'Forward March of Labour Halted?'

With the publication of Professor Eric Hobsbawm's 'The Forward March of Labour Halted?' in the September 1978 issue, *Marxism Today*, under Martin Jacques's editorship, launched its first major defining theme in Hobsbawm's critique of the labour movement, just days before the start of the annual conference of the Trades Union Congress.[3] Although Hobsbawm's article was based upon his talk at the annual Marx Memorial Lecture at the Marx Library in London six months earlier, it was only after MT published the lecture that it generated an intense debate across the left beyond the Communist Party of Great Britain: MT published contributions from leading trade unionists, SWP and CPGB activists, scholars and even a Labour MP. In the aftermath of the Labour Party's 1979 election defeat, which had been unexpected in some circles, Hobsbawm's thesis gained much greater prominence and influence on the left: it was no longer a matter of academic or theoretical debate but of 'immediate' political relevance. This turn of events was the beginning of MT's reputation for 'topicality' and challenging traditional left 'shibboleths'.

In his article, Hobsbawm confronted a widely-held belief on the left that the labour movement was gaining in strength and marching inexorably forward to socialism, which he argued was not true because labour and the left were weak and history was no longer pressing forward in favour of the working class, evident in its changing composition and declining electoral support for Labour. He also challenged the dominant view on the left that industrial militancy, often based upon the struggle for better wages, could be equated with political militancy: economic struggles could not be seen as indicating even a vague commitment to socialism, let alone as a foretaste of struggles for social change.[4]

Hobsbawm contrasted Labour's 'forward march' from 1900 to 1950, when its share of the vote hit a high of nearly 14 million in the 1951 general election before declining to 11.5 million in 1979,[5] except for a temporary hiatus in 1964–66.[6] Labour's electoral fortunes had been dependent upon the movement of

---

3   MT had a stall at the TUC promoting the September 1978 issue with Tony Benn and Hobsbawm on the cover.
4   Hobsbawm 1978. This section draws from Hobsbawm's original article and the revised book chapter as well as those then contemporary contributors, such as Pat Devine, who supported his critique.
5   It was to sink even lower in the 1983 general election.
6   Hobsbawm 1981, p. 169.

voters between the Conservative and third parties rather than winning over non-Labour voters.[7] As the composition of the working class and union membership was changing, with barely half of the population classed as manual workers in 1976 and with more women and white-collar workers than ever before, it was no longer enough for Labour to rely solely on appealing to a particular conception of the working class (if it ever did) since the manual working class, as narrowly understood and defined, made up a shrinking proportion of the population; it had never voted as 'a whole' for Labour at any point previously.[8] Implicit in Hobsbawm's assumption is the equation of the traditional image or stereotype of the working class as white, male, blue-collar, manual or industrial workers rather than the diverse, multi-racialised and gendered working class, a twenty-first-century reality. Although the working class was already in the process of being transformed during the postwar boom, it was this conventional image that was used to criticise the 'Old Left', Marxists and 'union militants' well into the 1980s and 1990s.

In addition, Eric Hobsbawm also pointed to the increasing divisions *within* organised labour, as indicated by such practices as 'sectionalism', which is when sections of the working class, particularly skilled workers, pursue their own interests irrespective of the consequences for other workers. The left was criticised for defending sectional interests 'as if they were class interests' without 'demonstrating any connection between the two'.[9] Those sections of workers able to exert the most pressure usually wound up targeting, 'directly or indirectly, the political will of the government' rather than the profitability of private employers.[10] If industrial militancy led to 'socialist consciousness' as opposed to 'trade union consciousness', than one gauge would surely include party memberships, which should have been increasing; however, membership rolls of the two largest parties, CPGB and Labour, had been declining since the 1950s, which was probably true of smaller parties despite a brief upturn in the late 1960s and early 1970s. Indeed, a high proportion of new recruits to the CPGB and other Marxist organisations consisted of 'new socialist activists', who were primarily students, white-collar workers and professionals, rather than industrial or manual workers.[11] Despite the upturn in industrial militancy in 1968–74, union activism overall was beginning to decline under Labour in the second half of the 1970s, even in sectional struggles.

---

7   Hobsbawm 1981, pp. 177–8.
8   Hobsbawm 1978, p. 280.
9   Devine 1980, p. 12.
10 Hobsbawm 1978, p. 284.
11 Hobsbawm 1978, pp. 285–6.

This analysis interestingly, and seemingly unknowingly, flagged a debate that had been taking place in the United States about the 'professional-managerial class' in this same period, 1977–79. The PMC was occupying a new 'middle ground' in the social relations of production of more technological advanced and service-based economies, where scientists, nurses, computer programmers and other technical personnel were required along with managers, human resource advisors and other, white-collar, para- and professional occupations, many of which required advanced training and learning, provided by another sub-grouping of the PMC, college and university lecturers. This new middle ground was mediating between both the industrial proletariat and the employer class. While there was not an agreement on the US Marxist Left about whether the PMC constituted an actual class or merely a stratum or sub-stratum of existing classes, it at least did recognise a shift taking place in class composition, as many of the daughters and sons of the industrial proletariat were graduating with postsecondary education, and moving into white-collar and public-sector occupations, and acquiring middle-class lifestyles.[12] This demographic shift in the UK constituted the new 'urban new left' in London.[13]

The earlier illusions about union militancy, encouraged by the 'Winter of Discontent' in 1978–79, were set aside after 1979 and replaced by a more 'dangerous set of illusions', according to Hobsbawm and others: that a Labour Party dominated by the left and committed to a socialist manifesto would guarantee victory at the next general election because, as many on the left believed, Labour had lost previous elections (1970, 1979) because voters felt it had betrayed its manifesto.[14] This is precisely what appeared to be driving activists to join Labour in the aftermath of Thatcher's first general election victory. However, while the crisis was not inevitable, the failure of Labour governments led by Harold Wilson (1964–70, 1974–76) to deliver on their promises had led to a loss of 'faith and hope in the mass party of the working class'.[15] Hobsbawm argues that people did not refrain from voting Labour because they failed to live up to their promises in office but because they had been unable to handle the economic crisis and acted in a way which was 'very nearly the opposite of

---

12 Ehrenreich and Ehrenreich 1977 wrote the original article that sparked the US debate (Walker 1979). They argue, decades later, that that the PMC is dead (Ehrenreich and Ehrenreich 2013). See also Offer 2008 on the transformation of working-class 'producers' into 'consumers'.
13 E.g. Curran et al. 2005.
14 E.g. Gill 1978; Costello 1979; Harrison 1979.
15 Hobsbawm 1978, p. 286.

what Labour voters and trade unionists expected'.[16] It was, after all, then Prime Minister James Callaghan's Labour government that brought in the first International Monetary Fund loan that compelled the government to institute three billion pounds worth of cuts to public services.[17] Thus, even as Labour's traditional electoral base was shrinking, significant numbers of this core group were alienated as a result of its policies in government: Labour had failed to achieve and maintain political hegemony 'on the basis of successful policies' and it had appeared to have even lost the electoral support of a majority of the working class.[18]

The shift to the left *within* Labour developed around trade union resistance to the Labour Government's policies in 1976–79 and led to a renewed interest in socialism, albeit mostly among political and union activists.[19] As the struggle for the Labour Party intensified, Hobsbawm warned against assuming that winning positions inside Labour could be equated with gaining popular support for socialist policies amongst the public: this was an illusion 'that *organisation* can replace politics'.[20] It is not enough to have 'the most left-wing party ... if the masses won't support it in sufficient numbers'.[21]

This failure of the left to appeal beyond the ranks of activists and supporters was not investigated by Hobsbawm beyond recognising that Thatcherism was more popular, at least in electoral terms. In contrast, Raymond Williams identified how significant the right-wing shift in the national newspaper market was during the 1970s, which was to have a significant negative impact on Labour's ability to reach out to the general public beyond its own base because of the limited access to these necessary means of communication; access was generally much more available to the New Right.[22] Hobsbawm's identification of the misdirected focus on Labour's internal battles by sections of the left was partly motivated by his emphasis on electoral appeal rather than a 'war of position', which would have meant a substantially different approach (e.g.

---

16   Hobsbawm 1981, p. 178. Yet, Hobsbawm's point here appears to have been overlooked or misunderstood, given Williams's critique discussed below in this section. Since the 2008 crisis and the imposition of austerity, a growing interest in the 1970s has brought back accounts of 1970s alternative economic ideas that were under consideration by labour and the left (e.g. Medhurst 2014; Guinan 2015).
17   Jackson and Saunders 2012.
18   Devine 1980, p. 15.
19   Devine 1980.
20   Hobsbawm 1981, p. 173 (original emphasis).
21   Ibid.
22   E.g. Williams 1978. This is dealt with in more detail in the section on the hegemonic apparatus.

the struggle over 'common sense' and populist rhetoric as part of a counter-hegemonic strategy). It is Stuart Hall's emphatic use of Antonio Gramsci's theory of hegemony that meant the latter's 'war of position' tended to get elided with increasing Labour's electoral appeal (discussed below).

In Hobsbawm's analysis, however, Labour's loss of support from even amongst the unemployed, who should have been one of its natural constituencies, demonstrated that 'the ideological commitment to Labour had been undermined', and some inner London areas with high unemployment were lost to other parties including the Tories.[23] Although such reactions from among the unemployed and manual workers do not necessarily mean that they were won over to the Conservatives, since those who did vote might also have done so as a protest against whichever party was in government at the time, there was no other way to account for such shifts beyond ideology (whether or not you believe in false consciousness or the populist appeal of Thatcherite discourse). Even the anti-authoritarian, anti-political or apathetic attitudes amongst working-class youth subcultures, such as punk, might also have influenced some of these voting patterns, such as ignoring or refusing to participate in the electoral process.[24]

The crux of Labour's electoral failures, according to Hobsbawm, was its inability, not to win over voters, but to hold onto those who had already been won over at previous elections. Labour's 1970 election defeat was a result of the loss of 800,000 votes they had gained at the 1966 election: it was 'the reactions of people who ought perhaps to have been Labour voters, *but no longer were*'.[25] How is this emphasis on 800,000 or more of the 'wayward' voters, who had once voted Labour and no longer did so, any different to the kinds of emphasis that New Labour put on reaching out to 'swing voters', twenty years later, in imitation of the US Democratic Party's electoral strategy in the 1990s of targetting these niche audiences? Of course, there is also the presumption that these are the same 800,000 voters who were won at the 1966 election and lost at the 1970 election. Even if it were so, is it for the same reasons that they were voting Labour in 1966 as in 1970? Do voters' reactions to political parties not shift as events and contexts shift? Are there not new voters coming in and older ones dying? Certainly, there must have been a number of reasons for a shift in supporting Labour from 1966 to 1970, which probably requires a more nuanced understanding of why so many did not vote for Labour in the 1970 election compared to the one in 1966. Nevertheless, whether or not these were

---

23   Devine 1980, p. 16.
24   E.g. Hebdige 1979; Willis 1977.
25   Hobsbawm 1981, p. 178 (original emphasis).

the same voters who were 'lost' in 1970, Labour as the incumbent party had attracted fewer votes. To win power, Labour would have had to build up support for its policies, which became more crucial as its share of the vote was declining, even amongst union members. Therefore, Labour had to appeal to other constituencies before it could move forward, which meant broadening its appeal: it could, in Hobsbawm's view, only do so as a 'people's party' not a 'class party'.[26] The legacy of the influence of the Popular Front on Hobsbawm's thinking is clear even if, in its own way, Labour itself was and has always been a coalition or 'broad church'. Whether attempting to retain the voters the Labour Party had won over in 1966 and lost in 1970 (assuming that they were one-and-the-same), or whether it needed to focus more on promoting its policies when in office or opposition, the discussions about Labour's appeal failed to acknowledge the need to focus on its own means of persuasion and rhetorical strategy.

By 1981, although none of the contributors to the 'Forward March' debate[27] disagreed with the essence of Eric Hobsbawm's thesis, including members of the Socialist Workers' Party,[28] there was no agreement on its implications which led to the increasingly bitter debates over Labour's strategy and, ultimately, its political trajectory. The subsequent split within Labour, with the establishment of the Social Democratic Party in 1981, lent support to those arguing that Conservative electoral victories were the result of a divided opposition.[29] The actions of the Labour Right contributed to the party's internal divisions, both real and psychological, and gave the Tory press lots of ammunition with which to attack Labour.[30] The Labour Right certainly appeared more intent on pursuing its vendetta against the left than in fighting the Tories.[31]

Part of Hobsbawm's emphasis on the rise in the strength and militancy of public sector unionism, which helped to make up for de-unionisation in the private sector, was an area of labour struggle which directly affects ordinary members of the public adversely rather than the capitalist class. The attacks on public sector unions, in the nearly four decades since Hobsbawm's thesis was published, is because they remain the last line of defence for the working class as the only organisations with sufficient staff, resources and networks

---

26 Hobsbawm 1981, pp. 175–9.
27 Jacques and Mulhern 1981b.
28 E.g. Jefferys 1981.
29 Panitch and Leys 1997. On Labour Right factionalism, see Meredith 2007, 2008. For a view from the Labour Right, see Hayter 2005.
30 Thomas 1998, 2007.
31 As can be seen in the attacks on Jeremy Corbyn once he became Labour leader in 2015 and again in 2016.

to provide the means to organise and lead the working class for the political (rather than workplace) struggles against neoliberalism and austerity policies, including the funding of single-issue campaigns and social movement organisations.

The 'Forward March of Labour Halted?' became more or less accepted as proven before Thatcher's second general election victory in 1983. Amongst those who contributed articles elaborating on this theme, was Stuart Hall, who in some of the articles published after his 'Great Moving Right Show' in the January 1979 *Marxism Today*, reinforced aspects of Hobsbawm's argument. For example, in Hall's third feature article for MT, 'A Long Haul', published in the November 1982 issue,[32] he warned that there was little likelihood that mass unemployment would play into the left's strategy against Thatcher. Since the greatest swing (14.5 percent) to the Tories in 1979 had been from those who had been unemployed between 1974 and 1979, during Labour's most recent period in office, one could not expect mass unemployment to be the 'magical "material factor"' that would subvert 'Thatcherism's ideological ascendancy' because it 'failed to deliver any such unequivocal political result'.[33] Hall also builds upon Hobsbawm's argument about the negative impact of 'sectoralism' on the labour movement by pointing to the 'division of grades, crafts, skills ... [which] has helped to strengthen and deepened the internal sectoralism of the class, and thereby its reformism'.[34] It is this 'real, empirical experience of the class', that is clearly evident in the hierarchies and divisions within the labour movement, that Hall argues means that 'class in its singular, already unified form, is really a political metaphor'.[35]

As Raymond Williams argued in response to Hobsbawm's 'Forward March', however, virtually all labour struggles begin as 'sectoral' struggles or what Willimas preferred to call labour's 'militant particularism'.[36] Like Hobsbawm, Williams wanted to get away from the simple equation of 'militancy with *socialism*', since '[p]eople recognise some condition and problem they have in common, and make the effort to work together to change or solve it', which means that it

---

32 Hall 1982b. A version of Hall's argument was published in *New Socialist* (May/June 1983) before the June 1983 general election (Hall 1982b, 1983b).
33 Hall 1982b, pp. 17, 16.
34 Hall 1982b, p. 18.
35 Hall 1982b, p. 18. Hall reduces working-class struggles to discourse contrary to Williams's approach in *Keywords* (e.g. 1983c). As Miller points out: 'There is no abstract struggle over language, only a struggle over power and resources of which ideological battles form part' (2002, p. 251).
36 Williams 1989e [1981].

is not limited by class because we can look to the 'militancy of stockbrokers or of country landowners or public school headmasters'.[37] What is special is that:

> the unique and extraordinary character of working-class self-organisation has been that it has tried to connect particular struggles to the general struggle in one quite special way. It has set out, as a movement to make real what is at first sight the extraordinary claim that the defence and advancement of certain particular interests, properly brought together, are in fact in the general interest. That, after all, is the moment of transition to an idea of socialism.[38]

However, Williams also points out that that even the 'struggle for that moment' is not a 'once and for all' moment but comes 'many times' as these moments can be lost, 'at least temporarily', and they have 'to be affirmed and developed, continually, if it [the struggle to socialism] is to stay real'.[39] Although he was 'broadly in agreement' with Hobsbawm's thesis and even thought that his criticisms were actually 'very restrained', Williams nevertheless identifies some important differences, including a problem with using the military metaphor of a 'forward march' for labour, which can then be commanded to 'halt' or be directed this way and that.[40] This metaphor tells us something about how some on the left, and in Labour and the CPGB saw unions, at a time when many CPGB activists had moved into union leadership and staff positions.

Many contributors to the debate saw the Thatcher government's attacks on unions and the working class as an 'offensive'.[41] In *The Thatcherite Offensive*, Alexander Gallas marks out clearly that rather than a 'forward march' being halted due to a decline in the labour movement, the Thatcher government's class politics were very clearly orchestrated 'by stealth' to gradually restrict unions through changes to labour law.[42] Although some critics pointed to the use of force or coercion against the labour movement, much of the incontrovertible evidence was not revealed until much later.[43] For example, the Thatcher government's willing use of force to defeat the most militant and powerful union during the miners' strike, must not be under-estimated ideologically and

---

37 Williams 1989e, p. 249.
38 Ibid.
39 Ibid.
40 Williams 1989e, pp. 249, 251, 247.
41 Gallas 2015, p. 61, n. 120.
42 Gallas 2015 makes a compelling case to see Thatcherism as a 'class political regime'.
43 For example, with the opening up of government papers to public scrutiny 30 years later.

materially in demoralising the labour movement and the left, as with Seumas Milne's account of the campaign and use of the intelligence services against the National Union of Mineworkers.[44] This was clearly a part of the class war where the state's 'Repressive State Apparatus' was deployed against the organised working class, something that Tory ministers and supporters were not keen to admit publicly.

In 1983, two years after the 'Forward March' collection was published, Williams's last monograph was published in his lifetime, *Towards 2000*, which elaborated further on his critique of the 'Forward March' thesis, which included rejecting some of Hobsbawm's assumptions.[45] Williams suggests that while Hobsbawm's perspective 'emphasises correctly, an *increasing* correlation between class and electoral politics, broadly from after 1918, to the "peak" of 1951', its 'ideological assumption ... extrapolates a continuing rising line', which then feeds the attempts to find 'short-term reasons' rather than to abandon the assumption underlying the thesis.[46] As Williams points out:

> However, it seems more probable that what really failed was the concept of an all-purpose radical party, nominally but always ambiguously socialist, which temporarily succeeded within a two-party system but then fell back within a multi-party system. This does not invalidate an underlying concept of a long march. It means only that the march was much longer than was supposed under the spell of this apparent 'short cut to socialism'.[47]

Interestingly, it appears that Williams, the 'humanist' and 'culturalist', according to Hall's widely accepted categorisation, offers a more developed, class-based, and cultural and historical materialist understanding than Hobsbawm, the ostensible 'Marxist' historian and CPGB intellectual.[48]

One of the key issues on the left was whether wage demands were fueling inflation or to what degree were unions responsible and how should socialists respond. It is worth noting that many socialist economists, including a number affiliated with the CPGB, had accepted the contention that wage demands were fueling the inflationary rise in prices by the second half of the 1970s.

---

44   Milne 2010.
45   Williams 1983a, pp. 153–74.
46   Williams 1983a, p. 155.
47   Ibid.
48   Williams 1983a, pp. 153–74. See McGuigan's reassessment of *Towards 2000* (McGuigan 2015).

Thus, within the CPGB you had divisions between the Industrial Department, which characterised the Labour government's attempt to orchestrate a 'social contract' between capital and labour as a 'social con-trick' for imposing wage restraint, and those who first gathered around dissident intellectuals, such as Dave Purdy and Mike Prior, and later MT, for not trying to work within the social contract and give it 'a socialist content'.[49]

However, while Purdy et al. go on to criticise the sectionalism of the labour movement, Roger Seifert and Tom Sibley point out, just as Williams had during the debate,[50] that all groups start out this way and to keep pressure on the Labour government to institute policies in a social-justice or socialist direction, it is necessary to engage in wage struggles to encourage militancy and ultimately the broader agenda.

> Furthermore, without being challenged by militant struggle on traditional union issues the Labour government had no political incentive to listen to the movement's wider agenda. And without the wages struggle the union movement could not generate the necessary mass political support particularly among its own members for its broader progressive agenda. It was one thing to get demands for an alternative economic strategy accepted at Labour Party conference but quite another to win the understanding of union members of the need for a radically different approach to Britain's economic problems.[51]

But, if Labour is in government and attempting to restrict or constrain the demands of militant unionists, it is going to create a tension that not everyone in the labour movement will see as sectional. It is just such reactions of a Labour government that might well provoke a backlash amongst workers, who might have decided to punish the government by voting against it.

Eric Hobsbawm 'nowhere discussed "seriously" how the actions of the Labour Party in office might have fostered the crisis of Labour', even though Stuart Hall's May 1982 article points to the 14.5 percent swing to the Tories amongst those who were unemployed between 1974 and 1979, i.e. under Labour governments.[52] Hobsbawm's thesis raised concerns about Labour's role as the political representative of the working class. It also drew attention to whether the working class can be expected to behave in particular ways, due to consciousness

---

49 Seifert and Sibley 2010, p. 121.
50 Williams 1981.
51 Seifert and Sibley 2010, p. 122.
52 Blackledge 2009, p. 213; Hall 1982b, p. 17.

of its own class interests, to support those entities that claim to represent its objective interests, *and* whether or not such organisations as trade unions can act as the working class's legitimate representative in the struggles against the state and capital.

Although Hobsbawm, Williams and others, recognised that workplace, sectional or economic struggles might not translate into socialist or class-oriented engagement in the political sphere, it does not necessarily mean that class consciousness or class solidarity were lost either. Three scholars, for example, who collected 'ethnographic shop-floor evidence' from the lock industry during the Conservative Party's 18-year reign, found that class consciousness, at least on the factory floor, contributed to a recognition of shared interests and the need for security provided by workers' solidarity.[53] Two other scholars who studied grassroots struggles in the Scottish coalfields under Thatcherism also point to a continued sense of class consciousness.[54] Although such consciousness or awareness might have grown out of the more immediate concerns workers faced in the workplace, it is also not necessarily clear that this would have translated into the broad support for the Labour Party at the local, regional or national level either.

Unemployed workers might well have considered not supporting an incumbent government in an election, especially when it had 'overseen' their loss of employment. Since Labour was in power, it might well make sense to not vote at all or to vote for others to punish the Labour government, even if it meant voting Tory. Of course, one could still argue that this is still a form of 'false consciousness' since Thatcherism would ultimately impose an enormous defeat upon the working class. The problem is in knowing exactly why working-class voters either turned up and voted for parties other than Labour (or Communist), spoiled their ballots or failed to even turn up to cast a ballot. Can such behaviour be understood as the loss of 'class consciousness'? Or is it simply what can be seen on the surface: electoral defeats for reasons that cannot necessarily be explained as working-class and union voters lacking in 'class consciousness'? Or was it because the appeal of Thatcher and the Tories in 1979 resonated in some ways after years of stagflation, unemployment and the 'British disease'?

There is one final consideration of the influence of Eric Hobsbawm's political interventions on the left. This is not to say that such interventions should not be made nor critiques of the labour movement acted upon. The traject-

---

53   Black, Greene and Ackers 1999.
54   Brotherstone and Pirani 2005.

ory of the global economy and the impact of Thatcherite legislation ensured that the general perception of the labour movement lacking a vision for the future and acting as a 'rearguard' defending 'an old way of life' became widely held. What was neglected, however, was the Thatcher government's ongoing attacks on working-class organisations that forced them onto the defensive while Hobsbawm claimed that there was no future for labour. Despite the promotion of feminism and the new social movements, via the 1977 *British Road to Socialism*, as key to a counter-hegemonic strategy, MT never incorporates such a focus into its thinking beyond the discrete contributions of a few individual activists and organisers. Thus, MT effectively removes any agency, whether unions or the NSMs (beyond the electoral mass party, i.e. Labour), around which the left can mobilise as a movement to engage in a 'war of position'.

2 'Thatcherism'

When Martin Jacques went to hear Stuart Hall speak at one of the annual Communist University of London events during the latter half of the 1970s, he was already aware that Hall was one of very few scholars on the left who was studying the rise of the right. Hall's work at this point already included public engagements, which had been going on since the mid-1960s in dealing with racism and black immigration to the UK, as well as with the politics of the left and especially the first New Left, since its formation in the aftermath of 1956. Impressed by his talk, Jacques subsequently commissioned Hall to write what would become, *Marxism Today*'s second, and most fiercely contested, thesis: 'Thatcherism'. Hall's analysis of 'Thatcherism' grew directly out of his collaborative project with four graduate students, *Policing the Crisis: 'Mugging', the State and Law and Order*, and was published in the January 1979 issue four months after Eric Hobsbawm's 'Forward March of Labour Halted?' feature and four months before Margaret Thatcher's first general election victory as leader of the Conservative Party.[55]

'Thatcherism' was a political project which aimed to construct a hegemony of the New Right in British politics with an agenda for that historical conjuncture of the late 1970s and early 1980s, in which three trends came together: the 'long-term structural decline' of the UK economy combined with a deepening world recession; the disintegration of the postwar consensus; and the 'resump-

---

55   Hall et al. 1978; Hall 1997.

tion of the "new Cold War", and a Britain sliding ... into a mood of intense, bellicose, patriotic fervour'.[56] In his analysis, Hall concentrated on political-ideological rather than economic aspects and on the domestic context, even though Thatcherism was seen as a 'global intervention', an indication of its hegemonic nature.[57]

Arguing against a then dominant view on the left, Hall stated that the '"swing to the Right" was not a reflection of the crisis but a *response* to the crisis'.[58] He argued against the kind of expectation that the working class was 'inevitably' and 'inexorably' moving towards socialism, which is why he insisted that Thatcherism was a 'response', not a 'reflection', of the crisis: Thatcherism signalled a qualitative shift in the political leadership of the right. It was opposed to traditional 'One Nation' Toryism and the Conservative Party's adherence to the postwar consensus (e.g. Keynesianism, welfare state, full employment); it incorporated both authoritarian elements, such as the 'hang 'em and flog 'em brigade', and libertarian strands, such as those represented by free-market ideologues.[59]

Thatcherism was also 'unquestionably a form of class politics, dedicated to the reconstruction and strengthening of the capitalist order'.[60] It represented not just the old ruling class in a new guise, but also a qualitatively new social historical bloc dedicated to remaking society as well as restructuring the economy, which drew its support from across all social classes and articulated a philosophy on all aspects of life. It was this ability to graft the free market idea onto 'organic patriotic Toryism', articulating the resentment and alienation of the 'man-in-the-street' against 'big government' and trade unions, with a strong state meting out punishment to criminals and 'the feckless', that was 'authoritarian populism'.[61] The discourse of Thatcherism had to disconnect the links of popular concerns and issues to left or social democratic discourses, as part of the process of dismantling the postwar consensus, to create a new authoritarian populist 'common sense' around which these concerns and issues could be rearticulated with and to the New Right discourse. As with other ideologies, Thatcherism was never a coherent whole, but contained contradictions that proved to be 'productive', which enabled it, for example, to make contradictory

---

56   Hall and Jacques 1983a, p. 9.
57   Hall 1980, p. 26.
58   Hall 1979, p. 15 (original emphasis).
59   Hall 1979. See also: Barker 1992; Hall et al. 1978.
60   Gamble 1987b, p. 122.
61   Hall and Jacques 1983a, p. 10.

claims, such as calling for economic freedoms but more restrictive civil liberties through law, as encapsulated in Gamble's phrase: 'the strong state and the free market'.[62]

The contradictions that constituted Thatcherism were represented through the connections with the Old Right's political traditions and projects, such as the proponents of the free market, supporters of the authoritarian state (e.g. law-and-order, censorship), 'Powellism',[63] Ted Heath's 'Selsdon Man' policies[64] and Sir Keith Joseph; these 'backwoods elements' of the Conservative Party had always existed but had been obscured by the postwar consensus.[65] Powellism articulated a potent mix of racism and anti-immigration appeals, calls for law-and-order and a growing hatred of 'collectivism' and the 1960s social movements.[66] These different tendencies 'all addressed populist elements and recidivist instincts inside and outside the party' which Thatcherism sought to turn into a 'moral-political force'.[67] Thatcherism rallied these tendencies against the 'neo-Keynesians, creeping collectivists and fellow-travelling social democrats everywhere', who were to be found not only in bureaucracies, unions and the Labour Party, but also 'lurking within the Tory Party itself'.[68] This authoritarian populism was an 'exceptional form of the capitalist state', in which all the formal aspects of representative democracy were maintained, while an 'active popular consent' was constructed around repressive measures taken by the state against oppositional groups, including the women's movement, anti-

---

62   Gamble 1987b p. 122. It is interesting to read some of the contending accounts that offer different or more nuanced responses than Hobsbawm and Hall, though both were reacting to developments as they were occurring and attempting to shape the left's response. A recent collection of perspectives on Thatcherism, for example, demonstrate a range of possible ways of understanding Thatcher and the Tories both in and out of power during the 1970s and 1980s (Jackson and Saunders 2012). It includes a fascinating account of how a peculiarly 'English rugged individualism' existed in the working class which Thatcherism exploited (Lawrence and Sutcliffe-Braithwaite 2012), although it can be contrasted with research on workers' class consciousness during the 1980s and 1990s (e.g. Black et al. 1999; Brotherstone and Pirani 2005).

63   Enoch Powell's infamous 'rivers of blood' speech on 20 April 1968 attacked non-white immigration and he became a figure appealing to a right-wing, 'nativist' populism, which also incorporated other reactionary ideas with free-market ideology, for which it was named 'Powellism' (e.g. Hall et al. 1978).

64   The 'Selsdon Man' policies of Ted Heath's government, 1970–74, were a partial move to what would become Thatcherism, but were abandoned in 1972 amidst industrial unrest.

65   Hall and Jacques 1983a, p. 10.

66   Hall 1979, p. 16; Hall 1980, p. 26.

67   Hall and Jacques 1983a, p. 10.

68   Ibid.

fascist groups and black organisations.⁶⁹ *The Sun*, *Daily Mail* and *Daily Express* helped to articulate this authoritarian populism, via the continuous everyday interpellation of the working- and middle-class readers, into an 'active popular consent'.⁷⁰

The analysis of Thatcherism that Stuart Hall offered demonstrated that the project of the New Right was not just about the extension of the rights of capital and an attack on the welfare state and trade union rights: it set out to use political power to roll-back the 'nanny-state' and the postwar consensus on which it was built, and to replace it with another 'entirely new type of social order'.⁷¹ It operated a total programme of reform based on a:

> political struggle conducted on many different fronts at the same time, with an intellectual, a moral, a cultural and a philosophical cutting edge, as well as an economic strategy.⁷²

Its success was due to winning consent around which it constructed a social bloc that predominated. Part of that success was the (re)articulation of key aspects of Thatcherism in a rhetoric circulated via the establishment media that appealed to enough voters to ensure electoral victory.⁷³ For example, if no more than 40–44 percent of voters, at any one time, subscribed to Thatcherism, then it was never completely dominant, although its acceptance by a substantial minority was sufficient to secure a parliamentary majority.

Hall's critique of the left, like Hobsbawm's, not only promoted a particular characterisation of the left, but also contributed to a representation of a type of 'left-wing activist' that resonated with right-wing portrayals of left-wing activists (e.g. 'rent-a-mob') in the national press (which made the greatest rightward political shift since the 1920s),⁷⁴ which amplified the right's influence on the public's imagination. Of course, such a representation coming from the left and, indeed, from a Communist periodical, is all the more persuasive with both its readership and the broader public.⁷⁵

The left's tendency to read off political affiliation through social class was a form of economic reductionism or 'economism', Hall claimed, which could

---

69   Hall 1979, p. 15.
70   Ibid.
71   Hall 1994, p. 170.
72   Hall 1994, pp. 170–1.
73   This assumes a voter who is an all-knowing 'subject'.
74   Williams 1978.
75   See Chapter 6.

not explain why millions of workers, including trade unionists, had voted for Thatcher. The only coherence in Tory economic policies, on the other hand, was their *ideological* adherence to the ideas of Milton Friedman and Friedrich von Hayek.[76] Therefore, Thatcherism's success could only be explained by its dominance in the political-ideological realm where it disarticulated different moral, political and cultural discourses from their original social-democratic and liberal sources, and rearticulated them into a new 'philosophy' or 'common sense', in which its values became dominant. The diverse elements of the New Right were constituted into a:

> radical political force, capable of setting new terms to the political struggle, and effectively condensing a wide range of social and political issues under the social market philosophy, a process vital in securing hegemony for Thatcherism.[77]

Since a popular discourse had to be constructed which would appeal beyond the narrow economic interests that Thatcherism represented, it had to deploy the 'discourses of "nation" and "people" against "class" and "unions" with far greater vigour and popular appeal' than Heath had managed to do in the early 1970s.[78] Simply replacing Keynesianism with monetarism or neoliberalism was not enough in itself to win votes.

However, it was the 'doctrines and discourses of "social market values"' that provided Thatcherism with a powerful repertoire of images and ideas that resonated with the population, such as 'the image of the over-taxed individual, enervated by welfare coddling, his initiative sapped by handouts by the state' and that of the welfare 'scavenger' as folk-devil.[79] It also articulated people's 'deep and profound disillusionment ... with the very form of social democratic 'statism' to which previous governments ... have been committed', which had grown out of people's real lived experiences as 'passive recipients' of the state; Thatcherism succeeded in identifying itself with 'the *popular* struggle against a bureaucratically centralist form of the capitalist state', while 'socialism' came to be associated with 'bureaucratic statism' in the public's eyes.[80] Thatcherism was, therefore, able to draw upon strong undercurrents of 'anti-statism', which also resonated with the libertarian left and the existing counter-culture (iron-

---

76 Hall 1988b, pp. 2–3.
77 Hall 1980, p. 26.
78 Hall 1979, p. 17. See also Lawrence and Sutcliffe-Braithwaite 2012 and Ortu 2008.
79 Hall 1979, p. 17.
80 Hall 1980, p. 27 (original emphasis).

ically), despite the government's strengthening of the repressive powers of the judiciary and police while eroding individual civil liberties.

Thatcherism's contradictory nature did not adversely affect its ability to articulate undercurrents of nation, authority, standards, self-reliance, family and duty into a 'set of discourses which are [were] then harnessed to the practices of the radical right and the class forces' they sought to represent.[81] This, for example, is represented in Margaret Thatcher's rhetoric as the negative characterisation of Labour as 'enemies'[82] and of industrial relations as 'a battle'.[83] To 'retain the loyalty of its working-class supporters', the Conservative Party represented disputes between workers and employers as 'a battle between workers' rather than as a 'simple class war'.[84]

The contradictions faced by social democracy in power came about because the Labour Government had to find solutions to which it could win key sections of capital, since it operates within the contract between government, capital and labour. The solutions that Labour's modernisation programme offered were inadequate because it misjudged the scale of the problem and it was involved in an attack on its own social base: the unions and the working class.[85] Labour used its 'indissoluable links' with unions 'not to advance but to *discipline* the class and organisations it represents' which helps to explain why Labour had declined as 'a popular political organisation' after 1966,[86] and why the Labour government lost the election as it reaped the animosity of the organised working class because of its policies and actions. Hall recognised this as a possible line of reasoning, that might influence union members and working-class people to vote against the Labour government, although he does not develop this line of thinking, despite the results of the 1979 election.

The Labour governments of 1966–70 and 1974–79 used the rhetoric of the 'national interest' against the 'sectional interests' of the organised working class, which was the 'principal ideological form' in which they imposed a series of defeats on the working class.[87] The rhetoric of the 'nation' and the 'British people' was opposed to that of 'class' and it is this rhetoric that Thatcherism appropriated and turned effectively against the organised working class

---

81   Hall 1979, p. 17.
82   Charteris-Black 2011, pp. 173–6.
83   Charteris-Black 2011, pp. 170–3.
84   Charteris-Black 2011, p. 172.
85   Jacques 1979d, p. 11.
86   Hall 1979, p. 17 (original emphasis).
87   Ibid.

and its institutions.[88] Indeed, it was this particular class inflection of the rhetoric of 'nation' and the 'British people' that enhanced Thatcher's appeal to a broader, cross-class public. At the same time as the rhetoric was being propagated via various media channels, workers and families would have encountered all sorts of problems and issues for which the incumbent Labour government would have been blamed and away from which, no doubt, many working-class supporters would have turned because of the straightened economic circumstances in which many of them found themselves.

Despite not attracting much attention initially, Stuart Hall's thesis was propagated through *Marxism Today* and, to a lesser extent, *New Socialist* (Labour's rival 'theoretical and discussion' magazine), and via public meetings hosted by CPGB branches and MT discussion groups and events, and it was eventually taken up in a series of debates through other left periodicals, such as *New Left Review* and *International Socialism*. At the start of the debate around Thatcherism and in the aftermath of the debate over Hobsbawm's 'Forward March' thesis, there was a general recognition of the need for debate on the left. There had even been a sense of unanimity of purpose and resolve across the left to support Tony Benn in his bid for the deputy leadership of the Labour Party. The establishment of the Socialist Society in January 1982 had been part of an attempt to bring the different organisations of the normally fractured left together under one loose umbrella, from the Labour Left and CPGB to the SWP.[89]

Hall argued that the left could learn how to become a hegemonic force by examining Thatcherism's methods and strategies. There were 'two immediate lessons': one was that democracy was 'no longer marginal or tangential to the struggle' but at its very heart, in which the left had to reconstruct a popular force which was able to articulate 'the crisis to the Left ... *intrinsically* linked with the struggle to deepen, develop and actively transform the forms of popular democratic struggle'.[90] Hall's ideas represent a shift away from the idea of the revolutionary overthrow of the state, or the 'war of manouevre', after the widespread

---

88   Hall 1979, 1983a. See also Lawrence and Sutcliffe-Braithwaite 2012.
89   Jacques 1982d.
90   Hall 1980, p. 28 (original emphasis). It is important to remember that there was widespread distrust of 'democracy' in its liberal, bourgeois, representative form on the left at the time. In Thatcher's first term, questions around democracy were raised and this challenged sections of the left over 'actually existing' Communist states, the so-called 'people's democracies', which the right used to tar all socialists as 'totalitarian'. But the right ignores the contrast to liberal democracy in the form of 'direct', 'proletarian' democracy (Williams 1983b, 93–98). MT published Williams's 'Marx Memorial Lecture' on 'Parliament and Democracy' (Williams 1982).

failure of '1968' and the turn to the 'long march through the institutions'.[91] The other lesson was that, since the working class and other social forces were unsuccessful in deflecting 'the long-term and deep currents and movements towards the right',[92] necessary defensive struggles would ultimately get the left nowhere if it proposed to return to the way things were before 1979. This meant formulating 'a new conception of socialism', not just to stop the crisis, but actually to turn it in a 'positive direction', which meant developing 'a sounder and fuller set of alternatives', which meant that the left had to become a 'modernising' rather than a 'conservative' force: Thatcherism's programme of 'regressive modernisation' was not the only way out of the crisis.[93] Therefore, to respond effectively, the left had two practical activities to engage in: unify the working class and build an 'historical alliance' around a new 'popular-democratic' consensus between labour and the new social movements, which could 'turn the tide of Thatcherism'.[94]

In the aftermath of the 1983 general election defeat, however, where Labour's near disastrous second place win with just 28 percent of the votes cast, brought out the differences in the debate over the implications of Thatcherism and the debate became increasingly vituperative and acrimonious during the rest of the decade. These developments renewed and deepened the older, pre-existing divisions on the left, which had partly been overcome in the broad support for Tony Benn's bid for the Labour Party's deputy leader position. After 1983, Labour's internal divisions became increasingly bitter in the debates over the defeat alongside internal manoeuvring for control of different party bodies. As the 1980s progressed, one's position on Hall's Thatcherism thesis became a veritable litmus test of one's position on the left and on MT. In particular, both Hobsbawm and Hall lined up behind the need for changes to the Labour manifesto, including jettisoning the 'Alternative Economic Strategy' and accepting of a number of Tory government policies already made into law.

---

91 The year '1968' is marked not so much for its chronological significance *per se* but as a signifier for the revolutionary upheavals that were happening around the world from Paris to Prague to Mexico City.
92 Hall 1980, p. 26.
93 Ibid.
94 Hall 1980, p. 28.

3   Thatcherism: Critiques

In this section, we examine several significant critiques of, and subjects of omission in, Stuart Hall's Thatcherism thesis because of the pervasiveness of its influence on the academic and political left, and contributions to trying to develop a (counter-)hegemonic strategy. Drawing upon several important analyses, the following section will cover six broad themes: the bracketting off of 'the economic'; alternative political explanations for Thatcherism; the focus on election results, polling and public opinion; problems with 'common sense'; Hall's (mis)understanding or (mis)use of Gramsci's theory of hegemony; and the neglect of Gramsci's concept of the hegemonic apparatus and the social production of ideologies.

4   Separation of 'The Economic'

Hall's emphasis on political-ideological themes was a challenge to the left's economism, where people's political-ideological beliefs could be read off of their positions within the social relations of the capitalist mode of production.[95] Hall noted in 1982, during Thatcher's first term, that 'people are not wholly convinced that unemployment is attributable exclusively to Tory mismanagement or monetarist dogma' and that unemployment had contradictory impacts which both encouraged 'some growth in militancy' and yet 'helped the Government to hold the line on wages, [and] damped down industrial militancy'.[96] Although Hall's emphasis on mass unemployment points to both material and ideological influences, since the political consequences had helped bring Thatcher to power in 1979, he claims that 'it underscores the point that, in general, there is no automatic transfer from the "material" to the "ideological" poles'.[97] The general expectation was that, with a massive increase in unemployment, the working class would move decisively to the left; however, when that did not happen, economism could not explain it. Hall's point challenges those who think that as things get worse, there will be a large shift towards a revolutionary situation, which the history of the rise of fascism in the 1920s and 1930s refutes.

Thatcherism's attempts to secure the support of some sections of the lower-middle and working classes was only the latest manifestation of a long Tory

---

95   Peck 2001, pp. 231–2.
96   Hall 1982b, p. 16.
97   Ibid.

tradition of seeking the subaltern vote via patriotism, paternalism and self-interest. The Tories had adopted a:

> revived neoliberalism, touching the daily realities of competition and individualism: 'the sharpest weapon against the proletariat in the hands of the bourgeoisie', as Engels once said.[98]

Hall's inclusion of Engels's quote resonates with Raymond Williams's point about how the 'movement of so many trade unions and so many wage-earners towards the principles of economic competition has radically weakened the idea of an alternative' to the current set up of the social relations of production.[99] The loss of working-class support for Labour, however, is not necessarily the same thing as Thatcherism demonstrating an ability to secure their consent. One does not necessarily beget the other as Liberals and the SDP gained lost Labour votes in the 1983 election, while the Tories lost nearly 700,000 votes compared to their tally in the 1979 election, if we accept electoral tallies as evidence for shifts in ideological beliefs. The Westminster electoral system of 'first-past-the-post' ensured the Tories a majority of seats, regardless of lost votes.

In an insightful overview of Hall's thinking, Janice Peck argues that, although he downplays the role of the economic, even when he claims it is 'determinate in the last instance', Hall nonetheless promotes a form of 'economism', albeit (and rather ironically) without emphasising the economic: 'Within such a formulation, capitalism is external and prior to thought, discourse, practices, and social relations'.[100] Peck criticises Hall for his 'fetishisation' by removing the economic and treating it as if it was somehow a 'force of nature':[101]

> ... rather than a historically determinate system of social relations within which, individually and collectively, we daily produce and reproduce both the conditions of our existence and ourselves through our practical activity.[102]

Peck suggests that Hall's conception of the economy is the same as how bourgeois economists conceive of the economy as 'the market'; it contributes to

---

98   Hall 1982b, p. 17.
99   Williams 1983, p. 172.
100 Peck 2001, pp. 238, 236.
101 Peck 2001, pp. 238–40.
102 Peck 2001, p. 236.

the divide between economy and culture, which reinforces the separation of ideas from their material base.[103] Against the determination of the economic and with the mode of production as 'only partially determinant', Hall proposed 'the (relative) autonomy of language, consciousness, and culture'. Equally significant in Hall's thinking is the individual subject who becomes the individual of classic liberalism, 'the modernist ideal of the subject who always exceeds any external legislation', who is somehow able to think outside of the social-economic forces that shape society and is, therefore, not subject to 'false consciousness' or being 'misled'.[104] Thus, the critical, negative concept of ideology in Hall's work also wanes.

The 'vulgar Marxism', that Hall and others had opposed, was seen to 'dispatch to the superstructure the social relations of production that, for Marx, had properly constituted the "economic structure" of society', the consequences of which 'was to make class struggle a superstructural phenomenon', which as Peck points out, is 'a problem that was conserved by cultural studies in its conception of "ideological struggle"', which ultimately becomes 'idealist'.[105] Hence, where the emphasis is on the economy as separate from culture, politics and society, the emphasis on ideological struggle maintains its separation from economic causes and the capitalist mode of production. Thus, as with 'vulgar Marxism', cultural studies retains a separation of the base from the superstructure in a way that provides a mirror image of the crude, reductionist image that Hall and others claimed about their opponents' economism.

This was an important concession to Thatcher's government and Thatcherism, once Labour failed to form any kind of challenge to neoliberal ideas on the economy and economic 'regeneration', after parts of Labour's Alternative Economic Strategy were dropped from its manifesto after the 1983 election.[106] Other alternative ideas on organising the economy, such as those provided by the Institute for Workers' Control, were ignored or unceremoniously (and studiously) dispatched to 'never-never' land.[107] By the end of the 1980s, however, MT attempted to adapt its thinking to 'post-Fordism' by reconnecting political analysis to descriptions of (global) economic developments in its 'New Times' project. By conceding the economic realm to the New Right, however, there was

---

103   Peck 2001, p. 240.
104   Peck 2001, p. 236. This is the same subject in Hall's 'encoding/decoding' model (e.g. Philo 2008).
105   Peck 2001, footnote 2, pp. 243–4.
106   E.g. Callaghan 2004; Jobson 2015.
107   E.g. Medhurst 2014; Guinan 2015.

nothing to stop New Labour's later 'transformist accommodation' to Thatcherism that would preserve market domination in its economic thinking.[108] Thus, well into the 1990s, Thatcher and her successors could still claim that: 'There is no alternative'.

One of the consequences of conceding the economic front is that it undermines the possibility of thinking of discourse as having a material basis, since if 'there is no alternative', on what basis would or could a challenge be mounted? If being working class meant that you had particular interests in common with others, it still has to be articulated through language, and clearly Thatcherism articulated the class interests of the few to those of the many to persuade enough of the latter to vote Tory during elections. To counter Thatcherism, it would have been necessary to develop the language that connects common sense and everyday discourses to the material self-interests of the working class in a transformative political-economic programme.[109] Without attention to the economic, how could the left successfully propose a programme that could undermine the changes taking place in the economy that played to the Thatcherite 'common sense' of the day? Indeed, in any kind of critical materialist approach, including one influenced by Gramsci's ideas, the importance of engaging in an ideological war of position requires a basis in a society's political economy. Thus, a critical connection was lost in the ideological war of position that Hall's Thatcherism thesis offered to the left.

5   Alternate Political Explanations

One of the principal lines of criticism of Thatcherism on the left was the political economy approach of Bob Jessop, Kevin Bonnett, Simon Bromley and Tom Ling.[110] They argued that Hall concentrated too much on the political-ideological and neglected policies and the economy through which Thatcherism appealed to the economic self-interest of the upper and middle classes (e.g. tax and spending cuts); this focus is an important and necessary part because of the contradictory nature of Thatcherite ideology. Jessop et al. contended that Hall's thesis did not attend to the material base that underpinned Thatcherism as an ideology, whereby policies on home ownership and council house sales,

---

108   E.g. Pearmain 2011; McKnight 2009. For an account of a similar rightward shift in the language of the economy in the US context, see George 2013.
109   As shown in practical terms in Williams's analysis of the miners' strike (Williams 1989f).
110   Jessop et al. 1984, 1985, 1987, 1990.

for example, could explain at least part of the support for the Thatcher government from sections of the populace.[111]

The appeal to economic self-interest already had a longstanding basis with the Tories. The policy of expanding homeownership was one example of their approach. At the 1946 Conservative Party Conference, for example, Anthony Eden had:

> introduced the phrase 'property-owning democracy', by which he referred to widespread home-ownership, employee share ownership and profit-sharing. There was a serious attempt to make this a reality from the 1980s, with the express aim of destroying the social basis for collectivism based upon the defence of labour power. Home ownership in Britain was boosted by the Conservative governments of the 1980s and it has been calculated that expansion of such assets directly increased the Conservative share of the vote between 1964 and 1987 by 4.6 per cent.[112]

Thus, some researchers draw a direct line between the economic self-interest of some class strata of voters and the policies of Thatcherism. This demonstrates how one particular policy was developed to appeal directly on material grounds to the specific interests of different class strata. This approach had a precedent in the United States, where homeownership was expanded because it was thought it would work 'as an explicitly anti-socialist policy' because homeowners with mortgages are not likely to go on strike or engage in militant collective action.[113] In addition, socialist intellectuals were identifying how mass unemployment, or the threat of unemployment, was actually working to prevent labour disruption under Thatcherism. What is new, Williams argued weeks before Thatcher's second general election win, is 'the sheer discipline of employment', where workers have to consider mortgage payments and other debts before going on strike.[114]

Yet, Colin Leys, who had initially supported Jessop et al.'s critique, changed his mind by the end of the 1980s and agreed that Hall's analysis was necessary in identifying the importance of ideology and the rearticulation of common

---

111 Gallas 2015 draws upon the strengths and identifies the weaknesses of both Hall's and Jessop et al.'s approaches via his neo-Poulantzian analysis of the 'Thatcherite offensive'.
112 Mulholland 2010, p. 413.
113 Ross 2014, p. 181. Worth (2014, p. 484) makes a similar point on home ownership and the Tories.
114 Williams 1989g [1983], p. 170.

sense to right-wing authoritarian populism.[115] Leys argued that Hall's account of Thatcher's 'ideological success', rather than economic or policy successes, was important to recognise because Thatcherism had displaced:

> ... the 'common sense' of the postwar social-democratic 'consensus', [shown] its ability to 'lead the key sectors, win the strategic engagements ... [and] stay in front when challenged' – even when far from being universally accepted as 'common sense'.[116]

This description appears to be closer to the actual situation since Thatcherism was not universally accepted, although it does not necessarily mean that it was not 'hegemonic'. In his Thatcherism thesis, Hall developed:

> a rich problematic of ideological themes, repertoires, articulations, terrains, condensations and the rest, through which, in his hands, the newly emerging linguistic and philosophical theories of signification became potent *practical* tools of ideological understanding and struggle.[117]

Leys captures the sense that Hall's Thatcherism offered a role for those who wanted to 'educate, agitate and organise' to mobilise people as part of a broad 'anti-Thatcher' movement via deconstruction of ideological texts in the news, mass media and popular culture, even though there was not a sense of where that would lead afterwards.[118] This approach, which emphasised the ideological struggle against Thatcherism, had a general appeal for many media and cultural studies graduate students and lecturers, and cultural workers, who were part of a social-economic formation or class stratum, similar to the US PMC.[119]

The shift in Leys's perspective, published in NLR, identifies a greater shift of the widespread acceptance on the left of Hall's thesis. Leys recognises that Jessop et al.'s critique misses Hall's intention to put greater emphasis on the political-ideological in socialist analyses of the conjuncture. Nonetheless, as Hall and Jacques later conceded, they might have made Thatcherism look

---

115 Leys 1990.
116 Leys 1990, p. 125.
117 Ibid. (original emphasis).
118 It is this sense of ideological struggle that motivated myself (and others) to study media and cultural studies at Goldsmiths' College, which felt part of a larger, albeit vague, 'anti-Thatcherite' project.
119 Harris 1992, pp. 201–5.

'impregnable' and without challenge.[120] Political alternatives did exist, whether around Labour, the SDP or nationalist parties in Scotland and Wales, even if it would have meant having to work twice as hard to win over the public.

Another key to the critique of Thatcherism's hegemony is the role of political divisions in the parliamentary opposition to the Tory government, which recognises how FPTP outcomes in the Westminster parliamentary system means that a government does not need a majority of the votes cast to obtain enough seats to form a majority government. This aspect has led to the phrase, 'elective dictatorship', to describe the Westminster FPTP system: governments can therefore implement policies for which the majority had not voted.[121] Thus, it is not a question of whether or not Thatcherism was 'common sense' at the time so much as the Thatcher government was passing legislation because it dominated Parliament and could, therefore, legally and constitutionally pass almost anything it wanted, except where its own internal party divisions threatened its agenda. Thatcherism is, thus, more aptly described as Raymond Williams's 'constitutional authoritarianism' than Hall's 'authoritarian populism', since the Tories used the RSA (e.g. police, judiciary) to enforce its policies in the face of widespread public opposition (e.g. miners' strike, printers' strike).

Constitutional authoritarianism offers a plausible explanation for Conservative dominance under Thatcher's premiership, which challenges Hall's authoritarian populism thesis. Williams's thesis offers a plausible explanation for Thatcherism, even though it was first published in the 'Afterword' to the second edition of *Modern Tragedy* in 1979, only a few months after Hall's 'Great Moving Right Show' had been published and just around the time Thatcher began her first term as prime minister.[122] Although neglected or overlooked at the time, Williams's concept offers a way to explain Thatcherism and hegemony, a process that highlights *coercion* and not just consent, since most cultural studies scholars concentrated on consent and ignored coercion in Gramsci's theory of hegemony.[123] Other interventions by Williams were primarily circulated through *New Socialist* and NLR, but remained marginalised compared to the manner in which Hall's ideas were taken up via MT and other left

---

120 Hall and Jacques 1983a.
121 This is borne out by experiences of right-wing parties elected in the 'Old Commonwealth' (i.e. white settler) countries, such as Canada and New Zealand, since the 1980s. One example is the Ontario Tories' provincial election campaign known as the 'Common Sense Revolution' in 1995, in Canada's most populous and industrialised province (e.g. Kozolanka 2007).
122 Williams 1979b, pp. 207–19. In an interview in 1984, Williams reiterated: 'I don't agree with Stuart about authoritarian populism' (quoted in Jones 2004, p. 113).
123 Gallas 2015; Thomas 2009.

periodicals, and in media and cultural studies where Hall's preeminent position guaranteed the influence of Thatcherism in academia, not only in the UK, but also internationally.[124] The greater popularity of Hall's authoritarian populism can be attributed partly to the differences in the production and circulation of their respective analyses.

To weigh up the merits of constitutional authoritarianism and authoritarian populism, one has to assess the degree to which Thatcherism's success was dependent upon shaping common sense or in employing the RSA. There is considerable evidence for constitutional authoritarianism with, for example, Seumas Milne's account of the Thatcher government's 'secret war against the miners'.[125] This was certainly not a period of unity in the land and the Thatcher government imposed its will upon those particular sectors of the populace that opposed or resisted its policies.[126] The defeat of the miners by the spring of 1985 was a decisive, demoralising defeat for the labour movement as a whole because of the miners' position as the most militant vanguard of the working class and their pride of place within socialist politics. Such a fate was followed by the defeat of another leading section of the working class, the printers' unions, first at Warrington by Eddie Shah in 1983–84, and then by Rupert Murdoch's News International at Wapping in 1986.

Labour's internal divisions have usually been blamed on the Labour Left rather than on the Labour Right, although Hall did write about the secession of the 'Gang of Four' and the establishment of SDP for MT in 1981.[127] Some critics pointed to a divided opposition as a reason for Thatcherism's 'hegemony' during the 1980s,[128] as more recent scholarship also points to an effective Labour Right faction, which helped to keep the party divided.[129] The frequently overlooked role that the mainstream media performed, as part of the dominant 'hegemonic apparatus', in complementing and amplifying the Labour Right's attacks by goading, undermining and misrepresenting the Labour Left, contrib-

---

124   E.g. Hall 1988b.
125   E.g. Milne 2010.
126   Graffitti calling for opening the 'Second Front' during the miners' strike, for example, began to appear in some cities in southern England, such as London (a reference to when the Allies were urged to invade Nazi Europe before the Normandy invasion to help the USSR during the Second World War).
127   Hall 1981b. The 'Gang of Four', composed of David Owen, Shirley Williams, Bill Rodgers and Roy Jenkins, launched the SDP with the Limehouse Declaration on 26 March 1981. A similar kind of split appears to have occurred in the Labour Party under Jeremy Corbyn in the first months of 2019 with the departure of a number of right-wing MPs.
128   E.g. Curran 1984a, 1990.
129   Meredith 2007, 2008.

uted to and enhanced internal divisions, and influenced the public's perception of Labour as a 'house divided'.[130] A useful reason, no doubt, for right-wing newspaper owners to subsidise their 'organs of opinion'.

A final, but not insignificant, consideration is Thatcher's 1983 electoral triumph, which came in the aftermath of the military victory over Argentina in the Falklands War a year earlier, which helped to make what was a very unpopular government popular near the end of its first term. This particular context was ideal for Thatcher's use of 'the nation' or 'people' over 'class' in her 'two nations' discourse and enabled her government to appropriate patriotism to secure a second majority government via its association with military prowess and success.[131]

6 Elections, Polling and Public Opinion

It is also necessary to consider how election results were used as a means of supporting or attacking the different positions around Stuart Hall's Thatcherism thesis. Electoral tabulations were drawn upon as if they revealed where people stood; many did not vote and more than 50 percent of those who cast ballots consistently voted for parties other than the Tories.[132] As Raymond Williams pointed out in the March/April 1984 edition of *New Socialist*:

> The true context of any practical politics is always the general social and economic situation, and only secondarily the party dispositions and shares of the popular vote which follow from this. One obvious weakness of recent electoral analysis ... is that it treats current distributions of votes as if they were primary data from which the social and economic situation, or at least the main responses to it, can be inferred.[133]

Williams argues that the electoral data is taken as if it is fundamental to understanding the underlying socio-economic factors rather than seeing it as a one-off result: i.e. a symptom or result rather than a cause of, or explanation for, the current distribution of power.

Attempts to counter the idea that the vote distribution in general elections tells us what people think or believe were supported by surveys of public atti-

---

130   Curran et al. 2005.
131   E.g. Jessop et al. 1984.
132   Williams 1989c, p. 177.
133   Williams 1989c, p. 176.

tudes. Some of Thatcherism's critics argued that electoral success could not necessarily be equated with being 'popular' because the British Survey of Attitudes showed that there had not been a significant shift from the 'social democratic consensus', since there was a marked difference between the values held by the public and those promoted by Thatcherism, and between what people said they wanted and Thatcher's three consecutive general election victories.[134] Its success politically, at least, was due to divisions within the political opposition: 'Thatcherism only gives the appearance of populist success because of the weakness of the opposition it faces'.[135] Yet, there were some counter arguments using the same surveys to support the Thatcherism thesis, which demonstrates that the data was open to differing interpretations to some degree.[136] Nevertheless, the Tory failure to secure many more than two out of five voters, albeit enough in the Westminster FPTP system to secure a majority government, indicates problems with securing the hegemony that Hall's thesis claims for it.

Another example of the contradictions between what people appear to believe and the ideology of the party that wins the election is also documented in US political history. There is a stark contrast between large numbers of people who voted for Ronald Reagan, for example, and large numbers who held values and beliefs that were contrary to his government's policies.[137] This appeal to the middle and working classes worked against their own economic interests even as Reagan appeared to be 'popular' with them. This appearance of 'popularity' could be the degree to which such ideas were represented and popularised via mass media rather than demonstrating any kind of deep absorbtion or acceptance by the working and middle classes.[138]

Yet, there was a fundamental point of contention between different sections of the left over whether working-class Tories, who voted for Thatcher, were doing so as the result of 'false consciousness', mystification or misrepresentation, or were independent 'subjects' giving their consent knowingly? Regardless of perspective, the growth in political communication professionals using modern technologies, focus groups and polling methods to identify and target swing voters, and who then skilfully manipulate language, symbols and

---

134   E.g. Crewe 1988a, 1988b.
135   Curran 1985, p. 40. See also: Curran 1984b; Kelly 1984; Crewe 1988a, 1988b; Meredith 2007, 2008.
136   E.g. Bloomfield 1985a.
137   E.g. Lakoff 2004.
138   George 2013 shows how the primacy of key terms, such as management, over decades in the *New York Times* favours the dominance of the ruling class over subaltern classes.

other elements of human communication to win enough votes of these narrow target groups to secure a majority government in the FPTP system, is part of a tactical repertoire to produce the strategic goal of winning an election.[139] This is not securing 'intellectual and moral leadership' via popular culture, language and common sense, Gramsci's three dimensions for establishing moral-intellectual leadership and eventually securing hegemony over the subaltern classes.

The best-known example of an organic intellectual of the ruling bloc who exhibits this capability is Frank Luntz, who has been incredibly influential in the framing and shaping of US politics for the Republican Party. He is one of the great 'spin doctors' whose use of language as a weapon in the class struggle has enabled the US capitalist elite to dominate politics for the last 40 years. His use of language to manipulate working- and middle-class Americans into supporting such actions, for example, as the abolition of the 'estate tax', which he renamed the 'death tax', helped to mobilise the 'man in the street' to support the less than one percent of the wealthiest Americans and to vote for Republican presidential candidates from Reagan onwards.[140] Indeed, the Conservative Party benefitted enormously from the effective use of innovative professional political communication techniques.[141] Such an approach and outcome cannot be equated with Gramsci's theory of hegemonic leadership. Indeed, it might well explain why Thatcher's government often had a sense of being 'embattled', even as it pushed through its legislative agenda and deployed thousands of police against miners, printers and anti-nuclear protestors. The 'authoritarian' half of Hall's authoritarian populism thesis was not given enough attention by Hall after 1978 (as it was in the original PTC volume).[142]

Polling and voting do not necessarily prove whether a new, contested form of 'common sense' has become hegemonic or not because both forms of sampling public 'thinking' remain momentary and fragmentary. Nevertheless, there was a general shift rightwards in the UK's political direction, of which the election results provided snapshots at three- to five-year intervals, which nonetheless lagged far behind the national press' own significant political shift rightwards.[143] This was the war of position during the 1980s where certain ideas and ways of thinking became more common and accepted albeit never without

---

139   E.g. Scammell 1995; Kozolanka 2007.
140   Luntz's 2007 book, *Words That Work*, shows how the 'word doctor' 'spins' persuasively.
141   E.g. Scammell 1995.
142   Hall et al. 1978.
143   Williams 1978. See also: Glasgow University Media Group 1976, 1978, 1982.

challenge. Indeed, it was only in the 1990s and under Tony Blair's 'New Labour' Party that much of Thatcherism or neoliberalism would appear to have become hegemonic.

7   'Common Sense'

In these early years of neoliberalism, there was not a lot of understanding of just how far these New Right projects, within their various national contexts, could or would go. There was a general belief that they would not be successful because these aims were beyond what was thought acceptable, according to the 'common sense' of the day. How far neoliberalism has been able to shift policies of governance, privatisation, de-unionisation and de-regulation, and, ultimately, the common sense of the day, is the story of the last four decades.[144]

Thatcherism provides an explanation for neoliberalism's trajectory via its ideological dimensions but the weakness in Hall's thesis is not necessarily what it explains so much as the way it is explained. Since Hall's thesis includes the idea of articulation of aspects of New Right ideology with elements of common sense, thereby deploying it through everyday discourses that helped to make it hegemonic, it is necessary to consider Thatcherism's connection with common sense. Cultural studies's focus on common sense has meant examining the language and reception of media and popular culture 'texts' to determine how people might come to accept or reject particular beliefs, which contrasts with the more abstract discussions of ideology amongst other socialist intellectuals and cultural theorists. These approaches all contrast with opinion pollsters, statisticians and social science surveyors, who attempt to measure voting intentions and electoral results to provide empirical evidence for changes in attitudes. The battles fought on the left over its direction often pointed to election results or opinion polls to criticise opposing analyses and strategies.

Nevertheless, there is still a question to be asked about the opinions or beliefs that are taken as being expressed through these various kinds of 'snapshots' of public reactions: whether it is from electoral results or in-depth surveys of attitudes or random polling of public opinion. Thus, Williams's distinction between 'opinion and information' stresses an important difference that raises questions about the analysis of Thatcherism as securing the consent of the governed, if we consider that:

---

144   Although the literature on neoliberalism is vast, Harvey 2005 offers a good concise account while Mirowski 2013 provides an in-depth analysis that includes an incisive, trenchant critique of economics as an academic discipline.

> Some opinions are deeply grounded, with or without full information, but others, however confidently expressed at the time, are comparatively shallow and volatile, easily affected by the flow of current contexts and circumstances ... The aggregations without specific valuation, which now run through polling as through voting systems, flatten these real differences, stabilise the range of choices, and themselves become persuasive forms of apparent information, not only indicating, but at some levels forming 'public opinion'.[145]

Williams's account here precedes the focus by professional political consultants who devised new tactics and strategies for political parties to go after swing voters. This kind of slippage in percentages of the polling of public opinion means that it can really be 'comparatively shallow and volatile' expressions on different issues that then determine how political parties will appeal to such groups. Thus, there is a shift with political parties moving to employ professionals, who address persuasive appeals to entice a much smaller demographic of swing voters in target constituencies, which can help to secure a majority of seats in Westminster.[146]

There is another aspect to thinking about the ways in which public opinion polling fits into the dominant discourse justifying the rise of neoliberalism. As Justin Lewis has argued, it is not the right's success in capturing 'public opinion but the agencies that define it', that the 'unpopularity of welfare', which is reported and discussed, becomes the '"conventional wisdom" of media and political elites'.[147] However, the popularity of 'social assistance' programmes for the poor and unemployed, on the other hand, is just 'a scrap of polling data that is discarded, unused and unintelligible in the dominant framework', since such data does not fit into the usual frames used in media reports within the dominant narrative of the country shifting to the political right.[148] That is, the mainstream media have a determining position in the way that 'public opinion' itself is (mis)represented, neglected or omitted.[149] Although Lewis is writing primarily about the USA, he also considers its applicability to the UK:

---

145 Williams 1983a, p. 149. The differences between Williams' analysis of public opinion and Hall's 'subject' in his influential 'encoding/decoding' model are telling in terms of their respective understandings of ideology and its influence on publics (e.g. Miller 2002; Philo 2008).
146 See Scammell 1995 for developments in UK political communication in the 1980s and early 1990s.
147 Lewis 1999, p. 218.
148 Ibid. In the US, 'welfare' has very negative connotations but 'social assistance' does not.
149 For a fuller account of his argument, see Lewis 2001.

Thus when polls suggested a high degree of opposition amongst the British electorate to fundamental aspects of the Conservative Party's approach to taxation and spending during the 1980s and 1990s, this public opinion discourse was ignored by most journalists partly because it did little to explain a narrative in which the Conservative Party remained in power for 18 years.[150]

Would widescale reporting of such results, in contrast to the ideologically driven, campaigning 'journalism' of the Tory tabloids and broadsheets, have had an impact in galvanizing a majority of the electorate to vote for Labour? Or would it have led to more thoughtful, nuanced reporting of the issues and the subsequent impacts on voter intentions?

To take into consideration MT's approach where it appeared to neglect a potential strategic ground (with a few exceptions) on which the left could have both articulated another common sense and still be where the people are (or were) is that of the NHS, which was a key element in the establishment of the postwar welfare state and which remains popular with the people into the twenty-first century. Yet, as John Clarke pointed out, in the same year that MT closed:

> The New Times critique of statism seems to have paralysed thinking about the state's material role in protecting and enhancing the conditions of public and private life. This is slightly strange since one of the signal failures of Thatcherism has been its inability to unlock the forms of attachment which large sections of the population have to selected aspects of the labourist state ... Such failures suggest that there remain deeply sedimented domains of 'common sense' which counter-hegemonic strategies could be colonizing, rather than assuming Thatcherism has mined all the available veins.[151]

Clarke, who had been a graduate student at CCCS and a co-author of *Policing the Crisis*, was the most constructively critical of the 'cultural populist' trajectory of cultural studies.[152]

Thatcherism's articulation of capitalist interests to common sense was enhanced by the nature of public opinion polling and its coverage by mass media,

---

150   Lewis 1999, p. 208. See Taylor-Gooby 1995, pp. 1–18.
151   Clarke 1991, pp. 166–7.
152   Ibid.; McGuigan 1992.

which points to the neglect of the hegemonic apparatus by Hall and others. This news coverage of opinion polls helps to explain how the hegemonic apparatus helped to articulate Thatcherism's 'popular' appeal and rework common sense. This includes the crucial use of mass media to promote certain views and ideas while omitting or misrepresenting others, which made Thatcherism's 'hegemonic' explanations more 'common sense' than alternative perspectives. While *Marxism Today* focussed on dismantling left 'shibboleths' that appeared to be no longer 'popular' or contrary to the new common sense, it failed, in turn, to offer an alternative or counter-hegemonic ideology to challenge Thatcherism. Indeed, Raymond Williams actually offered a concrete example of how the left could 'rearticulate' the meanings of keywords during the miners' strike to a common sense associated with the left and the working class, to build crossclass support for the miners.[153]

Williams's emphasis on the 'processual-cultural' aspect, or practice, fits well with Gramsci's conception of hegemony as always in motion, in a continual process of negotiation: i.e. it is not static. For example, Williams argues against any idea of a fixed dominant ideology that 'can ignore or isolate such alternatives and opposition' and points out that 'any hegemonic process must be especially alert and responsive to the alternatives and opposition which question or threaten its dominance'.[154] Thus, Williams offers a more nuanced understanding than either the 'vulgar Marxist' approach or the contention that ideology is not somehow influential, which is paradoxically a claim of Hall's Thatcherism thesis, since consent to being governed is secured through determining the dominant common sense, which runs counter to Jessop et al.'s criticisms that Hall over-emphasised ideology. It is perhaps better to think of Hall reducing all aspects of Thatcherism, including its material social and cultural practices, to a 'discourse', which in turn became a strict focus on textual manifestations *of* ideology rather than a focus *on* ideology, including its means of social (re)production, and those agents responsible for such practices.

Antonio Gramsci's 'common sense' also gets taken up as if it is a 'popular democratic discourse' rather than a type of philosophy that needs to be made critical before it can become *buon senso* ('good sense'). The meaning conveyed in the Italian phrase, '*senso comune*' ('common sense'), is considerably different to the Anglophone cultural understanding of the term, which has much greater positive connotations.[155] Andrew Robinson also contends

---

153   Williams 1989f [1985].
154   Williams 1977a, p. 113. See also del Valle Alcala 2010, especially pp. 72–3.
155   See Thomas 2009, p. 16, n. 61.

that Gramsci's concept of 'common sense' is one that has been 'oversimplified or misunderstood', which contributes to problems as it has been taken up and used in particular ways, as with Hall's use of it, which differs considerably from Gramsci's predominantly negative, critical use of it.[156] Robinson also points out that Roger Simon's introductory textbook, an accessibly written and inexpensive resource for understanding Gramsci for lecturers and students,[157] published by the CPGB,[158] which 'treats common sense, not as a conception of the world to be overcome, but as an ahistorical field in which social struggles take place', which is how it is understood more broadly in media and cultural studies.[159]

The move towards equating 'common sense' with 'good sense' develops within media and cultural studies in part because of the influence of Hall's 'encoding/decoding' model. This model assumes that individuals are knowing, independent subjects (i.e. classic liberal subjects) who are able to accept, reject or negotiate representations of their own 'free will' and are, therefore, able to determine the degree to which they are influenced by media or other 'Ideological State Apparatuses'.[160] If people are not subjected to ideology, then they are 'free' to choose to accept, negotiate or reject dominant ideas, that works with Hall's use of a neutral definition of ideology, which is also easily (mis)understood and conflated as discourse. Such uses undermine the critical, negative meanings of concepts that Gramsci employed where they have been used as neutral descriptions of particular ideas, beliefs etc., without a sense of their class belongingness and hence material constraints on possible meanings. This is partly the result of Hall's failure to take up the emphasis on the *social production* of ideology that would make the neutral definition more useful by focussing on the process, rather than simply as an abstract, static concept, which has implications for developing a counter-hegemonic strategy.

Although Robinson points to the only two places where Gramsci accorded common sense 'such positive connotations', many academics, such as Chantal

---

156   Robinson 2005, p. 470.
157   Simon 1982. Greaves 2011 points to problems with Simon's assumptions about Gramsci. As a media and cultural studies lecturer in London during the 1990s, I used Simon's text to help explain some of Gramsci's concepts.
158   The revised second edition had a short introduction by Hall 1991d; a third was published in 2015.
159   Robinson 2005, p. 470. See the entry for 'common sense' in O'Sullivan et al. 1983, pp. 40–1.
160   E.g. Philo 2008; Hall 1973. Hall's article has been reproduced in numerous collections and used on countless syllabuses in academia in and beyond the UK.

Mouffe, have given his concept a 'positive political significance', which has consequences at both a tactical and a strategic level.[161]

> The attitude of certain readers of Gramsci can only lead to a tendency to pander to existing beliefs as a way to maximise conjunctural political advantages, which goes against Gramsci's goal of 'intellectual and moral reformation'.[162]

Hall's emphasis on the need for the left to go to 'where the people are' can begin to 'lead to a tendency to pander to existing beliefs', especially where ideology is understood as a neutral term equivalent to discourse, and common sense is seen as a positive grouping of beliefs held by ordinary people. There is no indication of how to (re)articulate common sense into good sense. This approach took place during the 1980s as if it was a more 'democratic' approach to political engagement than that associated with vanguard political organisations and this impulse also fed off of and into cultural populism that was then making an impact on the left. Thus, this particular reading of Gramsci spurs cultural studies contributors to MT and other periodicals, inside and outside academia, to put the emphasis on a democratic movement in contrast to the New Right's authoritarian populism and the organisational forms of democracy that were open to manipulation by party elites of both left and right. Common sense was understood as what was popularised via tabloids, TV and other forms of mass media, since the democratic 'voice of the people' and 'resistance' were being identified by cultural populist academics in some popular forms of communication. For those scholars with no practical or close organisational connection to the working class or social movements, this elision between 'popular belief' and 'popular culture' was perhaps more readily accepted as equivalent at least at the level of the text or discourse.

This 'democratic impulse' of cultural populism had a curious effect. Over the course of the 1980s, it would lead to both a validation of 'popular' beliefs and a belief in the ability of subaltern classes to 'choose' what they 'wanted', without seeming to recognise that these were not choices that could be made freely, since they were provided by the dominant hegemonic apparatus, and that this approach potentially elides reactionary with progressive views in a way that reinforces acceptance of the status quo. The common sense phrases propagated by advertising and other commercial bodies were taken up as if they were

---

161   Robinson 2005, p. 470.
162   Ibid.

unproblematic expressions of 'the people', although there were critical, oppositional expressions drawn from popular culture by the public, such as 'Giz us a job' from Alan Bleasdale's *Boys of the Blackstuff*; this phrase quickly became iconic of the time because of the way it captured the 'structure of feeling' of unemployment as it reached three million.[163]

8 Thatcherism's Theoretical Underpinnings: The 'Wrong' Gramsci?

Several recent studies on Antonio Gramsci challenge long dominant (mis)understandings or (mis)applications of some of his concepts in the English-speaking world,[164] including a number of scholars who have attempted to use, or have pointed to problems with, Stuart Hall's Thatcherism thesis.[165] The latter contributions highlight aspects of Hall's (mis)interpretation of Gramsci, including misrecognition of Thatcherism's 'passive revolution' as a 'mirror image' for a 'counter-hegemonic' strategy, the neglect of coercion and the misunderstanding of 'common sense' (some aspects of which were discussed above).[166] One consequence of this approach is that mainstream media come to be seen as a means through which to communicate one's ideas to others without recognising that these media play their role as part the dominant 'hegemonic apparatus'.

Many in cultural studies overlook or ignore Gramsci's roles as Marxist theorist, socialist journalist and revolutionary leader, who helped found the PCI, the 'modern prince', in the struggle to overthrow capitalism and establish socialism, and for which he paid with his life. Such revolutionary commitments have implications for understanding his theory of hegemony, which Hall and countless other scholars have drawn upon without recognising the integral connections of the 'modern prince' in any counter-hegemonic strategy. As Peter D. Thomas points out, the importance of the modern prince, which is Gramsci's term for the 'working-class political party as an "organisation of struggle"', is the 'point of departure and arrival of the *Prison Notebooks*'.[167] It is the working-class political party as:

---

163   Bleasdale 1982.
164   E.g. Filippini 2017; Frosini 2005; Harman 2007; Ives 2004a, 2004b, 2005; Thomas 2009.
165   Some of those who have attempted to apply Thatcherism as a model for analysing the present: Bruff 2014; Worth 2014; Hall and O'Shea 2013; some of those who have identified problems with it: Davidson 2008; Robinson 2005; Peck 2001; Wood 1998.
166   Davidson 2008; Robinson 2005; Thomas 2009; Peck 2001; Wood 1998.
167   Thomas 2009, pp. 438, 437.

> ... a collective body constituted as an active social relation of knowledge and organisation, the 'active and effective expression' of a process of formation of a 'national-popular collective will' and 'intellectual and moral reform', 'coherent and systematic actual conscience and precise and decisive will'.[168]

Thomas highlights this important component in Gramsci's theory of hegemony, which challenges the assumptions underlying Hall's use of Gramsci's concepts which differ to Gramsci's use, which clearly have implications for thinking through a counter-hegemonic strategy. For example, Hall replaces the working-class party as central with a focus on alliances in what became seen as political, not ideological, struggles to an electoral end, which determined these as 'party-political' struggles, due to Hall's understanding of 'civil society'. The concept of an alliance is different in organisational structure and coherence to that of a political party. Labour was the *mass* party of the working class in the 1980s, but it was not the same type of political organisation as a *revolutionary* working-class party, such as the PCI in the 1920s, which was also a *mass* working-class party, unlike the CPGB in the 1920s or 1980s (or any decade in-between). Rather than the revolutionary party becoming the 'organiser of knowledge' for countering the dominance of Thatcherism, there is no clear modern prince beyond, perhaps, the 'broad democratic alliance' and Labour's electoral presence.

This is where the misunderstanding of Gramsci's concepts of 'civil society', 'hegemonic apparatus' and 'modern prince' are related. If civil society is the territory upon which the modern prince is meant to operate as an 'organiser of knowledge' but Hall's understanding of civil society excludes the political realm and the 'integral State',[169] the mainstream media (and even the state) take over as the key 'organisation of knowledge'; since the latter is part of the dominant 'hegemonic apparatus', one has to work on hostile territory, i.e. mainstream corporate and state media, while trying to organise a 'war of position', which becomes reduced to a 'guerilla warfare' of 'pot shots' and 'occasional raids' (e.g. opinion columns, letters-to-the-editor). The use of 'ideology' in either of the two primary senses of the concept, as defined by Williams, as a system of 'illusory or false beliefs' or as the system of ideas associated with a particular social

---

168 Thomas 2009, p. 438.
169 The 'integral State' was Gramsci's attempt 'to analyse the mutual interpenetration and reinforcement of "political society" and "civil society" (to be distinguished from each other methodologically, not organically) within a unified (and indivisible) state-form' (Thomas 2009, p. 137). That is, the state was not just be reduced to government and legal institutions.

class or stratum, are not really incorporated in Hall's contributions to the political debate after January 1979.[170] Hall's use of 'ideology' comes essentially to the same meaning as 'discourse', with his use of the neutral definition of ideology as 'the processes of the production of ideas', which loses any connection to social class or material interests.[171]

The emphasis Hall placed upon 'civil society' as the primary consideration in the war of position meant that the takeover of the state and even considerations about 'political society' would have to wait until the ideological struggle over 'common sense' had been won. As Alastair Davidson points out, Hall and his CCCS colleagues think that:

> Gramsci gives pride of place to 'civil society', the realm where the economic structures and superstructures unite and where a struggle for political dominance between ideologies is conducted. This pride of place given to civil society relegates the concept of hegemony to what is fought for and either won or lost in civil society.[172]

Civil society is not just an aggregate of individuals loosely gathered in particular geographic locales, but is itself also constituted by various intellectual, social, political and cultural formations that structure it in ways that are constitutive of power differences. It is within this concept of Gramsci's that the awareness of the (counter-)hegemonic apparatus's role and function would have helped to articulate a left counter-hegemonic strategy. Hall's Thatcherism thesis provides one understanding of how a counter-hegemonic project should proceed.

> Before capturing the state, all the spaces of 'civil society', not just the economic spaces, should be occupied to secure the transformation of 'common sense' into 'good sense', developing the former into participation of the people in national life.[173]

This appears to suggest a far longer and more complete struggle than what was necessary for Thatcherism to secure hegemony. The capture of the state also requires 'all the spaces' of civil society to be occupied via the transformation of common sense into good sense, but in Hall's thesis working within common sense is integral to 'learning from Thatcherism' for a socialist, counter-

---

170 Williams 1977a, p. 165.
171 Ibid.
172 Davidson 2008, pp. 70–1.
173 Davidson 2008, p. 72.

hegemonic strategy. However, this understanding of common sense shifts to accepting it as if it is already a form of Gramsci's good sense, even though he never articulated how good sense could be developed out of common sense. There was (and is) a greater need for political-ideological work on common sense to create good sense as required for any counter-hegemonic ideology around which subaltern classes could form. It is Hall's explanation of Thatcherism that at least points to the need to analyse how ideology is working through language, common sense and popular culture to reinforce the status quo but, unfortunately, it does not succeed in identifying how to fight against it.

For Gramsci, civil society is the place where the subaltern classes 'remain disaggregated' and in which the modern prince provides the means to move towards counter-hegemony as it develops the 'hegemonic apparatus of the subaltern classes'.[174] Hall's approach to civil society, however, is actually based upon Gramsci's thinking about 'the party',[175] which might explain Hall's misreading of Thatcherism's 'passive revolution' as the model for ideological counter-hegemonic struggle: 'learning from Thatcherism'.[176] The question is whether ideological counter-hegemonic struggle is 'different from that required in a passive revolution where the existing traditional ideas are merely reordered and represented'?[177] However, it is ideological struggle without any kind of central body around which to coordinate strategy, which contrasts with how the New Right was able to orchestrate its own 'war of position', which was, in reality, a 'passive revolution', against Keynesianism.[178] The 'neoliberal thought collective'[179] secured hegemony from the top down by targeting academic and business elites first and then media elites. Only after securing the 'commanding heights' of the (dominant) hegemonic apparatus, did the neoliberals target the general public.

---

174 Thomas 2009, p. 438.
175 Davidson 2008, p. 70.
176 Thomas 2009, pp. 473–4. See also Pearmain 2011, pp. 18, 24–6, 85, 104.
177 Davidson 2008, p. 78.
178 E.g. Brock 2005; Gutstein 2009; Jackson 2012. In the USA during the 1990s and 2000s, for example, weekly meetings were held with national leaders of key right-wing groups, which enabled them to agree on strategies and messages to frame public debate, and to coordinate their activities which proved more effective than any loose association might have done (Brock 2005).
179 Mirowski 2013.

9 'Ideology' vs. 'Discourse'

Antonio Gramsci suggests that the Leninist strategy for the seizure of power during a time of unrest, the 'war of manoeuvre', would be unlikely to succeed in western democracies because the 'values and consciousness of the populace' are deeply imbued with bourgeois beliefs through cultural forms, common sense and so on.[180] As part of the move away from false consciousness[181] and the takeup of Gramsci's theory of hegemony, Stuart Hall's analysis meant that the emphasis was put on ideological struggles in civil society to establish 'moral-intellectual leadership' to secure the consent of the subaltern classes for the counter-hegemonic bloc. This understanding meant that, in turn, struggle was often reduced to the realm of discourse, in which the mass media become mere transmitters of ideas rather than shapers or persuaders of those ideas or agents in their own right. Yet, this condensation of the struggle to discourse also meant that the political half of the political-ideological dimension was reduced to the electoral contest while the ideological was simply used as a neutral definition for a system of ideas and interchangeable with discourse.

Jan Rehmann demonstrates that Hall's claim that Gramsci's conception of ideology was essentially a neutral one is incorrect.[182] Of course, with a neutral definition of ideology, discourse is much more likely to replace ideology as the primary concept thereby negating the effect of misrepresentation and mystification as possible contributory factors to shifts in public opinion and electoral results.[183] The move away from false consciousness led to a sense by which discourse determined everything, as if economics or the base was 'nothing'. If Gramsci's conception of ideology is not neutral, this would complicate Hall's Thatcherism thesis, as he makes the case for the consent of the subaltern classes to the ruling bloc via Gramsci's theory of hegemony without the concept of the hegemonic apparatus, which is critical for a counter-hegemonic strategy.

Since Hall's ideology as a neutral concept is easily elided with discourse, his concept has consequences for understanding how ISAs or the hegemonic apparatus influence people. Hall uses Gramsci's ideas to talk about how authoritarian populism dis-connects the economic interests of the working class from the Labour Party and trade unions to link them, via 'articulation' (using the metaphor of an articulated lorry), to the interests of the ruling elite. The ques-

---

180   Callaghan 1988, p. 227.
181   Common sense and false consciousness are not necessarily contradictory or mutually exclusive.
182   Rehmann 2015.
183   E.g. Purvis and Hunt 1993.

tion that Hall's concept of articulation raises is that, how can it work, even at a semantic level, to rearticulate working-class interests to elite interests, if one assumes that there are no necessary corresponding class interests? There would be no possibility of determination by the economic, no matter how broadly understood or narrowly defined, not even in the 'last instance', if there is no correspondence between socio-economic strata or classes and particular objective, political-economic interests common to those strata or classes. Only the elites appear to have material interests in this way of thinking.

There is also a neglect of, or dis-engagement from, the means by which these 'interests' are produced and circulated amongst the public, including the role of the mass media. This is the 'blankspot' of both the Labour Party and the left, and their failure to address the role of mass *and*, indeed, of alternative and oppositional media. The role of the mass media was critical for both concepts, false consciousness and consent, as the usually implicit means of mystification or representation (respectively) to achieve support or acquiescence from the middle and working classes. False consciousness had been a popular notion with parts of the left in the 1970s, which helped to explain why some working-class people supported Conservative governments. However, Hall, Williams and other cultural studies scholars sought to move away from what they rejected as 'vulgar Marxism' and associated concepts like false consciousness; many, including Hall, challenged this thinking by stressing consent over coercion in their use of Gramsci's theory of hegemony.

Is the answer to overcoming the question of false consciousness, however, to focus on consent? It was often pointed out that many trade unionists and unemployed workers were voting for Thatcher even as her government was making workers redundant and cutting their benefits as well as destroying their unions' abilities to function as agents of their interests. One does not have to accept the concept of false consciousness to recognise that there are policies that are *not* in the common or material interests of different classes. Hall offers no understanding of *how* Thatcherism became part of common sense, other than to urge the left to go to 'where the people are', which is not the same as challenging that which people accept 'as is'. But, by stressing consent, Hall and others ultimately overlooked the lines along which hegemonic processes might be disrupted.

Davidson sees 'Hall's failure to develop or explain adequately the Gramscian notion of "discourse"', because he drew from 'Althusser and Laclau when he attempted to discuss how a socialist hegemony is achieved'[184] and his under-

---

184   Davidson 2008, p. 78.

standing of Althusser and Gramsci was influenced by Ernesto Laclau's 1977 book, *Politics and Ideology in Marxist Theory*, and by participation in Laclau's discussion group (1982–84), which focused on 'expanding the concept of "hegemony" and the analysis of the present conjuncture'.[185] For Laclau, politics could be equated to the contradiction between the 'people' and the 'power bloc', but it was not about classes.[186] Laclau and Chantal Mouffe's 1985 book, *Hegemony and Socialist Strategy*, was influential in replacing the idea of class and the material basis to subjectivity and consciousness with a purely discursive understanding: the emphasis on discourse as constitutive and with no necessary 'belongingness' beyond what could be articulated via discourse.[187] Thus, in Laclau and Mouffe's analysis, 'the people' only exist as an 'articulation of political discourse', which by reducing all forms of subjectivity to discourse, might have gone 'too far' for Hall, even if his own position was quite close to theirs.[188] Jim McGuigan notably identifies this as 'a "culturalist"[189] argument: politics as the production of identity'.[190]

10   'Hegemony'

In his use of Antonio Gramsci's theory of 'hegemony', Stuart Hall fails to draw out *how* Thatcherism's influence worked via language and common sense, which could have contributed to the left's struggle to rearticulate common sense to a socialist, counter-hegemonic position. It is this failure that Raymond Williams's cultural materialism helps us to address via its conception of 'hegemony as culture', rather than Hall's 'hegemony as structure', since the latter's emphasis is 'a matter for textual decoding', whereas the former's emphasis is 'a matter of material production, reproduction and consumption'.[191] Hall's emphasis is one that naturally sets itself up for seeing all aspects of social relations and the mode of production as a 'text' rather than recognising that some things cannot be reduced to a 'text' for decoding. Williams's approach on the other hand draws attention to the material aspects of the cultural – and ideolo-

---

185   Hall 1988a, p. 160, n. 7. See also Peck 2001, p. 244, n. 11.
186   McGuigan 1992, p. 16.
187   Laclau and Mouffe 1985.
188   E.g. Peck 1998, 2001; Robinson 2005; Davidson 2008.
189   McGuigan's charge of 'culturalist' applied to Hall is ironic since Hall had classified (dismissed?) Williams as a 'culturalist' in his influential 'Two Paradigms' essay (Hall 1980c).
190   McGuigan 1992, pp. 15, 16.
191   Milner 2002, p. 115. See also Milner 1993, pp. 81–3.

gical – production of hegemony. It is Hall's textualisation of social and cultural practices that contributes to making Thatcherism appear invulnerable since the only way of intervening would appear to be linguistic or verbal rather than material.[192] This actually has consequences for counter-hegemonic practices. Andrew Milner has summarised this neatly as:

> If hegemony is a culture, then it is materially produced by the practices of conscious agents, and may be countered by alternative, counter-hegemonic, practices; if hegemony is a structure of ideology, then it will determine the subjectivity of its subjects in ways which radically diminish the prospects for counter-hegemonic practice, except in the characteristically attenuated form of a plurality of post-structuralist resistant readings.[193]

The latter approach might work more effectively in the university than in the workplace or on the street. This is why Williams's approach was more relevant to developing a counter-hegemonic strategy than Hall's thesis, which enabled critique but not any kind of strategising for effective counter-hegemonic engagement.

While recognising Hall's analysis of Thatcherism as an advance on previous forms of ideological analysis, Brennon Wood identifies some limitations in Hall's approach that he contrasts with Gramsci's.[194] For example, Wood points out that Hall's use of Gramsci's concepts of common sense and philosophy are restricted to 'political outlooks' rather than with the broader understanding of the relationship of these concepts to the everyday and their contribution to the social (re)production of ideology. The emphasis on political outlook becomes reduced to the electoral contest thereby undermining the longer term that Hall himself stressed in his analysis.[195]

A key weakness in Hall's Thatcherism thesis is in this limited understanding of how hegemony is produced. This understanding:

---

[192] Williams's 'formational analysis of the CCCS links the necessary social distance of academic – and especially theoretical – labour with the choice of an instrumentally calculative "textualisation" of social practices tied to an unmasking ... conception of ideology' (Jones 2004, p. 114).
[193] Milner 1993, p. 81.
[194] Wood 1998.
[195] Ibid.

reduces the dialectical complexity of Gramsci's concept, ultimately obscuring the novel analytical capacity assigned to it in the *Prison Notebooks*, its distinctively political focus and, above all, its consequence for the strategies of the organised working class.[196]

For Hall counter-hegemony is conceived of as a 'mirror image' of Thatcherism from which the Labour Party was supposed to learn rather than hegemony as a process understood from the perspective of the subaltern. The understanding of hegemony 'as seen by the hegemon' as a 'mechanism of mediated subordination' limits the strategy to the tactical engagement on a field of battle, which in the case of Thatcherism became the electoral contest, but which has been designed by the bourgeois domination of liberal representative democracy.[197]

Electoral responses are about the only possible response that a compromised social democratic left can make when attempting to develop a counter-hegemonic strategy, especially if ideology and common sense are seen as neutral or even positive concepts. The concentration on electoral strategy, however, did (and does) not need to develop a counter-hegemonic response in the Gramscian sense, if it was capable of articulating the kind of populist appeal via the skilled manipulation of language and imagery to secure sufficient voter support in swing ridings to obtain a majority of seats in the House of Commons.

As Andy Pearmain argues, the New Labour project was 'a "transformist" accommodation ... to the deeper epochal shifts in our economy, culture and society' that 'the broader "passive revolution" of Thatcherism' brought about.[198] For Pearmain, this explains New Labour's 'success' as the Labour elite adopted Thatcherism's lines of thinking around which they organised their policies and approach to governance. If Thatcherism is a 'passive revolution' in Gramsci's terminology, connected to 'transformist accommodation', then it is not likely to be an adequate model for a counter-hegemonic strategy since insurgent or resistant subaltern strata are constrained in their access to the hegemonic apparatus.

The crux of the issue is whether the working class can still be an agency of social change and revolutionary action, if sections of that class have already been recruited into the ruling historical bloc via language, common sense and 'folklore' (i.e. mass media and popular culture). Yet, if the only struggle is political-ideological via discourse and common sense, it does undermine any

---

196   Thomas 2009, pp. 160–1 and p. 161, n. 6.
197   Thomas 2009, p. 161.
198   Pearmain 2011, p. 18.

need for a social-economic, material basis to a counter-hegemonic movement's struggle to reform, transform or overthrow capitalism. It, therefore, also undermines any material basis, not only for the modern prince, the revolutionary working-class party, but also for the mass, social-democratic party of the labour movement.

11 Social Production of Ideologies

While Hall emphasised the importance of discourse for understanding Thatcherism's hegemonic influence, he at the same time neglected to analyse (or show) how that discourse (not just hegemony) is produced and circulated. In part, without some kind of recognition of the material basis to ideologies, the social or sociological dimension is easily ignored in favour of a purely textual or linguistic focus on discourse. Hall 'slides between the discursive and statist approaches, unable to mediate their contrary claims because *he subordinates social relations to political articulation*'.[199]

> By suggesting such an overarching political unity Hall himself minimizes the significance of both social diversity and cultural conflict. Hall's ambiguity over the state's role thus destabilises his interpretation of Thatcherism and undermines the distinctive character of his hegemonic approach.[200]

Stuart Hall's analysis of politics during the 1980s was part of the 'discursive turn' that led to a neglect of the sociological dimension of Thatcherism. For example, Brennon Wood argues that Hall's analysis of Thatcherism is weak where it cannot identify the social basis of its support beyond some general statements where certain phrases stand in for the types of supporters among the lower middle and working classes. As Wood states:

> Hall interprets hegemony as a complex discursive field that takes shape across various social locations. However, he also appeals to some notion of the state, a notion that devalues cultural mobilisation by stressing a much narrower site of power.[201]

---

[199] Wood 1998, p. 402 (original emphasis).
[200] Wood 1998, p. 404.
[201] Ibid.

This is ironic given Hall's role in founding cultural studies and his own particular emphasis on the importance of the *politics* of (popular) culture.[202] This much narrower site of power becomes the focus of establishing an alliance to win an electoral contest rather than attempting to win over people by working through language, common sense, and 'folklore' (i.e. mass media and popular culture). Since election campaigns are not considered the time and place to educate the electorate, the focus narrows to whatever tactics and strategy will secure the requisite number of votes to win. Thus, the outcome of Hall's Thatcherism thesis was 'petit bourgeois theorists making long-term adjustments to short-term situations': i.e. strategic adaptations to electoral contests.[203]

Ironically, where Hall had emphasised the importance of culture in the past, his political focus on Thatcherism narrows down to a struggle over which party controls the state, at least as articulated for a left, rather than an academic, audience. Thus, the broad counter-hegemonic struggle is translated into a much narrower focus on Labour's electoral struggle, which arguably could even be seen as a form of 'war of manouevre' rather than 'war of position' since elections usually involve direct confrontation and conflict with the opposing party or parties to triumph. Although this might not be the war of manouevre Gramsci had in mind, it does show how counter-hegemonic thinking can be reduced to a narrow track that turns all other types of positioning on issues into one seeking tactical advantage over one's (electoral) opponent in a short-time frame rather than through the long-term strategic focus of (counter-)hegemony.

Thatcherism overlooks how a particular social bloc, including fractions of the dominant class, was able to effect political-ideological change because it had secured the backing of agencies of the dominant hegemonic apparatus, such as the national press and broadcast programmes,[204] which helped to prepare the ground for Thatcherism. Establishment media, in general, and the campaigning right-wing tabloid press, in particular, do influence at least what people think is significant or neglect as insignificant.[205] As Wood argues:

---

202   Hall 1981a.
203   Williams 1986, p. 30.
204   E.g. Chignell 2012. The Tory press drove much of the ideological agenda across all media outlets, since broadcast outlets are supposed to be non-partisan and often respond to the agenda set by others, including the national press and government public relations practitioners.
205   There is an attitude amongst scholars teaching about media influence, many of whom are uncomfortable with the concept of a dominant ideology, which is not to appear 'anti-democratic' or 'elitist' in suggesting that people might have been 'duped' if they vote against their interests (McGuigan 1992).

> The mass media play a leading role in this process; they undertake 'the critical ideological work of constructing ... a populist common sense' ... Their attack on 'loony' councils, for example, revitalized the rhetoric of racial and sexual pollution that grounds Thatcherism in the everyday discontents of British life.[206]

This is particularly true of the right-wing press, which actively campaigned against several 'loony left' London councils and inflicted considerable damage on the Labour Party during the 1980s.[207] Thus, despite Hall's own contributions to the academic study of media and popular culture, he curiously pays little attention to the media in his analysis of Thatcherism beyond a few descriptive or anecdotal references.

For example, one aspect of the campaigns against the 'Loony Left' London Labour councils is that it is unclear how the 'encoding/decoding' model,[208] or the 'resistant readings' of the active audience model, would apply to how audiences resisted (or not) or negotiated (or not) such pervasive, systematic (mis)representation of, and false or distorted, information and images of the London Labour Left. The Tory tabloids also worked actively to reproduce consent to the dominant ideology via common sense. Despite Hall's studies of media influence and their role as 'primary definers',[209] he neglects to take into account his own analyses in his polemical engagements with sections of the left over Labour's trajectory in the 1980s.[210]

This means that Hall can describe aspects of Thatcherism's 'common sense' and make the assumption that these ideas are widely distributed and accepted, even though one would assume that there must be some 'resistant readings' of audiences 'decoding' the media's messages in a negotiated or oppositional way rather than simply accepting the 'dominant reading'. Even the dominant mass media are not able to secure the consent of all. As Phillip Schlesinger, for example, pointed out, *Policing the Crisis* underestimates 'the dynamic pro-

---

206 Wood 1998, p. 403.
207 Curran et al. 2005.
208 The three possible readings of media texts were seen as either a 'dominant' reading which means the message is accepted as the sender intended; a negotiated 'reading', means the audience accepts some aspects, but rejects others; and a 'resistant' reading is when the audience rejects the message (Hall 1980c).
209 E.g. Hall 1977, 1978; Hall et al. 1978, pp. 53–77, and especially p. 59. For some other criticisms of Hall et al.'s model, see the summary in Miller 1993.
210 Referring to *Policing The Crisis* (Hall et al. 1978, pp. 204–19) Wood writes that it 'is framed by some sort of Althusserian functionalism that effectively reduces the media to servants of established political forces' (1998, p. 412).

cesses of contestation in a given field of discourse' because of Hall et al.'s 'structuralist assumptions'.[211] This is an issue if it is thought that there are no possible entry points for the left to intervene in public debate and engage in developing a counter-hegemonic strategy or war of position.

However, such a war of position cannot be left to Labour's parliamentary leadership because of the compromises that are necessary to win over reluctant voters and media gatekeepers to reach those reluctant voters. Hall's Thatcherism:

> subsumes the state within Thatcherite populism, which thus inherits the functionalist overtones with which the former had been invested by *Policing the Crisis*. As a consequence, Thatcherite leadership acquires an air of invulnerability. The mass media, for example, are portrayed as indisputably Thatcherite agencies.[212]

It is not necessarily incorrect that the mass media were 'indisputably Thatcherite agencies',[213] even if, as some argue, some newspapers promoted 'market populism' rather than support for Thatcher's government *per se*.[214] Such a move means that not all of the right-wing press could be seen as uncritically pro-Tory and some might become *more* persuasive by appearing to be at some ideological distance from Thatcher's government. The mainstream media can be more effective at securing consent by permitting opposing views some representation versus a media system that would exclude all opposing views, and it is within those openings that a left counter-hegemonic strategy would have to engage. This would, therefore, require a more explicit and dedicated attention to both the organisation and mobilisation of class and social movement forces on the ground (e.g. in the streets, neighbourhoods, workplaces) and to the development of a (counter-)hegemonic apparatus of the subaltern classes to articulate the (counter-)hegemonic ideas by connecting to those aspects of 'good sense' contained within the available materials in the language, common sense and popular culture of the day.

---

211   Schlesinger 1990, p. 69, cited in Wood 1998, p. 412, n. 6.
212   Wood 1998, p. 404.
213   Ibid.
214   McKnight 2009.

12   The Hegemonic Apparatus

Although Stuart Hall emphasises the importance of Thatcherism's appeal to the public via the articulation of ruling class interests with the public's interests via authoritarian populism, he practically ignores the importance of the mainstream media's role, as part of the hegemonic apparatus, in articulating and popularising such interests, since his model of ideology elides the social production of ideologies with 'ideology in general', which leaves no way to understand how Thatcherite discourse is produced and, therefore, no way of identifying a strategy to get outside of its ideology or to challenge it within the media sphere.[215] Ironically, this shift in Hall's thesis occurred despite his own emphasis on the political-ideological dimension.[216] Yet, Hall's analysis of Thatcherism is undermined precisely because it lacks an understanding of how Gramsci saw the role of the hegemonic apparatus, since he draws upon Althusser's formulation of ISAs and RSAs that drew from Gramsci's concept.[217]

Since Hall does not offer a clear understanding of *how* Thatcherism became hegemonic, it might explain why Thatcherism is not an easy model to replicate or apply elsewhere, because in Hall's thesis 'the discursive reading so disperses meanings and locations that hegemonic power is rendered fluidly indeterminate'.[218] This neglect weakens Hall's understanding of Gramsci's theory of hegemony because the 'hegemonic apparatus', which is defined as 'any institution, place or agent that organises, mediates and confirms the hegemony of a class over other classes',[219] plays an integral role in the process of how hegemony is continuously negotiated.[220] (Indeed, the hegemonic apparatus is key also to the social production of ideologies: without it, there is no means for the production of ideology.) Of course, this concept includes much more than the media, such as educational, religious, legal and other institutions, and extends beyond material infrastructure and organisations to include consciousness and knowledge. As Stefan Bollinger and Juha Koivisto explain:

---

215   See Jones 2004.
216   E.g. Davidson 2008; Robinson 2005; Peck 2001.
217   Bollinger and Koivisto 2009. See Thomas 2009, pp. 242–4 for a fuller explanation of the hegemonic apparatus and the limitations of Althusser's formulation of the ISAs.
218   Wood 1998, p. 401. This corresponds to 'Hall's *style* of theorising' (Ibid., p. 409).
219   G. Francioni 1984, cited in Bollinger and Koivisto 2009, p. 301.
220   E.g. Thomas 2009, pp. 224–8.

The installation of an apparatus is equivalent to a 'philosophical reform': insofar as it 'creates a new ideological terrain, it effects a reform of consciousness and of methods of knowledge, its [sic] a fact of knowledge, a philosophical fact'.[221]

This is a critical concept for understanding the process by which social formations establish 'moral-intellectual leadership' in the war of position for (counter-)hegemony.

Although Hall neglects to identify how Thatcherism was made 'popular', despite the focus on the media as primary definers in *Policing the Crisis*,[222] the collaborative project from which Hall's Thatcherism thesis evolved, there is no way to see how to get outside of Thatcherism, except to somehow rearticulate those elements of its common sense from a right-wing inflection to a left-wing accent. Gramsci's work included an emphasis on the social production of ideologies, which Althusser's theory of ideology, as with Hall's Thatcherism, inspired in part by Althusser, did not: there appears no way out of the neat circle of 'ideology in general'.

The differences in the potential to direct society between a ruling bloc with control over a (dominant) hegemonic apparatus (and hence a partial explanation as to *why* it is a *ruling* bloc), and a formation of subaltern classes, which has to try to develop its own (counter-)hegemonic apparatus, are considerable and each requires a different strategy. Yet, Gramsci was not clear on how an oppositional subaltern formation would develop a hegemonic apparatus prior to becoming hegemonic,[223] since the (dominant) hegemonic apparatus enables a ruling bloc to maintain hegemony through audience reach and legitimation functions and, thereby, presents a major problem for a (counter-)hegemonic formation of subaltern classes.

The role of a (counter-)hegemonic apparatus is, therefore, critical for the left to be able to engage in a war of position to defeat Thatcherism. The role of radical and progressive alternative media and cultural production is crucial here. The period of the 1970s and 1980s was a period of increasing 'democratisation' of media and cultural production as the necessary costs and skills were lowered to the point of becoming more easily adopted by alternative, radical

---

221 Gramsci cited in Bollinger and Koivisto 2009, p. 301.
222 Hall et al. 1978.
223 Thomas 2009. Gramsci never used the term 'counter hegemony'. However, I use the term to signify a hegemonic strategy against a ruling or historical bloc by subaltern formations, which means that such a strategy could perhaps be best described by Gramsci's concept of 'integral hegemony', as explained by Joseph Femia (Ives 2004b, pp. 68–70).

and marginalised groups so that they could produce their own 'voices' and messages.[224] It was not just a period of the unprecedented global transformation of the economy; it was also a period when the working and lower-middle classes had the means to produce and distribute to some extent their own cultural output. This was a major shift in the means of cultural production by the subaltern classes that meant less reliance on trying to seek access via the dominant hegemonic apparatus.[225] It is impossible, therefore, to conceive of a possible (counter-)hegemonic strategy that does not include the means for the social production of (counter-)hegemonic ideologies, which means having access to the means of communication for the articulation, production and distribution of (counter-)hegemonic ideas to establish the moral-intellectual leadership of the (counter-)hegemonic bloc: i.e. a (counter-)hegemonic apparatus.

Stuart Hall's approach has been criticised for assuming that the New Right's hegemonic approach to the battle of ideas, Thatcherism's passive revolution, could simply be turned upside down or inverted for the left's (counter-)hegemonic strategy. Ultimately, however, Hall's approach led to an over-emphasis on electoral strategy, which meant adapting to what your prospective audience understands via mainstream corporate and state media, and their production of the dominant ideology and common sense.[226] This is the role for the (counter-)hegemonic apparatus: i.e. the social production of ideologies outside of the dominant hegemonic apparatus. To be fair, even here Gramsci's concept was not clear about how a hegemonic apparatus of the subaltern classes would be built or operate, except for the modern prince which would operate via civil society to organise the subaltern classes into a social bloc. Thus, the role of alternative and radical media, including *Marxism Today*, is overlooked, thereby compelling the articulation of (counter-)hegemonic ideas to the margins of mass media of the (dominant) hegemonic apparatus. What cannot be ignored is that the hegemonic apparatus was key for Thatcherism and it included the national press, some broadcast programmes and neoliberal think tanks.

Gramsci identifies the hegemonic apparatus as playing an important role in the process of a ruling bloc maintaining its hegemony or in facing challenges to its hegemonic rule. This is an omission in Hall's analysis that takes on a critical significance when thinking about the rise and dominance of Thatcher's Conservative Party from the late 1970s onwards, which has to be ascribed in part, at the very least, to the dedicated partisan role of a majority of the national

---

224   E.g. Pimlott 2014a.
225   Ibid. E.g. Atton 2002; Aubrey et al. 1979; Baines 2015; Cooper et al. 1980; Downing 2001.
226   Part of the success of Hall's thesis on the left was due to his rhetorical skills (Chapter 6).

press and to that of the think tanks (although he does make mention of both). Indeed, most left organisers, leaders and intellectuals were well aware of the limitations of a media system that favoured the dominant class and, therefore, required some kind of alternative, independent media that would be able to produce and circulate the left's critical views and ideas.

The growing strength of unions, real or imagined, public sector borrowing and inflation scared the ruling bloc, and as a concomitant contribution to the rise of Thatcherism, anti-socialist and anti-union propaganda was (and is still) carried via the mainstream media and, in particular, the national press, which acted as the 'party paper' for the Thatcherite or neoliberal ruling bloc. The Communist Party and other left groups did make some attempts to organise around media and popular culture issues, such as the fortnightly forum on 'Marxism and the Mass Media' organised by the International Marxist Group, which included presenters from other left parties in London in 1977–78, and which was published as a collection in 1979.[227] Another collection published a year earlier, *The British Press: A Manifesto*, presented a series of analyses of the national press, which included contributions from public socialist intellectuals and leading media scholars, including Stuart Hall and Raymond Williams.[228] Both Williams and Hall noted that owners, editors and journalists were unhappy about printers' unions interfering with 'controversial' editions, which were often disputes over anti-Labour messages on the front page.[229] This was both an indication of the willingness of union leaders and activists to act, and a recognition of their collective strength to intervene, much to the chagrin of owners and editors.

Williams's contribution bears closer examination because, as we know in retrospect with our 20/20 vision, it was prescient in identifying a key problem for both the Labour Party and the left: the rightward shift in the national press would (and did) have dire consequences, if the left refused to recognise (and it did) the extent of the problem, as Labour governments had also ignored it in the past. He recognises that the left often reiterates the idea that other factors play into how people respond to issues; yet even if the national press is not directly leading opinion, it is still influential in setting the agenda for national debate. Why else would newspaper owners sustain substantial losses, contrary to the claims of 'free market' ideology and neoclassical economic theory, to ensure

---

227 Gardner 1979. There were also numerous efforts in the mid to late 1970s to establish production groups, for example, around design and film.
228 Curran 1978. Hall's and Williams's chapters to this collection are often overlooked in the bibliographies of their contributions to politics and cultural studies.
229 Williams 1978; Hall 1978.

that right-wing newspapers remained rightwing, if it were not to ensure the circulation of conservative or neoliberal ideology?

This direction played well into the approach subsequently adopted by many cultural and media studies scholars, overlooking the directly influential aspects of right-wing newspapers in favour of 'resistance' and 'agency' as exemplified by audiences resisting the dominant ideology.[230] While the imperative was not to assume that ordinary people are 'dupes', which is an important and necessary corrective to the common misrepresentations of 'the people', it also did not mean, however, that they were or are outside of being persuaded of views that work against their economic interests. Therefore, it is necessary to consider Williams's analysis in some detail here because the national press, and especially Tory tabloids, were engaged in popularising Thatcherism and contributed significantly to its influence during the 1980s.

The first two of 'three distinct kinds of crisis' affecting the national press were 'a deep and persistent crisis of the press as a capitalist industry', and the 'longstanding ... set of problems about the relationship between the press and the state'.[231] Members of the establishment, from capitalist press owners to leading politicians of the major parties, offer 'orthodox diagnoses' for the first crisis, which emphasise 'such problems as overmanning, restrictive practices, the difficulties of rationalisation': all areas where unions exerted power.[232] The second crisis is problematic precisely because of the role of the press as a 'watchdog on power' in a bourgeois democracy, which raises questions about its relationship to and with the state, and indeed with working-class power given the first crisis, which explains the antipathy towards unions on the part of journalists and editors. Most solutions deal with the first two kinds of crises. The third, however, is 'quite another form of crisis, which can be summarised as a set of unsolved problems about the modern national newspaper as a social and cultural form', which are affected by, but not limited to, the first two crises; only by examining the newspaper's form can we identify what was wrong with the press.[233]

The work of the late James Thomas provides the analysis that supports Williams's prescient critique about the impact of the national press and especially

---

230 See, for example, two early critiques of cultural studies: Harris 1992; McGuigan 1992. The Glasgow University Media Group's critical analyses of news coverage of strikes and economic issues became marginalised within cultural studies by the mid-1980s (e.g. GUMG 1976, 1978, 1982).
231 Williams 1978, p. 16.
232 Williams 1978, p. 19.
233 Williams 1978, p. 16.

the tabloids.[234] The tabloids' 'unique hostility displayed … towards Labour between 1979 and 1992', Thomas argues, was partly a result of decades-long changes in the newspaper form, as most notable in 'the shift from broadsheet to tabloid format that occurred for the *Daily Mail* and the *Daily Express* during the 1970s'.[235] The shift in ostensible middle-class and middle-market newspapers, from broadsheet to tabloid during the 1970s, a format that lends itself 'much more easily to a straightforward propaganda message' than a broadsheet's format does, led to the 'emphasis on one-story front pages, screaming headlines and short punchy prose at the expense of more detailed text', which in turn helped to 'produce a change in the emphasis of political coverage, from news and opinion to opinion and propaganda'.[236] Since 1945, changes in political coverage in 'all national newspapers' have made 'a more general shift downmarket', 'from a reactive style of reporting', where the party favoured by the paper got proportionately more space than its opponents, 'to an approach that has become much cruder, simplified, personalised and negative than in the past', especially with the popular press, where more 'opinion and personality' meant 'that by the 1980s it was misleading to refer to the popular press as *news*papers'.[237]

Of the closure of national newspapers in the previous 30 years, Williams writes, 'the really significant losses are political', since two of the centre-left and left papers that were lost, *The Daily Herald* and the *News Chronicle*, together with two other middle-market 'populars', *The Daily Express* and *The Daily Mail*, had sold more than nine million copies daily in 1960: 'around 60 per cent of the market'.[238] The transformation of *The Daily Herald* into *The Sun*, was perhaps the greatest political shift to the right by any newspaper since the early 1920s as a labour movement newspaper became an anti-union tabloid. Although it had maintained loyal support for the labour movement for half a century (1912–64), its one to two million older working-class readers were not of interest to advertisers and *The Sun* was transformed into an instrument for popularising Thatcherism by the late 1970s.[239]

Williams observed that while the 'right-wing popular papers are, in general, on the right wing of Conservative opinion', even the papers that continued to

---

234   E.g. Thomas 1998, 2005, 2007.
235   Thomas 1998, p. 89; Williams 1978, p. 16.
236   Thomas 1998, p. 89.
237   Ibid. (original emphasis).
238   Williams 1978, p. 20; Laing 1992, pp. 78–9. The third centre-left paper lost was *Reynolds' News*.
239   The TUC had sold the *Daily Herald* to Odhams' Press in 1930 to save it but Odham's sold it to IPC in 1962, which sold it to Murdoch in 1969 (Richards 1997); Williams 1978, p. 20.

support Labour shifted to the right, such as the *Mirror*, which was 'supposed to be the countervailing force', was 'on the right wing of Labour opinion', which led to his conclusion that 'the popular press, as a whole, [had] moved in the last thirty years decisively to the Right'.[240] He argues, therefore, that the focus on the press should not be on capitalist re-organisation and consolidation, but on its political consequences: i.e. few newspapers have even a centre-left, let alone a left, orientation.

There had been a broad postwar trend between the circulation of right and left editorial (ideological) lines of newspapers, and the tallies of Labour and Conservative votes: it 'used to be said that aggregate circulations corresponded quite closely to the distribution of the votes between Labour and Conservatives', albeit with some anomalies, such as the February 1974 election.[241] But, such tallies overlook 'the crucial area of industrial politics', whereby there are no national media that advance the viewpoint of the organised working class or its unions, which represented some 11 million workers in the 1970s. The national media barely, if ever, represent the crucial arena of workplace struggle from the perspective of the workers; it is virtually always from the perspective of managers, investors and owners: 'In virtually all disputes the majority of the press is hostile to the workers' interests from the outset'.[242]

While this hostility is not unexpected, Williams said that there were 'two significant special factors' that needed to be considered.[243] The first is the willingness of newspaper owners 'to bear heavy losses to keep right-wing papers going' since market forces would have produced quite different results.[244] Obviously, right-wing press owners do *not* subscribe to the idea that if their views are not 'popular' (i.e. literally not *bought* by readers in the marketplace of ideas), they should provide different views that *are* popular with their readers. Capitalists do not believe in subjecting their ideas and ideology to competition unless they can subsidise them, which is, of course, contrary to their own 'free [sic] market' rhetoric and theory.[245]

The other special factor was 'the extraordinary indifference of the organised Left', and Labour governments that had continually ignored or rejected any attempt 'to redress or maintain some sort of political balance' in the national

---

240 Williams 1978, p. 21.
241 Williams 1978, pp. 21, 20.
242 Williams 1978, p. 22.
243 Ibid.
244 Ibid.
245 Since there was no guarantee that their ideas could be supported through peer-reviewed channels in academic disciplines, think tanks were established to produce the 'correct' studies to prove neoliberal theories work (Desai 1994; Gutstein 2009; Mirowski 2013).

press, although Labour governments had been persuaded to maintain capitalist employment.[246] This works as state support for the maintenance of employment of journalists, editors and printers in the capitalist production of newspapers, and of their owners, via state policies, such as tax exemptions to help subsidise newspapers' distribution and sales.

Williams stated that 'both the Labour Party and the trade union movement are likely to pay very heavily' for the national press' rightward shift, which, unfortunately, proved correct.[247] Yet, he also knew that many on the left would adopt a 'common way of evading this uncomfortable but inevitable conclusion' by claiming 'that people do not ... necessarily take their political opinions from the newspapers that they read' (which became an integral part of the 'cultural populist' trajectory in cultural studies), during a time in which the press 'was more hostile to Labour than at any time in the post-war period'.[248]

Thomas's historical research substantiates Williams's prescient observations: 'roughly 70 percent of the national press supported the Conservatives, or, more accurately, Mrs Thatcher's particular brand of Conservatism'.[249] This research also identifies anomalies that some readers did not realise or know which political party their newspapers supported. For example, 52 percent of *The Sun* readers voted Labour in 1979, which was consistent since 1976, despite *The Sun*'s own political shift earlier in the decade,[250] although as Thomas points out, even a newspaper's editorial or 'party line' is not always understood by their readerships, nor is it necessarily aligned with the actual views of their audiences. Nevertheless, Labour's third worst general election result since 1945 was in the 1992 elections after being subjected to the hostility of a majority of the Tory tabloid press, which was the culmination of the extreme rightwing shift in the 1970s that Williams had identified.[251]

Williams outlines the 'missing theme' in understanding Thatcherism's dominance, since the 'militant particularism' of those engaged in local conflicts over 'immediate interests' (work and working conditions), had little chance of receiving balanced press coverage, which could have shifted their struggles to a more general political level. 'Resistance to a policy can be generated where there are direct but then characteristically localised conflicts of immediate interest', which Williams argued had 'sharply increased' in the

---

246 Williams 1978, p. 22.
247 Ibid.
248 Ibid.; Williams 1983a, p. 137; Thomas 1998, p. 87.
249 Thomas 1998, p. 87.
250 Thomas 2005, p. 85.
251 Thomas 1998, p. 81.

1970s.²⁵² However, without the national press coverage that is necessary to connect the interests of local struggles to the more general policies of the government and competing parties, local struggles remain localised because of 'the deep political biases of the press – its effective consensus over and above party differences and specific issues'.²⁵³

The rightward shift of newspapers meant that there was no place for the views of trade unionists and workers, even if a left press might not shift the situation in the short run: 'the great majority of those who might even, on past record, be inclined to consider and support it [a left press], never hear, day in day out, any alternative perspective and policy'.²⁵⁴ Even worse, was that the national press' rightward shift happened under a Labour government and that its victory 'is so complete that even to mention it seems either banal, to insiders, or in public terms, utopian and impractical'.²⁵⁵

Also important was the significant growth in circulation for the 'more expensive newspapers' as 'broadly in line with the development of higher education, which in one way sets their readership, content and style', whereas the 'cheaper press, led notably by the Murdoch *Sun*, has if anything moved back towards older cultural styles'.²⁵⁶ Although there had been an expansion of topics covered across all types of newspapers that were directly linked to advertising (e.g. travel, food), since advertising's 'increasingly significant role' in financing newspapers reinforced this particular material basis for subsidising the retail price for the press, there had been little change in the 'treatment of political, economic and social news' by the popular press since the 1920s, despite the growth of a 'significantly better educated and informed' population: 'All the devices of sensational simplification and spurious personalisation are still regularly practised'.²⁵⁷

Despite the ongoing social crisis in the 1970s, 'the proportion of such [relevant] news in the total selection of content has remained remarkably low' with even the quality press 'rarely exceeding 25 per cent'.²⁵⁸ There was a greater emphasis on financial news, 'in which the concerns of the stock exchange, the banks and the insurance companies have come to be much more centrally represented', demonstrating the growth of the financial sector's influence, which

252 Williams 1978, p. 22.
253 Ibid.
254 Ibid.
255 Ibid.
256 Williams 1978, p. 24.
257 Ibid.
258 Ibid.

also meant 'that some readers, including some socialists, now find the *Financial Times* the most serious national newspaper'.[259] Amongst those socialists, were some CPGB economists and the new editor of *Marxism Today*, Martin Jacques, who read the FT regularly from the 1970s onwards and greatly admired the writing of one columnist in particular: David Watt.[260] There was a tendency to accept the 'economic explanations' as if they were more 'technically' correct or explained 'stagflation', a new economic development where a stagnant economy mixed with high inflation.

The acceptance of neoliberal economists' explanations fuelled the critique that public sector strikes only harmed the people, as recipients of public services, not the government or corporations.[261] The establishment, Conservatives and right-wing newspaper owners took advantage of these explanations to attack wage demands as against 'the national interest' and later used the 'Winter of Discontent' in propaganda campaigns with which to beat Labour well into the 1990s, despite questions about the actual impact during the winter of 1978–79.[262]

Not everyone overlooked the importance of mass media and their connections to the dominant institutions in society. The Glasgow University Media Group focused on the power of the news media to frame important political and economic issues, for example, in their studies published in 1976, 1978 and 1982.[263] Williams highlighted some key issues[264] and challenged socialist economists, who were persuaded by right-wing economists' claims that wage demands were driving inflation. GUMG's analysis highlighted that the representation of wage inflation on the BBC, for example, went from the 20 pence in the pound in the original economic analyses to news reports claiming 60 to 75 pence in the pound, three to four times the original figure![265] These figures were inaccurate and seriously misrepresented the impact of unionised workers' bargaining power and yet such inaccurate claims were also generally accepted by socialist economists as the primary cause of inflation.[266]

---

259   Ibid.
260   Jacques 1996c.
261   E.g. Hobsbawm 1978.
262   Hay 1996, 2010. It was also used by Tony Blair to attack 'Old Labour'.
263   GUMG 1976, 1978, 1982.
264   Williams 1989d [1980].
265   Ibid.
266   Even Adam Smith in the eighteenth century argued that higher wages were seen as the cause of higher prices but high(er) profits sought by 'merchants and master-manufacturers' were ignored or downplayed; he equates the difference between the two causes as that of simple and compound interest respectively (Smith 1976).

FROM 'NEW LEFT' TO 'NEW LABOUR' 163

The other key element within the hegemonic apparatus that contributed to the rise of Thatcherism and neoliberalism, which has only gradually become an object of study over the last two decades, is the 'think tank'. Think tanks had (and continue to have) a very important role in the New Right's strategy for hegemony as these organisations produced the necessary ideas, policies and language, to persuade others to adopt Thatcherism or neoliberalism.[267] The strategy of the intellectuals, propagandists and promoters, who gathered under the aegis of the Mont Pelerin Society and various offshoots,[268] was closer to understanding the role of a 'passive revolution' or *trasformismo*, which is quite different to a (counter-)hegemonic strategy or war of position for subaltern classes seeking revolutionary change.

Hall acknowledged the role of think tanks, as with leader writers of middle-market tabloids, albeit without a sense of just how crucial they were, not only for the development of neoliberal ideas and policies, but also for the necessary media strategies to promote the ideas, policies and values: their role as a part of the dominant hegemonic apparatus. Integral to the success of the MPS and its followers, was their involvement in the production and circulation of the ideology (e.g. myths, values, common sense) of neoliberalism, in a targetted, systematic fashion. These neoliberal propagandists, as 'second-hand dealers' in ideas, targetted people in such positions as teachers, journalists and civil servants, who could also act in disseminating neoliberal ideas in their work and through their networks.[269] Radhika Desai outlined the key role played by think tanks in the social production and circulation of Thatcherism; her study would have contributed immensely to Hall's analysis because it helps to show *how* Thatcherism became influential via the 'hegemonic apparatus'.[270] Hall's thesis ignores the need for the production and distribution of Thatcherite ideas and policies via the hegemonic apparatus, which is central to the social production of (neoliberal) ideology.[271] Since the hegemonic apparatus plays such an important part in the process of negotiating hegemony for Thatcherism and

---

267 Numerous accounts of neoliberalism in the USA, UK and Canada have identified the key role played by think tanks whereby small groups of intellectuals, backed by substantial financial resources from wealthy individuals and corporations, were able to make neoliberalism hegemonic. This Gramscianism of the New Right brought about political-ideological changes albeit via a 'passive revolution' or '*trasformismo*', rather than a counter-hegemonic struggle or war of position (e.g. Gutstein 2009; Kozolanka 2007; Mirowski 2013).
268 Mirowski's label, 'Neoliberal Thought Collective', beautifully captures the totalitarian nature of this formation's ideological 'groupthink' (Mirowski 2013 *passim*).
269 Desai 1994, p. 31.
270 Desai 1994.
271 Jones 2004, p. 85.

neoliberalism, it should have meant that for a (counter-)hegemonic strategy of the working class there would have been a need to focus on a different means of articulating socialism to common sense since the left lacked access to the (dominant) hegemonic apparatus. This is where the modern prince becomes a necessary organisation around which the (counter-)hegemonic apparatus can be built to help bring the subaltern classes together in a potential ruling social-historical bloc.

With the benefit of hindsight, we can see the systematic attack on working-class institutions and organisations by Thatcher's government was, at least in part, propelled by the threat that such subaltern organisations represented in supporting a (counter-)hegemonic apparatus (e.g. *The Sunday Correspondent*).[272] This threat was posed by the growth in the 'democratisation' of access to media and cultural production for subaltern groups, which provided the means of establishing a left (counter) public sphere, whereby demands and policies in the economic interests of the working class, even if it was not coordinated or organised systematically, might have challenged the dominance of the establishment's hegemonic apparatus.[273]

Neoliberal ideas came to dominate the public sphere of debate by the 1970s as the result of the establishment of neoliberal think tanks, such as the Institute of Economic Affairs, the Centre for Policy Studies and the Adam Smith Institute in the UK. They developed and circulated ideas and started targeting leading opinion 'influencers': journalistic elite; academics; policy wonks and political decision makers. The influence of neoliberal ideas grew amongst senior journalists and editors in the national press and even amongst public sector broadcasters, including then Prime Minister Jim Callaghan's son-in-law, Peter Jay.[274] As Ben Jackson argues, the think tanks purposefully targetted media and political elites, through the publication of reports and through public relations drives for news coverage. By the beginning of the 1970s, most of the right-wing press, or at least the editors and leading commentators were won over to the need for 'monetarism', the precursor to neoliberalism, with *The Economist* as a relatively late convert amongst the right-wing press when it turned to neoliberalism in 1974.[275] The 'popularisers of neoliberalism' were out, not to convert public opinion, but to first influence elites, especially leading academics and media commentators, who would in turn provide the 'second-hand dealers in

---

272 Chippindale and Horrie 1988. This was an attempt to launch a left-wing Sunday paper in the mainstream newspaper market but the experiment lasted only six months.
273 Pimlott 2014a.
274 Chignell 2012.
275 Jackson 2012, p. 55.

ideas', such as 'journalists, academics, teachers, publicists, public intellectuals, novelists, political advisors and so on', with the ideas that had previously been 'regarded as out-of-date and intellectually unfashionable'.[276]

This strategy's success was the establishment of neoliberalism's dominance through political-ideological struggle, which would have been impossible without think tanks playing their role. In the first few years after MT's closure, Jacques helped to found the think tank, Demos, in addition to his appointment as an associate editor at *The Independent*. In essence, MT had become a kind of 'think tank' and so Demos was an obvious outcome, particularly given how resolutely MT had maintained its independence from any organisational connections with the left in its last years.

13   'New Times': From New Left to New Labour?

The period of the 'New Times' project marks a break in the connection of *Marxism Today*'s ideas to the Communist Party of Great Britain's old programme, the *British Road to Socialism*, just as the older economy of heavy industries and the welfare state were giving way to the development of a new(er) 'post-Fordist' future with 'decentred' workplaces, a dominant service sector and a 'knowledge economy'. The combination of the pursuit for a 'popular-democratic' politics and a recognition of a rapidly changing world gave birth to the New Times project, which sprang out of the May 1988 weekend seminar on 'Rethinking Socialism for the '90s'. However, New Times was in many ways a continuation of MT's two earlier theses, 'Forward March' and 'Thatcherism', with its continued focus on a popular-democratic politics and popular culture, but which failed, nonetheless, to articulate a popular-democratic discourse to replace labourism.[277] According to MT, the left could only solve its crisis by developing the 'correct analysis' of the important economic, social and cultural changes then taking place in the UK and around the world; otherwise it would have to leave the battlefield of ideas to Thatcherism's 'regressive modernisation'. Thus, while New Times was attempting to go beyond conventional left analyses to construct a cohesive, wide-ranging theoretical analysis which could explain the global changes in the economy, society and culture, it never proved to be as successful nor as persuasive as either the Forward March or Thatcherism.

---

276   Jackson 2012, pp. 44–5.
277   Harris 1992, p. 183.

The left had proved incapable of stopping the New Right under Thatcher's leadership, which had been able to rearticulate people's concerns and desires into support for its project. However, MT admitted to mistakenly conflating Thatcherism with the world it 'claimed to represent and aspired to lead', which made Thatcherism appear omnipotent.[278] Thus, if it could 'prise Thatcherism and that world apart' and develop 'a new politics of the Left, a politics beyond Thatcherism, which [could] give a progressive shape and inflexion to New Times', it would be able to establish itself as a hegemonic force, as Thatcherism had done ten years earlier.[279] MT saw their efforts around New Times as 'a dramatic achievement of bringing coherence to a chaotic situation and transforming despondency into a new direction'.[280]

This phase was perhaps the most innovative because of its attempt to supersede what MT writers claimed was the left's more conventional thinking and acknowledge how much society had changed as a result of, not just Thatcherism, but also the restructuring of global capitalism, new technologies and changes in consumption. It also meant a recognition that the terrain on which the left would have to engage with the right had shifted, permanently. New Times was an attempt to 'modernise' the left's politics, updating its analysis of social, economic and cultural factors.

However, before we look more closely at the articles that were published under the New Times label, we should consider the similarity of their ideas to those from a political-intellectual formation three decades earlier: the first New Left, 1957–62. These had also come out of a long period of Conservative government (1951–64), when the Labour Party was faced with internal dissension as the supporters of Hugh Gaitskell sought to revise Labour's constitution and policies on such key issues as nationalisation, public ownership and the market, all forerunners to the changes that Tony Blair and New Labour revisionists were to bring about after taking control of the party in 1994. The New Times project was developing in the decade of Thatcherism and neoliberal regulatory changes, after Keynesianism had been dispatched to the 'dustbin of history' with the Labour government's acceptance of the IMF loan in 1976.

Some of the similarities in ideas between the 1950s and 1980s revolve around finding a third way between Labourism and Stalinism: 'socialist-humanism'; 'classlessness' and the growing affluence or *'embourgeoisiement'* of the working class (and the consequences for class loyalties and politics); cultural politics

---

278   Hall and Jacques 1989a, p. 15.
279   Hall and Jacques 1989a, pp. 15–17.
280   MTEB 1988b, p. 6.

and popular culture.[281] Just as the first New Left developed a decentralised network of New Left clubs, so, too did MT support the development of discussion groups around the UK. There are similarities in the attention to design, images and popular culture alongside politics proper in the pages of NLR, 1960–62, and MT's second format, 1979–86.[282]

The first New Left's criticisms of the CPGB's 'democratic centralism' and the Labour Party's machinery were part of the critique of the bureaucracy of modern society and the welfare state. Influenced by the writings of the early Karl Marx, their focus was on alienation and a critique of both Stalinism and Labourism, inflected by a moral, rather than an economic, focus. E.P. Thompson helped to articulate a socialist-humanism that was an attempt to set out a new worldview for this 'third way' beyond these two dominant, albeit 'stale', ideologies. Nevertheless, the first New Left did still engage in a somewhat hopeful, if distant and critical, debate with the Labour Party until disillusionment set in with the failures of Harold Wilson's government after 1966. Michael Kenny points out the paradoxes that characterised the first New Left:

> ... it wished to provide a new political identity for those disillusioned with the orthodoxies of socialism, yet it remained closely engaged with developments in the Labour Party; it set out to rethink orthodox socialist ideas but never abandoned socialism as a creed; and it developed an instinctive sympathy for the popular dimension of political and ideological struggle, yet was fascinated by the avant-garde and modernistic elements of British society and culture.[283]

It was the ambivalence in the cultural arena that also characterised MT. The overlap in concerns between the first New Left and cultural studies was no coincidence because they shared many of the same contributors, such as Hall, Thompson and Williams.

The first New Left encouraged an engagement with democracy and a left individualism, which were highlighted in concerns over civil society and democracy, and in their tradition of hostility to Stalinism and statist socialism: they 'foreshadowed the argument of feminists that the "personal is political" and

---

281 E.g. Compare Hall 1958, 1960, 1988a, 1989a. See also: Harris 1992; McGuigan 1992; Sparks 1996.
282 Chapter 4.
283 Kenny 1995b, pp. 198–9.

they rejected the "orthodox models of political behaviour" on offer'.[284] The New Left's emphasis on civil society was influential: it offered 'an alternative set of ideas about how the left ought to conduct its political struggles and where it needed to find allies for these'.[285] The first New Left was also convinced that, contrary to the economism of Stalinists and Labourists, 'socialism was a *conscious* democratic movement and socialists were *made*, not born or "given" by the inevitable laws of history or ... the mode of production alone'.[286] Yet, the first New Left did not make any inroads into Labourism: it only succeeded in confirming that political culture's current of anti-intellectualism. 'All the difficulties for socialist politics had been identified' by the mid-1960s:

> a conservative and corporatist working class, an anti-intellectual Labourist socialist party, a tiny Communist Party, inadequate theoretical resources to begin to analyse British capitalism or to understand its crisis.[287]

These are part of the roots of MT's political project, particularly New Times, with its 'socialist individualism' and commitments to liberal representative democracy and civil society.

Marxism Today's articles,[288] which made up the New Times project, represent 'an attempt to rethink Marxism in the face of economic, cultural and political changes which are seen as having outrun the analytical capacity of conventional Marxism'.[289] NT writers, therefore, tried to 'expand the means of analysis available' and develop a vocabulary that could help explain these changes.[290] Though these changes were seen as important, they did not represent 'an epochal shift', as in the transition from feudalism to capitalism, but a transition 'from one regime of accumulation to another, within capitalism, whose impact has been extraordinarily wide ranging'.[291] New Times charts the shift away from the public sphere to business culture, consumerism and individual choice reflected in the two great changes of the 1980s: the rise of the market and civil society.[292] These can be seen in the emphasis on citizen-

---

284 Kenny 1995b, p. 200.
285 Kenny 1995b, p. 201.
286 Hall 1989c, p. 36 (original emphasis).
287 Harris 1992, p. 175.
288 Reprinted in Hall and Jacques 1989b.
289 Clarke 1991, p. 155.
290 Hall 1989a, p. 125.
291 Hall 1989a, p. 127.
292 MTEB 1988b, p. 6.

ship, 'socialist individualism', the politics of identity and the decentralisation of power, the use of marketing and new technologies, and the politics of consumption. This included an emphasis on areas that had traditionally been regarded sceptically by the left, such as Europe, consumerism and the politics of identity.

The most important concept in New Times was 'post-Fordism', although this term applied to the changing organisation of the workplace, production process and product, to mark the shift from the mass factories that had epitomised 'Fordism'. NT writers, however, used the term to also signal other important changes beyond the 'shuttered' factory gates, just as Gramsci had used 'Fordism' in his works to signal equally significant changes in culture and society beyond the growth of massive factories of the early twentieth-century economy. Whereas Keynesianism was associated with Fordism, mass production, centralisation of state and capital, and the mass over the individual, post-Fordism signposted decentralisation of organisation and production, differentiated products, quality circles and individual control in the workplace, and the primacy of consumers over producers. 'Flexible specialisation' demonstrates the way capitalism responds, not just to its own needs but also to people's needs, to survive, an idea that helped to provide a more positive spin on consumerism, which was embraced by many along with the expansion of advertising and the output of the expanding cultural industries, as media and cultural studies expanded in further and higher education. The decentred nature of post-Fordist production was not only extolled in articles, for example, on Benetton (the NT exemplar of post-Fordism), but also in studies in sociology and cultural studies on leisure, consumerism and shopping, and media production.

In his first article for *Marxism Today* in 1985, Robin Murray, who worked for the Greater London Council's Enterprise Board, introduced readers to a foretaste of some of the 'new thinking', or rethinking, about changes in the economy that was developing out of a decade of de-industrialisation, privatisation and restructuring. With the passing of Fordism, it was argued that there was no longer any room for state intervention in the economy, as the global reach of capital and the rise of the 'free market' appeared to render the nation-state incapable of economic intervention by the late 1980s. It should also be recognised, however, that the state, contrary to neoliberal politicians' statements, often intervened to enable the expansion of markets, and to hinder, deter or disable the actions of the working class and its organisations, especially trade unions. This was clear from the 'crisis of restructuring' of British industry in the early 1980s to which Keynesianism offered no solutions: thus the widespread disavowal of Keynesianism, which left both the centre and the left without an economic strategy.[293] It was the rediscovery of 'market socialism', therefore, that became an important middle way between a centralised, planned economy and the unrestrained forces of 'free market' capitalism. It is a very different scenario, however, since the impacts of the aftermath of the 'Great Financial Crisis', that hit the world in 2007–08, have continued to roll out in different ways across the globe.

Despite the stress on new technologies, Murray argued that post-Fordism promotes skilled labour as a central asset in production, not machinery. This accentuates the importance of education and training, and the role of local agencies to act as 'enabling bodies', which meant that the left could play an active role by promoting 'adult education inside and outside the workplace', although this meant conceding the workplace to the employer (reinforcing concession of 'the economic' to the New Right), and putting much of the emphasis on the individual.[294] The GLEB was an enabling body rather than an administrator of local industries during the 1980s, and it provided a means for incorporating popular participation in economic planning and restructuring.[295] It was this combination of infrastructure, training and planning on a decentralised scale that was seen as being best suited to meet local needs.[296]

Post-Fordism has 'a broader social and cultural significance' because the term signifies the 'greater social fragmentation and pluralism' taking place alongside, and as a result, of economic restructuring. There is the breaking down of traditional social identities based upon the workplace and the weakening of class solidarity; a new subjectivity is offered in their place where identities are created through 'the maximisation of individual choices through personal consumption'.[297] MT's call for a new 'socialist individualism'[298] to be at the heart of a *new* left politics was an important attempt to shift thinking on the left about the individual and the collective, which was supposed to account for the pluralism and diversity of modern life and recognise the need for individual rights, both constitutional and consumer, to be protected and extended. Two reasons for this thinking were the fragmentation wrought by the 'free market' which threatened society's cohesiveness and the imposition of the poll tax in 1989, for example, against the wishes of an overwhelming majority of the population, which demonstrated how increasingly authoritarian, centralised and

---

293   Murray 1985.
294   Murray 1985, p. 49.
295   Ibid.
296   Murray 1985, p. 50.
297   Hall 1989a, pp. 118–19.
298   Leadbeater 1989.

remote the Conservative government had become. But, this also challenged the idea that the state was a neutral entity since Thatcher's employment of the RSA against the workers (and supporters) involved in the miners' and printers' strikes.[299]

The proposed replacement for the CPGB's programme, the *Manifesto for New Times*, made the argument that the old form of social-democratic and corporatist politics of party and state, based upon static notions of class, could no longer provide the basis for a politics that could defeat Thatcherism and deal with the New Times. This meant a shift from the broad democratic alliance to a new type of alliance based upon 'unity-in-difference'.[300] This idea:

> ... represents an advance ... because it recognises the need for unity around common concerns whilst also understanding that the basis for unity is not homogeneity but a whole variety of heterogenous, possibly antagonistic, maybe magnicently [sic] diverse, identities and circumstances.[301]

The 'politics of identity' was criticised for fragmenting the opposition and denigrating the importance of class, the workplace and economic struggles.[302] It was also criticised for creating 'silos' which did not enable different groups to necessarily share interests or goals, except for those that had been clearly and consciously articulated, if they met a more general interest. These forms of identity politics were not much different than the labour movement's 'sectional interests' for which different groups of organised workers were criticised by Hobsbawm and others around MT, and later New Labour, when they put their demands ahead of other sections of the working class and the public's needs.

This shift to the 'politics of identity' and the rise of 'individualism' went hand-in-hand with reassessing the role of the state, at least for those who would help prepare the ground for New Labour. Whereas the left at least had traditionally looked to the state as the means for implementing a redistributive form of social-economic justice, it was felt necessary to move the focus onto the importance of the individual's rights asserted *against* the state, particularly in light of the success of Thatcherism in articulating resentment against the wel-

---

299 E.g. Milne 2010.
300 Brunt 1989, p. 158.
301 Ibid.
302 E.g. Sivanandan 1991.

fare state or at least its bureaucracy.[303] The concept of the 'empowering state', where rather than suppressing individual differences into a collective whole, the state would open 'the way for individuals and groups to pursue their own purposes', was presented as 'a new kind of socialist individualism': its central feature is the empowerment of individuals to replace collective self-interest.[304] However, New Times stressed not only individual rights but obligations as well, which became a favoured phrase of politicians on all sides of the political spectrum from the 1990s onwards.[305]

The role of the market was recognised in the heightened importance of consumption in the consumer-led economic boom of the late 1980s. The 'retail revolution' led the expanding service sector with the introduction of its innovations in retailing, such as 'just-in-time' distribution, 'niche marketing' and the segmented consumer profile. This was evidence of the impact of 'changing class relations' and the cultural impacts of feminism and the recession.[306] This development of the market, however, was given a 'democratic' veneer by, not just New Right propagandists, but also by many on the left when trying to explain the market's appeal. For example, Hall was one of the first in his January 1984 article, 'The Culture Gap',[307] to talk about the market in the language of 'democracy' and 'accessibility'. Other articles followed which reinforced the idea that there were elements in which capitalism, or even Thatcherism, had become popular by being associated with the idea of giving consumers 'what they want'.[308] Such thinking developed out of the 'cultural populism' trajectory in cultural studies in which MT played an important role.[309]

However, it is important to note that there is a fundamental problem with consumerism since it can only meet half the equation of the market as a place that provides choices for individual consumers. Those individuals' choices are restricted by their income and, therefore, one can only think of a market provision as one that favours consumers with more disposable income over those with less (and especially the working poor, unemployed or retired). The marketplace for consumers is a 'democracy' of money, not of citizens or individual

---

303 This largely applies to the social-democratic and socialist left broadly conceived, but excludes anarchist, anarchist-syndicalist, council-communist and other libertarian socialist groups. Thatcherism's anti-bureaucratic, anti-statist rhetoric even appealed to some elements of the libertarian left.
304 Wright 1996, p. 132.
305 Hall and Held 1989; Leadbeater 1990.
306 Saville 1990, p. 41.
307 Hall 1984a.
308 E.g. Mort and Green 1988; Campbell and Wheeler 1988.
309 McGuigan 1992; Harris 1992.

humans, as the amount of money determines the number of 'votes' one has. For this reason, the attempt to build a socialist individualism on the idea of the marketplace and the consumer is flawed, regardless of any state oversight to level the asymmetry of the marketplace to ensure fairness for all players.

Yet, *Marxism Today* did not want to leave the 'politics of prosperity' to the right.[310] It was not just about spending power: 'It goes hand in hand with a *cultural* vision of lifestyle and social identities'.[311] Thatcherism's potency was in its championing of 'the values of individualism, difference, autonomy and choice' but it was an individualism based upon selfishness and greed: an 'atomistic individualism'.[312] To counter this success in these changing times, the left had to change its thinking and offer an alternative: a 'social individualism'.[313] Bringing the individual into the left's political thinking with 'lifestyle politics' and identity, and a move away from old class-based certainties, it was claimed, should not be seen as merely a resurrection of an old form of liberal pluralism.[314] The changes that, nevertheless, did come about, at least under New Labour, do not appear to have gone much beyond liberal pluralism regardless of the claims of New-Times-cum-New-Labour writers, such as Charlie Leadbeater and Geoff Mulgan. Yet, changes were taking place in British politics through campaigns around issues of concern to the 'individual': for example, Charter 88's campaign around civil liberties and the Anti-Clause 28 Campaign that targeted the Conservative attack on local government's alleged 'promotion' of homosexuality. MT saw the 'reinstatement of the individual as the centre of analysis' as one of the principal shifts in focus for the left.[315]

However, this shift to the individual did not mean that there were no forms of solidarity. While 'feminisation' of the workforce brought about the 'death of institutionalised class consciousness' as conventionally understood, since class has always been intersected by sex, class and race, there was a 'new class consciousness expressed in militant self-help'.[316] The clearest example of the connections between changes in global production, social fragmentation and forms of political struggle was the campaign against Union Carbide's proposed move to Livingston, Scotland, because of its disaster in Bhopal, India, that killed

---

310 Saville 1990, p. 41.
311 Mort and Green 1988, p. 30.
312 Leadbeater 1989, p. 148.
313 Ibid.
314 McRobbie 1996, pp. 241–3; Hebdige 1989; Mort 1989. See also Rustin 1994, p. 90.
315 MTEB 1988b, p. 6.
316 Campbell 1989, pp. 293, 294.

at least 5,000 children, women and men. Livingston's example, as one progressive model of a 'New Times Town', could be contrasted with another model, Basingstoke, nicknamed 'Thatchergrad'.[317]

Environmental movements were also seen as addressing a new, but fundamentally important, area of interest and conflict, which demonstrated the convergence of individual and collective values. The core values of environmental or green organisations and movements are about humanity and the long-term sustainability and harmony of the planet as opposed to the narrow, short-term industrialism of both ends of the political spectrum, left and right.[318] Green politics turned consumption into as important an arena of conflict as production, since consumption was a sphere where people as individuals and as collectivities could have an impact: through the marketplace, green consumers can force businesses to supply environmentally-friendly goods. The response of many corporations was the use of 'green-washing' (advertising, marketing, public relations) to overcome consumer eco-activism which undermined some of the enthusiasm for environmental politics since green consumerism also appealed across political divisions. This vision of green politics offered the possibility of reaching beyond the traditional divisions of Westminster party politics, although concern was also expressed on the MTEB that green politics 'sat very uncomfortably with New Times'.[319] Either way, green consumerism and the environmental emphasis on individual responsibility helped to reinforce the appeal to a 'progressive individualism' as a replacement for socialist collective action.[320]

The shift to the individual was clearly manifested in the limitations and problems of the mass party, even within the realm of electoral politics. The political party had its origins in the Fordist age of mass production: it demanded loyalty and was based on taking over and commanding the state to effect change. Yet, there was a loss of faith 'in the party, in the state, in politics itself – and in the masses' amongst the electorate; the fragmentation of identity could

---

317 Campbell 1989, p. 294. The use of the Russian word for city, 'grad', was a purposeful move to associate 'Thatcher' ('the Iron Lady') with 'Stalin' ('the man of steel'), with one of its most commonly known forms in English, 'Stalingrad', linking authoritarian connotations of Stalin with Thatcher.
318 Steward 1989, p. 70.
319 MTEB 1988b, p. 7.
320 Of course, this was at a time when climate catastrophe did not appear as an impending reality. It was at a time, however, when concerns about the potential harmful impacts of climate change were first raised that initially had support from the US Republican President, George H.W. Bush.

not be accounted for within the traditional mass party, which meant changing the way political parties and democracy were conceptualised.[321] This kind of reasoning did not foresee the impact of Blair's 'iron grip' over Labour as it 'neutralised' its activist base from moving the party in a direction different to what the leadership wanted.

One of the central political consequences of post-Fordism, according to NT writers, was the need for the left to take consumption on as a central part in their programme.[322] The left had traditionally concentrated on the politics of production, which meant seeing and thinking of people as 'workers', which MT criticised: it was necessary for the left to take consumer aspirations seriously, as some of the NT writers argued, especially as the nature of work (or its lack) was changing. Consumption played an equally important part in people's lives: this development was equally important in cultural studies as 'cultural populism' gained ascendancy over political economy and Marxism.[323] Jacques argued that the left only talked about 'basic provision and access'. The Labour Party:

> should be decisively in favour of a culture of consumerism, but one where access to it is not denied by the poverty of an underclass. If consumption now looms so large, then society has an obligation to ensure that everyone has access to certain social resources.[324]

The new socialist politics, that NT was meant to encapsulate, had to recognise 'consumer aspirations' to become successful.[325] But, this recognition, although perhaps important to the 1980s left 'populist' approach to politics, has come undone in the aftermath of the twenty-first-century global financial crisis, which reveals the accuracy of Williams's critique of Hall's Thatcherism thesis (and presciently New Times) as 'petit-bourgeois theorists making long-term adjustments to short-term situations'.[326]

At the same time that the New Times project was underway, there had been other developments taking place across the cultural sector, both in terms of those working in the cultural industries as well as those studying media and culture in the expansion of higher education. In particular, out of the grassroots

---

321 Benton 1989, pp. 337–8.
322 Murray 1985, p. 48.
323 McGuigan 1992, 1997.
324 Cited in Saville 1990, p. 39.
325 Mort and Green 1988.
326 Williams 1989a, p. 175.

cultural sector, people working in and around various projects, such as Robin Murray at the GLEB, also contributed articles to *Marxism Today* as well as *New Socialist*, *New Society* and other periodicals, which emphasised the importance of culture as an important part of the economy, which should be considered part of the means to develop and rebuild both the economy *and* the social fabric of civil society. This development parallelled that taking place in cultural studies and overlapped with those promoting the 'cultural populist' approach to popular culture.[327]

It is hard not to think about this stage of the theorising of New Times and the CPGB's MNT, not to sense some kind of political frustration on the part of these left groupings, including those around MT, with always being perpetually 'outsiders' and 'naysayers'. In a sense, the MNT and the NT project were ways for the left to be able to enjoy the 'fruits of capitalism', you could say, without having to feel guilty. The failure of NT to take root is due to neoliberalism's success, which Williams had identified five years earlier in *Towards 2000* as 'Plan X', and in which Williams had already (presciently) identified and criticised MT's New Times project.[328]

14 Part II: 'From Wars of Position to Cultural Politics'

As the impasse of economic issues and workplace struggles seemed insurmountable, where secondary picketing became outlawed and the institutions and agencies of the organised working class faced attacks from all sides, culture became an important focus in the trajectory of Communist politics in particular and left politics in general during the 1970s and 1980s, especially as the range of issues went beyond *just* the economic to include the personal, as raised by feminism, anti-racism and the 'new social movements'. In essence, culture becomes an organising element around which the left was supposed to establish moral-intellectual leadership via 'cultural hegemony' over 'civil society' before it could attempt to gain political power.

This 'Gramscianesque' approach to understanding of culture underpins the two complementary parts that explain *Marxism Today*'s trajectory: its drive

---

327 McGuigan 1992.
328 See McGuigan's introduction and revised chapter for the second edition of *Towards 2000* (Williams 1983a) in (Williams 2015). *Towards 2000* has largely been overlooked in part because of its unfortunate title which dates it despite its insights for the contemporary situation (McGuigan 2015). However, Williams and his critical perspectives were already sidelined by Hall, MT and others by the mid-1980s.

for a 'popular politics' and its focus on 'popular culture'. Whereas the former was driven by MT's political project, the second part drew upon the rise of cultural studies and the increasingly symbiotic relationship between this new academic field and those student and academic members and sympathisers of the CPGB. Both, of course, were driven by the examination and analysis of Thatcherism to understand why it appeared so 'popular' in order to develop a strategy of greater 'popularity' to defeat Thatcherism.[329] This focus on the forces that could coalesce as a 'broad democratic alliance' against Thatcherism, had begun in the 1970s with the expansion of the CPGB's specialist committees and journals, driven by an enthusiasm for Gramsci's ideas, while outside the party there was a blossoming in the growth of community and alternative papers, unemployed action centres, workers' writing groups and so on. A growing interest in feminism, lesbian and gay liberation, anti-racism, ethnic organisations and other NSMs contributed to a vibrant sense of community and purpose, would later develop unevenly into increasingly separated 'silos' that in some ways reinforced a sense of isolation rather than communal solidarity, at least in the ways in which 'identity politics' separated out different NSMs from the working-class organisations and economic struggles from the mid-1980s onwards.

15 'Popular Politics'

The search for a 'popular politics', implicit and explicit, was a development that grew out of Eric Hobsbawm's 'Forward March of Labour Halted' and Stuart Hall's 'Thatcherism', and which acted as a code word for the 'broad democratic alliance', which was influenced via cultural studies's focus on popular culture and by Gramsci's theory of hegemony. The latter, of course, was also encouraged by the political gains of Eurocommunist parties in France, Spain and Italy during the 1970s. There was even a sense by which it also evoked an older line of influence, that of 'Communist populism', which had evolved out of the 1930s, and for which there was considerable support amongst an older generation of party members.[330]

It was the continuation of this historic Communist populist strategy of seeking an alliance across the 'popular' or 'subaltern classes', as with the Popular Front, albeit to defeat the forces of Thatcherism rather than fas-

---

329 McGuigan 1992, pp. 35–41.
330 Schwarz and Mercer 1981.

cism,[331] a connection made most clearly in Hobsbawm's contributions. Composed of both academic and non-academic historians, most of whom were 'instinctively "popular fronters"',[332] the Communist Party Historians' Group, one of the party's most successful specialist groups, helped to develop Communist populism by uncovering a 'history from below' to demonstrate a 'continuity' between a native, radical democratic tradition and contemporary Communist struggles, with the CPGB as this tradition's 'natural' inheritor via the 1951 BRS.[333] The CPHG took on conservative historiography to communicate this radical democratic tradition of 'the people' beyond professional historians to the people, for which *Past and Present* was founded.[334] The clarity and accessibility of *Past and Present* was an integral part of what made the journal popular to a broader audience than just professional historians, something that was noted by the party.

Propelled by Hobsbawm's and Hall's analyses, MT's idea of 'popular politics' developed as a means to find new forces and new ways of engaging in political-ideological struggle as the 1980s progressed. Although couched within Gramscian, or Gramscian-inflected, terms, MT's search for a counter-hegemonic politics, which was meant to be a 'war of position' was often couched in the notion of the 'popular', as opposed to the 'populist', generally a negative term on the left, in seeking out other forces that could be engaged as part of the BDA.[335] MT identified concrete examples of popular politics constitutive or exemplary of the BDA: e.g. the 'People's March for Jobs'; 'Live Aid'; and the Greater London Council. A 1980s version of the Popular Front meant drawing together a possible majority via the BDA to oppose Thatcherism, as constructed through economic struggles, identity politics and single-issue campaigns: from the organised, industrial, male working class to women, sexual and ethnic minorities, to the unemployed and radical youth (sub)cultures, to the anti-racist, peace and environmental movements.

However, despite the desire for a popular politics among the Eurocommunist, Gramscian and reformist sections, the industrial wing and traditionalists remained committed to the shopfloor, the 'most important world', which meant that their:

---

331 There were some contemporary claims of equivalence between Thatcherism and fascism which reinforced a sense of an historic war of position (and manouevre?) to be re-fought.
332 Hobsbawm cited in Callaghan 2003, p. 100.
333 Schwarz and Mercer 1981, p. 148; Callaghan 2003, p. 100.
334 Dworkin 1997, pp. 19–20. The journal included party and non-party historians.
335 McGuigan 1992, pp. 9–44.

strategies for British socialism revolved around encroaching on managerial prerogative and ensuring left-wing victories in elections for the shop stewards' committee and union branch.[336]

This narrower emphasis on workplace struggles contributed to the divisions between those who wanted the labour movement to lead an alliance between the working class and all other progressive groups, including the NSMs, and those who felt that the labour movement was too rigid, bureaucratic and incapable of comprehending the importance of certain, non-economic issues to women, ethnic minorities et al.; the latter, therefore, argued that the labour movement should be a co-equal or partner, not the principal player, in such an alliance. The traditionalists and industrial wing emphasised 'class politics', which was used as a label to indicate their adherence to the organised working class as the primary agency of transformation, which they reasserted in reaction to the growth of Communist populism and cultural Marxism during this period of a 'retreat from class', which can be traced as far back as the 1950s and the first New Left.

Although the working class was still pivotal to the BDA, the alliance was not just for its or its representatives' benefit (i.e. CPGB, Labour, TUC) since it would also include groups that did not have clear socialist goals (the shift away from economism).[337] The massive rise in unemployment during Thatcher's first two years, 1979–81, provided the CPGB with the chance to put the BDA into action: the 'People's March for Jobs' was a month-long march in the spring of 1981 by a broad coalition promoting full employment as the top priority.[338] Though the PMJ was organised by the unions, 'the only force with the experience, strength and capacity to bring off such an initiative', Jacques argued that it appealed to the people as a whole and not just to the economic-corporate interests of the organised working class: 'it was an object lesson in popular, non-sectarian politics'.[339] To have a broad appeal, Jacques argued, meant making the PMJ as inclusive as possible and, therefore, all types of groups from unions and local authorities to churches and unemployed groups to ethnic organisations and cultural agencies, were invited to participate: this was the *realisation* of the BDA in practice. Its success was contrasted with Labour's unemployment marches, which were seen as party-political events and, therefore, much more limited

---

336   Fishman 1995, p. 120. See also Callaghan 2004, 2005.
337   Cutler et al. 1978, p. 358. The BDA also sought to include Scottish and Welsh nationalist parties, which had gained support in their respective nations during the 1970s.
338   Jacques 1996c.
339   Jacques 1981, p. 6.

in their appeal to the general public, which is why union leaders and march organisers resisted Labour's attempts to do the same with the PMJ.[340]

This 'new way' of responding to Thatcherism, Jacques claimed, had rendered many of the old methods 'ineffective'.[341] The PMJ demonstrated the possibility of building the BDA for a war of position against Thatcherism, according to Jacques, which would be undermined if it became too closely associated with the aims of a single political party: i.e. Labour. Yet, only two years later, the second PMJ ended in chaos as different groups turned on each other, which highlighted a key problem in seeking out as broad an alliance as possible. It failed to establish a means to act in a cohesive manner when disputes arose between different organisations within such an alliance, which could have been avoided if it had been under the lead or control of a mass working-class party. Nonetheless, MT began shifting its thinking about an electoral alliance as a counter-hegemonic strategy to defeat Thatcherism, which meant prioritising the building of popular alliances and winning public opinion, rather than engaging in, for example, sectional industrial struggles. Strikes, especially after the 'Winter of Discontent', were seen as evidence of 'undemocratic' union power, in pursuit of sectional over class interests, alienating public opinion and ultimately losing electoral support for Labour (no discussion of the undemocratic power of large multi-national corporations though). Therefore, it was vital that the labour movement took on board such a strategy, especially since the industrial working class was declining in size and importance, while its traditional methods, including secondary picketing, were being rendered ineffective through legislation.

The 1984–85 Miners' Strike was notable for the lengths to which the state went to defeat the miners: it exposed the Conservative government's willingness to use coercion to defeat the miners.[342] In essence, Thatcherism's 'authoritarian populism' was exposed as just 'authoritarianism' or, perhaps more precisely, 'constitutional authoritarianism'.[343] It also exposed the divisions on the left over the conduct of the strike. Despite *Marxism Today*'s support for the miners and the National Union of Mineworkers, it criticised its leader, Arthur

---

340 Ibid.
341 Jacques 1981. This early admission of Jacques highlights a tendency to keep moving away from earlier attempts at bringing about political change when they fail, rather than working on how to improve such organisations and campaigns. Thus, he abandons the PMJ after the second disastrous attempt in 1983, supporting the GLC until its abolition in 1986, and shifts to supporting 'Live Aid' events from 1986, as each organisation, site of struggle or campaign was defeated or dispersed in turn.
342 E.g. Milne 2010.
343 Williams 1979b.

Scargill, and the NUM leadership for not holding a ballot on strike action and not doing more to win over public opinion. It was argued that a 'potentially permanent anti-Thatcher alliance' was being built through the support groups and campaigns, which demonstrated the greater importance of the women's and peace movements, and even the churches, than that of most unions.[344] Halfway into the strike, *New Socialist* published one of MT's key contributors, Stuart Hall, in the September 1984 issue, who argued that the Greater London Council had 'become the most important front in the struggle against Thatcherism', despite the 'Battle of Orgreave' just weeks earlier and evidence of the depth of the divide over the strike as manifested across the country.[345]

Against these positions, Raymond Williams argued that the NUM strike was opening up possible ways of mobilising popular opinion.[346] Williams's position offered a 'third way' (sic) between what were seen as the only two possible positions: it would have meant that the left could have used the strike to articulate a position different to that offered by the Labour establishment's silence or the internal bickering over whether the NUM leadership should have balloted their members, an issue also exploited by the Tories and the press. Unlike others on the left who abandoned the labour movement as 'backward' or for its 'old-fashioned politics', Williams shows how 'keywords' in the miners' strike could have been used to rearticulate a 'common sense' to working-class interests beyond the miners and that could have reinforced ideologically and politically the necessity of defending mining communities against the government's repression.[347] This should have been a line along which Stuart Hall and others interested in engaging in the Gramscian inflected ideological struggle across language, common sense and 'folklore' or popular culture, could have employed their rhetorical and intellectual skills to attempt to craft a popular politics, especially one which could be taken up from the grassroots, and which could have been articulated against the dominant hegemonic apparatus of the media, government and other ISAs during a deeply polarising conjuncture.

Greg Philo notes that a few scholars have pointed to the failure of the Labour Party to produce any memorable phrases that criticised the Tories and promoted its ideas during the 1980s. The Conservatives were able to produce a

---

344 Francis 1985, p. 14.
345 Hall 1984c, p. 37, quoted in Milner, 2002, p. 117. The Battle of Orgreave at the pits outside Orgreave, South Yorkshire, took place on 18 June 1984 between some 30,000 strikers and 18,000 police, and was seen as a key turning point in the miners' strike of 1984–85.
346 Williams 1989f [1985].
347 Ibid.

number of phrases that resonated with the public that undermined Labour and promoted their party, such as the infamous 'There is no alternative'. TINA was first used in May 1980 initially to claim that Thatcher's economic policies were the only possible ones, even though there were members of her cabinet who could have suggested, or did suggest, alternatives.[348] TINA could be used to demobilise opposition or alternatives being proposed, particularly once Labour and the social-democratic left more generally conceded the economic ground to the Tories. For example, Colin Hay's analysis of the 'Winter of Discontent' points to its effective use by the Conservatives, long after the actual winter of 1978–79 had passed into history, as an ideological and political tool, the propagandistic impact of which was far greater than the strikes' actual impacts on the different communities directly affected during those winter months; the phrase was used most effectively as propaganda to undermine Labour in the public's eyes.[349] Labour's electoral wins in 1945 and 1950 were made possible because of 'memories' of the 1930s depression amongst voters; in a similar way, voters were influenced by the 'Winter of Discontent' phrase to invoke 'memories' during electoral contests in the 1980s and 1990s.[350]

There was an elision between the war of position, which includes the struggle over common sense, with winning public opinion in the mainstream media. Public opinion becomes the 'holy grail' replacing other aspects of the BDA, which itself is an understanding of the Gramscian idea of a social bloc capable of orchestrating a counter-hegemonic strategy, though the degree to which it was more than a (hopeful) phrase or an ideological totem appears hard to find, except for, perhaps, the RAR and PMJ campaigns. However, as such, public opinion is accepted unproblematically at face value, without any sense of the role of mainstream media, not only in influencing, but also in constructing or constituting, public opinion in the first place: indeed, the national media come to stand in for 'public' opinion. Obviously, such a position is problematic given that most of the national press supported Thatcher's anti-union legislation and ideology, which was again in evidence with the printers' strike against News International at Wapping the following year.

We can see how MT's coverage of other labour disputes changes after the miners' strike, when MT reinforced the idea that union leaders appeared unwilling to 'modernise', and to try and win over public opinion and the mainstream

---

348   E.g. Philo 1993; McLean 2003.
349   Hay 1996, 2010.
350   Ibid. Tony Blair would later use this phrase as a (continuing) negative trope about 'union power'.

media.³⁵¹ The ambulance and health workers' protests in 1988, for example, received more favourable coverage because of different tactics that helped to mobilise public support and, of course, nurses are one of the professions that hold a special place in the hearts and minds of most of the public.³⁵² These groups represented public sector, white-collar, technical and (para) professional workers that were part of the new 'professional-managerial class'.³⁵³ As the sixties generation of radicals, (former) students and (ex) hippies became engaged in the 'long march through the institutions', many became part of a key constituency within the PMC which was responsive to MT's appeals.

16 Feminism and the New Social Movements

The NSMs were identified as potential bases for popular unity by appealing beyond narrow economic or class interests: part of a 'popular politics' via the BDA. The feminist movement during the 1970s and 1980s was decentralised with a plethora of groups organised around different economic, ideological and personal issues: from campaigns for equal pay at work to women's refuges to raising awareness on chauvinistic male attitudes towards women. While both feminists and socialists had a lot to benefit from the overthrow of Thatcherism specifically, and capitalism and patriarchy more generally, their goals were not seen as necessarily the same: feminists asserted that they were more than a 'single issue' campaign because patriarchy 'is not just an "issue" but a fundamental contradiction in society'.³⁵⁴ Sheila Rowbotham, Lynne Segal and Hilary Wainwright's *Beyond the Fragments*³⁵⁵ in 1979 provided a critique of left vanguardism from libertarian, Marxist and socialist feminist perspectives, which in turn influenced the radical left's use of 'democracy' to signify 'participative democracy' in the 1970s and 1980s.³⁵⁶

Feminist analyses and demands were a key ingredient in MT's break with the advocates of 'class politics', even though feminism was never fully integrated

---

351 The majority of trade unions have since changed (e.g. Davies 2000), even if New Labour's criticisms did not.
352 E.g. Illiffe 1988.
353 E.g. Ehrenreich and Ehrenreich 1977, 2013.
354 Davis 1981, p. 22. Davis was also criticising patriarchal elements within the CPGB at the time.
355 Rowbotham et al. 2013.
356 Egan 2006; Rowbotham et al. 2013. *Beyond the Fragments* was first published by the Newcastle Socialist Centre and Islington Community Press. Merlin published a second edition in 1979 and the third in 2013, which included three new chapters by each co-author.

into, and often neglected or marginalised in, the periodical's content and politics. The role of working-class institutions within the BDA, which were seen as having the necessary experience and resources for leading struggles, was questioned. Feminists pointed to problems with the patriarchal practices of and sexist attitudes within trade unions, not just those sexist practices operating within capitalist organisations. MT, for example, published feminist criticisms of dominant masculine attitudes in trade unions and on the left around issues of 'low pay, lack of opportunity and conflict between paid work and domestic responsibilities'.[357]

Yet, MT never addressed any of the contradictions in its own organisational setup and operation. Patriarchal institutions, capitalist and socialist, were criticised for sidelining these issues from the mainstream of labour relations. Union leaders were criticised for seeing women's issues as supplementary demands on employers: maternity leave and equality at work were often the first demands to be dropped during negotiations because they were not seen as 'universal'.[358] Jean Coussins warned at the time that it is 'all too easy' to give up on fighting for 'positive, innovative policies' when the labour movement is under attack and to remain defensive about existing rights. Yet, at the same time, Asian women were on strike at Grunwick demonstrating leadership and resilience in taking on their employer and its supporters.[359]

The women's movement provided a working model of popular politics for the BDA and its slogan, 'the personal is political', linked individual attitudes and behaviours to the wider public and private spheres. Feminism's popular appeal was built across different areas and not just around economic issues; its activism did not rely on traditional trade union tactics (e.g. picketing, strikes), which in the aftermath of the 'Winter of Discontent', were seen much more negatively. Feminism operated with pre-figurative forms of organisation (e.g. collectives, cooperatives) and, thereby, provided one of the best examples of pre-figurative politics during the 1980s.[360]

Despite the periodical's uneasy relationship with feminism, some attempts were made to bring feminist perspectives into the magazine via contributors, section editors and the MT Editorial Board.[361] Feminism was a useful tool with which to launch a critique of opponents within the CPGB and across the

---

[357] Coussins 1980, p. 11. See Anitha and Pearson 2018.
[358] Ibid.; Davis 1983.
[359] Coussins 1980, p. 11.
[360] Davis 1981.
[361] Feminist interventions on the MTEB included using quarterly reviews to raise awareness amongst board members as well as about the periodical's content (e.g. Cockburn 1989).

left who emphasised class politics. MT criticised the left's reassertion of the economic as the determinant 'in the last instance' as in effect privileging a class analysis over other approaches and thereby sidelining racism, sexism and homophobia. Stuart Hall pointed to the need to confront these very issues, which 'social traditionalists', who were not confined to the Tory right or even to CPGB traditionalists, since they were to be found even amongst the left's most progressive sections. 'Social traditionalism', more frequently and better known as 'social conservatism', had survived into the late twentieth century because socialists kept to a narrow definition of the 'political' and they, therefore, did not notice how the old social and sexual 'ranks and bonds' continued to work in the crevices of society.[362] Hall argued that it had 'a deep and profound hold inside' the socialist and labour movements, and in the working class, more broadly, and that it continued 'to feed, inside the minds and consciousness and allegiances of working people': this type of 'socialism' would 'not transform society'.[363]

MT's promotion of rethinking the left's attitudes towards certain issues and groups, that were usually excluded, was a part of trying to reconnect the left with 'ordinary citizens' and their concerns over issues such as crime and education.[364] Readers were warned that parents' concerns over education or working-class anxiety about crime were real and not necessarily just an expression of 'reactionary' sympathies; the New Right was making good use of such cultural, rather than economic, arguments to win over sections of the 'popular classes' (i.e. middle, lower-middle and working classes). Some critics saw such rethinking as an attempt to make MT 'popular' rather than as an attempt to address legitimate concerns that were otherwise ignored by the left. Thus, MT argued that the left had to develop a popular politics by promoting the concerns of the BDA's different constituencies, even if it meant adopting commitments with which the left was otherwise uncomfortable. However, there was no theoretical or ideological framework within which all of the concerns of the BDA's different constituencies could be integrated without reducing them to particular facets that made them appear as appendages to the party or labour movement. In the search for examples of the BDA in action that could correct that problem, MT latched upon local governments led by the Labour Left in places like London and Sheffield.

---

362   Hall 1982a, p. 17.
363   Hall 1982a, pp. 17–18. Yet, Williams pointed out in 1983 that the women's and environmental movements were most popular 'in their weakest, least systematic forms', while the left was in its weakest position since the mid-1930s (Williams 1989g, pp. 168, 169).
364   E.g. Kinsey 1986; McRobbie 1987.

17   'Municipal Socialism'

One key area that became important to MT's idea of a war of position was 'municipal socialism' as exemplified in the GLC under 'Red Ken' Livingstone's leadership, 1981–86, but which was also manifested in other cities in the UK, particularly 'The People's Republic of Sheffield'.[365] Part of the early inspiration for municipal socialism for the CPGB's Eurocommunists came via the *Partito Comunista Italiano* in the mid-1970s, where it operated in cities, such as 'Red Bologna', where local PCI governments worked at extending popular democratic participation and a new style of management that supported the idea of revolution as a process. This inspiration was evident in the June 1978 MT review, which showed how the left could engage in a war of position at the local level as part of an effort of building a national counter-hegemonic bloc.[366]

Labour's record in government demonstrated a deep-seated resistance to popular democratic forms of control because of its reliance on the mechanisms of parliamentary democracy, including at the local level.[367] MT criticised Labour for its failure to mobilise public support for its objectives because it relied instead on party supporters being elected onto local councils whereas what Labour should have attempted was to build a 'mass politics' (party-speak for mobilising public support outside of election campaigns), as a countervailing force to the propaganda of the Tory press.[368] This was the CPGB's idea of a 'strategic approach' compared to the Labour leadership's emphasis on electoral efforts.

MT claimed Livingstone's GLC as *the* example of connecting the 'older forces of reform' with the new social movements as a notable alternative to Labour's 'managerial style' of politics.[369] It was a combination of 'Old Labour' (party activists, trade unions) working with the NSMs to produce a truly popular government at County Hall, the location of which, situated on the Thames opposite Westminster, was also powerful symbolically. This popular government chose to put into action a popular agenda to meet the demands of social movements, old and new. The BDA behind the GLC was the 'urban new left' which represented the 'values and concerns' of a new generation, reflected in and constituted

---

365   E.g. Payling 2017.
366   E.g. Jäggi, Müller and Schmid 1977 reviewed in Green 1978, pp. 195–8.
367   Leonard 1979.
368   Cook 1985, p. 28.
369   Hall 1994, p. 171.

by the NSMs, which made the radical politics of the London Left.[370] The GLC and similar Labour-controlled city governments, such as Sheffield, represented virtually the left's only popular alternative to Thatcherism as most working-class institutions and organisations were in the process of being constrained, neutralised or even 'smashed' by the state.[371]

The GLC's campaigns, such as 'Fares Fair', which sought to make public transport cheap and available to all throughout London, was seen as an example of how it was possible to articulate concerns which resonated across all constituencies (even though it was ultimately struck down by the courts): e.g. white working class, women, ethnic minorities, sexual and gender minorities, people with disabilities.[372] Livingstone's GLC was hailed as pioneering 'a new relationship between power and the people', promoting equal opportunities and making itself an enabling body rather than an administrative bureaucracy: MT's example of a popular left alternative to Thatcher's cuts and (Old) Labour's managerialism.[373]

Still a number of local councils controlled by the London Labour Left became subject to criticism for the manner in which they conducted their 'new politics': they 'use the power of the town hall to short-circuit the toil of creating a new consciousness'.[374] As Dave Cook wrote in 1985, the left's activities at every level became primarily 'locked within Labour Party structures', where they had little 'organic connection to extra-parliamentary forces and struggle', and where internal victories over the right in the struggle for positions within the Labour Party were seen as if they were 'the successful popular projection of socialist policies' to the public.[375] This form of politics led to such examples of the so-called 'Loony Left' London boroughs of Lambeth and Brent.[376] Thus, perfectly sound policies, like Brent's anti-racist strategy, looked like a local council defending its prerogatives in hiring and firing because the Brent Labour Party did not campaign to educate the local public on the merits of that policy.[377] The problem with Labour, according to MT's Gramscian lens, was that it did not know how to act as a political party: i.e. mobilising public support for its

---

370   Curran et al. 2005, p. 10.
371   E.g. Gallas 2015; Milne 2010; Payling 2017.
372   Hall 1994, pp. 172–3; Campbell and Jacques 1986; Curran 1987; Hipkin 1984. See Gilroy 1987 for an alternative critique.
373   Hall 1984a, p. 20; Campbell 1987, p. 13; Curran et al. 2005, p. 5.
374   Campbell 1987, p. 13.
375   Cook 1985, pp. 27–8, 28.
376   See Curran et al. 2005.
377   Campbell 1987, pp. 11–12.

actions. Yet, many of the critics that took the London Labour Left to task did not appear to recognise the impact of the ongoing systematic propaganda campaigns of the Tory press.[378]

18 The Communist Party, Popular Culture and *Marxism Today*

Marxism Today's engagement with popular culture, which was an important component of its political and journalistic projects, especially in its ambitions to articulate a 'popular politics', was just one of a number of entities within the Communist Party to emphasise or promote culture. Indeed, (popular) culture for the party during the mid-1970s was a productive and intellectually stimulating focus that led to a number of developments, including the expansion of specialist groups and journals in the years preceding MT's October 1979 launch.

In some ways, MT was one of the primary sites of political engagement and dissemination of cultural studies outside the academy, evident in its understanding of culture, which included anthropological and literary-aesthetic definitions. The influence of the Centre for Contemporary Cultural Studies was evident with many regular and occasional contributors, including most obviously Stuart Hall, but also Dick Hebdige, Ros Brunt, Richard Dyer and Angela McRobbie amongst others. Despite Jacques's limited interest in cultural coverage, MT's focus on culture grew considerably by the mid-1980s under his editorship, when contributions began to shift to a 'cultural populist' approach.[379]

In many ways, the focus on (popular) culture in MT had been influenced by the intellectual developments of 'Communist populism' and 'cultural Marxism', particularly with the influence of the CP Historians' Group and the latter by a growing interest in continental 'western Marxist' critiques of the cultural industries (e.g. Frankfurt School), which were not always necessarily compatible with the later trajectory of cultural studies. Indeed, 'cultural populism' itself was in many ways a logical outcome of the strands of cultural Marxism and Communist populism, marked by the influence of the first New Left.[380] This perspective also reflected the different set of values of the 1960s generation,[381]

---

378 Curran et al. 2005.
379 McGuigan 1992. For a critique of Gramscianism's influence on cultural studies, see Harris 1992.
380 The early NLR, 1960–62, edited by Hall, had interviews with jazz musicians next to articles on Soweto, a precursor to the political-cultural mix achieved by MT two decades later (Andrews 1995a; Hall 1997; Kenny 1995a, 1995b; Pimlott 2000a). For a more critical view, see Harris 1992.
381 Waite 1995.

who were already on their 'long march through the institutions' by the time of the second format launch in 1979. MT's cultural coverage frequently drew out the political connections of various products, practices and performances of high and popular culture in its pages. Nevertheless, in the decades preceding the 1980s, there had been debates within the party over the nature of popular culture and whether or not the party should engage with it.

During the 1960s, for example, Young Communist League leaders recognised culture as a form and space for a politics opposed to society's dominant values, and with the YCL leaders' more open views on sexual liberation, rock music and drugs, they challenged the traditional values of many older party members, highlighting inter-generational tensions over taste, values and attitudes: the Wembley branch, for example, had its own band and night club to attract local youth.[382] However, internal party critics, who were angered by the YCL's attempts to broaden its appeal via popular culture, claimed that it was losing its 'working class essence' and, thereby, debates over style became signifiers of more fundamental, internal political differences. These were precursors to later splits, which were evident, for example, in mostly negative responses[383] to the debate over the radical potential of youth culture, initiated by Martin Jacques in MT in 1973.[384] Many of MT's contributors and readers during the late 1970s and early 1980s had been part of that 1960s generation of YCL members, who were scornful of authority and appreciative of hedonistic aspects of youth culture.[385]

By 1976, when culture was becoming an important part of the CPGB's activities, Jacques argued that the party was well situated to play a 'unique role', since the class struggle was not just economic, but also ideological and cultural, and since the party was uniquely situated to bring together industrial and cultural workers.[386] Since culture is 'an increasingly important area of class conflict', there are three aspects to consider: access to, and control of, cultural facilities, and ideology. Those areas of culture that are 'easily exploited for profit ... have been expanded'; however, public provision 'has been relatively neglected', particularly outside of London.[387] Jacques pointed to a growing centralisation of control over both private and public cultural production, even though these bodies were not immune from popular pressure either; nonetheless, he did

---

382 Waite 1995, pp. 220, 218–19.
383 E.g. Boyd 1973; Cornelius 1974; Costin 1974; Fauvet 1974; Filling 1974; Mills 1974.
384 Jacques 1973.
385 Johnstone 1995.
386 Jacques 1976, p. 165.
387 Jacques 1976, p. 163.

concede that big business and the establishment had had a negative influence that led to the 'decline of many traditional, local forms of cultural activity'.[388] Jacques was also aware that a new 'intellectual strata', which were part of the PMC,[389] were making up a greater portion of the workforce than ever before, and this meant that there was a key question to be asked about 'the relationship between these new cultural forces and the labour movement'.[390]

The third aspect, ideology, was what Jacques emphasised and which was key to understanding how the ruling class rules, not just by coercion but also by consent: 'by the ascendancy of its values, ideas and beliefs. And these values are promoted not only within the economic and political spheres but also within culture'.[391] As cultural activity expands, so does its importance as part of the ideological struggle between commodity/commercialism and education/creativity, and between elite/individual and the mass/collective.[392] As ruling class ideas dominate in the cultural sphere, their effect denies people the chance to fully develop their talents or access the facilities that could make that possible, although by 1976 working-class people had greater access to (popular) culture than ever before.

This background of Jacques's interest and involvement in the Theory and Ideology Committee and in debates on youth culture preceded his editorship and the coverage that MT would institute of culture, both popular and high. This interest appears to have been the bringing together of the three influential strands of political thinking, cultural Marxism, Communist populism and cultural studies, which is clearly evident in the cover stories on cultural-political issues. For example, between 1977 and 1981, before the launch of MT's culture section, 'Channel Five', cover features included John Lennon, sport and royalty,[393] and in its efforts to publish contributions to debates for a broader audience on the left, as with the debate over the future of socialist theatre across radical left periodical (and ideological) lines, including *Leveller*, *Wedge* and *Socialist Review*.[394] That influence had become more evident in the new section's pioneering coverage of popular culture: political-cultural criticism which took popular culture seriously without condemning it out of hand for 'false consciousness' or 'escapism'.

---

388   Ibid.
389   Ehrenreich and Ehrenreich 1977, 2013.
390   Jacques 1976, pp. 164–5.
391   Jacques 1976, p. 163.
392   Ibid.
393   E.g. Frith 1981; Triesman 1980, 1981; Trickey 1981.
394   E.g. Chambers 1978. Colin Chambers was *The Morning Star*'s theatre critic.

There is a certain irony that although Jacques was interested enough in youth culture, to initiate a debate in 1973 on the issue and to recognise culture as a key area in the struggle for hegemony, he was not the one who oversaw or implemented its coverage in MT. This was primarily done through some of his closest collaborators on the MTEC in the years prior to the Channel Five section, which was organised and overseen by its founder and section editor, Sally Townsend, from the October 1981 issue, which marked the start of the periodical's national newsagent distribution. This was one of the principal sections of the magazine by which the politics of popular culture and cultural studies made their impact felt and which appealed to an important demographic of MT's audience by the mid-1980s.

The establishment of Channel Five was a significant move, not only because culture was often a secondary consideration in the left press, but also because their focus tended to be restricted to books and occasionally films. MT demonstrated a commitment to analysing all aspects of culture in this new section, from the mundane and everyday, such as street-style and plastic, to forms of high art, such as opera and painting. Making culture an integral part of the second format, was a shift that MT helped to lead on the left, so that by the end of the 1980s, culture had become an important part of most left periodicals at the same time as it was being recognised increasingly as an important part of the economy.

Channel Five was both a means to attract advertising *and* a demonstration of the BDA in action.[395] For example, the October 1983 interview with David Yip, star of the 'Chinese Detective', highlighted issues around race, the left and acting, when realistic TV representations of ethnic minorities were limited at best and frequently problematic or racist at worst.[396] These interviews, reviews, analyses and commentaries usually drew out the links between culture and politics in a way that encouraged readers to think more politically about popular and high culture, and their influences upon values, attitudes and beliefs. The contributions of cultural studies lecturers helped to popularise cultural studies as an explicitly political engagement, including such leading scholars as Angela McRobbie and Dick Hebdige.[397]

---

395 Davison 1985b; Townsend 1984.
396 Yip 1983; Cohen and Gardner 1982.
397 E.g. McRobbie 1987; Hebdige 1989.

19   From 'Rock Against Racism' to 'Designer Socialism'

The growth in and emphasis on 'cultural politics' was a fairly new development for most socialist organisations, including the CPGB, although such concerns and ideas had been around for a long while. Some of the anti-political stances of young people and especially those who felt alienated by all forms of authority, played into the growing unemployment and sense of despair and futility. One notable development during the mid-1970s was the ways in which the growing threat of racism and fascism began to threaten blacks and Asians on the streets and in their neighbourhoods. It was during this time of growing youth unemployment, that gave rise to 'dole queue rock', aka 'punk music', which was part of the rise of 'crisis music', which included the 'two-tone' ska revival, reggae and dub poetry, as black and white working-class youth faced a common enemy on the streets.[398]

The rise of racist and fascist organisations, such as the National Front, brought a response from the Labour left to the far left, including anarchists and Trotskyists, and included many disaffected white and black youths, during the late 1970s. The Anti-Nazi League, set up by the Socialist Workers' Party, brought people together to fight racism and fascism through demonstrations, rallies, festivals, gigs and concerts. It was connected to the Rock Against Racism campaign, one of the most successful, anti-racist and anti-fascist campaigns in mobilising youth in large numbers in the postwar period.[399] Drawing upon the anti-authoritarianism of punk, it brought together black and white in its musical events, which combined punk, reggae and 'two-tone' bands, the latter an inspiration of the ANL's slogan of 'black and white, unite and fight'. RAR was a political, street-level movement with a radical message that brought together black and white bands; even if the majority of the fans were 'white' and already 'converted' to the anti-racism message, its importance should not be discounted.[400] Though the effectiveness of RAR in stopping the NF may be difficult to measure, since the latter's loss in electoral popularity was attributed to Thatcher's incorporation of racist, anti-immigrant sentiment, it demonstrated the possibility of building a popular politics via popular (music) subcultures.[401]

---

398   Pimlott 2014a.
399   RAR had been inspired by Eric Clapton's drunken remarks about voting for Enoch Powell and 'keeping Britain white' at a concert in August 1976 in Birmingham (Goodyer 2009; Widgery 1986).
400   Frith and Street 1992; Goodyer 2009; Renton 2006; Widgery 1986, 1987.
401   Ibid.

Despite *Marxism Today*'s promotion of cultural politics, the RAR was not a primary focus for its feature coverage, outside of the August 1978 cover story, which also sported a photograph of a National Front rally, because of its obvious link via the ANL to the CPGB's rival, the SWP. Nevertheless, as other scholars have noted, RAR remained a model for MT's coverage of popular culture[402] because it was seen as a manifestation of the BDA in action.

However, as RAR faded from the scene, MT and others on the left called on the Labour Party to change its approach to the media and popular culture, especially as Labour had failed to appeal to first-time voters in the 1983 election. It was a time when many on the left, who still largely ignored popular culture, preferred to be mired in a 'residual economism', in one critic's words.[403] Only Gramscian hegemony theory, according to MT, appeared capable of explaining people's beliefs without succumbing to elitist or vanguardist pretensions to know what 'the people' or 'the working class' wanted or that they were labouring under 'false consciousness'. MT claimed that to reach 'the people', the left would have to rethink their policies, attitudes and values, as the New Right had learned to do, which enabled it to rearticulate common sense with its ideas and values: the essence of becoming hegemonic.

The debates over style and 'designer socialism' in the mid-1980s were merely the most obvious symptoms of a crisis in the shifting relationship between the left and popular culture. It was a debate essentially about the accessibility and popularity of socialism, and the left's neglect that had been clearly articulated by Stuart Hall in a feature in MT's January 1984 issue:

> The Left's resistance to cultural change is reflected in our everyday practices and languages. The style of propaganda, party political broadcasts, of much educational and agitational material locks us into very traditional and backward-looking associations. Our political imagery is even worse in this respect.[404]

Hall's criticisms highlighted problems with the left's language and imagery, although many retained a 'nostalgia' for the imagery of the 1920s and 1930s, which was not suitable for left politics in the 1980s, except perhaps in an ironic, postmodern manner and as a *chic* stylistic expression. For example, the popularity of MT's use of 'Bolshevik chic' in its design and merchandise in 1986–87 was connected to the popularity within the CPGB of Mikhail Gorbachev and

---

402 E.g. Smith 2011; Worley 2012, 2016.
403 Bennett 1986, p. 6.
404 Hall 1984a, p. 20.

his role in leading the changes in the USSR with the policies of *glasnost* and *pereistroika*. Yet, such uses could be no more than a superficial form of flattery as the USSR moved closer to the 'capitalist West'.

An important part of Thatcherism's appeal was its ability to represent people's aspirations in language and imagery that were tied to the New Right's interests. The left, it was argued, could learn from the New Right's approach and articulate a 'popular socialist politics' providing they understood people's aspirations and rearticulated them to a popular, accessible socialist discourse.[405] As Hall explains:

> A labour movement which cannot identify with what is concrete and material in these popular aspirations, and expropriate them from identification with the private market and private appropriation, will look, increasingly, as if it is trapped nostalgically in ancient cultural modes, failing to imagine socialism in twentieth century terms and images, and increasingly out of touch with *where real people are at*.[406]

Although the reasoning could appear to elide consumerism with popularity, the labour movement's and the left's lack of engagement with, not only people's material aspirations, but also 'attitudes and practices', was all-pervasive.[407] Sports, health and fitness are examples of areas of popular interest, that touch upon goods, services, attitudes and practices, that MT argued the left has traditionally neglected but where people were (engaged or active) and which Jacques had identified a decade earlier.[408]

Marxism Today was interested in the ways in which the 'Live Aid'-type spectacles, sparked by the 1985 famine in Ethiopia, demonstrated the ways in which broad coalitions could be mobilised around general concerns.[409] The Aid 'mega-events' were designed to raise consciousness and elicit public sympathy as well as money for the 'Third World'. MT argued that these events were not merely self-serving spectacles for rock stars and celebrities but also positive developments, which could take place outside of narrow political interests because they were able to articulate anti-Thatcherite emotions (e.g. caring and compassion), and introduce development and aid issues to large numbers of

---

405 See Hall 1981a.
406 Hall 1984a, p. 20 (emphasis added).
407 Hall 1984a, p. 20.
408 E.g. Jacques 1976.
409 Hall and Jacques 1986. For some responses, see: Beresford 1986; Coulter 1986; Lestor 1986; Palmer 1986; Wright 1986.

people who would normally be left untouched by traditional aid campaigns or news reports. A later event, 'Sport Aid', was singled out for its participative manner: anyone, who wished to contribute, could do so by watching or participating in local events anywhere in the world. The focus on sport included a supplement on cycling in that issue (a sport that would be advertised regularly in the magazine through the last half of the 1980s).

However, these 'Live Aid'-type spectacles, whether they were 'participative' on the ground and in real life or via TV and other media, were still a far cry from organising and mobilising subaltern classes, particularly in the aftermath of the defeats of the miners and printers, and especially workers at key points in the social relations of production and distribution, during the second half of the 1980s. Also, curious, is Hall and Jacques's argument which acknowledges the role that mass media play in consciousness-raising, but ignore the role of many of these same media in false or misinformed consciousness-raising by inculcating and promoting pro-Tory and anti-Labour messages.[410]

This omission or neglect of media and its influence was not necessarily happenstance. For example, Jacques gave a talk about the left and the media at a conference on MT on 30 June 1984 in which he laid out the difference in his approach to the media compared to a 'traditionalist left' understanding, which saw the media in Althusserian terms as part of the ISAs. Jacques's approach was more in keeping with someone wanting to work with and through the mainstream media. It was a notable shift in thinking by anyone on the (far) left at the time. That conference was in the middle of MT's third year of substantial national media coverage, with articles being reprinted or used as sources in a few broadsheets, but especially *The Guardian*, in the coverage of the crises within the Labour and Communist parties.[411] This meant, whether consciously or not, adopting similar values, protocols and procedures to those of the national media's standards of professional journalism to be included as serious commentators in, and contributors to, the mainstream media's coverage of political issues. Thus, we see how there was an ideological shift by the primary decision-maker, the editor, as increasing numbers of professional journalists contributed to MT and its national media coverage grew.

By the mid-1980s, *Marxism Today*'s cultural coverage was distinctive from the dominant approaches on the left, which had been wary of the dominant ideology and popular culture's 'escapism'. The influence of Marxism and critical theory during the 1960s and 1970s, led to a place where the modernist

---

410   Ibid.
411   See Tables 11A, 11B, 12 and 13 in Chapter 5.

avant-garde came to occupy a privileged position in cultural politics amongst most left intellectuals, in which immanent critique and experimentation – the 'avant-garde' as the *cultural* vanguard (party) – were given precedence over accessibility and popularity, which it should be noted was in stark contrast to the ambitions of grassroots media and cultural production,[412] the latter of which became a partial focus for both MT and cultural studies during the 1980s.[413] This emphasis on the avant-garde and immanent critique was part of a left debate that saw many dismiss popular culture as inherently propagating 'capitalist propaganda': i.e. the base-superstructure metaphor, where the ruling ideas of any era are the ideas of the ruling class. Inherent in this perspective, which had been criticised as 'elitist' and 'anti-democratic', was a refusal to acknowledge the importance of making the radical left press 'accessible' to the general public and why attempts at 'popularisation' were at times seen as 'selling out'. Yet, it is this emphasis on 'the popular', the popularisation of radical ideas and attitudes, and accessibility that becomes integral to changes in the radical and alternative press, aspects of which MT itself came to exemplify.[414]

Marxism Today's search to find and meet 'the people' on 'their own ground', to find them 'where they are', meant it sought out those popular culture products, performances and practices which were used by, or held meanings for, 'the people'. Cultural studies research in the 1980s demonstrated that the people as audiences were able to discriminate or read against the ideological line of the capitalist media and popular culture, which directly challenged traditional Marxist understandings of how the dominant ideology worked or its base-superstructure model for cultural analysis.[415] Terms, such as 'false consciousness', were seen as reflecting left intellectuals' biases about 'the people', which was seen as equivalent to the conservative mass society critics of the 1950s and a reflection of elitist and condescending or patronising attitudes towards the people. Explanations that included the mainstream media as responsible for Labour's electoral defeats were seen as the left's refusal to accept blame, which became increasingly untenable after Labour's 1983 election defeat. Political economic critiques of media ownership and its impact upon the ideas in the public sphere were rejected because they were seen as too economistic or determinist.

---

412 Roberts 1990, p. 66.
413 McGuigan 1992, pp. 48–61.
414 Landry et al. 1985.
415 McGuigan 1992 remains one of the best early critiques of cultural studies's trajectory in the 1980s.

20   Conclusion

At the core of *Marxism Today*'s political project were the three themes around the crisis of the left, the rise of the right and the shifting political-cultural terrain of the substantive socio-economic changes of new times. As the first of the two dominant ideological themes that line up almost with the start of Margaret Thatcher's reign as Prime Minister from 1979, Eric Hobsbawm's 'Forward March of Labour Halted' became fiercely debated as an intellectual formation coalesced around MT as the centre of these critiques during the 1980s. Its critique of the 'militant labourism' of the CPGB's Industrial Department and the Labour Left helped to spur on MT's search for a popular politics via the broad democratic alliance and by 1983 his analysis was accepted on much of the left. It is the second theme, Stuart Hall's Thatcherism thesis, the most important and pre-eminent theme, which was also the most fiercely contested. Thatcherism fed the drive for popular politics and contributed to popularising the work of Hall and MT across the left while MT became influential with many on the cultural and academic left. Integral to its successful promotion and popularisation across sections of the left and in higher education circles, especially in the relatively new academic fields of media and cultural studies, were the connections that were made to popular politics and cultural populism. In his Thatcherism thesis, Hall emphasises the political-ideological struggle to establish intellectual and moral leadership, with the emphasis on common sense, ideology/discourse, beliefs, public opinion and so on. These were areas of emphasis that the left had needed to attend to. However, Thatcherism's weaknesses also include a limited understanding of how its hegemony was produced, which points to a failure to examine its material base, such as popular support generated by specific policies for particular groups. Hall also overlooked the role of coercion in Thatcherism's hegemony, against which Raymond Williams's constitutional authoritarianism offered a corrective.[416]

Hall provides a persuasive, descriptive narrative of Thatcher's government's dominance and its engagement in rolling back the welfare state, privatisation and de-certification of unions, amongst other changes, and the use of particular terminology and phrases, but these do not in themselves prove that Thatcherism was hegemonic. It does demonstrate, however, the importance of language backed by coercive instruments of the state, the 'Repressive State Apparatus', that ensure the implementation of policies and legislation against substantive and vocal resistance. Perhaps, it is more accurate to speak of 'mar-

---

416   Williams 1979b, pp. 207–19.

ket populism',⁴¹⁷ whereby the state becomes more unpopular with the people because of the Thatcher government's use of the RSA; the market, in turn, appears more popular since it does not appear to be involved in constraining, but in meeting, the people's 'choices'.⁴¹⁸ The market comes to replace the state as the forum through which social change appears possible, via such activism as 'ethical consumerism' and consumer boycotts.

Yet, Hall's Thatcherism's real weakness was in terms of the implications of its analysis for counter-hegemonic strategies of the left in light of the misunderstandings or misreadings of Gramsci's theory of hegemony. Ideas matter but do not upon their own virtues or truths make themselves preeminent or hegemonic. This is dependent upon the means by which such ideas are produced and distributed. Over the next four chapters, we will see the importance of the material basis of social-cultural practices that are necessary to produce and distribute ideas.

417 E.g. McKnight 2009.
418 Of course, people's 'choices' in the marketplace are constrained by their position within the social relations of production, which determines the amount of money they have to spend via their employment (or lack thereof). Hall's discussion of the market is quite illuminating as he connects the 'choices' on offer for ordinary people with a sense of 'democracy'; this is opposed to the idea of the state as the sole alternative to capitalism (Hall 1984a, 1984b). This popularisation of the market is part of the trajectory of 'cultural populism' in cultural studies by the late 1980s (McGuigan 1992, 1997).

CHAPTER 3

'The Party Line versus the Bottom Line'? The Political Economy of Radical Magazine Production

Fundamental to *Marxism Today*'s move from the 'radical ghetto' of Communist publishing into the 'mainstream' of the commercial marketplace of magazines were changes in its production processes, organisation and funding: editorial leadership and the role of the editorial board; finances; printing, typesetting and subscriptions; and staffing. While the lack of financial resources is often a key obstacle facing the radical press in reaching a broader public, despite expenses often at a fraction of commercial media costs, it is only one, albeit necessary, part of the larger production and distribution process. There are some advantages that alternative and radical media have had, such as the contributions of 'free' labour by professionals and others who volunteer their own financial resources, skills and time. However, even here, corporate media have been increasingly able to exploit volunteer labour through what are now called 'internships'.[1] Of equal importance though are also questions around editorial leadership and institutional structures, technology and human resources, all of which have a concrete, material impact upon the efficiency and efficacy of radical media.

1   'Passive' and 'Active' Editorships, 1957–91

If many conventional periodical and newspaper histories tend to focus on the impact an editor makes, this individual can be even more significant for small-scale alternative or radical media because of the difference a single editor can make for a periodical where there are much greater constraints or limited resources, including quite simply fewer people to do the work. In a section on 'Italian intellectuals' in Antonio Gramsci's very first prison notebook, he recognised the importance of also studying individual editors: he wrote that 'due to the absence of organised and centralised parties, one cannot overlook the

---

1   For example, in 1991, the UK Press Gazette noted that entry into journalism jobs were increasingly beyond the ability of working-class youth, who could not be subsidised by their parents the way middle-class youth could, which enabled the latter to work for free as a form of 'apprenticing' into journalism.

newspapers' since they 'constitute the real parties', and in any 'study of newspapers functioning as a political party, one should take single individuals and their activity into account'.[2] Of course, Gramsci's recognition was based upon his own lived experience as an editor of a revolutionary periodical and as a revolutionary socialist thinker, organiser and leader. An important part of the analysis, therefore, has to recognise the editor's role in organisational decision making, cultural practices and social processes of production and distribution. Fundamentally, we need to rethink the two editorial regimes in terms of their editors' personalities, attitudes and actions: i.e. editorial leadership and practices. From the top editorial position, everything else flows downward, except for the editor's relationship with the MT Editorial Board and the CPGB's top leadership bodies: the Political Committee and the Executive Committee. Therefore, the editor inhabits a position of mediation and negotiation between leading party bodies and officers, including the MTEB, and those working on and contributing to the publication.

To the extent that MT was run by the editor with minimal secretarial support and little interest from the leadership, the journal clearly faced a daunting challenge when it was launched in late September 1957. Its aim, as the party's 'theoretical and discussion journal', was 'to promote Marxist thought over a wide-ranging field of interest and to encourage as much discussion as possible', including a broad range of opinions from party and non-party intellectuals.[3] MT was supposed to be the answer to the history of trying to balance the contradictions between the freedom of editors to air controversial opinions and the leadership's right to exercise control, even though such matters were always worked out in the latter's favour – at least until 1977.[4]

For most alternative and radical periodicals, like MT, no one person is more important in its day-to-day operations than the editor. It is usually because there is no other full-time paid person available to produce a periodical. In MT's case, it was also because the editor was responsible to committees and officials higher up in the party, and it was a full-time paid position. John Gollan was officially appointed as MT's first 'Editor' (1957–62) for symbolic and legal reasons: as the CPGB's new General Secretary (1956–75), he was expected to exhibit intellectual as well as political leadership. Since the party was responsible for whatever was published in MT, Gollan's appointment was also meant to reassure loyal party members that the leadership intended to exercise control over conflicting demands between 'promoting the party line' and publish-

---

2 Gramsci 1985, pp. 390–1, 395.
3 CPGB 1957, p. 1.
4 CIPD 1957; Pimlott 2000a, pp. 48–51.

ing 'opposing viewpoints'. James Klugmann's intellectual reputation made his appointment as 'Assistant Editor' necessary if MT was to have any intellectual credibility with the remaining party membership,[5] and to reassert the party's position on the left and towards a new generation of intellectuals.[6] Although he was editor *de facto*, since Gollan's lack of interest in MT was evident from his absence at board meetings,[7] Klugmann was only officially appointed as 'Editor' in 1962 and remained in position until 1977. Thus, I tend to refer to Klugmann as the *first* editor and my comparisons between editorships and formats is built around the idea that it was Klugmann, not Gollan, who acted as the editor and oversaw MT's production and distribution. Of course, political decisions remained the prerogative of Gollan and the leadership.

Despite similar backgrounds, albeit a generation apart, James Klugmann's editorial style was quite different to that of his successor, Martin Jacques. They were both party intellectuals, involved in the CPGB since their youth, who cultivated interest in ideas that went 'against the grain' of orthodox thought in the party: Klugmann, for example, promoted the dialogue between Christianity and Marxism during the 1960s,[8] and provided space for Jacques to initiate a debate on youth culture in the early 1970s, where he argued for a more progressive understanding against orthodox (and puritanical) criticisms.[9] Klugmann's education and experience in other languages and cultures, and a stint working with the international students' movement before the Second World War ensured MT's strong international focus under his editorship with the CPGB's connections to sister parties around the world.[10] Although Klugmann worked during the war for military intelligence, it was thought that he had spied for the USSR.[11]

Klugmann's editorship of MT evoked as little interest from the leadership as it did controversy. Only one formal report was made to the leadership in MT's first 15 years, although two more followed in the subsequent five years.[12] Few leading members and officials contributed, as writing for the party's 'theoretical and discussion journal' was seen as a lesser priority than political or industrial work. However, Klugmann was able to encourage a few to offer shorter

---

5   Klugmann's intellectual reputation suffered outside the party because it had been damaged from his party work writing 'hatchet jobs' (e.g. Andrews 2015; Hobsbawm 1995).
6   Andrews 1995b; Brennan 1996; Johnstone 1995; Matthews and Matthews 1996.
7   Klugmann 1976b, p. 3.
8   Bright 1977; Klugmann 1967; Lewis 1967b. See Andrews 2004, pp. 81–83.
9   Jacques 1973; Jacques 1975a.
10 Cohen 1977; Simon 1977.
11 Andrews 2015.
12 Klugmann 1960, p. 1; Klugmann 1973, pp. 2, 6–7; Klugmann 1976, p. 4.

pieces for the 'Editorial Comments' section, so that the party could respond more quickly to 'bourgeois' ideas and writers. This was one of the few innovations that he introduced, albeit with the support of the leadership, although MT had been launched without any published editorial statement as to its purpose: its subtitle was seen as self-explanatory.[13]

The EC 'Statement on Ideology and Culture' in 1967 had ensured that the party was opening up its line on a range of issues which helped to position itself to reach out to youth, students, white-collar workers and intellectuals. During the late 1960s and early 1970s, there was both a significant growth in radical left political organisations and a concomitant growing academic interest in Marxism that meant that MT was receiving scores more articles than it could possibly print, in addition to increasing volumes of correspondence to which Klugmann had to respond.[14] There were controversies amongst Communist intellectuals across sister parties and the CPGB, including a major controversy over structuralist Marxism between John Lewis and Louis Althusser during the early 1970s, in recognition of the latter's growing influence on the left (these debates Klugmann publicised but did not initiate).[15]

Loyal to the party line, Klugmann tacked to whichever way that line moved, in part because of his own awareness of his position as an upper-middle class intellectual in a working-class party. Although Klugmann was interested in broadening intellectual debate beyond the party line, he continued to circulate 'controversial' articles (i.e. those that appeared to challenge the party line), amongst party leaders and officers for their approval, even as the internal parameters of debate opened up after 1967.[16] He referred such 'controversial' articles to party officials, even if he supported their publication as a contribution to a debate he was promoting in MT; nonetheless, he also chose not to promote debate against particular policies once they had been decided upon by the party or its leadership.[17] For example, Klugmann sought advice over responses to an article on the excesses of Stalinism and an unpublished manuscript on socialist democracy in 1970–71,[18] and during the 1970s he deferred to Bert Ramelson, the Industrial Organiser, on articles about trade unions, 'the economy and industrial strategy'.[19]

---

13   Klugmann 1960, p. 2.
14   Klugmann 1973, 1976.
15   Lewis 1972a, 1972b; Althusser 1972a, 1972b.
16   Andrews 1995a, p. 237; Cohen 1977, p. 325; Johnstone 1995.
17   Heinemann 1977.
18   Carritt 1970a, 1970b; Feltham 1970, 1971; Klugmann 1971; Perkins 1970.
19   Andrews 1995a, p. 237. E.g. Klugmann 1973; MTEB 1973a, 1973b.

Monty Johnstone, an anti-Stalinist intellectual and lecturer in further education, who remained in the CPGB after 1956, submitted articles critical of the British and Soviet Communist parties which were consistently refused publication until 1967, when the party adopted a more open line on scientific, cultural and ideological matters.[20] In Johnstone's case, he followed up on the rejection of his articles, as the 1957 CIPD Report had recommended, with MT's editor, James Klugmann, who offered various justifications or excuses for non-publication or exclusion. By 1967, however, when Johnstone was sufficiently 'rehabilitated', he was given somewhat more freedom in his expository prose than the occasional 500-word contribution to pre-congress discussions,[21] which was all he had been permitted when his letters were not denied publication outright as with other critics.[22] As discussion was opened up to include reformists and anti-Stalinists, space was shut down to certain viewpoints, which had been favoured until the recent changes in the party line,[23] and to opponents of some policies of the leadership, such as the latter's public criticism of the Warsaw Pact invasion of Czechoslovakia in 1968, even as pro-Soviet articles were still published.[24]

The combination of intelligence and caution in Klugmann as editor, alongside the awareness of his upper-middle-class background, meant that while he was interested in debate he was more deferential to party authority than his successor would be. After more than a dozen years of the same basic design, for example, he began to test gradual changes to the front cover over a period of eighteen months. The changes that were adopted were minor and reflected tinkering rather than a wholesale transformation, as Martin Jacques would later undertake, not once, but twice. This cautiousness and deference also saw him engage in 'intellectually dishonest' tasks, such as writing the 'hatchet job' on Yugoslavia, *From Trotsky to Tito*, when the USSR's line shifted in 1948,[25] and a two-volume official history of the party that was supposed to 'satisfy both Moscow and those who did not believe in such a history'.[26] Hobsbawm

---

20 Johnstone 1995; MTEB 1966.
21 Over a period of months preceding the biennial party congress, all members were, in theory at least, permitted to express their views on any topic for discussion within designated party publications.
22 Johnstone 1995. See also the dispute between the MTEB and readers over the leadership's position on the Warsaw Pact invasion of Czechoslovakia (e.g. Laithwaite 1968; Klugmann 1968; Carritt 1970b).
23 E.g. the Lysenko case: MTEB 1966.
24 Their views were thought to be supported by about 40 percent of the membership. Klugmann 1968; Laithwaite 1968; Andrews 1995a, p. 237; Johnstone 1995; Thompson 1992, p. 154.
25 Beckett 1995, p. 116; Andrews 1995a, p. 242.
26 Hobsbawm 1995, p. 251.

remarked upon Klugmann's unwillingness to 'speak his mind' at a meeting with CPGB leaders in 1956, when he and Brian Pearce, on behalf of the CPGB's Historians' Group, argued for the need to write a 'proper history' of the party: Klugmann 'should have had the courage to refuse' to write such a history.[27] While some saw his attitude as 'political cowardice',[28] Klugmann, however, referred to himself as a 'trimmer', tacking to the political winds in the party.[29]

Although Klugmann might be seen as less of an 'editor' in the terms of professional, journalistic practice, Irene Brennan, a former MTEB member, said that he was a 'very democratic editor', drawing upon contributors and ideas suggested by others, incorporating their ideas into the journal; he frequently tried to encourage party members to write articles who might not otherwise have contributed.[30] While Klugmann did try to encourage contributors to write in a 'clear and limpid style', and he corrected poorly written or structured articles, contributions which exceeded the word length were often simply cut in half and published over two issues rather than being ruthlessly edited for the space available.[31] For example, Klugmann offered advice on rewriting an article in a more accessible manner to one prospective author, a graduate student inspired by Gramsci's ideas, who, in turn, thought Klugmann was 'mad on monosyllables'.[32] Under Klugmann's 'passive' editorship, MT was more a discrete collection of articles representing different interests and sections within the broad parameters of the party line and acceptable internal critical perspectives, than any kind of cohesive political or journalistic project.

Despite similarities in their backgrounds, Martin Jacques's motivation for taking on the editorship of *Marxism Today* was because he wanted to change the party.[33] As part of the second generation of Communists (what Americans call 'red diaper babies'), Jacques was much more critical of traditions and loyalties that his parents' generation held dear, which influenced his approach to both MT and the party.[34] Thus, when Jacques assumed the editorship in

---

27 Ibid.
28 Jacques speaks of Klugmann affectionately and of the latter's willingness to encourage people like Jacques to be critical of orthodoxy, yet unwilling to do so himself (Jacques 1996b). Klugmann was active with the CPGB at Cambridge University during the time of Kim Philby, Donald Maclean, et al., and there were rumours about Klugmann acting as a KGB recruiting agent (Beckett 1995, pp. 85–7; Andrews 1998).
29 Johnstone 1995.
30 Brennan 1996. E.g. MTEB 1973a, p. 2.
31 E.g. MTEB 1973a, 1973b; Brennan 1996; Johnstone 1995.
32 Klugmann 1977b, p. 2; Spours 1977.
33 Jacques 1996a.
34 Ibid.

September 1977, he also initiated, what he called, a 'journalistic project', which was integral to the 'political project', which came out of his involvement with the Eurocommunists, Gramscians and other reformists who wanted to change the party, the way it operated and its relationships with the 'new social movements'. They envisioned a political strategy for the CPGB as one which would enable the formation of a 'broad democratic alliance' between the labour movement and NSMs in a Gramscian 'war of position' to transform society. However, when the leadership, under pressure from traditionalists, backed moves to restrict the reformists' influence at the 1979 National Party Congress, the combination of internal political strife and declining membership reinforced Jacques's desire to reach a broader left audience outside the party, though he was not ready to give up on the CPGB.[35]

After Thatcher's second general election victory in June 1983, Jacques began to feel that this was both an appropriate and a necessary response to the continuing 'crisis of the Left' and the 'rise of the Right', since he envisioned MT's role as one in reaching out to the broad left and intervening in Labour Party debates. He argued that the logic of the revised CPGB program, the 1977 *British Road to Socialism*, meant that the party, through MT, should open up and address itself to the broad left, which necessitated the 'journalistic project'.[36] This shifting project was ideally aimed at inserting MT into the centre of political debate on the left to ultimately lead the BDA. Jacques has said that he had 'no interest in journalism' *per se*, except insofar as it would enable him, working with other CPGB reformers, to change both the party and the left. Thus, there had to be a transformation from an internal party 'journal' into a broad left 'magazine', which meant changes in format, design and layout, content, writing style and editing practices to make it more accessible to both party and non-party readers.

In spite of lacking any journalistic training or background, Jacques proved to be a rigorous, demanding and professional editor with exacting demands placed on staff *and* volunteers.[37] He almost never published unsolicited copy, preferring to ask those he thought to be the 'most knowledgeable people on a subject' to contribute.[38] Both editors repeatedly asked EC members to exercise 'leadership' by writing for MT, but neither editor was able to elicit much enthusiasm: writing for MT was seen as a lesser priority than other party work.

---

35   Andrews 1995a, pp. 239–43; Jacques 1996a.
36   Jacques 1978a.
37   E.g. Brown 1996; Johnstone 1995; Taylor 1995; Townsend 1996.
38   Andrews 1995b; Jacques 1996a.

Jacques's exacting demands were not limited to staff either. Contributors, who were paid nothing, were also not exempt from being asked to rewrite their feature articles two, three or more times, though Jacques was often forced to wait: 'When you're not paying them, and yet you are asking them to produce 3–4,000 words on a subject, you have to also be patient'.[39] Jacques insists that he did not rewrite articles: he briefed contributors on their topics and explained his comments on their articles, but they alone were responsible for rewriting.[40] Features were worked through discussions between contributors and Jacques. Rather than edit articles unilaterally, he would push authors to work through the political implications of their contributions during the revision process; even though he says he was not always certain about the outcome, he did have his expectations, which is why particular authors were asked to contribute in the first place.[41] The editing process was 'an intellectual process of clarification, of exploring the subject, of thinking it [through in] a new way' and, frequently, 'the best articles were the four-drafters'.[42] Different demands were made of contributors: for example, Eric Hobsbawm only ever had to write one draft, whereas Stuart Hall often had to rewrite four or five times, albeit producing some of his best work for MT in the process.[43]

Under Jacques's active editorship, *Marxism Today* developed its own house style, which thereby helped to establish its credibility as a political magazine (explored in Chapter 6). Since a magazine's claims to authority can be swiftly and comprehensively undermined by basic spelling mistakes, poor grammar and simple editing errors, scrupulous attention to detail is 'a critical part of the process of producing the right magazine'.[44] In the drive for perfection, Jacques had his staff pay close attention to detail in commissioning articles, editing, revising, proof-reading and sub-editing, which in turn enhanced MT's authority and professional standing, particularly after a politically embarrassing mistake on the November 1977 cover, which signposted an article on the 60th anniversary of the October 1917 Revolution as its 'Sixteenth' anniversary! This was the second issue of his editorship but the first one that Jacques edited, and he did not want such an obvious mistake repeated, especially if such mistakes were likely to encourage or provoke traditionalist opponents to push the leadership to intervene against his editorship (e.g. many traditionalists did not

---

39   Jacques 1996c; Edgar 1991.
40   Jacques 1996d.
41   Jacques 1996c.
42   Ibid.
43   Ibid.; Brown 1996; Hall 1997.
44   Morrish 1996, pp. 101, 106.

like seeing the party make public criticisms of the USSR).⁴⁵ Jacques was willing to draw upon anyone he felt had the requisite expertise, skills or ability, while still demanding the utmost from everyone including volunteers; he could also instill the necessary confidence in staff and volunteers to fulfill whatever tasks they were set.⁴⁶

The impact of professionalisation can be seen in differences between the editorial practices of both editorships, which began to exemplify MT's shift from an internal party 'journal' to a professional public 'magazine', with the attempt to develop its accessibility for an audience beyond the party. Considerable effort was expended through the production process to first establish and later enforce a new 'house style', to give MT a distinctive voice and identity. The writing had to overcome 'the diversity of style and language' and 'areas of relative incomprehensibility', if it was going to address two different audiences on the left: an internal party readership and an external readership of progressive, non-party activists and intellectuals.⁴⁷

MT's professionalisation was in part achieved through adopting conventions of the mainstream broadsheet journalism in terms of sub-editing, proofreading and house style. This included training up staff and volunteers in professional editorial practices, such as rigorous, standardised sub-editing and proofreading processes, in promotional skills, and in managing strict deadlines for each stage of the production process. As an integral part of this professionalisation process, a 'style sheet' for staff was adapted from the *Sunday Times* to ensure consistency in word usage and style, and to establish MT's distinctive voice.⁴⁸ A number of media professionals, including former MT staff who had moved onto working in mainstream media, provided additional help.⁴⁹

When Martin Jacques was chosen to replace James Klugmann as editor, he had already acquired a PhD from Cambridge University and had been lecturing in economic history at Bristol University for six years, from 1971 until 1977. He accepted the job because he believed it would be the only one that would offer him the chance of fulfilling his political ambitions of not only becoming part of a new, reformist leadership which would change and revitalise the party, but also succeeding as the party's General Secretary.⁵⁰ Jacques had been recruited to the party's governing body, the Executive Committee, at the age of

---

45   Jacques 1996c; MTEB 1977c.
46   Brown 1996; Davison 1995; Townsend 1996.
47   Jacques 1979a, p. 151.
48   Jacques 1996c.
49   Townsend 1996; Jacques 1996c.
50   Jacques 1996a.

22 years in 1967, as one of the youngest members ever, because he had been identified as a young intellectual of great promise and at a time when he still held, by his own admission, 'fairly orthodox views'.[51] Jacques's appointment as *Marxism Today* editor was a unanimous decision by the Political Committee,[52] though its decision also reflected the leadership's 'managerialism' in trying to balance the party's competing tendencies.[53]

Amidst the internal strife that began to tear the Communist Party apart in the late 1970s and 1980s, Jacques proved to be an effective 'political operator', drawing upon his years of experience as an EC member and connections within the party hierarchy. Upon commencement of his duties as a full-time party officer, he had to sit on numerous committees, boards and agencies beyond the MTEB.[54] These skills and his standing as a party intellectual, which helped Jacques manoeuvre around obstacles so that he could publish views more in keeping with MT's political project, gave him a distinct advantage over others seeking greater editorial autonomy. For example, Sarah Benton, the editor of *Comment*, 1978–80, had revamped its design and made it more accessible, but she was eventually forced to resign after making too many changes too quickly in her 'pluralistic and critical approach', which included a 'controversial account of the Party's links with Stalin'.[55] Since Benton lacked Jacques's connections and experience, there was little she could do, without support from leading party officials, to fend off the constant interference and criticisms.[56] Her fate served as a warning to Jacques to make changes cautiously.[57]

The differences between Benton and Jacques, and the leadership's responses to each of them can also be attributed in part to gender: Benton was characterised as 'fiery and impulsive', characteristics which are viewed differently when associated with women rather than men; Jacques was cautious, building support in leading committees and advisory bodies for changes before attempting anything too radical.[58] The leadership even sidelined Benton's role as editor by taking decisions over content without even consulting her, something which would be much harder to imagine happening to a male editor.[59] There were

---

51   Ibid.
52   Brennan 1996; Jacques 1996a; McLennan 1996.
53   Andrews 1995a, pp. 239–43.
54   Jacques 1996a; Andrews 1995b.
55   Andrews 1995a, p. 243.
56   Ibid.; Benton 1980.
57   Jacques 1996a; Andrews 1995a, p. 243.
58   Jacques 1996b.
59   Andrews 1995a, p. 243.

differences in the two publications' roles: as the internal party bulletin or 'party review', *Comment* was responsible for communicating EC and PC decisions, party announcements and providing space for the membership to respond on a regular basis. MT's function as the 'theoretical and discussion' journal, however, was specifically meant, in theory at least, to open up space for debate and disagreement and, to Jacques's advantage, at that time MT was not seen as important to the leadership as *Comment*. MT's frequency, subject matter and format, and audience of intellectuals meant that it was thought to have less influence on internal politics than the fortnightly *Comment*.[60]

As he settled in as editor, Jacques began gradually to put forward his proposed changes for MT's role, and its relationship to the party and the left in a series of biennial reports to the EC, whilst asking for suggestions from the readership.[61] The changes he felt were important included changing the types and subject matter of articles, and re-organising the journal's contents, format, and design and layout. Jacques argued that the logic of the newly revised BRS meant that the CPGB, through MT at least, should open up and address itself to the left and not just to the party.

The differences in their styles of editorship can be partly equated to how they perceived their own roles and positions within the party. James Klugmann was an editor whose sense of duty and responsibility to the party (leadership), combined with his caution and deference, translated into a journal which did not 'rock the boat', as the controversial debates were still within the boundaries of 'acceptable limits' of debate. Martin Jacques, however, is somewhat harder to characterise, although he was cautious, he was as autocratic as any editor could be and pushed gradually, but relentlessly, for political and journalistic changes. Like Klugmann, Jacques was part of the leadership and was primarily interested in the party, but he wanted to change it, in line with his Gramscian and reformist desires, rather than promote the party line. As part of a younger, second generation of Communists (both of Jacques's parents had been party members),[62] Jacques was much more critical of the traditions and loyalties that Klugmann's generation held dear, which influenced his role as editor and approach to party 'shibboleths',[63] including his commitment to high production values and certain editorial practices, partly borne out of his frustration with the blocking of party reforms. These differences in the conceptions and identities that editors have about themselves and their roles, have a corollary in

---

60 Cope 2016, pp. 157, 159. In the 1960s, *Comment* had been published weekly.
61 Jacques 1978b.
62 Jacques 1996b.
63 See Samuel (1985, 1986a, 1987) on generational differences in traditions and values.

the way in which mainstream journalists subscribe to a professional ideology, while journalists working in radical media are more likely to emphasise their commitment to political ideals or social aims over such professional ideals as 'objectivity' and 'competition', since the latter ideals tend to work in favour of the status quo.[64]

Both gave up promising academic careers for the less secure and financially-rewarding life of the party intellectual and official. Jacques left it as it disintegrated during 1990–91 and after revelations that the CPGB had been in receipt of 'Kremlin gold' until 1979.[65] After MT closed in December 1991, Jacques, who had never had much interest in journalism before MT, moved into a full-time career as a freelance journalist and writer, which included a stint as an associate editor of *The Independent* in the mid-1990s.[66]

2 'Editorial Control' or 'Cultural Circle'?

Launched in the aftermath of 1956, *Marxism Today* was the CPGB's 'theoretical and discussion journal' and while it was the direct successor to *Marxist Quarterly*, its formation was influenced by the 1953 Commission on Party Journals and the 1957 Commission on Inner Party Democracy. The battles between editorial autonomy and party control had manifested several times in disputes between editors and party leaders since the 1930s: e.g. *Left Review, Arena, Our Time*.[67] These disputes drew attention to the key organisational body between party leaders and editors: the editorial board. The editorial board's primary function was to oversee the editor and periodical on behalf of the publisher, i.e. the party, and the expectation was that the editor and editorial board would be in general agreement over a periodical's mission and overall direction.

The *Marxism Today* Editorial Board was engaged in reviewing issues usually on a quarterly basis and offering views on the treatment of various subjects, as well as suggesting improvements and future topics. Though it was not a mechanism to produce a periodical on a day-to-day basis, it was seen as the body that should provide strategic advice and direction for editor and staff, and provide

---

64   Downing 1984; Hackett and Zhao 1998; Atton and Hamilton 2008.
65   Anderson and Davey 1995. Morgan 2005 writes that 'Kremlin gold' was spread around the UK left more broadly than usually thought.
66   Jacques 1996a.
67   Croft 1995, pp. 97–9.

feedback on recent issues.[68] However, the degree to which an editor makes use of a board's suggestions may depend upon a number of factors including the editor's personality and political or professional disposition, the willingness of board members to dedicate time and efforts to make suggestions or interventions, and its position within the institutional framework, including support from those higher up in the organisation. Furthermore, an editorial board should lend intellectual weight to a periodical to provide its opinions with an authoritativeness beyond the gravitas of an individual author. Academic editorial boards will oversee or help carry out scholarly journals' peer-review process, by which they ensure that articles published meet the requisite standards in content, style and presentation; similarly, editorial boards of political periodicals perform a peer-review function, albeit on behalf of party or movement leadership, by which an article's political and theoretical suitability can be assured to fall within acceptable ideological boundaries, as with commercial and other ideological publications.[69]

The composition of the first MTEB was an attempt to meet these demands. It included some of the best known party intellectuals, such as Professors George Thomson and J.D. Bernal, Arnold Kettle, Maurice Dobb and Maurice Cornforth, which enhanced MT's intellectual profile. It also included leading party officers, such as Emile Burns, the CPGB's 'cultural commissar',[70] Les Burt and John Mahon, who ensured a strong ideological input as representatives of the party's working-class base to counter the potential 'revisionist' tendencies of middle-class intellectuals, since there was a suspicion that intellectuals could not really be trusted after 1956.

James Klugmann used the MTEB to review the two or three most recent issues, readers' comments and unsolicited articles. It would also discuss his proposals for future issues and make suggestions about possible issues to be covered. The MTEB gradually expanded despite the passing of an older generation of intellectuals (e.g. Bernal, Dobb, Thomson), with new members reflecting viewpoints developing inside and outside the party, such as those of the women's movement, although everyone brought on board were party members. Klugmann brought the first two women onto the MTEB in January 1973: Irene Brennan and Betty Matthews.[71] Matthews's appointment though, like Jack Cohen's, was to effect a closer link between the party's Education Depart-

---

68 Jacques 1978c.
69 It is often forgotten that most mainstream media are capitalist, for-profit corporations.
70 Burns had been involved in disputes over the editorial direction of previous party journals (e.g. Croft 1995, p. 97).
71 Brennan wrote for *Link*, the CPGB's women's journal (Brennan 1996).

ment and its theoretical and discussion journal: MT articles were used in education packs for branches and summer schools.⁷²

The MTEB's composition can be seen as a limited response to general social and political changes, and to internal tensions, as MT's role in providing 'intellectual guidance' began to give way to a greater range of debate. As interest in Marxism grew in relation to the social movements, political developments and industrial unrest in the 1960s, there was a cross-fertilisation with new ideas and the leadership opened up debate on the party line in science, religion, the arts, ideology and culture after 1967 through MT, albeit with a watchful eye on political and economic issues. The pluralism of the EC's 1967 statement was allowed because Marxism-Leninism provided no clear position on culture, science and religion, which cleared the way for the CPGB's more open attitude to new social movements and cultural questions.

Since the MTEB was an advisory body and the means by which the CPGB retained overall ideological and political control over MT, Jacques would need to focus on it as part of the journalistic project. The MTEB was an issue that he and his supporters would have to address since it could intervene and sack the editor, censor articles or engage in other forms of unwanted interference. From the first days of his editorship, Jacques began the process of redefining how the MTEB should operate: its role changed from exercising control over MT's general direction, to acting more as a discussion forum or Gramsci's 'cultural circle'.

Professor George Thomson, a member of the first MTEB, had suggested as early as November 1957, in MT's second issue, that part of the problems of previous party journals had been the failure of editorial boards to function as 'cultural circles'.⁷³ He argued that the cross-fertilisation of ideas, methods and approaches was actually more to do with the integration of Marxist theory into traditional academic disciplines than with creating a truly interdisciplinary scholarly approach. A board that functions as a cultural circle, as Gramsci articulated the idea, acts as a 'homogeneous group of intellectuals trained to produce regular and methodical "literary" activity' and it would integrate the contributions of each specialist to increase the average knowledge level of the other members, and thereby increase the 'collective competence'.⁷⁴ The cultural circle was an integral part in the production of ideas as the necessary prac-

---

72   Matthews and Matthews 1996. George Matthews was a former editor of the *Morning Star* and later a head of the CPGB's Press and Publicity Department.
73   Thomson 1957, p. 62.
74   Gramsci cited in Thomson 1957, p. 62; Gramsci 2007 [1957], pp. 126–32, especially p. 128.

tices of writing, editing and publishing could be shared and improved upon for a broader impact within the party and on the public beyond it.

Under Martin Jacques's editorship, the *Marxism Today* Editorial Board was responsible for overseeing MT's general direction and strategy, reviewing previous issues and discussing future topics, just as it had been under his predecessor. Unlike his predecessor, however, who approached MTEB members and Party Centre staff to help out, Jacques did not want board members involved in the daily production process, preferring instead to seek out people whose skills or abilities he wanted to draw upon. A group of volunteers and staff functioned as MT's 'editorial collective', as it was frequently referred to, which together with Jacques handled the daily production process.[75] The MTEB's functions were clearly demarcated from the daily production process in Jacques's proposals on MT's development, which would enable Jacques to exercise greater freedom to operate at some remove from oversight by the board.[76]

Since the MTEB was appointed by the Executive Committee, it was important for Jacques to secure its agreement with the changes he envisaged for it. Nevertheless, it 'operated in a relationship of some tension' with the editor between 1977 and 1985, because of the mixture of traditionalist, loyalist and reformist members. Therefore, unsurprisingly, Jacques sought to change the MTEB's composition because of the opposition to some of his ideas from some board members, even though he had instituted more frequent meetings during the first half of his tenure, 1977–86, which also meant that there had been more opportunity for opposition to be expressed than when Klugmann was editor.[77] Three members were removed (Gabriel Carritt, Nick Wright, George Wake) and five new members were selected with the MTEB's backing, while a further three names, without board support, put forward to the EC were not selected.[78] This new intake in 1979 reflected both Jacques's suggestion that the board had a representative function to perform and his wish that it would discuss strategic issues with a more favourable disposition towards Eurocommunist and Gramscian perspectives: the new intake included one industrial worker (Dan Connor), one feminist (Jean Gardiner), one traditionalist (John Hoffman) and two

---

75 Jacques 1996b. Jacques preferred to refer to the production process as 'collaborative' rather than 'collective', although the word 'collective' seems to have been the most commonly used term.
76 Jacques 1978c.
77 MTEB meetings were held every two, instead of three, months, although at least one meeting per year would have to be cancelled because of a political crisis or summer holidays.
78 MTEB 1979a, p. 1.

reformist (Eric Hobsbawm, Bob Rowthorn) intellectuals. Hoffman's inclusion reflected Jacques's continuing caution for the board to appear representative to ensure that he did not alarm his opponents.

The content was not seen as much of a problem in the first few years of Jacques's editorship until its profile became more public, particularly after its features on the Polish crisis as the independent trade union, Solidarity, challenged Communist Party rule in 1981–82.[79] Traditionalist board members, such as Irene Brennan, John Hoffman, John Foster and Michael Seifert, however, were becoming increasingly disgruntled and frustrated with MT's political trajectory, claiming that it was becoming 'too one-sided' in its presentation of issues, even though they acknowledged the improvements in design, format and distribution. Jacques was accused of using the MTEB to 'rubber-stamp' decisions that he had already taken and as 'a cover' for MT's role as a 'factional journal': these criticisms intensified after the Tony Lane affair in 1982.[80] However, after the purge of traditionalist opponents at the May 1985 Special Congress, Jacques was able to see through the personnel changes he wanted.[81]

This was a significant victory for Jacques in further securing the MTEB as a secure base of support prior to the third format launch in 1986, at least partly influenced by leadership's need for allies during the CPGB's 'civil war'.[82] The board was to be expanded to a maximum of 30, including non-party people, and the editor and deputy editor were to become full, voting members; section editors were to be included as non-voting, advisory members.[83] In July 1986, Jacques submitted a list of 24 new names for inclusion on the expanded MTEB,

---

79 Townsend 1996; Taylor 1995.

80 Brennan 1996. E.g. EC 1982a; Foster 1982a, 1984; MTEB 1981b; Seifert 1983.

81 Brennan says she left in 1980–81, though her name remained on the masthead until 1985; she tried to convince Seifert to leave because Jacques would only take their advice if and when he wanted to (Brennan 1996). Foster was no longer invited to board meetings after the 1985 Congress because he was amongst those purged (MTEB 1985a). Hoffman and Seifert were officially removed from the MTEB in 1986.

82 Dave Priscott criticised Jacques for presenting the EC with proposals for changes to MTEB's conceptualisation and its composition because it would not allow the EC or other bodies to make suggestions for board members (Priscott 1985a). In a separate personal letter, dated the same day, to Jacques, Priscott expressed his concerns about rumours that efforts were being made to promote Jacques as a 'future General Secretary' because it would affect attitudes to EC members and directives by polarising the EC into two camps (Priscott 1985b).

83 Priscott 1986, p. 1; MTEB 1985b. Increasingly, in the second half of the 1980s, volunteers who became 'staff' (whether paid or unpaid) were not necessarily party members (e.g. Julian Turner).

which included the first non-party members, including Stuart Hall, David Edgar and Robin Murray, and at least one ex-CPGB member, Fred Steward.[84] The leadership approved the new board.

With internal opponents removed and critics silenced, Jacques began to reshape the MTEB's role by making its function more clearly strategic and advisory: its meetings were switched from an evening every two months to one day every three months. The board was to 'influence and shape the longer-term direction' via discussions of 'ideas and themes', though Jacques also argued that it could not determine what went into MT on a monthly basis,[85] even though he never felt constrained by any decision taken by the MTEB.[86] A suggestion was made that the MTEB should replace the Theory and Ideology Committee because the latter no longer functioned effectively and the board's role in 'exchanging and generating ideas' duplicated functions. The party, it was argued, could make better use of resources by putting some TIC members onto the new MTEB.[87]

The new MTEB had three key functions. One was to discuss general strategy for the magazine and staff reports. Though the EC always dealt with MT's budget, the editor and staff reported to the board on marketing strategies, sales figures, debts, staff changes etc.: 'We shared our problems with the editorial board'.[88] For the editor and staff, this educative function with the MTEB ensured the latter's support for proposed changes or additional resources in Jacques's requests to the EC and PC. The board thus became a means of supporting the editor and periodical vis-à-vis the party rather than functioning as a means for the party to exert oversight of the periodical.

The second key function was as a forum for feedback through reviewing the two or three most recent issues, with different board members taking responsibility for preparing and leading each session: all aspects were considered including content, design, front covers etc., and how to redress editorial 'imbalances' or 'absences'. This provided an opportunity for Jacques's critics on the MTEB to make critiques about MT's political-ideological trajectory and changes in format and style. However, it would be incorrect to only read such traditionalist critics as opposing MT's content. For example, at the MTEB meeting of 6 June 1982, John Hoffman's review of the May and June issues was generally

---

84 Hall did not want to be the only non-party MTEB member and agreed to do it only if there were other non-party members invited (Hall 1997).
85 Jacques 1986a.
86 Brennan 1996; Jacques 1996d; Townsend 1996; Taylor 1995.
87 Priscott 1986, p. 1.
88 Taylor 1995.

supportive of content.[89] It should also be made clear that criticisms of substance or style did not necessarily always align alongside the two broad opposing tendencies within the party: i.e. traditionalist and reformist. For example, Ros Brunt and David Edgar disagreed over 'designer socialism'.[90]

The third key function was as a forum for bringing key people together to discuss issues around contemporary politics, culture and life. After 1986, non-party people, including Hall and Edgar, were invited to join the MTEB while others were invited on occasion for discussions with the board. It was through such discussions that the 1988 weekend seminar, 'Rethinking Socialism for the 1990s', turned into MT's third big political theme after the 'Forward March of Labour Halted?' and 'Thatcherism': 'New Times.'[91] Thus, the strategy for the new MTEB developed into a lively, productive forum of ideas, judging by the notes of the reviews: a 'cultural circle'.[92] Jacques and his allies had envisioned the MTEB as a forum for discussing ideas and exploring themes, a process by which the maneuverings inside the party created the space for MT to operate autonomously on a day-to-day basis without any party oversight.

Although not everyone on the MTEB was always in agreement, after 1986 such differences tended to be one of degree rather than of broader oppositional groupings or internal party manouevring. Most subsequent tensions on the board were productive of engagement with approaches, ideas or politics, as might take place on academic editorial boards. Nevertheless, by 1987 internal tensions began to emerge over MT's increasingly divergent path from the party as it was also changing. Leading intellectuals, such as Dave Priscott and Monty Johnstone, voiced concerns of both loyalists *and* reformists, that MT should play a closer, more supportive role for the party, since the traditionalists had been purged and the leadership was gradually being replaced with reformists.[93] Nevertheless, there were older party intellectuals and officers who maintained unconditional support for the magazine, which helped to persuade ordinary members to do likewise, even if they were otherwise uncertain about it.[94]

---

89   MTEB 1982a.
90   MTEB 1989b.
91   Jacques 1988c; MTEB 1988a.
92   E.g. Cockburn 1989; MTEB 1988a, 1989a, 1989b, 1989c; Steward 1990.
93   Although Priscott's dissatisfaction went back to 1982, McLennan had convinced him to stay on the MTEB regardless (Priscott 1988). Priscott and Johnstone both addressed their resignation letters to the EC rather than Jacques or the MTEB in recognition of the party's authority over MT (Johnstone 1990).
94   They included reformists (e.g. Hobsbawm) and loyalists (e.g. Kettle, George and Betty Matthews) (Hobsbawm 1997; Kettle 1985; Matthews and Matthews 1996).

The *Marxism Today* Editorial Board under both editorships, therefore, functioned as a forum for feedback and to discuss strategy. Both editors also limited their take-up of MTEB members' suggestions to those that were within the acceptable parameters of debate in Klugmann's case, or of MT's political project in Jacques's case, although Jacques used the board more consistently in generating and exploring ideas, especially after July 1986. In addition, the MTEB proved useful in supporting Jacques's proposals and ideas against internal opponents, shifting from the body overseeing MT on behalf of the party to one which functioned as a useful shield against, and support mechanism inside, the party. This last version of the MTEB also acted as a 'cultural circle' with weekend events for 'big thinking' (e.g. 'New Times').[95]

3   'Who Pays the Piper, Calls the Tune?' Financing *Marxism Today*

The radical media's neglect of their own organisational and economic requirements limits the potential for success from the outset and the financing of radical political publications has been subject to different considerations, often political as well as organisational. Almost always, such publications cannot simply be dependent upon support of the political organisation that produces it, or upon support from its location within a movement or milieu. Publications based within or addressing social, environmental or identity movements or milieux are often controlled and run by small circles of friends, groups or collectives, and while representative, or even constitutive, of a larger group or movement, there is no certainty of income or audience upon which to base any kind of long-term planning or strategy.[96]

Political parties, particularly those based upon the vanguard model or Leninist party-paper structure, usually have the organisational structure that can ensure the collection and distribution of resources and ideas while also providing a core audience. Published by the then largest political organisation on the Labour Party's left, *Marxism Today* was in a better position than its other far-left rivals because of the CPGB's size. During MT's first two decades, 1957–77, the party provided a potential audience of 25–35,000 members, against actual sales generally between 2,500 and 4,500 per issue, as well as the funds, staff and organisational nexus for production and distribution. MT was promoted

---

95   The one-off 'comeback' issue of October–November 1998 began as a weekend of ideas in Surrey.
96   Atton 1999; Khiabany 1997.

through party branches and committees, and the party agency responsible for party bookshops, national distribution for CPGB districts and branches, and subscriptions: Central Books.

Since left parties openly recognise publications as an extension of their work, the issue of finances is addressed differently to that of commercial publications: subsidy is seen as necessary 'and self-sufficiency was deemed desirable but unattainable', since it is difficult to compete in a marketplace when there are so many factors stacked against a radical left publication, especially 'in an advertising-based press system'.[97] Traditionally, very little had been done on the radical left in terms of market research and feedback to ensure sufficient interest (readers, advertisers) and income to sustain the periodical beyond the first few issues. Attempts to rectify this situation have most commonly adopted such tactics as: the 'fighting fund' (e.g. *The Morning Star*), where money is raised through various means (e.g. donations, benefits); the recruitment of 'supporting subscribers', who pay higher subscription rates than ordinary consumers (e.g. *The Leveller, New Socialist*); or where sellers encourage casual or regular buyers to pay 'solidarity prices', whereby the reader pays above the stated price as an act of solidarity.[98]

Finances for CPGB publications, including MT, were subsidies. It was not necessary to break even, let alone make a profit, because publications were absolutely essential to the party's ability to act politically. The CPGB, of course, benefited from 'Moscow gold,' though the USSR's contribution declined substantially after 1968 before ceasing altogether in 1979. The party's property provided it with substantial assets, which were sold off when financial difficulties became critical: the King Street headquarters in central London were sold in 1980; ten years later, the party sold its headquarters in St. John Street, London (which raised some three million pounds in 1990). When necessary, therefore, the CPGB could still raise revenue that enabled it to continue subsidising various activities including MT.[99]

The CPGB's financial control was, in Martin Jacques's words, a 'crude form of centralisation' because anytime the editor wanted to change anything he had to get the agreement of the PC and the EC: it undermined 'any sense of initiative'.[100] This attitude was reflected in MT's status as a sub-section of the Press

---

97 Comedia 1984, p. 98; Chippindale and Horrie 1988. Are right-wing propagandists aware of the irony (and hypocrisy) of 'free market' think tanks subsidising their publications (e.g. Lorimer 1993)?
98 Landry et al. 1985.
99 Thompson 1992, p. 206.
100 Jacques 1996b.

and Publicity Department: until the 1970s, it was just one line of expenditure in annual reports. This, of course, contrasted greatly with MT after 1979 with its launch of the second format.

All party publications faced financial pressures during the 1970s as inflation added to printing costs while declining party membership meant declining, actual and potential, readerships and revenues. Whatever could be done, therefore, had to be done at no additional cost to the party, which explains the importance of the free help and advice provided by friends and volunteers.[101] Until Jacques was able to acquire greater control over MT's budget, it was difficult to initiate changes in format, distribution, printing etc., without lobbying the leadership or engaging in other forms of internal politicking. Eventually, however, lobbying efforts paid off when MT was granted a separate bank 'sub-account' of the CPGB in October 1984, which brought greater flexibility in planning, strategy and budgeting, and it gave Jacques more control over MT's day-to-day finances.

Although MT no longer had to lobby party officials over hiring staff or making changes to its format, any changes which affected party enterprises, such as subscriptions and printing, still had to be ratified by the EC. Also, with its own 'sub-account' from October 1984 onwards, MT became responsible for costs previously paid for by Party Centre, such as office space and overheads (telephones, electricity, postage etc.), except for the 1.6 full-time equivalent staff, which the party had paid for since 1957. Revenue generated from advertising and sales was ploughed straight back into staffing, production and distribution, and MT was able to become more ambitious about its plans for merchandising, events or special issues etc.[102]

Marxism Today was also relatively unique in the way its high production values belied its shoe-string budget and it led the changes that most left publications would incorporate as technological changes began making it cheaper and easier to develop 'glossy', professional looking magazines. As with so many alternative and radical papers, MT also relied on the dedication of its editor, staff and volunteers to provide free labour in the actual production of ideas (i.e. writing, editing, proofing), as well as in promotion and publicity work to support distribution. Thus, finances tended to be directed primarily towards paper, printing and typesetting costs, which could not be avoided, and secondarily towards design, artwork, photographic reproduction and covers. Such investments were absolutely necessary to compete against rival periodicals on

---

101 Ibid.
102 Perryman 1994b; Turner 1994.

TABLE 1   Annual income and expenditure, 1977–91

	1978[a]	1979[b]	1982[c]	1983[d]	1984–85[e]	1987[f]	1989[g]
Income	13,115.00	15,524.00	60,406.62	77,740.00	120,580.98	210,850.00	241,321.84
Expenditure	-13,761.00	-15,817.00	-70,692.22	-90,271.00	-125,515.05	-262,918.00	-292,079.62
Profit/Loss	(646.00)	(293.00)	(10,285.59)	(12,531.00)	(4,934.07)	(52,068.00)	(50,757.78)

a   EC 1980.
b   Ibid.
c   PC 1984; EC 1983.
d   MTEC 1984d.
e   October 1984 to September 1985: the first full year when MT had its own bank sub-account.
f   PC 1988.
g   PC 1991.

the newsagent's shelf. Further costs arose with expansion, such as newstrade distribution, which requires higher print-runs to ensure sufficient supply for newsagents, and for promotions and publicity.

MT's success in achieving wider distribution, circulation and press coverage only paid off after extensive efforts had been made and resources expended. For example, the first full year of Jacques's editorship, which includes the original, first format and design, and being printed and distributed by CPGB enterprises, MT's income was derived overwhelmingly from sales and reached a modest £13,115 while its expenses, almost solely printing and typesetting costs, exceeded income by less than £650 (Table 1). Despite a fall in circulation during the first half of the following year, and increased production costs with the move to the second format (October 1979) and changes in typesetting, layout and design etc., MT actually incurred a smaller loss: the investment in these changes ensured increased sales and hence income. By 1982, however, despite nearly a four-fold increase in income, rising costs left MT with a deficit of just over £10,000. One major cost was the move to full-colour covers from March 1982, after only four months with four-colour printing, although the cost differences between four- and full-colour printing was minimal.[103]

The deficit increased by more than 20 percent in 1983 from increases in production costs and wage expenditures. Interestingly, the increases in both total revenues and costs are almost three times greater in 1987 as compared to 1983, which on the one hand, indicates that the costs of changes in production, promotion and distribution were substantial and yet, on the other hand, the

103   Townsend 1996.

TABLE 2   Finances (%) 1979–89[a]

INCOME	1979	1983	1985	1987	1989
Newstrade		16.5	21.8	23.4	19.2
CB Wholesale		22.9	12.0	6.0	5.0
Subscriptions		14.6	28.3	25.4	29.8
Misc. Sales		1.0		1.0	
Total Sales		55.0	62.1	55.8	54.0
Advertising		40.9	32.4	40.0	37.1
Miscellaneous		4.1	5.5	4.2	9.0
TOTAL (%)		100.0	100.0	100.0	100.1
TOTAL (Pounds)	15,524.00	77,740.00	120,580.98	210,850.00	241,321.84

EXPENDITURE	1979	1983	1985	1987	1989
Printing		48.0	31.2	26.0	22.9
Typesetting		11.0	10.3	6.8	4.8
Design		12.0	9.0	9.3	11.6
Promotion		5.3	4.0	7.6	8.2
Distribution		–	19.3	14.8	15.6
Wages		14.4	14.9	15.9	23.3
Office expenses		8.0	5.3	12.6	7.6
Miscellaneous		1.5	6.0	7.0	5.3
TOTAL (%)		100.2	100.0	100.0	99.3
TOTAL (Pounds)	15,817.00	90,271.00	125,515.05	262,918.00	292,079.62
Balance (Pounds)	(293.00)	(12,531.00)	(4,934.07)	(52,068.00)	(50,757.78)

a There is no breakdown for 1979, although sales would have accounted for at least 90% of income because there was very little advertising. The figures for 1985 are for October 1984–September 1985 and do not include a number of costs only charged to MT later in 1985 (MTEB 1989c; MTEC 1983a, 1984b, 1984d, 1986a; PC 1988, 1991).

returns of the limited circulation increases were nonetheless still substantial. Advertising for both these years, four years apart, is virtually the same (40.9 to 40) percentage of total revenue, despite income increasing by more than three times albeit with increased space via greater pagination and with the larger page format (Table 2).

The first increase in pagination for individual issues began with the October 1980 issue, which was published with 36 pages instead of the usual 32 (a 12.5 percent increase), at the start of MT's one-year trial run in selected London newsagents. The price was also increased from 50 to 60 pence (a 20 percent increase), to help retain revenue for MT while providing retailers and distributors with their share of the cover price. For the rest of the next 11 months, pagination was reduced to 32 pages until the national newsagent launch issue of October 1981, which increased its pagination by 50 percent to 48 pages and increased its price from 60 to 65 pence.

After national newsagent distribution began, its pagination varied between 40 and 48 pages until February 1986, with occasional special issues where pagination was increased to 52 pages (e.g. March 1983: Karl Marx special with 'vox pops'; October 1983: Neil Kinnock as superman cover; January 1984: special issue on '1984'), 56 pages (e.g. December 1983: Christmas; April 1985: special issue for Special Party Congress in May) and even 60 pages (e.g. October 1985: Labour conference). Some issues were published with supplements, such as the 48-page October 1984 issue, which included an additional 32-page supplement for the MT Event 'Left Alive' stabled into the centre (the issue was available a month before the event), or the 60-page October 1985 issue, which included another 16 pages in a 'Style' supplement, which (contrary to its title) focussed on how labour, grassroots and NSM organisations could communicate better and more persuasively.

One of the most significant financial years was MT's first full year of 'independence' with its own bank account, from October 1984 to September 1985, where the loss was less than £5,000, although some substantial costs only became evident in the last quarter of 1985. This explains why such figures, which excluded certain financial quarters, could be seen as hiding substantial losses (which critics accused them of doing so intentionally).[104] Though MT's losses soon reached around £19,000 for 1986 (the third format launch), it was only when a number of factors contributed to a serious deficit almost three times the 1986 figure (£52,068.00) that its debts became a potential political liability with the party. From 1987 until it closed in December 1991, its annual deficits averaged £40–50,000 or more, a level at which neither MT nor the (shrinking) CPGB could sustain for long. Even when the CPGB let MT go, it still put in £69,000 to help fund the magazine for a further 18 months.[105]

By examining the expenditures and revenues generated during the monthly production cycle, it becomes clear that reaching out to a broader audience to generate a higher income also incurs additional costs above a proportional rise in unit costs. These costs will almost always arise before increased revenues

---

104 These costs more than doubled the deficit (£12,000) for all of 1985.
105 PC 1991.

TABLE 3 Monthly averages of income and expenditure: selected years[a]

INCOME	1977	1979	1981–82	1983	1984–85	1987	1989
Newstrade		30.00	1,244.17	1,066.92	2,192.37	4,105.92	3,870.26
Central books	872.78	1,127.00	1,904.37	1,481.16	1,201.12	1,047.67	997.02
Subscriptions				946.58	2,839.53	4,467.00	5,983.88
Misc. sales				66.50		177.08	
Total sales	872.78	1,157.00	3,148.54	3,561.06	6,233.02	9,797.67	10,851.16
Advertising	85.00	435.40	1,331.82	2,793.33	3,260.67	7,035.08	7,459.05
Miscellaneous			256.47	123.94	554.73	738.08	1,799.94
TOTAL	957.78	1,592.40	4,736.83	6,478.33	10,048.42	17,570.83	20,110.15

EXPENDITURE	1977	1979	1981–82	1983	1984–85	1987	1989
Printing	898.33	1,426.00	3,804.96	£3,610.00	3,262.25	5,704.92	5,583.76
Typesetting			555.52	818.00	1,075.20	1,489.17	1,157.38
Design		140.00	670.86	1,012.00	940.29	2,040.50	2,832.49
Ads artwork		10.00			314.85	433.92	631.02
Production misc.						57.33	162.78
Promotion			311.89	487.00	410.75	1,668.00	2,001.87
Distribution					2,021.33	3,242.33	3,804.71
Wages			272.50	1,083.00	1,561.62	3,478.83	5,660.01
Office expenses			403.16	600.00	558.50	2,767.00	1,838.41
Miscellaneous	44.11		98.60		314.80	1,027.83	463.52
TOTAL	942.44	1,576.00	6,117.49	7,609.00	10,459.59	21,909.83	24,339.97

| BALANCE (P/L) | 15.34 | 16.40 | (1,380.66) | (1,131.00) | (411.17) | (4,339.00) | (4,229.82) |

a These figures are drawn from several documents submitted to the PC, EC and MTEB: 1977 figures are based on the first nine months (MTEB 1978a); December 1979 (second format) is used as representative for 1979; 1981 figures are averaged from six months, October 1981 to March 1982 (PC 1984); 1983 figures are from MT Accounts for 1983 (PC 1984); 1985 figures are based upon MT's first 'independent' year, October 1984–September 1985 (EC 1986a); 1987 and 1989 figures from EC (1988a, 1990).

can have an impact and these will have a greater adverse effect on undercapitalised publications. For example, almost all the first format (1957–79) costs were for printing and typesetting (virtually) text-only issues by Farleigh Press since the CPGB covered the costs for 1.6 FTE staff. The regular addition of photographs and graphics in the second format (1979–86) initially incurred costs of less than 10 percent of total expenditure, even as the proportion of images to text increased (Table 3). As printing and typesetting costs increased in absolute terms, they became an increasingly smaller share in relative terms of the total: Table 2 shows that between 1983 and 1989, printing and typesetting dropped from 59 to 27.7 percent; staffing rose from 14.4 percent to nearly one-quarter (23.3 percent); promotion increased by more than half, from 5.3 to 8.2 percent; and a new cost, distribution, rose from nil to 15.6 percent.[106]

However, these costs partially disguise the massive increases that were effected in some of these areas during the 1980s. For example, promotion costs averaged per issue, rose from less than £45 in 1977[107] to just over £2,000 by 1989, and even compared against 1983, this represented a four-fold increase in six years, with a noticeable impact upon media coverage.[108] But MT did not spend the same amount on publicity every month. October always exceeded other months because of a political and commercial convergence: it was always published ahead of the Labour Party conference and it is one of the most important months for magazine industry promotions. Table 3 figures for monthly expenditures for 1981–82 of £311.89 are a little misleading because these were six-month averages: MT spent £1,412.69 on promoting the October 1981 issue, the national distribution launch issue for W.H. Smith's, against an average monthly expenditure of less than £100 for the other issues.

Although MT ruthlessly exploited publicity in all forms, promotion costs played an important part in ensuring national media coverage. For example, when sales began declining in 1988, it was as necessary as ever to spend money attempting, not only to win back readers, but also to convince distributors and newsagents that MT was making the effort to promote sales so that they would continue to stock the magazine. If the promotional efforts fail, however, then the added costs and larger print runs (to ensure newsagents would be adequately stocked with copies), will only worsen the financial situation, although there might be no other choice in attempting to increase circulation to prevent the magazine's closure, since the party's decline also meant decreasing subsidies for MT. Monthly sales declined from an average of 13,388 in the first half of 1988 to 10,980 in the second half of 1990 despite spending more than £24,000 on promotion in 1989 alone. With the changes in Eastern Europe, the name became a partial drag on sales despite the increased interest in official Communism's demise.[109]

---

106 Distribution costs covered promotion to and around the newstrade (other than costs for other publicity), subscriptions, packaging etc.
107 Miscellaneous costs do not include cross-promotional copy (MT ran advertisements in exchange for other publications to run ones for MT).
108 Chapter 5.
109 Audited figures are averaged over six months and do not show monthly fluctuations.

MT's trade in ideas was not as expensive as with commercial periodicals, because it rarely if ever paid its writers. During the early years of MT's transformation, there was no expectation by contributors to be paid for writing, as this was a common practice for left and other alternative periodicals. However, such expectations changed with MT, since its high production values, voluminous media coverage and national distribution provided it with a public image at odds with its financial reality. Increasingly, it became more difficult to persuade potential contributors to write for nothing, especially if they were contributing to the features section where Jacques often demanded several rewrites. Some public figures agreed to interviews or discussions but not to *write* for MT because they were not paid.[110] However, this could be offset by the political *kudos* that became attached to writing for, or being interviewed by, MT: it was the promise of political and cultural capital, not financial, for contributors.[111]

The Communist Party paid for 1.6 full-time equivalent staff, the editor and one secretary three days per week, for the duration of *Marxism Today*'s existence, costs that were not included in MT's accounts. However, it did not begin with even such a minimal commitment being guaranteed because within his first year as editor, Martin Jacques had to make the argument that MT would need a dedicated part-time staff member at least. When he started he had four different women, two of whom were quite elderly, working part-time at party headquarters; one of the four he shared with *Comment* and another stopped showing up altogether, while a third wanted to retire in January 1978.[112] These part-time secretaries provided all sorts of help with the production and circulation, including handling advertising, correspondence and back orders, typing up articles, compiling indexes for the year and getting each year's 12 issues bound together as a single volume. In his argument against the Political Committee's cost-cutting measures, Jacques itemised and explained his assessment of the prospective financial costs of 'dropping the part-time position'. These costs were itemised as follows: the potential loss of £200–250 in advertising revenue per issue; additional typesetting costs of £20–35 per issue for text rather than ad space; loss of some of existing revenue based upon the sales of bound volumes ('difficult to estimate') but somewhere between £200–500 per annum; plus additional typing costs and potentially more 'proof corrections'

---

110   Jacques 1996c, 1996d; Taylor 1995; Townsend 1996.
111   Denis Healey refused to write for MT because it would not pay him; however, he agreed to be interviewed for MT (Jacques 1996c).
112   Jacques n.d. [1977].

worth up to £50–70 per issue; other aspects of cleaning up material for publication (i.e. 'approximately 15–20,000 words per issue'; 'the rest, 10–15,000 arrives clean/tidy').[113]

These two early memos of Jacques's are also useful in identifying the various duties that the assistant provided to the editor and their basic economic importance: in his summary, Jacques points out the costs to MT will amount to £260 to £375 a month against a savings of £176 (which is the cost of the job): 'a net loss ... £84-£199 a month'.[114] This cutting of the part-time position would have meant: 'Physically, the production of the journal in its present form would be seriously jeopardised'.[115] Without these early efforts at soliciting the PC's support for funding editorial assistance, Jacques's might have had a much more difficult position to focus on developing MT in his first two years as editor. His experience and position in leadership committees were important in securing this initial support that enabled the periodical to survive its immediate future.

Additional staff meant the wage bill increased from 'nil' in 1977 to more than £5,600 a month by 1989, although wages were below market rates for all types of skilled workers. Such increases in wage costs, to pay for fairly minimal staffing levels, were absolutely crucial to MT's ability to recruit ever greater amounts of advertising, secure distribution networks and outlets, expand promotion, increase editorial space and pagination, experiment in design and layout, and manage large numbers of volunteers. That overall low wage costs belied MT's high production values highlights one of the few areas where alternative media retain an advantage over many of their commercial (and ideological) competitors: free labour. However, this comparative advantage has changed dramatically since the 1990s, as capitalist organisations are utilising interns and unpaid labour to replace paid labour and therefore making use of what was once alternative media's singular advantage.[116] Nevertheless, many mundane but vital tasks would have remained undone without paid staff, particularly on the business side, such as recruiting advertisers and processing subscriptions, which are usually of the least interest for alternative and radical media volunteers.[117]

The financial viability of any media organisation is also dependent upon efficient and effective administrative structures that can compensate for the loss of experienced staff. The massive 1987 deficit was the result of a number of factors

---

113   Jacques n.d. [1978]; Allison 1978.
114   Jacques n.d. [1978], p. 1.
115   Jacques n.d. [1978], p. 2.
116   E.g. Perlin 2011.
117   Landry et al. 1985.

including: Jacques's absence (due to ill-health); the loss of three of MT's most experienced staff; the lack of administrative procedures for controlling financial transactions that would have allowed MT to deal with additional ventures (e.g. merchandising); and staff incompetence, due to inadequate training and experience. A combination of these factors, for example, led to lost revenue when advertisers were not billed and increased costs when MT paid some of its bills twice.[118] Similarly, where the role of a single, powerful individual in a small media organisation, such as the editor, can be quite critical to its success, that same media organisation becomes vulnerable when that individual editor is absent or unable to perform his or her usual role; thus, the fate of the periodical is inextricably intertwined with the fate of the editor, something which is not likely to happen with larger capitalist and state media.

Even though *Marxism Today*'s budget was 'centralised' and the Political Committee and Executive Committee were involved in agreeing to every new staff member hired, Jacques was often able to obtain what he wanted. Nevertheless, sometimes it was politically expedient to hire a party member rather than another applicant to placate MT's opponents: e.g. the hiring of the new circulation manager in November 1982 in the aftermath of the Lane affair.[119] All staff in the CPGB[120] and at MT received the same pay, regardless of skills, experience, training or responsibilities. However, in December 1988, workers at Party Centre learned that MT's advertising staff received higher wages than other party workers and complained to Gordon McLennan.[121] Julian Turner, managing editor (1987–91), defended the move to pay advertising staff commissions on the money they brought in because of the difficulty of recruiting advertising staff on the low CPGB/MT wage rates, and to offer incentives for these staff to try and meet targets; he pointed out that commissions on income recruited was the standard way of paying advertising staff.[122] Nevertheless, with the massive debt in 1988 and under pressure from the PC to cut costs, MT made redundancies for the first time: the equivalent of six working days per week were cut. These were reduced even further during 1990: Jacques was reduced to three days per week; the deputy editor to four days per week; and a commissioning editor was appointed for one day per week.[123] Of all the forms of labour,

---

118   Jacques 1988c.
119   Jacques 1996d.
120   District party workers were expected to raise their own wages (Samuel 1986a).
121   Apter et al. 1988.
122   Turner 1988.
123   In 1988, Jacques began earning money from freelance writing, which helped with the cut to his salary.

professional or otherwise, there was an acceptance by the party hierarchy that design, illustration and advertising work had to be paid for.[124]

Until 1977, income was overwhelmingly generated from sales, and although it never dipped below 50 percent of the total income generated, there were variations within sales. For example, Central Books provided the largest single source of sales income until 1983, when it accounted for 41.6 percent of all sales (22.9 percent of total) income. However, as party membership declined and its networks and bookshops closed, the income generated via CB declined from 12 percent of total income in 1985 to a mere five percent in 1989.

The most politically important revenue was that generated via the newstrade because of its significance for MT's public image. Despite a brief experiment with some newsagents in London's Soho in 1979, which netted £30 for one issue,[125] it was not until the autumn of 1981 that national newstrade generated significant revenue (over £1,200.00 per issue), which had more than tripled by 1987 (£4,105.92 per issue), though these amounts represented increases that were more or less still incremental rather than immediate substantial increases in revenues (Table 3). Newstrade income peaked in 1987, with 23.4 percent of total revenues (£49,271.00) and declined to less than 20% in 1989 (under £47,000) even though distribution and promotion costs rose, indicating that despite efforts to promote sales and public interest, newstrade sales were not picking up.

There were continual battles to maintain newstrade sales and distribution, which meant spending on promotional campaigns and other forms of support to ensure newsagents would carry the magazine. By the late 1980s, while newstrade sales declined, subscriptions picked up, with income from the latter rising from £11,359.00 to £71,806.60 over six years, 1983–89, an increase of nearly five-and-a-half times: the subscriptions' percentage of the total income doubled from 14.6 to 29.8 percent. Subscriptions not only bring in a greater proportion of the cover price for the publisher, even though they usually have to offer an incentive (i.e. a discount on the cover price) to encourage potential subscribers to commit to one or two years in advance, but they also receive the revenue a year or more in advance which enables longer term planning and a financial base upon which one can build. This trend became more important to magazines in the 1990s with pressure on shelf-space.[126]

---

124   Townsend 1996.
125   Probably sold about 100–120 copies at just a few newsagents based on the new cover price of 50 pence with the launch issue of the second format, October 1979, and with at least 40–50% of cover price going to the retail agent.
126   See Logan 1996; Campaign for Press and Broadcasting Freedom 1996a, 1996b.

'Miscellaneous income' became an important element of MT's income by 1989 when it accounted for nine percent of the total. This income was from 'Friends of MT', merchandising, events and fees for article reprints, while 'miscellaneous expenditures' rose to consume nearly five percent of costs in 1987, including bank charges incurred by the deficit. MT moved into merchandising as one of its strategies for raising money and promotion. Its initial success in producing promotional material led to a merchandising off-shoot called 'Central Committee Outfitters', the brainchild of a couple of MT volunteers, which turned out a regular production of t-shirts, filofaxes, mugs, boxer shorts, etc., including a 'Bolshevik Chic' line of goods.[127] While this practice demonstrated that the left could also use other means for promotion and increase revenues, it also provoked accusations of 'selling [sic] out'.

The 1987 debts only minimally restricted MT's ability to operate independently because of continued support from key older members of the leadership, who were crucial in sustaining its autonomy, even as Jacques and MT were compelled to work more closely with the PC to get their finances in order. Though financial difficulties caused friction between McLennan and Jacques, the former continued to support the latter because McLennan says he was in agreement politically with MT's project.[128] Others assert some other *quid pro quo* between the two because Jacques had had ambitions to lead the party and they claim that McLennan had wanted to retire earlier than he did. These critics were reformists who had wanted MT to work more closely with the party, especially after the 1985 purge of many traditionalist opponents.

Further professionalisation occurred with the separation of editorial and business: Julian Turner took over the business side as 'managing editor', the equivalent of the magazine industry's 'publisher', in 1987, enabling Jacques to concentrate on editorial. Turner's task was to separate MT's finances from the party's so that it could operate independently. He also helped to establish a number of initiatives, such as 'Friends of *Marxism Today*', at the beginning of 1988 to help raise money to pay off debts and plan for future developments. Similar to 'launch subscribers' schemes, 'Friends' provided additional low-cost perks, such as invitations to openings and special newsletters, to those willing to pay extra money by standing order or direct debit. Within five months, when a meeting of 'Friends' was held at 'The '68 Show' in May 1988, the scheme

---

127 There was even an attempt at a cabaret (Taylor 1995). Mark Perryman, circulation manager and fundraiser, went on to co-found Philosophy Football, a t-shirt company, in the 1990s.
128 McLennan 1996.

was raising around £500 per month.[129] However, the legacy of bitter infighting meant that such initiatives as 'Friends' also generated complaints from some party members.[130]

Various fundraising ventures were undertaken, such as local MT events and standing order campaigns, to recoup the 1987 losses. In 1988–89, the promotions drive was linked to turning newstrade sales into subscriptions to maximise a stable income base.[131] Subscriptions increasingly became the single most important source of income during the last four years because they provided stable funding through the peaks and troughs of a magazine's annual cycle, even though it is more characteristic of journals than magazines. Thus, as MT developed it became again more dependent upon subscriptions, except this time it was to ensure a better financial return than newstrade sales could.

Jacques was fortunate that his editorship coincided with a 'remarkable turnaround in the fortunes of magazine publishing' during the 1980s, which was 'by all standards remarkable given the parlous state of print publishing in the late 1970s'.[132] Unfortunately, once MT's debts from 1987 were, at least, difficult to overcome, the 'collapse of advertising revenues' in 1991, sealed any possibility of MT preventing its own closure (and especially as the CPGB dissolved itself).[133] The recession's economic impact across the magazine industry helped to put paid to Jacques's ambitions for a new periodical, after MT's closure.[134]

4   Advertising

Advertising's role in driving consumption in the production-distribution-consumption cycle is also ideological, acting as capitalism's propaganda arm, which fuels the left's suspicions, including its role as a potential censor of, and influence on, editorial in periodicals that depend upon advertising for revenue. This influence also affects magazines' visual presentation. Thus, radical publications tend to neglect advertising as a significant source of revenue and rely upon sales or subsidies as their principal means of income.[135]

---

129   Jacques 1988b, p. 2.
130   EC 1988c.
131   MTEB 1988b.
132   Driver and Gillespie 1993, p. 183.
133   Ibid.
134   MT 1991. *Agenda* was the working title for one periodical proposal.
135   Curran 1977; Richards 1997; Williams 1980, pp. 170–95. For a history of the establishment and running of a non-advertising-supported (and mainstream!) newspaper, see Stoltzfus 2007.

Alternative publications in the 1970s and 1980s tended not to seek out advertising beyond that which was in line with their general political outlook or aims, nor to accept advertisements from any organisation considered to be 'politically incorrect' (e.g. companies investing in apartheid South Africa). Until the 1980s, advertisers had little interest in reaching left-wing readerships and were put off by the low circulation and anti-capitalist politics of the radical press.[136] However, things began to change in the early 1980s when some periodicals, such as *New Internationalist* and *New Socialist*, began to attract advertising beyond radical bookshops and political groups.[137] By the mid-1980s, *Marxism Today* was recruiting more mainstream advertising, although the first non-political ad had been published as early as the October 1982 issue, where its back cover sported a full-page ad for futons, which became a defining consumer item for the metropolitan 'trendy lefty' reader, a potentially desirable, urban consumer with disposable income (and recognisable as a member of the 'professional-managerial class').

During its first 22 years, all the advertising in MT was from either a CPGB agency or an entity which was sympathetic to the party: the party's publishing company, Lawrence and Wishart, and Central Books, or Collet's, an independent left bookshop.[138] Advertising was mostly text-only display ads of English-language publications by and about the USSR, the CPSU and Communist bloc. As sales of the July issue rose during the Communist University of London events during the mid-1970s, MT was able to recruit major academic publishers wanting to advertise books with Marxist or radical themes. After 1979, advertising became an increasingly important source of revenue, accounting for between one-third and two-fifths of all revenues until MT closed in 1991, but reaching its maximum percentage at just over 40 percent of revenues in 1983. However, regardless of the percentage of total income, advertising revenues continually increased in absolute terms (Tables 2, 3). There was at least a four-fold increase in advertising income over 1977 (Table 3) and it indicates how substantially important advertising revenues had become to the magazine, albeit not just in terms of money, but also in terms of its look (Chapter 4).

---

136 Atton 1999; Khiabany 1997.
137 Comedia 1984.
138 Collet's had originally been Hendersons' 'Bomb Shop' in Charing Cross Road, and run by two old-timers from the Independent Labour Party, who sold it to the CPGB, with the wealthy Communist, Eva Collet Reckitt, putting up the money. Although officially not a party bookshop, all the managers were party members and 'so were many of the staff' (Cope 1999, p. 11).

It was only after Jacques was able to recruit more staff that he was able to consider a wider range of advertisers. The part-time editorial assistant had to recruit advertising as well as carry out office and production work: few volunteers were interested in soliciting advertising.[139] This reluctance is not uncommon among radical periodicals, since their views are usually very critical of advertising (note the telling phrase, 'selling out', used as a criticism when alternative papers are successful). Between December 1981 and January 1986, no less than eight people held the post of advertising manager (all of whom had been left-wing, male graduates).[140] In March 1985, an additional part-time worker was hired which increased substantially the amount of advertising sold in the subsequent nine months of 1985 compared to the same period in 1984: an increase in revenue of 48 percent (April–June), 73 percent (July–September) and 41 percent (October–December).[141] The first quarter of 1985 had dropped in advertising revenue from the last quarter of 1984 by nearly 20 percent, which hastened the need to recruit extra advertising staff, though the first quarter of every year was usually the least profitable.[142]

Marxism Today's name also made it difficult in securing advertising even from other left-wing groups, since many would not advertise in rival journals.[143] However, this changed as MT's public profile rose through newsagent distribution and media coverage: some groups, such as the Socialist Workers' Party and the Revolutionary Communist Party, sought to tap into an audience that they otherwise might not have been able to reach. Although trade union advertising was a new area opened up by MT from March 1986 onwards, there was a lot of political resistance to it from the unions.[144] This is not surprising because of the connections between the 'militant labourist' tendency and traditionalists, many of whom were closely affiliated with the Industrial Department and involved in unions, who saw MT as 'anti-union'.

Besides advertisers' political orientations, there is a more prosaic concern for some advertisers: whether a publication covers interests relevant to an advertiser's business. For example, although MT had succeeded in attracting some mainstream film and theatre advertising as early as 1982, problems arose in attracting other arts advertising because many were not convinced that MT

---

139   Townsend 1996.
140   MTEC 1986b, p. 1.
141   Ibid.
142   MTEC 1986a; EC 1986a.
143   Townsend 1996.
144   MTEC 1986b, p. 4.

had a 'significant arts input'.¹⁴⁵ However, MT was able to expand its advertising revenues from local authorities, and especially the Greater London Council: during 1985, it rose substantially from £250 for the first quarter, to £2,258 for the second and £1,900 for the third. The GLC knew its time was limited as it was facing abolition the following year, and MT had also promoted the GLC as one of the 'major fronts' operating against Thatcherism.¹⁴⁶

Increased advertising meant either losing editorial space or increasing pagination, although one-off supplements absorbed some of the increased demand for advertising space. MT did increase its pagination over time, with the most important months (in order of importance: October, September, March) being accorded the most pages. The rapid increase in MT's advertising space in the first half of the 1980s was not unwelcome even by the party because there had always been calls at EC meetings, for example, for increasing ad revenue in other party publications to help pay for their production and distribution costs (e.g. *Comment, Morning Star*).¹⁴⁷ However, by the mid-1980s, MT had to devote 50 percent of additional pagination for advertising to pay for its ongoing transformation. Advertising had become an integral part of MT's identity, especially as it reached beyond the usual entities to commercial and non-political outlets, which also acted as a 'lightning rod' for critics.

5 'Private Enterprise or Political Commitment?' Printing and Subscriptions

For most magazines, typesetting and printing decisions are simply financial decisions about selecting the best or cheapest companies based upon the quality, services, costs etc. These types of decisions became the sites of important battles, however, in establishing *Marxism Today* on a more commercially viable and 'production-sensitive' footing (overcoming the limitations of older technologies and bringing in newer ones), and in establishing its political-editorial independence from the Communist Party, as it was transformed from a 'journal' into a 'magazine'. Printing MT, therefore, became as much about the editor's struggle for autonomy as it was about the production process.

---

145   MTEC 1986b, p. 3; Townsend 1984. Its frequency was not ideal for advertising many forms of entertainment.
146   E.g. Campbell and Jacques 1986; Griffith 1982; Hall 1984b; Hipkin 1984; Livingstone 1984, 1985.
147   E.g. EC 1977, 1979d, 1981b.

Farleigh Press, a CPGB enterprise, printed MT for its first 29 years, from the October 1957 to September 1986 issues. MT was always published around ten days before the beginning of the cover date: e.g. the October issue was published in late September. The production routine allowed for a long lead-time for articles (of months!) which enabled James Klugmann to consult with leading party officers and committees over 'controversial' contributions and FP to typeset articles well in advance. Like older printing houses, FP had provided its own proofreaders, saving MT time and money. Despite the quality of proofreading and printing, Martin Jacques and MTEC staff claimed that it was neither the most efficient means nor sufficiently flexible for producing an increasingly topical, monthly periodical. Despite the changes in printing techniques and technology between the mid-1960s and the mid-1970s, the 'Offset Litho Revolution',[148] which was an important contributory factor in the rise of the alternative press during this period, FP continued to typeset and print MT with hot-metal printing technology.

When Jacques took over as editor in September 1977, he claims that he inherited nearly four issues worth of articles already set in hot-metal type, but he continued to rely on the older, hot-metal printing until he had MT redesigned for its second format relaunch with the October 1979 issue.[149] Hot-metal type was more expensive: articles set in hot-metal type had to be broken up after they had been set whether they were used or not. For example, MT had to pay FP to break up those four months' worth of articles that had been typeset, since Jacques was not interested in publishing the articles received or commissioned by Klugmann. The newer photolithography process was better for preparing layout and more manageable than hot-metal technology, where each individual letter had to be stamped out, and set in rows and clamped together. Photolithography meant that copy was typed out and cut into strips and set out on sheets as 'camera-ready copy' before being photographed and then printed. It was easier to layout artwork and photographs around the text (or vice versa) and implement other changes and, thus, images, and graphic and design innovations became an integral part in attempting to reach new readers via newsagents. The phototypesetting image did not produce as clear and distinct reproduction of type as the hot-metal process; however, it provided the requisite, rapid reproduction of words without 'setting them in stone' (or lead).

Offset photolithography contributed to MT's transformation by enabling 'maximum flexibility in production' because: it gave editorial control over the

---

148   Marshall 1983.
149   Hammarling 1996; Jacques 1996d.

layout 'right up to the last minute'; the technique was easy to learn; and it was 'ideally suited economically to small radical papers', printing 1,000–10,000 copies, whereas 'hot-metal typesetting and the rotary letterpress, only becomes economically worthwhile on longer print runs'.[150] The editor's greater control over content and last-minute changes was especially important for the 'Focus' section, which tried to always publish topical material, which was a difficult task for a monthly with 7–10 days lead time before arriving on newsstands or in people's homes.[151]

The new editor's first step was to use the new typesetting technology. For the 1979 relaunch, MT went to an outfit called Dessett Graphics Limited. It had not been hard for Jacques to convince the leadership to allow MT to transfer its typesetting to Dessett because it was half-owned by Farleigh Press. However, FP decided to pull out of Dessett in the autumn of 1981, and Jacques was told then that he would have to move back to FP since it was installing new typesetting equipment. However, Jacques said that he did not want a repeat of the hassles and problems which he had already gone through during his first two years as editor.[152] He indicated that he had worked hard to get MT to the position it had achieved by October 1981: new format and design, more sections, visuals, wider distribution and increased circulation. More importantly, MT had just been launched into newsagents nationwide via W.H. Smith's: the pressure to meet the deadlines of national commercial distribution was far greater than for the CPGB's distribution arm, Central Books. So great were the difficulties that Jacques claimed he expected to re-encounter if he was forced to have MT typeset again by FP, that he threatened to resign. By this time, Jacques had invested so much of himself, intellectually, politically and socially, into MT that he felt that, since the magazine was positioning itself to really take-off with national newsagent distribution, he could make that threat since he was so closely associated with its success. Jacques only made the threat known to the General Secretary, Gordon McLennan. It was the first of two occasions he says when he threatened to resign during his fourteen years as editor.[153] The matter was resolved in Jacques's favour and MT moved its typesetting to a non-party firm,

---

150   Aubrey et al. 1980, p. 6.
151   In the twenty-first century of 24/7 livestream coverage, such a lead-in time seems almost 'prehistoric'.
152   For example, one major difficulty was trying to rearrange changes in copy between MT, based at Party Centre in London, and FP in Watford, north of London, as there was only one delivery to, and one drop off from, FP per day (Jacques 1996c).
153   Jacques 1996c. However, there appears to be some sense that Jacques might have made the threat more than twice and that he did so in front of others (e.g. Priscott 1985b, 1986; McLennan 1996).

Advantage Filmsetting Limited, demonstrating that McLennan's relationship with Jacques was key to the editor retaining control of MT.

Behind *Marxism Today*'s typesetting, which was done out of house between 1979 and 1989, was a thorough proofreading of all copy, two to four times for each issue. At first Jacques used editorial board members as proofreaders until his editorial working group or 'editorial collective' (MTEC) acquired sufficient volunteers. By 1980 there were usually three to four volunteers, party members, who were professionals, who proofread everything for MT, as part of their connection to the party.[154] MT's proofreading process was considerably more rigorous than most alternative and, indeed, mainstream commercial publications, including the national press.[155] Jacques's drive for producing the best possible results with limited resources played an important role in MT's 'professional look' and establishing its credibility as a source of left news and views.[156]

As part of Julian Turner's initiatives to make MT's third format more cost-efficient, typesetting was moved in-house during 1989 because of the developments in desk-top publishing, which were revolutionising the production of small periodicals.[157] While the move to DTP enabled MT to cut typesetting costs, the staff never got to the point of being able to do layout on the computer, so that the actual production of the proofs still had to be done by outside typesetters. Initial savings in 1989, nonetheless, did help, although they were only about 15 percent of total monthly typesetting costs for 1987 (approximately £330) (Table 3).[158] While in-house typesetting sped up the production process and ensured that staff were not having to work all hours[159] to get MT ready for the printers by the last possible moment, all the artwork and photographs were still pasted in by hand until the last issue.[160]

Printing was another area where Jacques also fought an intermittent five-year battle to have *Marxism Today* printed outside the Communist Party: from December 1981 until September 1986. The costs that Farleigh Press charged MT were 'paper' charges insofar as they were costs which were incurred within the party. The leadership tended not to be concerned with what Jacques did as long as any proposed changes would not incur costs greater than the year before. Jacques sought quotes from other printers, notably Development Workshop,

---

154   Townsend 1996.
155   Ibid.; Taylor 1995; Morrish 1996, pp. 101, 106.
156   Taylor 1995; Townsend 1996.
157   Taylor 1995.
158   MTEB 1988b.
159   Although they still worked very long hours (Brown 1996; Taylor 1995).
160   Brown 1996.

and used them as evidence to demonstrate that cheaper printing was available elsewhere. Reuben Falber, Assistant General Secretary, with overall responsibility for all party enterprises, reiterated certain points which explained FP's difficulties and advantages:[161] its labour costs were constant whereas DW's would increase after April 1982; it provided longer term credit, worth 'more than £1,000 p.a. in borrowing costs'; and it provided greater flexibility because it could expand MT's pagination in increments of just four pages to DW's eight pages.[162]

At the MTEB meeting in February 1982, the board agreed that MT should switch to web offset printing 'as soon as possible in order to maintain the development that has taken place (and its viability)', which Jacques communicated to McLennan.[163] Gerry Cohen, Secretary of the London District CP, wrote to McLennan detailing their vote of 16 to 12 (and 4 abstentions) opposing any attempt by the Executive Committee to withdraw the printing of MT from FP and arguing that it was vital to maintain 'Party-owned printing facilities' and FP's viability.[164] The involvement of other groups in what would normally be a 'business' matter indicates the possible actions which Jacques's opponents would undertake to try and exert control over MT's political trajectory via business decisions; however, the nearly fifty-fifty split in the LDCP leadership vote reflected the wider internal party divisions. The Political Committee decided to maintain the printing and other arrangements as they stood until September 1982, at which point they would review them again. The PC also decided to postpone employing a full-time circulation manager until the September review, 'subject to being possible to continue with its present arrangement'.[165]

Successful enterprises were expected to pay a rebate to the party and, though Farleigh Press had not made any profit in the previous two years, it had consistently paid rebates for 16 out of the previous 20 years (1964–84) 'totalling over £100,000'.[166] FP argued that the loss of an important customer, such as MT, would affect the services it provided for the CPGB. This would have com-

---

161 Falber was one of the four key men who knew about 'Moscow gold', Soviet subsidies paid to the CPGB: the other three were John Gollan, David Ainley, chief executive of *The Morning Star*, and George Matthews, one of its former editors. During the 1960s the subsidy amounted to around £100,000 per annum but it was reduced to £14–15,000 after 1970 and ended in 1979 (Anderson and Davey 1995, p. 33; Andrews 1995a, p. 245; Beckett 1995, pp. 216–21).
162 Falber 1982.
163 Jacques 1982b.
164 Cohen 1982.
165 Woddis 1982.
166 Blatt 1984.

pounded FP's problems that were a result of a failure to invest in technology, which in turn had affected its ability to provide competitive prices and extra features. The CPGB's principle of having its own printing press had become secondary and FP had 'been vilified because it is unable to compete with some of the cheapest printers in the trade'.[167] FP's prices were subjected to trying to meet the quotes provided by the competition. Jacques kept up the pressure on FP while highlighting MT's annual losses (and hence the size of party subsidies) when submitting accounts by presenting the difference between what FP charged and what DW or Chesham Press would have charged had they done the work: FP's actual charges were always higher than the quotes cited by MT. In the build up for the third-format launch issue, Jacques and Paddy Farrington, circulation manager, lobbied for changing the printers through June and July of 1986. The disputes were over paper quality and the quotes used to negotiate against FP's charges. But the crux of the matter for Jacques was not just financial nor even a question of editorial autonomy: it was the changing nature of MT's printing needs. It was argued that FP was overstretched and could no longer meet MT's needs in pagination, supplements, print run and timing, which would adversely affect its ability to meet growing demand.[168]

Farleigh Press's response to *Marxism Today*'s criticisms was to claim that the alternative printers cited by Jacques were unreliable, even if they provided the cheapest prices, and that MT might be forced to go elsewhere and pay considerably higher costs for its printing. For example, FP cited problems with the 'Women Alive' programme, which it had to sort out, but which MT's non-party printers should have done. FP argued that its production process, using sheet-fed machines, took no longer than the web offset printer's machine because FP printed the periodical section by section as they received the copy, usually over seven to ten days. Thus, there was little time difference between when FP received the final copy from MT to when it was ready, and the three days the web-offset printer needed, because not only would MT have had to submit all their copy at once, but they would have had to still allow time for pre-press operations, like typesetting, which would have taken up the same amount of time.[169] MT's production process meant it worked with an older printer because much of its copy was ready in advance of production dates, with other sections being printed at later dates, thereby negating an advantage of the web-offset printing process.

---

167 Ibid.
168 Jacques and Farrington 1986.
169 Shackleton 1986.

Jacques also submitted an outline of the issues and problems the periodical faced and why it needed to move to a web offset printer.[170] MT was also looking to expand its print run to 28,000 for the October 1986 relaunch, up from the October 1985 print run of 21,100. Whereas a magazine needs thousands of extra copies to ensure an adequate supply for the newstrade for possible sales at newsagents across the country, the October print run was the most numerous as it was considered the most important for reaching and retaining new readers in the annual periodical publishing cycle. MT had used Chesham Press for printing their supplements, such as the 'Left Alive' programme, and Jacques suggested that they could not keep on going back to Chesham Press for quotes against which FP would have to pitch its prices. FP had even agreed two years previously, in 1984, that MT was 'cheaper to print web than sheet-fed'.[171] While Jacques claimed that, contrary to FP's claims, MT had been paying its bills regularly, albeit four months behind; FP's Liz Shackleton pointed out that few, if any, commercial printers would allow such a situation.[172] The party leadership agreed in the end to MT's move: the third-format launch issue of October 1986 became the first printed by a non-party press, Birmingham Printers, although MT had to switch printers yet again when it moved from sheet-fed to web-offset printing.

Yet, the dispute did not end there. Less than two years later, another dispute about printing costs for MT event programmes resurfaced. FP raised the issue with the EC that a company, Shadowdean, had received this work over FP even though the other company's quote had been higher than FP's, a point which appeared to undermine Jacques's claims about FP. The matter was taken up by the EC and MT replied to FP's accusations but the matter remained unresolved.[173] The issue was obviously a matter of some concern for FP, when MT provided a substantial portion of its work, particularly as other party work dried up, which undermined its ability to invest in new technologies and remain competitive. Thus, we can see how the party as publisher is directly affected by changes in membership, where its decline affected the capacity of its agencies and departments to operate. FP and its precursors were an integral part of the CPGB's political viability, since its founding in 1920, when non-party printers refused their business for reasons of either state intimidation or politics, and CPGB enterprises, such as FP, became integral to providing the very infrastructure that enabled the party to reach out beyond itself. MT was the one 'bright

---

170   Jacques 1986b.
171   Ibid.
172   Shackleton 1986.
173   EC 1988a.

spot' on the CPGB's roster of publications in the 1980s because its needs for printing increased, in terms of both pages per issue and print runs to support national newsagent distribution.

The struggle over typesetting and printing, however, was not the only ongoing battle over *Marxism Today*'s autonomy in commercial decisions over production and distribution costs. Since Central Books was a party agency responsible for all elements of distribution (outside of the newstrade), from supplying party branches, and party and independent bookshops, to handling domestic and international subscriptions, any changes had to have the agreement of the PC and the EC. CB used a newly installed computer in 1982 to try and monitor MT's subscriptions more effectively. Part of the key to a successful subscription service is to ensure that subscribers receive renewal reminders prior to their subscription lapsing and that they are cut off when their subscriptions lapse or are terminated. However, MT found itself dealing with a series of problems between 1982 and 1984:[174] subscribers being 'suspended' even though they had paid; other subscribers continuing to receive copies well after their subscriptions had lapsed; MT did not receive an adequate, ongoing and up-to-date flow of information; problems in maintaining a properly organised system for tracking and following subscriptions (which appeared to stem from the computer); no break-down of information to better target subscribers; and the need for better liaison and accounting.[175] MT complained to the EC that these problems were exacerbated by CB's failure to respond to an earlier request for a meeting to solve them.

Each and every change in typesetting, printing and subscriptions required the extensive collection of information and data, backed by lobbying and politicking, to make a persuasive argument for changes. Thus, the MTEC was forced to spend considerable resources and time on researching subscription services and garnering the necessary information to present to the PC and EC about the need for a better service.[176] MT staff argued that they did not feel that CB's responses (or lack thereof) to their ongoing queries and criticisms reflected a very efficient operation nor did they feel that CB was taking their concerns seriously.

As the negotiations in May 1984 represented a culmination of two years of disputes over subscriptions (as well as printing and finances), Jacques threat-

---

174 MTEC 1984a. A compilation of the documents on finances, subscriptions and printing presented to the PC during this period are contained in PCSub 1984a.
175 MTEC 1983a, pp. 1–4. MT checked out the list of lapsed and suspended subscribers sent by CB (MTEC 1984b; PCSub 1984a).
176 MTEC 1983a, pp. 1–4; MTEC 1984b; PCSub 1984a.

ened to resign (again) if these changes were not enacted, as did his opposite number at Central Books, Reuben Falber, a very important member within the party hierarchy, in a counter-threat.[177] In the end, Jacques won a partial victory: in July 1984, the EC granted MT permission to move its subscriptions to an outside agency.[178] MT began using Punch as its subscriptions agency from October 1984, which had already taken over MT's newstrade distribution from Moore-Harness the year before, because it was felt that the latter was 'not doing a satisfactory job'.[179] Decisions over commercial enterprises could be taken much more readily than they could with CPGB enterprises, especially once MT had control over its own budget, which the move to a bank 'sub-account' of the party in September 1984 enabled. When MT was dissatisfied with the service, price or income, it switched agencies without having to make extensive notes and collate data, and engage in negotiations with members of the EC or PC, nor with members of the party agency involved: the decision could be made and acted on quickly, if, as and when MT saw fit.

6 'A Little Help From My Friends': The Process of Magazine Production

A key part of the production process is the availability of staff and volunteers, which may depend upon some (self) financing or enthusiasm, in terms of the motivation of volunteers. Historically, radical and alternative media had access to a greater preponderance of free labour than corporate and state media outlets at least during the 1970s and 1980s, although this is a resource increasingly being exploited by mainstream media outlets, which use unpaid interns and graduates seeking experience to obtain paid employment eventually in the media industry.[180] Volunteer labour was one of the most important advantages of radical media over corporate and state media.

As with the production of academic journals, *Marxism Today* required a long lead-time because of limited resources, human and financial, and the necessity

---

177   PC 1984; PCSub 1984b.
178   EC 1984b. Counter motions to shift this back for yet more discussion were defeated. These kinds of counter motions were usually lost by the same tally of votes by which the first vote had been won.
179   MTEC 1984d, p. 2.
180   During a stint as an assistant manager in the early 1990s, I observed a daily average of four to 12 letters asking for an opportunity to shadow professionals working in television post-production.

of circulating unsolicited articles, thought to be controversial or in contravention of the party line, to party officials for approval. James Klugmann often appealed for contributions from MT Editorial Board members, the Executive Committee and other leading bodies, whose articles would have promoted the party line and demonstrated intellectual leadership.[181] Klugmann tried to use the MTEB as part of the production process: involving some board members on an informal basis for proofreading articles and providing advice on unsolicited manuscripts. During the 1960s and 1970s, while some board members helped out occasionally, Jack Cohen, head of the Education Department, MTEB member, and Klugmann's friend, provided regular help by acting as an assistant editor.[182] By the early 1970s, Klugmann was requesting further help with production to free up time for theoretical work and writing the party's history.[183]

Martin Jacques relied upon the support of an editorial collective, which was known initially as the 'editorial working group', and often accepted their advice. There was never any question of Jacques's ultimate control over any and all decisions affecting MT, however, even though he did encourage those staff and volunteers with the skills, aptitude or ability to take on different responsibilities for its production and distribution. The existence of MTEC was acknowledged, though never formally constituted; however, at his suggestion MTEC members were allowed to attend board meetings in an advisory capacity.[184] Though Jacques would use suggestions for contributors from both the MTEB and MTEC, he maintained total control over who wrote for and what went into the features section until 1987.[185]

Though there was no question that Jacques ran MT as he saw fit, he had to rely more on his closest advisors to maintain editorial control as the number of helpers increased during the 1980s and especially during two periods of ill-health in 1983 and 1987; after the second bout of M.E. (nicknamed 'yuppie flu'),[186] he had to slow down his pace and he shared some of his duties with senior staff: deputy editor, Jane Taylor, was given responsibility for editing one

---

181   Klugmann 1960.
182   Johnstone 1995. Cohen's help was mentioned in EC reports.
183   MTEB 1973a; ECSub 1976.
184   MTEB 1979a, p. 1.
185   Taylor 1995.
186   M.E. stands for 'Myalgic Encephalomyelitis', which is an illness that was known for at least a century before its media profile in the 1980s, when it acquired the pejorative label of 'yuppie flu'. Information from the National M.E. Centre and Centre for Fatigue Syndromes, 'Non-Sufferer Guide', available at: http://www.nmec.org.uk/menonsuffererguide.html (accessed 19 August 2013).

feature per issue, which had previously been Jacques's exclusive preserve, and managing editor, Julian Turner, took over the financial side.[187]

Marxism Today's transformation was produced with volunteers, and unpaid and paid staff. The notion of 'unpaid staff' recognises differences between volunteers who 'lend a hand' and those who play important roles in MT's production and distribution.[188] Despite frequent changes in job titles in the 1980s, there were three basic staffing areas: editorial (including office and production); advertising; and design. For the first twenty years, all three areas had been the responsibility of the editor and his part-time secretaries: one full-time editor, as the position of assistant editor was dropped after James Klugmann took over as editor in December 1962, and one part-time secretary working three days a week (1.6 FTE paid staff).[189]

There were few paid production staff: Jacques occupied the only full-time editorial post for the first five years. The only other paid position at first was the three-days-a-week editorial assistant, who replaced the part-time secretaries. Besides some production and advertising work, this position involved basic administrative and secretarial tasks. Illustrators and artists, like designers, however, were usually paid for their work, even if it was below regular or market rates. For example, the cost to reuse an illustration that has already been commissioned by another publication is considerably less. Early in the second format, Peter Hammarling enlisted John Minnion, who had been working for *New Statesman*, as an illustrator to do work for the periodical that began with his third piece for *New Statesman* being reused in MT's February 1980 issue.

Since MT's budget was limited and all additional expenditures had to be negotiated with the EC, Jacques set about bringing in people who were knowledgeable about magazine production or design, but they also had to be willing to help out with basic tasks, such as selling advertising and proof-reading. During the early years of Jacques's editorship, he drew upon the help of people he knew, such as Sally Beardsley, a professional designer, and David Triesman, a sociology lecturer who had worked on the short-lived, lively and accessible, radical weekly, *7 Days*.[190]

---

187   Jacques 1996d; Taylor 1995.
188   Townsend 1996; Taylor 1995.
189   When Jacques first took over the editorship in 1977, there were three different part-time secretaries: one worked two days, another one day and a third a few hours per week (Jacques 1996a).
190   Not to be confused with the party review of the same name launched in 1985. Triesman prepared a document that identified potential changes for MT's second format (e.g. MTEB 1978a, 1978b).

When Jacques established the MT editorial collective, it initially consisted of four 'unpaid staff' overseeing key areas: David Triesman (Design/Books), Paul Marginson (Circulation/Promotion), Jon Chadwick (Advertising) and Colin Roberts (Production).[191] MTEC was invaluable: it consisted of people who helped with the day-to-day tasks and who Jacques knew and trusted, including, among others, contributors, who were or became prominent contributors on the left: Sarah Benton, editor of *Comment*, 1978–80, and later a *New Statesman* journalist; Beatrix Campbell, a socialist-feminist and party journalist, who went on to work for *City Limits*, a radical listings weekly in London, and a freelance writing career; Dave Cook, a leading Eurocommunist and party officer, and close friend of Jacques. MTEC members would suggest contributors for both features and short pieces.

As the culture section editor, Sally Townsend had her own mini-collective to help with production, contributors and generating ideas for 'Channel Five',[192] which included Chadwick (CPGB), a theatre literary manager, and Richard Dyer (non-CPGB), a film studies lecturer and one of the three contributors to *Comment*'s TV column. All volunteers were trained to proofread and follow-up on press releases; however, they were not kept on if they did not perform well.[193]

> Volunteers had to just pitch in, and whoever had enough 'nouse' to be trusted to do something did it, and whoever didn't was given envelope-licking to do … the sorts of things that the volunteers did were not very high-powered, but were absolutely essential to the production process in particular, which was a monthly nightmare every single month.[194]

The recruitment of volunteers from basic tasks into a higher level of responsibility or even into the inner core was a process by which your worth was identified and judged. For example, Alan Lawrie was:

> involved in organising a couple of 'Moving Left' shows and afterwards I was told I could come to the 'collective'. You always felt you were being moved onto another platform. There was always a process of talent spotting or a league table. There was a collective of people who organised it, but it had no correlation at all to party organisation.[195]

---

191 MTEB 1978c.
192 Townsend 1996. See Chapter 4.
193 Jacques 1996b; Townsend 1996.
194 Taylor 1995.
195 Pearmain 2011, pp. 132–3.

As much as MTEC had a constant need for volunteers, because it used them up at 'an alarming rate' in production and promotion, recruitment became easier as its reputation and public profile grew as well as its extensive list of contacts.[196]

Often volunteers were not as useful in expanding MT's networks beyond recruiting more volunteers because they tended to be young, inexperienced graduates. However, some volunteers and staff continued to offer help and advice after they left. For example, Paul Webster worked on MT in 1979–80, but continued to help over the next decade while working for *The Morning Star*, *Sunday Times* and *The Guardian*; he was a valuable source of contacts, contributors and interviewees.[197] This was actually not dissimilar to the production of *The Daily Worker* during the 1930s and 1940s when Communist journalists and printers, working on other commercial or labour movement publications, would commit to helping out *pro bono* by providing invaluable professional advice and help (even if it was not always appreciated).[198]

During the initial period of MT's transformation, most of the production process was handled by MTEC, which sits 'below' the MTEB in its organisational diagram.[199] By 1983 the MTEC was becoming too big to operate as a single entity. As the number of regular helpers grew to thirty by 1984, they were organised into 'mini-collectives' responsible for different areas of work, which included the four paid staff, 'unpaid staff', section editors, some MTEB members and designers; all staff and section editors were usually members of more than one group. The MTEC had ten separate sub-groups by 1985: 'section editors'; 'C5 collective'; 'Press Group'; 'Colour Supplement Group';[200] 'cover group'; 'promotion collective'; 'circulation collective'; 'designers'; 'trade union group'; and 'business group'. Although 'unpaid' or paid staff led every MTEC group, either the editor or deputy editor still exercised oversight and control by attending all meetings of every section. The breakdown of the production, distribution and promotion processes run by these different groups contributed to what was referred to as MT's 'meetings culture'.[201]

---

196 Turner 1994.
197 Townsend 1996. *The Guardian*'s relationship with MT is discussed in Chapter 5.
198 Pimlott 2006b, 2013. There was quite a debate at times over the direction of the *Daily Worker* (Morgan 1995; Pimlott 2013).
199 MTEC 1984c.
200 This was a one-off group formed specifically to produce a response to earlier congress resolutions (and internal critics), the *Marxism Today Colour Supplement, Congress Special* (MT's eight-page report for the 1985 Special Party Congress). Its title is an indication of its irreverence (MTEC 1985, pp. 1–2).
201 Brown 1996.

With growing revenues, MT was able to increase to four full-time staff by 1984: editor; deputy editor; advertising manager; and circulation manager. There were also two additional part-time staff who made up one full-time equivalent staff: an office/business manager employed three days per week; and an advertising executive hired for two days per week. In addition, a freelance graphic designer was contracted for ten days per month to oversee production and layout, commission artwork and photographs, and do picture research.[202] By 1985, MT's success, which at least in terms of satisfying the party leadership and its own supporters, had meant that the magazine had raised its national public profile, that it had been able to expand its paid staff to five FTE, since MT was permitted to reinvest all of its income back into itself. Thus, MT had nearly doubled its paid staff to nine FTEs by 1987 as it put the money from the growth in sales and advertising into hiring staff, even as the use of volunteers saved money.[203]

Part of the ability of MT to retain such key staff was due to the editor's personal qualities. There was something of the 'Leninist' about Jacques and his leadership qualities in the ways he could obtain such deep commitment from staff and volunteers, as those interviewed expressed similar ideas about his persuasiveness with themselves and others. Although Jacques was very demanding to work for, one interviewee said it was nonetheless rewarding because you learned to push yourself and see what you could accomplish, despite limited resources and time.[204] By the mid-1980s this was beginning to develop into an inner core that Jacques could reach out to, who were referred to as 'Martin's boys' by Geoff Andrews.[205] These were young men who were:

> all variously competent and intelligent, ambitious and irreverent, heavily committed and enthusiastic. They were also available and reliable, not to say compliant and biddable.[206]

Some staff members who started out as volunteer section editors and were promoted to paid positions (which only happened if it was felt that they could do the job), would still have responsibility for overseeing their section in addition to their paid staff responsibilities. For example, Jane Taylor continued to edit

---

202   MTEC 1985.
203   Jacques 1991.
204   Brown 1996.
205   Pearmain 2011, p. 156.
206   Ibid. Pearmain continues: 'Again the parallels with New Labour are startling, especially in its latter-day Brownite manifestation' (Ibid.).

the 'Focus' section as an 'unpaid staff' responsibility, even after she was promoted into a paid staff position.[207] Others started out as staff and ended up with voluntary duties: Sally Townsend was an editorial assistant before setting up and editing 'Channel Five'.[208]

During the first half of Jacques's editorship, volunteers were attracted by MT's ideas and they often shared a commitment to its politics, even joining the CPGB if they were not already members. However, as MT's public profile and reputation rose and it acquired more *cachet*, the motivation of volunteers shifted as they increasingly came more out of an interest in acquiring media experience than out of any commitment to MT's ideas or politics. It might be identified for its early exploitation of 'interns'.[209] For example, Julian Turner, who became MT's first managing editor in 1987, was a doctoral student in medaeval history; he volunteered at MT because he wanted to see if he would like a career in journalism, instead of academe: after leaving MT, he went on to work on the business side of *The Guardian* and *The Observer*.[210]

There is a drawback to volunteer labour. As long as the volunteers can be self-sufficient, supported by others or survive on welfare payments or part-time work, then the skills and expertise they acquire can be retained for the periodical they work for, though such expertise also increases the likelihood of their finding paid or better employment elsewhere.[211] Jacques, though, was persuasive enough to convince key people to stay on or even to return, an invaluable contribution for maintaining MT's high production values. Art editor, Jan Brown, for example, was persuaded to stay on after returning to MT for only one issue, while deputy editor, Jane Taylor, wanted to leave some six months before she finally did leave.[212] Even among paid staff, commitment beyond thirty years of age was difficult to sustain because, with the pay rates well below equivalent jobs elsewhere, it was difficult for staff to meet their personal and career needs, especially beyond people's late twenties (the age when most students are studying for their graduate degrees).[213]

---

207   Taylor 1995.
208   Townsend 1996.
209   For the US context, see Perlin 2011.
210   Turner 1994.
211   Ibid.
212   E.g. Townsend 1996; Brown 1996; Taylor 1995.
213   Jacques 1996c.

7 The Production Process

The production process quickened as *Marxism Today* was transformed, step by step, from a journal into magazine: finding experts; commissioning articles and artwork; researching pictures; designing covers; proofreading; and editing. One continual difficulty was getting contributors to work to deadlines, particularly as they were not being paid. Under James Klugmann, contributors had been party members with only occasional contributions from non-members and non-party Marxists.[214] During Martin Jacques's editorship, the number of non-party contributors increased, shifting gradually from the CPGB and labour movement to the broader left and new social movements to established centre-left journalists and scholars, as well as public political figures (Chapter 5). This shift in contributors played an important role in the transformation of MT's production process, which began each month with a meeting.

Under Jacques, each issue's production cycle began at the MT editorial collective's monthly meeting, where each staff member took a turn to lead the review of the latest issue, 'hot off the press', but only with 'a weekend to look at it'.[215] Similar to the MT Editorial Board's quarterly meetings, except with less time devoted to reflection, MTEC meetings involved discussion of the issue's strengths and weaknesses, and suggestions for improvements. The second half of these monthly meetings involved brainstorming ideas for the next issue. In addition, staff, MT discussion groups and the MTEB were all seen as key audiences providing feedback for making changes and improvements, although these varied in terms of the nature and depth of the reflections and critiques.

Section editors often discussed ideas with Jacques before co-ordinating their own groups' work: e.g. discussing possible topics, suggesting contributors.[216] This was especially critical for 'Focus', the news section, because of a possible overlap of its stories with features. Each section editor would explain MT's requirements and send copies to potential contributors if they were unfamiliar with it; there was clearly a difference before and after MT obtained sufficient national public recognition, as the first word of the title did have the potential of putting off prospective contributors who were unfamiliar with its contents.[217]

Staff and volunteers were asked for their suggestions on leading authorities for particular topics, and one of the experts would be invited to contribute.

---

214 E.g. Lindop 1971.
215 Taylor 1995.
216 Ibid.
217 Ibid.; Townsend 1996.

If the person asked could or would not contribute, they were asked to suggest someone who might be able to do so. The collective also provided alternate contacts. After MT's national public profile was established, many journalists were flattered to be asked to contribute and proved to be quite willing to write on their specialisms for MT, even if only because they could take a different tact from their regular positions. Indeed, 'you could find small nests of left-wing journalists nestled in the unlikeliest of places', including the *Sunday Times*'s sports desk.[218] This is also an indication of the difficulty of trying to 'read off' contributors' political biases from their occupations, since what they were paid for professionally, on right-wing newspapers, for example, usually meant having to hide or leave out their political beliefs (if they were left-wing). As production values improved and MT appeared increasingly like a glossy, professional magazine during the 1980s, contributors began asking to be paid.[219]

Once Jacques indicated how many pages an issue would have (e.g. 32, 48, 64), the designer or art editor would begin a provisional mapping out of the running order, advertisements and features, in addition to the pages allocated to the different sections, over which section editors sometimes had to fight to maintain their allotted pages. From its first issue in 1957 until September 1981, MT was almost always 32 pages. From October 1981, however, pagination increased by fifty percent, from 32 to 48 pages, which became the minimum within six months. Of course, the increase in pagination was also meant to account for increases in advertising, which in turn was meant to pay for the increased pagination. Subsequently, pagination increased up to 64 pages plus occasional supplements, which were printed and overseen by a separate group of the MTEC. With pagination agreed, Jacques would still only have a rough idea of which articles would run, but this was enough to get advertising sales under way and for the front cover to be worked out in terms of which feature topic to highlight.[220]

Front cover meetings, as with the Channel Five section editor's remit, were meant to make up for Jacques's particular weaknesses: his lack of visual imagination or ability to think through ideas in a visual way, and his particular focus on the feature articles on political issues to the detriment of arts, culture, sports etc. Jacques was aware that he did not understand visual communication and would defer to others even when questioning suggestions, for example, for the front cover. Cover meetings included Jacques, the deputy editor, the designer or

---

218 Townsend 1996.
219 Ibid.
220 Brown 1996.

art editor, the cover designer and, occasionally, someone special; later, the circulation manager was also brought in to attend these meetings, since the front cover's role as a marketing and promotional tool is also integral to publicity strategies.

Despite criticisms that MT was driven by style rather than editorial content, cover page meetings involved a lot of negotiation over what would go on the cover because of the differences between those involved with ideas literally (i.e. editorial staff and writers) and those who worked with ideas visually. Nevertheless, an idea would be agreed upon without necessarily consulting the designer(s) first, since Jacques would rely on those with more expertise in visual communication, but often after the idea of what the cover should focus on had been agreed.[221] However, the evolution of the thinking around the role of the cover for each issue was influenced by marketing considerations and commercial decisions as well as political and ideological decisions: the cover was seen, not just as a means to make a 'statement', as the radical left press has traditionally understood it, but also as a 'marketing tool'.[222]

The MTEC produced a one-page circular for the '*Marxism Today* Conference', on 30 June 1984, which laid out the timeline for the production process for one issue: 'How Marxism Today is Organised'.[223] This document is useful for understanding the production cycle via a series of deadlines that are necessary for an alternative radical magazine to meet when producing for national newstrade distribution. After noting the 10 sub-groups that constituted the different areas for production, from front covers to circulation to design and promotion, the production cycle for the July 1984 issue was outlined, which was just 'hot off the press' for the conference.

The circular outlined that the MTEB and the MTEC began discussing ideas for articles for the July issue as early as March 1984 and writers were sought out and commissioned. By the middle of May, the process of selling advertising space had begun. The end of May was when the cover group met to work out the front cover and the deadline of 29 May 1984 was set for two of the features and for MT's different sections: 'Focus'; 'Viewpoint'; 'Reviews'; 'Channel Five'.

As provided in the outline, the rest of the timing provided below indicates the degree to which the production cycle was labour intensive with tight deadlines to meet distribution commitments to ensure that the magazine made it onto the newsagent shelves on time (failure to do so could mean losing distribution agreements):

221 Brown 1996; Hammarling 1996; Perryman 1994; Minnion 1996.
222 Perryman 1994.
223 MTEC n.d. [1984]. See also MTEC 1983c.

'THE PARTY LINE VERSUS THE BOTTOM LINE'? 251

> 4 June: [type]setting begins
> 5 June: design starts: graphics and picture research
> 6 June: dummy (plan of magazine) made up
> 8 June: deadline for cover, cover ads, copy for all ads, titles for features
> 11 June: BERLINGUER[224] DIES. Last minute decision to commission a piece on his life and contribution.
> 12 June: All ads in. 'Update' in. Print run set.
> 13 June: printing starts
> 14–15 June: rush to get the setting finished, corrections made, etc.
> 16–17 June: rush to finish design.
> 22 June: printing ends. Copies packed and sent to Euston and Central Books.
> 25 June: copies dispatched to wholesalers.[225]

As the July issue hits the newsstands by 27 June 1984, the August issue is already 'well under way'.[226] It is important to recognise that each issue's production process and timeline is not neatly confined to one single month when it comes to all the material cultural practices involved from selling ads to identifying potential contributors and commissioning articles, to writing, revising and editing, as well as preparing promotional and publicity materials.

It is an intense, time-consuming process that requires discipline, time and people management skills especially since only a few are paid and most are volunteers. Their political commitment underpins their discipline to labour under professional and industry pressures to ensure the product hits the shelves on time every month. By the second half of the 1980s, the political commitment becomes more of a media industry 'apprenticeship' and yet MT's volunteer labour remained disciplined enough to ensure MT met its deadlines.

One final comment is worth making about the production process, which is related to, but different from, MT's 'meetings culture'. Most forms of self-managed or prefigurative alternative or radical media involve production and editorial meetings (which tend to be much more democratic than those conducted within capitalist corporate and state media). In this way, MT was no different to other alternative and radical media. However, the way its production was organised meant that there were numerous meetings and yet:

---

224   Enrico Berlinguer was the PCI's national leader 1972–84 and its most popular with Italians.
225   MTEC n.d. [1984].
226   Ibid.

> Martin [Jacques] would never consider himself bound by any decision of any meeting, however firmly and decisively it was taken, and so, if he wanted to change anything he would just do so. It was also a good way of avoiding taking difficult decisions.[227]

According to Jane Taylor, MT deputy editor, 'the meetings culture' was 'Martin's fetish ... [as] there tended to be a constant stream of impromptu meetings for this that and the other'. Regardless of Jacques's refusal to accept the decisions made by others, whether by the MTEB or MTEC, this 'meetings culture' offered a sense by which volunteers could feel included in the process of decision making. Taylor though believes that this was a means of avoiding making a decision or deferring or hiding responsibility: 'It was really a kind of a charade of democratic involvement and input when it didn't do any of that because of the personalities involved'.[228]

8   Conclusion

Marxism Today demonstrates benefits from aspects of the dominant models for radical and alternative media, Bolshevik and Comedia, in addressing the financial, organisational and production issues facing the left press. On the one hand, MT enjoyed the advantages of being published by a political party, which meant it was assured a minimal audience and income; party subsidies clearly ensured its survival, while even its efforts in the marketplace were helped by the party's organisational and financial support, which ensured a stable base and means of distribution especially until the early 1980s. For example, many of MT's discussion groups and promotional events were supported by local party members and branches, which provided some of the infrastructure for the dissemination of its analyses and criticisms at local levels, especially within the greater metropolitan area of London and some cities, such as Birmingham. Critics, who argue against relying on the market, identify the importance of finding ways, such as subsidies, whether via personal, party or other benefactors, for the radical press.[229]

On the other hand, MT's experience *also* demonstrates the financial benefits that the market can offer, enabling it to professionalise its production process.

---

227   Taylor 1995.
228   Ibid.
229   E.g. Atton 1999; Bambery 1996; Khiabany 1997.

As MT engaged in competition in the marketplace, it became more 'production-sensitive': the improvement of production quality (e.g. design, new technologies) which was, in turn, necessary to engage in market competition (and on the newsagent's shelf) and bring in greater revenues, including from advertising, which in turn helped improve the quality and even the credibility of the magazine, at least in terms of its newer readers and national media pundits. In effect, use was made of the marketplace and its requisite mechanisms, adapting to the processes and routines, but relying on the party to make up for bad decisions or 'market failures'. This was the 'best' of both worlds as the editor and his acolytes could extoll the virtues of engaging with the marketplace and yet rely upon the party to bail them out when necessary.

The changes in financing and production fed into each other in a symbiotic relationship between commercial and political decisions (an oft-cited but seldom examined relationship). However, some party members resented *Marxism Today*'s autonomy when Communist Party enterprises lost out to private companies, which combined with internal party strife over MT's political project, made it difficult for Jacques to make certain commercial decisions without having to engage in internal lobbying and politicking. All of these activities absorbed considerable energies of editor and staff, and furthered the drive to increase MT's autonomy from the party. On the other hand, Jacques's relationship with the General Secretary seems to have been critical to ensure a political-cum-financial lifeline for MT, especially as the crisis in its finances and the reformist takeover of the leadership threatened its autonomy (reformists wanted the magazine to begin working more closely with the party).

It might be argued that, whereas *Marxism Today* and other party publications subsidised the CPGB's enterprises, such as Farleigh Press, by giving them work rather than an outside firm, party enterprises at least ensured such money circulated within the party and, more importantly, ensured that MT could be printed and distributed before it succeeded in gaining national newstrade distribution. It might even be considered an example of the kind of 'internal market' (such as that promoted by New Labour in the late 1990s) that is supposed to be of such a great benefit as a means of ensuring greater efficiencies for public institutions and non-profit organisations.

While difficult to measure practically, an editor's leadership and personal qualities can have a tremendous impact upon the success or failure of small periodicals. MT's success was actually a result of the publisher, i.e. the party leadership, allowing the editor, over time and via considerable negotiations and trade-offs, a great degree of operational autonomy, editorial and financial. Jacques had arguably greater freedom to operate than most editors of the corporate or so-called 'free press' do in their relationships with press owners[230] and, in turn, MT was ruled by Jacques's 'Leninist'-style command, which is not unlike editors overseeing capitalist publications. Directing the periodical as he saw fit, he used all sorts of friends, volunteers, MTEB members, et al., to provide ideas, financial help and production support, drawing upon advice liberally, if he wanted to, motivating staff and volunteers, but also lobbying board members and party leaders. The magazine also benefited greatly from the support of paid and unpaid staff and volunteers. The organisational structures set up in the 1980s enabled MT to make the most of the free labour that was available which worked through various smaller collectives, the working practices of which were harnessed for its benefit, where final decisions remained the prerogative of the editor or those he appointed in his place.

There is an important relationship between an editor's style and degree of independence, and the type of periodical that can be produced, even within financial limitations. The differing editorial styles of James Klugmann and Martin Jacques and their particular relationships with *Marxism Today*, the editorial board and the party leadership, parallel the two forms, of a journal and of a magazine, respectively. The changes to finance, organisation and the production process were crucial to MT's transformation from a journal into a magazine, all of which were intertwined in turn with its focus on developing an image and organisation that appealed to newsagent browsers. The next chapter assesses MT's transformation from the first through the second and third formats, examining its editorial organisation, structure and visual developments. All of these aspects of production and format change were what enhanced its ability to gain access to the public sphere, and as MT's access to the public sphere grew, so too did its public profile and the pace of transformation. A key part of this move from the 'margins to the mainstream' was the ruthless promotion of all that MT published which, as we will see in Chapter 5, was a key component of the magazine's identity and public profile, albeit a process over which it was not necessarily the master.

---

230 Chippindale and Horrie 1992; Neil 1997.

CHAPTER 4

'From the Party Line to the Politics of Design': *Marxism Today*'s Cultural Transformation

In its first format, 1957–79, *Marxism Today* did not undertake any substantial changes in the layout and design, imagery or format. Indeed, it was more than a decade before some effort was made to make changes. MT's staid layout and functional design was similar to other Communist Party publications in the 1950s and 1960s, which were not unusual given technical and financial constraints faced by most literary and political periodicals at the time. However, as the technical constraints began to ease with the development of new (and cheaper) printing and photographic technologies, with the introduction of new graphic design techniques and the expansion of innovative, colourful publications, especially by commercial presses with their greater resources, most alternative and radical periodicals quickly began to look dated in comparison.

There were some adventurous uses of graphic design, photography and printing techniques made by individuals and groups with limited resources in the 1960s underground press, but these again only served to reinforce the boring look of the rest of the radical press. The counter-culture's brilliant and vibrant coloured posters, leaflets and papers, however, did have some impact upon the party's posters, which could be adapted more easily and quickly to changing aesthetic and design techniques, technological developments and popular cultural influences in their one-off print runs for a general public (versus ongoing production of several periodicals with limited audiences).[1] Introduction of punk aesthetics in the mid-1970s, also made many left papers look dense and staid by contrast, although there were notable exceptions, such as *7 Days* and *Socialist Worker* in its 'punk phase'.[2]

The changes in MT's design, layout and imagery during Martin Jacques's editorship, 1977–91, were influenced by developments in the periodical marketplace and on the left. Although Jacques did not know exactly what he wanted, he did know that he wanted to reach a larger audience and, therefore, MT had to become more accessible. From Jacques's earliest memoranda to the party

---

1 The production and distribution demands of posters and other kinds of 'disposable literature' are different from those of periodicals (Pimlott 2011).
2 Allen 1985. *7 Days* was a lively radical left weekly published in the early 1970s.

leadership, he emphasised the importance of making it more attractive to prospective readers.³ This was the 'journalistic project'⁴ that Jacques articulated as part of MT's political project: making the periodical 'accessible' for a new audience meant thinking about changes in format, design and layout, and the use of images as well as changes in rhetoric and writing style.

Marxism Today's attempt to move from the margins into the mainstream would have been practically inconceivable without the *transformation* from its 'journal' form into a 'magazine'.⁵ This is not simply a case of semantics: it is about differences in political aims and the ideal audiences expressed through these different cultural forms. Left publications are usually targeted at either a mass audience (e.g. working class, general public, popular front appeals to 'the people') or a narrow one (e.g. intellectuals, artists, scientists). The combination of a periodical's role and target audience should determine its format, design and writing: yet in spite of the expressed desire of many radical left groups to reach a wider audience, their publications in the 1970s and early 1980s usually made few concessions in format, design and layout, or rhetoric and writing style. Therefore, MT's journalistic project was absolutely integral to its political project to combat Thatcherism, by building the 'broad democratic alliance' via access to the national public sphere and the mainstream media to reach a larger audience outside the Communist Party. MT made changes in the format, design and layout, imagery, rhetoric and writing style to convince potential non-party readers and the commercial mass media to take it seriously in spite of its name and affiliation. While Chapter 6 examines MT's rhetoric and writing styles, this chapter begins with an examination of the theory of the periodical before analysing changes in MT across formats from design and layout to editorial sections to visual imagery.

1   The Theory of the Periodical and Magazine Design in the 1980s

The 'periodical' is a ubiquitous, serial, cultural form with which one need not be familiar to understand its appeal and which is marked by time (hence, its name); it is a more open-ended cultural form than the book, which is a single, discrete volume.⁶ Developments in the late twentieth century led to clearer dif-

---

3   E.g. Jacques 1977, 1978e. However, it was not until the third format that the editorial staff kept insisting to volunteers to refer to MT as a 'magazine' (Taylor 1995).
4   Jacques 1996b, 1996e.
5   Pykett 1990, pp. 12–13.
6   Beetham 1990, p. 29.

ferences between types of periodicals, with the journal as a periodical form closer to the book with its emphasis on text and a linear conceptualisation of its ideas moving from beginning to end. Technological limitations also meant that the 'journal' was isolated from wider cultural influences, frequently found in the imagery, advertising, and design and layout of commercial 'magazines' because of the latter's greater sensitivity to the marketplace's competition for readers' attention and money.

Since periodicals need to build and maintain a readership, they have to develop 'continuities in format, shape and pattern of contents' to offer 'readers a recognisable position in successive numbers', and to continually reproduce the popular sections to keep readers coming back to buy the next issue.[7] The periodical that is read in smaller, 'bite-sized' pieces, where the shorter stories can be 'digested' more easily and quickly is known as a 'magazine'. Equally important is the recognition that each of these sections can offer prospective advertisers the potential to more precisely target readers that fit their ideal demographic profiles, an important innovation in print media long before the development of more precise methods for identifying audiences for advertisers in the latter half of the twentieth century and since. Thus, the form itself is predicated on the idea of specific subject matter offered in different editorial sections (or 'compartments') at regular intervals to retain a particular readership that can be justified in economic terms by advertisers' costs and publisher's returns. This requires the introduction of designers to bring about those desired changes to reach a broader audience, or at least one with enough disposable income sought by advertisers, which would increase the likelihood of boosting revenues.

Design played an important role in transforming *Marxism Today* into a more attractive periodical for browsers and prospective purchasers, and accessible to those not usually inclined to read a Marxist periodical or (more specifically) journal. There are no particular attributes of visual presentation, design or format that predetermine what makes a socialist or Marxist magazine. Most of the (pejorative) characteristics that are assumed by readers and critics alike are what have come to be conventionally associated with left periodicals. In magazine design, for example, there are 'no immutable principles [that] can be applied' to each and every magazine nor are there problems common to all: the magazine 'has no definite visual form',[8] although different types of periodicals are often instantly recognisable as either a journal or a magazine, or by such categories or adjectives as 'glossy', 'gossip', 'current affairs' or 'news'. It

---

7   Beetham 1990, pp. 28, 26.
8   Owen 1991, p. 126.

is the combination of available editorial, technological and aesthetic priorities that act as constraints on the look of a journal or magazine, via layout and design, typography, images and format. As with other radical media, financial issues limit what a periodical can implement in its design, imagery and overall presentation or look. However, MT's connection to the CPGB ensured that it had access to greater resources than most non-party publications until the 1980s and it was also able to draw upon the expansion of advertising revenues during that decade.

The innovations in MT's design, format and imagery in its second format, 1979–86, were in keeping with some of the contemporary developments in magazine design. As William Owen outlines, the shift from 'the defensive conformism of the 1970s' was due in part to the 're-emergence of editorial-led magazines which [did] not fit conventional marketing categories' and was partly spurred on by the 'vitality of independent and underground publications, combined with the comparative wealth of the 1980s', all of which 'undoubtedly weakened the influence of marketing professionals and the preference for lowest common denominator of mediocrity'.[9] In part, therefore, it was timing that also benefitted MT and other periodicals that started publishing at that time, such as *New Socialist*, *i-D* and *The Face*, all of which would have benefitted the newstrade at a time when 'gaps in the market' meant new audiences were being sought while other commercial publications were seen as having reached their limits.

Nevertheless, MT and other radical competitors were just beginning to discover the potential offered by some marketplace mechanisms, such as promotion and national newsagent distribution, which enhanced the Comedia model for left periodicals.[10] The economic and technological developments in the 1980s contributed to the growth in the importance of the designer, due to the greater flexibility provided 'by new pre-press technologies' and 'the influence of television on readers' expectations and habits of perception'.[11] Together these developments enhanced 'the designers' position in the editorial process, as both initiator and communicator of ideas', which in turn was boosted by a 'decade of high economic growth' that helped to encourage further 'experimentation and innovation'.[12] These developments, which were 'observable if by no means universal trends', did benefit MT, *New Socialist* and other left periodicals, and influenced the rise of 'designer socialism'.

---

9   Owen 1991, p. 130.
10 E.g. Comedia 1984; Landry et al. 1985; Mulgan and Worpole 1986.
11 Owen 1991, p. 130. E.g. Baker 1982.
12 Owen 1991, p. 130.

It should come as no surprise that *Marxism Today*, in its attempt to reach out beyond the 'radical ghetto', underwent redesigning and reformatting efforts since the crisis of English magazine design in the 1970s quickly gave way to a decade of design innovation and experimentation, and a tremendous growth in the volume and range of periodicals. Developments in new printing and reprographic technologies, as well as the greater accessibility with lower skill levels and costs, led to rapid innovations in magazine design. As Owen has suggested, such specialist magazines as *The Face* and *i-D*, both launched in 1980, drew upon 'more liberal definitions' of their remits 'to create the freedom to explore outside their declared subject area', with 'equally individualistic and provocative visual presentation – and sometimes in spite of restrictive budgets', which meant that *The Face* became more than 'just a music magazine' and *i-D* became more than 'just a fashion magazine' reflecting 'the fragmentation of life'.[13] With the possibilities of innovations for even traditional newsmagazines opening up, MT sought to go beyond conventional expectations of a Communist journal's look.

Since most magazines are driven by their content, it is necessary to bring some balance by emphasising the role of design in making editorial attractive and accessible. *Marxism Today*, which was committed to its political ideas, commentary and analysis, and was, therefore, similar in emphasis to centre-left newsweeklies (e.g. *New Statesman*) or left monthlies (e.g. *Socialist Review*), retained the dominance of ideas vis-à-vis images, and layout and design, an emphasis which designers understand.

> For most magazine designers ... the journalistic imperative is dominant. That is, maximum exploitation of resources and materials to the end of clear communication – to tell a story – to a closely defined readership; a problem which is overcome at the most basic level by a formalised design structure.[14]

It is important to recognise that MT's material transformation was integral to its appeal to, and success with, a left public beyond the CPGB. Prior to the 'designer socialism' debate in 1986, the appeal of marketplace mechanisms to improve public outreach was a key shift in thinking on the left and the growing popularity of the Comedia model over the self-managed and Leninist models.[15]

---

13 Owen 1991, p. 131.
14 Owen 1991, p. 126.
15 Comedia 1984; Landry et al. 1985.

The visual power of a magazine is important and can be persuasive to a certain extent but cannot replace, dominate or surpass the *raison d'être* of a 'journal of opinion' or 'a magazine of ideas', although one needs to distinguish between those which are simply commercial vehicles for debate, as with the bourgeois press, or are part of a counter-hegemonic 'war of position'. Although MT was commonly associated with the idea of 'designer socialism', it was *New Socialist* that permitted the primacy of design over content with Neville Brody's redesign of *New Socialist* in 1986. This provided a tiny font for the main text that created a background sea of type, that was difficult to focus on and read, thereby, undermining the text's legibility and accessibility. The new design conveyed a very different sensibility than its first format, 1981–86, where NS's role as the Labour Party's 'theoretical and discussion' magazine was clearly delineated in the subordination of design to its mission to make ideas accessible: 'the nature of the material and the readership [should] govern visual expression'.[16] The new design negatively affected accessiblity for NS's readership, even though designers are meant to use the available tools 'to amplify, relate, or simply present a story, and to maintain interest'.[17] Successful magazine design can be assessed simply by asking, 'does the result obstruct or assist the communication of the message?'[18]

2   Format: 'From a Journal into a Magazine'

The format is a key component of understanding how journals and magazines work and how they organise their ideas based upon particular assumptions about their target audiences. The transformation of *Marxism Today*'s format, from a 'journal' into a 'magazine', was an integral part of the process of becoming accessible to a new generation of readers, which was connected to changes in production, distribution and promotion and thereby to its success in gaining (partial) access to the national public sphere. Although the words, journal and magazine, were often used interchangeably, there was an implicit, if not always explicit, understanding of the differences in format and strategy amongst MT staff.[19] A journal is written for a limited readership, often specialists, and can therefore draw upon a complex vocabulary or jargon in long articles with few, if any, illustrations, except perhaps for occasional tables or charts. A magazine,

---

16   Owen 1991, p. 127.
17   Ibid.
18   Owen 1991, p. 128.
19   Jacques 1984b; MTEB 1983.

however, tends to be published more frequently, with a greater degree of attention to design and visual presentation of editorial content, and an accessible writing style in shorter, more compartmentalised or defined editorial sections, to reach a broader readership.

The differences in MT's journal and magazine formats are key to their roles and appeal: the journal relies upon postal and party distribution, which does not require newsagent display, to reach its audience and often has only two or three editorial sections; the magazine is compartamentalised into separate editorial sections to appeal to different readerships to maximise the potential audience, especially via retail newsagent distribution. These differences were realised after the second format was introduced in 1979 and its evolution moved from an implicit into an explicit understanding via changes in production, distribution, images, design and layout, and writing (staff were adamant about calling it a magazine by the late 1980s).[20]

3   The First Format: 1957–79

The first format's small size (7.25 by 9.75 inches) and standard 32 pages per issue, from 1957 until 1979, was no hindrance to its circulation amongst the membership via the party network or by post. The two-section format of the 'theoretical and discussion journal of the Communist Party of Great Britain' was as functional as its subtitle was literal: one section was for theory, the other for discussion. As outlined in Chapter 1, *Marxism Today* took the place of a number of journals and their functions, with primary responsibility for making the party's theoretical work public by providing a space for party intellectuals to discuss Marxist theory and political issues. Its secondary purpose was to win over progressive intellectuals to Marxism and the party,[21] though the layout, writing and design reveal little effort in attempting to appeal to potential non-party readers.

When it was launched in 1957, MT's format was not so different compared to other literary and political periodicals of the 1950s, though clearly different to some of its rival intellectual periodicals of the time, such as *The New Reasoner*, the format and structure of which was closer to that of a book than a periodical, and *Universities and Left Review*, which was closer to that of the larger A4 format of many contemporary periodicals. All three period-

---

20   Taylor 1995.
21   Johnstone 1995; Matthews and Matthews 1996; McLennan 1996.

icals faced different financial constraints. One can argue perhaps for a homology between the 'gravitas' of TNR, its format, editorial team (e.g. John Saville, E.P. Thompson) and subject matter (e.g. international politics, political economy), and between ULR, its format (with its 'bold modernist lines'),[22] editorial team (e.g. Stuart Hall, Raymond Williams) and subject matter (e.g. culture, politics, education). Interestingly, both Hall and Williams were involved in the first two years of *New Left Review* and would later become leading contributors to *Marxism Today* and *New Socialist* at the start of the Thatcher decade. NLR, the result of the merging of the editorial and political trajectory of TNR and ULR, at least for the early period of the first New Left, was itself closer to a magazine than a journal in terms of format and approach during its first two years under Hall's editorship. For example, it had photographs of Soweto in the aftermath of the uprising alongside interviews with jazz musicians. After Perry Anderson took over the editorship in 1962, NLR moved closer to that of the journal as it promoted continental Marxist theories and a more complex, sophisticated approach to politics belied by its functional, if textually dense, format.

Fundamentally, the approaches of left periodicals, such as *New Statesman*, *Socialist Review* and *Red Pepper* in the twenty-first century, are not very different to the left political newsmagazines of the 1980s in terms of format, imagery, and design and layout, other than the greater flexibility with imagery and design, at a much lower cost and with a lower level of necessary skills because of developments in photographic reproduction and desk-top publishing. Differences are more about how electronic and digital formats offer alternatives to putting time-sensitive information into print that needs a shelf life of one or two weeks compared to one or two months in the early 1980s and the complementarity of electronic media providing additional materials and resources. Thus, while periodicity matters more for print media, websites and e-mail listservs can complement them by providing the immediate communication of timely information for meetings, book launches and other events in-between print editions.

MT's first format encapsulates the 'common sense' representation of the conventions of a Marxist journal and, in turn, contributed to this image, especially with the longevity of an unchanging look: pages of dense prose unrelieved by photographs or advertising, set inside cover images, if any, of Communist icons or social unrest. The primacy of ideas is evident in the emphasis on the text and the design's functional nature, although it should be noted that post-war

---

22   Kenny 1995, p. 103.

English design in general took time to mature. As with most journals in the 1950s, MT was simply 'a medium for communicating words'[23] and, therefore, its format, design and layout were static because all 'editorial design was constrained by the need to conserve paper and so artistry was measured by the ability to pack the page'.[24] As long as English magazine design was dominated by literary journalism and graphic design was 'immature', the visual communication of ideas would remain undeveloped.[25] The problem with the layout and design of most left periodicals at the time was that the emphasis on content was driven by the need to pack in as many words as possible on the page to keep costs down. Thus, they began appearing increasingly static and dated, especially as other (i.e. commercial) publications adopted newer production technologies that enabled them to incorporate colour and images, and achieve greater flexibility with layout and design.[26]

A homology can be discerned in this relationship between the political-ideological status quo within the Communist Party, James Klugmann's 'passive' editorship, the format's static nature and the production process. This top-down approach was reinforced by the hot-metal type printing process which needed sufficient time and space for the preparation of articles, which included the highly skilled process of making and setting the type. The two-column grid did not permit much flexibility for integrating visuals and text that also contributed to the page's 'boxy' shape (7.25 by 9.75 inches). This steadfastness in layout and design matches the conformity to the party line and restricted parameters of debate, particularly in light of 1956 and the question of 'inner-party democracy', which were reinforced by expectations as much as by editorial policy. As one discussant put it:

> We accept in the *British Road* the existence of opposition parties ... [and] the possible existence of more than one trend in the Labour movement ... We couldn't possibly accept more than one trend within the Communist Party however.[27]

---

23 Hammarling 1996. Hammarling's comments arose while examining copies of the first-format MT.
24 Owen 1991, p. 80. This was, at least, partly a legacy of postwar paper rationing.
25 Owen 1991, p. 83.
26 See Owen 1991 and Crowley 2003 for examples of the changing nature of magazine design and innovation in front covers prior to and during the 1980s.
27 Kelsey 1965, p. 125.

The possibility that such an attitude combined with suspicion of that which was unfamiliar in the Cold War era meant that even stylistic changes or design innovations would have been seen as *literally* breaking from the party line or, at the very least, they would have been seen as suspect in journals such as MT. Klugmann's cautious approach to innovation was, therefore, in keeping with expectations. Hot-metal printing technology, which was being superseded by photolithography, remained the determining feature of the first format: 'Even if *Marxism Today* [in the late 1970s] was no longer being produced by hot metal, it certainly looked as though it was'.[28]

Alongside MT's name and subtitle, the cover signposted all the articles and authors, repeated on the inside front cover with prospective titles on forthcoming features, the list of board members and contact information. Editorial was simply divided between an unlabelled features section (minimum 4,000 words) followed by responses in 'Discussion' (maximum 2,500 words). The more infrequent 'Reviews' (around 2,000 words) were usually situated in-between the two sections. Articles were run one after the other in the same sequence listed on the cover, encouraging a linear reading of the articles as set out in order of importance. The pagination encouraged each year's twelve issues to be seen as instalments of one volume, from January to December, pages 1 to 384, that were subsequently bound together as a single 'book'.

The first major innovation was the introduction of 'Editorial Comments' on the first page of each issue from the July 1960 issue until the second format launch with the October 1979 issue. This new section was introduced because the leadership recognised a need to respond more quickly to topical issues, instead of waiting months for a properly formulated analysis, and for space to announce upcoming events, publications etc.[29] The MT Editorial Board could publish its views 'on new books, progressive and reactionary, [and] ... participate in current polemics and discussions in the field of politics, culture and science'.[30] Although readers were invited to suggest topics to be covered and could even include 'a rough draft of the proposed commentary', the editor retained the right to reject anything thought 'unsuitable'.[31] This provision of shorter, topical items was to encourage party members to read MT as it would also address current issues, since its circulation was declining even as party membership was growing.[32] The journal's frequency of publication still required something

---

28 Hammarling 1996.
29 Klugmann 1960.
30 MT 1960, p. 193.
31 Ibid.
32 Klugmann 1960.

more than just longer features to draw readers in, especially if such articles did not address contemporary issues or topical subjects.

However, as the ideological parameters of features and discussion in MT gradually opened up and shifted from 1967, with the opening up initiated by the Executive Committee's 'Statement on Ideology and Culture',[33] material changes also followed gradually. The design had begun to look staid by the mid-1960s because no attention was paid to the use of white space, graphics or images while other periodicals were using new technologies and processes to radically transform their look as both television and the 1960s' youth culture made their influences felt.[34] As a journal targeted at members and distributed by post and party networks, MT's appearance was of little consequence. Only minor changes to typefaces and layout were introduced gradually during the first format in tandem with the party's gradual ideological shift: content still took precedence over accessibility and presentation.

After experimenting with different typefaces for each article in the November and December 1969 issues, a new format style was adopted for the January 1970 issue.[35] The primary design innovations were: illustrated covers, variations in size and style of typefaces, and subheadings and rules.[36] Typefaces and rules provided the only visual boundaries between editorial sections. An attempt was made to set each feature on separate pages, as if to suggest individual contributions were self-contained and no longer part of a seamless, monolithic worldview. Once single issues were no longer separate entities, when they were bound together into one annual volume, they became individual chapters of a single 'book', especially where those features sparked months-long discussion contributions enhancing connotations of a book's singular focus.[37]

The introduction of illustrated covers in 1969 was the first major innovation since 1960, although the inside pages remained largely the preserve of text. The few images used were only deployed as illustrations of the text's subject, usually in articles about art or artists: captions were unnecessary since visuals performed primarily an illustrative or ornamental function only and were therefore thought to be self-explanatory. An article on Russian painting in the February 1965 issue, for example, contained three pages of photographs without any text or captions,[38] while an article on George Grosz ten years

---

33 EC 1967.
34 Owen 1991.
35 Klugmann 1969, p. 356.
36 Rules are lines used to demarcate sections and articles from each other.
37 Pykett 1990.
38 Niven 1965, pp. 47, 48, 51.

later, in the February 1975 issue, included three reproductions of his work set within the text, captioned only with their titles:[39] their meanings were already 'anchored'[40] by the (con)text.

However, it was not just competition with other left periodicals or the transformations taking place with magazines that were exerting pressure on MT's look. Newspapers, 'as a form', were moving 'towards the magazine and away from the *news* paper which is still taken as its central definition', as Williams pointed out in 1978, due in part to 'the significant development of television as an alternative source' of news after 1945.[41] Newspapers also came to offer more contributions in the area of arts and culture that periodicals like MT were already providing by the second half of the 1980s. Popular culture's influence would manifest itself more concretely in the second format when 'Channel Five' was introduced in 1981.

4 The Second Format: 1979–86

The launch of *Marxism Today*'s second format with the October 1979 issue, published five months after Margaret Thatcher's first general election victory as Tory Party leader and nine months after Stuart Hall's Thatcherism thesis was published in the January 1979 issue, should also be seen as MT's response to this particular historical conjuncture via the integration of its journalistic and political projects. The journal's transformation into a magazine, even as it was not always formulated as such, was integral politically to attempting to address the left more broadly, including the Labour Left, and in addressing new social movements.[42] In Martin Jacques's vision, MT was attempting to open up space to address other readers besides party intellectuals: the broad democratic alliance of trade unionists, progressive intellectuals, and political and social activists, in line with the 1977 *British Road to Socialism*. To address this new audience, Jacques had argued that MT had to transform itself from a party journal into a 'broad left' magazine to make it accessible to and persuasive with non-party readers.

From 1979, all major changes in format, layout and design were introduced in the October issue, although the March issue was sometimes used to introduce minor changes. October became the largest issue because it was the most

---

39   Watkinson 1975, pp. 58, 59, 60. The cover carried a fourth work.
40   Barthes 1977.
41   Williams, 1978b, p. 24 (original emphasis).
42   E.g. Downing 1980, pp. 180–99.

important for MT politically, since it was published shortly before Labour's annual conference with topical features of political analysis, and economically, since October was one of the two most important months in the annual commercial magazine cycle for reaching new readers and greater potential revenue via advertising, sales and subscriptions (the onset of autumn is the ideal time to recruit new readers as people start spending more time indoors due to inclement weather). With MT's move to national newsagent distribution in 1981, it became vital to invest heavily in publicity and promotion for the October issue to persuade wholesalers and retailers that the magazine would sell.

Jacques had initiated the process of working out a new format, soon after becoming editor in September 1977, because he found its design a 'source of embarrassment'.[43] He made it clear to the readers that design was 'as important as the ideas' because how ideas are presented determines MT's image, and thereby 'who reads it, how and why'.[44] The second format was bigger (8.4 by 10.75 inches) with nearly 28 percent more space for graphics and advertising in addition to text, though ideas retained priority as there was an increase of almost 20 percent in wordage (in part due to a smaller font): from the first format's 26,500 words per 32-page issue (840 words per page) to the second format's 31,500 per 32-page issue (980 words per page), which was the equivalent of adding one additional feature.[45] The editorial sections were doubled to six and were usually broken down per 32-page issue as follows: 'Contents' one page; 'Focus' four pages; 'Features' 20 pages; 'Discussion' four pages; 'Reviews' two pages; and 'Notes' one page (all pages include space for ads). When editorial is broken into sections, it helps to make a magazine's content more accessible and generate expectations to keep readers coming back.[46]

There is a homology between this process of compartmentalisation found in the magazine form and the CPGB's BDA strategy, as each editorial section was self-contained in focus to appeal to different interests of different readerships, even as political features retained their dominance alongside the primacy of the mass working-class party as the key agency for change.[47] Periodical theory

---

43   Jacques 1996b.
44   Jacques 1978b, pp. 269–70.
45   Jacques 1978e, 1979i; MTEB 1979b. All discussions of pagination exclude front and back covers (inside and out), inserts and supplements, which provided more advertising opportunities and revenue.
46   Beetham 1990; Owen 1991.
47   While members saw their party at the heart of the BDA, they recognised that Labour had mass working-class support and was, therefore, necessary to any strategy. In the eyes of

fits with the BDA strategy, although it can also be read or understood as a form of fragmentation, as each section appeals to different groups without necessarily bringing them together. Since the audience is less integrated by magazine content, a journal is differentiated by a greater singular editorial focus. MT had to maintain a balance between adding new sections with different subject matter to appeal to potentially new constituencies while retaining existing audiences with the original sections and subject matter as part of a cohesive identity.[48] A socialist or Communist periodical seeks to ensure the (ideological) integrity of the different sections to overcome any sense of fragmentation between, or lack of connection across, editorial sections via its general political line (which need not be narrow nor prescriptive).

To make MT more accessible, other innovations were introduced, such as magazine paratextual elements, which help to guide the reader.[49] Amongst the first paratextual elements introduced were 'quotes'[50] and 'stand-firsts', which generally had not been used in the first format, except for the occasional stand-first introducing an author assumed to be unknown to readers. MT's assumption that readers would be familiar with authors, for whom there was no stand-first, such as Communist leaders and intellectuals, highlights the closed nature of the journal's audience. The use of paratextual elements was improved incrementally in recognition of a more diverse readership. The layout of quotes, for example, moved from seemingly random placement throughout features to more systematically designed linkages of quotes to the page from which they were excerpted. These kinds of developments signalled to both readers and the newstrade that MT was a 'magazine' produced by professionals similar to others on the newagent's shelf.

The combination of topical black-and-white, and later colour, cover photographs, the second format's size, which was similar to that of the *New Statesman*, newsagent distribution and the reprinting of articles in *The Guardian* all worked at a connotative (and literal) level to contribute to the perception of MT as a 'newsmagazine' by the early 1980s. As there were few radical and socialist publications being sold in newsagents, and there were even fewer that succeeded in having dozens of articles reprinted or used as 'primary sour-

---

its supporters, the CPGB was the one political organisation, however, that could provide the analysis and leadership necessary for a transition to socialism. Hence, its attempts to affiliate to Labour (e.g. Callaghan 2005).

48   E.g. Olive 1983; Taylor 1989b.
49   Keeble 1994, p. 369.
50   Short, provocative or interesting excerpts are laid out in a much larger font on the page, often emboldened and with rules or borders, to draw in the newsagent browser.

ces'[51] by national media, these associations helped to persuade others to take notice of MT as a 'serious' periodical, especially amongst *Guardian* readers.

An important part of the strategy, to gain access to the national public sphere and expand MT's potential readership was to play down its link to the CPGB, while simultaneously ensuring that MT fit in with similar types of left newsmagazines and yet posed an attractive choice against its competitors on the shelf. For example, the October 1981 issue incorporated important changes to the front cover for nationwide distribution, including a cover price increase from 60 to 65 pence and a 50 percent increase in pagination (from 32 to 48 pages) and the introduction of a special section on culture called 'Channel Five'. The title was shifted from its position on the centre-top of the cover to the left-hand corner to be seen on the newsagent shelf, as magazines usually overlapped one another physically on the right-hand side to enable a greater range of publications to be displayed. With its subtitle permanently removed from the front cover and printed on the contents page in a tiny font perpendicular to the listings, where it was easily overlooked as the fine print, MT's direct connection to the CPGB was intentionally obscured until its closure in 1991.

5 The Third Format: 1986–91

The October 1986 launch of *Marxism Today*'s third and largest format (8.9 by 11.7 inches)[52] was a triumph of considerations of design and layout over financial concerns. For example, Keith Ablitt's proposal for the change to the third format was selected despite being considerably more expensive than the others.[53] This was MT's response to its leading competitor, *New Socialist*, which had hired Neville Brody for its redesign, in the visual debate over 'designer socialism' that the two socialist magazines represented. This final format reveals a greater degree of influence from contemporary innovations, such as style, music and women's magazines, as MT's transformation from a journal into a magazine continued.[54] Competition for readers increased as the number of consumer magazines grew, newspaper supplements expanded after 1986, and Saturday turned into a 'newspaper day' in 1988: all of which threatened the survival of

---

51   The definition of 'primary sources' is part of the analysis of national press coverage in Chapter 5.
52   The size is close to 'the most favoured' format which 'printing presses are designed to handle' (Davis 1988, p. 21; Brown 1996).
53   Jacques 1996d; Brown 1996; Minnion 1996.
54   Brown 1996; Jacques 1996d.

monthly political-cultural magazines and 'weekly journals of opinion'.[55] Newspapers, such as *The Times* and *The Guardian* (and the latter's *G2* tabloid section), provided arenas for 'good writing' and writing across 'semi-political' (i.e. socio-cultural) issues that magazines like MT, NS and *New Society*, had already staked out.[56]

MT attempted to keep abreast of developments in new technologies and graphic design to compete with other magazines on the newsagent's shelf. The influence of popular culture was also becoming more apparent in its layout, design and images, as it learned from different magazines, including 'style mags', such as *The Face*, and current affairs magazines, such as *The Economist*. Professional magazine designers, such as Simon Esterson and Michael Lackersteen, who had been involved with *Crafts* and *Blueprint*, and Pearce Marchbank, who had worked on *Time Out* in the 1970s, were hired to work on covers.[57] These designers were amongst the first contributors paid for their work on MT (though frequently, but not always, below market rates). They experimented with different elements of graphic design, such as 'drop caps',[58] typesetting in bold, and employing 'quotes' and 'floating columns',[59] to make the pages less forbidding.

With the largest format, the page was divided into four columns to permit greater flexibility with visuals and text. The features section, however, only used three of the columns for text while the fourth, floating column was used to break up the page with white space and quotes to make the features more accessible and less visually forbidding (as a wall of text might appear). Boxes and graphics were also used to make 'terminally turgid writing' and complex material more accessible.[60] Other sections used all four columns, such as 'Focus', to make the most of the available space as well as to differentiate other sections from features. Moving from the format to consider the different aspects of the periodical, we should begin with the periodical's most obvious and public aspect: the front cover.

---

55 Tunstall 1996, pp. 163–69.
56 Tunstall 1996, pp. 168–9.
57 Brown 1996.
58 'Drop caps' are when the first letter of the first word in different sections of an article are several sizes larger than the rest of the letters of the first word of the opening sentence of the article.
59 The 'floating column' is an extra column used for images, captions or quotes, but not for the text; it can be moved around to enable greater flexibility for laying out text and images on every page.
60 Taylor 1989b.

6 Front covers

There is no better way to judge a magazine than by its cover, which is often vital to its success in reaching out to (or attracting the attention of) prospective readers and integral to its persona, politics and position, especially vis-à-vis its competitors. Front covers play an important role for political periodicals, though their purpose will vary depending upon the particular editorial approach and ideological line. Political journals have in the past used the cover as a statement of their ideas, whereas commercial magazines use it as a marketing tool, though it can work for both those reasons. For most, if not all, left periodicals, the emphasis on their ideas usually translates into using the front cover as a means for promoting their politics rather than marketing their publication. *Marxism Today* was no different in its first two formats.

The first format under James Klugmann's editorship did little with the front covers other than list the contents of the articles contained inside in the page order in which they were printed. For the first 12 years, the only variety that MT's front covers demonstrated before 1969 were alternating background colours and the introduction of a white background for the cover's table of contents since the text was barely legibile with some of the darker background colours. The first illustrated front cover was the September 1969 special issue on 'The National Liberation Struggle' with a two-tone image of Vietnamese guerrillas. Socialist icons like Marx and Lenin were also used, as were those of students, police, demonstrations etc., which expressed both a seriousness in terms of the content and a topicality befitting the industrial and social unrest of this period, 1968–74. These images were also similar to the standard repertoire of other far left groups, which frequently used various iconic thinkers and leaders, such as Marx and Lenin, from the pantheon of leading Communists, on their covers as signifiers of their politics: where the exclusion of one or more icons often signified a particular ideological line.

Nevertheless, many cover images did not reproduce well and text-based covers remained fairly common until 1973, after which they were gradually phased out. There were only four between 1974 and 1977, though all contributions were still listed on every front cover. Out of the 121 issues from September 1969 to September 1979 (inclusive), 33 were text-only, two were facsimiles of text-based posters, 43 were facsimiles and reproductions of illustrations and drawings, nine were two-tone photographic images and the remaining 34 used photographs on their own or in combination with drawings or cartoons. These changes were part of an attempt to reach a wider audience both inside and outside the Communist Party, fed by the growing interest in Marxism and the expansion of post-secondary education. Equally important, though, was the ideological and aesthetic competition from other far left groups and the alternative press.

There was not a lot of change in the nature of front covers in the first two years after Martin Jacques took over the editorship in September 1977. In the last two years of the first format, Jacques brought in some designers and socialists for advice, including personal acquaintances and the politically committed, to help prepare covers (and take on other production tasks). David Triesman, for example, who had been involved with the innovative radical *7 Days* weekly in 1971, helped out in this early period. In addition, to writing a number of articles on the politics of culture and sports, he designed several front covers, including six of the 12 issues in 1978. He also helped prepare some of the key documents for rethinking MT's design and form(at).[61]

It was only with the second format's launch with the October 1979 issue's front cover of a black-and-white photograph of a portrait of Margaret Thatcher looking outwards and upwards from in front of a microphone (outside No. 10?), that we really begin to see a systematic approach to the front covers. A difficulty in picking front covers was ensuring that the image used to highlight a key feature article was also timely and topical, i.e. 'newsworthy', for a couple of weeks at least since events changed quickly while a long lead time was required for the feature articles' commissioning, writing and editing process. With the second format, for example, the lead time was initially six weeks before the publication date because of the demands of the production process.[62]

A series of illustrated, cartoon and black-and-white photographic images were published on MT's front covers during the first two years of the second format, although the preference for photographs began to predominate. These covers began signifying a 'newsmagazine' with black-and-white photographs of public figures and celebrities in the news: for example, Thatcher (October 1979, July 1983), Tony Benn (October 1980, May 1982) and John Lennon (January 1981). Celebrities and public figures are often used to draw readers to the magazine; they also signify news values via relevance and contemporaneity or topicality, and are more likely to draw less committed readers in. Documentary-style photographs helped to reinforce connotations of MT as a newsmagazine; during the second format's first years, many cover photographs lacked captions because of their generic, non-specific nature.

---

61 The authorship of some of the documents of Jacques's rethinking of MT's format and design, marketing and so forth were unclear: Jacques 1978c and 1978d are likely Triesman's authorship.
62 Jacques 1996d.

The October 1980 issue, for example, was the first issue available outside of party networks and radical bookshops via the trial run at selected London newsagents. The front cover's photograph of Tony Benn and Eric Hobsbawm promotes Benn's interview as the cover story,[63] and its appeal to attendees at the Labour Party Conference and to the left-leaning browser in the trial newsagents is on news values: e.g. topicality; timeliness; 'unexpectedness' or 'journalistic surprise'.[64] Although the interview took place in July, it was only published in the October 1980 issue to appeal to potential readers at the Labour Conference where Benn was running for the deputy leadership. It was of great interest to the existing MT readership and anyone else interested in left politics. The second appeal was to Communist Party members and sympathisers because of the role of Hobsbawm, a leading party intellectual, as interviewer of a Labour ex-cabinet minister and Labour Left leader despite the CPGB's proscription from affiliation to Labour.

The second format's first topical pop cultural cover was also newsworthy, although this was not the first issue which featured a cultural topic, as there were several produced prior to January 1981 under the editorships of both James Klugmann and Martin Jacques.[65] As a result of his murder, the January 1981 cover carried a photograph of John Lennon with a line from one of his songs in red type across the top of the image: 'A working class hero is something to be'. The phrase would have appealed to audiences around two possible interpretations. First, it would have been read as a statement on Lennon himself, his class background and politics, which would have appealed to fans with similar politics, including many of the 1960s generation, who had grown up with the Beatles. Second, the phrase also would have addressed party members with no interest in popular music but who would have found the line politically acceptable.[66] The story, written by sociologist and *Melody Maker* contributor, Simon Frith,[67] was short for a feature article in MT, composed of barely three pages including photographs, but it had the broadest appeal of all that issue's features and it was the most newsworthy. The other three features included the 'Alternative Economic Strategy', an interview with Ted Knight, Labour leader of Lambeth Council (London), and socialist strategy. This cover was also a significant move for a left periodical because it signalled that popular

---

63   Hobsbawm 1980.
64   E.g. Richards 1997, p. 5.
65   E.g. February 1975; June 1976; November 1978; June 1980.
66   This cover might have aroused enmity among traditionalists who had opposed the Young Communist League's use of Lennon on its journal's cover in the 1960s (e.g. Waite 1995).
67   Frith 1981.

culture was being taken seriously and it shows how MT attempted to appeal to a younger, more media-savvy generation with a fusion of politics and popular culture.

The October 1981 issue that launched MT officially via the national news-agent distribution made the most of its two 'news scoops': interviews with both the Polish Prime Minister, Mieczyslaw Rakowski, and the leader of the independent trade union, Solidarity, Lech Walesa, during the Polish crisis that preceded the military takeover and dictatorship. These two interviews justified the word 'exclusive' across the two extreme closeups placed side-by-side on the front cover (and reproduced in a couple of national newspapers).

From November 1981 to February 1982, there was some experimentation with using four-colour printing but it proved to be almost as expensive as full-colour printing.[68] The move to using full-colour printing for the second format's front and back (and sometimes inside) covers helped MT to compare more favourably with other left newsmagazines. Frequently, between the introduction of full colour with the March 1982 issue and the October 1983 issue, practically every issue used colour photographs with human figures on the cover. David Crowley says that the 'the image of the face and the body' dominate magazine front covers, which 'aspire to take on human form, "speaking" to us with their cover lines ... and staring out at us ... through the eyes of the "headshot"'.[69] Some of these were clearly recognisable politicians of the time whereas other covers depicted issues, such as the women's camp at Greenham Common or Apartheid South Africa. The latter issue's problem for the white minority in South Africa was concisely and starkly depicted on the January 1983 front cover, with a medium shot of a white policeman standing at the head of dozens of partially undressed black South Africans (prisoners or police recruits?).

Humour was also an important tool in transforming the front cover from a statement into a marketing tool to reach out to prospective buyers and play off against the seriousness of the title's first word, 'Marxism'. An early example of MT's provocative style and humour was the April 1982 cover with a photograph that signposted the interview with the Chief Constable of Devon and Cornwall, John Alderson, who favoured 'community policing' in the aftermath of the 1981 inner city riots. It portrayed a smiling policeman with an ice cream in each hand, under the title, 'Policing: The Cornish Approach'. This image played a pun on Cornish ice cream and Alderson in contrast to policemen armed with

---

68   Hammarling 1996; Townsend 1996.
69   Crowley 2003, p. 7.

truncheons attacking strikers or protestors, an image with greater currency with the left, which is why many left activists read it as uncritical of the police. However, this cover image also plays on the right's dislike of community policing, playing on the associations of ice cream as 'soft' or a 'treat', and 'rewarding' rather than punishing offenders. The reaction of the Tory press was easy to predict, as with *The Sun*'s read of Alderson's interview in a 'Marxist rag' as proof of the 'suspect' nature of community policing.[70]

It prompted, for example, at least one respondent to compare MT unfavourably to the *TV Times*, in the newly instituted 'Letters' page, albeit alongside another letter praising MT for having short pieces on fashion.[71] Communist periodicals did *not* carry interviews with people in authority, least of all the police, and to do so with humour upset many readers' expectations, as it also challenged the radical left's more common representations of (and experience with) police and other agencies of state control. However, two issues later, another letter writer challenged earlier criticisms by saying that the left complains that the establishment will not talk to it, but here was an authority figure speaking to the left in one of its magazines.[72]

This particular cover can be seen as the start of a move away from the more didactic, conventional or historical covers of an older MT, towards an increasing ambiguity in meaning and imagery as many front covers lacked text. This development was an experiment (or a necessity) to try and reach browsers in newsagents with a more popular and complex aesthetic, even if it was only used on the front cover as a marketing tool. The October 1983's innovative graphic, 'tongue-in-cheek', front cover, which depicted Neil Kinnock as 'Superman' flying to Labour's 'rescue' after its disastrous June election, available at Labour's post-election conference, was an early example of these front cover experiments.[73] Most covers subsequently attempted to draw out the time-sensitive, relevant news values, such as public figures, like the 'vox pops' style of commentary from politicians, pundits and intellectuals on the centenary of Karl Marx's death (March 1983);[74] timeliness, with the 'British on holiday' (Au-

---

70   Bond 1982; *The Sun* 1982. There was enough media coverage that the policeman holding the two ice creams in the photograph contacted MT to get a copy (Townsend 1996; Jacques 1996c).
71   Baker 1982; West 1982.
72   Hodgson 1982.
73   Brown 1996; Perryman 1994b. The 'Gone with the Wind' poster of Reagan, Thatcher and a nuclear mushroom cloud in the background was used for a cover of *New Socialist* (January–February 1982).
74   Townsend and Webster 1983.

gust 1983); and public events, such as the Greenham Common[75] roundtable on the women's peace camp (February 1983).

To reach other potential readers, *Marxism Today* was willing to play on a cover's ambiguities, especially in the third format. It could also mean a more direct statement of ideas, an approach that complemented the shift into using covers as more of a marketing tool than a political statement: however, these changes provoked some readers to complain. For example, the January 1988 cover, designed by Keith Ablitt, signposted the abortion roundtable[76] with a photograph of a foetus on a sky-blue (heaven?) background; pro-choice readers complained that MT was playing into the hands of anti-abortionists with such a controversial image, even if it was only intended to attract attention.[77] At the time, Parliament was debating a private member's bill to restrict abortion, which appealed to the Tories' social-conservative wing. It was not just a 'marketing ploy', according to MT's art director at the time, Jan Brown, who claimed that the cover was an example of the magazine's 'realistic' approach to presenting issues 'as they are' and not as we (the left) would wish them to be: the image of the foetus constituted the essence of the abortion debate.[78] Such an explanation, however, can be seen as and is reductive: it plays to the emotions with an image which itself is not necessarily representative of why abortion is at times necessary and at other times a 'choice'. The contradiction that appeared to keep everyone 'happy' was that, while the pro-choice respondents complained about the front cover, they also thought that the roundtable discussion was very good; a majority of the MT Editorial Board also thought the cover was a mistake.[79] Yet, in the end it did work as a marketing ploy for the magazine and its persona: newsmagazines, like newspapers, 'thrive not on predictability, but on surprise'.[80]

For a more systematic comparison of the front covers between the second and third formats, I have chosen to focus on a quantitative overview of the 60 issues of the second format that were distributed nationally, October 1981 to September 1986, and the 63 of the third format, October 1986 to December 1991. Indeed, one-in-six, or 10 issues, of the second format only used text

---

75　Greenham Common was a women's peace camp set up outside a US air force base in Berkshire in September 1981 which became famous after an April 1983 gathering of tens of thousands of protestors.
76　Savage et al. 1988.
77　E.g. Lee 1988; Wright 1988.
78　Brown 1996.
79　Lee 1988; Wright 1988; MTEB 1988c.
80　Richards makes a similar point about *The Daily Herald* (1997, pp. 5, 137).

to identify one feature or theme. Except for the exclusive news scoop of October 1981, which clearly warranted no distracting text, the other nine included eight that were published from January to September 1983, excluding June, a period of some tension on the left leading up to and just after the June 1983 election. Out of these 60 second-format issues, there were 43 front covers (nearly 72 percent) that focused upon one or two people, of which 27 (45 percent) were of notables (e.g. politicians, celebrities); 16 (nearly 27 percent), or more than one-in-four (including both graphic and photographic images), were of Thatcher (five), Kinnock (four), Benn (three), Michael Foot (two) and Ken Livingstone (two). Other than Thatcher, the emphasis in the second format was clearly upon Labour politicians.

There were some shifts in topics on the front covers from the second to the third format. For example, nearly half of the (30 out of 63) third format's front covers, were graphic or abstract illustrations versus the second format's one-third (19 out of 60), which might have been the influence of better-known designers attempting to create the most evocative or provocative covers with limited resources, even as the third format increased its revenues substantially over the second format's. In keeping with MT's focus in the earlier format on politics, a total of 46 out of 63 covers focused upon politics in one form or another: 28 on domestic UK politics (and economics); seven on Gorbachev, the USSR and Eastern European Communism; six on Europe; and five on such international political issues as Nelson Mandela and Apartheid, and the Gulf War. Another 16 focused upon such social and ecological issues as sex, masculinity, abortion, the 'demon drink' and global warming. The one remaining issue was the final issue, 'The End' (December 1991), the cover of which was composed of several miniature front covers from the previous 12 years.

The third format's front covers included a number of striking or provocative images used to catch the eye of the newsagent browser. These covers included extreme close-ups of the human body, as with a photographic image of a foetus (January 1988) and a graphic image of a hand (October 1986), and one with a four-letter word, 'aids' (January 1987). The latter issue had the acronym 'aids' in a lower case font in large, white letters (taking up the lower quarter of the page) set against a simple black background, with a flame as a 'dot' above the 'i', to represent and not just signify the candles used in vigils.[81] The April 1988 front cover for a special issue on 'men' used a bare male torso in the background with two fists tattooed with 'love' and 'hate' in the foreground, which was set in a metallic steel grey colour tint, which captures something of masculinity at a

---

81   Designed by Keith Ablitt.

time of the rise of the 'new lad' in reaction to the 'new man'.[82] Another cover was the one that promoted Eric Hobsbawm's 'strategic voting' article, which simply used a 'dotted red circle' on a yellow background, to signify Labour's rosette, with Hobsbawm's name followed by the statement that the only 'way of defeating the Thatcher government' is to vote 'for the candidate who is best placed to keep out the Tory'.[83] (Tory was written in white on a blue circle signifying their 'rosette' and outside the 'dotted red circle'.)

Despite some of these provocative and striking covers, it was actually the abstract front covers that sold best, according to Mark Perryman, a former circulation manager for MT. Although it cannot perhaps be put down to front covers alone, since the two best-selling issues were the October 1988[84] 'New Times' launch issue and the January 1989[85] 'Postmodernism' issue, which corresponded more to the growing popularity of 'new thinking' about contemporary political, socio-economic and cultural changes, and especially with the interest of lecturers and graduate students.[86]

As the magazine shifted away from conventional expectations, it undermined a significant portion of its audience base without necessarily guaranteeing a new audience. Of course, the growing interest and public profile of MT enabled these later issues to attract greater attention than earlier ones, especially after seven years of national newsagent distribution and with the then recent intensive coverage of MT in the national press. The greater integration of visuals and text, use of graphic design and the expansion to four columns in many sections made the magazine more accessible, even though ideas remained MT's primary purpose and *raison d'être*.

7   Visual Communication, Advertising and Design

The changes in the visual presentation of *Marxism Today* through the second and third formats was not only about making the periodical more attractive to prospective readers-cum-purchasers, but also to make it more accessible in presentation for audiences. While design and photography played an important role in the changes in MT's look and visual communication, the role of advertising and cultural coverage were equally significant. Advertising was not

---

82   Designed by Jan Brown.
83   Designed by Keith Ablitt.
84   Designed by Jan Brown.
85   Designed by Simon Esterson and Michael Lackersteen.
86   Brown 1996; Perryman 1994b. This excludes the 1998 one-off, 'comeback' issue.

only about increasing revenues, but also about improving MT's presentation, since ads can also help to attract readers while enhancing a periodical's look to the casual browser. With the growing visual influences of advertising, marketing, television and film throughout society from the late 1970s, the use of images in the second format began to look ornamental or pedantic, which is why it became necessary to bring in an art director, designers and illustrators, host cover meetings and develop a greater degree of innovation in the use of imagery to transform MT's look.

The second format's design was a definite improvement upon the first format, even though it appeared to still be a fairly functional and unadventurous approach, at least in comparison to the third format, although it was not that unusual compared with many of its contemporary competitors on the left. This was due in part to the limited flexibility for laying out text and images, which were constrained by the two-column grid, although the second format's larger page size did help. The integration of text and images improved as the design was upgraded and columns were increased from two to three. Between 1979 and 1981, MT tried to have at least one photograph per article and even introduced them onto the contents page.[87] These images were essentially decorative for stories in the same way that clip-art provides ubiquitous images for electronic communication: simple, generic illustrations of subject matter, rather than images specifically connected to each story. Yet, gradually MT was able to increase the range and type of images despite limited financial resources because of sympathetic press officers, and social and political activists, who supplied relevant images for its features.[88]

However, as MT's income increased, it was able to invest more resources into the images and design, and it no longer had to rely upon sympathetic publicity staff or personal connections to social movements, non-profit organisations or political bodies. This is expected of a magazine distributed nationally because it has to invest in its presentation on the shelf against the competition, so that newsagents and distributors know that it is more likely to sell than if it had remained static in look.

The move from two-column to three- and four-column pages during the 1980s increased the flexibility to arrange text, graphics and images. From 1981, variations of two-, three- and four-column pages also helped to differentiate editorial sections, alongside the use of rules or borders as well as differentiating type or fonts (e.g. bold, italics). Three or four columns permit flex-

---

87 Hammarling 1996.
88 Ibid.

ibility for integrating images, charts, sidebars and tables, all of which contributed to MT's compartmentalisation and transformation into a magazine. With the shift to the third format and an increase in wordage for features, it also meant a greater integration of white space and images to help make the ideas and commentary more accessible to the average centre-left newsagent browser.

While graphics and illustrations were used to help 'make its content more accessible and available',[89] illustrations can draw out the essence of an article, the way a headline encapsulates the primary focus, if not the perspective presented therein. As art editor, Jan Brown sent copies of articles with notes in the margin to the illustrator(s) who was (were) commissioned for artwork for each issue. As an illustrator, John Minnion, points out, that even the most imaginative creative editor of a periodical, like *New Statesman* or MT, can be 'too much of a word-minded person to be a good commissioner of illustrations'[90] (i.e. 'too literal');[91] it is important for editors to understand how imagery works, which is why good editors will recognise the necessary role that art editors or directors provide. Although Jacques recognised his own limitations, it did not stop him from rejecting suggestions, even though he solicited ideas for cover images from anyone attending cover meetings as well as Channel Five's section editor, since there was a potential greater variety of material for illustrations and graphics drawn from its coverage.[92]

Beginning with his image of Ayatollah Khomeini in the February 1980 issue, Minnion's line-drawn caricatures of other leading politicians of the day, including Thatcher and Norman Tebbit, many of which were commissioned especially for MT, became a regular visual feature, but not all caricatures were restricted to MT, since most illustrators, like other freelance artists and writers, often sold work on commission to different outlets. These satirical and humorous images contributed to its appearance as a contemporary political magazine, in part because of commissioned images adding to MT's appeal and some unique or distinguishing features vis-à-vis its competitors.[93] Minnion was the first of a number of artists and illustrators, such as Paul Bateman, Jane Smith and Clifford Harper, whose work appeared in MT during the 1980s and which might have appealed to or created a sense of familiarity for those newsagent browsers who had encountered their work elsewhere. Images were either dir-

---

89   Jacques 1978b, p. 270.
90   Minnion 1996.
91   Brown 1996.
92   E.g. Brown 1996; Jacques 1996d; Perryman 1994b; Taylor 1995; Townsend 1996.
93   Minnion 1996.

ectly commissioned or adapted for MT's use, which contributed to its topicality and visual appeal, and increased costs.

As illustrations, graphics and photographs became more integrated with the text, they became part of the very fabric of the magazine. Images were no longer just illustrations of the subject matter, but were used to add something more than what was in the text.[94] For example, as Brown explained, the image of Joan Crawford facing the reader from the front seat of the Ford motorcar, which was laid out over the two pages of the third format (a space of 17.8 by 11.7 inches) as part of Stuart Hall's introduction to the 'New Times' issue,[95] signified the hope and forward looking vision that 'modern times' had embodied for an earlier era. This was a period when people were facing significant shifts in society, culture and the economy, and to which the 'New Times' analysis was attempting to point to this earlier conjunctural shift as on a parallel to that of the late 1980s.[96] This image fit in with the sense of a shift in 'sensibilities' as a result of a number of leading debates taking place across the left and in the academy, not only about Thatcherism and the future of Labour, but also around the new intellectual and political developments associated with postmodernism and identity politics.

The change to offset photolithography and the innovations in layout and design together enabled the greater use of photographic imagery and graphic illustrations in the second and third formats, which helped to transform MT into a magazine. Even the advertisements in the first format, for example, used images sparingly and were laid out in the conventional manner of display ads, while most ads for books and journals were text only. It is really the use of advertising, however, that becomes a core element in the second and third formats that clearly distinguishes their look from the first-format's journal form. The use of advertising added a sense of colour and even 'dynamism', in terms of meeting the requirements of those seeking space for their 'goods for sale' in the magazine, which helped to connotate a sense of affluence or prosperity.[97] The use of more commercial, colourful advertising helps to connotate professionalism and a similarity to other magazines on newsagents' shelves, thereby enabling MT to compete against other left magazines for readers.

---

94 Brown 1996.
95 Hall 1988d.
96 Hall and Jacques 1989a. Brown indicated that it had been a difficult image to find (Brown 1996).
97 Consumer magazines convey these connotations just through the colours of their images, let alone the content of those images, such as beautiful models and luxury items (e.g. Owen 1991).

Advertising was a key element in MT's transformation from a journal into a magazine, not only as a major source of revenue and visual engagement, but also as a means to appeal to prospective readers. While advertising is integral to commercial magazines because it keeps the cover price down by helping to pay for production and distribution costs, it requires a substantial proportion of space, usually between 40 and 60 percent of pagination. This in turn helps to define the appearance of a magazine and will even draw in browsers, since readers will often read particular magazines for their ads.[98] Non-political, consumer advertising brought MT some legitimacy in the eyes of the magazine trade as it suggested that its readership was a valuable source of potential consumers of commodities rather than just audiences for political ideas.

Back cover ads for Soviet bloc and CPGB publications from Central Books or Collet's (an independent left bookshop close to the CPGB) comprised most of the advertising in the first format. Advertising varied from a half-page to a maximum of one-and-a-half pages on the inside, accounting for only two percent of space by 1973 (Table 5). From that year, Klugmann was able to recruit commercial publishers, such as Penguins and Macmillan, wanting to advertise their expanding lists of books on Marxism and by Marxists, since MT was reaching a niche market through the Communist University of London in the 1970s.[99] Most extra advertising was for the July issue, reproduced weeks in advance, when the annual CUL took place. Advertising remained, nonetheless, a minor, even negligible, part of the journal until its transformation into a magazine with the October 1979 issue.

Advertising's importance grew during the 1980s, although initially in the second format it was still seen as an adjunct to editorial: a means to supplement MT's income and not integral to its image and identity. Only 1.75 of the 32 inside pages were allocated for advertising at first and these were primarily near the back of each issue, reinforcing the idea that advertising was secondary and an add-on or after-thought and not integral to the journal. However, with the interest of commercial and academic publishers, in part due to the growing success of the CUL by the mid-1970s, advertising came to include the inside front cover and both sides of the back covers, which altogether brought the total number of pages dedicated to advertising to 4.75 by 1979. Although miniscule by the standards of MT's later two formats (let alone commercial magazines), this was still a dramatic increase of more than double the total space between the first format's last two sample years of 1973 and 1978 (Table 5).

---

98   Perryman 1994b.
99   Klugmann 1976d.

As the importance of advertising to the periodical's professionalisation and transformation was recognised, MT increased its efforts to recruit a broader range of advertising which helped to enhance its image. To expand editorial space and increase revenue to meet rising production and distribution costs, advertising was rapidly expanded as a significant proportion of total space: from 4.8 percent in 1978 to 18.8 percent in 1983 to 28.5 percent in 1988 (Table 6). Advertising was gradually expanded throughout MT: ads were integrated into features by the mid-1980s, with whole pages set aside for ads by 1988, allowing MT to retain a visual separation of advertising and editorial. In addition, advertising inserts were included in increasing numbers into the third format, although initially they were used for promoting MT and its events, and later for other periodicals, such as *Feminist Review* and *New Left Review*, and for campaigning organisations, such as the African National Congress and the War on Want, and even non-political outlets, such as bicycle shops.

Marxism Today's recruitment of consumer and non-political advertising alarmed many party members. Traditionally, the left has been suspicious of the influence of advertisers since the level of influence they exert can be directly related to the level of their financial contributions to commercial media, which in turn exerts pressure on other (state, public and non-profit) media, directly and indirectly, via competition for readers, listeners and viewers (even when the latter are not technically 'competing' for audiences to sell to advertisers). Advertisers provide subsidies for magazines to keep cover prices low, or lower than what would otherwise be necessary for the reader to pay, so that the publisher could still recover the full costs of production and distribution. Thus, advertisers help to subsidise publications for better-off audiences with a greater amount of disposable income in the hope of gaining a profitable return on their investment.[100] The covert and overt links between advertising and editorial in commercial magazines is not surprising: editorial texts constitute a continuum of a 'commodity-based culture' because the editorial promotes products that are actually being advertised elsewhere within the magazine.[101] Similar links can be found in left publications, where articles or reviews (of books, plays etc.) are placed next to related advertisements, including throughout MT's first format. Such practices are not seen as insidious

---

100 E.g. Curran identified how the radical working-class press was censored and put out of business by a capitalist press that was (and is) subsidised by advertising and could thereby offer cheaper newspapers to working-class readers (Curran and Seaton 1991). Williams's critique of the extreme rightwards shift of newspapers during the 1970s also highlights this aspect (Williams 1978).
101 McCracken 1993.

because there was no threat of subverting a periodical's ideology or editorial line, if the advertisers hold the same or similar views or there is no single advertiser (or group) that supplies a substantial part of the periodical's revenue. Nevertheless, the imperatives for recruiting advertising may wield a general influence over topics, interviewees, contributors, design, formats and writing styles to attract ideal audiences for advertisers.

Of the second format's 60 back covers, from the October 1981 to the September 1986 issues, which provided a prime advertising space, 34 were of books, bookshops, publishers and magazines (57 percent connected to print), and 20 (or one-third) of which were connected in some way to MT or the CPGB (eight were for Collet's Bookshop). In addition, three advertised MT events and one was for a Labour Party festival. Another eight were for campaigns or political organisations with four more for (political) educational media outlets. There were some non-political consumer ads, including one for a futon company, another for an electronic interactive database and a third for a musical instrument shop.

The third format's back covers, from October 1986 to December 1991, continued with some of the same advertisers, such as Progressive Tours with 11 out of 63 back covers, compared to the three out of the 60 second-format back covers, and eight for MT merchandising, including four for Central Committee Outfitters and two for MT's 'Cred Card'. Of course, Progressive Tours specialised in Communist countries and also frequently advertised on the inside covers when it was not using the back cover. There were 15 out of 63 back covers used for campaigns, rallies and organisations, such as the National Union of Public Employees or the ANC. Unlike the second format, there were only eight (13 percent) for print (related) media (including bookshops) versus the 34 (57 percent) in the second format. However, 13 third-format back covers were used to advertise theatre, films, art exhibits and music, which is four times more than the second-format's three back covers for arts. There were also more non-political consumer goods, such as five back covers advertising bicycles and related merchandise, one for an electronic interactive database (which frequently advertised on inside covers), and one for a mortgage broker who used the same background as the October 1988 'New Times' issue and framed the ad with 'New Times' for (re)mortgaging a home!

8   Editorial Sections: Features

All types of periodicals target audiences through the presentation of content via the formatting of editorial into sections, which clearly highlight a publication's priorities and the accessibility of content. By examining the percentage of editorial devoted to different subjects over the course of *Marxism Today*'s history, we see shifts in priorities and changes in accessibility (Tables 4, 5, 6). Both editors, James Klugmann and Martin Jacques, retained features as the single largest and most important editorial section throughout their editorships, although content, approaches and subject matter shifted, as did their ideological trajectories and political strategies. The differences between and within formats arose in part as features shrunk as a proportion of total space over time, which was especially evident in its last 12 years.

These shifts as outlined through the analysis of the breakdown of editorial content, however, demonstrate Jacques's actions as editor, as he sought 'to banish' at least two of the three basic types of features that he identified that had been published by Klugmann. The first type was what he called 'legitimation and apologist' features, i.e. official Communist Party speeches and documents, including from the CPGB's sister parties, since they would have reinforced MT's position as an official party channel. The second type was what he called 'esoteric Marxist', such as those published around the 'dialectics of nature' debate, because they were intelligible only to a small group of intellectuals.[102] Both would have limited MT's room for manoeuvre by restricting its editorial autonomy (and content) while also limiting its appeal to non-party readers.

The third type of feature, the 'political-analytical', provided what Jacques called 'a conjunctural analysis' of contemporary political, social and economic developments, which he claimed were the 'creative application of Marxist and Gramscian ideas to British politics' and had a broader appeal (not least because they tended to deal with contemporary issues more than just historical, official or esoteric matters).[103] Jacques reiterated this point in his memos to the PC and EC in the two years leading up to the second format.[104] This focus was meant to enhance MT's appeal, which was the means for increasing the audience for Gramscian and Eurocommunist ideas, and its influence in the 'war of position' *within* the party.

Under Klugmann, features remained the single most important editorial section in the journal, proportionately retaining a minimum of 60 percent or more of annual pagination (Table 5). The first format's single greatest change was the introduction of the 'Editorial Comments' section in the July 1960 MT. It reaches nearly one-in-five pages (18.5 percent) of the twelve issues' 384 pages

---

102   Jacques 1996b. E.g. Alce 1977.
103   Jacques 1996b.
104   Jacques 1996a. E.g. Jacques 1977, 1978c, 1978d, 1978e, 1979f, 1979g, 1979h, 1979i.

in volume 12 (1968), for example, but which declined to 11.8 percent (of total pagination) in 1973 and 9.3 percent in 1978 (Table 5). Since the latter year was Jacques's first full (calendar) year of his editorship, this shift to less than one-in-ten pages reflected his concern that 'Editorial Comments' would be seen as the party's 'voice' on any issues discussed therein and opponents would have been alert to any political or ideological 'deviations', which could have made his position as editor more tenuous.[105]

Interestingly, the number of features under Klugmann's editorship range from a low of 38 (1973) to a high of 58 (1958) in the first format, and under Jacques's editorship, from a low of 42 (1978) (less than four per issue) to a high of 61 (1983) in the second format and 60 (1988) in the third format (Table 6). Three out of four sample years in the first format, 1968, 1973 and 1978, and all within the first format's second (and last) decade, published almost the same number of features each year (41, 38, 42 respectively), which points to a certain regularity of production within the limitations based upon the size and format. The first sample year, though, has almost the same number of features as the sample years for each of the second and third formats, without the same high level of pagination (58 versus 60 and 61) (Table 6).

Yet, even though the first format's first full calendar year, 1958, includes the most features of that format and the most features of more than 4,000 words (36) and which accounted for three-quarters (76.8 percent) of pagination, it includes almost the same number of discussion items, 27, as the next two sample years, 28 each in 1973 and 1978, which account for almost the same proportion of pages (17.7, 17.1, 18.1 percent) in all three sample years under Klugmann's editorship (Table 5). The 1958 tally was before the 'Editorial Comments' section was introduced, which absorbed 10 to 20 percent of pagination per annum. Even though MT was only launched in October 1957, there was more or less the same amount of discussion items in that first full calendar year, 1958, as there were in the following sample years of 1968 and 1973, demonstrating a certain consistency in Klugmann's attempts to encourage a sense of debate and readership participation in the discussion section. This demonstrates what critics from opposing tendencies, such as Irene Brennan and Monty Johnstone, saw as Klugmann's 'democratic' or supportive commitment to debate, even if he was not willing to take a stand himself against the shifting, parameters of sanctioned debate.[106]

---

105 E.g. Jacques 1978e.
106 Brennan 1996; Johnstone 1995.

Despite doubling the number of sections with the second format, Jacques retained the emphasis on having four features (3,500 to 6,500 words) per issue, rather than expanding any other section.[107] The number of features shown in Table 6 that are 4,000 words or more drops to 40 percent of all features by the third format sample year (1988), albeit with nearly an equal number (i.e. 23) that are just under or close to 4,000 words. This compares to fewer features, albeit with a greater percentage of 4,000-plus word features, in the remaining sample years, with 1978 as the worst, with 76.8 percent of features (33 out of 42), which also had the greatest percentage of 'Marxism and Political Theory' features (which matches the same number for 1958: eight). Although 1968 has the greatest number of 'CP Reprints' of all sample years, 21 out of 41 features, it was a significant year for the Communist world with Czechoslovakia's 'Prague Spring' and the 'Tet Offensive' in Vietnam. Although MT included statements from CPGB and sister parties, 1968 had only the third largest percentage of 4,000-plus features of all six sample years (at 63.4 percent, slightly ahead of 1958's 62 percent). Given the 'common sense' expectations of Communist prose, it is perhaps surprising that many of these statements appear to be less verbose than one might expect.

While the actual number of features remained fairly consistent during the 1980s, they declined as a proportion of total pagination to barely more than one-third (36.6 percent), albeit with a larger format and a much greater number of available pages: e.g. the total pagination for sample years 1983 and 1988 increased by more than 54 and 67 percent respectively over the first format's standard 384 pages per annum. Features retained their importance and centrality to Jacques's editorship while expanding the range of editorial sections to appeal to other (and not necessarily competing) audiences and their interests. This proportionate decline of features was a result of the expansion of the total available pagination, which enabled a shift towards compartmentalisation as part of MT's ongoing transformation from a journal into a magazine, as compartments separate editorial into discrete 'bites' for easier 'digestion' by readers. Ideally, this process encourages a range of different readers to buy the magazine, while using such 'fragmentation' of interests to attract a broader range of potential advertisers. Although the editorial structure in 1978, just a year before the second format launch, was still essentially identical with MT's launch issue two decades earlier, it was virtually unrecognisable with the third format launch less than seven years later.

---

107   Jacques 1979g, 1979i.

The shift in topics was more pronounced by 1988, where British politics and social issues dominated (50.8 percent) as priorities for *Marxism Today* (Table 4). However, Tables 4, 5 and 6 together indicate that the changes in topics cannot simply be read as indicative of an ideological shift *per se* between the editorships of Klugmann and Jacques. If you look at the breakdown in Table 4, the percentages indicate that there were similarities between all three formats across three decades in some subjects. There are between two and five features for every sample year, except for 1988 (none), with a primary focus on the CPGB, for example, although the variation in percentages ranges from 3.3 to 12.2. On the other hand, in 1988 there were four features (6.6 percent) on 'International CPs', with the impetus of the massive political changes taking place in Eastern Europe that were of general interest beyond the Communist Party, the same as 1973 and 1978 (four features each), but more than in either 1958 or 1983 (two and one features respectively). Only 1968 had more feature coverage of 'International CPs' than any other year (seven articles or 17.1 percent) because of that year's significance for the Communist world.

TABLE 4   Breakdown of feature articles by topic in selected years, 1958–88

Percentage of features by topic	1958	1968	1973	1978	1983	1988
TOTAL (No of features)	58	41	38	42	61	60
1. International CPs[108]	3.4	17.1	10.5	9.5	1.7	6.6
2. CPGB	3.4	12.2	5.3	9.5	3.3	–
3. Labour Party	3.4	–	–	4.8	8.3	8.2
4. British politics[109]	6.9	4.9	7.9	9.5	16.7	21.3
5. Industrial relations & trade unions	3.4	12.2	–	7.1	5.0	4.9
6. Economics	12.1	–	7.9	–	1.7	4.9
7. International politics	27.6	19.5	21.1	7.1	21.7	8.2
8. Feminism/Women	–	2.4	–	2.4	10.0	4.9
9. Marxism & political theory	13.8	7.3	13.2	19.0	3.3	1.6
10. Arts & culture[110]	8.6	4.9	7.9	9.5	11.7	6.6
11. Education	1.7	–	–	2.4	1.7	1.6
12. Peace	1.7	2.4	2.6	–	5.0	–

---

108   1988 is the only year in this category which does not include any official party documents or speeches.

109   For 1988, this category includes 'New Times' articles.

110   The figures for 1983 and 1988 do not include any 'Channel Five' coverage.

TABEL 4   Breakdown of feature articles by topic in selected years, 1958–88 (*cont.*)

Percentage of features by topic	1958	1968	1973	1978	1983	1988
13. Science & technology	1.7	–	5.3	4.8	1.7	–
14. History	6.9	9.8	10.5	7.1	–	1.6
15. Social issues, racism, psychology, religion	5.2	7.3	7.9	7.1	8.3	29.5
TOTAL (due to rounding, may not add up to 100.0)	99.8	100.0	100.1	99.8	100.1	99.9

Actual numbers of articles	1958	1968	1973	1978	1983	1988
TOTAL (No of features)	58	41	38	42	61	60
1. International CPs	2	7	4	4	1	4
2. CPGB	2	5	2	4	2	–
3. Labour Party	2	–	–	2	5	5
4. British politics	4	2	3	4	10	13
5. Industrial relations & trade unions	2	5	–	3	3	3
6. Economics	7	–	3	–	1	3
7. International politics	16	8	8	3	13	5
8. Feminism/Women	–	1	–	1	6	3
9. Marxism & political theory	8	3	5	8	2	1
10. Arts & culture	5	2	3	4	7	4
11. Education	1	–	–	1	1	1
12. Peace	1	1	1	–	3	–
13. Science & Technology	1	–	2	2	1	–
14. History	4	4	4	3	–	1
15. Social issues, racism, psychology, religion	3	3	3	3	5	18

Some differences arise in the feature coverage if the two categories, 'International CPs' and 'CPGB', are included together: 1968 has the most coverage (29.3 percent or 12 features), with two-thirds of that in 1978 (19.0 percent or eight features) and half that level for 1973 (15.8 percent or six features). The other three years are minimal with 1983 (5.0 percent) beating out 1958 (6.8 percent) and 1988 (6.6 percent) for the fewest features, although 1988 included coverage of the reforms championed by Mikhail Gorbachev in the USSR. If 'International Politics' is also examined, although 1983 rates high with 21.7 percent, when 'International CPs' is factored in, the years 1958 (31.0 percent), 1968 (36.6 percent) and 1973 (31.6 percent), reflecting Klugmann's international

Communist connections, beat out all three of Jacques's sample years: 1978 (16.6 percent), 1983 (23.4 percent) and 1988 (14.8 percent).

There are some interesting differences over the thirty years between the different editorships that we can see by focusing on Table 4 more closely. For example, the focus on 'British politics' is much greater under Jacques's editorship, rising from 9.5 percent of features in 1978 to 21.3 percent by 1988, including some 'New Times' features. More specifically, if we examine the features that focus on the CPGB, Labour Party and 'British politics', then Jacques's MT consistently has had about one-in-four features on domestic and party politics in each of the three sample years. There was minimal (two out of 58 in 1958) to no coverage in features on the Labour Party in the sample years of Klugmann's editorship,[111] whereas Jacques's editorship shifted from 4.8 percent to around eight percent in the second and third formats (two features in 1978 and five each in 1983 and 1988).[112]

Another aspect of the shift that is evident is the focus on a broad miscellany of interests and concerns categorised under the 'social, psychological and religious issues', and not otherwise covered by the other categories in Table 4. This includes topics such as abortion, racism, masculinity and alcoholism, and accounted for nearly 30 percent of all features (18 stories) in 1988, but which outnumbers in absolute terms all previous sample years combined (17 stories). While this category of features gradually increased in terms of the share between 1958 and 1983, from 5.2 percent to 8.3 percent respectively, this works out to three features per year except for the five in 1983. In some ways, this shift in focus away from party politics in 1988 spoke to the demoralisation that gripped the left in the aftermath of Labour's third consecutive general election defeat in 1987 by Thatcher's Tories.

What we can ascertain from this breakdown is that the focus in 1978 had been on the Gramscian influenced ideas adopted by the CPGB and supported by MT in the aftermath of the 1977 Congress. Thus, we can see that of all sample years, 1978 has the greatest focus on 'Marxism and Political Theory' at 19 percent of features. Since 1983 covers the critical general election year, it should be no surprise that the feature topics on 'British politics' and the 'Labour Party' are at their greatest coverage to date, particularly as the second

---

111   It is perhaps a chance occurrence in the years sampled since amongst active CPGB members there was considerable interest in the UK's largest working-class party.
112   The focus on the CPGB drops to virtually nothing in 1988, even though the 'New Times' project did become part of its 1989 manifesto, a copy of which was bundled with the June 1989 MT.

format was much closer to a newsmagazine, which was important as it moved into national distribution by 1981, where there was a broader potential audience for Labour, rather than Communist, politics.

The focus on topics, such as education, is minimal which is somewhat surprising given the readership for MT's second and third formats. The sample year, 1983, is the only one that rates over 10 percent for features on 'Art & Culture', even though Channel Five, introduced in October 1981, was dedicated to covering arts and culture, indicating that some stories on culture were considered important enough to receive 'feature treatment'. That same year, 1983, also has the greatest focus on 'Feminism/Women' at 10 percent (six features), which is twice as many as in 1988 and one feature more than all the other sample years combined (with none or one story in each year: 1958, 1968, 1973 and 1978). 'Peace' came in at five percent (three features) in 1983, which is the total for all three of Klugmann's sample years combined and no coverage in Jacques's other two sample years.

For the BDA, 1983 had the best coverage of all the sample years and demonstrates that despite claims to the contrary, the focus remained on domestic politics and Labour (and even the CPGB) over new social movements. The number of features in Table 4 that focus on 'Economics' and 'Industrial Relations & Trade Unions', however, are greatest proportionately in the sample years 1958 and 1968, respectively, and neither topic exceeds five percent in the second and third format sample years. Yet, when we consider the actual number of features just on 'Industrial Relations & Trade Unions', we see a consistency in Jacques's editorship of three features per year which combined (nine) outnumbers the seven features from all three of Klugmann's sample years. While these might be an anomaly, it is clear that in certain categories that one expects a Marxist theoretical journal to cover, Jacques's editorship sometimes was not far off the mark. It is also contrary to then contemporary criticisms that Jacques's editorship was not as committed to covering labour or union issues, though MT did promote perspectives that challenged traditionalist perspectives on unions.

Jacques did mostly dispense with features primarily concerned with history, despite his own academic background in economic history. This does not take away from the historical background provided in other articles primarily concerned with more contemporary topics. While proportionately the number of historical features published under Klugmann's editorship varied between 6.9 and 10.5 percent, there were four features every sample year, three times as many as Jacques published in all sample years (i.e. 12 to four). This difference speaks to Jacques's focus on making changes to the party and to the political directions of Labour, whereas Klugmann's more cautious approach meant his-

TABLE 5 Breakdown of editorial contents,[a] 1958–88

	1958	1968	1973	1978	1983	1988
Total number of pages	384.0	384.0	384.0	396.0	592.0	644.0
Advertising[b] (%)	0.1	0.8	2.0	4.8	18.8	28.5
Features	76.8	60.5	68.1	72.6	49.2	36.6
Discussion/Viewpoint/Comment	17.7	17.1	18.1	5.9	1.4	0.5
Letters	–	–	–	–	1.3	3.0
Editorial comments	–	18.5	11.8	9.3	–	–
Focus	–	–	–	–	8.1	7.5
Notes/Update/Classifieds[c]	–	–	–	–	2.0	2.5
Reviews[d] (Books)	5.3	3.1	–	7.3	5.6	4.1
Channel 5/Culture[e]	–	–	–	–	11.6	12.2
Postmark[f] (column)	–	–	–	–	–	1.4
Close-up[g]	–	–	–	–	–	1.9
Table of contents[h]	–	–	–	–	2.0	1.9
Totals	99.9	100.0	100.0	99.9	100.0	100.1

a These figures do not include cover pages, supplements or inserts.
b This category includes exchange advertisements, and CPGB and MT promotional copy.
c Includes space for contributors' backgrounds.
d Includes 'review articles'.
e This includes the 18-page 'Review of 87' which focused on arts, culture and sports, but it does not include book reviews (26.5 pages) which are separated for this chart.
f It started with the April 1988 issue and there was always a different person writing about a different place, such as Glasgow or Malaga.
g A one-page profile of someone in the news.
h The first format's inside front cover listed the table of contents and is not included in the editorial breakdown.

tory might have been a safer topic than contemporary political issues (or any article dealing with the history of the party).

Feature articles were MT's primary content and *raison d'être* through all three formats, even as their share of the periodical eventually shrank to 37 percent by 1988 (Table 5). However, it should be kept in mind that under Jacques there were increases in the number of pages and their size, and in the second format, typefaces were initially smaller when compared against those used in the first format, which meant that features under Jacques were allotted at least an equal amount of space and wordage in absolute rather than relative terms.

TABLE 6 Comparison of selected modes of presentation, 1958–88

	1958	1968	1973	1978	1983	1988
Total number of pages	384.0	384.0	384.0	396	592	644
Features (percentage)	76.8	60.5	68.1	72.6	49.2	36.6
Features (total)	58	41	38	42	61	60
Features (4,000+ words)	36	26	26	33	30	24[a]
Discussion items	27	28	28	11	6[b]	4
Reviews (books)	5	2	1	9	24	38
Non-CP reprints[c]	–	1	1	3	1	2
CP-related reprints	7	21	10	7	2[d]	1
Interviews (feature)	–	–	–	3	6	6
Interviews (C5)	–	–	–	–	9	12
Roundtables (features)	1	–	–	–	5	6
Vox pops	–	–	–	–	1	1

a However, there was nearly an equal number of features (i.e. 23) just under 4,000 words, indicating an achievement of professionalisation by the greater uniformity in length.
b Half were published in 'Viewpoint' in November and December 1983.
c Reprints include articles based upon talks and reports adapted for MT.
d This includes a short statement (about 250 words) on Iran adopted at the 38th National Congress.

9   Features: Alternative Modes of Presentation

Two important innovations within the features section that provided alternative presentational modes to the essay, to make ideas and issues more accessible to the general reader, were those of interviews and roundtable discussions, especially since dialogue often reads more easily than scholarly or journalistic prose. Although neither innovation was completely new to MT (although there are no interviews in the first format's three sample years), it was only under Jacques's editorship that they were systematically developed and used to promote (reformist) ideas on issues that challenged traditionalists' perspectives (e.g. Thatcherism, miners' strike).[113] This contrast in the alternative modes of presentation from the standard argumentative essay for 'journals of opinion' helps to reinforce the idea of the differences between the journal and magazine form(at)s as identified via the theory of the periodical.

---

113   E.g. Baker et al. 1985; Jenkins et al. 1982 (Pimlott 2000a, pp. 184–6).

The roundtable developed in tandem with the upsurge in social movements and industrial struggles in the early 1980s,[114] and they were, at first, attempts to bring in those normally excluded from participating in public debates because of a lack of time, skills or confidence. However, as the demands of the production cycle shifted, with formatting and design changes from second to third formats, so, too, did MT's political line and the types of roundtable participants and contributors: from union and CPGB members, to socialist scholars, and social and political activists, to public figures (e.g. mainstream journalists, Labour politicians) (Chapter 5).

It offered a different way of appealing to and addressing prospective readers. These dialogues also appeared 'spontaneous', despite the labour-intensive selection, transcription and editing processes that were necessary to make them accessible within the constraints of a feature article; however, it also meant that there was no need for participants to be able to write.[115] It was important to promote dialogue between different perspectives in the second format, if the broad democratic alliance was to have meaning, and it was equally useful as a tactic against accusations of bias, if different viewpoints on an issue were literally coming out of the mouths of others.

The roundtable's conversational format enabled participants to engage with each other's ideas, although the display of dialogue also performed a highly symbolic function in representing opposing positions, with which readers might identify, and conveying to all readers, party and non-party, MT's self-promoted 'open politics', which was part of its promotional and publicity efforts.[116] Individual photographs contributed to this material representation of different roundtable participants as individual perspectives being (re)presented rather than something dictated by the editor or editorial line. Nevertheless, some participants felt that their own viewpoints were not being represented as well as others: John Hoffman, MTEB member and roundtable participant, said the roundtable on Marx (March 1983) worked very well, although he felt that the 'old-fashioned Marxist point-of-view should perhaps have had more representation'.[117]

The format also enabled Jacques to present critiques of orthodox left or traditionalist positions while remaining ostensibly 'neutral' to protect his and MT's

---

114   MT's very first roundtable was one in name only because contributions were summarised and written up in essay format defeating the mode's purpose (MT 1957a, 1957b).
115   Taylor 1995.
116   E.g. MTEB 1981b, 1983, 1985a. A quote from Peter Jenkins, a *Guardian* columnist, about MT's 'open politics' was used in publicity efforts in the early 1980s.
117   MTEB 1983, p. 3.

positions from internal opponents. Thus, roundtable features could be used to signal critiques of Arthur Scargill and the National Union of Mineworkers, as with the miners' strike roundtable in the April 1985 issue, for example, without Jacques and MT being seen as too closely aligned with such a position.[118] Despite the 'plausible deniability' that Jacques's position represented, opponents made the connections in their criticisms since the choice of participants, host(s), transcription and editing were all under the editor's control.

When interviews and roundtables were well received, there was pressure from readers, party leaders and/or the MTEB to use these formats more frequently. Sometimes, however, it was 'too much of a good thing' and complaints were made that MT was making too much use of roundtables or interviews.[119] Roundtables and interviews, however, did not always work due to any one or more of the various factors or processes involved, such as the selection of participants, chairing or editing. It was not always easy to know ahead of time whether or not roundtables or interviews would work and provide good copy.[120]

There are three interviews and no roundtables out of 42 features in the initial full calendar year of Jacques's editorship. Interviews, like roundtables, become a possible alternative mode of presentation for ideas in the second and third formats, doubling to six each in 1983 and 1988, while 12 interviews were published in Channel Five in 1988, which was an increase of one-third from nine in 1983. This increase is accounted for by the shift in contributors for Channel Five, where increasing numbers of journalists from mainstream media outlets are likely to have greater access to prominent figures in the arts and politics, especially compared to volunteers and staff from a small 'leftist rag'. This was especially true for access to high-profile interviewees, like Ted Heath, the former Tory Prime Minister, 1970–74, who was interviewed by Hugo Young of *The Guardian*.

The interviews of various individuals for the Channel Five section did not necessarily make MT much different from other contemporary arts, media and culture magazines, although the fact that prominent mainstream and alternative artists, broadcasters and other cultural producers were being interviewed, did ensure that there was a topicality in keeping with developments in the arts and culture, and an opening towards advertising for different kinds of cultural products and programmes, all of which helped to make MT feel more contemporaneous alongside commercial magazines on the newsagent's shelf. The combination of feature interviews and Channel Five interviews contributed to

---

118 Baker et al. 1985. See also Ackers 2014.
119 E.g. Jacques 1984b; MTEB 1981b.
120 E.g. MTEB 1981b, 1983, 1985a.

a greater sense of a multiplicity of voices in the magazine against traditionalists and other left critics, who claimed that it was promoting a singular or particular worldview.

10   Modes of/for Discussion

While there was a multiplicity of perspectives on a range of issues, to which the interviews contributed, the left critics' claim against *Marxism Today* was in terms of the way the periodical promoted a particular perspective across the left via other means than features and interviews, such as via the 'Discussion' section and letters-to-the-editor contributions. It was the second defining adjective in MT's subtitle, the party's 'theoretical and discussion journal', that made clear that contrary views would be published.

There is an annual average of more than two 'Discussion' items per issue, which drops by more than half, from more than two per issue or 27 or 28 in the three preceding sample years, to just under one per issue in 1978 (11), six in 1983 and four in 1988, partly because the section was renamed and subsequently eliminated during the 1980s in the transition via the second to the third formats. The 'Discussion' items were, however, an integral part of journal's first format, by which regular readers could be contributors to debates initiated by a feature or discussion article, or expect to read responses to features in the 'Discussion' section, which contributed to a general expectation that the audience would be overwhelmingly composed of party members as regular readers and subscribers, who could therefore be expected to follow discussions over months and even years. This is not what one would expect with a magazine, especially one distributed to newsagents nationwide. However, under Jacques's editorship, roundtables, letters and other sections, such as 'Viewpoint', became replacements for 'Discussion', part of MT's *raison d'être* since 1957.

The role of 'Discussion' in the first format was to provide a space for responses to features, though MT set out the topics to be discussed which were often linked to party issues or Marxist theory. A topic could last for months or a year or more,[121] when the editor allowed it, but such an expectation for ongoing contributions to 'Discussion' requires a stable readership, such as that provided via membership-only or subscription-based journals. It is not appropriate for a magazine sold via newsagents, whereby the incentive is to reach

---

121   E.g. The 'Trends in Youth Culture' debate initiated by Jacques in September 1973 was completed 19 months later (April 1975), although not every issue published responses (Jacques 1973, 1975a).

as many readers as possible with discrete or self-contained issues, so that new readers do not feel left out of the conversation of some kind of in-group audience. As James Mills wrote about contemporary Victorian periodicals in the nineteenth-century marketplace: periodicals must flatter, not challenge, their readers and they must make an immediate appeal to prospective readers (i.e. purchasers) of their texts.[122]

Under Jacques, 'Discussion' initially remained an integral part of the periodical's first format, which was used to encourage debate and draw in traditionalists, loyalists and reformists, although the longest debate took place before the second format's October 1979 launch issue.[123] There was even an attempt to develop a system, 'The Grid', to ensure all relevant topics were covered through each annual cycle.[124] With the second format, Jacques wanted to have 'structured debates' only, clearly not wishing to open up discussion to just any topic or contributor and to set the agenda for debate in influencing the CPGB's political trajectory. Responses to features that were part of the 'Discussion' section were only published for a few months after the initiating article was first published.[125] The move to national newsagent distribution mitigates against carrying on debates beyond a couple or three issues because of casual purchasers of a periodical. It is difficult for occasional readers to follow responses published months after the initial appearance of the feature to which contributors are responding. This requires structuring debates in a different manner and including contributors from differing perspectives in the same issue or in the issue immediately following where the first contribution is published.

In 1983, there was only one 'Discussion' contribution (published in the August issue) in the seven issues from April to October (inclusive): the first three of those months would have been during the general election campaign in which the left was still broadly unified to try and elect Michael Foot's Labour Party. The 'Discussion' section returned as 'Viewpoint' in the November 1983 issue, providing space for, as the name change connotes, particular individual perspectives on different issues. 'Viewpoint' implies the possibility of contrasting perspectives by those holding a different 'point-of-view' without any implication that it is endorsed by the periodical.

---

122   Pykett 1990, p. 12.
123   The 'Forward March' debate spanned 13 issues (September 1978–September 1979) and both Hobsbawm's initiating feature and final response were each published in the September issue for the annual TUC conference over two successive years (Hobsbawm 1978, 1979b).
124   Jacques 1978d.
125   Jacques 1979i, p. 2.

As the venue for structured debates, 'Viewpoint' was replaced by 'Comment' with the third format launch issue of October 1986, whereby space was usually provided for just a single observation or discussion of some topic. Since 'Comment' means adding to or offering something, it need not have any kind of connection to the rest of the editorial content, a position which was reinforced by its location near the back of the magazine. Therefore, rather than being seen as an integral part of *Marxism Today* in the way in which 'Discussion' had been in the first format, 'Comment' was set up more as a newspaper's guest opinion column, whereby someone outside the editorial staff or regular columnists provides commentary on a topic or issue. 'Comment' was located near the back between 'Channel Five' and 'Notes'/'Update', and laid out alongside a number of display advertisements and classifieds, marginalised, like many of its contributors.[126] In the aftermath of the CPGB's 'civil war' and a large loss in membership, Jacques argued that there was no need to give space to certain views (e.g. Leninists, traditionalists) because one 'knew' already what they were going to say.[127] 'Comment', thus, quickly declined in importance: only six items were published in 1988 and the section was subsequently discontinued. Yet, one could also claim to know what MT was going to say, especially given the persona that had been created via its promotion and publicity; by excluding certain perspectives, Jacques removed other lines of criticism of MT's political project.

As with mainstream newspapers and periodicals, the letters-to-the-editor section provides a means by which a sampling of 'public opinion' can be presented where newspapers or periodicals have clear political-ideological or editorial lines. In the same way, MT introduced a letters page to be able to better account for a range of criticisms and compliments for what the periodical was doing. The May 1982 issue introduced the 'Letters' page to provide space for (shorter) responses than 'Discussion' had provided,[128] and for a potential greater range of, albeit shorter, viewpoints. In fact, 'Letters' was expanded regularly to two full pages to accommodate additional responses during times of intense debate, such as that which occurred on the left during this period of intensive strife around the 1984–85 miners' strike.[129] The cutbacks to the 'Discussion' section and its successors increasingly limited MT's role

---

126 E.g. Samuel 1986b; Wainwright 1988.
127 Jacques 1988a.
128 The MTEB had been more or less evenly divided over introducing 'Letters' since 1978 (e.g. MTEB 1981b).
129 Beginning with the January 1985 issue, the 'Letters' section was expanded to two pages which included room for responses to other issues in addition to the miners' strike.

in internal party discussion, which became of less importance with the third format launch in 1986 as party membership continued to decline and internal opponents left or passed away. The letters pages provided a space for internal critics and supporters who were able to make their views known, including those in stark contrast to MT's position or persona. In belated recognition of its role change, 'Letters' was renamed 'Forum' with the October 1989 issue: it had become the primary space for views that differed to those promoted by MT within the parameters of its editorial-ideological line.

11 Other Editorial Sections

To reach readers on the left outside the Communist Party and to aid in forming the broad democratic alliance, Martin Jacques argued that it was necessary for *Marxism Today* to not be seen as an official party channel. The 'Editorial Comments' section was published at the front of the journal, where discrete topics, issues and events appeared without by-lines, which suggested that it was an authoritative expression of the editor's and publisher's (i.e. the CPGB's) position, which is a common expectation of most other periodicals, commercial or Communist. The style implied a single, 'anonymous ... omniscient author'.[130] Its removal would ensure that there would be less need for the leadership to intervene, if the periodical published anything that contradicted the party line.

The section's functions were divided into two in the second format: 'Focus' and 'Notes'. Located at the front right after the 'Contents' page, the average of two to four pages of 'Focus' were composed of short, current news items on domestic and international events and campaigns, which would not otherwise have been covered by news media and which did not require feature treatment or for which there was insufficient time within the production cycle to prepare a longer piece. Ideally, the 'Focus' section was conceived as dealing with items that would be political, 'but not decisively so', *and* controversial.[131] For example, some of the early suggestions in the section's development included such topics as the 'ultra-left press' and 'monetarism'.[132]

Despite being one of the longest running sections under Jacques's editorship, ten full years from the October 1979 to September 1989 issues, there was a constant debate over the appropriate style, topics and approach in the 'Focus' section because of competition from the expansion of media outlets and news

---

130   Jones 1980; Jacques 1979i; MTEC 1978.
131   Jones 1980.
132   Ibid.; MTEB 1980, p. 2.

coverage during the 1980s, and the difficulties of maintaining the relevancy of news items for upwards of two months due to the production schedule. For example, it took six weeks of writing, editing and printing, and, as a monthly periodical, one had to plan for the issue to sit for at least two weeks on the news-stand.[133] By 1981, however, the timing had been cut to four weeks for the short 'newsy' articles in the 'Focus' section, with two weeks allocated for the production process and two weeks for sitting on the newsagent's shelf.[134] As technological changes speeded up the production process, time pressures intensified for staff to identify issues and contributors, and to meet tight deadlines.

'Focus' items seemed to date even more quickly by the end of the 1980s when a number of important political and social events began unfolding more rapidly than the production process could meet (e.g. the collapse of the Communist regimes in Eastern Europe). However, developments in new technologies, such as desktop publishing, in the late 1980s helped to speed up MT's ability to respond to the rapidity of events by scheduling last-minute 'breaking news' later in the production cycle, and contributed to higher production values, such as making reports more accessible through the integration of other visuals beyond photographs or line drawings, such as maps, charts and graphs. In 1989, 'Leader'[135] and 'Preview' (upcoming events) replaced 'Focus', and new sections were also added, such as 'Europhile' (column) and 'Eye to Eye' ('personality' interviewer, Beatrix Campbell). These changes were seen as necessary to be able to compete visually and materially, in layout, design, images and colour, with other left-of-centre periodicals because of the growing influence of the 1980s trend towards 'lifestyle' journalism and 'personality' columnists: such changes were evident even in the listings section.

The listings service of events, campaigns, publications etc., provided by 'Notes' was seen as the connection between theory and practice: a practical realisation of the BDA in the second format. It included publishing contributors' names with the announcements for campaigns, events and rallies to help maintain MT's distance from various advocacy groups, political organisations and social movements. For example, from the October 1979 issue, with the very first 'Notes' section on the last page, there are two announcements, including one for Ruskin History Workshop and another for CPGB conference on opposition to Tory cuts to the NHS: each begins respectively as follows: 'Raphael

---

133 Jones 1980; MTEB 1988b; Taylor 1989a.
134 Jacques 1996d.
135 Note the use of the conventional term, 'leader' for the 'editorial' or 'party line' of a newspaper or periodical. Any complaints against MT had little hope of succeeding by this time.

Samuel writes' and 'Steve Illiffe writes'. 'Notes' expanded from just politics, books and campaigns to include discussion groups, consumer items and leisure activities to romantic personal ads, in the third format. This wider remit revealed the influence of London listings magazines, *Time Out* and *City Limits*, which was expanded again with 'Update', the successor to 'Notes'. Their influence is not a surprise since MT drew upon designers, such as Pearce Marchbank, who had worked on *Time Out*, and writers, such as Beatrix Campbell, who was involved with *City Limits*.[136] 'Update' drew in new readers and extra revenue, and it provided a space for the relaunch of MT discussion groups, which had been stopped by the party leadership in 1979. The introduction of personal ads in the classifieds provoked controversy over 'alternative sexualities'.[137]

However, the introduction of the 'MT Leader' in October 1989, which focussed on the Eastern European revolutions,[138] raised the possibility of a clash between the party leadership and the periodical. Whereas Jacques claimed that the 'MT Leader' was a way of intervening publicly in the aftermath of the launch of the New Times project, the party's leading body, the Political Committee, expressed concern that MT's 'editorialising' would be seen as the CPGB's position, which ironically had been Jacques's position when he wanted to dispense with the 'Editorial Comments' section back in 1979.[139] A discussion between the PC and the MT Editorial Board resolved the issue in Jacques's favour: the 'Leader' was continued.[140] This was the symbolic embodiment of MT's editorial autonomy, after it had been achieved politically and practically. It also demonstrates how little influence the leadership was able (or willing) to wield over Jacques and MT, despite the party's ongoing subsidies for its production and distribution.

12 Cultural Coverage: From 'Reviews' to 'Channel Five'

Books remained the primary focus of 'cultural' coverage from 1957 until 1981.[141] That *Marxism Today* did not have to qualify the title of its 'Reviews' section with any kind of adjective, emphasises the importance that books held during

---

136 *City Limits* was started by a number of left-wing journalists and staff after a strike at *Time Out* in 1981 over changes to the arrangement of equal pay.
137 Some personal ads were fictitious, though this did not stop controversies from arising (or perhaps being encouraged?) due to their content (Perryman 1994b).
138 Jacques 1989b.
139 Jane Taylor 1989b; MTEB 1989c.
140 MTEB 1989c.
141 The 'trends in youth cultures' debate in 1973–75 was seen as political rather than cultural.

this period, not only in the left's understanding of 'culture', but also more generally across most other journals of opinion in their understandings of 'culture' (excluding specialist periodicals). Books retained a preeminent place within the coverage of both popular and high culture well beyond 1981, however, since most publications on the left neglected popular and high culture, outside of literature, into the 1980s. Nevertheless, James Klugmann actually published fewer book reviews in the respective sample years than Martin Jacques did, alongside a few reassessments of important cultural figures, such as the writer, Rudyard Kipling, which stirred controversy amongst some readers.[142] Early problems identified in 'Reviews' during Jacques's editorship, included the lack of an organised approach in the selection of books to be reviewed, the timeliness of reviews, which were frequently published long after their initial publication date, and the general inaccessibility of writing and presentation.[143]

The 'Reviews' section was regularised after the second format launch in 1979, with a span of the last four pages of each issue, which was provided as a space for the exploration of books covering contemporary issues, such as feminism, Nicaragua's Sandinistas and Poland's Solidarity movement.[144] To improve accessibility, MT sought to improve the writing style and broaden the range of publications to include non-academic, union and 'non-socialist theoretical material', and to include trade unionists and activists as reviewers.[145] Despite various improvements or attempts to redress the section's weaknesses, some concerns were still being expressed in 1985, halfway through Jacques's editorship, that books were being reviewed singly rather than thematically. Part of the problem was that there were too few reviewers available who had the expertise to cover several subjects in the way that MT wanted.[146] The breadth was supposed to reflect 'all aspects of the BDA, and a wide definition of political culture' and to comment on topics not otherwise covered, but space was limited: the topics covered best were those with which the 'Reviews' editor was most familiar.[147] Although the 'Reviews' editor at the time, Sally Davison, attempted to avoid the 'famous name syndrome' by using activists as reviewers in the second format, she did think that this approach made the section feel 'slightly ghettoish'.[148]

---

142   E.g. Ash 1965; Dunman 1965; Hill 1965.
143   Webster nd (but probably 1979).
144   E.g. February 1982, March 1982 and April 1982 issues.
145   Webster nd.
146   Davison 1985c.
147   Davison 1985b, p. 1.
148   Davison 1985b, pp. 1–2.

Contrary to John Saville's criticisms published in the 1990 *Socialist Register*,[149] Table 6 demonstrates that in 1988 MT had actually published the most book reviews ever, even if, as a percentage of the total space, its share had declined, while the size and number of pages had increased: Jacques's first sample year had more book reviews than all three of Klugmann's sample years combined. Saville's criticisms were based in part upon assumptions of what books were appropriate for a socialist periodical to review: during the 1980s, the range of books expanded from those covering politics and history to books on culture, and literary and popular fiction.

The greatest editorial innovation in the second format was the section on popular and high culture, 'Channel Five'. The section's importance grew as popular culture was recognised as having an important contribution to make to MT's counter-hegemonic strategy: its notion of 'popular politics'. Channel Five drew out or made explicit the links between culture and politics, moving beyond the traditional separation of the two found in left periodicals, including social democratic or mainstream publications (e.g. *New Statesman*)[150] and the more traditional Marxist view of culture or the Frankfurt School critique, which saw popular and even high culture as part of the 'superstructure' and an instrument of alienation or indoctrination; yet, other socialists saw it as a means of liberation (e.g. *Socialist Review*). Seen as 'one expression of the BDA', which is key to understanding MT's transformation into a more accessible periodical, Channel Five broadened its coverage to include individual television programmes, exhibitions, fashion etc.: culture as both a way of life and as an artefact.[151] The influence of cultural studies on MT can be seen in the definitions of and discussions over culture.

When culture was taken seriously in Klugmann's MT, it was in reference to abstract concepts, such as 'freedom', or its instrumentality as 'a weapon' in the class struggle.[152] This was considerably different to how integral culture became to Jacques's MT. For example, Channel Five played a key part in transforming the journal into a magazine by making it 'more accessible and attractive' to new readers and because this culture section was also the most effective way to secure more advertising.[153] In the MT editorial collective's discussion on Channel Five, it argued that this section had to be different in its coverage from *New Statesman* or a Sunday broadsheet, in part because of MT's

---

149   Saville 1990.
150   Smith 1996.
151   Townsend 1996.
152   E.g. Bush 1963, 1964; Carritt 1965; Green 1973.
153   MTEC 1981, p. 3.

less frequent periodicity; it had to be able to offer something not otherwise available; *and* it was not supposed to (solely) focus on high culture. *Time Out* was seen as a useful model because of its 'broad democratic approach to culture': covering everything from punk, fashion and soap opera to classical opera, art exhibitions and theatre.[154] MT's cultural coverage also had to avoid too narrow a focus on a particular radicalised artistic or musical subculture, such as Rock Against Racism, even though, as some scholars have pointed out, RAR was a standard against which other cultural campaigns were frequently judged, since it offered a model of the BDA in action.[155]

Its name signified the democratic impulses of the BDA: Channel Five not only invoked television, then popular culture's dominant medium, by playing upon the forthcoming Channel Four (which had been first raised as a possibility in 1964),[156] and its remit to cater for all those ignored by the BBC-ITV duopoly. These impulses pushed MT to try and avoid the 'elitism and pretentiousness' of upmarket cultural criticism and find a unique 'style, range and approach' in 200 to 800 word pieces.[157] The editor of *Comment* set an example for MT to emulate with the cultural criticism provided in the innovative 'Television Review' column that was shared by three cultural studies lecturers.[158] A friend advised Jacques that the cultural section should be in the 'manner of *Comment* rather than *Melody Maker*, or *Screen* or *Formations*' and articles should be 'thoughtful but readable and even low-key', and Jacques was urged to not assume that readers were London-based, middle-class socialists, feminists and ecologists: 'A sort of lefto-cultural-studies-but-not-high-falutin'-crap-journalistic-but-not-uncritically-populist framework'.[159]

The growth in the use of photographs, graphs and line-drawings was also spurred on by Channel Five, which, because of its subject matter, had to be 'visually very interesting'.[160] The section editor, Sally Townsend (1981–88), organised a small collective to supply ideas and contributors. At first, Channel Five was allocated only three pages, less than 10 percent of total pagination, because features had priority and the pressure to increase advertising cut into the remaining available space.[161] Although it took until 1984 before Channel Five's suc-

154   MTEC 1981, pp. 1, 2–3.
155   E.g. Smith 2011; Worley 2016.
156   Although Channel 4 launched on 2 November 1982, its Welsh 'cousin', S4C, was launched one year earlier.
157   MTEC 1981, p. 3.
158   They were Ros Brunt, Ian Connell and Richard Dyer (only the latter was not a CPGB member).
159   Stewart 1981, pp. 2, 3.
160   MTEC 1981, p. 3 (original emphasis).
161   MTEB 1979b, 1981b.

cess was acknowledged, MT did eventually realise that it had found a 'glaring gap' in most left periodicals' (lack of) coverage of popular culture and media. Of course, this coverage coincided with MT's own interest in cultural politics, which could be seen as a continuation of the interests of the first New Left, cultural Marxism and cultural studies. This coverage appealed to many of the 1960s generation who had grown up 'in' popular culture. Despite Channel Five's secondary or tertiary position within the hierarchy of ideas, it was nonetheless an integral part of increasing MT's appeal to both readers (including increasing numbers of cultural studies students and lecturers) and advertisers, in attempting to break away from other magazines' cultural coverage in focus and writing style.[162]

13   The Politics of Form and the Form of Politics

For a useful example to see how these different aspects of the editorial format, imagery and layout came together in the form of *Marxism Today* and its political project, the April 1985 issue provides probably the best single issue to demonstrate how these worked together. This also enables us to see how MT operated in the 'marketplace of ideas' in terms of how it deployed its resources in the 'war of position' against its internal party opponents. This issue was chosen because it was a critical political struggle for both the CPGB and MT that took place mid-way in Jacques's editorship when MT was still engaged with the CPGB and the left.

While April was not usually one of the periodical's most important issues during the year, in 1985 it was of special significance, because of the increasing intensity of the 'civil war' between the reformist and traditionalist tendencies, with a large contingent of loyalists in the middle, that was ripping the CPGB apart in the run-up to the 39th Special Party Congress (18–20 May 1985). These internal battles were paralleled in the struggles within the Labour Party between the so-called 'hard' and 'soft' lefts, which were particularly intense in disputes, such as those over the strategy and tactics of the miners' strike, part of a wider struggle over the 'realignment of the left', and this issue is a good example of how the BDA was manifest in MT's form(at).

What was important for MT and its allies was to ensure that it could win over those within the CPGB who were either uncommitted or loyal to the leadership to back both the leadership and MT in the upcoming congress. These

---

162   Townsend 1984, p. 1.

party members, most of whom were steadfastly loyal to trade unions and especially the miners, who had played a key part in the labour movement's long history, had to be won over to a point-of-view that was critical of the National Union of Mineworkers' leadership in an atmosphere that was rife with recriminations and accusations of 'betrayal' in the immediate aftermath of the defeat of the NUM's year-long strike.

At the same time, MT also had a readership, both party and non-party, which *was* critical of unquestioning loyalty to unions and the working class, as well as those non-party, left-of-centre readers who might have been more sympathetic to a critical albeit supportive position of the miners. Thus, MT had a mixed audience to reach and convince; the way this position is achieved is illuminating for understanding the way in which all the elements that make up a 'magazine' could be persuasive. MT was aware of the success of the GLC in bringing together a coalition of seemingly disparate groups, including white working-class men, and mobilising public opinion in its favour.

These issues were also being debated in the period leading up to this issue, an intense time to which the second MT event, 'Left Alive', in October 1984, brought together the debates between Ken Livingstone and Beatrix Campbell (published in the December 1984 MT), and Tony Benn and Stuart Hall (published in the January 1985 MT) over the direction and 'realignment' of the left. Similarly, the position of traditionalists within the CPGB was being criticised in Tricia Davis's review of *Class Politics* (January 1985) and Dave Cook's 'No Private Drama', which was about the impending split in the party (February 1985). Responses from Ben Fine, one of the authors of *Class Politics*, and John Foster, a member of MTEB, were printed in the 'Viewpoint' section of the March 1985 issue, in an issue that included an interview with David Blunkett, Labour leader of Sheffield City Council on 'Ratecap Resistance', an article on developments in the USSR by the anti-Stalinist party intellectual, Monty Johnstone, and an assessment of the miners' strike by the CPGB's Industrial Organiser, Pete Carter, a reformist and MT ally.

This was the context for MT's April 1985 issue. With the lead-up to the SPC in May, MT had to ensure winning over support within the party to defeat its opponents. MT had to appeal in these areas for its own perspective in a way that would win over the leadership, or at least those loyal to the party leadership. If the leadership had been won over by the traditionalists, the outcome for MT would have been very different. It was into this critical juncture, where both the leadership's and MT's positions were dependent upon each other, that the April 1985 issue was launched.

The first thing about the issue that confronts you is, of course, the front cover with a photograph of a miner (head and shoulders) with a helmet and a dirty face and a determined (inscrutable?) look against an out-of-focus background.[163] On the cover in white upper case letters is the phrase 'Down but not out', which stands out against the background and could also be read as the politically neutral 'colour' white (truce, surrender?), which is attempting to appeal to both sides: if MT's position could have been read on the cover as, either with those who argued that the miners had been defeated, or with those who said they had won, its sales potential and ability to reach those who were on either side of the fence would have been reduced. To this end, the phrase indicates a setback or defeat, but acknowledges something as to the spirit of the miners and their communities in this bitter dispute. It was very important for MT not to be seen as insulting to, or patronising of, one of the most respected sections of the organised working class.

To the left is MT's logo in a box, so that it will be seen when overlapped by other magazines on the newsagent's shelf, and below it is the date and price (75 pence). In a black diagonal space in the right-hand corner of the cover is a signposting of the features in red font, with the most important feature, Eric Hobsbawm's 'Retreating into Extremism' set out on a 45 degree angle in upper case letters (red on black) as is the next line: 'The Miner's [sic] Strike: An Assessment'. The next line signposts 'Bea Campbell Interviews Frances Morrell',[164] followed below by 'CND and the Next Election'. The final line announcing two Focus and two Channel Five items in this issue, which include: 'Gorbachev', 'Fashion', 'Aids' and the film, 'A Passage to India'. One can see different interests or potential constituencies of the BDA highlighted as the advertising also demonstrated.

Out of a total of 56 inside pages plus the four extra pages provided by the covers, there are thirteen and one-third pages of advertising plus one-half of a page of classifieds (a proportion of 23 percent of the total pages including covers or just under 20 percent of the total of pages available, close to the annual average for advertising in 1983).[165] Significantly, however, just over four-and-one-third pages of advertisements (approximately one-third of all advertising) were messages of support for the miners and their families from thirteen trade union bodies and two non-union groups (Welsh Congress in Support of Mining Families and 7:84, the radical theatre company); a fourteenth message was from the NUM Scotland thanking MT readers for their support on behalf of Scottish

---

163   Designed by Lee Robinson.
164   Morrell was the leader of the Inner London Education Authority, which was abolished in 1990.
165   Only three of four cover pages were available for ads: inside front cover and both sides of the back cover.

miners' families (p. 27). Two of the three NUM leaders listed on this advertisement, Michael McGahey (President) and George Bolton (Vice-President), were supportive of MT's position (Bolton was a participant in the roundtable on the miners' strike in this same issue). However, there was also an advertisement from another union, TASS, which was led by a vocal opponent of MT, Ken Gill. Two of the unions providing messages of support came on the pages of Channel Five: Actors' Equity and the Association of Cinematograph, Television and Allied Technicians (ACTT).

In addition, Central Books had a list of books on the miners' strike filling up the whole of the inside back cover as well as a number of advertisements for publishers, various left, gay, Latin American and movement events, journals and bookshops, a 7:84 play (their second advertisement), design and printing co-operatives (there was a 'Focus' item on 'The New Workers Co-operatives') as well as 'Progressive Tours' (to Cuba, Nicaragua, Eastern European city breaks) on the inside front cover and Francis Wheen's book on 'The Battle for London' (Pluto Press) between the GLC and the central government. This latter advert was important in MT's thinking because of how Stuart Hall and others saw the GLC as the 'the most important front in the struggle against Thatcherism'.[166] There were even two ads for postgraduate programmes (political economy, sociology) and one for overseas vacancies with a United Nations aid organisation. The ads were clearly targetted at an audience that would have included a high proportion of readers interested in their content, which testifies to the broadening audience that advertisers sought.

Importantly, advertisements for CPGB membership and MT subscriptions occupied two and one-half pages. More importantly though was the way in which these ads addressed the readers, especially the one for party membership. This one-page advert is a drawing of four cartoon characters carrying ancient stone tablets up a hill (the biblical association to Moses on the Mount with the 'Commandments' is immediately apparent) underneath a caption asking, 'Tablets of Stone?' (in large, upper-case letters). Below the hill, there is the continuation of the question in 14-point type in lower-case letters: '... or politics for Britain in the 80's?' The implications are clear as to which is more important, the 'orthodoxies' of yesteryear or the development of politics for today (something to which MT consistently laid claim). It disparaged those who would argue for a left and a political party that is based on 'go-it-alone attitudes' or 'the belief in Unchanging Truths about the working class'. The ad continues: 'We need to build an alliance of *all* the progressive forces in Britain. Mass, pop-

---

166 Hall 1984c, p. 37, quoted in Milner, 2002, p. 117.

'FROM THE PARTY LINE TO THE POLITICS OF DESIGN' 309

ular movements hold the key to socialist change'.¹⁶⁷ The advert made it clear where the CPGB leadership stood on the issue vis-à-vis the traditionalist opposition.

MT's Development Fund called for 'supporting subscribers' (p. 50) with four short paragraphs next to photos of the last four covers, highlighting MT's 'pioneering role on the political scene', advertising how it 'launched key debates on Thatcherism, the labour movement's crisis, and the responses required of the left'. Indeed, MT's self-promotion extended further: 'It has hosted a broad range of writers, developed a new style of political journalism, aroused lively and creative controversy'. A vindication of MT's political impact could be seen in the 'regular increase in sales and the addition of new editorial sections' while its 'attention to style and design ensures that it gets pride of place on the newsstands'.

> Conscious of the need for development and renewal, we are constantly investigating ways of further expanding the magazine and overcoming its many weaknesses ... Resourcefulness has taken us so far; we also need resources (p. 50).

As with all other alternative and radical media, the familiar call for help with finances rings out with beautifully written copy.

This stress on moving away from orthodoxy, being willing to confront the world 'as it is', obviously appeals to this notion of being heretical, confronting authority and 'thinking the unthinkable'.¹⁶⁸ These ideas, which had particular appeal at a time of a major defeat of one of the leading sections of the organised working class, was hard to miss. Indeed, the actual content in this issue can be seen as the BDA in action. Two articles on the miners' strike, including an assessment by the Welsh CPGB historian, Hywel Francis, and a roundtable that included two NUM officials, who were also CPGB members, George Bolton and Alan Baker, and one NUM Branch Delegate from the Stillingfleet Colliery in Yorkshire, Ken Capstick, who was also a Labour Party member, and chaired by Dave Priscott (EC and MTEB member), were published as features. Eric Hobsbawm's 'The Retreat into Extremism' was a key feature article on the internal party strife in the leadup to the May Special Congress, and around which there was national media coverage. In addition, the articles on the NUM strike, a feature article on CND and a review of E.P. Thompson's *The Heavy Dancers* (an

---

167   All emphases in the original text.
168   This was not opposition to liberal or bourgeois orthodoxy but to left orthodoxy (Wilson 1997).

important review of interest to those interested in CND), a range of non-feature articles that included addressing issues around 'minority television' and the 'new morality' and the Eurocommunist and reformist sociologist, Alan Hunt, responding to previous contributors to 'Viewpoint' on the CPGB's internal conflict.[169]

However, while the advertisements themselves give us some clue as to the 'synchronicity' between the editorial content and advertising solicited for a particular issue, such as the union messages in an issue dedicated to assessing and debating the miners' strike, as do some of the contributions on the 'Letters' pages, there were still a range of topics covered which connotate a newsmagazine with compartamentalised interests, albeit somewhat more limited than in commercial newsmagazines. This particular issue stands out in the way in which its cohesion is built around a significant political issue, the miners' strike, and the CPGB's internal conflicts, all of which are meant to be seen as applying to the left beyond the CPGB.

14   Conclusion

The uneven, ongoing transformational process during Martin Jacques's editorship certainly made *Marxism Today* more accessible and persuasive than it had ever been to a potential readership beyond the internal party audience. These transformations in form, editorial sections and imagery usually worked well together, enhancing its intervention in debates on the left and in gaining partial access to the public sphere during the 1980s. After MT's 1979 relaunch in a newsmagazine format, the periodical began its transformation from the 'theoretical and discussion journal' into a hybrid magazine of three publication types, generally identified with the Leninist party: as with the daily or weekly 'party paper,' it sought to address a broader audience across the left and *not* just party members; as a 'theoretical journal,' its features retained an intellectual depth, although the focus shifted from arcane, historical and theoretical debates to discussions of contemporary political events; as with a fortnightly or monthly 'party review', it paid more attention to accessibility and format. It is the transformation into operating across these three periodical types of the Leninist party, which both constrained and enabled it to reach a wider audience than the one for which it had originally been conceived. This tranformation helped to establish MT as an increasingly separate entity from its publisher, the CPGB,

---

169   Hinton 1985; Davison 1985a; Hunt 1985a; Neverson 1985; Segal 1985.

while identifying key components towards constructing the BDA, which was integral to the transformation into the second format. The third format moved away from the idea of the BDA and came more closely to resemble opinion magazines (compartamentalisation of different opinions-cum-constituencies) associated with the centre-left.

Although MT's public profile rose because of increased distribution, publicity and press coverage, as examined in the next chapter, its transformation was integral in helping to secure at least some of that coverage. These changes, in turn, were aided by the combination of advertising, self-promotion efforts and press commentary from 1984 onwards. Although Jacques had benefitted from the 'remarkable turnaround in the fortunes of magazine publishing' in the 1980s, his ambitions were undercut by the 'collapse of advertising revenues' in 1991, subverting the Comedia model for the radical press.[170] A periodical that had started as an orthodox Marxist journal succumbed to the economic determinants of the capitalist marketplace.

---

170   Driver and Gillespie 1993, p. 183.

CHAPTER 5

'From the Margins into the Mainstream': Publicity, Promotion and Distribution in the Marketplace of Ideas

Explicit or implicit, the 'marketplace of ideas' remains the dominant metaphor for thinking about the relationship between the media and prevailing beliefs in western democracies, which accounts for idealist histories of political journals that provide accounts as if ideas could win on their own without an apparatus to support them. In the days before the public internet, advocates of the capitalist press argued that newspapers were 'subjected to the equivalent of an election every day', but did not entertain the possibility that the market might actually impede access for alternative views; they claimed that left-wing papers' small circulations were 'explained' as a result of their views being 'unpopular'. However, on the other hand, *Red Pepper*, the alternative magazine promoting a 'Red-Green' alliance of socialists, feminists and environmentalists since the 1990s, for example, has had little sales success, despite surveys that indicated a substantial audience for such 'news and views'.[1]

Radical papers, though, have more often ignored the marketplace because of the demands placed upon them by distributors and retailers, where the latter have often refused to distribute radical periodicals for legal reasons; however, once there was some liberalisation of laws around blasphemy and libel in the 1980s and 1990s, reasons for refusals have shifted to claims about space and turnover (i.e. a higher turnover of fewer magazines means greater profits), thereby acting as censors.[2] In this way, the market limits the range of ideas, as smaller magazines, without deep pockets for promotion, are squeezed out of retail space, thereby curtailing the circulation of some ideas. Without access to distribution mechanisms, such as wholesalers and newsagent chains, most periodicals will fold. The marketplace of ideas is thus a limited or misleading

---

1   Khiabany 2000.
2   The example of *Gay Times* in London in 1977 is a case in point (e.g. Berry et al. 1980, pp. 39–52; see also Cooper et al. 1980). In seeking greater profits in 1996, W.H. Smith's discontinued stocking some 350 small circulation magazines, which undermines the Comedia model when profitability drives the selection (and reduces the ideological-political diversity) of magazines against the numbers that can be sold (CPBF 1996a, 1996b; Logan 1996).

metaphor.³ However, it should be noted that corporate sponsored think tanks that promote free-market ideology appear to ignore the marketplace since they subsidise their own publications because it is more important to influence the media and academia than to worry about trusting something as manipulable or unreliable as the marketplace.⁴

The fundamental division between the two primary models for the radical press, 'Bolshevik' and 'Comedia', pivots on the question of the usefulness of the marketplace, which is directly related to different criteria for determining success or failure. Is success best determined by sales and circulation figures, or by the correspondence between a paper's means and ends?⁵ The Comedia model's emphasis on using market mechanisms is what many alternative periodicals did, such as *New Internationalist*, *New Socialist* and *Marxism Today*.⁶ Typical explanations, however, for MT's success during Thatcher's decade are based upon negative or positive ideological assessments, as either 'rethinking left shibboleths' or 'selling out'.⁷ Yet, neither view explains *how* MT gained access to the national public sphere. This chapter examines MT's circulation, readership and contributors, groups and events, promotion and publicity, and national press coverage to demonstrate how its use of market mechanisms enabled it to reach an audience beyond the 'radical ghetto'. An important starting point for investigating MT's access to the marketplace of ideas, is to start by examining its sales figures to gauge its success via distribution, before examining its promotion and publicity, and media coverage.

1 Party Distribution

Like other Communist parties, the Communist Party of Great Britain provided an organisational base, a mainstream audience and a publishing infrastructure for everything from leaflets to books, as an historical necessity borne of state repression and publishers' boycotts. Central Books oversaw party bookshops and print media distribution which included non-party bookshops and party branches.⁸ *Marxism Today* was also sold at CPGB events and occasionally in some university bookshops; its articles were included in education packs

---

3 Peters 2004.
4 E.g. Lorimer 1993; Gutstein 2009.
5 Downing 1984; Landry et al. 1985; Atton 1999.
6 Landry et al. 1985; McCrea 1989.
7 Bloomfield 1985; Callinicos 1985.
8 Cope 1999.

TABLE 7 Distribution, selected issues (% of total)[a]

Date	Party Sales	Central Book[b]	Subscriptions	Newsagents	Misc.	Total
Oct. 1957		77.0%	10.0%		13.0%	4,037
May 1958		61.7%	13.2%		25.1%	4,878
Nov. 1962		55.5%	13.3%		31.1%	4,179
Jan. 1972		56.5%	24.0%		19.5%	3,302
May 1973		57.0%	22.8%		20.0%	4,095
May 1979	53.0%	11.0%	23.5%		12.5%	4,705
Sept. 1979	52.0%	11.7%	24.8%		11.5%	4,579
Oct. 1979	56.3%	11.1%	21.0%	1.6%	9.9%	5,332
May 1980	49.4%	16.0%	23.5%		11.1%	4,914
Oct. 1981		40.2%	15.0%	44.9%		9,255
Mar. 1982		43.2%	16.8%	40.0%		9,324
Oct. 1982		39.3%	18.8%	40.3%	1.5%	10,639
Mar. 1983		41.9%	21.7%	33.7%	2.7%	11,692
Oct. 1983		33.6%	22.8%	39.5%	4.1%	11,870
Mar. 1984		31.4%	26.0%	39.7%	2.9%	11,762
Oct. 1984		29.1%	27.6%	39.8%	3.5%	12,803
Mar. 1985		24.9%	29.3%	43.2%	2.6%	13,927
Mar. 1986		22.7%	30.0%	44.0%	1.9%	14,388

a Klugmann 1960, 1973; MT 1986; MTEC 1984b. Gaps exist in total listings of figures.
b This figure includes 'party sales', except when there is a separate figure listed in that column.

for party schools. Distribution was not a problem as long as party journals addressed an internal audience, although it was supposed to try and reach progressive, non-party intellectuals.

After MT's launch in 1957, its circulation fluctuated between around 2,500 and 4,500 (with many core readers drawn from its precursor, *Marxist Quarterly*), with special issues hitting 5,000-plus.[9] For example, an issue which generated extra interest, was the General Secretary's speech on the twentieth anniversary of Soviet premier Nikita Khrushchev's 'secret speech', which sold out its print run of 7,500 (an extra 2,000 had been printed) in January 1976. A pamphlet[10] was also subsequently issued, which was another means of extend-

9   Klugmann 1976b.
10 Gollan 1976.

ing the reach of MT articles. During its first two decades, 1957–77, MT was never able to attract more than around 15–20 percent of total party membership; yet, there was not necessarily any correlation between membership and readership fluctuations. During MT's first five years, 1957–62, for example, monthly circulation remained at around 4,000–4,500 even as membership increased by 5,750 (21.5 percent) to 32,492, though the circulation figures also included monthly exports to the USSR (300) and China (400) (Table 7).[11]

After 1962, the editor, James Klugmann, had to work against a steady drop in membership, which threatened MT's potential audience and future income: any expenditure on improvements could not guarantee recovering costs, unless a greater proportion of members purchased it. Between 1967 and 1977, as overall membership declined, so did the party's composition change. There was an influx of white-collar workers, students and intellectuals into the party, attracted by the CPGB's more open approach to cultural, scientific, religious and social issues after the adoption of the 1967 Executive Committee 'Statement on Ideology and Culture', itself a response to the increasing competition from far left political organisations.[12] Such new members were more disposed towards reading MT and other party journals as their intellectual horizons broadened. MT's circulation started to climb back towards 4,000 and more by the mid-1970s, as more and more readers were attracted to Marxism and the ideas of Antonio Gramsci via the annual Communist University of London, as also reflected in changes in content and audience.[13]

The single greatest increase in sales occurred with the October 1981 issue, the first to have national newsagent distribution. The increase of 88.3 percent was nearly double the number of monthly issues sold: it increased from 4,914 (May 1980) to 9,255 (October 1981) (Table 7).[14] Obviously, the use of national newsagent distribution brought about a new audience, including casual readers interested in political events,[15] and ensured a new pipeline of funding *and* expenses. The share of sales of Central Books's distribution, which included copies sold via non-party bookshops, increased by March 1982 to 43.2 percent (4,028) of total sales, although it was not until March 1983, when sales via party

---

11   Jacques 1978; Klugmann 1973, 1960. Although China stopped taking MT soon after the Sino-Soviet split, MT and other CPGB periodicals continued to be purchased by pro-Soviet regimes.
12   EC 1967, pp. 134–8; Andrews 1995, pp. 226–7, 233, 243.
13   Andrews 1995a, pp. 233–4, 238–9; Johnstone 1995.
14   May 1980 is the issue with the highest sales closest to October 1981 that I have been able to find.
15   The subtitle, which identified its connection to the CPGB, was permanently removed from the cover with the October 1981 issue to avoid 'scaring off' non-party readers.

networks peaked at 4,900 copies, albeit at a slightly lower percentage of 41.9 (Table 7).[16] By March 1986, CB accounted for slightly more than 20 percent of sales, a consequence of the 'civil war' when hundreds left the party or were expelled which left fewer readers to reach.

Although MT had reached the limits of internal distribution and promotion by 1981, its party and bookshop sales continued to increase even after it secured national newsagent distribution, no doubt due to its growing public profile, which helped to increase interest in the magazine. By July 1984, more copies were sold for the first time via subscriptions than via the party, although it would take nearly a year before subscriptions consistently outperformed the latter; by 1986, subscriptions had increased to 30 percent of sales (Table 7). Subscriptions were important in establishing a solid base of readers and financing, since the money was paid up in advance, by one year or more, and because of the increasing irregularity and insecurity of party and newsagent sales. The party network became progressively less important until 1989, when it effectively ceased being of use. The decline in party membership had an impact on the utility of party networks that meant MT had to emphasise expanding external distribution networks.

2 'Out-of-Party' Distribution

Important changes in distribution outside of the CPGB enabled *Marxism Today* to expand its circulation substantially during the 1980s, which were partly enabled by its material transformation from a journal into a magazine. Martin Jacques had never considered selling MT via newsagents because of his background in academia and the party: 'the world of political ideas rather than journalism'.[17] His comment is telling because it indicates that Jacques became open to finding other ways of trying to reach a larger audience of potential readers than relying only on what the party could deliver. It was a combination of declining membership and internal political strife that forced Jacques to reach outside the party, to secure a future for MT. Dave Cook, a party officer and close friend, told Jacques when they and other reformists faced the leadership's blockage of change in 1979, that the best thing he could do was 'to keep sending MT onwards and upwards' because no one would be able to argue with its success.[18]

---

16   Jacques 1987b.
17   Jacques 1996b.
18   Ibid.

The second format launch in 1979 led to a slow but steady increase in sales and new outlets via independent bookshops and a few newsagents in central London. The first significant increase in sales, however, only came after a formal, trial agreement in 1980 with the national newsagent chain, W.H. Smith's, which brought a substantial increase in revenues, publicity and press coverage. Although W.H. Smith's did not distribute radical magazines at that time, Chris Hill, a Central Books representative, and Jacques eventually persuaded the company that MT 'wasn't the political rag that they thought it might be', by drawing attention to its editorial content, including the contributions of public figures writing in, or being interviewed by, the magazine: it was meant to be seen as 'serious' rather than 'scurrilous'.[19] Thus, MT had to work against mainstream perceptions of 'Marxists' whenever it was encountered in the field (general anti-Communist beliefs and stereotypes were widespread).

Since it is in the very nature of the capitalist marketplace to be persuaded by the potential to profit, MT sought to persuade its readers to take out subscriptions, introduce it to neighbours, friends and workmates, or try to get their local bookshops to stock it. Jacques made his appeal in the last issue of the first format (September 1979) about the 'new, enlarged format' where he wrote of 'more words and ... new regular features, including book reviews' and 'a more attractive and striking appearance', which meant a special promotion drive 'to present *Marxism Today* to a much wider readership' and 'we would be grateful for any assistance that readers can offer in helping to increase the circulation of the journal'.[20] Short news items in the two subsequent October issues highlighted readers' efforts to increase sales and MT's growth in distribution and circulation. The October 1980 issue announced that the second format's first year saw monthly sales 'consistently over 500 higher' than in the previous year. Sales and subscription numbers, newsagent trials and nationwide distribution, were all mentioned to encourage readers to become (more) active in promoting MT. It was also necessary to help persuade marketplace 'gatekeepers' to continue to distribute and sell MT where there was a demand for it. Readers, for example, were informed that the October 1980 issue, with a trial distribution in central London at selected newsagents, hit an all-time record of 'a print run of 10,000'.[21]

The October 1980 issue was given a three-month trial run in six W.H. Smith's outlets in London: three in railway stations and three in central London.[22] As

---

19   Townsend 1996.
20   Jacques 1979b, p. 264.
21   Webster 1980, p. 36.
22   Webster 1980. One manager was reputed to be a National Front member and for obvious

sales soared, the trial period was extended and distribution was expanded to 30 newsagents in London. Staff and volunteers checked outlets to make sure MT was properly displayed and newsagents were stocked. Jacques was advised to hire a proper distributor for nationwide distribution rather than trying to organise the deliveries themselves, although the circulation manager still had to accompany trade representatives to persuade newsagents to take it.[23] Despite this issue, the London trial run led to MT's breakthrough with a one-year, trial agreement for national newsagent distribution with W.H. Smith's, starting with the October 1981 issue. The trial's success secured distribution until MT's closure in December 1991.

The success of that trial year at 'selected W.H. Smith retail outlets … during which *Marxism Today* repeatedly sold out in a number of central stations' in London, the magazine secured nationwide newsagent distribution and the print run for the October 1981 issue was 20,000, double that of the previous October and 'nearly double that achieved for any previous issue'.[24] Paul Webster noted that it was the 'active contribution of its readers', without which MT 'could never have recorded the successes of the past two years', although 'much more can still be achieved'.[25] Thus, MT continued to ask readers for help in monitoring the availability of the magazine in newsagents while thanking them for responding 'far beyond our expectations', since increased sales were results of 'the efforts of many different people in Sheffield, Motherwell, Birmingham, Newcastle, Liverpool, Manchester, Bradford, London, Glasgow, Cardiff and a lot of other places'.[26] The readership base in the party was also concentrated in several of these cities and helped to create local demand for MT.

The October 1981 cover is particularly symbolic of MT's increasingly market-orientated approach for two reasons: the removal of a tag-line connecting it to the party, helping to distance itself from too close an association with the CPGB (at least on the cover); and 'scooping' national media on an international news story. First of all, while little could be done about the name, except for playing it off against the contents, the subtitle, 'the theoretical and discussion journal of the Communist Party', was removed from the outside cover and placed in tiny font on the masthead inside. Secondly, this was a particularly symbolic

---

reasons would not stock MT on the newsstand (he kept it behind the counter) (Townsend 1996).
23   Jacques 1996b; Townsend 1996.
24   Webster 1981, p. 48.
25   Ibid.
26   Grant 1982, p. 39.

move because it was carrying two exclusive, topical interviews: one with the then Polish Prime Minister, Mieczyslaw Rakowski; the other with his opponent, Lech Walesa, the leader of *Solidarity*, the first independent trade union in Eastern Europe. MT had 'scooped' the news media with Walesa's interview, which was carried by three national newspapers, and which ensured that mainstream media would take the magazine more seriously. Press cuttings of such stories helped persuade retailers of MT's public profile and therefore sales potential. Yet, such a news scoop did not grant MT ready and unfiltered access to the national public sphere.

With national newsagent distribution, sales nearly doubled overnight and it became the single most important source of new readers. Nearly half (44.9 percent) of 9,255 copies of the October 1981 issue were sold via newsagents, whereas only two out of five copies (40.2 percent) were sold via party branches and bookshops. MT averaged sales of 9–11,000 copies per issue in the early 1980s, edging up towards 15,000 by 1986. The October 1986 third format relaunch was an attempt to put MT 'decisively above the 15,000 mark' by securing 2,000 more sales per month.[27] Although it would never achieve this objective consistently, since there was considerable variation in sales between individual monthly issues and six-month averages, there was one six-month audit where MT did surpass this mark (July to December 1988), which included one of only two exceptional issues, selling 17–18,000 copies (October 1988, January 1989). Otherwise, its monthly sales averaged 13–14,000 in the late 1980s. However, sales started a decline in 1989 from which MT never recovered.

3   In the Marketplace of Left Periodicals

While *Marxism Today* was part of a range of social democrat, Labour, socialist, communist and anarchist publications that made up the left's counter-public sphere, under Martin Jacques MT moved towards targeting people on the 'broad Left', especially Labour Party supporters, while ignoring what might be called the 'vanguard' or 'Marxist Left'. Its primary competition, as Jacques and key MT staff saw it, became the independent, pro-Labour weekly, *New Statesman*, and Labour's own, bi-monthly (later monthly) magazine, *New Socialist*, which MT had inspired. One other important periodical was *New Left Review*, which was a theoretical journal that had been almost singlehandedly responsible for introducing continental European Marxist ideas to Anglophone audi-

---

27   Jacques 1986b.

ences. Despite NLR's limited engagement with domestic politics, MT's growing influence prompted NLR to publish a number of responses to MT's political themes, such as 'Thatcherism', and on the Communist Party's 'civil war' in the mid-1980s.[28]

The Labour Party's lack of a tradition of publishing intellectual journals reveals both a suspicion of ideas and intellectuals, and a limited understanding of the role that such journals can play. Instead, affiliated organisations took over the role, as the Fabian Society did when it launched the *New Statesman* in 1913, which was and is the preeminent social-democratic newsmagazine. To some extent, the NSS became a competitor with MT, especially after it took over *New Society* in 1988 and attempted to incorporate a stronger social-cultural mix covering popular culture, for which MT had gained a reputation.[29] However, NSS was a different type of magazine, well established and more news-orientated, and with a weekly production cycle, which meant it was better able to respond in a timely manner to political debates as they unfolded. Its decline through the 1980s, to around one-quarter of its all-time circulation peak of 100,000-plus in the early 1960s, was due in part to the fracturing of its primary audience by Conservative policies: the public-sector middle class.[30]

Recognising MT's growing influence, the Labour Party decided to launch a rival, *New Socialist*, its first (and only ever) 'theoretical' journal. The Labour leadership's limited vision of an intellectual journal would have confirmed expectations of limited circulation and audiences, if it had not been for the efforts of its first editor, James Curran, who had to fight for resources, when the leadership only put up £1,400 initially to launch a national magazine, and so he raised an additional £25,000. Curran also had to convince the leadership to increase publishing frequency and to have NS distributed through newsagents instead of bookshops.[31]

Launched one month before MT's national newsagent launch and at the peak of the Labour Left's influence, NS's potential was much greater because its affiliation gave it access to a much larger potential audience of Labour members and supporters. Although they were competitors in the marketplace, Curran and Jacques, nevertheless, co-sponsored debates on the left, and both publications, moved along similar political trajectories before the 1983 general election, and shared writers and readers.[32]

---

28   E.g. Hall 1985c; Jessop et al. 1984, 1985, 1990; Leys 1990; Samuel 1985, 1986a, 1987.
29   MTEB 1988a.
30   Smith 1995; Howe 1996.
31   McCrea 1989.
32   E.g. Curran 1984a; Curran 1997b; Jacques 1996a.

New Socialist's production schedule and distribution strategy were vindicated by its first Audit Bureau of Circulation figures of 27,324 per issue for January–June 1982, nearly three times MT's figures of 9,599 per issue (NS's launch issue sold between 47,000 and 'over 50,000').[33] Though NS was initially successful in influencing debates over the future of the left, it did so against a continually declining circulation. Despite out-selling MT at first, NS's sales and influence waned rapidly after 1984 and it ceased publication in 1987 (Table 8). With a change in editors and the intensification of 'realignment' across the left, NS's circulation and influence declined while MT's continued to grow, albeit slowly, for most of the rest of the 1980s. Interestingly, MT did not pick up most of the readers NS lost, even when allowing that some readers purchased both magazines (Table 9F).

The frequency of publication also has an impact upon the ability of periodicals to reach, retain or recruit readers. While NS's connections with the Labour Party enhanced its desirability to Labour members, its bi-monthly publication schedule during its first three years put it at a distinct disadvantage since MT was published monthly. MT, in turn, was at a disadvantage against NSS's weekly editions.

New Socialist's and *Marxism Today*'s circulation successes in gaining access to a broader audience and the national public sphere should not be forgotten because both helped to raise the level of debate across the left. Their successes highlight the contributions that market mechanisms can make, but as MT's history shows, these mechanisms are not as straightforward as they might first appear. For example, in the first half of the 1980s, MT's circulation was significantly less than rivals NS and NSS, and yet MT was ultimately more influential. By 1985, MT had become *the* agenda-setter for debate on the left, two years after it had already eclipsed, in influence and importance, the CPGB's first two most important publications in the basic typology: the daily newspaper, *The Morning Star*; and the monthly internal party review, *Focus*. The latter's predecessor, *Comment*, which had been weekly before becoming a fortnightly in the 1970s, had been shut down as it lost circulation; *Focus* was in turn replaced by *Seven Days*. No party review ever achieved the level of influence that *Comment* had during the 1960s and 1970s, in part when the membership was much greater and the CPGB was still the largest party to the left of Labour. As the NS's readership declined and other CPGB periodicals closed, and as party funds dried up, MT's readership numbers did not pick up anything close to 'the slack'.

---

33 Lawrence 1982. See NS's second issue.

TABLE 8 Periodical circulations in averages for selected years, 1977–89[a]

	1977 (Jul–Dec)	1978 (Jul/Dec)	1979 (Jul–Dec)	1981 (Jul–Dec)	1982 (Jan–Jun)	1982 (Jul–Dec)	1983 (Jan–Jun)	1983 (Jul–Dec)	1984 (Jan–Jun)	1984 (Jul–Dec)
MT	4,843	5,033	4,976	10,255	9,599	10,018	10,598	10,978	12,043	11,882
NS	–	–	–	–	27,324	25,113	25,145	23,666	24,232	24,609
NSS	38,922	37,489	40,331	37,577	33,986	29,849	30,432	30,109	30,001	27,808

	1985 (Jan–Jun)	1985 (Jul–Dec)	1986 (Jan–Jun)	1986 (Jul–Dec)	1987 (Jan–Jun)	1987 (Jul–Dec)	1988 (Jan–Jun)	1988 (Jul–Dec)	1989 (Jan–Jun)	1989 (Jul–Dec)
MT	13,153	13,798	14,023	13,715	14,195	13,927	13,388	15,649	14,254	13,208
NS	17,273	17,382	16,491	16,102	13,011	–	–	–	–	–
NSS	29,006	28,375	26,129	25,865	29,442	25,374	–	–	–	–

[a] ABC supplied the figures for MT 1984 (Jan–Jun) to 1990 (Jul–Dec) and for NS and NSS. The other figures are based on averages of the figures cited in reports and documents discussed at MTEB and MTEC meetings (MTEB 1979a, 1981a; MTEC 1984a, 1984b); monthly averages for 1978 and 1979 are based on despatch figures (not sales) for the whole year (Jacques 1979i).

4 'Cadres to Consumers': Changes in Readership, 1957–91

The composition of *Marxism Today*'s readership was tied to its position within the CPGB, especially in its first format, from 1957 to 1979. As the party's social base changed, so too did MT's readership. The events of 1956, for example, preceding the establishment of MT in 1957, led to the loss of nearly one-third of party members, although there was a brief upturn in recruitment by the early 1960s. In 1962, only one percent of party members were students.[34] By the mid-1960s, declining membership numbers affected the CPGB's ability to carry out political action, which was not always apparent in the resolutions passed at the National Party Congress. However, this was not just about numerical decline but about a change in social composition and values.[35]

The recruitment of middle- and working-class students was complemented by an increase in professional recruits and a *rapprochement* with older dissident intellectuals. Their absorption into the party's hierarchy was symbolised by Jacques's election to the Executive Committee in 1967.[36] Nevertheless, the industrial working class remained at the heart of CPGB strategy: intellectuals were expected to stick to their specialisms and leave strategic planning to party leaders and officers.[37] Within a decade of the start of this influx, the CPGB began losing members from all sides: one-quarter of its membership left between 1977 and 1981.[38] Membership decline quickened again after the volatile 1985 Special Congress and again with the adoption of the *Manifesto for New Times* in 1989,[39] which indicated that the leadership's managerial style of balancing two opposing tendencies was no longer of use. Despite this decline, MT's social base of intellectuals, (para)professionals, students and white-collar workers helped to recover sales lost during the internal strife of the 1980s.

While the move to national distribution was significant and did contribute to some changes in its audience, overall MT's readership was and remained, like its contributors, primarily white, middle-class, university-educated men and, prior to the 1980s, party members. For the first twenty years or so, the level of writing that dealt with theoretical issues and discussions required a high standard of reading and comprehension, if not actual familiarity with the ideas of Marxism-Leninism (Chapter 6). Nonetheless, there was a minority of

---

34 Andrews 2004, p. 31.
35 Thompson 1992, p. 153.
36 Andrews 1995a, p. 228; Jacques 1996b.
37 Andrews 1995a, pp. 229–30.
38 Andrews 1995a, p. 243.
39 Fishman 1994, p. 157.

working-class readers who wanted to learn about Marxist theory and history, who formed a much smaller fraction by the 1980s.[40]

Party leaders viewed MT's new audience as potential recruits, especially as its circulation grew rapidly while membership was declining. Prior to the October 1981 issue, MT did not carry advertisements for the CPGB because most readers were assumed already to be members. The first advertisements suggested that if readers 'enjoyed' MT they might want to join the organisation that publishes it. Between October 1981 and May 1982, these ads attracted a mere 83 applications and enquiries out of a monthly circulation of 10,000-plus. Readers were either already party members or not interested, regardless of its relationship to MT.[41] Yet, these miniscule recruitment figures bettered all other party agencies, including *The Morning Star*, thus confirming the party's limited appeal. By the end of 1983, and after opening up debate about Labour's future after its second general election defeat, these ads began to play upon the 'iconoclastic' and heterodoxic attitude towards the left's key policies and core principles (pejoratively labelled 'shibboleths'), for which MT was beginning to acquire a reputation.[42]

The November 1983 advertisement (p. 46) for MT subscriptions, for example, pointed out that it had 'taken readers far beyond the traditional realm of socialist politics', including a focus on the Derby, interviews with a monk and a chief constable, while highlighting how its 'cultural coverage read like a who's who … Its original and stimulating insights into politics … one of the most interesting glossies on the book-stands'. The December 1983 issue promised 'No more skating around those thorny political problems'; you could 'Subscribe now, and join the mainstream of political debate' in the January 1984 issue, a message meant to support the idea that MT was where political debate happened. An advertisement in the March 1984 issue contained the first endorsements from the mainstream media (rather than individuals): 'Essential political reading', according to *The Guardian*; and the *Sunday Times* claimed that MT was: 'A bright well written glossy'. The 'Left Alive' event programme in the October 1984 MT included a quote, from David Rose of *Time Out*, the London weekly listings magazine, which captured how MT saw itself: 'one of the most important forums for left-wing writing, both theoretical and empirical. Painstakingly edited, free from jargon and beautifully produced'.

---

40   Johnstone 1995. Impression corroborated by McLennan 1996. Such workers were not a novelty, since the CPGB had a long tradition of worker education (e.g. Samuel 1985, 1986b; Thompson 1992).
41   McKay 1982.
42   Some ads were written by MT staff (Perryman 1994b).

As befits the Comedia model, *Marxism Today* made use of market research to learn about its readers to better target them, increase sales and help sell advertising. Two readership surveys were conducted: one in 1986 by Comedia; the other in 1990 by Summertown Research Consultants, which included at least one former Comedia researcher.[43] These surveys are useful in providing a picture of readers in the second half of the 1980s, although one has to be cautious because these surveys depended upon respondents self-selecting. Nonetheless, these surveys do provide a useful picture of both continuities and changes in the readership's composition, and the second survey had a high response rate of around 15 percent.[44]

The readership was made up of well-educated, managerial, administrative, white-collar and professional workers (i.e. ABC1),[45] which coincides with the 'professional-managerial class' identified by the US New Left[46] and which was associated with MT.[47] The PMC could have described the sons and daughters of the working and lower-middle classes in the UK, whose opportunities for social and economic advancement arose out of the expansion of post-secondary educational opportunities and professional, administrative and managerial positions, and who were subjected to the tensions and insecurity of their contradictory location in-between labour and capital. This is an apt description of a majority of MT's readers by the latter half of the 1980s.[48] Also, the PMC represents a particular postwar development to which the welfare state contributed, with greatly increased social and occupational mobility and contrasts significantly with the twenty-first-century situation of white-collar and (para) professional workers, whose jobs have become increasingly proletarianised in income, status and working conditions.[49]

---

43 This chapter's readership tables draw from Comedia's 1986 survey results, which were included in the MTEB summary, and the 1990 figures draw from the SRC report (MTEB 1986; SRC 1990).

44 There were 1596 responses out of a circulation of about 10–11,000.

45 ABC1 and C2DE are six categories of readers, according to occupation, which are often split into two groups: C2DE include semi-skilled and unskilled manual workers, pensioners and the unemployed.

46 Though the term was disputed, changes in the social composition of the workforce was less contentious (e.g. Ehrenreich and Ehrenreich 1977, 2013; Walker 1979).

47 Harris 1992, pp. 186–94.

48 For other accounts of this 'new class', see Mallet 1975 on France or Gouldner 1979 on the US.

49 For example, the situation of precarious scholars, a section of the PMC, is known in the twenty-first century in the UK, USA and Canada (e.g. adjunct and contract faculty; 'zero-hours contract' academics). On the 'death' of the PMC, see Ehrenreich and Ehrenreich 2013.

Although women readers increased by about two-thirds to 24 percent by 1990 and made up 28 percent of new readers, men remained predominant. Nevertheless, this increase in female readers was a significant increase over 1986 and reflects some of the shifts in content. While readers remained overwhelmingly young, with 'under 45s' declining slightly from 84 percent in 1986 to 82 percent in 1990, those under 35 years declined more quickly in the same period, from 70 to 58 percent. These percentages reflect a proportion of readers growing older with the magazine, though the numbers of readers still with MT for five-plus years dropped 31 percent. Thus, nearly one-in-four readers were 35–45-year-olds in 1990; these were the postwar 'baby-boom' generation, chronologically and socially, who had come of age, politically, in the late 1960s and early 1970s: the generation of '68. Both this grouping and the post-war generation were more sympathetic to cultural politics, and the mix of 'agit-prop' and rock'n'roll. These readers were most likely to be libertarian in their attitudes towards social and lifestyle issues, to be interested in popular culture and to have studied at the new universities and polytechnics. Their political attitudes were shaped by opposition to the Vietnam War and support for national liberation movements as well as by the anti-authoritarian currents of May '68, which meant that many new readers had a more critical attitude towards party hierarchy and traditions (including Labour's) than the older generations of party members and MT readers.[50]

Education provided a nexus for the vast majority of MT's readers: either as the percentage of readers with a first or higher degree, which increased by 10 percent from three-in-five readers (61 percent) in 1986 to two-in-three (67 percent) by 1990, of which those with a post-graduate degree made up more than one-in-five readers (22 to 24 percent); and those who were students made up more than one-in-five readers (22 to 21 percent).[51] Indeed, the number of respondents without educational qualifications declined from a mere four percent in 1986 to nought in 1990, a sign of MT's consistent appeal to well-educated readers and the complexity of its writing (Chapter 6).

The educational and occupational profiles demonstrate a strong overlap between readerships of both *Marxism Today* and the *New Statesman*: nearly two-thirds of full-time employees, who were readers of MT, which was one-third of all its readers, were public employees (Tables 9B, 9C, 9D). Given the importance of a periodical's readership base to its circulation and possible influence, as that base comes under threat or begins to decline, the periodical's

---

50 Andrews 1995a, pp. 226–9.
51 SRC 1990, p. 17.

TABLE 9A   Age and gender (% of total)

	1986	1990
Age (under 35 yrs)	70.0	58.0
Age (under 45 yrs)	84.0	82.0
Male	85.0	76.0
Female	15.0	24.0

TABLE 9B   Education (% of total)

	1986	1990
No qualifications	4.0	–
First degree (Bachelor's)	39.0	43.0
Postgraduate degree	22.0	24.0

financial viability and longevity is threatened. It helps to explain the decline of *New Statesman*'s circulation from its peak of 100,000 in the mid-1960s, when public sector employment had expanded considerably with the rise of the post-war welfare state.[52] While one-in-three readers remained in the public sector by 1990, there was a shift within from local government and education, which usually have been well represented amongst Labour and left readerships, to 'other' areas. Interestingly, there was a near doubling of readers employed in the private sector, perhaps due in part to the privatisation of public services and the rise of media and cultural industries.[53]

The survey indicates a significant shift in readership had taken place, as part of shifts in both content and form(at), and in production and distribution. By 1990, only 31 percent of the sample had been readers for five years or more, while 38 percent had been reading MT for less than two years: nearly 70 percent had not read MT before 1985. Thus, for example, by translating circulation figures with the sample that would mean that only 4,094 of the 13,208 readers per issue in July–December 1989 would have been readers before 1985, a

---

52   Howe 1996.
53   The 1986 survey indicated that 12.5 percent of private sector employees worked in media and computer industries (MTEB 1986). It is likely that this figure increased by 1990 in tandem with the changing profile of contributors. See also Harris 1992, pp. 187–8.

TABLE 9C Occupation (% of total)

	1986	1990
Full-time employees	51.0	55.0
Part-time employees	6.0	8.0
Self-employed	5.0	6.0
Pensioners, disabled	5.7	6.0
Students	22.0	21.0
Unemployed	8.3	4.0

TABLE 9D Full-time employees (% of total)

	1986	1990
Public sector:	33.2	33.0
Education	(13.9)	(10.4)
Local government	(7.0)	(3.3)
Health/Social services	(5.6)	(4.4)
Other	(6.7)	(14.9)
Voluntary sector:	3.6	–
Private sector:	12.8	22.0
Not Available:	1.4	–

TABLE 9E Newspapers (%)

	1986	1990
The Guardian	82	76
Independent	–	30
Financial Times	10	10
Morning Star	12	6

figure approximate to MT's better circulation figures under Klugmann's editorship, which indicates a substantial loss of older CPGB readers (Tables 7, 8). Therefore, MT's shift towards the political centre did mean losing a substantial portion of its earlier readership, albeit not just party members, since others left because they became disillusioned with politics or MT. After 1985, increases in

TABLE 9F   Periodicals (%)

	1986	1990
New Statesman	46	41
New Socialist	40	13
New Left Review	19	14
New Internationalist	18	18
City Limits	18	12
Private Eye	28	19
Viz	–	16

TABLE 9G   Party members (% of total)

	1986	1990
Percentage of total readership	58	48
Labour Party	39	31
CPGB	17	10
Other parties	2	7

sales had to draw in enough new readers to make up for those who had left the party and stopped buying it, in addition to building up a substantial readership to sustain the magazine. Thus, during the mid-1980s, MT had to recruit hundreds of new readers to replace those hundreds who left, just to keep circulation at previous levels, and then recruit on top of that exodus, which was another reason why it had to invest so substantially in publicity and promotion.

A general sense of MT's shifting political trajectory towards the centre is reflected in shifts in readers' newspaper preferences. Between 1986 and 1990 the decline in *Guardian* readers is made up by a substantial portion of readers who indicated that they also read *The Independent*, launched in October 1986, which occupied a political niche between *The Guardian* and *The Times* and is one indicator of MT's rightward political shift.[54] The preference for Sunday newspapers, though, demonstrates a clear preference for liberal and centre-left, rather than right-wing, newspapers: 42 percent of readers chose *The Observer*, 33 per-

---

54   Tunstall 1996, p. 53.

cent the *Independent on Sunday* and 25 percent the *Sunday Correspondent* (a short-lived, centre-left broadsheet-cum-tabloid).[55] None of those surveyed, for example, chose either the *Sunday Times* or *Sunday Telegraph*.

During this period, those MT readers who also read the *Morning Star*, dropped by half to six percent of all readers surveyed, reinforcing the loss in traditionalist readers who were members of either the CPGB or the Labour Party, whilst gaining more non-party-affiliated centre-left readers. Readership figures demonstrate a general decline in 'political commitments' in two ways: of those who were members of a political party (from 58 to 48 percent); and of those who purchased a second political magazine. While there was a more than three-fold increase in readers who were members of 'other parties', the total remained marginal (from two to seven percent). There was a loss of more than one-quarter of readers who were members of either the CPGB or the Labour Party (from 56 to 41 percent): Labour members had dropped by 20 percent to less than one-in-three readers, while CPGB members had dropped by over 40 percent to just one-in-10 readers. While the loss of CPGB readers was clearly a result of the fallout from the internal power struggles or disillusionment with the party or MT, the drop in Labour readers also indicates a dissatisfaction of others outside the party with MT's political trajectory.

However, when readers were asked which parties they would consider supporting (respondents could choose more than one party), 81 percent said Labour, seven percent Social Democratic Party/Social and Liberal Democrats, 28 percent Greens and 22 percent the CPGB. Since the latter tended to be readers of MT for more than five years, it points to a significant part of the magazine's core audience as party members who ensured a small, but not insignificant, and stable base of income support. Despite the overwhelming intention amongst readers to support Labour in the next election, the choices offered indicate a rightward political shift from 1986, aligning with changes in MT's position.

The readers' choices of the other magazines that they read in the two surveys also helps to identify a shift away from the left amongst *Marxism Today*'s audience. For example, although there were three magazines that were read by more than 25 percent of MT's readership in 1986, *New Statesman* (46 percent), *New Socialist* (40 percent) and Private Eye (28 percent), only NSS retained a similar level of popularity by 1990 (41 percent). There were notable decreases in NS (it had been discontinued by the Labour leadership) and *City Limits* (in financial difficulty), slight decreases in *New Left Review* and *Private Eye*: only readers of *New Internationalist* remained constant. This fragmentation was reinforced

---

55 See Chippindale and Horrie 1988 for an account of its all-too-brief and fraught existence.

by the results for newstrade readers, who were more likely to be under 25 and consider supporting non-left parties (e.g. SDP, Greens); while the 28 percent who bought *most* months tended to be younger, students and read the *Financial Times* or *The Economist*, an indication of the shift in politics towards the centre and right.[56] However, nearly half (47 percent) of the newstrade readers who bought MT *every* month tended to be older, male CPGB members, which no doubt reflected also the breakdown of party distribution via Central Books. The breakdown in the party distribution network meant that, while CPGB readers had to buy their copies at the newsagent, it ensured that there was a greater demand for MT at newsagents than might otherwise have been the case.

By the latter half of the 1980s, it was clear that the social strata that were an integral part of MT's core readership were from the PMC.[57] Between 1986 and 1990, MT readers were a mixture of primarily middle-class, university-educated, male professionals and (graduate) students; the overwhelmingly majority of whom were under 45 years. They tended to read the centre-left broadsheets and mostly vote Labour, although more than one-in-five readers worked in the private sector by 1990. There were essentially two types of reader: an older one, who had aged with MT at least since 1981, and most likely a member of either the CPGB or the Labour Party; and a new younger MT reader, more lifestyle-oriented and interested in social and cultural issues, and more likely to vote Green or SDP, or even be apolitical, and open to criticisms of the left. These surveys demonstrate a rightward political shift in MT's readership.

5 Contributors

Promotion and publicity for *Marxism Today* were helped by a shift in the types of contributors during the 1980s that raised its public profile. Under James Klugmann, contributors were mostly party officials and academics with occasional contributions from rank-and-file, working-class party members. A significant shift took place in the early 1980s, as Martin Jacques recruited both party and non-party scholars, and political and social movement activists; by the late 1980s, this mix contained increasing numbers of professional journalists and non-CPGB (primarily Labour Party) politicians, including Tony Blair in October 1991 (Table 10). Changes in contributors were justified by claiming to seek

---

56 Jacques had been reading the FT since the 1970s (Jacques 1996d).
57 The collection in Walker 1979 provides a range of contrasting positions on the PMC. Ehrenreich and Ehrenreich initiated the debate in 1977 and wrote about its demise 36 years later (1977, 2013).

TABLE 10   Breakdown of contributors by occupation in sample years (% of total)[a]

Primary occupation of contributors	Feature articles			Other contributions		
	1975	1983	1988	1975	1983	1988
Academics[b]	34.2	52.6	35.2	40.7	37.5	32.3
Journalists[c]	7.9	7.7	37.4	–	30.4	53.3
CP officials[d]	44.7	5.1	3.3	33.3	0.9	0.6
Other parties' officials	–	1.3	3.3	–	–	0.6
Trade unionists	2.6	11.5	2.2	3.7	7.1	1.2
Social movements[e]	2.6	12.8	1.1	–	10.7	3.6
Labour MPs, PPCs	–	1.3	4.4	–	2.7	0.6
Professionals[f]	2.6	3.9	8.8	11.1	8.0	3.6
Workers	–	–	–	–	0.9	0.6
MT staff	–	1.3	2.2	–	–	3.0
Misc./Unknown	5.3	2.6	2.2	11.1	1.8	0.6
TOTAL[g]	99.9	100.1	100.1	99.9	100.0	100.0
(Absolute numbers of contributors)	38	78	91	27	112	167

a   Contributors' primary occupations were determined by the listing in MT, unless otherwise known. The final numbers tabulated do not indicate the numbers of contributors because some will have contributed more than once, nor do they indicate the exact number of articles because some were authored by two or more or included several participants (ie roundtables).
b   This includes academic-related occupations, such as researchers, but not school teachers.
c   This includes all media-related occupations, although journalists predominated.
d   The category 'CP officials' includes international Communist Party officials and documents (counted as one 'official'). No documents were carried in 1983 or 1988, although the CPGB's MNT was carried in 1989.
e   This includes representatives and employees of social movements and pressure groups, such as CND.
f   This includes white collar employees, including teachers and nurses.
g   Due to rounding, numbers might not add up to 100.

the 'best qualified' people, including public figures, to write on various topics; recruiting the public figures became easier as MT's public profile rose nationally, which was helped by public figures who wrote for it.[58] Media contacts were used to help generate responses to articles, which included being commissioned to write letters to the editor of MT (a not uncommon practice for commercial magazines but not common with left and alternative periodicals), or to write short pieces for the news and cultural sections, such as 'Focus' and 'Channel Five'; although many, who agreed to write, did so because it gave them the opportunity to write longer, in-depth articles that they did not get to do in their paid work for the mainstream media.[59]

As MT under Jacques began to address the broad left rather than the Communist Party, left-leaning politicians, union leaders, cultural figures and social activists replaced the speeches of, and interviews with, domestic and international Communists. Gradually, leading international and domestic public figures became more common, particularly as MT's profile rose in the national press. Yet, many of these interviews were only secured through nationally or internationally renowned contributors or professional journalists with national newspapers: e.g. Hugo Young, *Guardian* political columnist, interviewed former Conservative Prime Minister, Ted Heath; Stuart Hall, a cultural studies scholar of international repute, interviewed Jesse Jackson, an African-American leader of the US 'Rainbow Coalition' (of ethnic groups and new social movements).[60]

MT increased the total number of contributors year on year during the 1980s because of new types of articles, such as discussion roundtables, and the expansion of space with larger and extra pages with format changes and incremental increases in pagination in most years.[61] Media professionals became the largest occupational group of contributors by 1988, contributing to all sections including features, where they ranked ahead of academics, in part because they are trained (and required) to write to deadlines, which ensured meeting distribution needs on time and was part of MT's professionalisation process.

The contributions of academics and media professionals ("journalists") prevailed over that of party officials and activists. In 13 years, media professionals' contributions went from less than one-in-20 (4.5 percent or three out of 65)[62] to nearly half (48 percent or 123 out of 258), while academics' contributions

---

58   Jacques 1996c.
59   Ibid. Townsend 1996.
60   Heath 1988; Jackson 1986.
61   Pages per issue increased from 32 to 64 by the late 1980s.
62   The numbers in this paragraph combine 'features' and 'other sections' from Table 10.

slipped a little, proportionally, from 37 percent (24 out of 65) to 33.3 percent (86 out of 258) (Table 10). Together, however, both types of contributors nearly doubled, from two-fifths (41.5 percent or 27 out of 65) to four-fifths (81 percent or 209 out of 258). There was a substantial increase in the absolute numbers of contributors because of an increase in features and shorter pieces for successive issues in larger formats with more pages, even if 50 percent of additional space was earmarked for advertising.

In 1975, all three professional journalists, who contributed to MT, were party members employed on party publications. The first non-party, professional journalists who began contributing in 1983 were from two of the UK's leading national broadsheets: the FT and *The Guardian*. They were the first media professionals to help raise MT's public profile and lend an aura of mainstream 'respectability' and 'credibility' to the periodical. By 1988, nearly 60 percent of the 49 professional journalists, who accounted for almost 40 percent of features, were affiliated with liberal and centre-left broadsheets: nine each from *The Guardian* and FT; four from *The Observer* and seven from *The Independent*. These included such leading journalists as Neal Ascherson, John Lloyd and Charlie Leadbeater (though Leadbeater was also a party member).[63] Though these same contributors provided sympathetic coverage for their newspapers' readers and raised MT's profile with a broader public, it enhanced their standing with MT's readers, and thereby reinforced mainstream media perspectives within a medium for the (counter) public sphere.

While the professionalisation of contributions was in part made possible by increasing numbers of media professionals, and especially journalists from the centre-left broadsheet press, the magazine in turn was expending a great number of resources, human and financial, in publicity and promotional efforts to reach out to mainstream media outlets for coverage. The broadsheets' coverage became a bridge for these liberal and centre-left journalists to address the left, via MT, on such topics as rethinking socialist and Labour 'shibboleths'. Thus, those, who already had access to national media, gained access to a channel to the left's counter public sphere.

This major shift to media professionals amongst contributors during the 1980s is notable because many media managers, news editors, executives and commentators, had felt 'besieged' by print unions and talked about making journalism a 'closed shop' during the late 1960s and 1970s.[64] Journalists also played a role in promoting monetarism and Thatcherism, for example, even via public or state broadcasters, such as BBC Radio Four's current affairs pro-

---

63 Leadbeater went on to become an important New Labour advisor and propagandist.
64 Jackson 2012, p. 53.

grammes, such as *Analysis* and *File on Four*, in the late 1970s, all of which targetted the academic, business and political elites. Journalists, themselves, might have felt particularly vulnerable after Wapping when the printers' unions had been defeated, and it might explain why the media were rarely a focus for analysis in the pages of MT during Thatcher's decade, as journalists might be rightly shy of criticising their (actual or potential) employers. Two years after Jacques's publicly stated shift in his view of the mainstream media,[65] media professionals were becoming the largest group writing for MT during the third format, which was particularly noticeable in the massive increase in interviews because of mainstream journalists' access to important public figures.

6   Book Publishing

Book publishing proved to be another useful vehicle for promoting the ideas in *Marxism Today* and contributing to the counter public sphere. There were three published collections of MT articles, including critiques of its positions, on the three key themes that were part of MT's political project during the 1980s. While James Klugmann's MT had provided articles for occasional special pamphlets or booklets produced for party schools and special events, it was the ideas in Martin Jacques's MT that continued to have an impact through book-length collections of articles, which continued to sell even after the magazine's closure. Although the CPGB publisher, Lawrence and Wishart, had already published three collections of papers from the Communist University of London, it was not interested in a collection based upon the debates over Eric Hobsbawm's 'Forward March of Labour Halted?', published in MT over a year and a half. After Frances Mulhern, of New Left Books,[66] NLR's book-publishing arm, had suggested the idea for the first collection, Jacques approached Lawrence and Wishart first, since it was the party's publisher, but with no success.[67] NLB published *The Forward March* collection in 1981, in association with MT, at a time when there was still a feeling of unity on the left.

Lawrence and Wishart's publication of three collections of papers that had been presented at the annual CULs in 1977, 1978 and 1980, included not just CPGB contributors, but many others outside the party, including Stuart Hall and Chantal Mouffe.[68] Out of the three collections, Hall contributed two papers,

---

65   Jacques 1984a.
66   It was renamed Verso in 1981.
67   Jacques 1996d; MTEB 1980.
68   Bloomfield 1977; Hibbin 1978; Bridges and Brunt 1981.

the second one of which, '"The Whites of Their Eyes": Racist Ideologies and the Media', from the 1980 CUL, was reprinted and republished numerous times for post-secondary courses on race and media.[69] The contributors and topics in the collections reflected the attempt to intellectually engage the broad democratic alliance. The 1981 *Silver Lining* collection contained the most effective demonstration of the BDA 'in action' intellectually and theoretically in demonstrating the link between the 'war of position' beyond the party and with cultural politics.[70] It covered: feminism; race and media; gay cultural politics; Northern Ireland; national liberation (for the UK); 'socialist welfare'; the CPGB and the BDA; popular politics and Marxist theory; and Gramsci on hegemony and the 'integral state'.[71]

The popular interest in both 1981 collections, *Silver Linings* and *The Forward March*, spurred Lawrence and Wishart, the party publisher, to express an interest in publishing a collection of articles on Thatcherism. *The Politics of Thatcherism* came out in 1983. It also published *Marxism Today*'s third collection, *New Times: The Changing Face of Politics in the 1990s*, in 1989.[72] A fourth collection, *The New Soviet Revolution*, focusing on *glasnost* and *perestroika*-related developments in the Soviet Union and edited by a Eurocommunist party member, Jon Bloomfield, was also published in 1989.[73] However, though it appealed to MT supporters in the party, Jacques claimed it was not part of MT's political project, which is why it did not receive the same kind of promotion and acknowledgement as the other three collections had. Jacques wanted to maintain as great a distance as possible from the CPGB's erstwhile ally and supporter.[74] In addition, both Stuart Hall and Eric Hobsbawm had collections of essays published by Verso (formerly NLB) in association with MT in 1988 and 1989, which included many of their contributions to MT.[75] These books continued to circulate MT's ideas long after it had ceased publishing, through book-

---

69   Hall 1981d. All three collections include authors, besides Hall, who were part of the then growing field of cultural studies: e.g. Ian Connell, Elizabeth Wilson, Richard Dyer, Colin Mercer, Chantal Mouffe.
70   Bridges and Brunt 1981. Around the same time, Jacques was arguing that the first People's March for Jobs was the BDA 'in action' politically (Jacques 1981b).
71   Bridges and Brunt 1981.
72   Jacques and Mulhern 1981b; Hall and Jacques 1983b, 1989b.
73   Bloomfield 1989. Bloomfield was the editor of the first CUL collection (Bloomfield 1977).
74   Jacques 1996d. Although Jacques expressed this sentiment in an interview with the author in 1996, MT had sponsored a special event to watch (via satellite transmission from Moscow) the 70th anniversary parade in 1987, just two years before *The New Soviet Revolution* was published.
75   Hall 1988a; Hobsbawm 1989c.

shops, public libraries and university courses because the book form provides a durable means of making ideas available and ensuring the continuity of these particular perspectives into the future.

7   'The Art of Talking': Discussion Groups, Talks, Events, Conferences

Discussion groups, public talks, including those sponsored by local party branches, and weekend events were an integral element of *Marxism Today*'s promotional efforts for pushing its ideas across the left and to the broader public. These groups, talks and events also acted as an 'audience-feedback' mechanism, by engaging with the readership face-to-face, and encouraging participation in the discussion of ideas in the periodical, all of which helped to generate more income and sales.

In its first two decades, MT sponsored talks as part of the process of trying to engage with other progressive intellectuals on behalf of the Communist Party as per its *raison d'être*. James Klugmann gave lectures and talks, published occasional collections of MT articles as CPGB pamphlets,[76] and helped with preparing party educational materials. The journal was seen as a vehicle for the party line even if it was 'open' to discussion with others on the left, which might have deterred non-party members from attending such forums. As early as 1962, MT sponsored talks, debates and events, including the 'Forum in London', spurred on by the activities of the NLR and New Left clubs; it also organised a 'Week of Marxist Thought' a year later, inspired by an event held by the French Communist Party in 1961.[77] However, these early forms of outreach never acquired anything close to the influence and publicity of either the CUL in the 1970s or MT events in the 1980s.

The interest and dynamism of the Communist Party's cultural outreach with the annual CUL had grown substantially and intellectually from the 100 in attendance at its first, politically orthodox 'school' in 1969 to 300 attendees at CUL 5 in 1973 to 630 at CUL 6 in 1974 and 737 at the CUL 7 event in July 1975.[78] MT benefitted from the annual CUL events. In the July 1976 issue, for example, Klugmann reported on the 'increasing support for the activities of the specialist groups of the Communist Party', which included: history, philosophy, psycho-

---

76   E.g. CPGB 1974.
77   E.g. Griffith-Hentges 1962; MT 1962a, 1963. See Chapter 3 in Callaghan 2002 for more detail on the CPGB's 'cultural front' in this period.
78   Klugmann 1976c, p. 201.

logy, Esperanto, built environment, music, law and science.[79] The literature and sociology groups were even more successful because they had 'broken out of the pattern of regular but small meetings'.[80] Klugmann also pointed out that the 'Moving Left Show'[81] in 1975, a year earlier, had put on two sessions with 500 people each, and 300 people, including many non-party people, attended 'Foco Novo' in Birmingham. The 'Marxist Discussion' week in September 1975 included over 400 participants. All of these examples were areas of intellectual and cultural interest that appealed to both party and non-party people, and increasingly to higher education students and lecturers. In 1977, CUL 9 was the peak year with some 1,500 party and non-party scholars, students and activists, after which attendance dropped until it closed in 1981.

The CPGB specialist committees, such as the Theory and Ideology Committee, were another important party nexus that brought together intellectuals and ideas. These committees prepared reports, ran seminars, published papers and advised the party on their areas of expertise. Many committees followed their own dynamics in which ideas were developed, to a limited extent, beyond what might be deemed acceptable: some members of the Economic Committee, for example, supported the idea of an 'incomes policy' when most of the left, including the CPGB, opposed it.[82] These ideas evolved out of a combination of the political practice of holding public meetings with non-party speakers (in part to attract non-party people) with the academic practice of discussing ideas in a seminar-type manner, rather than simply as a lecture masquerading as a 'talk'. Of equal significance is the invitation of the public to participate in discussions at party branches over the new draft of the BRS in 1976–77, although it caused some headaches for the leadership.[83] MT incorporated a similar practice into its discussion groups and events, which meant that organisers in some areas had to establish discussion groups outside of party branches to host meetings with MT contributors or about its ideas.[84]

Martin Jacques used party publications and groups to promote MT to party members and sympathisers, even hosting a national conference on promot-

---

79 Klugmann 1976c, p. 202.
80 Ibid.
81 The title appears to have 'inspired' both Hall's first feature title in MT's January 1979 issue, 'The Great Moving Right Show', and MT's first big event in the autumn of 1982, 'The Moving Left Show'.
82 Andrews 1995a; Pearmain 2014.
83 E.g. PC 1977.
84 For example, some members of the Cardiff branch worked separately to organise a Gramsci event in 1987 (Andrews 1998).

ing the periodical in 1983 attended by over 60 party activists.[85] The conference encouraged party branches to invite contributors to address their members and the local public. These local events, meetings and seminars helped to spread MT's ideas outside of large urban centres and even attracted local press coverage, such as in Gloucester and Dudley, West Midlands, though these were more the exception than the rule.[86]

During the 1980s, *Marxism Today* established itself as *the* promoter and sponsor of discussion groups, conferences and events over and above the party itself. MT events, which began in 1982, were an attempt to take the best of the CUL without the connotations of either 'Communist' or 'University'.[87] This was even reflected in the terminology: MT organised 'events' not 'conferences', with *activist* rather than *academic* connotations.[88] The infrastructure of dissent played an important part in supporting a culture of public meetings, fora and events, something which can be traced back to a range of different influences both educational and political, including the Workers' Educational Association,[89] the 1930s Left Book Clubs and left newspapers, such as *Reynolds News* and the *Daily Herald*, the New Left clubs (1957–62) and journals (e.g. ULR, TNR), and the practice of radical academic journals in the 1970s.[90] For example, *Screen*, a radical film studies journal, sought to extend its 'theoretical effectivity' and influence by encouraging participation via readers' groups, events and summer schools.[91] In the pre-discussion period before the 1977 Congress, party branches were encouraged to hold public meetings on the proposed revisions to the BRS, although the leadership did express concerns about some speakers.[92]

Just as the CPGB had an established tradition of party education, specialist groups, many of which had grown up during the 1970s alongside the CULs, fed into the demands for discussion over such areas as 'actually existing socialism' in Eastern Europe or a Marxist approach to art. Just as many party members and

---

85   Farrington 1983.
86   Dudley was where Mark Perryman established a MT group prior to being recruited to join MT in London (Perryman 1994b). The author attended a few MT group discussions in north London during the late 1980s, one of which overwhelmed the seating capacity of the local library.
87   Townsend 1996.
88   Ibid.
89   WEA included many CPGB and ex-CPGB members during its time: e.g. E.P. Thompson, John Saville, Raymond Williams.
90   E.g. Chun 1993; Easthope 1988; Lemahieu 1988; Samuels 1966.
91   Easthope 1988, p. 233.
92   Townsend 1996; Johnstone 1995. See the story of the South Essex District CP in Chapter 1.

sympathisers would have been well disposed towards discussion, so too many of MT's readers were well-disposed towards seminar-type political discussions, especially amongst the great proportion of students and graduates, two-thirds of whom had university degrees, including one in five with postgraduate qualifications. The idea of the seminar or debate, rather than a lecture, would have had a particular kind of appeal to such a readership, as did the appeal of the writing styles and rhetorical strategies of key contributors, like Stuart Hall.

The annual, weeklong Communist University of London hit a high point in the mid-1970s. By 1979, however, it was rapidly losing money and participants, as the party's influence in student politics waned.[93] The Communist Party had also held a 'People's Jubilee' in 1977 as a counter-rally to the celebrations for the 'Queen's Jubilee' (which the Sex Pistols' immortal 'God Save the Queen' was meant to 'commemorate'), marking the 25th anniversary of Queen Elizabeth II's ascension to the throne, which attracted 11,000 people to Alexander Palace in north London. The only notable party event of a similar nature and size was the 'Marx with Sparx' day event in 1983 on the 100th anniversary of the death of Karl Marx.

While the Socialist Workers' Party carried on the tradition of the CUL, after the last one was held in 1981, with their own annual 'Marxism festival', *Marxism Today* replaced the CUL with its *own* biennial events, the three largest of which were: the 'Moving Left Show' in 1982 (1,700 people); 'Left Alive' in 1984 (2,500 people); and 'Left Unlimited' in 1986 (3,500 people). Smaller events were organised and held locally, as were some events which targetted different constituencies, such as 'Women Alive' in 1986 (1,000 people) and 'Gramsci 87' (on the 50th anniversary of Gramsci's death). The last major event was the 1988 'Re-Thinking Socialism' (aka 'New Times') weekend (a 'working seminar'), which specifically targetted a much smaller group unlike other MT events.

The 'Moving Left Show' was considered a great success and generated the first positive comments about MT in the national press: participants were described as 'open-minded', of 'moderate disposition,' and not as 'myopic' as the Labour Party, as the event's connections to the CPGB were identified.[94] Such a contrast, no doubt, helped to support the representation of Labour in the media as 'extreme' and 'too left-wing', particularly with descriptions of a 'Marxist' or 'Communist' event including 'open-minded' participants. Rhetorically

---

93   Jacques 1996c.
94   Jenkins 1982; Rutherford 1982. Rutherford was not actually the first FT journalist to participate in an MT event. Twenty years earlier, Klugmann's MT had hosted a forum entitled, 'Man on the Screen: What Shall We Make of Him?', which included the FT's film critic, David Robinson (MT 1962b).

and politically, this situated MT in a position to be sought after by mainstream media commentators and journalists, although it was not all supportive commentary or coverage (see below).

The second weekend event, 'Left Alive', expanded its remit to include extracurricular activities, such as 'jazz dance, jogging and rock climbing', in addition to the usual fare of political debates: a notable change in left political conferences.[95] Big draws, such as the debates between Ken Livingstone, the popular, left-wing Labour leader of the GLC, 1981–86, and Beatrix Campbell, a leading Communist and feminist writer, and between Stuart Hall and Tony Benn, were carried in subsequent issues of MT. The 'Women Alive' event in July 1986 was part of a strategy to attract women, a key constituency in the BDA with which MT identified itself, even as it was slow in bringing more women writers on board and incorporating feminism into its political project.[96]

'Left Unlimited', MT's third national weekend event, was used to promote the third format, but only attracted 70 percent of the expected 5,000 attendees that left the magazine with substantial debt. It might be that, with the end of the CPGB's 'civil war' and the impact of the 'realignment of the left' fracturing the left, the pool of potential attendees became shallower than before. 'Left Unlimited' sparked a political intervention by Third World First (TWF) over development issues, which had become increasingly marginalised in MT under Jacques (Table 4). TWF distributed a leaflet at the event criticising MT for its exclusion of non-white speakers, and race and development issues. TWF suggested that a representative of an African aid agency should have been invited to represent the views of the recipients of 'Live Aid'.[97] Nonetheless, the EC considered the event an 'outstanding success', despite losing a lot of money.[98] MT events also elicited criticisms from others across the political spectrum. Leading media commentators criticised media celebrities, like news presenter Anna Ford, for participating in the 1982 MLS because the event was sponsored by a Marxist publication, while party members criticised MT for inviting right-wing personalities, such as anti-abortion campaigner Victoria Gillick, to 'Left Unlimited' in 1986, and complaints were heard from MT supporters in the party.[99]

---

95   MT 1991, pp. 18, 21.
96   See 'Moving Forward on Feminism', which includes notes of a report on 'Women Alive' and local follow-up, by Sarah Gasquoine and a report on MT and feminism by Tricia Davis, submitted to the EC in 1986 (EC 1986b). See also Cockburn's review of MT for the MTEB (Cockburn 1989).
97   TWF 1986.
98   EC 1986b.
99   PCSub 1986.

An important, but less high profile, aspect of MT's public interventions were the readers' discussion groups, which Jacques conceptualised as a means to 'assume an increasingly "interventionist" role' and to establish 'a more "living" relationship' with both party and non-party readers.[100] Although three MT readers' groups had been established as early as January 1979, the leadership only moved to suppress them in September 1979, under pressure from traditionalist opponents, who suspected that this was the beginnings of a parallel network for reformists outside of formal party structures (and control).[101] MT was subsequently forced to rely on supporters in party branches to host talks by contributors and discussions, seminars and meetings on the ideas published in the magazine: these took place in colleges, libraries, town halls and other public arenas around the country.[102] For example, MT groups worked with the local party branches in Birmingham and Teeside, sharing members and resources.[103] But where MT faced hostile party branches, supporters had to organise outside local party networks. In Cardiff, for example, a local party activist set up an MT discussion group outside the party because the local branch was controlled by traditionalist opponents and Stalinists; he went on to help organise other forums and regional talks, including the Cardiff forum on Gramsci in 1987, a regional supplement to the national MT event on the 50th anniversary of Gramsci's death.[104]

As *Marxism Today* was transformed into a magazine, however, its sponsorship of talks and readers' groups took on a more 'factional' position, as groups were increasingly sponsored outside the party structure, even though MT's opponents were less of a problem as they were purged from or left the party. In fact, this 'factional' position was not necessarily internal *to the party* but more broadly (and generally) part of debates on the broader left. This independent de-centralised approach to participation in MT's political project was taken up by its readers, a practice most familiar with those with some post-secondary education or experience of political meetings and public discussions. In fact, those with student and academic connections would find feedback or 'talking back' to be a vital part of these experiences and is most closely linked to the university seminar. Unlike party-controlled groups, MT groups were set up and run by their members, and it also meant that they did not have to accept MT's

---

100 Jacques 1978b, p. 270; Jacques 1978e.
101 EC 1979c.
102 Townsend 1996.
103 Andrews 1998; Jacques 1996d; Perryman 1994b.
104 Andrews 1998. Geoff Andrews also organised an MT group at Ruskin College, Oxford University.

ideas or themes uncritically. One group used MT as a basis around which to organise discussions that often took a critical line on its political project, while another group focused on sexual politics because this was an important topic that they felt the magazine neglected.[105] Such independence makes the resilience and appeal of these forms of participation stronger, while also having consequences: for example, *Screen* was influential at its peak in the mid-1970s, but as its readers' groups and summer schools declined, so too did the journal's influence.[106]

Many people's desires to discuss issues differed to what the party offered in many of its branch meetings. Meetings offer a means for disseminating ideas, but they can also offer a means by which people can challenge the same ideas and argue against them. Although in higher education, the seminar differs from the lecture as a mode of learning, it does not mean that one is necessarily more 'democratic' than the other. Yet, the seminar is probably a better means for engaging others because it can prove to be a non-hierarchical pedagogic mode which can help to validate the ideas of others, while still pulling people closer into the seminar host's ideological orbit. It probably did not hurt MT that so many of its readers were higher education students and graduates. However, the appeal of these forms of political engagement might also limit MT's, or its readers' groups', appeal to those not so closely linked to higher education.

8 Promotion

The differences between the two editorships of James Klugmann and Martin Jacques could not be more starkly delineated than in their respective approaches to publicity and promotion, both of which, in the last two formats, were intricately linked to Jacques's fervent desire for the ideas to circulate in the national public sphere. Although the CPGB sent out a press release announcing the launch of *Marxism Today* on 21 August 1957, publicity and promotion under Klugmann remained primarily focused on reaching an internal audience of party members and sympathisers, and through that focus developing discussion across theory, politics and other areas that linked the CPGB to its sister parties around the world.[107] When Klugmann did try to reach out to other left publications, most publicity material consisted simply of listings of forthcoming articles and authors; nothing was used to target national papers.

---

105 Osler 1996; Rutherford 1997.
106 Easthope 1988, p. 233.
107 CPGB 1957c.

Promotion and publicity would not have been as big a concern for Klugmann because of how the Communist Party conceived of MT's role. As a sub-grouping of the Press and Publicity Department, it merited only a single line in congress reports as a minor part of party literature that was distributed to branches and bookshops. Even the CPGB's need to address the means of communicating to new audiences amidst rapid political and social change, little attention was applied to promotion. For example, after the CPGB held a conference on 'Party literature' in 1965, it did not bother to hold another one until 1979, 14 years later when the CPGB was facing a much different and more critical situation. Outside of the daily newspaper, this oversight or neglect demonstrates the low priority the party's literature, never mind promotion and publicity, held for both leadership and staff: as if the ideas would distribute themselves.

In January 1979, the Press and Publicity Department prepared a seven-page report on the good and bad news facing party publications, from leaflets to books. Although the CPGB's membership and *The Morning Star*'s circulation had been declining, and the circulation of party journals was static or falling, there had been an increase overall in the sales and circulation of 'Party literature', which included the Lawrence and Wishart's book list. The party literature distribution network, however, was becoming increasingly less important as many members were subscribing via the post or purchasing Communist literature directly from the party's bookshops rather than ordering them via their local party branches. This points to the growing inactivity of local party organisations despite a growing public interest in Marxist and socialist ideas.

The difference with promotion efforts under Martin Jacques's editorship, on the other hand, could not be more stark. From the beginning, he made consistent and ever increasing efforts at publicity and promotion, especially once the second format was launched with the October 1979 issue.[108] While developing his approach, Jacques used cross-media promotion with party publications, via listings of future articles, as Klugmann had done, and with other left papers, via exchange ads.[109] This was an integral part of his move to have MT address an audience on the left outside the party as well as within it, and he was aware that there would be internal opposition to such a plan. However, if the party and MT were to have any chance of establishing influence across the broad left, then it was necessary to try and reach out to those who did not normally read

---

108   In the two years before the second format launch, Jacques was more selective about which issues he actively promoted because he wanted something of which he could be proud (Jacques 1996b).

109   Jacques 1979h, p. 1; Farrington 1983.

CPGB publications. As mainstream press coverage increased during the 1980s, it helped MT to begin to move some way out of the 'radical ghetto'.[110]

Timing was an important part of *Marxism Today*'s promotional efforts. To achieve the political influence with the Labour Party that Jacques desired for MT,[111] the October issues became the most important because they were always published at the start of Labour's annual conferences, with key articles reprinted on *The Guardian*'s 'Agenda' page. Richard Gott, 'Agenda' editor, saw it as an opportunity to engage in the then current debates on the 'crisis of the Left' and the 'rise of the Right'.[112] Also, it was fortuitous for MT that October is seen as the most important month for magazine sales because, as autumn weather approaches people spend more time indoors, and with the start of the university and school years, reading and the demand for reading material increases substantially, making it the best possible time to reach out to new and, potentially, regular readers until the following summer.[113]

Jacques's strategy began to have an impact one year after the second format launch in 1979, with the October 1980 issue's cover story, an interview with Tony Benn, leader of the Labour Left: it was MT's first article to be reprinted in a national newspaper, *The Guardian*.[114] After the Labour government's defeat in May 1979, Benn represented the hopes that the left would finally get its chance to turn Labour into a socialist party. His interview garnered national media attention and raised MT's profile as an important periodical where the issues affecting the left, and not just the CPGB, were being debated. There is an irony here since the CPGB had been excluded from the April 1980 'Debate of the Decade' to which all other left parties had been invited.[115] This first reprint, and the attention that it garnered for MT across the left, marked the start of a close, productive relationship between MT and *The Guardian*, and spurred on the former's publicity and promotional efforts across all national media outlets. As this exposure became a key motivational factor, MT would invest increas-

---

110   Jacques 1996b; Perryman 1994b.
111   The CPGB's efforts to influence the labour movement included (always) unsuccessful efforts over decades of trying to affiliate to the Labour Party (Andrews 2004; Callaghan 2005; Thompson 1992).
112   Gott 1988.
113   Townsend 1996.
114   Hobsbawm 1980. This analysis is based upon the MT press clippings file that Jacques collected during his editorship which he made available to me in 1996 (see Pimlott 2000a, 2000b).
115   Hain 1980. The organisers were criticised for not inviting a speaker from the CPGB, although some party members, who spoke from the floor, had their comments published (Campbell 1980).

ing amounts of time and resources into publicity and promotion to, not only increase sales, but also (and more importantly in Jacques's eyes) raise MT's public profile nationally and, thereby, gain influence on the left and within the Labour Party.[116]

Changes in technology, funding and distribution were made possible by and contributed to MT's promotional efforts, which were evident in the differences between the launch issues for the second and third formats in 1979 and 1986 respectively. With a publicity budget of only £250 for the October 1979 second-format launch issue, MT used free and exchange (or cross-) advertising deals with alternative listings, feminist, socialist and Labour publications to target non-CPGB, left-wing and progressive audiences: e.g. *Time Out*; *Spare Rib*; *Socialist Worker*; *New Statesman*; *Tribune*.[117] Follow-up promotion included party publications, *Morning Star* and *Comment*, universities, conferences, festivals, and even a press conference for left publications. All of these efforts did bring MT to the attention of others on the left in the lead-up to its trial distribution deal in London and later nationwide.

For its October 1986 third-format launch issue, MT paid for ads in Labour Left (*New Statesman*, *New Socialist*, *Tribune*), CPGB (*Seven Days*), women's (*Spare Rib*, *Women's Review*) and alternative listings and youth magazines (*The Face*, *Manchester City Life*). Marxist Left publications were excluded, indicating a shift away from trying to appeal to radical left audiences, especially in the aftermath of the CPGB's 'civil war', although Marxist organisations continued to advertise in MT to reach a potentially larger readership for their publications. In addition, MT ran six ads in *The Guardian*, plus news stories and ads in the trade press (*Newsagent*, *Media Week*), backed by a promotional campaign with 200 posters in London underground stations, 3,000 fly-posters, 250,000 promotional folders, a press conference and party, and a weekend event, 'Left Unlimited' (which attracted 3,500 people, but not the expected 5,000, adding to MT's financial woes). This promotional campaign, which would have been impossible without the increased revenues and greater public profile from national distribution, highlights MT's investment in promotion as well as its shift from targeting socialists to searching for a broader, non-party, progressive audience.

---

116   Jacques 1996b.
117   Jacques 1979h.

9   Publicity

Marxism Today's small budget constrained both its promotional and publicity efforts at first: press releases, for example, were initially delivered by hand to save on postage.[118] By the mid-1980s, as revenues increased and volunteers multiplied, its publicity efforts expanded considerably. Between 100 and 400 copies of each issue were sent out with separate press releases, tailored for the relevant desk editors and specialist reporters (e.g. politics; health; arts; architecture; music).[119] MT issued more press releases than any other left periodical: from a minimum of two to as many as six different press releases per issue. This contrasts with *New Socialist*, for example, where its first editor only ever sent out one press release per issue.[120]

Press releases followed four basic themes in descending order of importance. First priority was given to promoting the ideas and analysis in the features section, which Martin Jacques hoped would have the greatest degree of influence on Labour and the left, while contributing to the magazine's public profile and increasing sales. Second priority was given to MT's interviews with leading political and cultural figures. Third priority was given to playing off the contradictions between the title and content, such as highlighting a Conservative minister on the cover of a 'Marxist' magazine. The last priority was on promoting spin-offs, such as the products of 'Central Committee Outfitters'.[121] The last two priorities were seen more as a means to gain exposure and challenge public misconceptions about MT and only became more possible after 1986 as MT became more 'iconoclastic', at least in terms of its 'Marxism'.

A typical example of MT's publicity strategy is that of the March 1988 issue. Three press releases emphasising three different topics were targeted at the relevant contacts in the national press. In order of importance, these were: a press release aimed at political editors highlighting the cover feature, an 'exclusive' interview with Michael Heseltine, Conservative MP, who was seen as a rival and possible successor to Thatcher at that time; a second press release on the 'Social Side of Cancer' targetted medical correspondents; and a third release for arts editors covered a debate about modern architecture (including *The Guardian*'s critic). Despite these efforts, only five news items appeared, all of which referred to the Heseltine interview, including a reprint in *The Guardian*. Although professional journalists contributed all three features promoted

---

118   Taylor 1995; Townsend 1996.
119   Taylor 1995.
120   Curran 1997a.
121   Jacques 1996d; Perryman 1994b.

by MT, only one article was used by the national press, which indicates that even contributions from mainstream media professionals gave no guarantee for media coverage of MT or its content.[122]

Less typical, albeit nonetheless illustrative, of the tensions between MT and its public persona, is the promotion of the June 1989 issue which carried a Communist Party document, *The Manifesto for New Times*, contradicting Jacques's usual efforts at maintaining a distance between MT and the party in public. MT's reliance on CPGB funding as circulation stagnated meant separation was much harder to maintain in practice than it had been, but Jacques and MT had more of a stake in supporting the CPGB's manifesto, MNT, because of their own ideological stake in it (i.e. it demonstrated the closest *ideological* connection between the party and MT's political project as it was at that point). The June 1989 issue was also the culmination of a three-month promotion by MT's distributor. Publicity efforts for June 1989 generated 17 news items and articles: none dealt with the Kenneth Clarke interview,[123] then Conservative Health Secretary, but seven covered the CPGB and its manifesto without actually mentioning MT. This seems a curiosity given the frequency with which the magazine was identified with East European Communist regimes by mainstream media seeking commentary on the 'fall of the Wall'. Of the remaining ten items, six were responses in the trade press. Despite all the effort put into promoting one issue over another, there was no way of ensuring national news coverage. While trade news was important, it was national news coverage that was the most sought after for its potential to raise MT's public profile, recruit more readers and increase sales, and ultimately extend its influence at the national level. It is this attempt to move beyond the left into the national public sphere that takes us into examining more systematically national press coverage of MT.

10   National Press Coverage

A defining characteristic of *Marxism Today* was the exposure it received in the national press during the 1980s, becoming the best-known left magazine, by reaching out beyond the 'radical ghetto' to a broader audience. The national broadsheet press provided the most important coverage because they often

---

122   However, the second press release promoted the medical feature to medical trade journals which did provide coverage.

123   Though there was some coverage of the interview in non-news and non-trade publications.

set the national political agenda.[124] National press coverage, however, was not unproblematic. As broadsheets followed their own agenda, MT could not always guarantee securing their attention, let alone being able to influence *how* the press would cover or frame the issue(s) being promoted.

Total broadsheet coverage during Jacques' editorship, 1978–91, amounted to over half of the period's press clippings: 507 out of 961 items (52.8 percent) (Table 11A). *The Guardian* accounts for nearly half of this total (45.3 percent); three other broadsheets that provided significant coverage are: FT (10.7 percent); *The Observer* (9.9 percent); *The Independent* (9.0 percent) (Table 11B). *The Independent*'s share, however, was more concentrated in part because it only started publishing in October 1986, but we can see a shift in MT to the right as *The Guardian* gives way to *The Independent*.[125] Liberal and centre-left broadsheets, therefore, account for three-quarters (74.9 percent) of all items that made reference to MT in some capacity, indicating that newspapers closest to the left politically were most likely to cover the magazine.

Just over three-quarters (76.5 percent) of the total coverage related to all types of political matters: nearly one in four items (23.3 percent) focused on the Labour Party and/or movement; two in five (39.8 percent) dealt with the CPGB and/or MT.[126] Coverage of MT in relation to the 'Labour Party and movement' was greatest between 1984 and 1987, a difficult and bitter period of internal strife for the left: 70 out of 118 news items (59.3 percent).[127] This figure increases to 82 items or nearly 70 percent if we include 1983. Of course, this is the period when MT was recognised by the national media and others for its willingness to engage in criticising left 'shibboleths'. Only 22 items (18.6 percent) were published between 1988 and 1991, indicating that reforms in the Labour Party, initiated under Neil Kinnock's leadership, 1983–92, and the Labour Left's marginalisation, had made MT's interventions of less interest to the national press.

Internal CPGB strife was another motivation for broadsheet coverage between 1984 and 1987, with two *Guardian* journalists favouring opposing sides in their stories. Over half (55.8 percent) of the coverage of 'CP or Communism', however, took place between 1988 and 1990 (58 items) with the launch of 'New Times' and its adoption as its manifesto by the CPGB, and the collapse of Communism. However, after the 1988 peak, and despite the Eastern European

---

124   Tunstall 1996.
125   Jacques would go on to become an associate editor at *The Independent* in the mid-1990s.
126   All numbers in this paragraph are drawn from Table 12.
127   The national press coverage helped to fan internal strife in both the CPGB and Labour, with particular columnists and reporters favouring one side or the other.

TABLE 11A Print media coverage of *Marxism Today*, 1978–91

Publication[a]	1978	1979	1980	1981	1982	1983	1984	1985	1986	1987	1988	1989	1990	1991	Totals
Broadsheets	1	–	2	8	29	40	42	64	45	64	73	45	45	49	507
Middle market daily & Sunday tabloid papers[b]	–	–	–	2	4	–	3	1	5	18	6	3	3	2	47
Down market daily & Sunday tabloids	–	–	–	2	6	–	2	–	2	3	3	–	–	–	18
Centre-left periodicals[c]	–	–	–	2	7	13	15	14	5	7	3	2	1	1	70
Right periodicals[d]	–	–	–	1	1	3	3	2	4	2	1	–	–	1	18
Left press[e]	1	–	–	4	11	4	6	1	4	7	10	10	–	2	60
Trade papers	–	–	–	–	4	–	2	4	4	6	1	1	1	1	46
Listings magazines[f]	–	–	–	2	4	9	7	10	5	8	1	23	6	1	53
Regional & Local papers	–	–	–	1	5	3	2	4	1	2	4	9	1	1	33
Cultural weeklies[g]	–	1	–	–	–	–	2	1	–	–	–	–	1	2	7
Feminist periodicals[h]	–	–	–	–	1	–	–	1	–	–	–	1	–	–	3
Fashion/Style magazines	–	–	–	–	–	–	–	–	2	5	3	–	–	–	10
Trade Union periodicals	–	–	–	–	3	–	1	–	–	–	–	–	–	–	4
Scottish press[i]	–	–	–	–	1	–	1	3	1	1	18	5	–	–	30
Foreign press[j]	–	–	–	–	4	5	4	2	4	2	5	4	4	3	37
Miscellaneous	–	–	–	1	–	–	2	1	2	3	–	4	3	2	18
TOTAL	2	1	2	22	81	77	92	108	84	128	128	106	65	65	961

a These were all the cuttings from MT's press file for 1978–91 that was made available to me by Jacques.
b Middle Market Daily & Sunday Tabloid Papers include *London Evening Standard* and *London Daily News*.
c Centre-Left Periodicals = e.g. *New Statesman, New Socialist, Liberator*.
d Right Periodicals = e.g. *Spectator, The Economist*.
e Left Press coverage is incomplete.
f Listings Magazines includes *New Musical Express*.
g Cultural Weeklies includes bi-weeklies.
h Feminist Periodicals = *Spare Rib, Everywoman*.
i Scottish Press includes Scottish listings magazines.
j This collection in the MT Press Clippings file was not complete.

TABLE 11B National broadsheet coverage of *Marxism Today*, 1978–91 (number of articles)

BROADSHEETS	1978	1979	1980	1981	1982	1983	1984	1985	1986	1987	1988	1989	1990	1991	Total
Guardian	–	–	2	5	18	11	22	33	29	24	34	17	17	18	230
Financial Times	–	–	–	–	3	6	9	8	5	4	9	2	3	5	54
Times	1	–	–	3	3	2	6	10	1	4	3	2	4	1	40
Telegraph	–	–	–	–	1	1	3	3	1	5	1	5	3	1	24
Independent	–	–	–	–	–	–	–	–	2	13	9	3	10	10	47
Sunday Times	–	–	–	–	4	7	–	2	–	5	8	8	1	4	39
Observer	–	–	–	–	–	11	2	7	5	8	8	3	2	4	50
Sunday Telegraph	–	–	–	–	–	2	–	1	2	1	1	2	–	–	9
Independent on Sunday	–	–	–	–	–	–	–	–	–	–	–	–	5	6	11
Sunday Correspondent	–	–	–	–	–	–	–	–	–	–	–	3	–	–	3
TOTAL	1	0	2	8	29	40	42	64	45	64	73	45	45	49	507

revolutions in 1989–90, overall press coverage began to ebb. This also made the play on the apparent contradictions between MT's title and its content less 'newsworthy': *The Guardian* reprinted only two articles in 1989–91. Press coverage only picked up at the end of 1991 in response to MT's impending closure.

Marxism Today itself became a focus of national press coverage, pushing it ahead of Labour Party issues after Labour's third general election defeat in 1987. As the left's morale fell sharply, feature articles moved away from a narrow definition of 'Politics' to focus more on social and cultural issues, such as abortion, masculinity and consumerism, with topics, perspectives and contributors that also reflected the influence and spread of cultural studies.[128] Between 1986 and 1989, MT was also surfing a wave of international and domestic interest in 'designer socialism', interviews with Conservative politicians and MT events, such as 'Left Unlimited'.

A breakdown of news clippings, by the degree to which MT's ideas and information constitute each news item, demonstrates that more than two-fifths (43.8%) of all mentions of MT in the broadsheets, or 222 items out of 507, were 'brief': anything from an event listing or a mention in a column, to a short one- or two- paragraph news item (Table 13). These references, however 'brief', nonetheless helped contribute to MT's public image and persona through sheer repetition, most frequently, of the contradictions between a 'Marxist' publication and the promotion of its own wine, filofaxes or interviews with Tory MPs. The three most important article types were those that provided the most space for MT's ideas: 'MT Reprints', 'MT Source' (40 percent or more of content drawn from MT) and 'Important Reference' articles, which totalled 189 (37.3 percent) for all broadsheets in 1978–91 (Table 13).

A clear indication of the significance of an MT article is whether it was chosen for reproduction on the opinion-editorial pages, where a newspaper's own political position or 'editorial line' is made explicit, and where pundits' opinions and readers' letters are published. This is where debate across the left and with others is encouraged and it represents a space for intervention, albeit shaped by the newspaper's staff. As the leading centre-left daily, *The Guardian* was responsible for 30 out of the total of 43 reprints, published on its 'Agenda' page. The liberal broadsheet, *The Independent*, launched in 1986, reprinted 10. Of *The Guardian*'s 30 reprints, ten were articles or interviews, by or with, Eric Hobsbawm. He occupied a privileged position in critiquing left 'shibboleths' because, as a lifetime Communist Party member and a respected Marxist his-

---

[128] E.g. Campbell and Wheeler 1988; Cockburn 1986, 1988; Hebdige 1989; McRobbie 1987; Mort 1989; Mort and Green 1988.

TABLE 12   National broadsheet press coverage by subject, 1978–91

SUBJECT[a]	1978	1979	1980	1981	1982	1983	1984	1985	1986	1987	1988	1989	1990	1991	Total
CP or communism	–	–	–	–	4	10	7	14	4	7	17	20	19	2	104
Labour Party and movement	–	–	1	3	10	12	18	23	11	18	9	5	6	2	118
On MT[b]	–	–	–	2	4	3	–	5	6	13	9	10	3	16	71
Culture	–	–	–	–	2	2	1	1	1	8	3	–	3	4	25
General politics[c]	–	–	–	–	4	8	–	10	12	6	4	8	5	11	68
MT events	–	–	–	–	3	–	2	–	7	3	10	1	–	1	27
Interviews[d]	1	–	1	3	2	3	10	2	4	7	16	1	6	11	67
Miscellaneous	–	–	–	–	–	2	4	9	–	2	5	–	3	2	27
TOTAL	1	–	2	8	29	40	42	64	45	64	73	45	45	49	507

a   The 'subject' is defined as the primary focus of the reference to MT within the item concerned.
b   This refers to items that focused on MT.
c   This refers to the area in which articles would discuss Thatcherism or intellectuals in politics, etc.
d   This is the one area in which the subject of the interview, the person, is of primary importance rather than the topic.

TABLE 13 National press coverage by article type and/or use, 1978–91

BROADSHEETS	1978	1979	1980	1981	1982	1983	1984	1985	1986	1987	1988	1989	1990	1991	Total
Editorials	–	–	–	–	1	2	2	5	2	1	2	–	2	3	20
Reprints	–	–	1	1	3	1	3	8	4	4	6	2	5	5	43
MT source	1	–	–	1	11	8	15	6	5	6	7	–	–	2	62
On MT	–	–	–	1	4	5	4	2	3	6	9	4	1	9	48
Important reference	–	–	–	3	5	11	5	8	5	9	9	16	9	4	84
Brief reference	–	–	1	2	4	9	10	30	23	35	34	23	25	26	222
Letters	–	–	–	–	1	4	3	5	3	3	6	–	3	–	28
TOTAL	1	0	2	8	29	40	42	64	45	64	73	45	45	49	507

torian of international repute, whose work was published in a CPGB journal, his analyses carried enormous authority and *gravitas*. His critiques of Labour and the left were at least nominally *from*, not just the left generally speaking, but specifically the Communist Party, which is supposed to be to the left of Labour. Thus, Hobsbawm's criticisms of Labour were invaluable to those pushing Labour to change its orientation on key issues, such as nationalisation and Europe, because of the greater weight accorded to a 'Marxist' intellectual over that of centre-left or liberal politicians and pundits, since it is the 'far left' concurring with the Labour Right.

Interviews with topical individuals in *Marxism Today* were popular as reprints or sources for news stories for newspapers of all political views, even predating the 1979 second format launch. For example, the September 1978 issue included a cover story, an interview with Bob Wright, a left-wing union leader, which was drawn upon by the Labour Left's *Tribune* as well as two national newspapers, *The Times* and *The Guardian*, later that autumn in the run-up to the 'Winter of Discontent'.[129] These were followed by interviews with such important Labour figures as Tony Benn, Neil Kinnock and Ken Livingstone. National newspapers used these interviews to show either how much the leadership was changing from 'Old Labour' or not. For example, an interview with Roy Hattersley, then Labour's deputy leader, was used by *The Times* to demonstrate that Labour still favoured nationalisation.[130]

But even as right-wing newspapers used MT as a source, they were often contradictory in their reactions. Opposed to those who saw it as a 'left-wing rag' or as part of an 'international Communist conspiracy', were others who contrasted Communist 'reasonableness' to Labour's 'radical extremes',[131] including asking if the CPGB would be the saviour of the left: the arch-Conservative *Telegraph* was asking if 'Professor Hobsbawm's logic alone [would] be sufficient to offset' the 'Trotskyist militant mood' that was gaining ground on the left 'out of sheer despair'.[132] This was a major achievement given the Thatcherite newspapers' penchant for otherwise ignoring the left and its ideas. For example, one journalist condemns Kinnock for his association with the Marxist Hobsbawm: guilt by innuendo; another, by contrast, points out how 'large sections' of Labour were to the left of the CPGB, and also lacked that party's discipline and commit-

---

129   I did not find a copy of *The Times*'s reprint or article (partial reprint?) in the MT Press Clippings File and therefore did not include it in the tables but found references to it elsewhere.
130   E.g. Times 1987.
131   Paterson 1985.
132   *The Telegraph* 1984a.

ment to the 'parliamentary road'.[133] *The Times*'s political editor suggested that Benn and Arthur Scargill, National Union of Mineworkers leader, should 'ponder' the miners' strike roundtable published in the April 1985 issue.[134] These dailies continued to express a contradictory mixture of either 'pleasant surprise' at MT's 'moderate' stance or suspicion of its, and the CPGB's, underlying 'motives'.[135]

There were similarities in the analyses in the liberal and centre-left press with those put forward by *Marxism Today*: the FT, as early as December 1982, points out that MT's Gramscian analysis of postwar British society 'may be surprising to readers of the *Financial Times* only because of its source'.[136] Other commentators pointed out that Labour could learn from the 'moderate', 'open-minded' and 'sensible' types who peopled MT's events; its articles expressed 'realistic' and 'sensible' ideas.[137] Peter Jenkins's views, for example, were an early indication of the support that MT began to attract from liberal commentators, opposed to both Thatcherite Right and Bennite Left, who urged the left not to become bogged down in winning positions inside the Labour Party. However, internal divisions, within both Labour and the CPGB, hardened over rival interpretations of the significance of Labour's 1983 general election defeat and this led to interest in Hobsbawm's hard-hitting criticisms of Labour, which led the 'realignment of the Left' through *The Guardian*, with such provocative headlines as 'Change the Party, Not the Workers' and 'Labour Must Go Forward with the Masses', rather than MT's more cautious titles, 'Labour's Lost Millions' and 'Labour: Rump or Rebirth' respectively. The titles' differences in emphasis signify MT's caution due to internal opposition.[138]

A good example of the way different newspapers drew upon MT's articles is the way that Tony Benn's speech at the November 1984 MT event, 'Left Alive', was taken up.[139] It was used as a source to criticise and ridicule Benn's ideas, taken as representative not only of the left, but also of Labour, in *The Sun*, *Express*, *Telegraph*, *Times* and even the *Mirror*.[140] Interestingly, it is only the FT that draws upon the text of Stuart Hall's speech, published in the same issue right next to Benn's, to criticise the latter for underestimating the scale of Labour's

---

133   *The Telegraph* 1984a, 1989; Walden 1988.
134   Jones 1985.
135   *The Times* 1982; Walden 1988.
136   Rutherford 1982.
137   Jenkins 1982.
138   Hobsbawm 1983b, 1983c, 1984a, 1984c.
139   Benn 1985.
140   Kavanagh 1984; Warden 1984; *The Telegraph* 1984; Jones 1985; Langdon 1984.

defeat; it also indicated that he was being criticised *by* the left and, therefore, Benn's position was *not* necessarily representative *of* the left. Two pieces in *The Guardian* covered Benn's speech, including an editorial criticising Benn. The rest of the mass media's neglect, including the apparently pro-Labour *Mirror*, that Benn could be criticised from the left can be read in three possible ways: either it was an elitist understanding that their audiences would not have been able to understand such 'nuance'; it would have undermined a particular image, even caricature, of the left that these media would not have wanted to disrupt since such long-standing stereotypes can be useful; or it simply did not fit into journalists' preconceived ideas or stereotypes of the left and was therefore disregarded.

As *The Guardian* was the only left-of-centre daily broadsheet throughout the Thatcher decade (1979–90), its relationship with MT is of special significance to understanding the latter's influence on Labour and the left. After Labour's 1979 electoral defeat, when it became wracked by internal struggles, *The Guardian* appeared to be anxious to distance itself from, not just the left, but also the Labour Party. *The Guardian*'s managing director in *Campaign* magazine in April 1981 stated: 'If the newly constituted SDP really takes off, then the *Guardian* is ideally suited to champion the new party's cause as the centre-party voice in the 1980s'.[141] Labour Party divisions were felt within *The Guardian*: some staff were angered by its coverage of Benn's campaign for deputy leader and expressed concern that some senior staff 'were using their position to push the Alliance [SDP-Liberal] ticket in the leader columns'.[142]

The Guardian and *Marxism Today* established a reciprocal relationship because of the former's position on the centre-left and the latter's desire to expand its readership beyond the CPGB. A key figure was Richard Gott, editor of the 'Agenda' page, 1978–88, who recognised that Jacques wanted to interrogate the left's shibboleths, especially after the 1983 election when it was split between 'traditionalists' (or 'hard left') and 'realists' (or 'soft left') in both parties. MT followed a conscious strategy of publishing important critiques of the left's 'orthodox' ideas, many of which Gott had reprinted in *The Guardian* at the start of Labour's annual conferences, encouraging the maximum impact on conference debates and amongst sympathetic *Guardian* readers (since a large proportion of *Guardian* readers also voted Labour).[143] The primary theme reiterated for public debate was Labour's failure to recognise shifts in social, political and

---

141   Cited in Hollingsworth 1986, p. 16.
142   Hollingsworth 1986, p. 58.
143   Gott 1988.

cultural values, as expressed in popular attitudes, and to adapt to this changed environment. In the view from many centre-left commentators and intellectuals, Labour could no longer rely on material interests or 'class belongingness' to automatically deliver working class voters and, therefore, it had to appeal to a larger public than its traditional supporters, and to do so meant developing policies with popular support.[144] Again, the ways in which these values were discussed were as if they do not have a point of origin or as if there was not a particular group or class interest that would have benefitted from promoting them: as if ideas are wholly a product of the 'heavens' (Chapter 2).

However, it should be noted that polls at the same time identified that people's social attitudes had not really changed during the 1980s; a number of analyses offered a different position from which to criticise those who argued that there had been a significant shift to the right.[145] Yet, while voting results are indicative because of a greater number of participants in elections than in opinion polls, both indicate only a particular picture in time of people's allegiances. Thus, while Stuart Hall is correct in suggesting that there had been a shift in public opinion, he fails to recognise the role of establishment media in propagandising an ideological worldview that not all people were capable of resisting.[146]

The Guardian reiterated points that *Marxism Today* was making: Labour had to win public opinion, jettison 'unpopular' policies, and rethink how it could establish an anti-Thatcher coalition. This included lessons from the miners' strike of 1984–85, drawn from the roundtable debate between party and NUM officials, as *The Times* had done, and a suggestion that the union should have made winning public opinion its central objective. Yet, at the same time, support for the strike was a 'litmus test' for everyone who identified with the left and against Thatcherism. MT raised money and public support for miners' families even as it criticised the NUM leadership.

Of equal significance were the topics that were ignored despite MT's publicity efforts. For example, when Jacques's MT did cover international issues, such as analyses of US interventions in Latin America, these were usually ignored: the exceptions include the Walesa interview (October 1981), the Gulf War issue (March 1991) and some commentary on the collapse of Communist regimes after 1989. The broadsheets also ignored analyses of the SDP/Alliance, and art-

---

144 Hobsbawm 1983b, 1984a.
145 E.g. Curran 1984b.
146 Hay has provided quite important insights into how the phrase, 'Winter of Discontent', has been used to attack the left, including by Blair and New Labour, long after 1978–79 (Hay 1996, 2010).

icles on feminism and women, except for occasional public figures interviewed in MT (e.g. Edwina Currie, Tory MP). Other social issues, such as AIDS, peace and apartheid, were also ignored despite the expertise of MT contributors. The national press seemed uninterested in contributors writing on areas of expertise from positions within their respective social movements; clearly, for the national press, MT's criticisms of Labour and the left were especially significant and 'remarkable' because of its connections to the CPGB. However, that connection could also work in reverse: for example, the Campaign for Nuclear Disarmament was denounced as a 'Soviet front' because a leading member of CND had written a feature article for MT.[147]

One area that all broadsheets commented on was the contradictions between their expectations and *Marxism Today*'s contents, from subject matter, interviewees and images, to its intellectual respectability and success. They saw that MT provided a standard against which the rest of the left could be measured: its willingness to criticise the left was particularly appealing, not so much for its criticisms as for their source: 'Coming out of the pages of *Marxism Today* this has a lot more force ... than when it emerges from the mouths of the Shadow Cabinet'.[148] Clearly, all broadsheets were primarily interested in left critiques of the CPGB, Labour and the unions. By 1988, Gott decided that there was no longer any point in producing the 'Agenda' page in *The Guardian* because the consensus that it had 'sought to go beyond' had been 'eroded by Mrs Thatcher and the zeitgeist': there was no point in debating about 'socialisms' and 'liberalisms' because the 'revolutionary times' in which they were living was not a 'revolution in which the Left or the Centre [could] take part'.[149] Thus, MT had been useful until the left was no longer a threat.

Quantitatively and qualitatively, *Marxism Today* was drawn upon for its criticisms of the Labour Party and its policies, while other contributions were generally ignored. Some journalists noticed that while MT's analysis coincided with their own, it was the latter's position as a periodical of the left, which was noteworthy and which helped substantiate their critique of Labour; yet, these mainstream journalists rarely if ever raised MT's critique of Thatcherism (i.e. the political right) and other issues for consideration by their readers. In this period of increasing rancour and division on the left after Labour's 1983 general election defeat, while MT was gaining greater national media coverage, it abandoned a critical (let along a Marxist) take on the establishment

---

147   *The Times* 1982.
148   Young 1985.
149   Gott 1988.

media (primarily the broadsheets, not the tabloids).[150] This shift in approach to the national media was also partly the result of including mainstream or establishment journalists as contributors and seeking national media coverage.

Since national newspapers help to set the agenda for public debate, their use of MT did help to extend its influence, albeit only on certain subjects, and to raise its national profile, but without necessarily increasing its sales significantly. As *the* centre-left newspaper, *The Guardian* helped to promote MT to a national audience as the left's leading agenda-setter, while enhancing its own position in the process; MT, in turn, was used selectively by *The Guardian*, and other national newspapers, to support criticisms of Labour 'shibboleths' and its 'traditionalists'. Although MT gained access to the national public sphere for its ideas, it had little control over which ones were selected and how they were framed and presented to the public. Thus, not only did the national press act as gatekeepers, permitting some ideas access to a wider public, but also they acted as agents in their own right, in helping to set the agenda for debates on the left, through critiques of left ideas and supporting centre-left ideas at the left's expense.

11   'Thinking the Unthinkable'

Marxism Today's task was to persuade both the left, including the Labour Party, and the national media to take its ideas seriously. The combination of ruthless self-promotion, advertising, publicity and media coverage all worked together to develop a persona for MT by the early 1980s. Press coverage was dependent upon its accessibility to non-Marxists, and especially journalists, achieved through changes to its house style, rhetorical strategies and journalistic practices (Chapter 6). MT set itself against popular expectations of Communist periodicals to reach a broad audience and the media, creating a unique 'persona' in the process that became a selling point for MT, though not always a welcome one.

By representing itself as a magazine willing to ask awkward questions about the labour movement, contradict the left's position on various issues and look for answers outside the left, such as arguing that the left could learn from Thatcherism, and 'to think the unthinkable', MT made itself 'newsworthy'. MT's willingness to question left orthodoxies contributed to its success in gaining

---

150   E.g. Jacques 1984a.

access to the public sphere as journalists took the magazine more seriously, aided by MT's analyses, which appeared prescient, which ensured that many of its ideas were attractive to the media.

At first, MT promoted itself only as a 'topical', 'informative' and 'controversial' periodical, an 'indispensable monthly read for all on the Left' (October 1980). However, as it grew in confidence, so did its self-advertisements: 'no simplistic answers to political problems, nor duck[ing] the difficult questions' (April 1982); and taking 'readers far beyond the traditional realm of socialist politics' (November 1983). By 1984, MT was promoting its agenda-setting role by promising to help subscribers 'join the mainstream of political debate' (January) and keep them 'firmly in the mainstream of today's debates' (March), which appeared plausible given that the March issue also carried MT's first national media (as opposed to individual mainstream journalists') endorsements from *The Guardian* ('Essential political reading') and *The Sunday Times* ('A bright well written glossy'). The 'Left Alive' programme in October was stamped with quotes from the FT, *Guardian* and other national newspapers extolling MT's 'open approach to socialist politics', 'beautiful production', and 'jargon-free' writing. These claims for MT's independent, iconoclastic, free-thinking image continued growing during the 1980s, fed by recognition in the national (and international) media.

However, MT's self-promotion contributed to its persona in a way different to media representations, and the public's 'common sense' understandings, of 'Marxism' and the left. The October 1985 issue carried the most direct claims of its persona, which was built around explicit and implicit criticisms of the left:

> If you expect to be told what to think – let us tell you now that you've got the wrong magazine. After all, *Marxism Today* is nothing if not open and pluralistic ... The fact is, the Left has a lot of hard thinking to do. The miners' strike, the rate-capping campaign, sexual morality, union ballots – all raise difficult questions. *Marxism Today* prides itself on facing them square on ...

MT's qualities are defined against right-wing populist assumptions about the left, who 'expect to be told what to think', which can be read as associating all tendencies on the left, such as democratic socialism, with authoritarian Soviet Communism. On the other hand, MT will not tell you 'what to think' because it 'is nothing if not open and pluralistic'. The left is either deceitful or evasive because it is unwilling to face 'difficult questions ... square on'.

With national distribution and press coverage raising MT's profile, the CPGB realised that the periodical was reaching new, non-party readers and wanted to recruit them so, as the party's 'theoretical and discussion journal' it reflected 'our attractive, committed and open approach to socialist politics' (January 1982). The CPGB continued to try and promote itself around MT's reputation, reiterating its 'open and pluralist approach' to socialist and democratic politics, though it stopped laying 'claim' to MT by 1988. The CPGB's lack of success is evidence that even MT's own promotional efforts were not enough to convince more than a relative handful of people to buy it nationwide (i.e. less than 20,000). This self-promotion worked well in enhancing a particular representation of the left that tied in to representations in the national press. However, it was not without foundation: many criticisms resonated with the experience of socialists. MT's self-promotion was part of its attempt to present an image that would attract a broad, progressive audience. The other contribution to its persona came from MT's 'rhetoric of realism' (Chapter 6).

12 Conclusion

Faced with an uncertain future as the Communist Party of Great Britain's decline meant a shrinking pool of readers, income and influence, *Marxism Today* gradually adapted to the marketplace, overcoming its limitations as a party journal by using non-party contributors, investing its human and financial resources heavily in publicity and promotion, and in adapting to newsagent distribution requirements and processes. Although academics predominated during the 1970s and early 1980s, by the late 1980s professional journalists had become the single largest occupational group of contributors, enhancing the magazine's potential access to a broader audience. MT and its discussion groups, sometimes working with supportive party branches, contributed to the promotion of ideas via seminars, meetings and events, garnering some local media attention as well. MT's rigorous and skillful use of publicity secured extensive news coverage that gained it widespread national (and international) exposure and raised its profile, enabling some contributors and their ideas access into mainstream media, from which the left is often excluded. Its intensive publicity and promotion campaigns also served to reinforce its own political narrative that was constructed against a particular view of 'the left', which was also shaped by the Tory press.

Access was also helped through national newsagent distribution, which introduced *Marxism Today* to new readers, whilst party networks continued to supply its long-time party members and bookshops, though these too declined, not only due to older readers' mortality, but also due to internal divisions. MT's marketplace success, which contributed to and was effected by its transformation from a party journal into a political magazine, extended its life as other party publications were forced to close during the 1980s. Despite competition from other left magazines and in spite of significantly lower circulation than its competitors, MT's influence was, ultimately, greater as its criticisms of the left were covered by, and promoted in, the national press that together helped to prepare the ground, ideologically, for 'New Labour'.[151]

The example of *Marxism Today*, however, also demonstrates the need to make some qualifications to the Comedia model, which promotes the use of marketplace mechanisms for alternative and radical media. The marketplace, on closer examination, does not simply provide access to the national public sphere. National press coverage constitutes a symbiotic, albeit highly asymmetrical, relationship between marginal alternative and radical media on one hand, and mainstream media on the other. MT's access to the national public sphere via the mainstream press was subject to the degree of correspondence between the latter's agenda and MT's ideas. *The Guardian*, for example, drew upon MT to support and promote its own agenda when it was strategically, ideologically and rhetorically advantageous. Although some of its contributors gained access to national media, MT's use of professional journalists, who already had national media access, provided access and legitimacy to those particular contributors to address the left within its own counter-public sphere rather than for the left to address others on the national stage beyond the radical ghetto. Thus, ironically, MT reversed access between mainstream and radical media providing a vehicle for *and* legitimacy to centre and right-wing journalists and their views, which would have, in turn, substantiated, at least to some extent, ideas about shifts to the right in public opinion.

151   Pearmain 2011; Andrews 1999, pp. 80–1; Andrews 2004; Pimlott 2000a, pp. 215–27.

CHAPTER 6

'Write Out of the Margins': Communist Ideology and Accessibility, Rhetoric and Writing Style

High production values, national distribution and important ideas are all integral to the success of a political periodical. However, the production of the ideas via the writing and editing processes still have to be accessible to the target audience(s): the ideas do not 'speak' for themselves, nor can they be influential if they cannot be understood, nor can they become important if they are not communicated clearly to an audience.[1] The language, rhetorical techniques and writing styles should address readers in a manner that conveys the complexity of these ideas without being lost in opaque jargon. The inability of radical organisations, such as the Communist Party of Great Britain, to 'speak' in an accessible manner to the general public helps to explain in part their limited influence, which contributes to and, no doubt, is influenced by the general perception of Marxist discourses as opaque and inaccessible, a situation which even Communist leaders recognised during the twentieth century.[2]

Despite the centrality of writing to the Communist articulation of arguments and analyses, and in their appeals to proletarians, peasants or 'the people', accessibility, rhetoric and writing have tended to be neglected in most analyses of Communist movements and Marxist parties. Too few draw from a historical or cultural materialist approach in analysing the accessibility, rhetorical strategies and writing styles used in Communist political appeals as part of understanding the successes or failures of political struggles. Of course, at the epochal level, the particularities of rhetorical appeals are of lesser importance perhaps in understanding shifts in modes of production and contending social formations. When dealing with shorter time frames, such as particular historical conjunctures of several years rather than centuries-long epochs, however, language, rhetorical techniques and writing styles are that much more integral to the success or failure of socialist forces on the stage of world (or national or local) history. Among the few key rhetorical scholars to approach this issue from a historical materialist perspective are the late James Arnt Aune and Dana

---

1 I am of course excluding those cult(-like) leaders and icons of the right who can sell millions of copies of their books but who often do not communicate clearly and are left to be 'interpreted' by readers.
2 For a concise overview, see Pimlott 2006b.

C. Cloud, in addition to Raymond Williams's cultural materialism which locates writing at the centre of understanding the material base for the production and distribution of ideas, and indeed 'the means of communication as the means of production'.[3] Aune wrote one of the first books in the English language to directly address 'Marxism and rhetoric', in which he locates communicative practices as those which mediate between 'structure and struggle'[4] and his focus directs our attention to linguistic connections between epoch and conjuncture through the speech and writing that underpinned and transformed ideologies of socialism, and that appealed to revolutionaries during times of crisis.

The improvements in accessibility, rhetorical techniques and writing styles was part of *Marxism Today*'s appeal, despite its subtitle as the Communist Party of Great Britain's 'theoretical and discussion journal'. This was due in part to a small but notable increase in its 'readability' or 'accessibility' as it moved through changes in language and writing styles, how its presentation of ideas and analyses eschewed common-sense expectations of Communist writing as abstract and jargonistic, though without ever fully becoming accessible beyond a first-year university level of education.

The book thus far has developed an understanding of how left publications can reach out beyond the 'radical ghetto' into the national public sphere by first analysing MT's relationship with its publisher, the CPGB, and by examining political and social forces, ideas and organisations throughout its history. Second, it has analysed the struggles over editorial autonomy, and over developing and financing technological and commercial mechanisms in production and distribution, which was followed by Chapter 4's examination of its form and transformation from a journal into a magazine by investigating its use of layout and design, imagery and front covers. Third, the previous chapter analysed the promotion of the magazine to, and its coverage by, the national media and this impact upon the development of MT's persona. This penultimate chapter develops the analysis further by closely examining changes in language, rhetorical techniques and writing style, under the editorships of James Klugmann and Martin Jacques, to see how such textual transformations might have contributed to winning over non-party readers and extending the influence of MT's ideas.

It is integral to understanding MT's influence to see how its ideas were represented via changes in accessibility, rhetorical techniques and writing style,

---

3 Williams 1980a [1978]. Aune 1994; Cloud 2003, 2009; Williams 1977.
4 Aune 1994, 2003.

which were key factors in reaching out to new readers beyond the party ghetto. This chapter will start with a comparative analysis of six sample years of MT's accessibility (i.e. comprehensibility) over its 34 years via a FOG Index analysis, after which we consider the shift between the house styles of Klugmann's and Jacques's editorships, and the various emphases placed upon 'plain style', jargon and other rhetorical techniques. The last section considers the rhetorical strategies and techniques, modes of address and metaphors, and writing styles of MT's two most prominent collaborators, Eric Hobsbawm and Stuart Hall, whose public positions and polemical interventions enhanced and extended the periodical's influence on the political and academic lefts. However, before we can engage more concretely with changes in MT's house style, we begin with a brief overview of aspects of Marxist and Communist rhetoric and its 'common sense' understanding, from which MT was attempting to differentiate itself by the early 1980s.

1   Twentieth-Century Communist Rhetoric

The best-known critique of bad political writing in English is George Orwell's ubiquitous 1946 essay, 'Politics and the English Language', one of the most frequently cited introductory essays about techniques of good writing, that is frequently reproduced for secondary school pupils and undergraduate students.[5] That Orwell cited Communist writing is no more a surprise than that he also included other political writing from Conservatives and anarchists. However, just as Orwell was a socialist journalist, so too were so many key organisers, theorists and leaders from socialist, communist and anarchist movements, whose ideas were popularised via the social and cultural practices of journalists, pamphleteers and (book) authors, and it is this integral connection between writing and complex ideas, critical challenges to dominant ideologies and accessible visions of alternative futures, which did help to make some counter-hegemonic ideas influential and popular among different social strata. And yet, it is paradoxical that some left political parties, like the Communist's, that were built upon the pillars of printing, journalism and education,[6] would end up as a cypher or cliché for bad writing and jargonistic prose.

At least since the start of the twentieth century, however, Communists have been warned about their approach to writing. Leading Communists, such as V.I. Lenin and Leon Trotsky, warned their followers against tendencies towards

---

5   On different, critical analyses of Orwell, see Williams 1971 and the collection in Szanto 2005.
6   E.g. Debray 2007.

dogmatic assertions, jargon-laden rhetoric and sloganeering, advice which, at least by the apparent necessity for its continuous reiteration at various times throughout the last century, appears to have frequently gone unheeded.[7] It must have been clear that there were problems with their rhetoric and writing style because as early as 1921, leading Communists, including one of the first theorists of the Communist Press, Adalbert Fogarasi, recognised the need 'to raise the level of intelligence and imagination of communist press writers', while others stressed the importance of writing clearly and concretely to reach a working-class audience, including advice offered in the CPGB's own handbooks.[8]

The paucity of analysis of Communist journalism, propaganda and pamphleteering in terms of accessibility, rhetorical strategies and writing styles is remarkable when considering the importance of a publication's readability.[9] Communist literature is usually targeted at either a 'mass audience', though that is frequently narrowed down to the most politicised sections of the working class, or a 'narrow audience', such as party intellectuals. Yet, in spite of the expressed desire of many radical and Marxist groups to reach a wider audience, their publications have seldom made concessions in their rhetoric and writing style, limiting their appeal to those who are already ideologically predisposed towards their ideas or identified with their movements. Indeed, Marxists have usually denied the rhetorical nature and needs of their own proselytising activities, which is somewhat ironic given Karl Marx's own interest in rhetoric as a young man and his own considerable literary and rhetorical skills, including his time employed as an editor and journalist.[10] Many of his pamphlets, such as *The Communist Manifesto* and *The Eighteenth Brumaire*, were written in an accessible, persuasive manner for a broad audience which speak to his power as a writer.[11] Yet, few Marxists consider the importance of language, rhetorical techniques or writing styles to the success or failure of political struggles, with the notable exception of Antonio Gramsci's emphasis on language, 'common sense' and 'folklore' in his theory of hegemony.[12]

---

7   Lenin cited in Hobsbawm 1984a, p. 9; Trotsky 1973a; 1973b. See Pimlott 2006b, 2013.
8   Fogarasi 1979, p. 153; Beauchamp 1945; Dunne 1928; Hutt 1956; Workers' Life 1979 [1928].
9   E.g. Aune 1994; Burgchardt 1980; Downing 1984; Pimlott 2006b; Protz 1979; Williamson 2002.
10 E.g. Aune 1994; Hutt 1966; Ledbetter 2010; Prawer 1976; Wilkie 1976; Wolff 1988.
11 E.g. Blackledge 2009.
12 See Aune 1994; Le Cercle 2009; Volosinov 1971; Williams 1977, 1983c. For Gramsci's writing on journalism, see Gramsci 1985, pp. 386–425, and on Gramsci's linguistics as integral to his thinking, see Ives 2004a, 2004b, 2005.

An early key problem for Communists was in addressing their audiences in a persuasive manner because sometimes the language of class struggle was foreign to workers who had not yet been radicalised.[13] The use of a Marxist vocabulary, which clearly marked out Communist publications, could appear strange, obfuscatory and alienating to the uninitiated, even though the use of a specialised vocabulary or jargon to communicate complex ideas precisely was the intention of Marxist propaganda. Many concepts, which might have had a particular resonance in their original language, were often simply translated by English-language Communist parties in a slavish imitation of Russian or Chinese parties[14] (known by some as 'translationese').[15] Such concepts connotated 'elitism' and 'foreignness' in their awkwardness as they distanced potential, non-Marxist audiences.[16] This practice, however, was also criticised by Communist journalists and activists[17] because this 'strangeness' made Marxism seem more like 'a rhetoric by and for intellectuals rather than workers',[18] and it often did not appeal to those they claimed to address.[19] Yet, this issue did not get the attention it deserved.

Given this history, it is understandable that the common sense understanding of 'communist journalism' would equate it with dense, 'lifeless' prose and 'torturous' jargon that would help to explain the general lack of success of Communist parties trying to reach out to working-class readers.[20] It should be noted, however, that Communist writers also have to work harder to persuade non-Communists because of long-standing, negative biases and the legacy of pejorative stories about the USSR and Communism promoted via mainstream media.

2   Accessibility

A useful quantitative method of analysis is provided by the 'FOG Index' analysis which determines the general level of reading comprehension required for an article: it is a practical approach used by both scholars and journalists, which is why it is useful to draw upon this quantitative method for analysing a sample of

---

13   Fogarasi 1979, p. 152.
14   E.g. Burgchardt 1980; Chairman 1932; Protz 1979; Williamson 2002.
15   Williamson 2002.
16   Burgchardt 1980, pp. 380–1; Williamson 2002.
17   Chairman 1932, p. 249; Pimlott 2006b.
18   Aune 1994, p. 26.
19   E.g. Kazin 1988.
20   E.g. Burgchardt 1980; Pimlott 2006b.

more than one hundred articles over some three decades.[21] The FOG index formula provides a number that comes from counting the number of words of a specified length (three-plus syllables albeit with some qualifications) and sentences for an average 100-word section (it sometimes takes several attempts). The lesser the FOG index number, the greater the number of short sentences and simple words (of one or two syllables), the lower the level of educational attainment necessary to comprehend the article and, therefore, the greater the number of people who can read it. The opposite is true when the FOG index number scored is higher; it means a greater number of complex words of three or more syllables, and usually long, compound sentences with one or more dependent clauses. A figure of '10' on the FOG index, for example, is considered accessible to the 'average 15-year-old secondary school pupil', between '14' and '16' requires an average university-level education, and over '18' is considered 'too difficult for newspapers'.[22] Some benchmark figures are: a mid-market tabloid like the *Daily Mail* rates 9.5, while down-market tabloids, such as *The Sun*, usually rate less than 9.0; *The Times* measures 18.0.[23] Despite limitations, the FOG index at least provides a snapshot of accessibility during MT's history.[24]

The FOG index formula was applied to a sample of six years, three each from James Klugmann's and Martin Jacques's editorships, selected at five- and ten-year intervals between 1958 and 1988. Two articles, one feature and one non-feature, per issue have been selected from each of 12 issues per sample year, for a total of 72 articles from all three sample years for each editorship for a total of 144 articles (Tables 14, 15). Regular contributors were selected over occasional ones, although no writer was selected more than once within any given year, to provide the broadest range of contributors in the sample years.

Tables 14 and 15 reveal considerable variation in readability levels between *and* within individual issues. For example, the November 1958 issue has the most accessible article of all sample years, a feature at 8.8, which is accessible for working-class readers of *The Sun*, whereas that same issue's non-feature measures at *The Times*'s level of 18.0, the establishment's 'quality' or broadsheet newspaper. The second most accessible article is a July 1988 discussion, which at 9.7 is comprehensible for mid-market tabloid readers, whereas that issue's feature, at 18.7, is considered difficult even for broadsheet readers. The sample, nonetheless, suggests a gradual shift towards greater accessibility from 1958 to 1988, from an average of 18.4 to 16.0 in features, although 1983 is the most access-

---

21 E.g. Fulkerson 1993; Hennesey 1997.
22 Hennesey 1997, p. 22.
23 Ibid.
24 E.g. Gunning 1968; Shelby 1992.

TABLE 14   FOG index rating for features, 1958–88

	1958	1968	1973	1978	1983	1988
January	23.1	19.6	23.1	16.4	25.1	17.1
February	17.7	17.6	13.2	11.5	11.3	14.5
March	16.1	16.6	17.0	16.9	11.2	20.6
April	17.3	13.2	12.4	16.6	13.3	15.9
May	17.5	25.6	16.1	17.7	14.3	11.9
June	25.4	14.8	12.8	16.6	15.0	12.3
July	18.0	18.4	18.0	15.4	15.0	18.7
August	25.2	18.0	18.1	20.3	14.2	15.9
September	18.2	19.2	17.9	20.0	16.7	16.3
October	17.1	17.0	16.4	22.8	13.3	13.6
November	8.8	11.6	21.0	16.1	20.4	20.9
December	16.7	13.4	17.8	25.6	13.1	13.7
AVERAGE	18.4	17.1	17.0	18.0	15.2	16.0

TABLE 15   FOG index rating for non-feature contributions, 1958–88[a]

	1958	1968	1973	1978	1983	1988
January	14.6	15.1	15.7	20.3	12.4	21.7
February	10.5	20.9	16.5	20.4	19.3	11.8
March	27.0	16.1	27.2	20.8	14.6	16.0
April	13.3	14.0	19.2	13.9	25.6	19.1
May	17.6	27.0	19.4	15.3	15.4	11.9
June	13.4	18.3	13.4	22.1	11.8	18.9
July	12.8	14.5	13.5	21.2	20.4	9.7
August	26.6	20.4	16.6	17.9	13.8	16.1
September	19.7	19.7	13.4	19.6	18.0	9.8
October	16.3	18.3	15.9	17.3	15.5	14.0
November	18.0	19.9	20.8	11.9	19.7	10.9
December	11.3	11.0	11.9	13.0	11.9	21.7
AVERAGE	16.8	17.9	17.0	17.8	16.5	15.1

a   If no discussion contribution was available then a non-feature article was selected (e.g. alternately from 'Focus' and 'Channel Five'/'Culture' in 1983 and 1988).

ible for features at 15.2, and 16.8 to 15.1 in non-features, with features being more difficult than shorter non-feature articles: an overall drop down to a general university educational level during Jacques's editorship. While the shift in accessibility was not as great as MT's promotional material claimed, it is still notable.

On closer inspection, other patterns can be discerned. If we consider all articles that are below 14.0, the sample years of 1983 and 1988, the decade of MT's greatest influence, are the most accessible of all. This shift in readability is supported by a decrease in the total number of articles requiring more than a general university education by 30 percent or more: sample years 1958–78 averaged 62.5 to 75 percent measuring 18.0 or higher, as opposed to 33.3 and 41.7 percent in 1983 and 1988 respectively (both of which have 17 out of 24 total [feature and non-feature] articles below 18.0).

There is a correlation between the quantitative FOG measurements and the shift in the subject matter of articles. For example, there is a high level of complexity for 1968 with 75 percent of 24 articles sampled registering above 16.0 and 50 percent (12) features at or above 18.0 that are becoming difficult even for broadsheet readers. This complexity can be partly explained by the record number of features published that year that were 'CP reprints' (i.e. official speeches and documents from the CPGB and its sister parties), 26 out of 41, which is two-and-a-half times the number of 'CP reprints' (i.e. 10) for the next highest year, 1973 (Table 6). The difficulty of official Communist discourse clearly restricts accessibility to those with a familiarity with the jargon or higher education (and the patience to read at length).

There was also a decrease in accessibility from 1973 to 1978, however, due to the growing popularity of continental Marxist theory and Eurocommunism amongst contributors that Jacques published in his first calendar year as editor: articles by Ken Spours and Stuart Hall, for example, were singled out by the MT editorial board for their difficulty.[25] This influx of new ideas and concepts had to be balanced out with the desire to reach readers beyond its current audience *and* the marketplace pressure to sell as many copies as possible to pay for improvements in production and distribution, pressures which were felt especially after 1981 with nationwide distribution. Financial issues increased the pressure for accessibility, especially after the third format launch in 1986, to ensure its articles would be comprehensible to a wider newsagent audience and thereby increase its potential for more sales.

---

25   E.g. MTEB 1977c, 1979a. Hall's writing was highlighted on a few occasions for its difficulty.

Nonetheless, there is considerable variety in the accessibility of feature and non-feature articles within all sample years, including the last two. For all features included in the 1983 sample, the FOG index ranges from 11.2 to 20.4, if we discount the highest score of 25.1 as an anomaly (as it was the only one at such a high level), and for non-features for the 1988 sample year are 11.9 to 20.9. Interestingly, whereas non-feature items drop in FOG Index ratings from an average of 16.5 to 15.1 from 1983 to 1988, increasing their accessibility for readers, features' difficulty actually increased, which was likely the result of the shift to include 'New Times'.

While the FOG index provides an overview of changes in MT's accessibility over three decades, these are only broad brushstrokes of the changes in accessibility rather than a closer, qualitative comparison of language (choices), rhetorical techniques and writing styles, and therefore a better understanding of the degree of persuasiveness or not. Thus, it is necessary to provide a closer textual analysis of selected articles over MT's 34-year history to reveal how the changes in writing styles might have contributed to reaching a broader left public, and the transition from the first to the second and third formats and MT's increased influence and higher public profile in the 1980s.

3   *Marxism Today*'s Defensive Rhetorical Strategy 1957–77

It is necessary to register that *Marxism Today* was an intellectual, theoretical and analytical periodical that was engaged in a type of thinking that requires a different type of writing to that which is used in agitation or even propaganda, at least as defined in the Leninist conception of these two communication practices, discussed in the Introduction. As the third type of Communist Party publication, it was involved in the explication and analysis of Marxist theory across a range of subjects and its application in different areas of thought, particularly as the CPGB's particular interpretation of 'Marxism-Leninism' shifted and necessitated explanations for its readers.

For those who were receptive to the ideas of the (pro-Soviet) Communist movement, its propagandists 'did not have to invent explanations' for political and social developments because Marxism 'provided a system comprehensive enough to support the convictions of the group; it answered all questions and quelled all doubts'.[26] The importance of ideology is clear:

---

26   Burgchardt 1980, pp. 382–3.

Statements of ideology must provide definition of that which is ambiguous in the social situation, give structure to anxiety and a tangible target for hostility, foster in-group feelings, and articulate wish-fulfillment beliefs about the movement's power to succeed.[27]

Marxism has also acted as a 'moral critic' of generations of workers who chose 'social-democratic reformism instead of "socialism"',[28] which explains why its rhetoric 'doesn't so much assume that the reader agrees with what is being said, but, rather, implies that those who disagree are engaged in self-conscious heresy'.[29]

As *Marxism Today* promoted its 'realistic' view of contemporary struggles, in which there were no assurances of the 'inevitable' triumph of socialism, it interrogated and undermined many standard Communist and Labour beliefs. It is in this latter approach to questioning left beliefs that MT worked against the designated function of its first format, which explains in part why it drew such ire from many CPGB readers: 'one's ideology constrains the arguments one uses and colors [sic] the presentation of those arguments'.[30] Nevertheless, it still did offer a 'tangible target for hostility', e.g. 'Thatcherism', which became a focus for thinking about a strategy to defeat it. As ideological constraints loosened, and MT gained greater autonomy and control over the production process, it gained greater flexibility in rhetorical strategies, which nonetheless also attracted criticisms of some contributors' writing styles. MT's appeal beyond party members to lecturers, (graduate) students, white-collar workers and Labour supporters was based upon its shift from Marxist terminology to something approximating mainstream political discourse, although not all Marxist terms were eliminated, nor were the Gramscian-inflected cultural studies approaches necessarily more accessible, as demonstrated in contributions from Stuart Hall and others.

Communist rhetoric uses Marxism 'as a philosophical underpinning and as a source of evidence', quoting Marx and his successors as 'proof'.[31] For example, the definitions of and proposed solutions to political, economic and social problems depend upon the 'pervasive role of Marxist theory in their arguments', and it is safe to assume that these were not very convincing except

---

27   Simons 1970, p. 5.
28   Aune 1994, p. 26.
29   Edgar 1991, p. 35. MT contributors were discouraged from writing in that manner (Jacques 1996b; Taylor 1995; Townsend 1996).
30   Solomon 1988, p. 184. See also McGee 1980.
31   Burgchardt 1980, p. 380.

to those already predisposed to Communist beliefs.[32] There was a hierarchy of evidence and proof evident in Klugmann's MT: in descending order, writers drew upon Marx, Engels, Lenin, (former) CPGB leaders Harry Pollitt and John Gollan, other Communist and Marxist figures, and finally party publications and members. Most non-party sources were academics, and government and trade union statistics, which were cited to demonstrate the veracity of Marxist analyses; these were all followed at a distance by government, mainstream media and big business as 'proofs'.[33] These sources were valid as long as MT addressed party members and sympathisers; however, once the magazine addressed audiences that included non-party or non-Marxist readers, many of these sources would no longer be as persuasive or credible.

Assertions were made and truisms invoked, but little or no proof was forthcoming because it was felt to be unnecessary since the assumptions upon which they were based were already widely held by Communists. CPGB writers in MT could make assertions and know that party members, at least, were not likely to challenge them. For example, the five following excerpts are typical of the writing or house style in Klugmann's MT; they were all published between 1964 and 1975, before and after the CPGB opened up its party line on culture, science and ideology:

> Marxist ideas cannot be ignored. Millions of words are written against them, but they continue to be a growing source of attraction to non-manual workers.[34]

> The Marxist truism that monopoly drives even its own middle strata into alliance with the working class ...[35]

> Most consistent, constructive and far seeing in the struggle against right-wing domination has long been the Communist Party with its campaign for an alternative, socialist policy for the labour movement.[36]

> They [the people] want an analysis of our society, a definition of the socialist alternative and the forces which can drive towards it. A study of the *British Road to Socialism* shows how effectively it meets this need.[37]

---

32   Burgchardt 1980, pp. 377–8.
33   E.g. Egelnick 1964; Illiffe 1975; Pearce 1971.
34   Egelnick 1964, p. 242.
35   Illiffe 1975, p. 10.
36   Mahon 1968, p. 241.
37   Pearce 1971, p. 6.

> The stronger the Communist Party ... the stronger will be the fight for ... fundamental social change ... Hence the fight to build the Communist Party ... is not the private affair of Communists, but is of direct concern to every militant and fighter for socialist change.[38]

The 'Marxist truism' in the second excerpt, from Steve Illiffe, a party activist, is a 'truism' only for Marxists and perhaps only in effect a 'truism' for CPGB members and by no means all Communists, let alone all Marxists. The evidence offered by two leading party officials, Max Egelnick and John Mahon, in the first and third excerpts respectively, for example, is simply asserted as is the answer provided by the party's programme. Of course, when writing for those who believe in the CPGB worldview, certain assumptions can be made. This, however, is not true for non-Marxist and non-party readers; to have been able to persuade non-party socialist readers, the authors would have had to have changed their sources and their writing styles and rhetorical techniques. Bert Pearce, another party official, in the fourth excerpt assumes his statement's validity is self-evident without recognising that non-party readers might need to be persuaded to accept such a view. The tautological validation of Marxist analysis leads to the solutions proposed by the CPGB, as both Mahon and Reuben Falber, another leading party official, make clear in the third and fifth excerpts respectively. Yet, both Mahon and Falber are attempting to appeal to non-party socialists and union militants that the CPGB was the party to lead the fight for 'socialism': i.e. transformative political change. Claims, such as theirs, however, often ran up against the actions of other Communist parties: reality versus rhetoric.[39]

This approach persuaded few outside the party because this writing style says more about the conviction in one's beliefs than in any understanding of the need to win over others. Their writing was more about reassuring party members that MT was trying to address, non-party readers than in actually doing so, especially since most readers were already party members. Such a reassurance would have gone some way to persuade the CPGB readers that both journal and party were on the right track, while any readers from outside the party might have been persuaded given that they were, at least, reading it. However, even as the CPGB engaged in the process of 'solidification', not all party members who were readers were persuaded of the necessity of MT's language choices. For

---

38 Falber 1970, p. 49.
39 For example, the *Partie Communiste Français* tried to act as a brake on student actions during the 'events' of May 1968 (e.g. Fišera 1978; Cohn-Bendit and Cohn-Bendit 1969).

example, in 1967, party member Margaret Cohen complained about the arrogance of party rhetoric (the first format's tone and house style as indicated in the excerpts above), in which 'we know all the answers' and claim that there 'must be a "line" on everything'.[40] Klugmann felt her complaint was sufficiently important, and perhaps representative of a constituency of discontented readers, to publish it (even though there was no 'letters-to-the-editor' section until 1982) in the July 1967 issue, only two months after the EC 'Statement on Ideology and Culture' was published, highlighting the necessity of making the writing more accessible, even for an internal audience, but especially so since the party was opening up its thinking on a wide range of topics.

4   'Solidification'

The 'solidification' process helps to explain the rhetorical strategies and writing styles in *Marxism Today*, especially in its first decade, 1957–67. Solidification is a rhetorical process of addressing internal audiences within an organisation in an attempt to sustain and reinforce the commitment to that organisation and its leadership, beliefs and values as a counter to external factors that undermine the integrity of the organisation.[41] This type of rhetorical process becomes important during periods of isolation, and of internal and external threats, such as, for example, during periods of official proscription or around periods of 'moral panic', as in the 'Red scare' of the 1950s, or after periods of internal divisions and crisis, such as that of 1956. These substantial threats to the CPGB's unity and existence compelled the party to make the rhetorical efforts to maintain organisational cohesiveness by focusing on retaining and solidifying the support of those members remaining. This rhetorical process of solidification would have taken precedence over attempts to encourage vigorous internal debate or recruit new members.

The consequences of belonging to 'an alienated group' is that these tendencies do have an important role in maintaining an organisation's unity in the face of external threats, such as those faced by the CPGB with the start of the Cold War. Thus, Communist Party rhetoric has usually been 'self-directed': orientated to solidifying group membership rather than persuading the public.[42] Solidification is the rhetorical processes 'by which an agitating group produces or reinforces the cohesiveness of its members, thereby increasing their

---

40   Cohen 1967, p. 221.
41   Bowers et al. 1993, pp. 23–34.
42   Burgchardt 1980, p. 382.

responsiveness to group wishes'.⁴³ These tactics include specific words and phrases (jargon), slogans, songs and 'in-group publications', with names that are usually 'themselves esoteric symbols' (e.g. *Marxism Today, World Revolution*) and content that is 'likely to stress in-group symbols, stories, and biases' and serve polarisation and promulgation functions.⁴⁴ The solidification process dominated the early years of Klugmann's editorship in 1956's aftermath, making its role to win over progressive, non-party intellectuals a secondary consideration.

The rhetorical practice of solidification did pay off as the CPGB began to recover by the early 1960s when its membership started growing again. By the late 1960s and 1970s, there was a growing engagement with heterodoxic ideas, including competing understandings of Gramsci's theory of hegemony⁴⁵ and a more critical understanding of 'actually existing socialism' (i.e. Communist states). This opening up of the party line in turn brought criticism from both those who reacted against such shifts, as it had the potential to undermine their beliefs and the party's special relationship with the USSR, and those who wanted the party to distance itself more definitively from these same authoritarian governments.

By the second half of the 1960s, less jargonistic phrases, such as 'crisis of monopoly capitalism', 'mass actions' and 'right-wing', which had a wider appeal outside the party because of the growing popularity of radical ideas, became constant refrains in resolutions, speeches and publications.⁴⁶ These were terms that were adopted by the CPGB and were also used to try and attract non-party left intellectuals, who were turned off by the policies and stances of Harold Wilson's Labour government, 1964–70.

Jargon or specialised vocabularies can play an important role through the rhetorical strategy of solidification, as an in-group positive term or slogan, or of polarisation, whereby 'invented derogatory jargon' is used against establishment groups.⁴⁷ Aggressive language and name-calling help 'to maintain' or even increase 'group cohesiveness' and unity during 'periods of stress and frustration', especially as 'the perception of danger increases', but it can make it more difficult to appeal to the general public: internal unity and cohesion

---

43 Bowers et al. 1993, p. 24.
44 Bowers et al. 1993, p. 33.
45 The take up of Gramsci by Hall and others around cultural studies or the CPGB's Eurocommunist wing was much more 'reformist' in interpretation compared to others who pointed to Gramsci's thinking as that of an active Communist revolutionary leader and philosopher (e.g. Anderson 1976; Hall 1987; Harman 1977a, 1977b; Simon 1982).
46 Andrews 2004, pp. 103, 97, 99.
47 Bowers et al. 1993, pp. 24–8, 34.

or reaching out to build bridges to others.[48] This is a necessary aspect of any political organisation because jargon is the means by which both division and unity can be made by establishing clear lines of differentiation between 'us' and 'them': between the 'in' and 'out' groups. Jargon therefore plays a role in solidifying group membership, such as the CPGB's during times of crisis. The repetition of party phrases, as a means for maintaining the party's identity in the face of external threats, was of a higher priority for members than for persuading the general public.[49]

What makes *Marxism Today* under Martin Jacques's editorship interesting is that its rhetorical strategy appears to be the opposite of solidification, at least in the minds of MT's critics in the early 1980s and increasingly in reaction to its public persona by the mid-1980s. The crisis of the left after the 1983 election, provided Jacques and MT with an opportunity to persuade both its readership and the party leadership (which provided the necessary subsidies for its production and distribution) of its approach and arguments.

5   Principles of Good Style

This overview of accessibility indicates a shift at the level of the text and this means examining changes in language, rhetorical techniques and writing styles. The qualities of effective style are essentially 'variations of the theme that language should be correct, clear, appropriate and vivid'.[50] Correctness in style means, at the most basic level, using words accurately and being grammatically correct; at a more complex level, it takes into account 'whether the speaker's words are faithful to the speaker's thoughts and to the world of facts'.[51] Clarity refers to the degree to which an author's intended meanings are conveyed accurately to the audience and this 'necessitates using words that are familiar to the audience and typically words that are specific and unambiguous': i.e. 'concrete' words.[52] Therefore, clarity and accuracy in the use of language can provide vivid imagery via figures of speech, which are important to good journalism and writing, as vivid metaphors 'can be tremendously

---

48   Burgchardt 1980, p. 383.
49   Simons 1970, p. 5.
50   Most authorities on style agree on these aspects, including those, like Aristotle, who see 'correctness' as part of 'clarity' (Cohen 1998, p. 37).
51   Cohen 1998, pp. 37–8.
52   Cohen 1998, p. 38.

persuasive'.[53] Words used in imaginative and non-literal ways, as with figures of speech (e.g. simile, metaphor), can be very persuasive, but should involve a 'clear and precise vocabulary, an active rather than passive grammatical structure, and examples marshalled as evidence'.[54] In this section, we examine changes in MT's house style, including word choice, imagery and figures of speech according to the tenets of effective style.

There appears to have been no attempt with the first format to adopt a more suitable language or rhetorical strategy to persuade people even within the constraints of the party ideology. Thus, we can say that MT's writing style was not adapted to its ambitions, which included addressing non-party intellectuals on the left. Although James Klugmann did attempt to make articles more readable, he did not promote any conscious house style beyond the expectation that contributors would have read articles in MT and followed the styles of published articles.[55] Since this was not the daily newspaper trying to reach a broad audience, readers could be and were addressed as party members, who were expected to be familiar with Marxist concepts and interested in deepening their understanding of Marxism. Thus, there was no need to adopt a more persuasive language and writing style because anyone who was interested was expected to learn the necessary vocabulary as part of their commitment to acquiring a deeper knowledge of Marxism. The party discourse, 'Anglo-Marxist humanism', was 'a rhetoric with which any interested party members could acquaint themselves and even become conversant'; one such dedicated group of working-class party members in London attempted to do just that by studying the monthly issues of MT.[56] As with literacy, there is an apprenticeship that requires time and effort to acquire different levels of competency in Marxist thought. The preponderance of party officers and academics as contributors points to the material burden of acquiring the necessary skills to be able to write for MT.

These readers were comfortable with being addressed as 'comrades', an identifiable Communist term of address, the use of an 'in-group' vocabulary and the liberal use of collective pronouns, such as 'we' and 'us', especially in articles that addressed political strategy and the labour movement.[57] Readers were, thus, invited to identify with the author/journal/party in part because the authors

---

53   Cohen 1998, p. 40; Cockcroft and Cockcroft 1992, p. 119. These and similar points are often reiterated in journalism and public relations handbooks.
54   Cohen 1998, pp. 39–40.
55   Johnstone 1995.
56   Fishman 1994, p. 157; Johnstone 1995.
57   E.g. Pearce 1971, 1973; Simon 1968.

were readily understood as interchangeable with the Communist Party itself: for example, the party's manifesto, *The British Road to Socialism*, was referred to as 'our programme', and references to the 'international movement' did not include the adjective, 'Communist', as it was understood as obvious given MT's subtitle and position within the CPGB.[58] Whereas such elements might appear obvious, it is an apparent lack of awareness of such potential 'alienating affects' of a writing style or editorial presentation that excludes potential non-party readers, even when the writing is accessible. By the mid-1970s, even Klugmann's closest associates, such as his *de facto* assistant editor, Jack Cohen, pointed out that there were too many articles on theoretical Marxism or written in party jargon at a time of growing public interest in Marxism and socialist politics.[59]

The Communist approach to writing does explain at least part of the complexity of Klugmann's MT, which is implicitly built upon, paradoxically, the marketplace of ideas metaphor, where the best ideas or 'truths' are supposed to win out against false or misleading ones.[60] This metaphor reinforces the idea that one does not have to worry if a specialised vocabulary is inaccessible, since the truth is supposed to win out; since Marxism-Leninism was seen as 'scientific socialism', its language therefore was seen as more accurate in describing reality. However, the reality of the mainstream media marketplace belies this idea(l), as most clearly demonstrated through the US corporate media's unquestioning dissemination of the US government's claims about 'weapons of mass destruction' in the lead-up to the 2003 invasion of Iraq.[61] This metaphor is primarily a mid-twentieth-century trope common in US legal decisions and in western democracies, despite the distortions created by power imbalances in corporate media markets that militate against the truth winning out over error or falsehoods unless there is a profit to be made.[62] Klugmann's house

---

58 E.g. Pearce 1971, p. 7.
59 Cohen 1978.
60 The CPUSA used the metaphor in its fight to be heard in the 1950s (Peters 2004) in contrast to Marx and Engels's 'ruling ideas' trope in *The German Ideology* (1970 [1845–46]).
61 E.g. Rampton and Stauber 2003. The misleading propaganda of US and UK governments pushing for war against Iraq were revealed years too late in corporate media to stop the bloodshed and 'blowback'. For an early account of US 'liberal' media acting as cheerleaders for US foreign interventions, see Chomsky and Herman 1979.
62 The issue around 'fake news' and Donald Trump's 2016 election campaign and his administration make it clearer that it is not just 'fringe' elements involved in promoting falsehoods and misrepresentations in the mass media. In an Ipsos Mori poll in 2013, for example, people were most likely to hold views on such areas as immigration, crime and benefit fraud that greatly diverged from reality and facts, a fault of both politicians and mainstream media (Paige 2013). Perhaps, critical communication scholars have been too quick to dismiss 'false consciousness' as a useful concept?

style plays into the Marxist belief that they merely need to reveal the reality behind the façade of capitalism, which should be sufficient to demonstrate the need for revolution, rather than seeing any need to try and persuade workers and intellectuals that it is in their interest to join together with the party. The workers' direct experiences of life under capitalism should 'automatically' lead them to socialism, a belief evident in the tautological patterns of arguments presented in Klugmann's MT.[63]

Articles which appeared to challenge the party line were still well within the party's ideological parameters, though they were not above appearing controversial to some party members, and such controversies were used to draw readers in, a tactic that Jacques's MT also used. For example, Jack Dunman's August 1965 reappraisal of Rudyard Kipling generated mixed reactions.[64] William Ash was adamant that the party line was 'correct'. Contemptuous of contrary views, he called Dunman's article 'a re-estimation of imperialism' and reduces Kipling the author (and attendant aesthetic, cultural, social and political issues) to a mere cypher of British imperialism.[65] There is little hope for open debate if differing views are seen as tantamount to betrayal: 'It is the proper task of *Marxism Today* to help combat imperialist ideology in Britain, not to give currency to imperialist apologetics'.[66] The tone of this reply, which demonstrates an unwillingness to consider other views, including those of a fellow party member and MT reader, whose assessment of a writer, who was at one time popular with the working class and whose writings were seen by some as ambiguous about the 'white man's burden', makes it clear that such views have no place in a 'Communist' publication. The tone of Ash's article represents a significant proportion of published responses to those supporting challenges to the party's more orthodox ideas in the first format.[67] This position saw such arguments as already occupying a place in public discourses propagated in commercial mainstream publications outside the party and, therefore, such perspectives did not need a forum for debate within the party as well.

Articles in the first format usually ended up pointing out the position of the Communist Party or the labour movement and what might happen without the left's attention; sometimes there was a proposal about the best position for the

---

63   Aune 1994, pp. 33–4.
64   Dunman 1965.
65   Ash 1965, p. 311.
66   Ash 1965, p. 312.
67   E.g. See similar types of responses to the mid-1970s youth culture debate: e.g. Boyd 1973; Fauvet 1974; Filling 1974.

left to take.⁶⁸ This was not unlike Jacques's approach as editor and for which he was criticised.⁶⁹ Many Communists expected to see explanations and analyses that demonstrated their veracity by references to Marxist theory: 'the belief that, if you get a political line right, everything else will fall into place'.⁷⁰ This had developed under the party's bureaucratic practices into the maxim that 'once the political line is decided organisation decides all'; political debate, subsequently, becomes secondary to the party once 'the line' is agreed.⁷¹ This also reinforces the secondary or tertiary position of intellectual journals such as MT. This self-justificatory approach, in which the analysis and strategy put forward by the party is always correct, becomes tautological as the author assumes that the reader does not need to be persuaded of its underlying premises or proof.⁷² However, eight years after publishing one complaint of the inaccessible nature of many articles in the journal, James Klugmann published another short contribution, this time from a Young Communist League member: 'Why is it that the articles must use such complicated sentences, and long, obscure words'?⁷³ The same point about the inaccessible nature of the writing style and language choices, which was followed up by another letter writer directly addressing MT's editor around the time of transition between the two editors.

Julie Alce wrote to complain that 'Party funds should not be spent on the indulgent few', if they could not write in 'plain layman's English', since this writing style made ordinary people 'feel inhibited' about contributing as even the Marxist vocabulary can alienate party members; the writer expressed her lack of surprise why 'some party members are anti-intellectual – we are ignored by these articles' and therefore wanted Jacques to consider making MT 'more readable'.⁷⁴ Taking over as editor, Martin Jacques promised to deal with her complaint provoked by the journal's 'Dialectics of Nature' debate,⁷⁵ and to start the periodical's transformation to overcome 'the diversity of style and language' and 'areas of relative incomprehensibility' immediately.

In the first two years as editor, Jacques continuously reiterated in internal memos and published pieces to party leaders and readers respectively that it was necessary to change all aspects of the journal, including its writing or

---

68 E.g. Hawthorn 1973; Lindsay 1958; Simon 1968.
69 E.g. Callinicos 1985; Saville 1990.
70 Jacques quoted in Chesshyre 1987.
71 Andrews 1995a, p. 242; Cook 1978b.
72 See the five examples quoted above near the beginning of this chapter.
73 Lucas 1975.
74 Alce 1977.
75 Ibid.

'house' style.[76] He argued that its writing style had been marked by mistaken ideas of what a theoretical journal was: theory was thought of 'as either the legitimation of the [party] line in flowery marxist jargon, or the discussion of relatively abstruse issues with no obvious bearing on the practical tasks of the party'.[77] This separation is in part a function of the lack of connection to its readership as well as the party's own understanding of MT as separate, secondary and something abstract, at one remove from political organising. Inspired by Gramsci's ideas, Jacques wanted to make MT more relevant to building the 'broad democratic alliance' which also meant theory had to be made more 'practical', which in turn meant that the periodical had to be accessible to readers: i.e. a *broad* democratic alliance. The accessibility of theory was seen as inseparable from its application to political struggles, i.e. its practicality, which meant therefore changing the writing style to reach more readers on the left.

Jacques saw *Marxism Today* addressing two left audiences: one for an internal readership; the other for a broad readership of activists and intellectuals.[78] This required finding writers who could address the two audiences by increasing the range of contributors (e.g. from party officers and intellectuals, to feminists, unionists and social activists, to journalists and politicians) and concerns (e.g. politics, popular culture, lifestyle). There was a third audience of progressives outside the organised left, who would be targeted by Jacques with the third format in 1986, as increased costs meant finding more readers to cover costs *and* to sustain MT financially.

Despite attempts to gradually eliminate the use of jargon, many new writers in the early 1980s adopted a style and vocabulary that they assumed was in keeping with the periodical given its subtitle.[79] The complaints about jargon later in the 1980s are also an indication of the audience's changing social composition: new non-party readers drawn in by reprints in *The Guardian*, or by encountering MT on the newsagent's shelf, might respond negatively to older unfamiliar terms, while newer jargon was more likely to provoke older CPGB readers wanting the reassurance of party prose. Yet, both editors did receive compliments for tackling subjects often ignored by the left and Jacques was praised especially for making them more accessible.[80]

Linking writing style to political openness and practical activities, Jacques argued that MT had to be a journal open to party *and* non-party contribut-

---

76 E.g. Jacques 1978a, 1978b, 1979a, 1979b, 1979c.
77 Jacques 1979a, p. 151.
78 Jacques 1996b.
79 Townsend 1984, p. 1.
80 Ibid.

ors, because the Communist Party was 'not the fount of all wisdom'[81] and such a move would require changes in house style, as well as other complementary changes for which he argued.[82] Jacques says that MT offered a space for journalists to write in greater depth, while academics were offered a platform to try and reach an audience outside the university. He wanted writing that was 'conjunctural and strategic',[83] which he defined as analysing the current situation with an understanding of how to move forward. This, he claimed, could best be effected by combining the best aspects of journalism and scholarly writing. Whereas journalists were good at writing, they were not very good at organising deeper arguments; academics, on the other hand, could organise and develop arguments and think in a strategic sense, but because they tended to write about the abstract, their writing was often not concrete enough for the general reader.[84] Academics can get away with a more obtuse writing style because, professionally, their audiences, as limited as they might be, have to read their articles; journalists, however, have to be able to interest people in what they are saying.[85] Scholars have been seen as 'suspect' if their writing was too accessible or published in formats other than the academic journal.

With a tight command over the periodical, Martin Jacques engaged in forms of interventionist editing, which were crucial to the development of *Marxism Today*'s house style and credibility with establishment media and non-party readers. Since 'nothing destroys a magazine's claims to authority more swiftly and comprehensively than spelling mistakes ... grammatical ineptitude and sub-editing errors', scrupulous attention to detail is 'a critical part of the process of producing the right magazine'.[86] Jacques's approach to editing began with working through a feature article in consultation with a selected contributor; rather than correcting the copy himself, he would push the contributor to work through the article's political implications during the revision process.[87] Two leading contributors illustrate practically the different levels of input that was required from Jacques in terms of what he wanted out of his contributors:

---

81   Cohen 1967. Such published criticisms appear to have had little impact on the writing in the first format.
82   Jacques 1979a, p. 151.
83   Jacques 1996b.
84   Ibid.
85   For two different views of academic and professional writing, see: Cohen 1993; Kostelanetz 1995.
86   Morrish 1996, pp. 101, 106.
87   Jacques 1996b.

Eric Hobsbawm was a 'one draft writer', while Stuart Hall 'often had to work through four or five drafts', as Hall himself readily admitted.[88]

In a column for the final issue, David Edgar lays out what he saw as the typical approach expected of an article for the magazine under Jacques's editorship.

> A proper *Marxism Today* article began by identifying a left shibboleth, and then proceeded to a sober (and often numerated) listing of those factors which might incline the reader to a more flexible and iconoclastic view of the matter, concluding with the statement that the Left had ignored this issue for too long (and would continue to do so only at its peril), lightened perhaps by a short list (again most likely numerated) of pointers towards future socialist policy on the question in hand.[89]

Although Edgar captures the sense by which MT was understood by both opponents and supporters alike, its 'flexible and iconoclastic view' of various topics was partly a result of the expectations of the audience, influenced in part by the mainstream media's characterisation of the periodical in contrast to what older readers had grown to expect from reading the first format. Edgar's concise and generalised picture of the feature article's structure does miss out on some important aspects.

First of all, this structure of MT's features is not uncommon for journalistic and academic articles, particularly when they seek to challenge conventional wisdom or orthodox views about a topic, issue or policy, or in a scholarly field or discipline, nor is such an approach limited to MT or the left. As editor, Jacques oversaw the identification of topics for feature coverage and liaised with editorial staff over suggestions for possible contributors.[90] Even if Jacques did not know exactly what he wanted from a contributor's article initially, he would work with the contributor to help them develop their ideas through the writing and editing processes. The process of listing or enumerating factors or questions is but one important rhetorical device that is meant to aid in the persuasion of audiences. Indeed, one can see this sort of writing in the first format as well.

Second, feature writing in MT's second and third formats was not as accessible as one might expect from encountering journalistic or opinion writing in mainstream media outlets, as its transformation was never what was claimed for it nor did contributors' writing styles change overnight. The features section

---

88   Ibid.; Hall 1997.
89   Edgar 1991, p. 35.
90   Jacques 1996b.

retained an academic feel, which makes sense since writers delved into issues in some detail, as Jacques himself admits, and the language was therefore not always accessible either, even as a specialised Marxist vocabulary was largely excised from the magazine by the late 1980s.[91]

6 Language

One of the most obvious differences in house styles between the two editorships can be found in word choice that was constrained by the party's ideology. Although the specialised vocabulary used in *Marxism Today* enabled writer and reader to engage in an in-depth examination of capitalism, it also meant that people who were unfamiliar with Marxist terminology would have found the journal a difficult read. The CPGB's Marxist rhetoric could at least have been seen as a partial 'distortion and exaggeration' because party prose failed to depict reality in the same ways as those dominant public discourses expressed via professional journalism and mainstream political-party communication. This contrast between the ostensible 'reality' as understood by non-party readers and that described by party writers, especially in the ambiguity of meanings of words between the specialised Communist terminology and everyday usage, was ultimately an unbridgeable gulf.

The word choice and use in James Klugmann's *Marxism Today* appears to have worked against clarity, an important principle of good style. Not only does the frequent use of foreign, specialised or academic terms put off ordinary readers, including party members, but so too does the use of everyday, concrete and unambiguous words to signify specific meanings different to their commonly understood meanings. The full meanings of phrases, such as 'building the broad alliance', 'homogeneous reactionary mass', or 'isolating monopoly and curbing its power', were understood fully only by those familiar with party discourse. 'Peaceful co-existence', for example, referred specifically to the CPGB's support for the USSR against its military and diplomatic isolation by western powers, and 'monopoly' was short-hand for 'monopoly capitalism', which was the (late) stage of capitalism, as identified in the CPGB's analysis, where the class enemy was reduced to a tiny coterie of big business owners and top executives, a terminology used to differentiate the CPGB 'from the Labour mainstream'.[92]

---

91 Ibid.
92 Andrews 2004, pp. 77, 86–9.

The use of jargon by CPGB officials and intellectuals had a tendency to be repeated, particularly as specific terms were invoked around the party line on different issues. Although repetition has a function in terms of the solidification process, there are problems that also arise from such language use. As we will see in the examples below, constant repetition contributes to awkward syntax and redundancy (sic), which in turn contributes to a dull, unimaginative and ritualistic style.

In the first excerpt below, Max Egelnick writes about the 'strengthening of the unity of non-manual and manual workers', but the sentence's subject is somewhat unclear and obscured, even if implied; he invokes the party phrase, 'advance to socialism', twice in that one sentence, illustrating the awkward style that arises from repetition and jargon, including CPGB's version of 'socialism' at that time (c. 1964). The nature of the question being asked is illuminating:

> Will monopoly win back the support of the non-manual workers and so retard the advance to socialism, or will there be a strengthening of the unity of manual and non-manual workers, so vital to isolating monopoly and curbing its power, thus building the broad alliance and advancing to socialism?[93]

Abstract terms, especially party phrases, have precise meanings that may not be properly understood by the uninitiated and, in turn, can be easily misunderstood by non-party readers because of broader or less precise definitions acquired through general public usage. Party terms need to be supported by examples and concrete words, including using broadly understood words in the same way as the public, to be accessible to those unfamiliar with party discourse.

The awkwardness of the writing in the next example is a direct result of the repetition of 'to the/that extent' four times in two sentences, which is compounded by a lack of clarity because of the imprecision of the author's language. The problems of repetition, whether for rhetorical, political or organisational reasons, become clear in the following excerpt:

> On the contrary, to the extent that the struggle for peaceful co-existence mobilises the masses of the people against imperialism, to that extent does it weaken imperialism and win allies for the national liberation movement. And to the extent that the national liberation movement

---

93 Egelnick 1964, p. 242.

> scores successes, to that extent is imperialism weakened and the fight for peaceful co-existence advanced.[94]

At the time this article was published, the author, Tony Chater, was the editor of *The Morning Star*, which would be criticised five years later for its inability to appeal to a broader public than the party faithful and its lacklustre approach to daily journalism.[95] Since this was to be one of only two resolutions that were passed that went against the wishes of the CPGB leadership, the motion clearly highlights members' frustrations with the paper that was supposed to be their 'public voice'. What hope could the party have to reach the public, if even its own members found the party's principal means of communication, the daily newspaper, unappealing or alienating?

The next example is taken from a pattern of long sentences with a series of dependent clauses, providing a ready comparison to a common expectation with academic writing styles. The sentence is composed of 99 words and four dependent clauses.

> Those who have already written off the Labour Party and all trade union leaderships as a homogeneous reactionary mass have failed to see what the ruling class has not failed to see, a contradiction about which *The Times* is entirely clear, the contradiction between the leftward movement of the trade unions, reflected in Congress policies as well as in mass actions, the leftward movement of the Labour Party as reflected in Conference decisions and National Executive elections as compared with the entrenchment of the Right in the Parliamentary Labour Party, the Shadow Cabinet and the machinery of the movement.[96]

It appears that the author, Ron Bellamy, a leading party official, added the dependent clauses to provide illustrations or examples, and to clarify, rather than weaken, the meaning and veracity of his analysis. However, from my understanding, it appears that the author is trying to point out that:

> The ruling class recognises the contradiction between the leftward movement of the labour movement and Labour Party members, and the 'entrenchment of the Right' amongst leaders, MPs and party 'apparatchiks'.

---

94 Chater 1973, p. 229.
95 *Morning Star* Sub-Committee 1978.
96 Bellamy 1973, p. 26.

Here I have tried to express the same meaning in one compound sentence of just 30 words, although I have left out some of the references (e.g. *The Times*) or evidence (e.g. 'Congress policies', 'mass actions'). Despite the best intentions to the contrary, his use of language and syntax undermines the very accessibility and clarity that the author intended.

The combination of dependent clauses, abstract terms and party jargon written in the passive voice make these articles torturous reading and difficult to follow for the uninitiated (if not for many party members too), which was only exacerbated by the length of features, many of which were more than 4,000 words. Dependent clauses provide qualifying passages in sentences but at the same time they may be more likely to confuse or mislead the reader because of the need to keep track of what exactly is being qualified by each successive clause (as with this sentence!). Qualifying phrases make it harder for a reader to get through a piece without re-reading passages over and again.

A notable benefit, you could argue, of this kind of language and writing style is that any important changes in the CPGB's political programme was clearly marked by the use of particular phrases, such as the succession of 'broad democratic alliance', over two earlier phrases, the 'anti-monopoly alliance' and 'broad popular alliance', which was adopted at the 1977 National Party Congress. All of these phrases act as codes identifying party policy, aims or strategy that also reflect shifting degrees of internal factional influence. While all three phrases incorporated the word 'alliance', the difference between the last two terms and the BDA signified the success of the Gramscian-influenced, reformist wing. The 'alliance' called for in the AMA and the BPA was one in which the working class, and by extension the 'most advanced sections' of the labour movement (i.e. CPGB, Labour Left), would have the 'leading' role in any coalition. The BDA signalled a qualitative shift since there was no 'leading' role for labour in an alliance with new social movements and it was used to justify MT's editorial line during the 1980s.[97]

As ideological constraints loosened and MT gained greater autonomy from the party, there was greater flexibility in language choice and use. Jacques recognised the limitations of party beliefs that constrained questions asked and answers offered. He began a gradual process of explicitly questioning many truisms, not only of the CPGB, but also of Labour.[98] MT's more 'realistic' view of contemporary struggles, in which there were no assurances of 'ultimate victory' (i.e. a rejection of Communism's teleology) and it critically interrogated tradi-

---

97 Andrews 2004, pp. 160, 195; Pimlott 2000a, pp. 22, 26.
98 Jacques 1996b.

tional Communist and Labour orthodoxies, was an integral part of establishing its credibility with non-party readers and establishment or mainstream media. While MT continued to offer a 'tangible target for hostility' (i.e. Thatcherism), which offered an organising focus for its counter-hegemonic strategy (i.e. the BDA) for party members, it was also working to intervene in debates about the direction of the Labour Party, especially as divisions hardened over interpretations of the 1983 defeat, as MT attempted to appeal to a broader left readership.[99]

Even after eliminating a lot of Marxist and CPGB terms after its relaunch in 1979, however, MT was still not 'jargon-free'. For example, in the April 1985 issue on the 1984–85 miners' strike, Hywel Francis and Eric Hobsbawm do not refrain from using Marxist terms in their writing.[100] The continuing influence of continental theorists and cultural studies researchers on contributors meant that some readers also found some of the writing in the 1980s almost as opaque as others had found many of the earlier 'esoteric Marxist' debates. Complaints shifted from the 'inaccessibility' of Marxist debates because of their specialised language, though not the use of Marxist terms *per se*, to the 'incomprehensibility' of Gramscian and cultural studies concepts or academic writing styles. Non-Marxist progressive rhetorics have drawn upon academic discourses of postmodernism and multiculturalism, which have also appeared to be less flexible and more stilted than that used by neoliberal pundits and propagandists. These attempts to use a vocabulary, which is more inclusive and non-discriminatory, led to an apparent awkwardness at times in the language used, making it appear somewhat artificial and less accessible to the common reader. This jargon provoked traditionalists wanting the reassurance of older party prose, and some editorial board members and social movement activists who complained of its difficulty (the latter indicative of a shift in readership).[101]

By eschewing most CPGB and Marxist terminology, *Marxism Today*'s writing style began to move closer towards the 'plain style' of national broadsheet journalism in the 1980s, due to the increasing numbers of broadsheet journalists writing for it and other contributors' attempts to address the shift in readerships. For example, there are no discrepancies between the denotations and connotations of words used in MT articles and those used in the leading centre-left broadsheet, *The Guardian*, which was engaged in covering similar subject matter and reprinting, with other broadsheets, 43 MT articles while drawing

---

99 Pimlott 2005, pp. 182–3.
100 E.g. Francis 1985; Hobsbawm 1985.
101 E.g. Ackers 1987; Alce 1977; Hadjifotiou 1984; Kennett 1987; Klugmann 1977; Knifron 1984; Lucas 1975; MTEB 1977b, 1977c, 1979a, 1979b.

extensively upon scores more as sources for news stories, as highlighted in the previous chapter.[102] Yet, despite the overall improvements in its house style, the academic passive voice prevailed nonetheless, including in articles by broadsheet journalists.

7   Plain Style

It is not just the use of awkward language choices or specialised vocabularies that put off readers, but also the way such language contributes to awkward syntax, which helps to explain the apparent unwieldiness of some Communist rhetoric and its frequent lack of appeal on the page. As part of the attempt to make *Marxism Today* accessible to a broader public beyond the Communist Party of Great Britain, there was a growing interest, under Martin Jacques's editorship, in moving towards the 'plain style' of professional journalism, even if this was not consciously expressed as such, but was nonetheless imitated in contributors' bids to become more accessible to non-party readers. Plain style is an approach to writing where language is understood as a 'transparent' mediator of reality, as with traditional, broadsheet and literary journalism, and it is more persuasive and successful ideologically because it offers itself as being 'outside' ideology; it is an approach with which George Orwell is closely associated.[103]

In his essay, 'Politics and the English Language', Orwell points to the use of clichés or dead metaphors as a problem with all kinds of political and academic writing, and not just with Communist texts.[104] Two themes arise in discussions of the use of metaphors in political language: one is that they can be used 'in rhetorically effective ways to create new meanings and to challenge previously established ways of understanding'; and the other is that they 'can function as routine idioms in political discourse in ways that deaden political awareness'.[105]

While repetition in rhetoric plays a role in solidifying members' allegiance to the party, the constant use of the same figures of speech for communicating party ideas means they cease to have much persuasive power, at least outside the party, as both the common meanings and the imagery originally invoked are lost, and the metaphors turn into idioms which 'deaden political aware-

---

102   Pimlott 2000b, 2004.
103   E.g. Cameron 1995; Kenner 1990; Matheson 2003.
104   Orwell 2004b.
105   Billig and MacMillan 2005, p. 459.

ness'. They are only likely, therefore, to appeal to those for whom such idioms retain meaning, such as party members or sympathisers.[106] It should be noted that such figures of speech, when they are used to signify a specific political meaning, will become used frequently precisely because they signify that specific meaning, and therefore any changes in those figures of speech will be used to signify a shift in the party line or policy, and for members and observers (e.g. 'Kremlinologists') such changes will indicate shifts in the influence and power of different factions.

According to the advice of professional journalists and rhetorical and communication scholars, vividness is about creating images in the minds of the audience and it is an important, integral element in good writing and professional journalism.[107] Words are to be used in imaginative and non-literal ways, as with figures of speech (e.g. metaphor, simile, metonymy, synecdoche), which can be very persuasive, but can also involve a 'clear and precise vocabulary, an active grammatical structure, and evidence in the form of examples'.[108] The lack of imagination or vividness in much of the writing in MT's first format is evident with the use of clichés or mixed metaphors and idioms: 'the whitewashing of British imperialism'; 'watering down of legal code article'; 'that this poison is exposed and rooted out'; 'boundaries are narrowing between office and factory workers'; and 'a revealing window on to wider social and political affairs'.[109] The last sentence fragment highlights a 'revealing window', providing an apparently redundant adjective for the noun but which raises a question about windows that they might equally be 'obscuring' or 'blocking out' views of what exists on the other side of 'the pane of glass'? It also implicitly challenges that old dominant metaphor of language (and news) as 'a window [on] to the world', which highlights its invocation of words as a 'transparent' medium of communication. The redundancy of the metaphor (or the literal meaning perhaps) draws attention to itself and away from the subject that the sentence is intended to communicate to the reader.

A comparison of the lead paragraphs covering the same topic and written by the same author, albeit 13 years apart and in two different formats, illustrates differences in tone and style between the two editorships. Steve Illiffe's first piece on the NHS, written in 1975, also demonstrates that by the mid-1970s some attention was being paid, even in James Klugmann's MT, to drawing readers in.

---

106 Billig and MacMillan 2005.
107 Evans 1972; Keeble 1994. See also Aune 1994, 2003; Cohen 1998; Phillips 1996, 1998.
108 Cohen 1998, pp. 39–40.
109 Cohen 1958, p. 369; Green 1966, p. 205; Jeffery 1970, p. 362; Egelnick 1964, p. 242; Illiffe 1975, p. 68.

> At one time or another the whole question of health care is of personal concern to us all. That alone makes it a topic worth close attention. More specifically, the current conflicts within the health service are a revealing window on to wider social and political affairs. The Marxist truism that monopoly drives even its own middle strata into alliance with the working class can be critically evaluated by a close look at the health professions; and the consequences of the Social Democrat's [sic] careful complicity with the ideology of the dominant class are charted by the progressive crisis in the National Health Service.[110]

There is an attempt to draw the reader in by working back from the broad issue of health care in the opening sentence, as the 'us' is inclusive of all, whether or not you are a party member, and justifying the topic. The third sentence, as pointed out above, uses an awkward trope around the 'revealing window' which might make more sense as a 'portal' 'on to wider social and political affairs'; clearly Illiffe is signifying that the NHS's situation has broader implications, since it was established in 1948 by a Labour government, so how the NHS fares nearly three decades later under a Labour government is of particular concern to socialists. However, the fourth sentence uses Communist concepts which are not likely to be a 'truism' for anyone other than Marxists.

The second example of Illiffe's writing published in MT's third format, on the other hand, reveals a very different style. The standfirst's short sentences set an initial breathless pace, hoping to draw the reader in: 'All hell has broken out in the NHS. It is open revolt. But where will it lead?'[111] Unlike the first format, the third format has a standfirst of 17 words in three sentences, creating a sense of rapid movement, which is set out in a larger font than the body of the article, to draw the newsagent browser's attention. The introductory paragraph, working off of the standfirst, changes tact, tone and even, momentarily, topics: the sense of 'urgency', in the standfirst, gives way to 'reflection', as sentences lengthen, as the NHS gives way to the 'news'.

> Odd thing, news. Most probably babies have died waiting for heart operations before this autumn, but only recently did one catch the PM's eye. Perhaps the close attention of media lenses sharpened her vision. At long last, the NHS is turning on the government. Health authorities are

---

110   Illiffe 1975, p. 68.
111   Illiffe 1988, p. 10. Although Illiffe might not have written the standfirst (since this is usually the responsibility of a sub-editor), the writing in the lead paragraph is also different to his earlier style.

threatened with legal action by their professional employees, copying mutiny from porters and cleaners. Stern surgeons, flanked (as ever) by nurses, spread petition pages for cameras, with Downing Street as the backdrop.[112]

The introductory paragraph in the 1988 article is more than twice as long as the 1975 one (182 words to 79). Illiffe provides detailed descriptions of different responses, particularly of those who are not usually 'on the barricades', which helps to make concrete the severity of the crisis and acts as proof. The author sets out to explain why the present focus on the NHS is news and presents the reasons by describing the escalation of the crisis since 1983. Even though his metaphors are not always imaginative (e.g. clinics 'whittled away'), Illiffe uses descriptions that are vivid, clear and even poetic, as they build image upon image of 'petitions by the hundreds', 'sad stories of treatment refused' and angry protests, fleshing out each step before clearly stating his argument.[113]

This second writing style is closer to that of broadsheets: all the words, phrases and acronyms are ones with which most broadsheet readers would be familiar. This writing style is more successful ideologically because, as with professional journalism, it conveys meanings via the plain style.[114] For example, there are no discrepancies between denotations and connotations of words used in the 1988 article and those used in a centre-left broadsheet like *The Guardian*.[115] This use of plain style language and journalistic writing techniques increased the possibility of national media coverage.

A closer comparison of two articles, published in *Marxism Today* 20 years apart, under the different editorships of Klugmann and Jacques, illustrate other differences in jargon, function and style. These articles by occasional contributors cover the composition of the working class and its relationship to socialist politics, and provide a useful comparison of some important differences in rhetorical techniques and writing styles. Beginning with the same subject matter, Max Egelnick's focus is more political-economic and structural, whereas Gregor McLennan's focus is more social and cultural.[116]

---

112 Illiffe 1988, p. 10.
113 Ibid.
114 Cameron 1995; Kenner 1990; Lanham 1974.
115 A style sheet had been adapted from a copy of *The Sunday Times* (Townsend 1996). By 1988, there were more journalists than any other occupational group contributing to MT (Table 10).
116 Egelnick 1964; McLennan 1984.

First, a general sense of the differences in accessibility between the two styles is provided by the FOG index: Egelnick's article rates 20.4, a level which is usually considered too difficult for broadsheets, to McLennan's 14.4, a level in-between *The Daily Mail* and *The Times*. Nonetheless, the expectation that readers would have had some type of higher education, facility with language or education in Marxism, is something that readers themselves would have certainly been aware of picking up a periodical that is described as the CPGB's 'theoretical and discussion journal', at least until its subtitle was removed from the cover from October 1981.

Second, there are differences in the sources of information, evidence and quotations in two articles covering the same topic. Only one quote out of nine in Egelnick's feature, for example, is from a 'primary definer' (government), in terms of mainstream or professional news media processes,[117] three are from trade union officials and the remaining five are Communist sources. All but one of the longest quotes (15 lines plus) are from party documents and speeches, cited uncritically as evidence to support the author's thesis and the 'correctness' of the party line. McLennan, on the other hand, draws upon government statistics and makes reference to survey data and MT contributors (e.g. Hall) and themes (e.g. 'Forward March', 'Thatcherism') from the second format, in effect referencing previous articles from the same periodical. His analysis is largely qualitative, discussing different interpretations and developing persuasive images of his ideas and criticisms.

To begin a more detailed analysis, we start with the feature's title. 'Non-Manual Workers in the Sixties', published in August 1964, defines Egelnick's topic at its most basic (in contrast to its FOG level). This was standard for features in the first format, with declarative statements of subject matter: e.g. 'The Function of Film in Working Class Struggle'; 'Health Care and the Medical Profession'.[118] On the other hand, McLennan's April 1984 article, 'Class Conundrum', not only gives some indication of its content, but it is also a creative word play, which is more likely to pique a reader's interest via rhetorical devices such as alliteration, which play with common phrases or create oxymorons, as with such titles as 'Sixteen: Sweet or Sorry?' and 'The New Nostalgia'.[119]

---

117   E.g. Hall et al. 1978. The term 'primary definer' refers to the dominant institutions, such as police, judiciary, parliament and large business organisations, from which representatives set the agenda and frame the issues covered by professional journalists in corporate and state media.
118   Green 1973; Illiffe 1975.
119   Cockburn 1986; Edgar 1987a.

Egelnick's article consists of 114 paragraphs separated into 13 sections over eight pages; the article's fragmented look is reinforced by several one-sentence paragraphs of between nine and 60 words. These are used inappropriately: one idea is often separated into two or three paragraphs, a feature more common in newspapers than intellectual journals and curiously contradictory to the FOG index level; long compound and complex sentences are ubiquitous. By contrast, McLennan's article has 33, mostly long, paragraphs, with the shortest one consisting of 44 words; broken into seven sections over four pages, it also includes three quotes, two advertisements and one untitled photograph of workers.[120] The paragraphs appear to be a little long for the second format because of narrow columns, which demonstrates a contradiction between the desire for a magazine-like format and the continuance of journal-style articles, at least in the layout.

The lack of imagination in much of the writing in the first format is evident in the use of dead metaphors and clichés: e.g. 'official Labour' is 'at one' with 'monopoly' because it believes that its policies must be 'watered down' to win over non-manual workers. Even when there are attempts to revive them, they often fall flat. For example, Egelnick extends the metaphor, 'delivering the goods': non-manual workers saw 'that Labour was not delivering the goods and even that deliveries [sic] had got worse'. In trying to express that, not only was Labour failing to carry out its promises, but also its policies were actually worse (than expected), Egelnick's metaphor is a poor choice, which becomes obvious once he extends it: if Labour is 'not delivering the goods', how can they get 'worse'?[121] The 'goods' are either delivered (late, early or on time) or they are not: it is not a question of degree. However, as the metaphor moves away from a simple transference of the qualities of one term to another into a more attenuated relationship, it undermines the metaphor's vividness or clarity.

Egelnick's article also demonstrates the consequences of the Marxist belief in 'showing' rather than 'persuading'. Since it is assumed that workers' direct experience of life under capitalism will 'automatically' lead them to socialism, Egelnick reasons that one only has to 'show' them that socialism will meet their 'needs': 'Whoever shows, by policy and example, that there is a solution to their problems, will win their support'.[122] This form of economic-determinist logic,

---

120   The integration of photos and ads in each issue was still at an early stage of MT's transformation into a magazine.
121   Egelnick 1964, p. 245.
122   Egelnick 1964, pp. 246, 245.

i.e. the 'base determines superstructure', is more about conviction in one's own beliefs than in any attempt to persuade others.[123] It also dictates a mode of reasoning which neglects to explain its own evidence. Three long quotations from Communist Party documents from 1926, 1937 and 1951 are included to demonstrate the 'correctness' of the party's position on non-manual workers at critical junctures for the labour movement: no additional interpretation or context is offered or provided because it is 'self-evident'. Egelnick appears to be at 'a loss', whether to provide more background or to explain some of the context, when introducing some quotations. For example, when introducing the 1937 resolution, for example, he writes: 'Its resolution on Unity contained the following words'.[124] Thus, it is no surprise that Egelnick is not trying to challenge the party line. In fact, he is trying to persuade party members and MT readers to accept the party line and overcome their prejudices against non-manual workers (assuming that they are manual workers or Communists with a suspicion of 'intellectuals', especially in the aftermath of 1956).

Both articles also tend towards the passive voice, as with most academic writing styles and most types of feature essay writing including those published in commercial magazines. Equally, this should be no surprise within the context of editorial practices where the editor is ultimately the final arbiter of what goes into the publication. In the case of both writers, the proliferation of dependent clauses in compound sentences intensifies the awkwardness of the prose, which is particularly true of Egelnick's sentences, even though they are grammatically correct. The constant repetition of particular phrases performs an important role in the solidification process and in demonstrating the veracity of the analysis compared to party policy, but it also contributes to awkward syntax and repetition, making the article dull and unimaginative.[125] For example, the phrase 'the advance to socialism' is used throughout Egelnick's article, including twice within one sentence. However, it is not always the words that he uses that are necessarily difficult, but that particular word combinations or phrases signified something different from their common usage. For example:

> Will monopoly win back the support of the non-manual workers and so retard the advance to socialism, or will there be a strengthening of the

---

123   Cockcroft and Cockcroft 1992, pp. 84–5.
124   Egelnick 1964, p. 245.
125   Egelnick 1964, p. 242. This was also true of many frequent contributors (e.g. Pearce 1971, 1973).

unity of manual and non-manual workers, so vital to isolating monopoly and curbing its power, thus building the broad alliance and advancing to socialism?[126]

This excerpt demonstrates that even when using concrete and unambiguous words, it was not necessarily comprehensible except to the initiated. Phrases, such as 'building the broad alliance' or 'isolating monopoly and curbing its power', often had specific meanings or connotations beyond their denotations. Both 'monopoly' and 'broad alliance' were concepts closely related to the analysis and strategy of the CPGB's manifesto and programme. The writing style comes across at times more like a collectively produced statement from a committee or party agency than as a particular intellectual's voice.

The differences with Max Egelnick's writing style are readily apparent in Gregor McLennan's feature article 20 years later, as we can see in the following excerpt:

> Non-class issues, let me say, are eminently issues which working class people rank as important. But they are not best described as class issues, because they affect everyone regardless of class, and they are important to working people as *citizens* rather than as workers.[127]

Like Egelnick, McLennan uses concrete words but the meanings are those generally accepted through common usage, so that even if some phrases are a little awkward, such as 'working class people', their meanings can still be commonly understood. McLennan's phrases are less ambiguous and abstract because they emphasise humanity (e.g. 'people') over more abstract aspects, such as socio-economic stratification or function (e.g. 'working', 'workers', 'class'), and McLennan ascribes agency to 'working class people'. This latter phrase is also more inclusive because 'people' does not preclude the non-working members of workers' families. It is also sounds less jargonistic to those readers who are not familiar with left discourses around class, although the 1970s was a decade where class was a commonly used term on both the left and the right.[128] The 'working class' moves from being a noun and a key subject with agency in the earlier feature to an adjective for describing the 'appearance' ('lifestyle'?) of the core 'human subject' of 'people'. It is also part of the slippage away from locat-

---

126   Egelnick 1964, p. 242.
127   McLennan 1984, p. 32 (original emphasis).
128   Lawrence and Braithwaite-Sutcliffe 2012.

ing the agent of revolutionary social change within the relations of production as 'people' is a broader term that is not designated by any position within the production process.

McLennan's use of basic compound sentences and occasionally the active voice (e.g. in the second sentence) to convey his ideas in a simple and relatively straightforward fashion, also known as the plain style's '1,2,3 syntax',[129] contributes to making his article more accessible and, thereby, potentially more persuasive with non-CPGB members than Egelnick's. The dependent clauses, abstract words and party phrases composed in the passive voice make Egelnick's piece an awkward, if not torturous, read. In places, the meaning is unclear: exactly who is doing the 'strengthening of the unity of non-manual and manual workers'? Is it workers themselves, trade unions, the Labour Party or the CPGB? The problem with the rhetoric of Klugmann's MT is that agency is either the prerogative of an abstract entity (e.g. monopoly, vanguard party) or it remains unstated. Egelnick's writing is grammatically awkward (e.g. inappropriate use of pronouns), mixes its metaphors (e.g. 'boundaries are narrowing between office and factory workers') and has poor syntax throughout (although there are no spelling mistakes or typos).[130]

Informal writing and speech patterns were more apparent in 'Editorial Comments' and 'Discussion' items than in the features published under Klugmann's editorship, except for lectures that were published as articles,[131] whereas under Jacques's editorship informal phrases and patterns of speech were much more common, although that does not mean that the later articles were all more accessible than those published in the first format. For example, McLennan uses colloquialisms and other signs of informality to make his article more accessible to non-party readers: his interjections with pragmatic particles, such as 'you know' and 'let me say', perform four tasks: they reinforce his writing as an individual, rather than a collective or institutional, voice; they simulate dialogue, as if he is responding to hesitations or doubts as part of a 'conversation' with the reader; they appeal directly to a reader's feelings; and they help emphasise the 'feeling' of the writing.[132] The interjections connote a sense of dialogue or a process of thinking through ideas, a process which by implication appears more open and informal than formal academic, journalistic, polemical

---

129 Kenner 1990.
130 Egelnick 1964, p. 241. The metaphor might have read better as 'the gap is narrowing' or 'boundaries are disappearing', but since the meaning is not clearly made, it draws attention to itself; it is not a 'window pane' on 'reality'.
131 E.g. Hutt 1966.
132 Lakoff 1990, p. 227.

or propagandistic writing and, therefore, more conducive to engagement with readers. This allows potentially controversial points to be qualified as his personal view (and not necessarily MT's): 'I want to focus on the basic idea of class politics in the context of socialist strategies'; 'I have certainly not been arguing that class or class interests are no longer relevant'.[133] Clearly, there is a homology here between the writing style and MT's 'seminar' practice in its discussion groups and in the MTEB quarterly reviews of issues, whereby the arguments that challenge the party's conventional ideas and approaches are set out in a conditional and qualified manner, akin to conversational structures. It is also the necessary interjections in the writing that attempts to pre-empt critics, who might have accused McLennan of ignoring class. Indeed, the author exhibits this important principle of good rhetorical practice in anticipating questions and potential responses of critics.

The interjections that Gregor McLennan employs also reinforce the 'reasonableness' of his view that there is something wrong with 'class politics': this was a tactical necessity because of the increasingly vociferous opposition to MT's political trajectory and especially in the middle of the CPGB's 'civil war'.[134] Argument by degree (probability) is persuasive, particularly if one can show that which was '*less* probable has actually happened, the *more* probable case is (proportionately) much more convincing'.[135] For example, rather than say that those who believe that 'a spontaneous class politics arising from a typical kind of labour' are wrong, McLennan is *more* persuasive by suggesting that this interpretation 'is much less convincing' than it once was; or that the 'working class, contrary to popular myth on the Left, has never been intrinsically socialist. And the myth is even less true today'; 'In all probability, then, coalitions are going to have to play a greater role in political life'.[136] The interjections and qualifications make McLennan's position appear to be more open and conditional in terms of what he is suggesting because it is a significant political shift if the working class moves from its leading position at the core of the Labour Party or the left, to becoming one of several partners in a coalition with other movements. Thus, his ideas come across as reasonable despite their implications for the *raison d'être* of both the CPGB and Labour: if little of any consequence can be determined by 'being' working class, then for what purpose does a working-class party exist? This was especially critical for the CPGB, which despite its

---

133   McLennan 1984, pp. 29, 31.
134   Some older party members might have realised that he was the General Secretary's son.
135   Cockcroft and Cockcroft 1992, p. 68 (original emphasis).
136   McLennan 1984, pp. 30, 31.

mild form of 'Marxist-Leninism' and its attempt to affiliate to Labour, it was still committed to some idea of being a vanguard party to justify its separate existence.

Under Martin Jacques's editorship, the writing style began to change, which played an important part in communicating through *Marxism Today* the critique of the 'orthodox' left, in both the Labour and Communist parties, which included identifying problems with the 'older' more traditionalist approaches to problems and policies.[137] MT's influence was enhanced by an ability to provide vivid, memorable images via the effective use of new or refreshing figures of speech that were also sometimes difficult to resist or refute. The strong negative reactions of sections of the left can be explained by some degree of veracity conveyed in these representations, although they do not take away from the ways in which MT promoted itself off of, and against, those same representations, frequently in its own promotional and publicity efforts. For example, criticisms of 'middle class socialists' has been a lucrative ground for drawing out the contradictions between material desires and utopian ideals, and between working-class conservatives and middle-class socialists, at least since the 1960s. MT's two most prominent and important contributors, Eric Hobsbawm and Stuart Hall, also penned some of the more memorable examples.

Marxism Today's house style incorporated ways of connotating 'openness' in the writing it published. Contributors used colloquialisms to make their articles seem more accessible to non-party readers. Interjections, such as 'you know' and 'let me say,' emphasise the individual voice and personalise the writing in a way that also simulates dialogue, as if they are responding to their own doubts or those of their readers. This sense of 'thinking out loud' signifies a process which, by implication, and as with oral communication in general and conversation in particular, is more open and conducive to engaging readers than more formal academic, Marxist or even journalistic discourses because it does not appear to 'command' or present itself as *the* authority. It is clearly different to formal or standard academic writing which can be less hospitable or accessible to others. Controversial ideas were therefore qualified as personal views, and not necessarily representative of MT's editorial line, which was an absolute necessity during the first years of Jacques's editorship. In case they were misunderstood by internal opponents, contributors used various caveats in their conclusions:

---

137 Pimlott 2000a, pp. 110–32.

> ... I have certainly not been arguing that class or class interests are no longer relevant;[138]

> ... the failure of even the gloomiest among us to appreciate the rate and distance of Labour's imminent retreat;[139]

> ... I am not suggesting that the Left can survive without a sense of history. Our own people know too little, not too much history.[140]

Within the context of the intense internal party strife, it was important for Jacques's tenure as editor to maintain a sense of separation between MT and contributors especially when ideas were seen as challenging fundamental party beliefs or policies. Thus, Jacques's MT could be seen as encouraging a broad(er) range of discussion without being seen as endorsing controversial ideas or challenging the party leadership. It was also a process of developing a more 'personalised', 'individualised' style that was similar in approach to mainstream broadsheet and magazine journalism.

8   *Marxism Today*'s Top Two Contributors: Eric Hobsbawm and Stuart Hall

Without a doubt, Eric Hobsbawm and Stuart Hall were *Marxism Today*'s two most important and preeminent contributors, whose respective theses became complementary themes of MT's political project, and whose political interventions, in turn, helped to promote MT and its project to a much broader audience than what the periodical might have been able to reach otherwise. Both Hobsbawm and Hall represent two constituencies that were key to MT's success and survival through the late 1970s and 1980s, and both were equally important in terms of its public face, social constituencies within MT's readership, and political-ideological positions. Their contributions were central to MT's public persona, and its political and cultural influence across the left and in the academy, in and beyond the UK, to which their writing styles, lexical choices and rhetorical techniques were critical.

---

138   McLennan 1984, p. 13.
139   Hobsbawm 1983b, p. 7.
140   Hall 1984a, p. 20.

9   Eric Hobsbawm and the Rhetorical Style of 'Realistic Marxism'[141]

Although Eric Hobsbawm's contributions to social and economic history are widely recognised, his political interventions in the struggles of the left during 'Thatcherism' are less well known. In total, Hobsbawm made 30 contributions to *Marxism Today* between 1978 and 1991, as author, interviewer, interviewee, and roundtable participant.[142] Hobsbawm exercised considerable influence through his interventions in public debates, as popularised through MT, which exerted influence in the Labour Party, even though he was a CPGB member. Indeed, Hobsbawm was referred to as 'Neil Kinnock's Favourite Marxist', despite having no close intellectual or personal relationship to the Labour leader in the early 1980s, a statement of his alleged influence on Kinnock's 're-making' of Labour. In addition, Hobsbawm was a central figure in contributions to MT's coverage of socialist parties and communist governments in its last three years.

To understand Hobsbawm's rhetorical appeal and the persuasiveness of 'realistic Marxism', it is necessary to first explicate the rhetoric of 'realism'.[143] In the worlds of international relations, economics and politics, the rhetoric of 'realism' is a powerful tool of persuasion. It works to limit debate because it presents itself as offering 'facts' which are, by definition, not open to dispute. Facts make it impossible to dispute realism's framing of an issue. Realism is a 'generally available discursive practice', that is 'a familiar, pervasive, and often pre-eminent way of speaking' which disciplines 'comprehension and conduct', which limits and constrains the possibilities for change.[144] As the narrative of realism 'sets the scene', it effectively 'structures subsequent argument'.[145]

Realism, thus understood, has played a particular role in Western liberal democracies, particularly in the realm of international politics and public debates over economic policy. For example, the appeal to realism, or *realpolitik*, in discussions around the support of western democracies for dictatorships is

---

141 The following section draws almost wholly from Hillary Pimlott [Herbert Pimlott], "From 'Old Left' to 'New Labour'? Eric Hobsbawm and the Rhetoric of 'Realistic Marxism'", Labour/Le Travail, 56 (Fall 2005), 175–97. Reprinted by permission of the publisher.

142 Hobsbawm 1978, 1979a, 1979b, 1980, 1982, 1983a, 1983b, 1984a, 1984b, 1985, 1986a, 1986b, 1987a, 1987b, 1987c, 1987d, 1988a, 1988b, 1989a, 1989b, 1990a, 1990b, 1990c, 1991a, 1991b, 1991c, 1991d; Blackburn et al. 1989; Campbell et al. 1990; Hobsbawm et al. 1983. In addition, Hobsbawm (1981) contributed an extra chapter to the book based upon this theme (in Jacques and Mulhern 1981).

143 In this section, I have drawn upon the work of Francis Beer, Robert Hariman and James Arnt Aune.

144 Hariman cited in Aune 1994, p. 60.

145 Beer and Hariman 1996, p. 3; Hariman 1996.

often made upon such grounds.[146] Used in this way, realism is an approach to the world that takes it 'as it exists' and does not put expectations upon other human actors in non-Western or non-democratic countries.

Realism is more powerful than other theories and ideological frameworks because it works by self-justification: in only presenting that which 'is', drawing upon the obvious, 'objective reality', the 'world of facts', it claims to represent the essences of global, national or class politics without any distortion or misrepresentation. It is 'eternal' and 'timeless' because it can account for any situation in political affairs of the past, present or future.[147] Realism's effectiveness is due to its pervasiveness as a way of reasoning or thinking within Western societies. Indeed, realism is so embedded in our language and thinking that 'it can operate effectively in fragments', being invoked in short phrases and even offhand comments (as with 'common sense'),[148] rather than through any kind of coherent political discourse. Its ubiquitous nature means that the entire code of 'political realism' 'can be activated any time we are reminded, e.g., that people are by nature self-interested, that law is useless without enforcement, or that testaments of common ideals are mere rhetoric'.[149] Realism is, therefore, in effect an ideology, or at the very least a mode of thinking, which supports the status quo, and has its corollary in the writing style known as 'plain style', which has considerable variability nevertheless, and for which the socialist, anti-Communist writer, George Orwell, was a well-known advocate.

A realist's understanding of politics is one in which the facts of political competition 'are grounded in human nature and confirmed by political history'. A realist in world, national or class politics would argue that it is necessary 'to see things as they are rather than as we would want them to be'. One can claim that one's arguments are based in 'objective' reality rather than in 'fantasy', 'slogans', 'ideals' or 'mere rhetoric'. The realist does not want to see things according to a vision of human nature, that is the 'alternative [or Marxist] account' and understanding of human beings in general and workers in particular, which lauds them for their inherent, political radicalness (i.e. revolutionary potential) and the dignity of their labour. Realists would argue that Marxist conceptions of the working class or humanity are not common-sensical or grounded in real human nature, but are in a way wanting to see a particular type of human being. These '[a]lternative accounts are either delusions ... or special pleading',

---

146 Western democratic governments use this kind of rhetoric to justify selling military hardware to dictatorships, since it appears that the pursuit of profit trumps all other values.
147 Beer and Hariman 1996, pp. 3–5; Hariman 1996, p. 35.
148 Ives 2004b, pp. 77–81; Green and Ives 2009.
149 Beer and Hariman 1996, pp. 3–5; Hariman 1996, p. 35.

whereas realism, by contrast, is only too aware of 'the fatal limitations of human nature'.[150] That, the 'road to socialism' leads to 'Stalinist gulags', for example, should come as no surprise, which is part of a right-wing canard about how the 'road to hell is paved with good intentions'.[151]

Realism, therefore, is not a term that is commonly applied to Marxists, especially not in reference to their ideals and values, whether expressed in or by party manifestos, histories or thinkers. It is a term that has been challenged by Marxists, particularly as they have demonstrated that capitalist societies and their precursors have often ensured their rule over the people by processes of 'mystification', of masking 'reality' from the oppressed, of engendering 'false consciousness'. The 'scientific method' of Marx and Engels, as understood by their followers, is necessary to reveal the actualities behind the façade of capitalism: to make clear humanity's real conditions of existence. Thus, there are those who argue that some forms of Marxism or Leninism are also forms of 'realism' and are 'realistic' in their understanding of the world and what needs to be done.[152]

Yet, realism is best understood as the justification of fatalists who accept the status quo, things and people 'as they are', and is largely determined by the dominant class as a means for understanding the world 'as it is' and, ultimately, thereby accepting, legitimising and justifying the present status quo in terms of the distribution of power, wealth and so on. As James Aune has argued:

> It is the discourse of realism that emerges as the source of the fundamental contradiction in Leninism: a realist rhetorical stance is essential to revolution, but realism by its nature is best suited to authoritarian statism rather than democracy.[153]

Even if it is realism that is claimed by those who are inclined to ask for incremental changes rather than revolutionary transformations, this does not make such people more democratic and less authoritarian.

---

150   Ibid.
151   However, no one appears to invert this phrase as: 'the road to heaven is paved with bad intentions'. That is, if only bad can come from good intentions, does that mean then that only good can come from bad intentions? This obvious inversion of a right-wing phrase shows just how ludicrous the thinking behind it is. What is not discussed is how this is usually used against those who strive for a better, more inclusive, just society, which one could argue is the only way we have been able to progress despite the profit motive's negative impact upon people's living and working conditions.
152   Aune 1994, pp. 58–62.
153   Aune 1994, p. 59.

Realism also points to a fundamental division on the left between 'idealists' and 'realists', or as more commonly labeled amongst socialists themselves, between 'reformists' and 'revolutionaries', or 'social democrats' and 'revolutionary socialists'. This division is based upon a fundamental difference in terms of both strategy and tactics: 'realists', reformists and social democrats see the value and importance of working within the system, of using the tools of capitalism to make it more humane, whereas the revolutionaries and idealists are more committed to a fundamental shift in power relations and argue that the ruling class will not give up power without a fight (something which they argue, by contrast, is a 'realistic' assessment of capitalist society).[154] It was on this division that Hobsbawm premised his appeal to Labour supporters and CPGB members alike, castigating the so-called 'hard left' for its refusal to see things 'as they are', just as Stuart Hall also frequently argued for seeing things 'as they are', which is implicitly another way of being 'realistic'.

Eric Hobsbawm's Marx Memorial lecture, 'The Forward March of Labour Halted?', was the opening shot in a series of interventions that *Marxism Today* published where realism was used as a trope, as Marxists and socialists alike had used it in the past to win arguments over tactics and strategy. Between Hobsbawm's political writings and MT's self-promotion and persona, realism became the dominant discourse. His straightforward realistic story of the decline of the British working class, provided the only possible narrative of Labour's limitations and ostensible solutions. Hobsbawm's representation was and is difficult to argue with because he presents his interpretation of the crisis of the left as just the 'facts', the situation 'as it is'. He recognised that to defeat the Conservatives electorally there was a need for an alliance and compromise because, as Hobsbawm made clear, the masses 'must be taken as they are, not as we should like to have them'.[155] The subsequent invocation of realism in every MT article he wrote quickly became an integral part of his rhetorical tactics to win over the undecided and defeat his critics. As with the construction of realism in international relations and economics, Hobsbawm's discourse was also self-validating through appeals to earlier 'realist' Marxists, such as Lenin and Dimitrov.[156]

As the primary articulator and rhetorician of 'realistic Marxism', Hobsbawm's *ethos* is crucial to understanding part of the persuasiveness of his critique of the labour movement. Ethos is one of the three primary forms of

---

154 E.g. Aune's account of the rhetoric and politics of Eduard Bernstein and Lenin (1994, pp. 52–62).
155 Hobsbawm 1984a, p. 10.
156 Ibid.

proof in the Aristotleian approach to rhetoric, when analysing the degree to which a rhetor (the speaker or writer) is successful in persuading others in their address, with a focus on the rhetor's credibility, authority and character. Hobsbawm's credibility as a life-long CPGB member and Marxist scholar gave him an almost unassailable personal position from which to launch his critique of the left. His engagement with anti-fascist politics during his youth in the Weimar Republic was an experience that coloured his views on the issue of alliances and which provided him with a strong moral position from which to criticise the left. Second, he remained a long-standing member of the CPGB after his arrival in Britain in the 1930s, even after 1956. Despite his loyalty to the party, Hobsbawm was critical of Stalinism and some CPGB policies,[157] and as part of the party's renowned CPHG, he was also critical of any attempt to write a history of the party for decades after 1956. Over several decades, his credibility as an historian was built via his multiple publications, which included international recognition as arguably one of the most wide-ranging social and economic historians, who uncovered the 'unwritten' history of peasants and workers, rebels and revolutionaries. Thus, Hobsbawm's ethos was considerably persuasive given his party, professional and personal histories lending *gravitas* to his challenge to orthodox beliefs.

Hobsbawm claimed to offer a 'realistic' and 'concrete' application of Marx's methods to the conjuncture of the late 1970s 'as it is'. The Marx Memorial Lecture provided him with the place 'to survey some developments in the British working class during the past 100 years', recognising that Marx himself had little to say a century earlier. He suggested that 'our task as marxists' was to apply Marx's methods 'concretely to our own era'.[158] If the labour movement is to recover 'its historical initiative', Hobsbawm argued that:

> ... we, as marxists, must do what Marx would certainly have done: to recognise the novel situation in which we find ourselves, to analyse it realistically and concretely, to analyse the reasons, historical and otherwise, for the failures as well as the successes of the labour movement, and to formulate not only what we would want to do, but what can be done.[159]

As the last phrase implicitly suggests, Hobsbawm references Lenin's best known pamphlet, *What is to be Done?*, to a 'realistic assessment' of 'what can be

---

157   Thompson 1992, p. 111; Dworkin 1997, pp. 10–23; Andrews 1995, pp. 225–50; Williams 1999, pp. 144–67.
158   Hobsbawm 1978, p. 279.
159   Hobsbawm 1978, p. 286.

done' (i.e. within limits). His emphasis on the 'failures as well as the successes' implied that the workers' movement's successes had received much greater attention than its failures.

Hobsbawm's rhetorical invocation of 'realism' limited the horizon of possibilities for the Labour Party to 'what can be done' rather than attempts at something more transformative. This tactic was an integral component of his rhetorical scaffolding in appealing to party leaders, thinkers and members via his use of key adverbs (e.g. realistically, concretely) and adjectives (real, concrete), to position the arguments of MT's opponents as 'unrealistic' and not based on 'concrete reality'.

For Hobsbawm, this was the logical outcome of recognising the shortcomings of Labour's situation and making the best of it, and to persuade the left of this idea, he increasingly invoked realism as part of his rhetorical strategy. It was used to devastating effect on the traditional left, increasingly painted into corners of 'un-realism', contributing to its eventual defeat. Hobsbawm did not best such opponents by his arguments alone; the persuasiveness of his claims became all the greater as some aspects of his analysis were increasingly borne out by events, and drawn on and promoted by individuals and institutions inside and outside the labour movement, including *The Guardian*. There is perhaps an irony here that century-old Marxist debates about the 'correct' interpretation of a conjuncture should end up being adjudicated by a centre-left commercial newspaper with a middle-class readership. *The Guardian*'s republication of Hobsbawm's arguments gave them considerably wider circulation than MT could ever have accomplished on its own or through the party, and thereby reinforced his arguments' pervasiveness and popularity. It thus appears as 'realistic' and 'common sense' since it is echoed via the mainstream media's repetition (a tautological form of reasoning and proof).

It was necessary for Hobsbawm to cite the writings of Marx, Engels and Lenin, not only to justify his perspective as a 'Marxist', especially for older traditionalist CPGB members, but also to reinforce the idea that his 'realistic Marxism' was in keeping with a Marxist, and even a Marxist-Leninist, analysis. These citations helped to demonstrate that it was prudent to make compromises and work in coalitions against critics for whom such positions were anathema. In this argument over 'compromise' and 'coalitions', Hobsbawm attempted to distinguish between two types of Marxism: one, 'which is exhausted in a few agitational phrases or a few simplified formulas and denunciations', clearly implying a very limited and inflexible scope in thinking, would not provide the necessary leadership; the other, more adroit, Marxism drew its strength from 'the realistic analysis of the historical situation, the developments in capitalism –

and socialism – and the actual state of the movement, however unexpected or unprecedented'.[160] This latter Marxism was presented as engaging with reality, the 'actual state of the movement', rather than in promoting 'a few simplified formulas ... [and] a few agitational phrases'.[161]

These key words and phrases that Hobsbawm used to invoke the new 'realistic Marxist' discourse were adopted by MT supporters, which included: 'concrete', 'concrete analysis' or 'concrete situation'; 'reality' or 'realism'; and 'confront', especially to 'confront reality'. These terms can be seen in the following excerpt, which had become a familiar form by 1985:

> *Marxism Today* has made it its business to confront reality and suggest ways of changing it. This is what comrades should recognise as the Leninist procedure of giving concrete analysis of a concrete situation.[162]

The citation of the 'Leninist procedure' in this excerpt was a common rhetorical tactic used by and in MT in the 1980s, particularly in its internal political interventions and promotional efforts that targetted party critics and traditionalists.

Critical to re-establishing common ground on which Hobsbawm could challenge orthodox beliefs among Communists of the 'forward march of labour' towards socialism, was the rhetorical use of Karl Marx and 'Marxist' to buttress his arguments and analysis: 'our task as marxists ... as applying Marx's methods and general analysis concretely to our own era'.[163] In providing an analysis which, arguably, would later challenge the very basis of a separate Communist Party, Hobsbawm claimed that his analysis was in keeping with a Marxist analysis. He claimed that Marx and Engels 'would have been neither very surprised nor very disappointed by the tendencies of development in the British working class' because 'they did not expect very much from the British working class beyond what actually looked like happening': i.e. they saw 'things as they are' since the establishment of a mass working-class party was the logical outcome of this development. Here Hobsbawm elides Marx and Engels's outlook on the likely future of the British labour movement in the late 1800s with his analysis and presents it as a 'natural' or 'inevitable' unfolding of events: a 'realistic' assessment of the situation. In his presentation, Marx and Engels are 'realists', 'like you and me' (MT's readers), and this was linked to a stringent cri-

---

160   Hobsbawm 1982, p. 15.
161   Ibid.
162   MTEC 1985.
163   Hobsbawm 1978, pp. 279, 285–6.

tique of Callaghan's Labour government and of the belief in the possibility of a radical class-conscious working class, at least prior to the 1983 election.[164]

Other Marxist thinkers were also marshalled by Hobsbawm to support his positions. References to Lenin were particularly important because he was the foremost Marxist on the 'hard left', and his citations worked to undermine a key thinker usually associated with the traditionalist camp, since his writings were normally understood as a 'guide to action' for the revolutionary (or 'hard') left. Lenin's words, which appeared to support Hobsbawm's argument for a 'people-based' rather than a 'class-based' party, were important in discrediting those who claimed the mantle of 'class politics':

> 'To march forward without compromise without turning from the path' – if this is said by an obviously impotent minority of workers ... then the slogan is obviously mistaken.[165]

Such appeals became much less important by the second half of the 1980s, since most traditionalists had stopped reading MT by then and the divisions on the left had become virtually unbridgeable.

An important and persuasive part of Hobsbawm's appeal to the left was his insistence on a 'common language' as a necessary part of the 'broad democratic alliance' strategy to reach out to 'the people'. Hobsbawm makes the case that this had been the policy of the Communist Party during the Popular Front era, which can be marked from Georgi Dimitrov's speech at the International Writers' Congress in 1935 for the need to use a 'common language' to make 'common cause' with the 'common people' to establish a 'common front' against fascism and in defence of democracy. Dimitrov is a figure with credibility for CPGB traditionalists because he was responsible for codifying the Popular Front strategy for the Comintern and he was a hero for standing up to the Nazis at a show trial, where they tried to frame Communists for the burning of Germany's Reichstag. Hobsbawm argues in a similar fashion for the role of a common language to make common cause with others who want to achieve the same immediate goals; in the 1980s, it was to defend the welfare state and defeat Thatcherism, which would necessitate an alliance or coalition to prevent isolation and ultimately failure. Dimitrov is cited as a leading Communist who articulates a 'realistic' position because he insisted that the masses 'must be taken as they are, not as we should like to have them', which, Hobsbawm argued, 'made

---

164 Ibid.
165 Lenin cited in Hobsbawm 1984a, p. 9. Lenin was referring to the British labour movement of 1919–20.

sense then and still makes sense'.¹⁶⁶ This was the formative period for Hobsbawm's politics, when as a youth he was forced to flee Germany with his family in 1933; drawing upon personal experiences and political lessons, the appeal of the Popular Front and its strategic direction resonated as the high-water mark of Communist success and progressive political advance for Hobsbawm as expressed in his political writings.¹⁶⁷

10 Rhetorical Strategy and Writing Style

Eric Hobsbawm's rhetorical intervention was clearly built around the need to appeal to two key audiences. The first audience was narrower and composed of CPGB members and sympathisers in the labour movement, including both traditionalists and reformists. The second was a broader, general audience composed of Labour Party members and supporters, which included a division between so-called 'hard' and 'soft' lefts, a division to which Hobsbawm and *Marxism Today* contributed.

Hobsbawm's rhetorical strategy was particularly effective in its constant binary of possibilities, in which, of two opposed positions there is always only one that is 'realistic'. For example, in 'Labour: Rump or Rebirth?', Hobsbawm's title itself captured two possible futures for the Labour Party. The first position, always the 'unrealistic' one, was that of a minority on the left, mostly Marxists (although even these were a minority) who would write off Labour and form a separate, 'mass' *socialist* party, such as that of the Trotskyist SWP. History demonstrated that this was a 'non-starter', Hobsbawm argued, because there has been no political organisation between 1900, when the Labour Party was formed, and the present, that has 'got anywhere' because Labour remains the single, mass, left-of-centre party over which everyone else is fighting for influence. One cannot argue with history because history just 'is'. The second view of the Labour Party was one which '[m]ost socialists, and ... [a] majority of Marxists, have accepted ... as a fact of life', and since one cannot argue with 'a fact of life', it follows that 'the future of socialism is through the Labour Party'. Even the CPGB recognised this, as it 'was implicit in its policy since the middle 1930s' and made explicit in its political programme in 1951.¹⁶⁸ Even just through the rhetorical process of 'depiction',¹⁶⁹ Hobsbawm and others helped to create the very divisions between the two lefts.

---

166 Hobsbawm 1984a, p. 10.
167 Hobsbawm 2002, pp. 218, 322–4; Dworkin 1997, pp. 14–15.
168 Hobsbawm 1984a, pp. 7–11.
169 Osborn 1986.

The informal style of Hobsbawm's writing helped to simulate dialogue as if he was responding to or expressing the same hesitations or doubts being expressed by the reader, or thinking through ideas, a process which took on the trappings of being more 'open' and conducive to engagement with readers than more abstract or academic writing. Colloquialisms, first-person pronouns, interjections and other signs of informality, associated with spoken rather than written communication, were integral to Hobsbawm's writing style. These pragmatic particles, asides and interjections were important aids to his persuasiveness. While making his writing more accessible, such stylistic forms reinforced statements as individual, even if authoritative, views, rather than the more emphatic and exhortative statements produced in manifestos or by the party. These aids to persuasion simulated his interpretation as dialogue or discussion, which was part of MT's broader attempt, under Martin Jacques, to modify its more abstract or obtuse aspects.

Despite his position as both a public and a party intellectual from which he could mount critiques, Hobsbawm still had to be cautious in putting forward controversial ideas or challenges to orthodox beliefs. As part of the dissemination of his views via MT, it was necessary that he at least appear to be putting forth his own views rather than those of any party faction. This caution eased as his interventions became more clearly targetted against traditionalists.

Hobsbawm was well aware of the 'political implications' of his analysis. During the period of his interventions, he had to be careful because those who challenged party orthodoxy, especially the 'leading role' of the working class, were liable to be accused of 'betrayal'. His interjections reinforced the 'reasonableness' of his view that there was something wrong with 'class politics': this was a tactical necessity because of the growing intensity of internal opposition to MT by 1984 and their opponents' appropriation of the term, 'class politics', in a pamphlet of the same name, which challenged the trajectory of the left as evident in MT[170] and which was meant to undercut the credibility of Hobsbawm's argument. Thus, his ideas were resolutely presented as realistic despite their (ultimate) implications for the *raison d'être* of both the CPGB and the Labour Party: i.e. for what purpose does a 'working class party' exist, if there is no 'working class' to represent?

Hobsbawm's interventions in public debate on the left began to take on a more urgent appeal after Labour's second general election defeat in June 1983. This defeat, he argued, indicated that a majority of the British electorate would not vote for Labour even though it had its most socialist programme ever, since

---

170   Fine et al. 1984.

Labour had only received 28 percent of the vote, barely two percent ahead of the third party, and it did not even win a majority of those groups which traditionally supported Labour, such as industrial workers and the unemployed. This meant that Labour could no longer rely on material interests to automatically deliver the working-class vote. This was a reaction against the 'vulgar Marxist' idea of reading off politics from people's social-economic position. To address a larger public, Labour had to develop policies that could gain popular support via the national media. Thus, the implications of Hobsbawm's analysis, published as 'Labour's Lost Millions' in the October 1983 issue, was reprinted in *The Guardian* at the start of Labour's annual conference with the more provocative title: 'Change the Party, Not the Workers'. This was followed a year later with Hobsbawm's October 1984 feature, 'Labour: Rump or Rebirth?', which was provocatively re-titled as, 'Labour Must Go Forward with the Masses', on *The Guardian*'s Agenda page.[171] Both articles and *Guardian* excerpts were published for the start of the Labour Party Conferences in 1983 and 1984.

As Hobsbawm's impatience with opponents on the left grew, he painted critics as incapable of recognising the obvious 'facts' of the situation or seeing things 'as they are'. Two things were now obvious as he surveyed the debates of the late 1970s:

> ... *first*, the sheer refusal of some of the Left to look unwelcome facts in the face, even though they were already obvious to any unblinkered observer, and *second*, the failure of even the gloomiest among us to appreciate the rate and distance of Labour's imminent retreat.[172]

The metaphor of limited or partial sight is a leading trope linked to the 'hard left', contrasted with the clarity of Hobsbawm's realism which 'looks' such 'unwelcome facts' 'in the face', which many on the left refuse to see. From this excerpt, we can see how the dominant metaphor is a simple one contrasting clarity of vision to limited or no sight.

Hobsbawm's negative characterisations of opponents on the left were particularly effective in preempting and derailing their criticisms. These were usually launched in the opening paragraphs of his articles, where he would make it clear that those who failed to recognise the 'reality' of things 'as they are and not as they would wish them to be', were 'blinkered' and cannot 'face up to the facts': unwilling 'to confront reality', the 'unseeing' left was already retreating behind

---

171   Hobsbawm 1983c, 1984c.
172   Hobsbawm 1983b, p. 7 (original emphasis).

screens to protect itself from 'the grim sight of reality'.[173] When opposition to Hobsbawm's critique continued, he became more insistent on how 'not even the most blinkered of sectarians' were prepared to claim that Labour had *not* 'suffered a disastrous defeat' or, at least, they were not willing to do so 'in public'.[174] Secondly, to emphasise just how bad things were, he said that the election results were *worse* than expected because 'even the gloomiest', i.e. pessimistic 'realists' like himself, failed to anticipate that Labour's vote would 'suddenly collapse' as much as it did, thereby, reinforcing the gravity of the situation.[175]

In constructing his rhetoric of 'realistic Marxism', it was necessary for Hobsbawm to present a plausible image of opponents on the left, which would help to explain *why* sections of the left were not 'realistic'. The effectiveness of his rhetorical strategy and writing style can be attributed to his use of metaphors that created 'freshly minted images'[176] in the minds of the audience that resonated with the opponents of traditionalists in both the CPGB and Labour, who saw the latter as 'unwilling' to change or even to recognise 'reality'. His invention of new figures of speech created vivid, memorable images of his opponents as either 'misguided idealists' or 'mindless zealots', drawing from popular and highly ideological caricatures of the so-called 'hard Left', that had been influenced by decades of the widespread, pejorative common-sense understanding of Soviet Communism promoted through the mainstream media. Two particularly striking tropes from Hobsbawm's strategic intervention in the debates over the 1984–85 miners' strike, for example, published in the April 1985 MT cover story in the run-up to the contentious May Special Congress, were: 'building the New Jerusalem like a 1960s tower block'; and 'the ready-made set of slogans chanted by photo-fit hard-liners'.[177]

The simile, 'building a New Jerusalem like a 1960s tower block', is used to associate the qualities of the 1960s tower block with 'socialist utopia'. By the 1980s, the 1960s tower blocks were widely recognised as unpopular: 'socialist utopia' is equated to an aesthetically unappealing architectural form created for the working class by middle-class professionals, who did not have to live in such buildings. Using the nineteenth-century phrase for socialist utopia, not only invokes religious references to socialism as a 'faith', with its negative connotations of doctrinaire political 'theology' for which 'facts' and 'reason' are ignored when they threaten 'belief', but also reinforces the connotations of

---

173   Ibid.
174   Hobsbawm 1983b, p. 9.
175   Hobsbawm 1983a, p. 7.
176   Cockcroft and Cockcroft 1992, p. 119.
177   Hobsbawm 1985, pp. 10, 12.

'socialism' as an ideology connected to an outdated and outmoded past. The simile rather neatly associates the traditionalists' programme with the 'qualities' of the tower block, the result of elitist, unrepresentative and undemocratic planning, which were unappealing to the working class for whom it was built. The implication is that 'socialist utopia' ignores the *real* desires of the working class and imposes what 'outsiders' think is best for them.

The second trope focuses on the 'hard left' and 'Trotskyists', usually caricatured in right-wing tabloids as a 'rent-a-mob', but more bitingly lampooned by Hobsbawm as 'photo-fit hard-liners'.[178] The notion of 'photo-fit' came from the then current police practice of using a combination of different, stock photographic images of facial features to put together a possible 'fit' for a criminal suspect. This places traditionalist opponents in a particular position: those who are, by transference and connotation, 'suspect' and interchangeable, assembled from 'stock' or generic images, as with mannequins or robots, and attend demonstrations or protests as rote behaviour, whatever the issue. They 'chant' in an endless recitation, a 'ready-made set of slogans': thinking is unnecessary because it is already done, 'ready-made' for every situation in which such leftists find themselves. Such imagery is richly suggestive of mass-produced popular caricatures of 'mindless Marxist militants', promoted by national newspapers and especially Tory tabloids.

These vivid images were difficult to resist or refute: the strong negative reactions of sections of the left can be explained by a general understanding that these representations had some basis in reality, as does any stereotype that resonates to some extent with an audience. Hobsbawm's criticisms were scathing and provocative, especially as the animosity, tension and polemics heated up between the two broad tendencies within both the CPGB and the Labour Party. Those on the left who argued that Labour's difficulties were part of a painful transition from Labourism to Socialism were likened to 'oarsmen being congratulated on their rowing much better than ever before while the boat is being swept to the rapids'.[179]

Despite his skills at propagating such vivid imagery, Hobsbawm did use mixed and dead metaphors, similar to those of the earlier *Marxism Today*, which were much less persuasive: e.g. 'glimmer of comfort'; 'making the best of a bad job'.[180] He would use party jargon when attacking critics, for example, as demonstrated in his March 1984 article:

---

178 Hobsbawm 1985, p. 12.
179 Hobsbawm 1984a, p. 9.
180 Hobsbawm 1983b, p. 9; Hobsbawm 1984a, p. 11.

'Labour's Lost Millions' ... was not a call for retreat into opportunism making the best of a bad job, but a call for advance. It did not even see the broad anti-Thatcherite front which is surely essential today, as a mere defence against encroaching reaction.[181]

The awkwardness in Hobsbawm's prose is evidence that the legacy of party jargon, and the awkward syntax that often followed from its use, was not dispensed with overnight: e.g. 'retreat into opportunism'; 'defence against encroaching reaction'. It was also a means to try to undermine his traditionalist opponents' claims to party authority or 'class politics' by using such jargon.

Thus, we can see that even as some writers were more accessible to non-Communist audiences, it was not always done simply or immediately, as traces of earlier rhetorical techniques and writing styles were often present. Eric Hobsbawm's writing style did not prevent publication in the national press, particularly if it was felt to be relevant, timely or perhaps ideologically aligned with the newspaper's editorial line. Hobsbawm's 'realistic Marxism', which became popularised via *Marxism Today* and *The Guardian*, served as a stick with which the Labour leadership could beat the Bennites and others who strayed outside the Labour Party's line; it also helped the CPGB leadership's ideological pushback against its (and MT's) internal opponents.

11   Stuart Hall: Socialist Public Intellectual and Polemical Rhetorician

Whereas Eric Hobsbawm represented an older constituency amongst both contributors to and readers of *Marxism Today*, Stuart Hall represented a newer constituency amongst both writers and readers as MT began its transformation into a magazine from 1979 onwards. Unlike Hobsbawm, however, Hall also became a key collaborator with Martin Jacques on MT's political project and critical to its success. Although Hall is well known for his focus on the rise of the new right and the populist appeal of Thatcherism, he is less well known for his contributions to the division of the left via his rhetorical strategy and tactics, especially around his characterisations of the left, but which also played into mainstream media's characterisation (caricaturisation?) of the so-called 'hard left'. As part of this analysis, it is first necessary to consider his role as a public intellectual engaged in the on-the-ground political debates about the direction of the Labour Party.

---

181   Hobsbawm 1984a, p. 11.

Through his close association with MT, Hall helped to increase its influence in cultural politics in the 1980s as his writings popularised areas that traditionally had been neglected until then: popular culture, media and ideology. The emphasis that Hall and others placed on what was understood as the Gramscian 'war of position' through 'civil society' ensured an important role for the intellectual in whatever way she might be defined. Yet, despite Hall's exhortations to those on the left, *academic* cultural politics became one of the defining elements around MT's political project, even as the magazine helped to pave the way politically for New Labour.

Hall's early career as a left intellectual had indeed begun in the aftermath of '1956', i.e. the Suez Crisis, Khrushchev's 'secret speech' and the Hungarian Revolution, in which he and other New Left intellectuals attempted to find a 'third way' beyond Washington and Moscow. Some of the issues Hall raised as the first editor of *New Left Review*, 1960–62, would be brought up again in his own writing in the 1980s in *New Socialist* and *Marxism Today*, including his focus on the politics of popular culture. While working in secondary and adult education in the early 1960s, he co-authored a book with Paddy Whannel on the same topic,[182] which drew Richard Hoggart's attention and an offer of the position as assistant director at the newly established Birmingham University Centre for Contemporary Cultural Studies in 1964, taking over as director in 1969. In 1979, he departed the CCCS for the position of Professor of Sociology at the Open University, a post he held until his retirement in 1997. The positions that Hall held before and during his collaboration on the MT's political project contributed substantially to the latter's influence.

Throughout Stuart Hall's career, from around the start of his work at the CCCS, he participated in or contributed to a number of studies, commissions and other projects of civil society organisations, from local and national immigrant and anti-poverty groups, such as the National Committee of Commonwealth Immigrants and the Joseph Rowntree Social Services Trust, to national and international organisations, such as the Runnymede Commission on the Future of Multi-Ethnic Britain and the United Nations Education, Social and Cultural Organisation. A good example of his participation in extra-academic commitments was Hall's involvement in co-presenting the 30-minute video, *It Ain't Half Racist, Mum*, broadcast (1 March 1979) on BBC 2, produced by the Campaign Against Racism in Media[183] with the BBC's Open Door Community Unit. It examined racism in popular television programming and took its name

---

182   Hall and Whannel 1964.
183   Comedia with CARM published an anthology on racism in the media (i.e. Cohen and Gardner 1982).

from a then popular situation comedy broadcast on BBC.[184] In reaching out past the narrower audiences of political periodicals and academic courses, the programme's focus was not just educational but also political because of street demonstrations, festivals and rallies against the National Front's presence on the streets of England at the time; the NF's decline after 1979 was attributed in part to Thatcher's incorporation of aspects of 'popular racism' into her speeches (e.g. the infamous 'swamped by an alien culture' speech in 1978).[185]

Hall's work as a professor at the OU, 1979–97, on broadcast and educational documentaries, presenting TV programmes and courses on popular culture, and preparing textbooks for OU courses, contributed to his influence as these texts were frequently adopted for courses in the polytechnic sector, where media and cultural studies programmes were growing rapidly, all of which brought together audiences and authors for the ideas in MT and NS. These academic contributions via debates, conferences and articles promoted his Thatcherism thesis within the academy, which contributed to Hall's growing influence.[186] These academic contributions also helped to popularise and extend his influence beyond his political contributions in the (counter) public sphere of left debate via various socialist magazines, conferences and talks, including those hosted by MT and the CPGB. For example, during the second half of the 1970s he attended the annual Communist University of London. Two of his presentations were included in CUL collections, including the widely reproduced article, '"The Whites of Their Eyes": Racist Ideologies and the Media'.[187] After hearing Hall speak at one of the CULs,[188] Martin Jacques decided to get him to write for MT and his January 1979 feature would mark the beginning of the productive collaboration between Hall and Jacques, which would continue past MT's demise, even though Hall was a Labour Party member and never a member of the CPGB.[189]

It is also necessary to consider why Stuart Hall was more influential in cultural studies *and* left politics than other leading intellectuals of the political and cultural left, particularly Raymond Williams, who had been seen as

---

184 *It Ain't Half Hot, Mum*, was a 1970s sitcom about British soldiers in a depot in India in 1945.
185 Schofield 2012, pp. 105–7.
186 E.g. Hall 1982a, 1988b.
187 Hall 1981d. Hall presented this chapter at the penultimate CUL in 1980, when it was well past its peak.
188 The MTEB had discussed asking non-CPGB contributors, including Hall, to write for MT in December 1976 (e.g. MTEB 1976a).
189 Hall was a willing participant in CPGB events back in the 1950s (e.g. Hall and Back 2009, p. 674).

the left's leading cultural thinker in the 1960s.[190] If we weigh up Hall's contributions against Williams's and their reception on the left prior to the latter's death in January 1988, for example, we can get some sense of difference between these two socialist public intellectuals and former collaborators in the founding of the first New Left and cultural studies. Terry Eagleton makes the case that by 1979 Williams's books had sold more than 750,000 copies, which indicated that his work was reaching far beyond the 'ivory tower', but without an organised counter-public sphere there was no space within which his writing could be taken up and debated, which he contrasts with the example of the Weimar Republic, where a vast range of organisations on the left contributed to a dynamic (counter) public sphere.[191] Eagleton's contention needs to be qualified by the recognition that there was a left (counter) public sphere, but that it was fractured by sectarian divisions and, thus, Williams's critiques of Hobsbawm's and Hall's theses, which offered different analyses to better known counter arguments on the left, were sidelined or overlooked.[192]

In total, Stuart Hall was involved in contributing or participating in 25 articles published in *Marxism Today* between January 1979 and December 1991. Hall is the single author of 18; in the remaining seven articles, he is either co-author, interviewer, interviewee or roundtable participant. Sixteen out of 25 were published in MT's last six years (1986–91), including six of the seven articles where Hall is one of multiple participants, almost all within the period of Hall's membership of the editorial board.[193] During the 1980s, Hall also wrote for *New Socialist*, *New Left Review* and a range of other fortnightly, weekly and

---

190   E.g. Williams mentions how people assumed that Harold Wilson's government would contact him after coming to power in 1964 (Williams 1979a, p. 371).
191   Eagleton 1984.
192   An interesting difference is their approaches to analysing language. Whereas Hall quickly moves to writing and speaking about discourses, Williams had engaged in a fully 'historical semiotics' by which individual words and phrases were analysed for their meanings as evidence of the various shifts that have taken place in class rule and power struggles historically (Williams 1983b). Hall works at the abstract, general or meta-level of discourse, whereas Williams focuses on the particular and details the relationship between language, media and politics, as, for example, in his analysis of the miners' strike (Williams 1989f [1985]).
193   They are (in chronological order): Hall 1979, 1980a, 1981b, 1982b; Jenkins, Hall and Aaronovitch 1982; Hall 1984a, 1984b, 1985a, 1985b; Jesse Jackson [interviewed by Hall] 1986; Hall and Jacques 1986; Hall 1986, 1987b, 1987c, 1987, 1988c; Hall and Jacques 1988; Hall 1988d; Hall and Held 1989a; Jameson and Hall 1990; Hall 1990; Hall and Jacques 1990; Hall 1991a, 1991b, 1991c.

monthly periodicals, and he edited and/or contributed to collections of articles on Thatcherism and the challenges facing the left.[194]

The first and most influential article that Hall wrote for MT was 'The Great Moving Right Show' (in which he named 'Thatcherism'[195] four months before Thatcher's first general election victory), which was published in the January 1979 issue. His second was a response to three other features responding to his article, which provided Hall with an opportunity to clarify the 'swing to the Right'.[196] His two subsequent contributions in the next two years focussed upon the Labour Right, after the defection of the 'Gang of Four' to form the Social Democratic Party, and the relationship between class and party, particularly as affected by the impact of unemployment and the 'new recession'.[197] 'A Long Haul', Hall's third feature for MT, reinforced the message that being working class, including the long-term unemployed, did not automatically translate into support for Labour, and even where it did, it did not offer the promise of growing support because of structural changes in the economy. Hall's final contribution in Thatcher's first term was to a roundtable on the political map prior to the 1983 election with a leading CPGB intellectual, Sam Aaronovitch, and Peter Jenkins, a centre-left opinion columnist with *The Guardian*, and the first mainstream journalist to contribute to MT's feature section.[198]

During 1983, Hall's two contributions associated with *Marxism Today* were not actually published in the magazine, but were part of the collection on Thatcherism Hall co-edited with Jacques, published on 1 May 1983 by Lawrence and Wishart in association with MT (even though both entities were funded by and part of the CPGB). The two contributions included the co-authored introduction to the collection and the key chapter in the collection, the substantially revised version of 'The Great Moving Right Show'.[199]

In 1984, Hall focused on two key areas for *Marxism Today*, both articles played into critiques of the left that were identified in the Thatcherism thesis. The first one published in the January 1984 issue, 'The Culture Gap', emphasised the importance of culture and the market's 'democratic' appeal to consumers, where Hall makes connections between 'the market' and the idea of

---

194 E.g. Curran 1984b; Hall and Jacques 1983b: The first reference is for a collection published under the auspices of *New Socialist* and the other one was published in association with MT.
195 Hall was not the first to use the word but his was definitely the first that named right-wing authoritarian populism that was taken up on the left. For a different view, see Vinen 2010.
196 Hall 1979; Hall 1980a. The three articles were: Corrigan 1979b; Leonard 1979; Jacques 1979d.
197 Hall 1981b, Hall 1982b.
198 Jenkins et al. 1982.
199 Hall and Jacques 1983a; Hall 1983a.

'choice', and links it to everyday practices of living and its appeal to middle- and working-class consumers.[200] The other article, published in the November 1984 MT, 'The State: Socialism's Old Caretaker', highlighted how most on the left saw the state as the *defacto* means through which socialism, in some form, would have to be implemented, and how socialists were closely associated with the (capitalist) state in the minds of many, because of the social democratic left's close association with Keynesianism and support for the capitalist welfare state.[201] Bookending the following year, 1985, mid-point in Thatcher's second term, Hall's contributions, in the January and December issues, pushed back against 'Old Labour' and the left's apparent 'refusal' to abandon key tenets of traditional socialism. Hall's polemical interventions in the debate over Labour's trajectory also played into the divisions within both the Labour and Communist parties.[202]

As the decade progressed, Hall's contributions continued his critique of the left's and Labour's responses to Thatcherism and contributed articles on Gramsci and to the 'New Times' project.[203] These also included an interview with the black US politician, Jesse Jackson, who was attempting to establish a 'rainbow coalition', and his co-authored piece on 'People Aid' (with Jacques), both of which sought a new approach of building alliances across social movements, single-issue mobilisation and identity politics.[204] Hall's work became more closely identified with MT, particularly after he joined the editorial board just a couple of months before the launch of the third format in 1986.

In addition to Hall's contributions to MT, there were a series of important academic and non-academic articles, in which there was considerable overlap with subjects covered in his work for the periodical.[205] His writings were distributed via other periodicals and political anthologies, including Labour's *New Socialist, The Socialist Register* and *Silver Linings*, alongside academic collections, such as *People's History and Socialist Theory*, and *Marxism and the Interpretation of Culture*, all of which contributed to the influence of Hall's version of Gramsci's theory and concepts as developed in his Thatcherism thesis.[206]

---

200 Hall 1984a, 1984b.
201 Ibid.
202 Hall 1985a, 1985b.
203 E.g. Hall 1986, 1987a, 1987b, 1987c, 1988c, 1988d, 1990; Hall and Jacques 1990.
204 E.g. Jackson 1986; Hall and Jacques 1986.
205 E.g. Hall 1978, 1980b, 1981a, 1981c, 1981d, 1982a, 1986b, 1986c, 1988b.
206 Harris 1992 provides a scathing critique of 'Gramscianism' in cultural studies; other recent critiques see problems with Hall's understanding of Gramsci's concepts (e.g. Davidson 2008; Thomas 2009, pp. 44, 161). See Chapter 2.

It is not a surprise then that Hall's ideas contributed to the divide within cultural studies that mirrored the divisions of the left's (counter) public sphere.

Although Hall's position as a socialist public intellectual and leading cultural studies scholar contributed substantially to the popularisation of MT amongst the academic left, the coverage of his MT articles in *The Guardian* and other media, in turn, contributed to extending his influence on and across the left beyond the academy. Interestingly, the corporate daily and Sunday press picked up almost none of Hall's key articles analysing Thatcherism, but they took up some of his other articles that focussed on critiques of the left, such as 'The State: Socialism's Old Caretaker'.[207]

12   Stuart Hall's Rhetorical Techniques and Writing Style

The only theory worth having is that which you have to fight off ...[208]

∵

Stuart Hall's writing style in *Marxism Today* is characterised by a combination of memorable or pithy quotations, lucid characterisations and vivid metaphors in addition to an increasingly informal and conversational syntax, in part based upon political talks he was giving at MT events and in part based upon a 'strategy of qualification' and conditionality. All of this contributed to Hall's political persona and public profile during the 1980s. His articles for MT varied from the more formal or academic style to the more informal conversational mode, his tentativeness and qualification was part of his attempt to persuade readers of the veracity of his critique of the left and analysis of Thatcherism.

In contrast to the conventions of academic discourse and left political analysis at the time, Hall frequently made use of the first-person mode of address in both singular and plural forms (e.g. 'I', 'we'), in his contributions to draw readers in to identify with the positions he stakes out and claims he makes. The first-person, plural mode of address is a conventional rhetorical device to help draw the reader into identifying with the author's position, even as it also contributes to a more informal writing style. The use of first-person pronouns, when bal-

207   Hall 1984b.
208   Hall 1992, p. 281.

anced against the third-person mode of address, commonly found in writing in MT in all three formats, would become more common under Martin Jacques's editorship, although political journalism more broadly was also changing during this period. This mode of address also made it clear to the reader that the ideas were the author's own rather than the position of MT, its editorial board or the Communist Party. This was of considerable importance early in Jacques's editorship since Hall was not a member of the CPGB and because of the internal power struggles that had the potential to make Jacques's position as editor vulnerable.

Hall's rhetorical use of the first-person plural mode of address also contributes to the classic 'us-versus-them' means of division and unity. Hall's identification of 'them', the so-called 'hard left', was at first vague and clearly intended for his audience in MT to be read as the 'other left': e.g. the SWP or *The Morning Star* faction. In the aftermath of Labour's June 1983 election defeat, as divisions deepened, Hall's criticism became harsher and targeted CPGB traditionalists and Labour's Bennite wing, and his rhetoric became more confident and assertive, calling out the 'hard left' for its unwillingness to 'learn from Thatcherism'.

While Hall's 1979 article introducing Thatcherism to MT readers prior to the 1979 general election was more cautious in its criticisms of the left, the substantially revised version, published as the first defining chapter after his (co-authored) introduction to the 1983 collection on Thatcherism, is much more forceful and direct in its critique. Hall's critical depiction of the left had shifted into a more overt attack on the resistance amongst socialist intellectuals to his Thatcherism thesis and on a continued resilience of 'economism' on the left. One of Hall's objectives in his critique of economism was to get past the blockage that this thinking had on perpetuating a kind of 'vulgar Marxism' that MT claimed its opponents on the left propounded. His rhetorical strategy was an attempt to shift the left away from this economism. Yet, Hall's polemics, like many on the 'soft left', targetted a straw man of 'vulgar Marxism', which was not always a true representation of his opponents but more of a popular 'myth-conception', which complemented and reinforced Tory tabloid misrepresentations of the left in general.[209]

---

209 The play on 'misconception' is intentional since Barthes's concept of 'myth' shows how ideological ideas become naturalised as if they are universal eternal 'truths' that lie outside of ideology (Barthes 1973).

13 Qualification and Conditionality

As with any good rhetor, Stuart Hall anticipated likely points of contention and attempted to pre-empt his opponents' expected lines of criticism particularly in his early contributions when the great majority of MT's readers would have been Communist Party members. To encourage those readers to be open to his ideas, Hall frequently presented his critiques, analyses and prescriptions in ways that could be seen as conditional and qualified, an approach common in academic writing. Hall's third article for MT, for example, in the April 1981 issue, still demonstrates an awkward writing style.[210]

This is a most common characteristic of Hall's prose in MT in the early 1980s, in which one finds the modesty or humility of the scholar, who either does not appear to know more, or better, than his audience and who appears to be engaged in a 'dialogue' with readers.[211] The use of qualifications, hesitations, interjections and conditional statements convey both this modestness *and* a sense of speech or dialogue. Hall was an exceptional orator and his work on television and other media programmes for the Open University, no doubt also contributed to the almost dialogic nature of his style, although it can also contribute to ambiguity in meaning. As Brennon Wood has pointed out: '[p]art of the problem is Hall's *style* of theorising' because 'his work is explicitly partial, he relies on a strategy of repeated qualification'.[212] Other critics have complained that his ideas can be both 'right and wrong' as they 'can be stretched in different ways according to circumstances'.[213]

This latter observation complements David Harris's critique of Hall and other MT contributors, and especially those writing from a cultural studies or cultural populist perspective, who drew upon particular conventions and techniques of academic writing that helped to make their contributions more persuasive, which he calls 'academic realism'.[214] This approach allows authors to 'display their flaws to the reader, while a privileged account is allowed to emerge as "more real"', while other writing conventions enable a writer 'to conceal' his or her work 'from the readers so as to encourage a sense of involvement, or to appear to maintain a certain "balance", while setting agendas'.[215]

---

210 Hall 1981b.
211 This approach draws from Hall's approach at CCCS, where faculty and students worked collaboratively as part of a new way of engaging in research (Connell and Hilton 2015; Brunsdon 1996; Sparks 1996).
212 Wood 1998, pp. 409–10 (original emphasis).
213 Jessop et al. 1988, p. 72, cited in Wood 1998, p. 410.
214 Harris 1992, pp. 203–4.
215 Harris 1992, p. 203.

This more 'realist' or 'academic realist' narrative emerges, Harris suggests, and is 'maintained by the use of personal interventions and asides, disclosures and apologies' which do much to strengthen 'the authorial voice'.[216] The conditionality of the claims Hall makes in his analysis is part of his strategy of repeated qualification. It is this very 'style of theorising', however, which might make Hall's audience more open to his ideas because of the expression of tentativeness, hesitation and even uncertainty in his writing.

Those of us who inhabit the left or the academy are well aware of the contradictions between the claims made by different theories, and the actual historical events and political developments that they seek to explain, as well as the challenge of the egos of many of those involved in these debates. Hall's tentativeness conveys our own sense of tentativeness with theory: the extent to which we believe it actually explains the real world out there and how those things that do not fit into our theory can be explained. Yet, Hall is much more certain than he intimates through his use of language since he wants to draw in and persuade sceptical readers.

Immediately following the opening sentence in his first feature for MT, Hall qualifies his position as still tentative as there is much yet to be learned and Thatcher had not yet won her first general election as leader of the Conservative Party. This tentativeness was also rhetorically apt since Hall was not a CPGB member, which put him in a minority of MT contributors and readers in 1979. Yet, he also deploys the first-person plural, 'we', to draw in the sceptical reader:

> We may not yet understand its [Thatcherism's] extent and its limits, its specific character, its causes and effects. We have so far – with one or two notable exceptions – failed to find strategies capable of mobilising social forces strong enough in depth to turn its flank. But the tendency is hard to deny. It no longer looks like a temporary swing in the political fortunes …[217]

Of course, his explanation for Communist readers remains tentative in terms of where the analysis will go and it is this tentativeness that is noticeably different to many, perhaps most, political commentators on the right or left, whether journalists, pundits or scholars. It is conditional: Hall acknowledges that there has been some successful resistance but they are 'one or two notable exceptions'.[218]

---

216   Ibid.
217   Hall 1979, p. 20.
218   These must not have been *that* 'exceptional' since even that reference is excised from the

The apparent conditionality of Hall's prose plays into his use of contrasting the 'hard left', which he sees as opposed to his ideas, with those who can see the shift that has taken place in the political landscape. For example, in Hall's first feature he writes: 'Certainly, there is no simple, one-to-one correspondence between a "correct" analysis and an "effective" politics'. Qualifying one's analysis is standard practice for most academics and it can then be used, however, to point out the 'obvious lack of political perspective which now confronts the left'. Although by pointing out the 'obvious', Hall flatters those readers who align with him and can, therefore, identify as not being amongst the 'blinkered left'.

There is also the construction of a particular idea of the 'left' that is not open to change or taking on board challenges to its way of thinking, especially if some of its key ideas are threatened. It contributes to the idea of the 'left' as a single, monolithic entity. Indeed, Hall's rhetoric depicts a 'left', and especially a 'hard left', that was more robust, stronger, monolithic and united than it actually was. It is not that Hall's critique was without merit: it resonated with many who felt that members of some or all far left groups were 'know-it-alls', who patronised and attempted to dominate any alliance or coalition in which such groups participated. These groups' belief in the 'inexorable' movement towards socialism, often exhibited in their rhetoric, which confidently expressed their particular perspective with an 'aura of absolute assurance', made it appear as if they had all the answers.

This type of rhetorical technique contrasted starkly with Hall's claims that were couched within qualifications and conditionality. That the rhetorical style of many Marxist organisations became more about retaining the loyalty of their own members (i.e. solidification), than reaching out to prospective members, belies at the same time the self-assurance in the correctness of their beliefs, that such organisations propagated in their rhetoric that brooks no room for doubt and usually becomes impervious to dialogue with others (as outlined above). This imperviousness, therefore, precludes any possible reassessment or changes to the party's worldview and beliefs that such a dialogue might provoke and thereby makes it an inhospitable environment to external or internal audiences (i.e. party members) who express questions about aspects of those beliefs.

Such a space of discourse, contrasted with Hall's more 'open' rhetoric which exhibited some doubt, qualification and conditionality of advancing its critique of the left and its strategy, was enough to open up many readers to Hall's

---

version published by Lawrence and Wishart, on 1 May 1983, five weeks before election day (Hall 1983a).

critique because of the apparent willingness to entertain doubt and not claim to have all the answers. As Harris argues, the use of expressions of self-doubt in one's work can help to persuade readers of the veracity of one's interpretation or perspective, as can the appearance of representing other viewpoints for consideration, since it offers a 'balance' and does not appear to be privileging one view over another.[219] Hall did not just criticise the Labour Left and Tony Benn; he also criticised the Labour Right, including the 'Gang of Four', and later Neil Kinnock's leadership (and even in the 1990s with Tony Blair's leadership, even though Blair had been dubbed the '*Marxism Today* candidate').[220]

'A Long Haul', published in MT's November 1982 issue, was clearly written at a time when there was still broad support for unity across the left in the run-up to the 1983 election, despite *The Morning Star*'s attack on Jacques and MT for publishing Tony Lane's article on trade unions three months earlier. Hall's writing had to take into account that MT's readership included a substantial proportion of CPGB members and sympathisers, many of whom were involved in unions. Thus, Hall strikes a note of caution in wrapping up his article. He writes that he is 'aware of gross over-simplification in order to make a point or give substance to an impression' because of the limitations of language:

> ... language hardly permits us to express things dialectically – in their true contrariness, double-side[d]ness, in their positive and negative – at the same time. *The picture is impressionistic, and I hope it might provoke those who are much better equipped to speak on each of its aspects to correct, disagree or counterpose* a different interpretation to the one I have given. I have offered the piece, essentially, for discussion and debate, not for polemic or to make a point.[221]

In his concluding paragraph, Hall has reiterated albeit with different words why he has 'offered' this 'impressionistic' picture to engage in 'discussion and debate, not for polemic'. Since those who are likely to offer a 'different interpretation' might present barriers to his argument, Hall's attempt here is to be heard. In making arguments against the left's labourism or workerism, Hall was careful not to offend those who were in positions of influence in the labour movement and he stakes out his position cautiously by pre-emptively justifying that it is difficult to get the analysis right and that what he has presented is not simplified or exaggerated.

---

219   Harris 1992.
220   Jacques and Hall 1997. See MT's one-off 'comeback' special issue (MT 1998).
221   Hall 1982b, p. 21 (original emphasis).

> It would be easy to simplify and exaggerate these trends. It is difficult to strike the right balance in assessing so complex a picture, especially when so much is at stake, politically.[222]

Hall is aware of how many of MT's readers would no doubt have read his comments in the aftermath of the Lane affair in August and the beginnings of the CPGB's 'civil war'. He acknowledges the labour movement's achievements to pre-empt his critics' expected line of attack.

> To refer to the relative decline of a particular sector of a class is not to launch a political attack on those who have sustained the labour movement for so long and without whose political and industrial muscle the working class movement would be hopelessly exposed. It is perceived as the leading fraction of the 'vanguard' of the class, because this is the role which it has played for so long.[223]

MT's opponents were responding to the 'threat' that Lane's criticism of union officials was meant to represent and, therefore, Hall was attempting to persuade the readership of the necessity of reassessing what had been accepted as 'common sense' in the past. While this article is an important response to the attack on MT, it nevertheless urges the readership to consider the importance of moving away from certainties that were no longer considered adequate to the changing socio-economic impacts of de-industrialisation and the political legislation undermining union protection.

Hall's articles included various types of utterances, interjections and phrases in the printed text that conveyed a sense of informal conversation or dialogue with the author, which was a key part of his writing style that complemented and enhanced the sense of tentativeness conveyed through the use of conditionality and qualification. Of course, such interjections were expected in those features based upon interviews, roundtable discussions or talks. For example, in the transcript of Hall's talk on a panel with Tony Benn at MT's 'Moving Left Show', the November 1984 weekend event, we can see clearly how his use of interjections and qualifications worked in print as well. The primary target of Hall's critique was the left and its response to Labour's 1983 defeat as outlined in the title. 'Faith, Hope or Clarity' highlights the ways in which Hall sought to represent his views as 'realistic', 'clear' and 'practical'. As part of that 'clarity',

---

222   Hall 1982b, p. 19.
223   Ibid.

his contribution is clearly marked by interjections expected in conversation: e.g. 'of course'; 'But, let me ...'; 'let me ...'; 'I do not ...'. It is as if Hall is preemptively responding to imagined or expected interlocutors in a debate throughout his talk, who would, of course, have been in attendance when he spoke. The decision would have been made in the process of editing the transcription for readers' comprehension and accessibility.

Paradoxically, out of the conditionality and qualifications of Hall's rhetoric come his exhortations. These exhortations are built upon that very conditionality and qualifications, which in retrospect appear as anything but because they do not appear to undermine his exhortations, especially after 1983. The persuasiveness of this rhetorical strategy is enabled, at least in part, by his use of the first-person plural mode of address to create a sense of solidarity and unity with those who are encouraged to identify with his views.

Although one might expect to hear exhortations from the so-called 'hard Left', where selling the paper every week is part of a member's commitment, a similar kind of call to commitment is being made to others on the left. The call to engage in one struggle or another can also be seen as part of a process of solidification.[224] Hall exhorts the labour movement and the left to do its 'duty' in facing up to the 'unpleasant reality' of the conjuncture: e.g. 'It *must* reflect'; 'It *must* discover'; 'It *must* not mobilise on its own account'.[225] The exhortations, however, of what 'must' be done are part of an intellectual, academic, analytical and theoretical understanding of the importance of self-reflexive criticism that Karl Marx had urged: 'the ruthless criticism of everything existing'.[226] And, when the left did not respond in the ways in which it was urged to act, Hall could then express his contempt for their failure to learn (especially as Thatcher's Tories remained in government throughout the 1980s).

Another example of Hall's use of one exhortation followed by another is for 'a more detailed account of the effects of particular policies', which is in turn followed by a list of three clauses, each prefaced by an exhortation, in the first-person plural, of necessity, 'we need', and each offering two subjective adjectives as qualifiers of analysis, alternatives and struggles: 'we need a better and deeper analysis ... we need a sounder and fuller set of alternatives ... and we need a detailed and sober assessment of how the struggles ...'.[227] In trying to 'unstick' people's conventional beliefs and the assumptions on which they

---

224 E.g. Bowers et al. 1993.
225 Hall 1982b, pp. 19, 20 (original emphasis).
226 Karl Marx, letter to Arnold Ruge, September 1843, published in the *Deutsch-Französische Jahrbücher*, February 1844.
227 Hall 1980a, p. 26.

rest, you have to work at bringing them on board, in part by reassuring them that they are not 'wrong', per se, but that the situation has shifted, the context has changed and the forces marshalling are composed of a greater range and variety of people than ever before (i.e. it is no longer just the working class).

14 Unity and Division on the Left: From 'Common Sense' to Caricature?

The shift in rhetorical style that takes place with *Marxism Today* in the 1980s was part of the shift in MT's political project and not so much about the accessibility of the writing, since many articles remained as difficult as others in the first format (including some of Hall's contributions). This was a move from the rhetorical strategy of solidification to one of division via representation and depiction. It is in the struggle over the direction of the Labour and Communist parties that such a political-ideological struggle inevitably leads to the kind of negative characterisation and depiction of one's opponents, for example, as Hall does persuasively in his vivid representation of a 'hard left'.

Through this process, the 'hard left' is opposed to that of the implied, if not always depicted, 'soft left'. Thus, 'realistic Marxism' comes to be a term which is used to separate out the 'hard left', in Hall's depiction, since it is not necessarily a 'realistic' left, the adjective which Hall uses as a term of criticism for the Labour Right during Thatcher's first term.[228] In the classic rhetorical style of political argument, there is a tendency to establish a division between only two possible positions, as Hobsbawm's 'realistic Marxism' did: for or against, the possible or the impossible. The process of appealing to others inevitably establishes a division between those who are with you or with your opponents. In the process of making an argument, a successful rhetor (speaker or writer) persuades their audience based upon their public credibility and standing (ethos), their appeal to the emotions of their audience (pathos) and the evidence and examples used in their arguments (logos).[229]

This process of division is an important one: there is no 'us' without 'them', no 'we' without 'they'. Thus, there is an apparent paradox in rhetorical appeals for 'unity' as such appeals create 'division' by maintaining 'unity' with 'us' and not 'them'. One cannot exist without the other. Both 'division' and 'unity' are terms that are deeply implicated in each other as antonyms. One begs the

---

228 E.g. Hall 1981b.
229 Aune 1994; Cockcroft and Cockcroft 1992; Cohen 1998.

other's existence since one cannot have 'division' without 'unity' and *vice versa*. As a result, the rhetorical appeal to and for 'us' creates 'them' against whom one is engaged in verbal, ideological, political, cultural and class struggle. So, for example, an attempt to unify all Marxists into one political organisation would mean a division of other, i.e. non-Marxist, socialists into other organisations and this is a process of separation and even perhaps of sectarianism (well known on the left).

The audience does not exist in a vacuum either. Their understandings of various texts and messages are also a factor that helps to determine an article's reception. Of course, the CPGB members and sympathisers were well aware of their differences with others on the left, and especially the Socialist Workers' Party, which had become the greatest threat to the CPGB's position on Labour's left by 1979. Many MT readers among the cultural and academic left would have recognised Hall's characterisations of the 'hard left', which would have resonated with some of their own encounters with some left groups. Since the focus of many Leninist organisations has been on building the party, to which everything else became secondary, this encouraged those around them to view the motivations for their actions with some suspicion.

15   Tropes and Metaphors

The use of metaphors to create vivid – and lasting – images in the minds of audiences is an important part of persuasive writing and Stuart Hall's writing demonstrated a skillfull use of metaphors in his contributions to *Marxism Today*. Hall's memorable, evocative phrases were the result of a combination of vivid metaphors and believable or plausible depictions of issues, events and opponents, all of which contributed to Hall's influence on the left as an important political analyst and cultural thinker. His discursive division of the left between 'us' and the 'hard left' had an inevitable impact upon the political-ideological struggle over the left's political trajectory. However, Hall's contributions to the deepening of the left's divisions, only really began from late 1984 during the miners' strike in his promotion of a 'counter-electoral', rather than 'counter-hegemonic', strategy.

Whether intentional or not, Hall's political writings helped to construct vivid images that played into and reinforced the negative depictions that were also promoted by the national press and especially Tory tabloids. Hall's and others' contributions to MT were being published in a context where the Conservative government had begun to expand its ideological war against local Labour governments (the so-called 'loony left' councils), especially after its abolition of the Greater London Council in 1986. This is not to suggest that Hall or other critics of the Bennite and 'hard left', were willing accomplices of Rupert Murdoch, Conrad Black and other right-wing press owners. Yet, it is not hard to see how such depictions reinforced the negative connotations of images created by right-wing newspapers to represent Labour as the so-called 'loony left'.

Hall's first use of the phrase 'hard left' is in the 1983 chapter version of his 1979 feature, which was published just four years after his original article in a book that came out five weeks before Thatcher's second general election victory. Some of the left responses to the rise of Thatcherism are described by Hall: where 'comrades' either welcome the crisis because 'worse means better', which is supposed to lead to the 'sharpening of contradictions' with the 'rising tempo of the class struggle ... [and] eventually guarantee the victory of progressive forces everywhere'; or others 'who dismiss the advance of the right as "mere ideology", which cannot be "real"' and therefore 'cannot become a material factor, let alone a political force'.[230] An extension of this latter position is that there are not any significant differences between Thatcherism and previous Tory ideologies. These three positions are 'especially characteristic of a certain hard headed response from the "hard" left'.[231]

Hall's characterisations of the left resonated with and reinforced certain understandings of far left activists, which is why it is necessary to understand his interventions via MT because they contributed to constructing a particular version of the 'hard left' to which others on the left were opposed. Hall was attempting to deal with an attitude and position on the left, which he helped to characterise as fundamentally committed to a belief that there was an 'inexorable' move towards socialism, as Hobsbawm had in his 'Forward March' analysis; however, for Hall it was encapsulated in the term 'economism'. The 'hard left', Hall argued, is 'to be found as much in the economism of Labourism ... as in the unquestioning support for the Soviet model of socialism'.[232] Economism could be identified as both the 'labourism' manifested in the Labour Party and trade unions as well as in the support for Soviet-style 'socialism' amongst the CPGB traditionalists, and the support of both groups for state intervention in the economy and a belief in the working class as 'automatic' supporters of 'socialism'. Hall, as with others of the first New Left, had opposed both Labourism and the CPGB's Stalinism and yet, here he is equating 'labourism' and 'actually existing socialism', just as Tory tabloids sought to equate Labour supporters with Communism's adherents.

---

230   Hall 1983a, p. 20.
231   Hall 1983a, p. 21.
232   Hall 1985b, p. 14.

The critical depictions of the left in Hall's articles also included, however, those 'types' later associated with *Marxism Today*. For example, in 'The Culture Gap', Hall sketches out the 'inverted puritanism' of 'middle class socialists' who, despite having all the modern trappings of consumer society, reject the idea of 'materialism' for the 'masses'. These middle-class socialists:

> heaving under the weight of their new hi-fis, their record collections, their videos and strip pine shelving ... sometimes seem to prefer 'their' working class poor but *pure*: unsullied by contact with the market.[233]

Hall conveys his critique through these vivid metaphors which construct an image which is both concrete and believable: his 'straw man' is explained by providing descriptions of goods ('new hi-fis', 'strip pine shelving') which connotate recognisable aesthetic tastes with a social-economic class stratum, such as the 1980s 'yuppie', with attributes applied to opponents that would have resonated with readers' depictions.[234]

This critical characterisation of one part of the left would have resonated with many older readers, and would also have been read as critical of the 'right on' trendies or left-wing 'yuppies' with whom the magazine became associated in the minds of more traditional party and union members, many of whom were increasingly opposed to what MT stood for. This is ironic as it is many of the newer, younger MT readers themselves who probably recognised their own 'guilty' selves in this image.

In his writing, Hall is usually working to qualify a previous statement with a more substantive understanding. For example, after his critical depiction of the 'middle class socialists', he writes:

> Yet the only tenable position for a true cultural materialist must be a deep sense of outrage that the fruits of modern industry, technology and know-how, which social labour itself has matured and developed, are still not available to the working people who produced them and need them![235]

---

233 Hall 1984a, p. 19 (original emphasis).
234 This characterisation of a 'yuppie left', while specific to a new 1980s stereotype, is nonetheless close to the historical stereotype of 'middle-class socialists', who were subject to attack and (mis)characterisation. For example, Orwell's biases about working- and middle-class socialists are visible in the contrast between his notes for *The Road to Wigan Pier* and the published version (Orwell 1987 [1935]; Williams 1971).
235 Hall 1984a, p. 19.

In the November 1984 issue, Hall's analysis of 'The State' also constructs an image of the left as limited in their thinking about the state, as part of his response to the debates that were taking place on the left. Increasingly the debate over the veracity of his Thatcherism thesis contributed to the left's divide, in which one's position was determined by whether one accepted Hall's thesis or not, although some critical left intellectuals who had originally sided with Bob Jessop et al.'s critique, such as Colin Leys, would later accept Hall's analysis.

As part of the growing intensity of attacks on parts of the left, a dominant caricature of the 'hard left' took on 'religious connotations', via both visual and verbal iconography, not only in Hall's writing, but also throughout the pages of *Marxism Today*, particularly as the 'civil wars' within the Communist Party and the Labour Party intensified in the mid-1980s. It is necessary to remember that religious and other faith-based ideologies were seen as conservative, if not reactionary, and which illustrate the regressive ideologies deployed against modernity and Enlightenment thought. Religion, because of its role as the ideological 'glue' for the *ancien regimes* of Europe, has been a major target for socialists, communists and anarchists in their struggles to overthrow the old order and build a new society. Yet, there had been a start at attempting to build some bridges between the left and some forms of religion with the Marxism-Christianity dialogue in MT under James Klugmann with the rise of liberation theology in Latin America from the 1960s. Religious metaphors raise particular connotations that emphasise associations of 'faith' over 'science', which might well have contrasted with the idea of Marxism as 'science'.

During the 1980s, as Hall's contributions to the divisive debates on the left became increasingly polemical, he used both religious and war metaphors, which are common on the left, to depict his opponents, since both religion and war are subjects on which the left has traditionally had quite strong critical positions. With the new 'Cold War' under Thatcher and Reagan, and the renewal of the peace movement in the 1980s, such metaphors would have had a greater purchase with a broader public, even beyond the left. Hall's technique is one in which he moves between faux deference and contemptuous sarcasm, as he begins by pointing out that he does not 'believe' that:

> ... posing difficult questions is necessarily a sign of the weakening of the faith. We should leave Faith to The Believers ... that profound sectarianism ... which I detect rising like the smog ... as those who dare to ... question ... our received wisdoms are instantly accused of treason, labelled as the enemy, or dismissed as 'pink professors misleading the Left' (in Tariq Ali's recent, immortal phrase) and despatched into outer darkness. So, braving

> the terrors of excommunication from the newly appointed guardians of orthodoxy, let us pose once more the question of where we stand on the question of the state.[236]

There is no need for quote marks in this excerpt, except for Tariq Ali's phrase, as Hall positions himself and others around MT as critics of the left's status quo, in which Hall extends the metaphor to one of religious exile and indeed 'expulsion' from the sect of 'True Believers'. However, it was Militant Tendency and other 'entryists' within the Labour Party, who were the targets for expulsion at that time. The association with 'heretics' or 'apostates', who have been expelled from 'the church' for questioning 'shibboleths', was attributed to those who were defiantly 'heretics' within Labour but which Hall depicts as the 'newly appointed guardians of orthodoxy'.

The actual 'guardians of orthodoxy', however, are the Labour Party and CPGB leaderships rather than those who espouse different, minority views of socialism within both parties. This is a fact about how a 'minority' is written about as if it is a 'majority' or that they somehow are holders of 'orthodoxy' who wield power to exclude or include. Those who are excluded are those who do not adhere to the particular understanding of say, Marx or socialism, which is why the roles are seemingly reversed. Thus, what really underlies this depiction is that Militant Tendency and other adherents of an 'Old Left' version of socialism are seen as dogmatic and sectarian 'true believers' attacking the 'apostates' for their failure to adhere to dogma which is where the depiction of the latter differs from the reality of their base within Labour or the CPGB. However, this reversal of positions was something that MT was in the position to foster and circulate within various circles of influence (e.g. media, the academy).

This was a period of bitter internecine strife in both the Labour and Communist parties and one in which disagreements over the analysis of Thatcherism became a hard dividing line. However, as Hall made clear in one of his two most important political interventions in 1985 to the 'realignment' of the left, he spoke of the 'hard Left' as not just a monolithic grouping within any one party:

> Rather, it is the 'hard Left' as a peculiar and distinctive political style, a set of habits, a political-cultural tradition, stretching right across the actual organisational sub-divisions of the Left, which is at issue. It is the 'hard

---

236 Hall 1984b, p. 24. The phrase is from the title of Ali's opinion piece in *The Guardian* (Ali 1984).

Left' as keeper of left consciences, as political guarantor, as the litmus paper of orthodoxy, which is the problem.[237]

'Hard Left', therefore, is more about an attitude and habits, rather than identifying a particular political faction or organisation. In explaining why realignment is a lengthy process which keeps 'running into the sand', Hall hits on a self-reflexive phrase: 'It is because there is a tiny bit of the "hard Left" inside *all* of us'.[238] This phrase was also used as a quote (in a larger font) in the centre column on the first page to pique the newsagent browser's attention. The phrase is provocative and, yet, it is also an admission of a weakness on the author's part, albeit increasing Hall's *ethos* with readers, who might not have identified as 'hard Left' but who would have recognised such sympathies, perhaps even in their own selves at one point.

This critical, self-reflexive part of Hall's writing style is important as a rhetorical technique to reach readers who might not be inclined otherwise to countenance what he is saying. As Hall deepens the explanation about the 'hard Left' that exists inside us all, he says it is:

> patrolling the frontiers of consciousness, repressing from memory certain profound but awkward facts, ruling certain questions 'out of court', keeping us all on the straight and narrow and thus helping to hold in place certain automatic and unquestioning responses.[239]

Only the responses of the 'hard left' are 'automatic and unquestioning' because no one will admit that their own thinking is similarly hard-line, which is what Hall views as a problem even with those opposed to the 'hard left'. Rhetorically, his criticisms are reinforced by his concession that he is also guilty of similar hard-line thinking.

16 Stuart Hall's 'Realism'

Stuart Hall's rhetorical appeal was built upon an ability to construct realistic images or rhetorical depictions that were persuasive. The degree of persuasiveness was dependent upon the degree of believability of his representations. In the process of engaging with arguments on the left, Hall had to represent

---

[237] Hall 1985b, pp. 13–14.
[238] Hall 1985b, p. 14 (original emphasis).
[239] Ibid.

his opponents in a way that would make his ideas more readily acceptable and believable to those who might not otherwise be open to his ideas. At the same time, Hall was trying to argue against those who assumed that the left was on this 'inexorable' path to 'inevitable' victory over capitalism. One part of his challenge, that begins in the 'Great Moving Right Show' and continues in subsequent articles in *Marxism Today* and *New Socialist*, is his depiction of the left and its 'optimism' in the 'inexorable' march to socialism's ultimate victory.

Hall identifies 'realism' as a way of selling out and as shorthand for critiquing the Labour Right, which is different to Eric Hobsbawm's 'realistic Marxism'. However, in another sense, Hall was a 'realist' because he urged the left to see reality 'as it is' and 'things as they are'. However, his use of 'realism' is different to how it is generally understood and this was probably the result of academic debates over realism and representations of class, gender and race in mass media and popular culture. For example, in his article on the state, Hall implicitly criticised the Labour Right when he wrote of 'realism' as 'often simply a code name for giving in'. Such a perspective placed Hall outside the divide between 'soft' and 'hard' lefts or 'traditionalists' and 'reformists', and was sufficiently important in the context of debates on the left that this sentence fragment was used as a 'quote' on page 14 next to another quote critical of the Labour Left: 'the leapfrog game of "lefter-than-thou"'.[240]

Many phrases that Hall and others around MT employed were about 'presenting things as they are', and approaching people 'as they are' and 'not as we would wish them to be', which (re)signifies the 1930s movement in documentary reporting and photography (which was at the time receiving considerable academic attention),[241] and the rise of journalism and news discourses with their emphasis on communicating 'reality' as it is and not as we want it to be.[242] The news had established itself as an authoritative discourse with a distinctive style by the 1920s.[243] In 'Why I Write', George Orwell wrote of the 'historical impulse': 'Desire to see things as they are, to find out true facts and store them up for the use of posterity'.[244] The combination of journalism and the documentary movement in the 1930s influenced the left's belief that, by merely exposing the public to the 'truth' or 'reality' of social, political and economic

---

240 The explicit association is made between childishness (leapfrog, a child's game) and the 'hard left'. Hall 1984b, p. 14.
241 E.g. see the collection in Gloversmith 1980.
242 Laing 1980, pp. 142–60.
243 Matheson 2000, pp. 557–73.
244 Orwell 2004a, p. 5. Orwell's experience in the Spanish Civil War fighting with a Trotskyist militia, who were betrayed by Stalinists, inspired both his commitment to democratic socialism and his work's anti-Communist 'historical impulse' (e.g. Orwell 1984 [1938]).

issues, people will be won over to socialism. While this appealed to many on the left over the decades, by the 1980s this approach of seeing people 'as they are' contributed to the dangerous elision of appealing to people by pandering to their beliefs while not attempting to counter ideologically the populist appeals of 'free marketeers'.

If you can claim that you are looking at things or people as they 'are', your 'realism' is given. If, however, you are looking at people as you would want them to be, that is 'idealism' or even 'delusional', since it means seeing people different to how they are 'in reality'. Hall highlights 'revolutionary optimism' and 'revolutionary pessimism' as two variants on the left. To the latter, who think that 'we mustn't rock the boat', 'one can only reply with Gramsci's injunction: to address ourselves "violently" towards the present *as it is*, if we are serious about transforming it'.[245] The optimists identify 'points of resistance' to counter and Hall concedes that 'they are right' at least 'in one sense': 'We must look behind the surface phenomena, we must find the points of intervention, we mustn't underestimate the capacity for resistance and struggle'.[246] Yet, despite not underestimating this capacity, Hall still warns against ignoring the 'realistic' assessment of where we, the left, are at politically.

> But, if we are correct about the depth of the rightward turn, it means that our interventions need to be pertinent, decisive and effective. Whistling in the dark is an occupational hazard not altogether unknown to the British Left.[247]

17 Conclusion

Changes in language, rhetorical techniques and writing or house style were an integral part of *Marxism Today*'s material transformation from an internal party journal into a left newsmagazine, which increased its accessibility to both journalists and the general public. The changes in accessibility were related to the change in editors, from one who was deferential to party authority, to one who was willing to push the limits of party discourse, and to the changes in language, rhetorical techniques and writing styles, as MT sought to make its ideas more accessible to reach more people beyond the Communist Party. MT's shift in accessibility under Martin Jacques's editorship follows a basic ideological

---

245 Hall 1979, p. 14 (original emphasis).
246 Hall 1979, p. 15.
247 Ibid.

trajectory via its material transformation and relationship to the party, which itself was undergoing substantial changes in both composition and ideology.

While Jacques avoided the worst excesses and the writing achieved greater clarity, there could only ever be a partial shift from abstract to concrete words since abstract words are necessary in most kinds of intellectual endeavours. However, was it possible that, what was 'a more flexible and iconoclastic view' for socialist, social-democratic or Communist readers might be a more conventional view for the mainstream media's typical reader, reinforcing traditional, anti-socialist prejudices or working within the hegemonic 'common sense'?

Although MT became somewhat more accessible than it had been in the first format, it remained mostly limited to those with some university education. MT's autonomy from the party leadership meant a relaxation of the ideological constraints, which enabled MT to become more flexible with its language, rhetorical techniques and writing style, and, therefore, more likely to be persuasive with non-CPGB readers. Jacques's aim to establish a 'new style of political journalism', however, by combining the best aspects of journalism and scholarship was only partially realised because, ultimately, MT remained wedded to ideas rather than journalism.[248]

Despite the limitations in accessibility and complaints about some of the (new) jargon in MT, the magazine did reach new audiences outside the Communist Party, as it began to adopt some of the conventional uses of language as codified within the style sheets and journalistic conventions of the mainstream broadsheet press. The attempt to rejuvenate its house style with the use of vivid imagery and figures of speech to communicate critical ideas, which helped its accessibility to some extent, moved MT part way towards the plain style, even though many articles remained difficult for the average reader.

An integral part of *Marxism Today*'s successful appeal to others within and beyond the party was the contribution of Eric Hobsbawm and Stuart Hall during Jacques's editorship. First, both had public profiles as left scholars, which provided them with platforms to speak to the left, one with a basis in history and the other within the rapidly growing media and cultural studies fields. Hall in particular had a broader exposure through his role as a professor with the Open University and via his contributions to course textbooks.

Second, both of their interventions were often persuasive because of their rhetorical techniques and writing skills, which contributed to the defeat of the (so-called) 'hard left' within both the Labour and Communist parties. For example, Hobsbawm's rhetoric of 'realistic Marxism' undermined countervail-

---

248 Taylor 1995. This is similar to Jacques's assessment (Jacques 1996b).

ing arguments by offering only two choices, one of which was always 'unrealistic', and which contributed to the classic 'us versus them' division within the left. There was a Marxist position that was 'realistic' because it worked within the confines of what was deemed as 'acceptable', at least as understood via national media. (Of course, the implied opposite, 'unrealistic Marxism', is never systematically criticised beyond labelling certain intellectuals as 'hard left' and dismissing their ideas as 'wrong-headed'.) On the other hand, Hall's rhetorical interventions worked differently, in part because they were targetted at a different and newer consituency for MT. For example, Hall's rhetorical techniques used informal aspects of speech and his claims were often qualified or made conditional, which conveyed a sense of exploration and openness as if engaged in a dialogue with the reader. This approach contrasted considerably with most MT contributors, particularly (but not only) under James Klugmann's editorship, who offered solutions in a language and writing style that were frequently awkward and unimaginative but which engaged in the solidification process during times of the CPGB's isolation or crisis, particularly after 1956. In a manner that evoked the 1930s documentary movement, Hall called for going to 'where the people are' and to see things 'as they exist' (as did Hobsbawm), which played into Hall's exhortations to the left to 'address ourselves violently to the present' (attributed to Gramsci), and if the other side is not seeing things 'as they are', they must, therefore, be blinkered, misled or just wrong. This was the other side of Hall's conditionality and qualification which appeared more as a means to draw in the reader before exhorting them to rethink their traditional views.

Third, both Hobsbawm and Hall used vivid metaphors that resonated with audiences and which were effective at negative depictions of opponents on the left, and these kinds of phrasing and the arguments of 'realistic Marxism' were sometimes picked up and promoted by the national press to criticise the left. Hall's ethos helped to reinforce these critiques because of the way he would include himself as a target of self-reflexive critique, which increased his credibility with readers. While both of their critiques of the 'hard left' resonated with mainstream media depictions, it was the latter that in turn helped to substantiate Hobsbawm's and Hall's characterisations, albeit not necessarily with mainstream audiences, but more so (and significantly) with the academic and activist audiences that made up MT's readership.

This chapter's focus on the relationship between ideology and jargon, accessibility language, rhetorical techniques and writing styles are an important part of understanding how MT sought to appeal to a broader left public and through that process also divided the left in its polemical interventions across the organised left. The importance of the relationship between audience and ideology is mediated via the use of language, which in turn is made possible through the production and distribution of the periodical in which those ideas are manifest and through which they are made (in)accessible.

CHAPTER 7

'W(h)ither the Party Paper'? What Lessons for the Left Press?

In this book, I approached the transformation of *Marxism Today*, from a 'journal' into a 'magazine', within those aspects of its production that illustrate how it changed in its relationship with the party and its appearance, funding, staffing, writing, design, editorial structure and form(at), its relationship to distribution, publicity and media coverage, and its ideas and presence on the left. This approach recognises the importance of the material 'base' that enables the actual production and distribution of ideas, as it offers a way to develop richer historical analysis necessary to develop Marxist cultural theory. But, the material 'base' is not just the physical resources and forms, finances and labour but also the social processes and cultural techniques that are the socio-cultural practices through which those ideas are produced and distributed. That is, the 'base' is not distinctively 'material' in the way in which 'vulgar' Marxist definitions of the 'base/superstructure' model work. Yet, the approach of cultural materialism enables us to see that certain structural and structuring factors inhibit and favour different means of communication and different forms of cultural and media production: that is, what is produced is done within limits that are determined and determining (to paraphrase Raymond Williams).[1]

The material production and distribution of ideas via print media have been the most common basis for the development and circulation of political ideologies around which organisations and movements are built.[2] It has been and continues to be print media's fundamental role to provide sustained, systematic, serial analysis and argument, particularly when developing ideas to counter the dominant ideology and 'common sense' of a conjuncture. Historically, this role for print media has been consciously articulated on the left, although such media can be used to bridge differences and 'unify the left', they can also help to fragment the left or deepen sectarian divisions. The role of a 'theoretical and discussion' journal as the third basic type of CP publications was an important part of the party itself in the development of ideas and analyses as well as dealing with potential challenges to its ideas as explored in the first chapter.

---

1 Williams 1977a, pp. 83–9.
2 E.g. Debray 2007; Pimlott 2006b, 2011.

The transformation of *Marxism Today* means that we need to recognise that the typology of Communist periodicals is no longer valid to the same extent as it once was since the type of Leninist party that those publications served has more or less ceased to exist in the same way as it once did. The nature of forms of communication has also changed without necessarily eliminating the ways in which print addresses audiences, if one compares the differences in writing, imaging and editing processes for producing for social media platforms such as Twitter or Instagram versus electronic or print publications.

Print media can either be intimately tied to a political organisation, as with *Marxism Today*'s situation during its first 25 years (first and second formats), or it can have a more diffuse relationship with its readership via the marketplace, as the centre-left, weekly newsmagazine, *New Statesman*, does. Those two periodicals, however, have had different roles and functions as well as different relationships with the CPGB and Labour Party respectively. MT's cultural form was not 'new' so much as it incorporated innovations, via an eclectic mix of professional advice and influences, as necessitated via its entrance into the periodical marketplace and its publicity, promotion and engagement with prospective and actual readers.

The Comedia model became a model for left and alternative media during the 1980s. This model stresses the advantages of adopting marketplace mechanisms, although such mechanisms often require adequate finances to pay for longer print runs to ensure wholesalers and retailers have enough stock to meet demand and to ensure publicity to boost sales, which means more profit for wholesalers and retailers when maintaining a broader, more diverse, range of magazines.[3] It involves investing time and resources into the necessary but ancillary aspects of a periodical's relationship to the marketplace in terms of supporting publicity and promotion, subscription drives and constant innovation in design and printing.

In its move from 'the margins into the mainstream', *Marxism Today* became incorporated into the dominant mainstream system of 'literary' representation of the political left in the national public sphere, in which MT's development was indicative of the transformation of a section of the left intelligentsia of the

---

3   This has created problems when distributors and retailers want to stock more copies of best-selling magazines to increase profit, while cutting the rest: that is, cutting the choices available for the customer for the sake of profit. Here the profit drive works against the claims made for the so-called 'free market' or even the 'marketplace of ideas'. In the mid-1990s, W.H. Smith wanted to cut 350 small magazines from its shelves (e.g. CPBF 1996a, 1996b; Logan 1996). This kind of threat to small periodicals is why there was also an attempt to set up radical alternative distributors in the late 1970s and early 1980s.

'professional-managerial class' that sought political, social or cultural change. Its success in the national public sphere rested partly upon its public persona, promoted as the inverse to conventional expectations of a 'Marxist' periodical, which was useful in attracting interest and attention, to speak through mainstream media to the general public. However, with the fall of the Berlin wall, this persona was of less interest since mainstream media and centre-left magazines covered similar material and shared contributors, overtaking MT's unique position or 'selling point'.

The CPGB provided the necessary infrastructure, funding and audiences for *Marxism Today*, not just within its first two decades, but even during its second format when the party distribution network system was breaking down, as more and more party members turned to their local newsagents to buy their copies, even as others were turned off of the magazine. Yet, the more developed its autonomy from the CPGB, the weaker its potential for pursuing a 'war of position' (to the extent that this was ever a viable strategy on behalf of the party let alone MT), since it lacked a base inside the Labour Party to which it could attach itself, albeit providing a platform for those in the LP that it supported or wanted to engage in debate. MT could only recruit its diffuse audience of readers via newsagents and promotional campaigns, demonstrating that it could not survive on the basis of its ideas in the marketplace. It was the cultural and political studies academics and students, as well as other interested members of the public, including strata within the PMC, who drew upon MT in discussion groups in local libraries or at meetings organised by supportive local party branches. These groupings were not influential, however, beyond their own small constituencies, akin to the first New Left and Signs of the Times (a successor to MT discussion groups), and their fates.

It is the development of a new discourse of 'realistic Marxism' that begins the process of dismantling what Eric Hobsbawm and others promoted as a 'logjam' of thinking on the left. The 'realignment of the left' involved rethinking traditional approaches to issues such as nationalisation, social housing and welfare because they no longer appeared to be popular with the public. One can appreciate how far New Labour shifted by comparing the 1983 manifesto to Tony Blair's policies in office.[4] Hobsbawm's interventions were persuasive because of his ability to situate the only two possible options for the left in such a way that, 'there is [was] no alternative' (to quote Margaret Thatcher's

---

4   See Andrews 1999 and Cockett 1991, esp. 78–81, 103. On MT's role in the 'rethinking', see Panitch 2002, pp. 63–5, and Callinicos 2002, pp. 78–80. Callinicos contrasts Labour's leftward shift between 1979 and 1983 with 'New' Labour's rightward shift back to where ('Old') Labour had been originally!

infamous phrase), and which Hobsbawm put into effect rhetorically against the left. By implication, there was no future for 'class-based militancy', particularly if it was understood as led by the organised industrial working class. For if the core industrial working class was in decline, if its 'forward march' had indeed been halted, relying on its strength as central to any counter-hegemonic strategy was obviously a 'dead-end'. Yet, such a conclusion neglects the economic core that Gramsci's theory requires for a (counter-)hegemonic project (and, indeed, which the neoliberal trajectory of inequality growth, not only in the UK but throughout almost all, if not all, countries suborned to global capitalism, provides).

In addition, Stuart Hall's rhetorical interventions in political debates through *Marxism Today* contributed to the kinds of characterisations of the 'hard left' that reinforced certain mainstream or conventional depictions and contributed to the divisions on the left for which the 'hard left' was most frequently criticised. Hall's writing style, as with attempts to make changes in the traditional ways of writing employed in MT did help to some extent to make MT more accessible to its readers. Nonetheless, even when dispensing with one kind of jargon, another one was frequently deployed, such as that provided via the language of academic cultural studies or postmodernism. The shifts in writing styles and rhetorical strategies was also indicative of changes that were taking place in terms of the occupational categories of many of the contributors themselves, as the shift from predominantly party intellectuals and officials in the first format, to establishment journalists and academics (only some of whom were loosely affiliated with a political party) in the third format.

The critiques of Thatcherism outlined in Chapter 2 highlighted problems with misunderstandings and misapplications of Gramsci's concepts, including both hegemony and common sense. This includes Hall's understanding of hegemony which was limited because he neglected Gramsci's 'hegemonic apparatus', which is a critical component to hegemonic rule and which helped to make Thatcherism 'popular'. The neglect or omission of the (counter-)hegemonic apparatus, meant a failure of the left to think about how it could engage in ideological-political struggle, something which was made increasingly possible with the growth of grassroots radical media and cultural production during the 1970s and 1980s. With lowered costs and skills, there was potentially greater access for subaltern classes that meant that it would have been possible to establish a counter public sphere.

By ceding the economic to Thatcherism and the New Right, Labour and the social-democratic left effectively abandoned a central concern for a (counter-)hegemonic project, the economic interests of the working class and, therefore, made it easier to develop a 'popular politics' that would also concede the leading position of the organised working class in the broad democratic alliance, so that there would be no leading group or vanguard around which to formulate 'good sense' to counter the prevailing neoliberal 'common sense'. The struggle over the dominant common sense would have been more effective had it been part of a (counter-)hegemonic apparatus in which a more systematic, coordinated assault on Thatcherite hegemony could have been made. MT did not try to build bridges after the 1983 general election as divisions over the appropriate strategy for Labour to defeat Thatcher became the dividing line, and contributed to the polarisation and divisions on the left beyond the CPGB in the debates over analyses of the 1983 election. It is, nonetheless, important to recognise that in these debates Jacques and MT were also seeking to survive the intensifying internal party attacks from traditionalist opponents between 1982 and 1985.

Without a fuller understanding of the necessity of alternative and radical media, that can exist and function outside of the commercial marketplace, the attempt to establish a (counter-)hegemonic social bloc was doomed to failure because of the interventions of mainstream media outlets, which helped to structure the reception of *Marxism Today*'s ideas. At a time of the growing democratisation of the means of communication, via cheaper costs and lower skill barriers, there was a complementary fragmentation and dissipation of small left parties and organisations. It was no longer necessary to represent different constituencies, if they were able to represent themselves via their own loosely connected media, whereas some political organisations sustain their own means of communication to ensure their ideas will be produced and circulated, even if by hand or post because of limited or no access to the commercial 'marketplace of ideas'. Despite similarities in aims, sectarian divisions on the left also affect their media since there is no single (counter) public sphere where debates can happen across different political or ideological tendencies. It was not just the single-issue organisations that were operating in silos but arguably many (far) left organisations also operate inside their own silos despite claiming to speak to (or for) the broad public or the working class. As the left fragments and new social movements lacked access to mainstream media, Labour remained the only option, electorally and rhetorically, to defeat Thatcher.

Given the structure of the media at the time, the lack of recognition of the importance of independent radical media for the left to establish their own public sphere to articulate, debate and promote counter-hegemonic ideas, would have meant a shift from just attempting to access mass media to working with the range of socialist, Communist, Labour and other left organisations. As MT's own trajectory demonstrates, this lack of understanding demonstrates just how dependent radical and alternative media can become on establishment media and mainstream distribution networks to reach the public, compromising independence except, perhaps, where there is ideological convergence.

Thus, Hall overlooks and under emphasises the importance of the mainstream or establishment media's role as part of the dominant hegemonic apparatus that made Thatcherism what it was. This ignores how capitalists have invested heavily in newspapers, despite ongoing losses, to subsidise the production and distribution of their (far) right-wing views.[5] He also misses the significance of a (counter-)hegemonic apparatus that is integral to Gramsci's theory of hegemony, which is critical for the subaltern classes to mount a (counter-)hegemonic challenge. Ironically, although Hall stresses the importance of ideology, his political interventions via MT mostly ignore the influence of ideology and mainstream media (despite the origins of his Thatcherism thesis in the cultural studies magnum opus, *Policing the Crisis*).[6] The contribution of 'cultural populism' was to stand the strawman of 'false consciousness' on its head, as if to say that media and popular culture have little, if any, influence because people can choose what these 'texts' mean or that they do not 'buy' into these messages (i.e. they are able to 'decode' the messages in a negotiated or oppositional manner rather than accepting the dominant meaning and being ideologically interpellated by mass media and popular cultural messages).[7]

The popularity of two of MT's most important intellectual contributors, Eric Hobsbawm and Stuart Hall, was the result of their public profiles achieved through other forms of academic scholarship and activism, outside the CPGB, and via scholarly networks, groups and organisations as outlined in Chapter 6. In particular, Hall's popularity with the formation of cultural studies via the Centre for Contemporary Cultural Studies and the Open University, where his contributions, sometimes reproduced in videos, reached a much greater audience than any number of higher education classrooms could possibly reach at that time. Both appealed to two primary constituencies of MT's readership: the older, traditionalist party members, including but not limited to organised industrial workers, and a newer, reformist constituency in, but not limited to, the PMC.

Through cultural materialism, we can analyse the production of political periodicals and develop a better understanding of the connection between

---

5 Williams 1978.
6 Hall et al. 1978.
7 Hall 1980. While postmodernist interpretations are similar to many cultural populists', they can or do differ in some respects, since the latter can include those who adopt a materialist framework within which to understand popular culture and media messages.

political practice and cultural form (Table 16). *Marxism Today*'s transformation from a 'journal' into a 'magazine' was an important change that worked across a number of areas and practices in periodical production. The importance of the connections between cultural form and political practice can be identified across all three formats in Table 16, including distribution, design and layout, imagery, rhetoric and writing style, staffing etc.

TABLE 16   Marxism today: three formats, two periodical types, 1957–91

	First format 1957–79	Second format 1979–86	Third format 1986–91
Periodical Type	Political-Theory Journal	Political News Magazine	'Magazine of Opinion'
Relationship with Party	Dept of Press & Publicity	Editorial autonomy grows; but Party approval necssary	Editorial autonomy; finances reliant on Party
Editors	John Gollan, James Klugmann	Martin Jacques	Martin Jacques
Political Project	Develop Party Line, Anti-Monopoly Alliance	Broad Democratic Alliance, cultural politics	New Times, postmodernism
Exigency	Cold War, Colonialism, Vietnam, 'Stagflation'	Crisis of the Left (T'ism) & Rise of the Right (FMLH)	Thatcherism, Globalisation
Staff	1.6	5.0	9.0
Finances	1977 Income: £12,200 Expenses: £12,500	1983 Income: £77,700 Expenses: £90,300	1989 Income: £241,300 Expenses: £292,000
Printing	Farleigh Press (CP): hot metal type	Farleigh Press: lithography, photo-typesetting	Various: lithography, photo-typesetting, ltd DTP
Distribution	Party Branches, Mail, Bookshops,	Bookshops, Subscriptions, Newsagents	Newsagents, Subs, Bookshops
Non-Print Distribution (e.g. Events, Org'ns)	CP branches, schools & events, Communist University of London	MT events & conferences (e.g. *New Socialist*), Uni & left networks, CP branches	MT discussion groups & events, academic networks, CP branches
Circulation	2,500–4,500	4,500–13,000	11,000–15,000
Format Size	7.25″ × 9.75″; 32 pp avg @ issue (384 pages p.a.)	8.4″ × 10.75″; 48 pp avg @ issue (592 pages p.a.)	8.9′ × 11.7″; 56 pp avg @ issue (644 pp p.a.)
Cover	Table of Contents (primary), Illustrated ToC	Political Statement (primary) & Marketing	Marketing & Political Statement (secondary)
Layout	2-column grid	2- & 3-column: standfirsts, quotes, images	3, 4-columns: quotes, standfirsts, images
Editorial Sections	Editorial Comments, Features, Discussion	Features, Focus, Reviews, Interviews/Roundtables, C5, Letters, Viewpoint	Celebrity-interview/ers, Features, Culture, Letters Columnists, Comment
Features (4,000+)	68%	50%	40%
Ads (total space)	0.1–2.0%	19%	29%
Features	77%	49%	37%
Features: FOG	17.6 (1973)	15.2 (1983)	16.0 (1988)

TABLE 16   Marxism today: three formats, two periodical types, 1957–91 *(cont.)*

	First format 1957–79	Second format 1979–86	Third format 1986–91
Contributors	Party Intellectuals & Officials, some members	Lecturers; Political & Social Activists; Journalists	Journalists; Lecturers
Readership	Party Intellectuals, Officials & Members	56% CP & LP; 61% Grads; 24% Students; Activists; Lecturers	41% CP & LP; 67% Grads; 22% Students; Lecturers
Public Relations	Occasional press release	1–2 press releases/issue	3–6 press releases/issue
Key Newspaper	*Daily Worker/MorningStar*	*The Guardian*	*The Independent*
Press Coverage	Almost non-existent	205 broadsheet items	301 broadsheet items
Public Political Practice	Speech, Lecture, Branch Meeting, School	Public Talk, Open Meeting, Panel, Seminar, Event	Public Talk, Panel, Seminar, Event
Rhetorical Purpose	'Solidification'	'Us/Them' / 'Realignment'	'Intellectual Critique'
Rhetorical Style	Exhortation /Tautological	Realistic Marxism / Left Realism	Criticism, Commentary

For example, we can see that each of the three formats have something to indicate about the link between the party-as-publisher and the periodical-type: the first format, 1957–79, matched most closely to a definition of a 'political-theoretical journal', with its focus on developing and promoting the party-publisher's editorial-ideological 'party line'. This close link means that contributors and readers were most likely to be those who were closely affiliated to the party, such as officials and intellectuals, even if only a small proportion of party members were readers and, therefore, it is no surprise for this type of periodical to be less ambitious in its distribution networks, publicity and promotional efforts, or in its production processes, since contributors and readers were self-selecting and identified with the party-publisher. Therefore, distribution via postal and party networks meant that there was no need for bookshelf display nor hundreds or thousands of additional copies to supply newsagents.[8] Since the approach to this format and periodical type was straightforward and top-down, there was not as great a need for many staff to help in production as with the later two formats, since resources could be deployed as needed over greater stretches of time since articles were often produced months in advance. Distribution and sales efforts were helped by one-off and regular events, talks

---

8   While direct sales at events and conferences, and subscriptions bring in either all or a high proportion of the cover price paid directly to the magazine, selling via newsagents requires a substantial share of the cover price paid out to wholesale distributors and retail outlets.

and conferences held by either the party or the journal, although its highest circulation usually remained below, sometimes substantially below, 20 percent of the membership.

During *Marxism Today*'s first format as a journal, there was little change in the process by which the CPGB's printers, Farleigh Press, produced it with hot-metal type rather than with the newer, cheaper, more accessible, printing technology. There is a basic correspondence between the limited change in MT's production and the party line, as the leadership's control over development corresponded to the gradual changes in the format itself. As demonstrated in Chapter 4, changes in design, layout and imagery were also gradual. Some two-thirds (68 percent) of features were over 4,000 words while all features took up three-quarters (77 percent) of the available space with barely two percent devoted to advertising. MT's primary editorial focus on features exemplifies the journal within the party publications typology.

Little effort was put into promoting the journal to the media, as its front cover shifted from being simply a 'Table of Contents' to an illustrated 'Table of Contents', with images gradually integrated with the design. We can also see the political practice associated with this format was that of the speech, lecture, branch meeting and school, which are traditionally understood and practiced as top-down, linear and monologic means of communication, which fits in with the conventional understanding of the Leninist model of the party paper and the CPGB's attempts to dampen down or restrict the dissident challenges of *The Reasoner* and *The New Reasoner* in the years surrounding the 1957 launch of the party's 'theoretical and discussion journal' until after the 1967 Executive Committee's 'Statement on Ideology and Culture'. The manner of its format and public communication is tied to the rhetorical purpose of solidification and, at times, exhortation, while its underlying logic is frequently tautological, as the party is seen as the source and justification for the political trajectory, as demonstrated by its rhetorical techniques and writing styles. The limits of production and distribution correspond to the employment of the particular rhetorical techniques and writing styles that are possible within the editorial-ideological or party line.

In the second format, the front cover became a political statement *and* a marketing tool, rather than a simple listing of contents, with its imagery attempting to attract potential purchasers in the newsagent. Although not every front cover played with such emotional or provocative issues as abortion or strategic voting, the polysemic possibilities of MT's cover images demonstrates a willingness to risk complaints and overthrow expectations, as it engaged in using humour and inter-textual references to popular culture: a process driven by the need to differentiate MT from other glossy left magazines on the shelf. These kinds of developments often challenged expectations of the average party member or supporter and partly explains how both supporters *and* critics could understand the same periodical differently: as 'self-confident', 'lively' and 'irreverent'; or 'dismissive', 'divisive' and 'disrespectful'. The respective views of interpretation read the ideological attacks in their metaphorical gloves hammering them for their perceived and real flaws.

The move to lithography and phototypesetting during the second format meant that MT was more 'flexible' in its production schedules, which fitted in with its transformation into a format more closely aligned with the 'newsmagazine' in the commercial marketplace. The growth in sales was in part due to its transformation from a journal into a magazine with various self-contained sections that brought different readers back for those topics that interested them. Just as a shift was taking place with both contributors and readers, MT was scaling down the length of features, although about half were still 4,000 words or more in length and features took up half of the pagination of each issue. The second format enabled greater flexibility with the layout and design while advertising (excluding the front and back covers, inside and outside), took up nearly one-fifth (19 percent) of the increased pagination that made more space available for additional editorial sections. The types of contributors shifted as lecturers, activists and mainstream journalists began to replace party intellectuals and officials, while more readers came from what can be defined as strata from within the PMC, rather than traditional working-class occupations more commonly associated with the CPGB (and even the YCL) until the early 1960s.

More significantly, with the transformations into the second and third formats, *Marxism Today*'s attempts to interest or obtain national news coverage grew considerably. The one to two news releases per issue in the early 1980s and the CPGB's 'civil war', helped to secure press coverage by national broadsheets with 205 items during the period of the second format, 1979–86. During this period, *The Guardian* was the preeminent national newspaper with which MT became associated when it was closely connected to the CPGB's reformist wing and the Labour Left until 1983. This was closer to what MT's idea of the 'broad democratic alliance' to defeat Thatcherism became but equally its shift towards an ideological alliance to defeat the ideas of the Labour Left after 1983 saw its further transformation into a magazine.

Significantly, the second format also marks a transformation in the periodical type and format, whereby the increased flexibility with layout and the use of imagery corresponded to the ideological changes as MT was moving away from its close proximity to the Communist Party and towards the BDA (as it defined the idea). The last two years of the first format, which were the first two of Jacques's editorship, was the period in which MT launched the twin defining analyses of Hobsbawm's 'Forward March of Labour Halted?' and Hall's 'Thatcherism' theses. Alongside additional publishing ventures, pamphlets and collections of contributions to these theses, MT established its own events, such as biennial weekend conferences, replacing the annual Communist University of London which ended in 1981, and in promoting its ideas while working in tandem with other left publications, such as Labour's *New Socialist*, which was launched in September 1981, as part of an attempt to increase circulation of its ideas and influence to counter MT's influence on Labour's members and supporters. During the first half of the 1980s, NS and MT shared events, panels, contributors and ideas as there was a certain unity of purpose and direction in the lead up to the 1983 general election and in the immediate aftermath. Part of this trajectory was more than straightforwardly political: it was a challenge to the anti-intellectualism of much of the labour movement and the Labour Party. The unity of the left was at the heart of this transformation of the first format, a party journal, into the second format, a socialist newsmagazine, politically, ideologically and materially as outlined in Table 16.

The first format's monthly sales varied from between 2,500 and 4,500 for most of the first two decades or so, with occasional 5,000-plus sales for special issues, after which there was an increase in monthly sales with the second format, at an initially modest 500 sales or so per month, until the new, second format with national newsagent distribution more than doubled sales to 9,500. These eventually climbed to an average of 13,000 by the mid-1980s, as recorded by the Audit Bureau of Circulation, which was integral to MT's professionalisation process and the necessary transformation of its format to appeal to non-party readers in the marketplace.

Increased sales brought increased costs, as did larger page sizes, albeit while simultaneously providing more space for words. We saw the growth on both sides of the balance sheet from £12,200 in revenue and £12,500 in costs in 1977 to more than six times that in revenue (£77,700) and seven times that in costs (£90,300) by 1983, the year of Labour's second consecutive general election defeat and the second year of full-colour covers. Compared to the first format, the second format was larger with increased pagination and supplements, increased staffing and national distribution, plus additional costs for artwork, design and illustrations, as well promotional campaigns, all of which added to the ledger's debit side. Yet, such changes were necessary to compete against centre-left and left periodicals on the newsagent's shelf, a process which tended to be more in keeping with the social-democratic, rather than the socialist, left since these magazines had to appeal to as broad a potential public as possible. Nonetheless, such expenses enabled MT to continue to expand its reach and prepare for its third format launch in 1986.

The shift that took place in contributors became more pronounced to meet deadlines and the ruthless publicity efforts to secure national media coverage. In this respect, there is a greater degree of collaboration and an increase in contributions from journalists and media professionals, although post-secondary lecturers continue to provide articles in different areas. In addition, the third format saw columnists, like Suzanne Moore, who broke into mainstream media employment via MT.

The readership was also changing during this time, in part because of the internecine warfare on the left, which saw internal divisions within the Communist Party being mapped onto the Labour Party and movement. The first proper readership survey in 1986 revealed that nearly three-out-of-five readers were members of either the CPGB or Labour, three-out-of-five were graduates and one-in-four were students. By 1990, with the third format, a second reader survey found that readers' party affiliations had decreased to just two-out-of-five holding memberships in either the CPGB or Labour, two-thirds were graduates and slightly less than one-in-four were students. This high proportion of graduates and students highlights particular strata of the PMC and the influence of the academy via media and cultural studies. This shift in readership demonstrates the increasing academisation of politics that reflected in part MT's own repositioning as a current affairs or public commentary magazine without any kind of organisational basis from which it could intervene in politics, electoral or cultural, beyond the seminar or panel discussion.

The third format was the largest and most flexible in terms of the space on the page to play with text and images. Although revenue and expenses had both increased by more than 300 percent by 1989, the annual gap between income and costs had grown by nearly four times what it was in 1983 from about £12,600 to £50,700. There was a move with some editorial sections, which had started to copy mainstream periodical innovations, such as the 'celebrity-type' interview columns, and which marked a downward shift in some of the political coverage as features accounted only for 37 percent of the total space with 29 percent devoted to advertising by 1988, and only 40 percent of features counted 4,000 words or more. Interestingly, there had been something of an increase in difficulty in the FOG index from the second to the third formats, although still less in comparison to that recorded in the first format, even though all three formats retained a difficulty in reading that more or less required a first-year university level of education (as confirmed in the two readership surveys).

Overall, there is a transformation of the periodical's 'rhetorical purpose', from the 'solidification' of the membership and sympathisers in the first format, to the second format's attempt to persuade others via unity and division (i.e. 'Us/Them') tactics to create a 'realignment' of the left in the pursuit of an alliance to defeat Thatcher(ism), to the third format's attempt at some 'journalistic' distance via 'intellectual critique' as an 'independent', current affairs or public opinion magazine rather than as a periodical that is part of a broader movement. In effect, MT voluntarily neutralised its potential political impact by cutting its ties of association, at least publicly, with the party and to a certain extent the labour movement and the left. It was always associated with the left but sought to break away from any kind of overt connection, which was made more clear in MT's third and final format is where it was attempting to become a 'journal of opinion', albeit in a magazine format.

Yet, MT's weakness stemmed from a lack of connection to an organisation that could be a means of influencing social-political change. This was a key factor in limiting the influence of the first New Left.[9] Yet, MT's ability to influence the Labour Party was not due to cutting its ideological, political or organisational links to the CPGB. It is in part due to Labour's failure to have developed its own intellectual culture, which meant its members often looked elsewhere for more in-depth analyses that helped to explain the world and make connections across various disciplinary silos.

This transformation of formats is also linked to the attempts to sponsor external or public talks, events and seminars, a different sort of 'meetings culture' than that found within political organisations, but which is more commonly associated with higher education. This shift in seeking to reach new readers, build larger audiences and establish a public presence was in many ways quite successful, but not necessarily in the way determined by, nor under the control of, *Marxism Today*. Nevertheless, the national media coverage of MT did increase during the third format to some 301 broadsheet features, news stories and minor announcements. But, it was always within the ways in which these establishment media chose to draw upon MT rather than in the analyses or topics for which MT sought coverage.

1   A Perennial Question

It is the assessment of *Marxism Today* after its demise that we should go back to the period in which it was launched. In her book on the New Left, Linn Chun raises questions that are as equally pertinent to ask of *Marxism Today* as

---

9   Chun 1993.

they are of the New Left, especially when we consider the terms in which there were particular continuities in the respective conjunctures and crises between the 1950s and the 1980s: two periods of long Conservative electoral hegemony and left divisions, as substantial changes transformed working-class living and working conditions. The most important weakness that the New Left exhibited was its 'political incapacity': '[it] also failed to formulate any long-term programme for the future regeneration of the socialist movement'.[10]

And, as with the New Left, *Marxism Today* drew attention to 'the cultural dimensions of politics', but it 'never worked out the following question':

> [H]ow do radical thinking and theoretical analyses directly affect politics? Or, to put it differently, can a lively but solely intellectual force play any decisive role in bringing about social change?[11]

MT's vision was one that moved from rethinking the left's political (and especially electoral) strategy into one that was increasingly focussed on increasing sales and recruiting media coverage for its ideas: that is, the pressures of the marketplace and its expectations for the cultural form(at) began to predominate.

Unlike the first New Left, which had begun outside the existing party structures, even as it sought to connect to or organise a new, independent socialist movement outside of Washington and Moscow, MT moved away from its connections to the CPGB and its various bodies into a 'semi-autonomous' position half in and half out of the commercial marketplace: ideologically and politically quite independent and, yet, dependent to greater or lesser degrees, organisationally and financially upon party agencies and subsidies. Its connection to labour, women's and new social movements was primarily limited to personal contributors and connections, and it lacked an organisational basis beyond what it developed through its discussion groups, which were organised by discrete grassroots groups and supportive party branches, and MT's personal networks of contributors whose public profiles could attract attention, such as Stuart Hall or Eric Hobsbawm. Chun goes on to point out that the question is partly about 'how to translate theories into concrete political discussions' and about 'how these two levels of cultural struggle are to be communicated to the agencies or potential agencies of the actual movement'?[12] Since socialist intellectuals are outside the 'centres of power' and influence, how could

---

10   Chun 1993, p. xv.
11   Ibid.
12   Ibid. Chun also asks how is 'the theory that a socialist movement requires' produced? MT

they possibly secure 'cultural hegemony', Gramsci's moral-intellectual leadership, prior to securing political power and bringing about the 'transformation of the existing system'?[13]

> Given the complex relationships between ideas, ideological institutions and institutional power, by what means, in any case, could at least a major section of the population be not only won over culturally, but also mobilised politically?[14]

The pre-emergent, socialist counter-culture that was a result of the oppositional and alternative practices that had been developing through the 1970s and early 1980s was something of which MT was a part.

For a short time, MT and other socialist periodicals, such as *New Socialist*, explicitly recognised that there was a role to play in trying to build a counter-hegemonic coalition. MT was not the only left periodical that could have contributed to building this hegemonic apparatus but the individual fortunes of periodicals militated against building this hegemonic apparatus for the subaltern classes and socialist movement. The hegemonic apparatus is the missing connection or agency here because it provides the means for developing cultural (counter) hegemony as part of the process of seeking political power. Faced by what the dominant hegemonic apparatus has to offer, MT needed to connect more broadly across the left, as did the other left parties, to build such a (counter-)hegemonic apparatus, whether or not there was a modern prince around which socialists could gather.

Working through the ideas in this book has contributed to a shift in my own rethinking of the basis of the connection between the party organisation and the paper, under the idea of 'vanguard *media*' as part of a necessary process of rethinking 'strategic communication' for the left.[15] There are at least five different functions in which media are necessary to connect the relationship between the 'modern prince' and the socialist (counter-)hegemonic project in the twenty-first century, in essence the functions of a (counter-)hegemonic apparatus, including the function of the party paper.[16] These five functions are necessary to the modern prince because of the difficulty of trying to strike a bal-

---

      moved away from trying to address this question in practice as it became more topical in the commercial marketplace of ideas.

13   Chun 1993, p. xv.
14   Ibid.
15   Pimlott 2015.
16   Ibid. The other four are: organisation; the bridge; network; and public relations.

ance between 'open discussion and promoting the party line', especially within one publication, and we know that it was almost always resolved in favour of the party line. Yet, such a situation is not going to encourage a full range of discussion, especially over contentious issues, which was essentially unresolvable in theory or practice, as demonstrated in the postwar period and throughout MT's history.[17]

2   Epilogue

A fundamental matter for all political media, print or otherwise, is that link between organisation and communication. In *Marxism Today*'s case, for example, the desire to reach beyond the Communist Party to influence the Labour Party, meant removing itself from the network and apparatuses of the one without any guarantee of connections to the other. The process of constructing a strategy of (counter) hegemony, a (counter) public sphere needs to be created or developed where a range of different positions can be debated and discussed. Unfortunately, even as there were attempts by MT and *New Socialist*, for example, to provide a platform for debate across the left, their appeal remained limited to a left public. And this appeal remained the province of people in discussion groups and seminar rooms rather than within any kind of political network where 'action' could be taken upon these ideas.

While it is important to recognise the advantages that *Marxism Today* claimed through its connections to the CPGB were important and enabled it to thrive in a way that would have been more difficult without the party's organisational nexus, it is equally important to recognise that MT was able to move beyond the radical ghetto of party readers to a broader left audience only to a limited extent. MT was dependent upon what mainstream media wanted to report on which were not necessarily the same issues, let alone the same perspectives, that Martin Jacques or other MT staff and contributors wanted to promote. They could not control the ways in which their ideas were discussed in mass media outlets, even as MT provided a means for mainstream media commentators and journalists to access the left's (counter) public sphere and provide a legitimising channel for views that were more in accord with the social-democratic left or the centre-left of the political mainstream (i.e. Labour Right).

---

17   CIPD 1957.

Nonetheless, it is important to see that *Marxism Today* offers a way for rethinking how a radical left magazine might seek to reach out beyond its immediate organisational links and support networks to find a broader audience to try to win over. While we can see the difference that a generation or two can make, as with the all-too-brief rise of Jeremy Corbyn to Labour Party leader and the temporary switch away from a neoliberal-New Labour nexus, which was welcomed by Jacques himself in recognition that Corbyn was 'far from being a retread of a failed past' and 'more than any other leader – in tune with the times'.[18] However, MT remained unconnected to the means of extending class struggle to more than discourse: i.e. no practical vehicles to carry on the struggle. For MT, access to mainstream media became the *de facto* replacement for the modern prince.

MT was transformed in the process of changing its political economy (e.g. funding, sales, production, distribution) and editorial content (e.g. topics, analysis, rhetoric, writing style, layout, design, imagery) and, as it was transformed it was picked up by mainstream media and promoted, intentionally or not, via the pages of the broadsheet press, particularly *The Guardian* and later *The Independent*. Does MT's 'persona' and political interventions into left debates undermine the *raison d'être* of a socialist periodical of critical or radical ideas and discussion? Is it the desire to reach out to the general public which means that both content and form begin to change to meet the demands of such a desire, at least as mediated by the marketplace? MT's persona had an impact upon how it was received by prospective and existing readers.

These political-economic changes point to the tensions between the party and *Marxism Today*, between political and editorial autonomy, and between marketplace demands on one hand and those of the party-publisher on the other. On one level, these issues led to conflicts between commercial and political decisions: 'business' decisions became 'political' decisions, subjected to a lot of negotiation and politicking, and these 'political' decisions, in turn, had an impact upon the production process and commercial performance and, *ipso facto*, became 'business' decisions. It is in the very process of such decision-making processes that 'professionalisation' has its impact.

In future, market distribution will have to be as much a concern for radical media as advertising has been if they want to ensure access to a broader public *and* retain the integrity of their ideas. For a revised alternative media model, the desire for access to the national public sphere must take into account that such

---

18 Jacques 2017, p. 28. This was the only time in the recent history of the Labour Party where the left actually succeeded to the leadership, albeit briefly.

a move could open up access for, and confer legitimacy upon, establishment voices in radical media themselves. The marketplace of ideas metaphor may no longer be an apt metaphor, let alone a reality, for understanding the 'battle of ideas' in the Gramscian war of position because of its failure to recognise that the unequal relations in the marketplace between dominant and radical media contributes to the mystification of the market as subjecting all periodicals to the equivalent of 'an election a day'.

There remains a mistaken belief that any 'war of position' can be won in the capitalist marketplace of ideas, even though capitalists themselves subsidise segments of the (dominant) hegemonic apparatus, from think tanks and newsmedia to public relations companies and astroturf campaigns.[19] This belief overlooks the importance of the material conditions, which structure and limit what can be produced and distributed via whatever in-person, print, broadcast or electronic networks are (made) available, and thereby will misunderstand the complementary importance of both the means of communication and the political organisation necessary for a (counter-)hegemonic strategy. In essence, the only way in which radical left movements, from socialist to communist to anarchist, will be able to both control their own narratives and ideologies is through the subsidies and support that are achieved through political organisation of all social, economic, political, ideological and cultural struggles.

Despite all Jacques's, Hall's and other *Marxism Today*'s supporters claims to the contrary, MT's 'war of position' during the 1980s was not such an engagement as conceptualised by Gramsci. It was a 'staking of position' in the commercial marketplace of ideas and more specifically the UK's magazine marketplace and was therefore dependent upon the various forces that acted to constrain or permit access within that framework. This was not a war of position because there was no (counter-)hegemonic apparatus, of which MT was a part, for the subaltern classes without the political organisation of the modern prince, just as the party needs a means of cultural production, Gramsci's (counter-)hegemonic apparatus, to be politically effective. This means that cultural politics is not just about how culture is political or politics is cultural as it is about how cultural production is integral to political organisation and each require the other to succeed, especially in any (counter-)hegemonic struggle against neoliberal hegemony.

19   E.g. Brock 2005; Desai 1994; Gutstein 2009; Kozolanka 2007; Scammell 1997.

Illustrations: *Marxism Today* 1957–1991

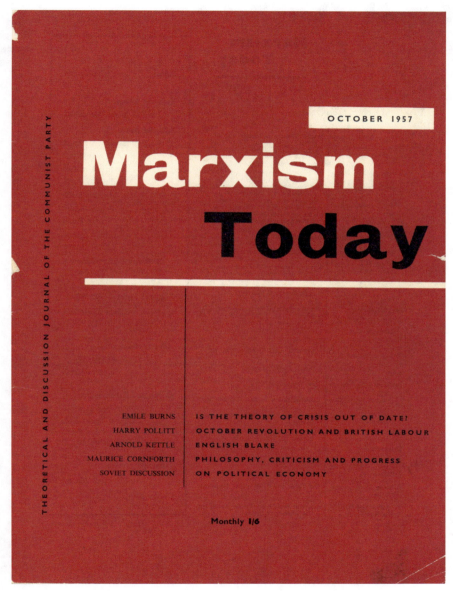

FIGURE 1   *Marxism Today* October 1957: The very first issue and first format
COVER DESIGN: FARLEIGH PRESS – *MARXISM TODAY*

Marxism Today

Theoretical and Discussion Journal of the Communist Party   February 1975   25 pence

Editorial Comments

Ray Watkinson   A Study of George Grosz

George Grosz: Toads of Property, 1921

George Matthews	The Wilson Government and Britain's Crisis
Georges Marchais	Report to the Twenty-First Congress of the French Communist Party — Part II
Maurice Dobb	Further Comments on Inflation
Judy Bloomfield	*Trends in Youth Culture*

FIGURE 2   *Marxism Today* February 1975: An example of a first format's front cover's use of art work.
COVER DESIGN: PAT COOK AND GEORGE GROSZ; PHOTOGRAPH COURTESY OF STUDIO VISTA – *MARXISM TODAY*

Marxism Today

Theoretical and Discussion Journal of the Communist Party   March 1976   30 pence

From the cover of
Lawrence and Wishart's
latest book on
The General Strike

Editorial Comments:

Jon Chadwick — Alternative Culture

Fidel Castro — Historical Analysis of the Cuban Revolution Part 1

Renzo Galeotti — On the Death of Paolo Pasolini

Discussion:

Gavin Mackenzie — Class and Class Consciousness: Marx Re-examined

Pat Sloan / Dorothy Friedmann — Socialist Democracy—Some Problems

FIGURE 3   *Marxism Today* March 1976: 1926 General Strike 50th Anniversary Issue.
COVER DESIGN: PAT COOK – *MARXISM TODAY*

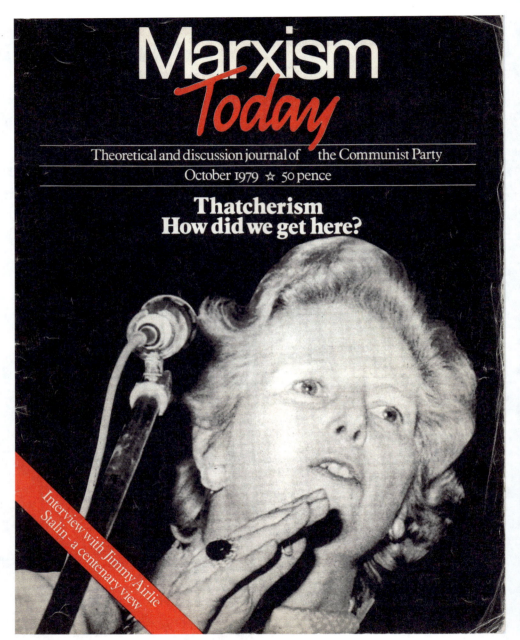

FIGURE 4   *Marxism Today* October 1979: Launch issue for the second format
COVER DESIGN: ANNA AUBREY AND PETER HAMMARLING – *MARXISM TODAY*

FIGURE 5 *Marxism Today* October 1979: 'Focus' section in layout in second format

DESIGN: ANNA AUBREY AND PETER HAMMARLING – *MARXISM TODAY*

FIGURE 6   *Marxism Today* October 1983: Neil Kinnock as Superman
COVER DESIGN: PETER HAMMARLING, KATHRYN TATTERSALL AND LEE ROBINSON;
COVER ILLUSTRATION: BRETT EWINS – *MARXISM TODAY*

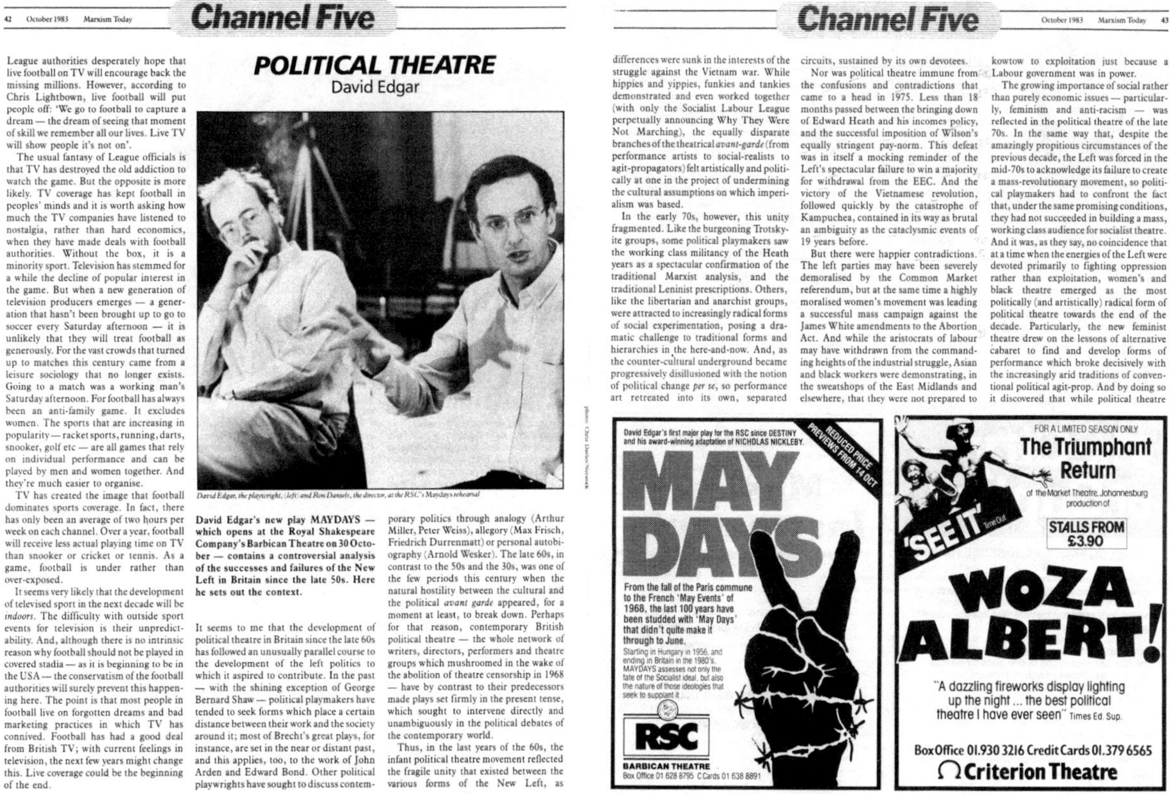

42 October 1983 Marxism Today **Channel Five**

League authorities desperately hope that live football on TV will encourage back the missing millions. However, according to Chris Lightbown, live football will put people off: 'We go to football to capture a dream — the dream of seeing that moment of skill we remember all our lives. Live TV will show people it's not on'.

The usual fantasy of League officials is that TV has destroyed the old addiction to watch the game. But the opposite is more likely. TV coverage has kept football in peoples' minds and it is worth asking how much the TV companies have listened to nostalgia, rather than hard economics, when they have made deals with football authorities. Without the box, it is a minority sport. Television has stemmed for a while the decline of popular interest in the game. But when a new generation of television producers emerges — a generation that hasn't been brought up to go to soccer every Saturday afternoon — it is unlikely that they will treat football as generously. For the vast crowds that turned up to matches this century came from a leisure sociology that no longer exists. Going to a match was a working man's Saturday afternoon. For football has always been an anti-family game. It excludes women. The sports that are increasing in popularity — racket sports, running, darts, snooker, golf etc — are all games that rely on individual performance and can be played by men and women together. And they're much easier to organise.

TV has created the image that football dominates sports coverage. In fact, there has only been an average of two hours per week on each channel. Over a year, football will receive less actual playing time on TV than snooker or cricket or tennis. As a game, football is under rather than over-exposed.

It seems very likely that the development of televised sport in the next decade will be *indoors*. The difficulty with outside sport events for television is their unpredictability. And, although there is no intrinsic reason why football should not be played in covered stadia — as it is beginning to be in the USA — the conservatism of the football authorities will surely prevent this happening here. The point is that most people in football live on forgotten dreams and bad marketing practices in which TV has connived. Football has had a good deal from British TV; with current feelings in television, the next few years might change this. Live coverage could be the beginning of the end.

POLITICAL THEATRE

David Edgar

David Edgar, the playwright, (left) and Ron Daniels, the director, at the RSC's Maydays rehearsal

photo: Chris Davies/Network

David Edgar's new play MAYDAYS — which opens at the Royal Shakespeare Company's Barbican Theatre on 30 October — contains a controversial analysis of the successes and failures of the New Left in Britain since the late 50s. Here he sets out the context.

It seems to me that the development of political theatre in Britain since the late 60s has followed an unusually parallel course to the development of the left politics to which it aspired to contribute. In the past — with the shining exception of George Bernard Shaw — political playmakers have tended to seek forms which place a certain distance between their work and the society around it; most of Brecht's great plays, for instance, are set in the near or distant past, and this applies, too, to the work of John Arden and Edward Bond. Other political playwrights have sought to discuss contemporary politics through analogy (Arthur Miller, Peter Weiss), allegory (Max Frisch, Friedrich Durrenmatt) or personal autobiography (Arnold Wesker). The late 60s, in contrast to the 50s and the 30s, was one of the few periods this century when the natural hostility between the cultural and the political *avant garde* appeared, for a moment at least, to break down. Perhaps for that reason, contemporary British political theatre — the whole network of writers, directors, performers and theatre groups which mushroomed in the wake of the abolition of theatre censorship in 1968 — have by contrast to their predecessors made plays set firmly in the present tense, which sought to intervene directly and unambiguously in the political debates of the contemporary world.

Thus, in the last years of the 60s, the infant political theatre movement reflected the fragile unity that existed between the various forms of the New Left, as

Channel Five October 1983 Marxism Today 43

differences were sunk in the interests of the struggle against the Vietnam war. While hippies and yippies, funkies and tankies demonstrated and even worked together (with only the Socialist Labour League perpetually announcing Why They Were Not Marching), the equally disparate branches of the theatrical *avant-garde* (from performance artists to social-realists to agit-propagators) felt artistically and politically at one in the project of undermining the cultural assumptions on which imperialism was based.

In the early 70s, however, this unity fragmented. Like the burgeoning Trotskyite groups, some political playmakers saw the working class militancy of the Heath years as a spectacular confirmation of the traditional Marxist analysis, and the traditional Leninist prescriptions. Others, like the libertarian and anarchist groups, were attracted to increasingly radical forms of social experimentation, posing a dramatic challenge to traditional forms and hierarchies in the here-and-now. And, as the counter-cultural underground became progressively disillusioned with the notion of political change *per se*, so performance art retreated into its own, separated circuits, sustained by its own devotees.

Nor was political theatre immune from the confusions and contradictions that came to a head in 1975. Less than 18 months passed between the bringing down of Edward Heath and his incomes policy, and the successful imposition of Wilson's equally stringent pay-norm. This defeat was in itself a mocking reminder of the Left's spectacular failure to win a majority for withdrawal from the EEC. And the victory of the Vietnamese revolution, followed quickly by the catastrophe of Kampuchea, contained in its way as brutal an ambiguity as the cataclysmic events of 19 years before.

But there were happier contradictions. The left parties may have been severely demoralised by the Common Market referendum, but at the same time a highly moralised women's movement was leading a successful mass campaign against the James White amendments to the Abortion Act. And while the aristocrats of labour may have withdrawn from the commanding heights of the industrial struggle, Asian and black workers were demonstrating, in the sweatshops of the East Midlands and elsewhere, that they were not prepared to kowtow to exploitation just because a Labour government was in power.

The growing importance of social rather than purely economic issues — particularly, feminism and anti-racism — was reflected in the political theatre of the late 70s. In the same way that, despite the amazingly propitious circumstances of the previous decade, the Left was forced in the mid-70s to acknowledge its failure to create a mass-revolutionary movement, so political playmakers had to confront the fact that, under the same promising conditions, they had not succeeded in building a mass, working class audience for socialist theatre. And it was, as they say, no coincidence that at a time when the energies of the Left were devoted primarily to fighting oppression rather than exploitation, women's and black theatre emerged as the most politically (and artistically) radical form of political theatre towards the end of the decade. Particularly, the new feminist theatre drew on the lessons of alternative cabaret to find and develop forms of performance which broke decisively with the increasingly arid traditions of conventional political agit-prop. And by doing so it discovered that while political theatre

FIGURE 7 *Marxism Today* October 1983: 'Channel Five' in layout in second format

DESIGN: LEE ROBINSON AND KATHERINE GUTKIND – *MARXISM TODAY*

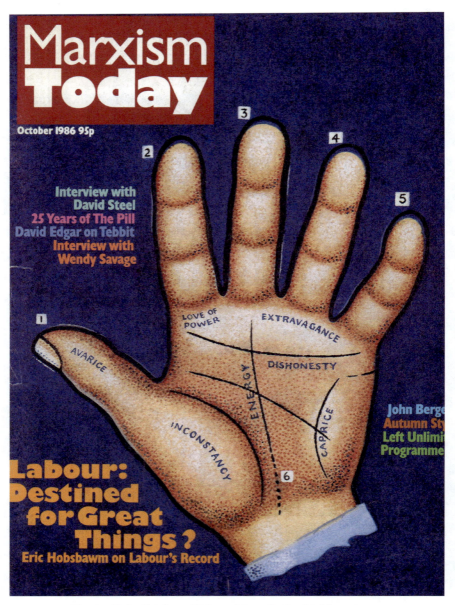

FIGURE 8 *Marxism Today* October 1986: Launch issue for the third format
COVER CONCEPT: KEITH ABLITT; COVER ILLUSTRATION: TONY MCSWEENEY – *MARXISM TODAY*

ILLUSTRATIONS: MARXISM TODAY 1957–1991

FIGURE 9   *Marxism Today* January 1987: 'aids'
            COVER DESIGN: KEITH ABLITT – *MARXISM TODAY*

FIGURE 10 *Marxism Today* April 1988: 'men'
COVER DESIGN: JAN BROWN; PHOTOGRAPH: ABEL LAGOS – *MARXISM TODAY*

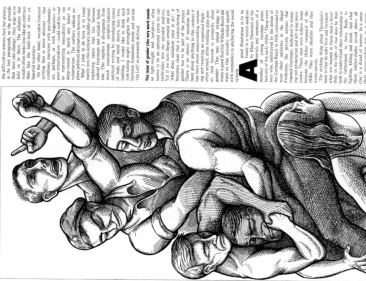

FIGURE 11 *Marxism Today* April 1988: 'Feature' article in layout
DESIGN: JAN BROWN; ILLUSTRATION: CLIFFORD HARPER – *MARXISM TODAY*

FIGURE 12 *Marxism Today* October 1988: 'New Times' launch issue
COVER DESIGN: JAN BROWN; COLLAGE: JAN BROWN – *MARXISM TODAY*

FIGURE 13 *Marxism Today* October 1988: 'Feature' article in layout

DESIGN: JAN BROWN; PHOTOGRAPH: NATIONAL MOTOR MUSEUM, BEAULIEU – *MARXISM TODAY*

FIGURE 14 *Marxism Today* December 1991-January 1992: 'The End' final issue
COVER DESIGN: PEARCE MARCHBANK – *MARXISM TODAY*

References

Primary Materials

Interviews and Personal Communication

Andrews, Geoff 1995b, Personal Communication, 18 July.
Andrews, Geoff 1998, Personal Communication, 1 May.
Brennan, Irene 1996, Interview, 13 March. *Marxism Today*, Editorial Board member.
Curran, James 1997, Personal Communication, 18 September. Editor, *New Socialist*, 1981–84.
Curran, James 1997b, Personal Communication, 25 May. Editor, *New Socialist*, 1981–84.
Davison, Sally 1995, Personal Communication, 1 July.
Hall, Stuart 1997, Interview, 21 January.
Hammarling, Peter 1996, Interview, 20 February.
Hobsbawm, Eric 1997, Personal Communication, 9 January.
Jacques, Martin 1996b, Interview, 2 September.
Jacques, Martin 1996c, Interview, 15 October.
Jacques, Martin 1996d, Interview, 7 November.
Jacques, Martin 1996e, Interview, 28 November.
Johnstone, Monty 1995, Interview, 23 October.
King, Francis 1994, Personal Communication, 15 September.
McLennan, Gordon 1996, Interview, 20 August.
Matthews, Betty and George Matthews 1996, Interview, 12 November.
Minnion, Jon 1996, Interview, 23 February.
Osler, Dave 1996, Personal Communication, 23 February.
Perryman, Mark 1994b, Interview, 14 September.
Perryman, Mark 1995, Personal Communication, 26 June.
Rutherford, Jonathan 1997, Personal Communication, 21 June.
Taylor, Jane 1995, Interview, 16 July, Deputy Editor, *Marxism Today*, 1987–90.
Temple, Nina 1994, Transcript of interview by Gareth Smythe, 25 July.
Townsend, Sally 1996, Interview, 5 March. MT's Deputy Editor, 1982–87.
Turner, Julian 1994, Interview, 26 September, MT's Business Manager.
Turner, Julian 1998, Interview, 15 March.
Wilson, Elizabeth 1997, Personal Communication, 19 December.

Periodical Articles (*Not from MT's Clippings File*)

Anderson, Paul and Kevin Davey 1995, 'Moscow Gold? The True Story of the Kremlin, British Communism and the Left', *New Statesman and Society*, 7 April, supplement.

Andrews, Geoff 1996, 'A Swing to the Bright', *Times Higher Education Supplement*, 16 August.
Campaign for Press and Broadcasting Freedom 1996a, '"WH Smenzies" and Press Freedom', *Free Press*, 92, p. 5.
Campaign for Press and Broadcasting Freedom 1996b, 'Press Distribution Campaign', *Free Press*, 94, p. 5.
Howe, Stephen 1996, 'Staggering On: Review of *The "New Statesman"*', *London Review of Books*, 18: 10.
Jacques, Martin 1996a, 'His Project for the Party is a Triumph, But What About His Project for the Country?', *The Guardian*, G2, 26 September.
Jacques, Martin 2017, 'A Leader for the New Times', *New Statesman*, 16–22 June, pp. 28–31.
Jacques, Martin and Stuart Hall 1997, 'The Great Moving Centre Show', *New Statesman and Society*, 21 November.
Logan, J. 1996, 'The Strong Get Stronger, the Small Go to the Wall', *Free Press*, 92, pp. 4–5.
Paige, Jonathan 2013, 'British Public Wrong About Nearly Everything, Survey Says', *The Independent*, 9 July.
Smyth, Gareth 1994, 'Marxism Yesterday', *New Statesman and Society*, 25 July.
Williams, Raymond 1977b 'The Paths and Pitfalls of an Ideology as an Ideology', *Times Higher Education Supplement*, 10 June, p. 13.

Newspaper and Periodical Articles (MT's Clippings File)

Ali, Tariq 1984, '"Pink Professors" Hinder the Struggle Against Capitalism', *The Guardian*, 24 September.
Anderson, D. 1985, 'Realistic, Ambitious – and Extreme', *The Times*, 1 October.
Bloomfield, Jon 1985a, 'Voters Who Can't Afford Labour's Wealth of Ideology', *The Guardian*, 3 January.
Bond, P. 1982, 'Riot Squad Risk, by Police Chief', *The Sun*, 22 March.
Brown, C. 1989, 'Marxist Backing for NHS Changes', *Doctor*, 9 March.
Chesshyre, R. 1987, 'Left Magazines Try for Right Path', *The Observer*, 11 October.
Culf, A. 1989, 'New Thinking for New Times', *The Guardian*, 27 November.
Express on Sunday 1982, 'Police Chief and Watchdogs', *Express on Sunday*, 21 March.
Gerard, N. 1986, 'Small Noises, Loud Voices', *The Guardian*, 11 March.
Gill, Ken 1985, 'Retreat to the Centre', *Morning Star*, 18 May.
Gott, Richard 1988, 'Goodbye to All This', *The Guardian*, 8 February.
Guardian, The 1984, 'Star Wars and Worker Warriors', *The Guardian*, 2 June.
Guardian, The 1985a, 'No Time for a Challenge to Kinnock', *The Guardian*, 4 January.
Guardian, The 1985b, 'The Vote and the Answers', *The Guardian*, 27 March.
Guardian, The 1990, 'A Name for the Party', *The Guardian*, 11 September.
Heffer, Eric 1982, Letter, *The Guardian*, 12 May.

Hobsbawm, Eric 1983c, 'Change the Party, Not the Workers', *The Guardian*, 20 September.
Hobsbawm, Eric 1984c, 'Labour Must Go Forward With the Masses', *The Guardian*, 20 February.
Jenkins, Peter 1982, 'The Present System Enables the Electorate's Wishes to be Largely Ignored, Even Treated with Contempt', *The Guardian*, 3 November.
Jones, Michael 1985, 'Fraticide on the Hard-Left', *The Times*, 31 March.
Kavanagh, Trevor 1984, 'Benn Calls for The Revolution', *The Sun*, 29 December.
Kettle, Arnold 1989, 'Comrades are Sinking Slowly in the West', *The Guardian*, 29 November.
Langdon, J. 1984, 'Put up, or Shut up', *Daily Mirror*, 29 December.
Lawrence, F. 1982, 'Political Magazines Show Their True Colours', *Newsagent*, 18 November.
Linton, M. 1990, 'Communists Vote for Party's Reprieve', *The Guardian*, 10 December.
Lloyd, John 1986, 'The Left Searches for a Voice', *Financial Times*, 12 April.
Mail, Daily 1982, 'MPs in "Marxist" Rumpus', *The Daily Mail*, 28 April.
Massam, A. 1989, 'Marxist Praise for Clarke's Reforms', *London Evening Standard*, 21 February.
News Trade Weekly 1989, 'First for *Marxism Today*', *News Trade Weekly*, 20 May.
Paterson, P. 1985, 'A Lesson From the Communists', *The Sunday Times*, 20 January.
Retail Newsagent 1989, 'New Times Ahead', *Retail Newsagent*, 27 May.
Rowbotham, Sheila 1989, 'Left out of the Argument by Ideological Gift-Wrap', *The Guardian*, 20 February.
Rutherford, Malcolm 1982, 'The Left Adapts to Thatcherism', *Financial Times*, 23 December.
Star, Daily 1982a, 'Riot Police Fears of Chief', *Daily Star*, 22 March.
Star, Daily 1982b, 'As you say, Tony', *The Daily Star*, 28 April.
Sun, The 1982, 'Odd Man Out', *The Sun*, 22 March.
Telegraph, The 1984a, 'Swept into the Rapids', *The Telegraph*, 25 February.
Telegraph, The 1984b, 'Britain Needs a Peaceful Revolution, says Benn', *The Telegraph*, 29 December.
Telegraph, The 1989, 'Communists Turn Right to Democracy', *The Telegraph*, 27 November.
Telegraph, The 1989, 'Fellow-Travellers' Rest', *The Telegraph*, 27 November.
Times, The 1982, 'Sheep's Clothing', *The Times*, 29 November.
Times, The 1987, Leader, *The Times*, 28 September.
van Hatten, M. 1984, 'Benn's Blueprint Attacked by Left', *Financial Times*, 29 December.
Walden, Brian 1988, 'Clear-eyed Communists Show Kinnock the Way', *Sunday Times*, 4 December.
Warden, J. 1984, 'Benn's New Year Threat to Kinnock', *Daily Express*, 29 December.

Webster, Philip 1984, 'Benn Wants Annual Elections', *The Times*, 29 December.
Wintour, Patrick 1985, 'Miners' Strike: A Study in Failure', *The Guardian*, 18 March.
Wintour, Patrick 1989, 'Stark Choices for Communists', *The Guardian*, 25 November.
Young, Hugo 1983, 'A Mirage of Coalition', *The Sunday Times*, 30 January.
Young, Hugo 1984, 'Enough of the Squabbling and Let the Real Arguments Begin', *The Guardian*, 31 December.
Young, Hugo 1985, 'The New Right Lesson the Left Must Learn', *The Guardian*, 12 December.

All Materials Drawn from Martin Jacques's Private Papers, Unless Otherwise Noted, and the Communist Party of Great Britain Archives at the People's History Museum

Materials drawn from the CPGB Archives (CPA) are listed according to its formula: e.g. CP/CENT/EC/15/08.

Alce, Julie 1977, Letter to the Editor, *Marxism Today*, October.
Allison, Doris 1978, Memo to Martin Jacques, 27 January.
Apter, R., et al. 1988, Letter to Gordon McLennan, 20 December.
Barron, J. 1978, Letter to the Executive Committee, 22 November.
Benton, Sarah 1980, Resignation Letter, 6 November.
Blatt, A. 1984, Letter to Nina Temple, 9 July.
Carritt, Bill 1970b, Letter to B. Findlay, 10 July.
Cockburn, Cynthia 1989, *Review of MT August, September and October 1989*. MTEB, 14 October.
Cohen, Gerry 1982, Letter to Gordon McLennan, 17 May.
Cohen, Jack 1978, Letter to Martin Jacques, 3 July.
Communist Party of Great Britain 1957b, *Report of the Commission on Inner Party Democracy*.
Communist Party of Great Britain 1957c, 'New Marxist Monthly', London: CPGB. 21 August. Press Release.
Congress Appeals Committee, 40th National Party Congress 1987, 'First Report', *Congress Document*, 14.
Davison, Sally 1985b, *Marxism Today Reviews*, *Marxism Today*, Editorial Board, 8 March.
Davison, Sally 1985c, *Notes from Meeting on Reviews*. MTEC, 23 May.
Davison, Sally 1985d, *Proposals for Marxism Today Reviews*. MTEB, 8 March.
Discussion Editorial Board 1937, 'Memorandum', London: CPGB, 3 May.
Executive Committee, CPGB 1958, *Minutes*, 10–11 May 1958.
Executive Committee, CPGB 1971, *Report to the 32nd National Party Congress*.
Executive Committee, CPGB 1976, *Minutes*, 8–9 March 1976. CP/CENT/EC/15/08.

Executive Committee, CPGB 1977a, *Minutes*, 12–13 March, p. 1. CP/CENT/EC/15/14.
Executive Committee, CPGB 1977b, *Report to the 35th National Party Congress*.
Executive Committee, CPGB 1978, *Minutes*, 11–12 November.
Executive Committee, CPGB 1979a, *Minutes*, 13–14 January.
Executive Committee, CPGB 1979b, *Minutes*, 12–13 May.
Executive Committee, CPGB 1979c, *Minutes*, 8–9 September.
Executive Committee, CPGB 1979d, *Report to the 36th National Party Congress*.
Executive Committee, CPGB 1980, *Minutes*, 12–13 January.
Executive Committee, CPGB 1981a, *Minutes*, 10–11 January.
Executive Committee, CPGB 1981b, *Minutes*, 9–10 May.
Executive Committee, CPGB 1982a, *Minutes*, 11–12 September.
Executive Committee, CPGB 1982b, *Minutes*, 13 September.
Executive Committee, CPGB 1982c, *Minutes*, 13–14 November.
Executive Committee, CPGB 1983, *Minutes*, 11–12 March.
Executive Committee, CPGB 1984a, *Minutes*, 12–13 May.
Executive Committee, CPGB 1984b, *Minutes*, 14–15 July.
Executive Committee, CPGB 1984c, *Minutes*, 8–9 September.
Executive Committee, CPGB 1984d, *Minutes*, 14 October.
Executive Committee, CPGB 1984e, *Minutes*, 23 November.
Executive Committee, CPGB 1986a, *Minutes*, 10 January.
Executive Committee, CPGB 1986b, *Minutes*, 8–9 November. CP/CENT/EC/22/12.
Executive Committee, CPGB 1987a, *Minutes*, 28 June.
Executive Committee, CPGB 1987b, *Minutes*, 11–12 July.
Executive Committee, CPGB 1987c, 'The New Challenge facing Britain's Labour and Democratic Movements', *News and Views*, Congress Special Issue.
Executive Committee, CPGB 1988a, *Minutes*, 14–15 May.
Executive Committee, CPGB 1988b, *Minutes*, 9–10 July.
Executive Committee, CPGB 1988c, *Minutes*, 10–11 September.
Executive Committee, CPGB 1989, *Manifesto for New Times*.
Executive Committee, CPGB 1990, *Minutes*, 14–15 July.
Executive Committee, *Morning Star* Sub-Committee 1978, *Report on the Morning Star*.
Executive Committee, Sub-Committees, CPGB 1976, *Report of the Sub-Committees*, 13 March.
Falber, Reuben 1977, Letter to Margaret Woddis, 16 January. CP/CENT/EC/15/14.
Falber, Reuben 1982, Letter to the PC, 28 January.
Farrington, Paddy 1983, 'Promoting Marxism Today Within the Party', MTEB, 21 June.
Farrington, Paddy 1984, *Campaigning with Marxism Today*, MTEC, 30 June.
Feltham, P. 1970, Discussion Contribution on 'Socialist Democracy'. Unpublished manuscript.

Feltham, P. 1971, Letter to Arnold Kettle, 17 April.
Fosker, R. 1991, Memo to Lynda Chalker, Minister for Overseas Development. Information Department, Westminster, 26 June.
Foster, John 1982a, Letter to General Secretary, 2 September.
Foster, John 1982b, Letter to Martin Jacques and the *Marxism Today* Editorial Board, 18 October.
Foster, John 1984, Letter to Executive Committee, 4 November.
Gardiner, Jean 1982, Letter to Martin Jacques, 19 October.
Hansard 1982, Order Paper, No. 105, Wednesday, 28 April.
Hobsbawm, Eric 1958, Some Notes About the '*Universities and Left Review*'. Report for the Executive Committee, 10–11 May. CPGB.
Jacques, Martin nd [1977], 'Additional Assistance for *Marxism Today*', Memo to the Political Committee.
Jacques, Martin nd [1978], 'Effects of Dropping the Part-Time Position', Memo to the Political Committee.
Jacques, Martin 1977, *Perspectives for Marxism Today*, Document for MTEB, 14 December.
Jacques, Martin 1978c, *The Development of Marxism Today*, *Marxism Today* Editorial Collective.
Jacques, Martin 1978d, *The Grid*, December, *Marxism Today* Editorial Collective.
Jacques, Martin 1978e, *Report on Marxism Today*, Executive Committee, February, Communist Party Archives.
Jacques, Martin 1979f, Notes of Arts and Leisure Committee Meeting, 3 February.
Jacques, Martin 1979g, *Redesign: Contents and Other Questions*. *Marxism Today* Editorial Collective.
Jacques, Martin 1979h, *Promotion of the New Format*. MTEB, *Minutes*, 20 June.
Jacques, Martin 1979i, *Marxism Today in New Guise*. MTEB, 20 June.
Jacques, Martin 1982a, Letter to the Executive Committee, 9 September.
Jacques, Martin 1982b, Letter to Gordon McLennan, 21 April.
Jacques, Martin 1982c, *Notes of Marxism Today Editorial Board Meeting*, 20 October.
Jacques, Martin 1982d, *Report to the Executive Committee*.
Jacques, Martin 1983, *Report to Executive Committee on Marxism Today*. CPGB: Executive Committee. 12–13 March 1983. CP/CENT/EC/19/05.
Jacques, Martin 1984a, *The Left and the Media*. Notes for a talk given at Oxford. March.
Jacques, Martin 1984b, *The Role of Marxism Today*. Speech, *Marxism Today* Conference, 30 June.
Jacques, Martin 1984c, *Strategies for Marxism Today*. Notes.
Jacques, Martin 1985, *Developments in British Politics and Perspectives for the Communist Party*. EC Report.

Jacques, Martin 1986a, *Report on Proposed Changes to* MTEB. EC, 11–12 January.
Jacques, Martin 1986b, Letter to the Political Committee, 22 July.
Jacques, Martin 1987a, Letter to Michael Heseltine, 27 January.
Jacques, Martin 1987b, *Report on Marxism Today*. Executive Committee, CPGB. 28 June.
Jacques, Martin 1988b, *Report on* MT *Finances*. EC, 15 May.
Jacques, Martin 1988c, *Notes on 'Rethinking Socialism for the 90s'* (20–22 May). MTEB, 23 July.
Jacques, Martin and Paddy Farrington 1986, Letter to Political Committee, 23 June.
John, G. and I. Field 1987, Letter, *News and Views*, 2.
Johnstone, Monty 1977, Letter to Gordon McLennan, 9 March. CP/CENT/EC/15/14.
Johnstone, Monty 1990, Letter to the Executive Committee, 26 January.
Jones, Mike 1980, *Briefing Notes on 'Focus'*, *Marxism Today* Editorial Board, 18 June.
Kettle, Arnold 1985, Letter to Martin Jacques, 26 October.
Klugmann, James 1957, *Proposals for New Theoretical Journal*. CPGB, 3 April 1957. EC files, CPA.
Klugmann, James 1960, *Proposals for the Development of Marxism Today. Marxism Today* Editorial Board. EC files, CPA.
Klugmann, James 1968, Letter to Reuben Falber, 27 November.
Klugmann, James 1971, Letter to P. Feltham, 1 April.
Klugmann, James 1973, *'Marxism Today*: Background Notes'. Political Committee, 12 June.
Klugmann, James 1976d, Letter to Reuben Falber, 10 February.
Klugmann, James 1976b, *Report on the Work of the* MTEB. EC, 10 February.
Klugmann, James 1977, Letter to Martin Jacques, 9 May.
Labour Party 1997, *New Labour: Because Britain Deserves Better*, London: Labour Party.
Laithwaite, W.H. 1968, Letter to James Klugmann, 25 November.
Lanning, Paula 1982, Letter to the Editor, *Marxism Today*, 30 August.
Lawrence & Wishart 1953, 'Publisher's Note', *Modern Quarterly*, 8, 3.
Marxism Today 1986, *Report on Marxism Today Relaunch*. MTEB, 19 July.
Marxism Today 1990a, *Summary of Setting Up Marxism Today Limited*.
Marxism Today 1990b, *The Feasibility Study*.
Marxism Today 1991, *The Agenda Business Proposal*, February.
Marxism Today 1988a, 'Building Blocks', Press Release, 19 February.
Marxism Today 1988b, 'The Tory Opposition', Press Release, 19 February.
Marxism Today 1988c, 'The Social Side of Cancer', Press Release, 19 February.
Marxism Today 1989a, 'Marxism Today Advertising Staff Changes', Press Release, 12 May.
Marxism Today 1989b, 'MT Binds On!', Press Release, 12 May.

Marxism Today 1989c, 'Patient as Punter', Press Release, 25 May.

Marxism Today 1989d, 'Kenneth Clarke interviewed in *Marxism Today*', Press Release, 25 May.

Marxism Today 1989e, 'Dear Friend', Press Release, 25 May.

Marxism Today Editorial Board 1966, *Minutes*, 28 October.

Marxism Today Editorial Board 1973a, *Minutes*, 19 September.

Marxism Today Editorial Board 1973b, *Minutes*, 12 December.

Marxism Today Editorial Board 1976a, *Minutes*, 15 December.

Marxism Today Editorial Board 1976b, 'The Discussion on Socialist Democracy', *Discussion on Socialist Democracy*. MT Supplement.

Marxism Today Editorial Board 1977a, *Minutes*, 19 April.

Marxism Today Editorial Board 1977b, *Minutes*, 22 September.

Marxism Today Editorial Board 1977c, *Minutes*, 14 December.

Marxism Today Editorial Board 1978a, *Minutes*, 21 June.

Marxism Today Editorial Board 1978b, *Minutes*, 13 July.

Marxism Today Editorial Board 1978c, *Minutes*, 20 September.

Marxism Today Editorial Board 1979a, *Minutes*, 21 March.

Marxism Today Editorial Board 1979b, *Minutes*, 20 June.

Marxism Today Editorial Board 1980, *Minutes*, 18 June.

Marxism Today Editorial Board 1981a, *Minutes*, 18 February.

Marxism Today Editorial Board 1981b, *Minutes*, 17 December.

Marxism Today Editorial Board 1982a, *Minutes*, 6 June.

Marxism Today Editorial Board 1982b, *Minutes*, 20 October.

Marxism Today Editorial Board 1983, *Minutes*, 11 March.

Marxism Today Editorial Board 1985a, *Minutes*, 6 September.

Marxism Today Editorial Board 1985b, *Minutes*, 2 December.

Marxism Today Editorial Board 1986, *Minutes*, 19 July.

Marxism Today Editorial Board 1988a, *Minutes*, 23 July.

Marxism Today Editorial Board 1988b, *Minutes*, 22 October.

Marxism Today Editorial Board 1988c, *Minutes*, 23 January.

Marxism Today Editorial Board 1989a, *Minutes*, 4 February.

Marxism Today Editorial Board 1989b, *Minutes*, 28 April.

Marxism Today Editorial Board 1989c, *Minutes*, 14 October.

Marxism Today Editorial Board 1990, *Minutes*, 27 January.

Marxism Today Editorial Collective 1978, *Current Design Character*.

Marxism Today Editorial Collective 1981, *October Revamp Report*. MTEB, 7 June.

Marxism Today Editorial Collective 1983a, *Marxism Today Subscriptions, Documents 1–9*. Submitted to the Political Committee.

Marxism Today Editorial Collective 1983b, *Notes on 'Notes'*.

Marxism Today Editorial Collective 1984a, *Perspectives for Marxism Today*.

REFERENCES   483

Marxism Today Editorial Collective 1984b, *Addendum: Update to March 1984*, Document B.
Marxism Today Editorial Collective 1984c, *How Marxism Today is Organised*.MTEB.
Marxism Today Editorial Collective 1984d, *MT Accounts Outline*, July.
Marxism Today Editorial Collective 1985, *Marxism Today Colour Supplement, Congress Special*. Report for 39th Special Congress, 18–20 May.
Marxism Today Editorial Collective 1986a, *MT Accounts October 1984–September 1985*. Submitted to the Executive Committee, 10–11 May.
Marxism Today Editorial Collective 1986b, *Perspectives on Advertising*, June.
Marxism Today Editorial Collective 1986c, *Brief for Redesign*.
Marxism Today Editorial Collective nd [1984], 'How Marxism Today is Organised', 30 June.
Marxism Today Redesign Group 1986, *Minutes*, 3 April.
Matthews, Betty 1982, Letter to the Executive Committee, 9 September. CPGB. CPA.
Matthews, George 1982, Letter to Gordon McLennan and the Political Committee, 31 August. CPGB.
McLennan, Gordon nd [1979a] Memo to Jacques, re: Dave Priscott's article.
McLennan, Gordon nd [1979b] Memo to Jacques, about article on 'Devolution'.
McLennan, Gordon nd [1979c] Memo to Jacques, re: Paul Corrigan's article.
McLennan, Gordon 1985, 'Speech Introducing the Main Resolution to Congress', *39th Special Congress Report*. CPGB.
MORI 1990, *Marxism Today: Market Potential for a Left of Centre Magazine*. Report for MTEB.
Mullen, P. 1978, Letter to the Executive Committee, 23 November.
National Party Congress, 38th, CPGB 1983, 'Composite Motion on Marxism Today', *Communist Focus*, 14.
National Party Congress, 40th, CPGB 1987, 'Composite Motion on Marxism Today', *Congress Document*, 10.
National Party Congress, 41st, CPGB 1989, 'CP Marxism Today', *News and Views*, 52.
Olive, P. 1983, *Marxism Today: Towards 1984*. MTEC, 25 February.
Perkins, J. 1970, Letter to James Klugmann, 25 July.
Perryman, Mark 1998, Personal Letter to Nina Temple, London. 25 October.
Political Committee 1957, *Political Letter*, May,
Political Committee, CPGB 1973 *Minutes*, 30 May.
Political Committee, CPGB 1977, *Minutes*, 11 March.
Political Committee, CPGB 1984, *Minutes*, 2 May.
Political Committee, CPGB 1988, *Minutes*, 2 May.
Political Committee, CPGB 1991, *MT: CP Account 1991*.
Political Sub-Committee, CPGB 1984a, *Minutes*, 25 April.

Political Sub-Committee, CPGB 1984b, *Minutes*, 5 May.
Political Sub-Committee, CPGB 1986, *Minutes*, 10–11 May.
Priscott, Dave 1980, Letter to the Executive Committee.
Priscott, Dave 1985a, Letter to Martin Jacques for *Marxism Today* Editorial Board, 2 September.
Priscott, Dave 1985b, Personal Letter to Martin Jacques, 2 September.
Priscott, Dave 1986, Letter to Political Committee, 6 February.
Priscott, Dave 1988, Letter to the Executive Committee.
Ramelson, Bert 1987, Letter, *News and Views*, 2.
Rodriguez, J. 1988, Letter to the Executive Committee, 31 August.
Rowthorn, Bob 1982b, Letter to the Executive Committee, 9 September.
Seifert, Michael 1982, Letter to the Political Committee, 9 September.
Seifert, Michael 1983, Letter to Martin Jacques, 10 March.
Shackleton, Liz 1986, Letter to the Political Committee, 21 July.
South Essex District Communist Party 1977, *The British Road to Socialism: Ideas and Problems*, No. 1, Ilford: South Essex District CP. CP/CENT/EC/15/14.
Special Party Congress, 39th, CPGB, 1985, 'Composite 19: *Marxism Today*', Congress Document, 25, London: CPGB.
Steward, Fred 1990, 'Marxism Today in the 1990s', MTEB, 16 February.
Stewart, G. 1981, Letter to Martin Jacques, 29 June.
Street, Colin 1976, Letter to Executive Committee. CP/CENT/EC/15/08.
Summertown Research Consultants 1990, *Marxism Today Readership Survey*, *Marxism Today* Editorial Board.
Taylor, Jane 1989a, 'Rethinking the Front End of the Magazine', *Marxism Today* Editorial Board, 28 April.
Taylor, Jane 1989b, '*Marxism Today* "Reviews" Meeting', *Marxism Today* Editorial Collective, 10 June.
Temple, Nina 1984, *Public Work and Party Membership*, Executive Committee Report, CPGB.
Third World First 1986, 'Open Letter to "Left Unlimited"'. London.
Thompson, Willie 1984, Letter to the Executive Committee, 11 June.
Thompson, Willie 1987, Letter to Martin Jacques, 11 June.
Thorneycroft, Bill 1976, Letter to Executive Committee. CP/CENT/EC/15/08.
Townsend, Sally 1984, *Report on Channel Five*, MTEB, 11 May.
Turner, Julian 1988, Letter to Gordon McLennan, 22 December.
Webster, Paul nd, *Report on the 'Reviews' Section*. MTEB.
Woddis, Margaret 1982, Letter to Martin Jacques, 24 May.
Woddis, Margaret 1977, Letter to the Executive Committee, 1 March. CP/CENT/EC/15/14.

MA Theses and PhD Dissertations

Diamanti, F. 1992, *Communist and Labourist Paths to 'New Times'*. Unpublished PhD thesis, University of Edinburgh.

Hubert, P.J. 1988, *On Party and Propaganda in the Newspapers of the Left*, Unpublished PhD thesis, University of Leeds.

McCrea, Joel 1989, *New Socialist Under J. Curran and Stuart Weir*. Unpublished paper.

Secondary and Scholarly Bibliography

Ackers, Peter 1987, 'Must Try Harder', *Marxism Today*, 31(11): 9.

Ackers, Peter 2014, 'Gramsci at the Miners' Strike', *Labor History*, 55(2): 151–72.

Allen, Peter 1985, '*Socialist Worker*: Paper with a Purpose', *Media, Culture and Society*, 7(2): 205–32.

Althusser, Louis 1972a, 'Reply to John Lewis: Part I (Self-Criticism)', *Marxism Today*, 16(10): 310–17.

Althusser, Louis 1972b, 'Reply to John Lewis: Part II (Self-Criticism)', *Marxism Today*, 16(11): 343–8.

Anderson, Paul and Nina Mann 1997, *Safety First*, London: Granta Books.

Anderson, Perry 1976, 'The Antinomies of Antonio Gramsci', *New Left Review*, I/100 (November–December): 5–78.

Andrews, Geoff 1990, 'Universal Principles', *Marxism Today*, 34(8).

Andrews, Geoff 1995a, 'Young Turks and Old Guard: Intellectuals and the Communist Party Leadership in the 1970s', in *Opening the Books*, edited by Geoff Andrews, Nina Fishman and Kevin Morgan, London: Pluto.

Andrews, Geoff 1999, 'The Three New Lefts and Their Legacies', in *New Left, New Right and Beyond*, edited by Geoff Andrews, Richard Cockett, Alan Hooper and Michael Williams, Basingstoke: Macmillan.

Andrews, Geoff 2004, *Endgames and New Times*, London: Lawrence & Wishart.

Andrews, Geoff 2015, *Shadow Man*, London: I.B. Tauris.

Andrews, Geoff, Nina Fishman and Kevin Morgan (eds) 1995, *Opening the Books: Essays on the Social and Cultural History of the British Communist Party*, London: Pluto.

Anitha, Sundari and Ruth Pearson 2018, *Striking Women*, London: Lawrence and Wishart.

Armstrong, D. 1981, *A Trumpet to Arms*, Boston: South End Press.

Ascherson, Neal 1987, 'End of an Era', *Marxism Today*, 31(5).

Ash, William 1965, 'Rudyard Kipling Re-Estimated', *Marxism Today*, 9(10): 311–12.

Atton, Chris 1999, 'A Reassessment of the Alternative Press', *Media, Culture and Society*, 21: 51–76.

Atton, Chris 2002, *Alternative Media*, Thousand Oaks: Sage.

Atton, Chris and James F. Hamilton 2008, *Alternative Journalism*, London: Sage.

Aubrey, Crispin, Charles Landry and Dave Morley 1979, *Here Is The Other News: Challenges to the Local Commercial Press*, London: Minority Press Group, Series 1.

Aune, James Arnt 1994, *Rhetoric and Marxism*, Boulder: Westview Press.

Aune, James Arnt 2003, 'An Historical Materialist Theory of Rhetoric', *American Communication Journal*, 6(4) (online) http://acjournal.org/holdings/vol6/iss4/index.htm.

Baines, Jess 2015, 'Nurturing Dissent? Community Printshops in 1970s London', in *Civic Engagement and Social Media: Political Participation Beyond Protest*, edited by Julie Uldam and Anne Vestergaard, Basingstoke: Palgrave Macmillan.

Baker, Alan, George Bolton, Ken Capstick and Dave Priscott 1985, 'The Miners' Strike: A Balance Sheet [A Roundtable Discussion]', *Marxism Today*, 29(4): 21–7.

Baker, G. 1982, 'TV Times', *Marxism Today*, 26(5).

Baluyev, Boris 1983, *Lenin and the Bourgeois Press*, Moscow: Progress Publishers.

Bambery, Chris 1996, *The Case for the Socialist Newspaper*, London: SWP.

Barker, Martin 1992, 'Stuart Hall, *Policing the Crisis*', in *Reading Into Cultural Studies*, edited by Martin Barker and Anne Beezer, London: Routledge.

Barker, Martin and Anne Beezer 1992, 'Introduction', in *Reading Into Cultural Studies*, edited by Martin Barker and Anne Beezer, London: Routledge.

Barthes, Roland 1973 [1957], *Mythologies*. London: Palladin.

Barthes, Roland 1977, *Image – Music – Text*, London: Fontana Press.

Beauchamp, Kay 1967, 'Racialism in Britain Today and How to Fight it', *Marxism Today*, 11(7): 197–206.

Beckett, Francis 1995, *Enemy Within*, London: John Murray.

Beer, Francis A. and Robert A. Hariman 1996, 'Realism and Rhetoric in International Relations', in *Post-Realism: The Rhetorical Turn in International Relations*, edited by F.A. Beer and R.A. Hariman, East Lansing: Michigan State University Press.

Beetham, Margaret 1990, 'Towards a Theory of the Periodical as a Publishing Genre', in *Investigating Victorian Journalism*, edited by L. Brake, A. Jones and L. Madden, Basingstoke: Macmillan.

Benn, Tony 1982, 'Democracy and Marxism', *Marxism Today*, 26(5): 6–14.

Benn, Tony 1985, 'Who Dares Wins', *Marxism Today*, 29(1): 12–15.

Benn, Tony and Chris Mullin 1981, *Arguments for Democracy*, London: Jonathan Cape.

Bennett, Tony 1986, 'The Politics of "the Popular" and Popular Culture', in *Popular Culture and Social Relations*, edited by T. Bennett et al., Milton Keynes: Open University Press.

Benton, Sarah 1989, 'Decline of the Party', in *New Times*, edited by Stuart Hall and Martin Jacques, London: Lawrence & Wishart with *Marxism Today*.

Beresford, M. 1986, 'Labour Aid', *Marxism Today*, 30(8).

Bernays, Edward 2005 [1928], *Propaganda*, New York: Ig Press.

Berry, Dave, Liz Cooper and Charles Landry 1980, *Where is the Other News? The News Trade and the Radical Press*, London: Minority Press Group.

Billig, Michael and Kate MacMillan 2005, 'Metaphor, Idiom and Ideology: The Search for "No Smoking Guns" Across Time', *Discourse and Society*, 16(4): 459–80.

Birchall, Ian 1980/81, 'The Autonomy of Theory', *International Socialism*, 2, 10: 51–91.

Birchall, Ian 1985, 'Left Alive or Left for Dead?', *International Socialism*, 2, 30: 67–89.

Birchall, Ian 1987, 'Five Years of *New Socialist*', *International Socialism*, 2, 35: 116–28.

Black, John, Anne-Marie Greene and Peter Ackers 1999, 'Clinging to Collectivism? Some Ethnographic Shop-Floor Evidence from the British Lock Industry 1979–98', *International Journal of Human Resource Management*, 10(5): 941–57.

Blackburn, Robin, Eric Hobsbawm, Colin Lucas and Laura Mulvey 1990, 'Vive Le Revolution' [Roundtable discussion on the French Revolution chaired by Martin Kettle], *Marxism Today*, 33(7): 24–9.

Blackledge, Paul 2004, *Perry Anderson, Marxism and the New Left*, London: Merlin.

Blackledge, Paul 2009, 'The *Eighteenth Brumaire* and Thatcherism', in *Marx's 'Eighteenth Brumaire'*, edited by Mark Cowling and James Martin, London: Pluto.

Blair, Tony 1990, 'Back Page: Tony Blair', *Marxism Today*, 34(7): 48.

Blair, Tony 1991, 'Forging a New Agenda', *Marxism Today*, 35(10): 32–4.

Bleasdale, Alan 1982, *Boys from the Blackstuff*, London: Comedia.

Bloomfield, Jon (ed.) 1977, *Class, Hegemony and Party*, London: Lawrence & Wishart.

Bloomfield, Jon 1985b, 'A Reply to Alex Callinicos', *International Socialism*, Series 2, 30: 107–15.

Bloomfield, Jon (ed.) 1989, *The New Soviet Revolution*, London: Lawrence & Wishart with Marxism Today.

Bollinger, Stefan and Juha Koivisto 2009, 'Hegemonic Apparatus', *Historical Materialism*, 17: 301–8.

Bowers, John W., Donovan J. Ochs and Richard J. Jensen 1993, *The Rhetoric of Agitation and Control*, 2nd edition, Prospect Heights, IL: Waveland Press Inc.

Boyd, J. 1973, 'Trends in Youth Culture', *Marxism Today*, 17(12): 375–8.

Brake, Laurel, Aled Jones and L. Madden 1990, *Investigating Victorian Journalism*, Basingstoke: Macmillan.

Bridges, George 1969, 'British Youth in Revolt', *Marxism Today*, 13(8).

Bridges, George and Ros Brunt (eds) 1981, *Silver Linings*, London: Lawrence & Wishart.

Bright, L. 1977, 'Tribute to James Klugmann', *Marxism Today*, 21(11).

Brock, David 2005, *The Republican Noise Machine: Right-Wing Media and How It Corrupts Democracy*, New York: Three Rivers Press.

Brotherstone, Terry and Simon Pirani 2005, 'Were There Alternatives? Movements from Below in the Scottish Coalfields, the Communist Party, and Thatcherism, 1981–1985', *Critique*, 33(1): 99–123.

Brown, A. 1987, 'The Gorbachev Offensive', *Marxism Today*, 31(6).

Brownlee, Jamie 2005, *Ruling Canada: Corporate Cohesion and Democracy*, Halifax: Fernwood Books.
Bruff, Ian 2014, 'The Rise of Authoritarian Neoliberalism', *Rethinking Marxism*, 26(1): 113–29.
Brunsdon, Charlotte 1996, 'A Thief in the Night: Stories of Feminism in the 1970s at CCCS', in *Stuart Hall: Critical Dialogues in Cultural Studies*, edited by David Morley and Kuan-Hsing Chen, London: Routledge.
Brunt, Ros 1987a, 'Why Currie', *Marxism Today*, 31(5): 12.
Brunt, Ros 1987b, 'Thatcher Uses Her Woman's Touch', *Marxism Today*, 31(6): 22–24.
Brunt, Ros 1987c, 'The Left's Hallelujah Chorus', *Marxism Today*, 31(12): 32–35.
Brunt, Ros 1989, 'The Politics of Identity', in *New Times*, edited by Stuart Hall and Martin Jacques, London: Lawrence & Wishart with *Marxism Today*.
Burgchardt, Carl 1980, 'Two Faces of American Communism: Pamphlet Rhetoric of the Third Period and the Popular Front', *Quarterly Journal of Speech*, 66: 375–91.
Bush, Alan 1963, 'What Does Music Express?', *Marxism Today*, 7(7): 204–9.
Bush, Alan 1964, 'What Does Music Express? A Reply to Discussion', *Marxism Today*, 8(4): 121–3.
Callaghan, John 1988, 'The British Road to Eurocommunism', in *Communist Parties in Western Europe*, edited by M. Waller et al., Oxford: Blackwell.
Callaghan, John 1993a, 'Endgame: The Communist Party of Great Britain', in *Western European Communists and the Collapse of Communism*, edited by D. Bell, Oxford: Berg.
Callaghan, John 1993b, *Rajani Palme Dutt: A Study in British Stalinism*, London: Lawrence & Wishart.
Callaghan, John 2002, *Cold War, Crisis and Conflict: The CPGB 1951–1968*, London: Lawrence & Wishart.
Callaghan, John 2004, 'Industrial Militancy, 1945–79: The Failure of the British Road to Socialism?', *Twentieth Century British History*, 15(4): 388–409.
Callaghan, John 2005, 'The Plan to Capture the Labour Party and its Paradoxical Results, 1947–91', *Journal of Contemporary History*, 40(4): 707–25.
Callinicos, Alex 1985, 'The Politics of *Marxism Today*', *International Socialism*, Series 2, 29: 128–68.
Callinicos, Alex 2002, 'Tony Blair and the British Left', in *Critical Political Studies: Debates and Dialogues from the Left*, edited by Abigail B. Bakan and Eleanor MacDonald, Montreal: McGill-Queen's University Press.
Cameron, Deborah 1995, *Verbal Hygiene*, London: Routledge.
Campbell, Beatrix 1980, 'Flexing the Body Politic', *Comment*, 18(8).
Campbell, Beatrix 1984, *Wigan Pier Revisited: Poverty and Politics in the 80s*, London: Virago.
Campbell, Beatrix 1987, 'Charge of the Light Brigade', *Marxism Today*, 31(2): 11–16.

Campbell, Beatrix 1989, 'New Times Towns', in *New Times*, edited by Stuart Hall and Martin Jacques, London: Lawrence & Wishart with *Marxism Today*.

Campbell, Beatrix and Martin Jacques 1986, 'Goodbye to the GLC', *Marxism Today*, 30(4).

Campbell, Beatrix and Wendy Wheeler 1988, 'Filofaxions', *Marxism Today*, 32(12): 32–3.

Campbell, Beatrix, Eric Hobsbawm, John Lloyd and Mario Telo 1990, 'The End of the Affair' [Roundtable chaired by Martin Jacques], *Marxism Today*, 34(1): 40–5.

Carlin, Norah and Ian Birchall 1983, 'Kinnock's Favourite Marxist', *International Socialism*, Series 2, 21: 88–116.

Carritt, Bill 1965, 'The Freedom of Art?', *Marxism Today*, 9(12): 376–7.

Carritt, Bill 1970a, 'Why Did It Happen?', *Marxism Today*, 14(6): 191–2.

Carter, Pete 1977, 'Tribute to James Klugmann', *Marxism Today*, 21(11): 325.

Chairman, London Communist Print Group 1932, 'A Popular Workers' Newspaper', *The Communist Review*, 4(5): 245–50.

Chambers, Colin 1978, 'Socialist Theatre and the Ghetto Mentality', *Marxism Today*, 22(8): 245–50.

Charland, Maurice 1987, 'Constitutive Rhetoric: The Case of the Peuple Québécois', *Quarterly Journal of Speech*, 73: 133–50.

Charteris-Black, Jonathan 2011, *Politicians and Rhetoric: The Persuasive Power of Metaphor*, Basingstoke: Palgrave Macmillan.

Chater, Tony 1973, 'The Strategy of Peaceful Coexistence Today', *Marxism Today*, 17(8): 229–37.

Chignell, Hugh 2012, 'BBC Radio Four's *Analysis* and the Third Way', *Media, Culture and Society*, 34(4): 488–97.

Chippindale, Paul and Chris Horrie 1988, *Disaster! The Rise and Fall of the News on Sunday*, London: Sphere.

Chippindale, Paul and Chris Horrie 1992, *Stick It Up Your Punter! The Rise and Fall of the Sun*, London: Heinemann.

Chomsky, Noam and Edward S. Herman 1979, *The Political Economy of Human Rights*, 2 vols., Montreal: Black Rose Books.

Chun, Lin 1993, *The British New Left*, Edinburgh: Edinburgh University Press.

Clarke, John 1991, *New Times and Old Enemies: Essays on Cultural Studies and America*, London: HarperCollins Academic.

Clarke, John 2010, 'Of Crises and Conjunctures: The Problems of the Present', *Journal of Communication Inquiry*, 34(4): 337–54.

Cloud, Dana C. 2003, 'Beyond Evil: Understanding Power Materially and Rhetorically', *Rhetoric and Public Affairs*, 6: 531–8.

Cloud, Dana C. 2009, 'The Materialist Dialectic as a Site of *Kairos*: Theorizing Rhetorical Interventions in Material Social Relations', in *Rhetoric, Materiality, and Politics*, edited by Barbara Biesecker and John Lucaites, New York: Peter Lang.

Cockburn, Cynthia 1986, 'Sixteen: Sweet or Sorry?', *Marxism Today*, 30(12): 30–33.
Cockburn, Cynthia 1988, 'Macho Men of the Left', *Marxism Today*, 32(4): 18–23.
Cockcroft, R. and S.M. Cockcroft 1992, *Persuading People*, Basingstoke: Macmillan.
Cockett, Richard 1991, 'The New Right and the 1960s: The Dialectics of Liberation', in *New Left, New Right and Beyond: Taking the Sixties Seriously*, edited by Geoff Andrews, Richard Cockett, Alan Hooper and Michael Williams, Basingstoke: Macmillan.
Cohen, Jack 1977, 'Tribute to James Klugmann', *Marxism Today*, 21(11): 325.
Cohen, Jodi 1998, *Communication Criticism*, Thousand Oaks: Sage.
Cohen, Margaret 1967, 'Writing', *Marxism Today*, 11(7): 221.
Cohen, Phil and Carl Gardner (eds) 1982, *It Ain't Half Racist, Mum: Fighting Racism in the Media*, London: Comedia in association with Campaign Against Racism in Media.
Cohen, Sandi 1993, *Academia and the Luster of Capital*, Minneapolis: University of Minnesota Press.
Cohn-Bendit, Gabriel and Daniel Cohn-Bendit 1969 [1968], *Obsolete Communism: A Left-Wing Alternative*, Harmondsworth: Penguin Books.
Combustion 1984, *Miner Conflicts, Major Contradictions*, London: Combustion.
Comedia 1984, 'The Alternative Press', *Media, Culture & Society*, 6(2): 95–102.
Commission on Party Journals, Political Committee 1953, *Proposals for Party Journals*, London: CPGB.
Communist International 1921, 'Thesis on the Organization and Structure of the Communist Parties', in Mattetlart and Siegelaub (eds) 1979.
Communist International 1979 [1921], Part VI, 'On the Party Press', in *Thesis on the Organisation and Structure of Communist Parties*, Red Ink.
Communist Party of Great Britain 1957a, 'Statement', *Marxist Quarterly*, 4(1): 1–2.
Communist Party of Great Britain 1974, *Class Structure*, London: *Marxism Today*.
Commission on Inner Party Democracy 1957, *Report on Inner Party Democracy*, London: CPGB.
Commission on Inner Party Democracy 1979, *Report on Inner Party Democracy*, London: CPGB.
Connell, Ian 1983, 'Commercial Broadcasting and the British Left', *Screen*, 24, 6.
Connell, Kieran and Matthew Hilton 2015, 'The Working Practices of Birmingham's Centre for Contemporary Cultural Studies', *Social History*, 40, 3: 287–311.
Cook, Dave 1978a, *A Knife at the Throat of Us All*, London: CPGB.
Cook, Dave 1978b, 'The British Road to Socialism and the Communist Party', *Marxism Today*, 22(12): 370–9.
Cook, Dave 1981, '"Rocky Road Blues": The Communist Party and the Broad Democratic Alliance', in *Silver Linings*, edited by G. Bridges and R. Brunt, London: Lawrence & Wishart.

Cook, Dave 1985, 'No Private Drama', *Marxism Today*, 29(2): 25–29.
Cooper, Liz, Charles Landry and Dave Berry 1980, *The Other Secret Service: Press Distribution and Press Censorship*, London: Minority Press Group.
Cope, Dave 1999, *Central Books: A Brief History*, London: Central Books.
Cope, Dave 2016, *Communist Party: A Bibliography*, London: Lawrence & Wishart.
Cornelius, J. 1974, 'Trends in Youth Culture', *Marxism Today*, 18(9): 281–3.
Corrigan, Paul 1979a, 'The Local State: The Struggle for Democracy', *Marxism Today*, 23(7): 203–9.
Corrigan, Paul 1979b, 'Popular Consciousness and Social Democracy', *Marxism Today*, 23(12): 14–17.
Costello, Mick 1979, 'The Working Class and the Broad Democratic Alliance', *Marxism Today*, 23(6): 172–80.
Costin, M. 1974, 'Trends in Youth Culture', *Marxism Today*, 18(12).
Coulter, P. 1986, 'By-passing the Left', *Marxism Today*, 30(9): 46.
Coussins, Jean 1980, 'Equality for Women: Have the Laws Worked?', *Marxism Today*, 24(1): 6–11.
Crewe, Ivor 1988a, 'Has the Electorate Become Thatcherite?', in *Thatcherism*, edited by Robert Skidelsky, London: Chatto & Windus.
Crewe, Ivor 1988b, 'Ideological Change in the British Conservative Party', *American Political Science Review*, 82(2): 361–84.
Croft, Andy 1995, 'Authors Take Sides: Writers and the Communist Party, 1920–56', in *Opening the Books*, edited by Geoff Andrews, Nina Fishman and Kevin Morgan, London: Pluto.
Croft, Andy (ed.) 1998, *A Weapon in the Struggle: The Cultural History of the Communist Party in Britain*, London: Pluto.
Crowley, David 2003, *Magazine Covers*, London: Mitchell Beazley/Octopus Publishing Group.
Cuevas-Wolf, Cristina 2009, 'Montage as Weapon: The Tactical Alliance between Willi Münzenberg and John Heartfield', *New German Critique*, 107: 185–205.
Curran, James 1977, 'Capitalism and Control of the Press 1800–1975', in *Mass Communication and Society*, edited by James Curran et al., London: Edward Arnold.
Curran, James 1984a, 'Reconstructing the Mass Media', in *The Future of the Left*, edited by James Curran, Cambridge: Polity Press and *New Socialist*.
Curran, James (ed.) 1984b, *The Future of the Left*, Cambridge: Polity Press and *New Socialist*.
Curran, James 1985, 'Rationale for the Right', *Marxism Today*, 29(2): 40–1.
Curran, James 1987, 'The Boomerang Effect: The Press and the Battle for London 1981–6', in *Impacts and Influences*, edited by James Curran et al., London: Methuen.
Curran, James, Ivor Gabor and Julian Petley 2005, *Culture Wars: The Media and the British Left*, Edinburgh: Edinburgh University Press.

Curran, James and M. Gurevitch (eds) 1991, *Mass Media and Society*, London: Edward Arnold.

Curran, James and Jean Seaton 1991, *Power Without Responsibility*, London: Routledge. Fourth edition.

Cutler, A., B. Hindess, P. Hirst and A. Hussain 1978, 'Marxist Theory and Socialist Politics', *Marxism Today*, 22(11): 358–62.

Davidson, Alastair 2008, 'The Uses and Abuses of Gramsci', *Thesis Eleven*, 95: 68–94.

Davies, Aeron 2000, 'Public-Relations Campaigning and News Production: The Case of "New Unionism" in Britain', in *Media Organisations in Society*, edited by James Curran, London: Edward Arnold.

Davies, Ioan 1995, *Fragments of Empire: Cultural Studies and Beyond*, London: Routledge.

Davis, A. 1988, *Magazine Journalism Today*, Oxford: Heinemann.

Davis, Tricia 1981, 'Stand by Your Men? Feminism and Socialism in the Eighties', in *Silver Linings*, edited by G. Bridges and R. Brunt, London: Lawrence & Wishart.

Davis, Tricia 1983, 'Feminism is Dead? Long Live Feminism', *Marxism Today*, 27(10): 14–18.

Davis, Tricia 1985, 'Retreating from Reality: A Review of *Class Politics*', *Marxism Today*, 29(1): 36–7.

Davison, Sally 1985a, 'An English Dissenter: A Review of *The Heavy Dancers*', *Marxism Today*, 29(4): 47–8.

del Valle Alcala, Roberto 2010, 'Towards Cultural Materialism: Criticism and Hegemony in Raymond Williams', *Estudios Ingleses de la Universidad Complutense*, 18: 67–76.

Debray, Regis 2007, 'Socialism: A Life Cycle', *New Left Review*, II, 46: 5–28.

Desai, Radhika 1994, 'Second-hand Dealers in Ideas: Think-tanks and Thatcherite Hegemony', *New Left Review*, I/203: 27–64.

Devine, Pat 1974, 'Inflation and Marxist Theory', *Marxism Today*, 18(3): 79–92.

Devine, Pat 1980, 'The Labour Party: Why the Decline?', *Marxism Today*, 24(1): 12–16.

Dickinson, Robert 1997, *Imprinting the Sticks: The Alternative Press Beyond London*, Aldershot: Arena/Ashgate Publishing.

Downing, John 1980, *The Media Machine*, London: Pluto.

Downing, John 1984, *Radical Media*, Boston: South End Press.

Downing, John 1988, 'The Alternative Public Realm', *Media, Culture & Society*, 10(2): 163–81.

Downing, John 2001, *Radical Media*, Thousand Oaks: Sage.

Driver, Stephen and Andrew Gillespie 1993, 'Structural Change in the Cultural Industries: British Magazine Publishing in the 1980s', *Media, Culture and Society*, 15: 183–201.

Duncombe, Stephen 1997, *Notes from Underground*, New York: Verso.
Dunman, Jack 1965, 'Rudyard Kipling Re-Estimated', *Marxism Today*, 9(8): 242–8.
Dunn, Robert 1991, 'Postmodernism: Populism, Mass Culture, and Avant-Garde', *Theory, Culture & Society*, 8: 111–35.
Dworkin, Dennis 1997, *Cultural Marxism in Postwar Britain*, Durham, NC: Duke University Press.
Dyer, Richard 1985, 'A Passage to India', *Marxism Today*, 29(4): 42–44.
Eagleton, Terry 1984, *The Function of Criticism*, London: Verso.
Easthope, Anthony 1988, *British Post-Structuralism Since 1968*, London: Routledge.
Edgar, David 1985, 'Why Aid Came Alive', *Marxism Today*, 29(9): 26–30.
Edgar, David 1986, 'Never Too Old: Learning from the Sixties', *New Socialist*, 38: 16–20.
Edgar, David 1987a, 'The New Nostalgia', *Marxism Today*, 31(3): 30–5.
Edgar, David 1987b, 'The Morals Dilemma', *Marxism Today*, 31(10): 20–5.
Edgar, David 1988, 'When the Hardline is Right', *Marxism Today*, 32(2): 30–1.
Edgar, David 1991, 'The Final Deadline', *Marxism Today*, 35(12): 35.
Egan, Daniel 2006, 'Bureaucracy and Radical Politics: The Case of the Greater London Council', *New Political Science*, 28(3): 377–400.
Egelnick, Max 1964, 'Non-Manual Workers in the Sixties', *Marxism Today*, 8(8): 239–46.
Ehrenreich, Barbara and John Ehrenreich 1977, 'The Professional-Managerial Class', *Radical America*, 11(2): 7–31.
Ehrenreich, Barbara and John Ehrenreich 2013, *'Death of the Yuppie Dream': The Rise and Fall of the Professional-Managerial Class*, New York: Rosa Luxemburg Stiftung.
Elms, Robert 1986, 'Ditching the Drabbies', *New Socialist*, 38.
Enzensberger, Hans Magnus 1976, 'Constituents of a Theory of the Media', in *Raids and Reconstructions*, London: Pluto.
Evans, Harold 1972, *Newsman's English*, London: Heinemann.
Ewen, Stuart 1995, *Spin!*, New York: Basic Books.
Executive Committee, CPGB 1967, 'Questions of Ideology and Culture', *Marxism Today*, 11(5): 134–8.
Fauvet, Paul 1974, 'Trends in Youth Culture', *Marxism Today*, 18, 3: 93–4.
Ffrench, Patrick 1995, *The Time of Theory*, Oxford: Clarendon.
Filippini, Michele 2017, *Using Gramsci: A New Approach*, London: Pluto.
Filling, Brian 1974, 'Trends in Youth Culture', *Marxism Today*, 18(9): 283–6.
Fine, Ben 1985, 'Class Politics', *Marxism Today*, 29(3): 44.
Fine, Ben, Laurence Harris, Marjorie Mayo, Angela Weir and Elizabeth Wilson 1984, *Class Politics: An Answer to Its Critics*. London: Leftover Pamphlets.
Fišera, Vladimir (ed.) 1978, *Writing on the Wall*, London: Allison and Busby.
Fischer, Ernst 1964, 'Art and Ideological Superstructure', *Marxism Today*, 8(2): 46.
Fishman, Nina 1994, 'The British Road is Resurfaced for New Times', in *Western Euro-*

pean Communist Parties After the Revolutions of 1989, edited by Martin Bull and Paul Heywood, London: St. Martin's Press.

Fishman, Nina 1995, 'No Home but the Trade Union Movement', in Opening the Books, edited by Geoff Andrews, Nina Fishman and Kevin Morgan, London: Pluto.

Fogarasi, Adalbert 1979 [1921], 'The Tasks of the Communist Press', in Communication and Class Struggle: Volume 1, edited by Armand Mattelart and Seth Siegelaub, New York: IMMRC/International General.

Forgacs, David 1984, 'The National-Popular', in Formations of Nation and People, edited by Tony Bennett, London: Routledge and Kegan Paul.

Forgacs, David 1989, 'Gramsci and Marxism in Britain', New Left Review, I/176.

Fountain, Nigel 1988, Underground: London's Alternative Press, 1965–1974, London: Routledge.

Francis, Hywel 1985, 'Mining the Popular Front', Marxism Today, 29(2): 12–15.

Frith, Simon 1981, 'John Lennon', Marxism Today, 25(1): 23–5.

Frith, Simon and John Street 1992, 'Rock Against Racism and Red Wedge', in Rockin' the Boat, edited by R. Garofalo, Boston: South End Press.

Frosini, Fabio 2005, 'Beyond the Crisis of Marxism: Gramsci's Contested Legacy', in Critical Companion to Contemporary Marxism, edited by Jacques Bidet and Stathis Kouvelakis, Leiden: Brill.

Fuchs, Christian 2016, 'Neoliberalism in Britain: From Thatcherism to Cameronism', tripleC, 14(1): 163–88.

Fulkerson, Richard 1993, 'Newsweek "My Turn" Columns and the Concept of Rhetorical Genre', in Defining the New Rhetorics, edited by T. Enos and S. Brown, Newbury Park, CA: Sage.

Galeotti, M. 1997, Gorbachev and His Revolution, Basingstoke: Macmillan.

Gallas, Alexander 2015, The Thatcherite Offensive, Leiden: Brill.

Gamble, Andrew 1985, 'Smash the State: Thatcher's Radical Crusade', Marxism Today, 29(6): 21–6.

Gamble, Andrew 1987a, 'Crawling from the Wreckage', Marxism Today, 31(7): 12–17.

Gamble, Andrew 1987b 'Class Politics and Radical Democracy', New Left Review, I/164: 113–22.

Gardner, Carl (ed.) 1979, Media, Politics and Culture: A Socialist View, Basingstoke: Macmillan.

Garnham, Nicholas 1983, 'Public Service versus the Market', Screen, 24(1).

Garnham, Nicholas 1995, 'The Media and Narratives of the Intellectual', Media, Culture & Society, 17(3): 359–84.

Gaunt, P. 1992, 'Distributing the News', Media, Culture & Society, 14(1): 89–109.

George, David 2013, The Rhetoric of the Right: Language Change and the Spread of the Market, Abingdon: Routledge.

Gill, Ken 1978, 'The Forward March of Labour Halted?', Marxism Today, 22(12): 395–6.

Gitlin, Todd 1991, 'The Politics of Communication and the Communication of Politics', in Curran and Gurevitch (eds) 1991.

Gitlin, Todd 1997, 'The Anti-Political Populism of Cultural Studies', in Ferguson and Golding (eds) 1997.

Glasgow University Media Group 1976, *Bad News*, London: Routledge and Kegan Paul.

Glasgow University Media Group 1978, *More Bad News*, London: Routledge and Kegan Paul.

Glasgow University Media Group 1982, *Really Bad News*, London: Writers and Readers.

Gloversmith, Frank (ed.) 1980, *Class, Culture and Social Change: A New View of the 1930s*, Brighton: The Harvester Press.

Gollan, John 1976, 'Socialist Democracy: Some Problems', *Marxism Today*, 20(1).

Goodyer, Ian 2009, *Crisis Music: The Cultural Politics of Rock Against Racism*, Manchester: Manchester University Press.

Gouldner, Alvin 1979, *The Future of Intellectuals and the Rise of the New Class*, Basingstoke: Macmillan.

Grace, Tony 1985, 'The Trade-Union Press in Britain', *Media, Culture & Society*, 7(2): 233–55.

Gramsci, Antonio 1971, *Selections from the Prison Notebooks*, London: Lawrence & Wishart.

Gramsci, Antonio 1981, Extracts from *Selections from the Prison Notebooks of Antonio Gramsci*, in *Culture, Ideology and Social Process: A Reader*, edited by Tony Bennett et al., London: Batsford Academic and Educational Ltd. with Open University Press, pp. 191–218.

Gramsci, Antonio 1985, *Selections from Cultural Writings*, edited by David Forgacs and Geoffrey Nowell-Smith, translated by William Boelhower, London: Lawrence & Wishart.

Gramsci, Antonio 2007 [1957], 'The Organisation of Education and Culture', in *The Modern Prince and Other Writings*, translated and comments by Louis Marks, New York and London: International Publishers and Lawrence & Wishart.

Grant, Dave 1982, 'Notes: *Marxism Today*', *Marxism Today*, 26(1): 39.

Gray, Robert 1982, 'Falklands Fallout', *Marxism Today*, 26(7): 8–12.

Greater London Council, Community Arts Subcommittee, 1986, *Campaign for a Popular Culture: A Record of Struggle and Achievement: The GLC's Community Arts Programme 1981–86*, London: GLC.

Greaves, Nigel 2011, 'Resisting Abstraction: Gramsci's Historiological Method', *International Gramsci Journal*, 3: 37–56.

Green, David 1978, 'Review: What Does Red Bologna Mean for Britain?', *Marxism Today*, 22(6): 195–8.

Green, John 1973, 'The Function of Film in the Working Class Struggle', *Marxism Today*, 17(2): 54–6.

Green, Marcus E. and Peter Ives 2009, 'Subalternity and Language: Overcoming the Fragmentation of Common Sense', *Historical Materialism*, 17: 3–30.
Griffith, J. 1982, 'The Law Lords and the GLC', *Marxism Today*, 26(2): 29–31.
Griffith-Hentges, P. 1962, 'Week of Marxist Thought', *Marxism Today*, 6(6).
Guinan, Joe 2015, 'Ownership and Control: Bring Back the Institute for Workers' Control', *Renewal*, 23(4): 11–36.
Gunning, R. 1968, 'The FOG Index After Twenty Years', *Journal of Business Communication*, 6: 3–13.
Gutstein, Donald 2009, *Not a Conspiracy Theory: How Business Hijacks Democracy*, Toronto: Key Porter Books.
Hackett, Robert A. and Yuezhi Zhao 1998, *Sustaining Democracy? Journalism and the Politics of Objectivity*, Toronto: Garamond Press.
Hadjifotiou, N. 1984, 'Anna Coote's Challenge', *Marxism Today*, 28(3): 46.
Hain, Peter (ed.) 1980, *The Crisis and the Future of the Left: The Debate of the Decade*, London: Pluto Press.
Hain, Peter 1987a, 'Popular Socialism', *Marxism Today*, 31(8): 9.
Hain, Peter 1987b, 'Soft-Left Sectarians', *Marxism Today*, 31(10): 53.
Hall, Stuart 1958, 'A Sense of Classlessness', *Universities and Left Review*, 1(5).
Hall, Stuart 1960, 'The Supply of Demand', in *Out of Apathy*, edited by E.P. Thompson, London: New Left Books/Stevens and Sons.
Hall, Stuart 1973, 'The Determination of News Photographs', in *The Manufacture of News*, edited by S. Cohen and J. Young, London: Constable.
Hall, Stuart 1977, 'Culture, the Media and the "Ideological Effect"', in *Mass Communication and Society*, edited by J. Curran, M. Gurevitch and J. Woollacott, London: Edward Arnold.
Hall, Stuart 1978, 'Newspapers, Parties and Classes', in *The British Press: A Manifesto*, edited by James Curran, Basingstoke: The Macmillan Press
Hall, Stuart 1979, 'The Great Moving Right Show', *Marxism Today*, 23(1): 14–20.
Hall, Stuart 1980a, 'Thatcherism: A New Stage?', *Marxism Today*, 24(2): 26–8.
Hall, Stuart 1980b, 'Encoding/Decoding', in *Culture, Media, Language*, edited by S. Hall, D. Hobson, A. Lower and P. Willis, London: Hutchinson Education.
Hall, Stuart 1980c, 'Cultural Studies: Two Paradigms', *Media, Culture & Society*, 2: 57–72.
Hall, Stuart 1981a, 'Notes on Deconstructing the Popular', in *People's History and Socialist Theory*, edited by R. Samuel, London: Routledge and Kegan Paul.
Hall, Stuart 1981b, 'The "Little Caesars" of Social Democracy', *Marxism Today*, 25(4): 11–15.
Hall, Stuart 1981c, 'Summer in the City', *New Socialist*, 1: 4–7.
Hall, Stuart 1981d, '"The Whites of Their Eyes": Racist Ideologies and the Media', in *Silver Linings*, edited by G. Bridges and R. Brunt, London: Lawrence & Wishart.

Hall, Stuart 1982a, 'The Battle for Socialist Ideas in the 1980s', in *The Socialist Register*, edited by M. Eve and D. Musson, London: Merlin.

Hall, Stuart 1982b, 'A Long Haul', *Marxism Today*, 26(11): 16–21.

Hall, Stuart 1983a, 'The Great Moving Right Show', in *The Politics of Thatcherism*, edited by S. Hall and M. Jacques, London: Lawrence & Wishart with *Marxism Today*.

Hall, Stuart 1983b, 'Whistling in the Void', *New Socialist*, 11: 8–12.

Hall, Stuart 1984a, 'The Culture Gap', *Marxism Today*, 28(1): 18–22.

Hall, Stuart 1984b, 'The State: Socialism's Old Caretaker', *Marxism Today*, 28(11): 24–9.

Hall, Stuart 1984c, 'Face the Future', *New Socialist*, 18: 37.

Hall, Stuart 1985a, 'Faith, Hope or Clarity', *Marxism Today*, 29(1): 15–19.

Hall, Stuart 1985b, 'Realignment for What?', *Marxism Today*, 29(12): 12–17.

Hall, Stuart 1985c, 'Authoritarian Populism: A Reply to Jessop et al.', *New Left Review*, I/151: 115–24.

Hall, Stuart 1986a, 'No Light at the End of the Tunnel', *Marxism Today*, 30(12): 12–16.

Hall, Stuart 1986b, 'Media Power and Class Power', in *Bending Reality: The State of the Media*, edited by J. Curran et al., London: Pluto.

Hall, Stuart 1986c, 'The Problem of Ideology: Marxism Without Guarantees', *Journal of Communication Inquiry*, 10(2): 28–43.

Hall, Stuart 1987a, 'Gramsci and Us', *Marxism Today*, 31(6): 16–21.

Hall, Stuart 1987b, 'Blue Election, Election Blues', *Marxism Today*, 31(7): 30–5.

Hall, Stuart 1987c, 'In Praise of the Peculiar', 'Gramsci Supplement' (April), *Marxism Today*, 31(4): vi–vii.

Hall, Stuart 1988a, *The Hard Road to Renewal*, London: Verso with *Marxism Today*.

Hall, Stuart 1988b, 'The Toad in the Garden: Thatcherism Among the Theorists', in *Marxism and the Interpretation of Culture*, edited by C. Nelson and L. Grossberg, Basingstoke: Macmillan Education.

Hall, Stuart 1988c, 'Thatcher's Lessons', *Marxism Today*, 32(3): 20–7.

Hall, Stuart 1988d, 'Brave New World', *Marxism Today*, 32(10): 24–9.

Hall, Stuart 1989a, 'The Meaning of "New Times"', in *New Times*, edited by Stuart Hall and Martin Jacques, London: Lawrence & Wishart with *Marxism Today*. [Originally published as Hall 1988d.]

Hall, Stuart 1989b, 'Politics and Letters', in *Raymond Williams*, edited by Terry Eagleton, Cambridge: Polity.

Hall, Stuart 1989c, 'The "First" New Left: Life and Times', in Oxford University Socialist Discussion Group (1989).

Hall, Stuart 1990, 'Coming Up For Air', *Marxism Today*, 33(3): 22–5.

Hall, Stuart 1991a, 'Chopping Logic: Jameson's Postmodernism or the Cultural Logic of Late Capitalism', *Marxism Today: Review of Books* (supplement): 35.

Hall, Stuart 1991b, 'Europe's Other Self', *Marxism Today*, 35(8): 18–19.

Hall, Stuart 1991c, 'And Not a Shot Fired', *Marxism Today*, 35(12): 10–15.

Hall, Stuart 1991d, 'Introductory Essay: Reading Gramsci', in *Gramsci's Political Thought: An Introduction*, by Roger Simon, London: Lawrence & Wishart.

Hall, Stuart 1992, 'Cultural Studies and its Theoretical Legacies', in *Cultural Studies*, edited by Lawrence Grossberg, Cary Nelson and Paula Treichler, New York and London: Routledge.

Hall, Stuart 1994, 'Some "Politically Incorrect" Pathways Through PC', in *The War of the Words*, edited by S. Dunant, London: Virago.

Hall, Stuart 1998, 'Great Moving Centre Show', *Marxism Today*, Special 'Comeback' Double Issue, October–November: 9–14.

Hall, Stuart and Les Back 2009, 'At Home and Not at Home', *Cultural Studies*, 23(4): 658–87.

Hall, Stuart, Chas Critchley, Tony Jefferson, John Clarke and Brian Roberts 1978, *Policing the Crisis: 'Mugging', the State and Law and Order*, London: Hutchinson.

Hall, Stuart and David Held 1989a, 'Left and Rights', *Marxism Today*, 33(6): 16–23.

Hall, Stuart and David Held 1989b, 'Citizens and Citizenship', in *New Times*, edited by Stuart Hall and Martin Jacques, London: Lawrence & Wishart with *Marxism Today*. [Originally published in *Marxism Today*: Hall and Held 1989a.]

Hall, Stuart and Martin Jacques 1983a, 'Introduction', in *The Politics of Thatcherism*, edited by S. Hall and M. Jacques, London: Lawrence & Wishart with *Marxism Today*.

Hall, Stuart and Martin Jacques (eds.) 1983b, *The Politics of Thatcherism*, London: Lawrence & Wishart with *Marxism Today*.

Hall, Stuart and Martin Jacques 1986, 'People Aid: A New Politics Sweeps the Land', *Marxism Today*, 30(7): 10–14.

Hall, Stuart and Martin Jacques 1988, '1968', *Marxism Today*, 32(5): 10–14.

Hall, Stuart and Martin Jacques 1989a, 'Introduction', in Hall and Jacques (eds) 1989b.

Hall, Stuart and Martin Jacques (eds) 1989b, *New Times*, London: Lawrence & Wishart with *Marxism Today*.

Hall, Stuart and Martin Jacques 1990, 'March Without Vision', *Marxism Today*, 34(12): 26–31.

Hall, Stuart, Doreen Massey and Mike Rustin 1995, 'Uncomfortable Times', *Soundings*, 1.

Hall, Stuart and Alan O'Shea 2013, 'Common Sense and Neoliberalism', *Soundings*, 54: 9–24.

Hall, Stuart and Paddy Whannel 1964, *The Popular Arts*, London: Hutchinson Educational.

Halpin, K. 1979, 'The Forward March of Labour Halted?', *Marxism Today*, 23(2): 63–64.

Ham, C. 1989 'Clarke's Strong Medicine', *Marxism Today*, 33(3): 38–41.

Hariman, Robert A. 1996, 'Henry Kissinger: Realism's Rational Actor', in *Post-Realism: The Rhetorical Turn in International Relations*, edited by F.A. Beer and R.A. Hariman, East Lansing: Michigan State University Press.

Harker, Ben nd [2019], *The Chronology of Revolution: Communism, Culture and Civil Society in Twentieth-Century Britain* [draft manuscript], Toronto: University of Toronto Press.

Harman, Chris 1977a, 'Gramsci *versus* Eurocommunism' (Part 1), *International Socialism*, 1(98): 23–26.

Harman, Chris 1977b, 'Gramsci *versus* Eurocommunism' (Part 2), *International Socialism*, 1(99): 10–14.

Harman, Chris 1984, 'The Revolutionary Press', *International Socialism*, 2(24): 3–44.

Harman, Chris 2007, 'Gramsci, the Prison Notebooks and Philosophy', *International Socialism*, 114: 105–23.

Harris, David 1992, *From Class Struggle to the Politics of Pleasure: The Effects of Gramscianization of Cultural Studies*, London: Routledge.

Harrison, Royden 1979, 'The Forward March of Labour Halted?', *Marxism Today*, 23(6): 188–91.

Harvey, David 2005, *A Brief History of Neoliberalism*, London: Oxford University Press.

Hawthorn, J. 1973, 'The Communist Party and Developments in British Culture', *Marxism Today*, 17(12).

Hay, Colin 1996, 'Narrating Crisis: The Discursive Construction of the "Winter of Discontent"', *Sociology*, 30(2): 253–77.

Hay, Colin 2010, 'Chronicles of a Death Foretold: The "Winter of Discontent" and the Construction of the Crisis of British Keynesianism', *Parliamentary Affairs*, 63(3): 446–70.

Hay, James 2011, '"Popular Culture" in a Critique of the New Political Reason', *Cultural Studies*, 25(4–5): 659–84.

Haynes, Richard 1995, *The Football Imagination: The Rise of Football Fanzine Culture*, Aldershot: Arena.

Hayter, Dianne 2005, *Fightback! Labour's Traditional Right in the 1970s and 1980s*, Manchester: Manchester University Press.

Heath, Edward 1988, '"No, Prime Minister": Edward Heath Interviewed by Hugo Young', *Marxism Today*, 32(11): 16–23.

Heinemann, Margot 1977, 'Tribute to James Klugmann', *Marxism Today*, 21(11): 321–2.

Hennesey, Brendan 1997, *Writing Feature Articles*, Oxford: Focal Press.

Hibbin, Sally (ed.) 1978, *Politics, Ideology and the State*, London: Lawrence & Wishart.

Higgins, John 1999, *Raymond Williams: Literature, Marxism and Cultural Materialism*, London: Routledge.

Hill, Albert 1965, 'Rudyard Kipling Re-Estimated', *Marxism Today*, 9(10): 312.

Hinton, James 1985 'The Case for the Defence', *Marxism Today*, 29(4): 15–18.

Hipkin, Brian 1984, 'Writing on the Wall for the GLC', *Marxism Today*, 28(8): 34–8.

Hirst, Paul 1989, 'After Henry', in *New Times*, edited by Stuart Hall and Martin Jacques, London: Lawrence & Wishart with *Marxism Today*.

Hobsbawm, Eric 1957, 'The Future of Marxism in the Social Sciences', *Universities and Left Review*, 1: 27–30.

Hobsbawm, Eric 1978, 'The Forward March of Labour Halted?', *Marxism Today*, 22(9): 279–86.

Hobsbawm, Eric 1979a, 'Intellectuals and Labour Movement', *Marxism Today*, 23(7): 212–20.

Hobsbawm, Eric 1979b, 'The Forward March of Labour Halted? A Response', *Marxism Today*, 23(9): 265–68.

Hobsbawm, Eric 1980, 'Eric Hobsbawm Interviews Tony Benn', *Marxism Today*, 24(10): 5–13.

Hobsbawm, Eric 1981, 'Observations on the Debate', in *The Forward March of Labour Halted?*, edited by Martin Jacques and Francis Mulhern, London: NLB/Verso with *Marxism Today*.

Hobsbawm, Eric 1982, 'The State of the Left in Western Europe', *Marxism Today*, 26(10): 8–15.

Hobsbawm, Eric 1983a, 'Falklands Fallout', *Marxism Today*, 27(1): 13–19.

Hobsbawm, Eric 1983b, 'Labour's Lost Millions', *Marxism Today*, 27(10): 9–13.

Hobsbawm, Eric 1984a, 'Labour: Rump or Rebirth', *Marxism Today*, 28(3): 7–11.

Hobsbawm, Eric 1984b, 'The Face of Labour's Future: Eric Hobsbawm Interviews Neil Kinnock', *Marxism Today*, 28(10): 8–15.

Hobsbawm, Eric 1985, 'The Retreat into Extremism', *Marxism Today*, 29(4): 7–12.

Hobsbawm, Eric 1986a, 'Past Imperfect, Future Tense', *Marxism Today*, 30(10): 12–19.

Hobsbawm, Eric 1986b, '1956: Eric Hobsbawm interview by Gareth Stedman Jones', *Marxism Today*, 30(11): 16–23.

Hobsbawm, Eric 1987a, 'Snatching Victory from Defeat', *Marxism Today*, 31(5): 14–17.

Hobsbawm, Eric 1987b, 'Ostpolitik Reborn: Eric Hobsbawm interviews Peter Glotz', *Marxism Today*, 31(8): 12–19.

Hobsbawm, Eric 1987c, 'Out of the Wilderness', *Marxism Today*, 31(10): 12–19.

Hobsbawm, Eric 1987d, 'Master of Arts [Obituary of Arnold Kettle]', *Marxism Today*, 31(2): 29.

Hobsbawm, Eric 1988a, 'No Sense of Mission: Rethinking Labour', *Marxism Today*, 32(4): 14–17.

Hobsbawm, Eric 1988b, 'Bush by Default', *Marxism Today*, 32(12): 18–19.

Hobsbawm, Eric 1989a, 'A Miller's Tale: Arthur Miller Interview', *Marxism Today*, 33(1): 40–3.

Hobsbawm, Eric 1989b, 'Another Forward March Halted', *Marxism Today*, 33(10): 14–19.

Hobsbawm, Eric 1989c, *The Politics of a Rational Left*, London: Verso.

Hobsbawm, Eric 1990a, 'Splitting Image: Eric Hobsbawm interviews Achille Occhetto', *Marxism Today*, 34(2): 14–19.

Hobsbawm, Eric 1990b, 'State of the Nations', *Marxism Today*, 34(6): 30–5.

Hobsbawm, Eric 1990c, 'Goodbye to All That: New World Order', *Marxism Today*, 34(10): 18–23.

Hobsbawm, Eric 1991a, 'Leader: The Follies of War', *Marxism Today*, 35(3): 4–5.

Hobsbawm, Eric 1991b, 'Out of the Ashes', *Marxism Today*, 35(4): 18–23.

Hobsbawm, Eric 1991c, 'Leader: The Centre Cannot Hold', *Marxism Today*, 35(9): 2–4.

Hobsbawm, Eric 1991d, 'We've Got Problems Too', *Marxism Today*, 35(12): 16–19.

Hobsbawm, Eric 1995, 'Afterword', in *Opening the Books*, edited by Geoff Andrews, Nina Fishman and Kevin Morgan, London: Pluto.

Hobsbawm, Eric 2002, *Interesting Times: A Twentieth-Century Life*, New York: Pantheon Books.

Hobsbawm, Eric, Ralph Miliband, Bob Rowthorn, and Anne Showstack Sassoon 1983, 'Karl Marx: 100 Not Out [Roundtable Discussion chaired by Alan Hunt]', *Marxism Today*, 25(11): 7–17.

Hodgson, D. 1982, 'Letter', *Marxism Today*, 26(7): 47.

Hoggart, Richard 1957, *The Uses of Literacy*, Harmondsworth: Penguin.

Holland, Patricia 2013, *Broadcasting and the NHS in the Thatcherite 1980s: The Challenge to Public Service*, with Hugh Chignell and Sherryl Wilson, Basingstoke: Palgrave Macmillan.

Hollingsworth, Mark 1986, *The Press and Political Dissent*, London: Pluto.

Hunt, Alan (ed.) 1980, *Marxism and Democracy*, London: Lawrence & Wishart.

Hunt, Alan 1981, 'Discussion: Is the Marxist Tradition Democratic?', *Marxism Today*, 25(11): 34–5.

Hunt, Alan 1985a, 'The Drama Unfolds', *Marxism Today*, 29(4): 51–2.

Hunt, Alan 1985b, 'What Price Democracy?', *Marxism Today*, 29(5): 25–30.

Hutt, Allen 1966, 'Karl Marx as a Journalist', *Marxism Today*, 10(5): 144–54.

Illiffe, Steve 1975, 'Health Care and the Medical Profession', *Marxism Today*, 19(3): 68–71.

Illiffe, Steve 1988, 'Thatcher's Achilles Heel?', *Marxism Today*, 32(2): 10–17.

Ives, Peter 2004a, *Gramsci's Politics of Language*, Toronto: University of Toronto Press.

Ives, Peter 2004b, *Language and Hegemony in Gramsci*, London and Winnipeg: Pluto and Fernwood.

Ives, Peter 2005, 'Language, Agency and Hegemony: A Gramscian Response to Post-Marxism', *Critical Review of International Social and Political Philosophy*, 8(4): 455–68.

Jackson, Ben 2012, 'The Think-Tank Archipelago', in *Making Thatcher's Britain*, edited by B. Jackson and R. Saunders, Cambridge: Cambridge University Press.

Jackson, Ben and Robert Saunders (eds) 2012, *Making Thatcher's Britain*, Cambridge: Cambridge University Press.

Jackson, Jesse 1986, 'Jesse Jackson: Stuart Hall Interviews America's Leading Black Politician', *Marxism Today*, 30(3): 6–11.

Jacques, Martin 1971, 'Notes on the Concept of Intellectuals', *Marxism Today*, 15(10): 307–16.

Jacques, Martin 1973, 'Trends in Youth Culture: Some Aspects', *Marxism Today*, 17(9): 268–81.

Jacques, Martin 1975a, 'Trends in Youth Culture: Reply to the Discussion', *Marxism Today*, 19(4): 110–16.

Jacques, Martin 1975b, 'Universities and Capitalism: The Present Crisis', *Marxism Today*, 19(7): 196–206.

Jacques, Martin 1976, 'Culture, Class Struggle and the Communist Party', *Comment*, 14(11): 163–7. [Report to the EC 8–9 May 1976.]

Jacques, Martin 1978a, 'Editorial Comments', *Marxism Today*, 22(1): 1–5.

Jacques, Martin 1978b, 'Editorial Comments', *Marxism Today*, 22(9): 269–70.

Jacques, Martin 1979a, 'Editorial Comments', *Marxism Today*, 23(6): 161–4.

Jacques, Martin 1979b, 'New Format', *Marxism Today*, 23(9): 264.

Jacques, Martin 1979c, 'The Forward March of Labour Halted?', *Marxism Today*, 23(9): 261–4.

Jacques, Martin 1979d, 'Thatcherism: The Impasse Broken?', *Marxism Today*, 23(10): 6–15.

Jacques, Martin 1979e, 'Theory in Action', *Comment*, 17(10): 150–1.

Jacques, Martin 1981, 'The People's March: A Turning Point?', *Comment*, 19(13): 6–7.

Jacques, Martin 1988a, 'Report for Executive Committee on *Marxism Today*', *News and Views*, 11: 8–11. [Report submitted to EC 10–11 September 1988. CP/CENT/EC/23/13.]

Jacques, Martin 1989a, 'Britain and Europe', in *New Times*, edited by Stuart Hall and Martin Jacques, London: Lawrence & Wishart with *Marxism Today*.

Jacques, Martin 1989b, 'Leader: Sunset in the East', *Marxism Today*, 33(10): 3–4.

Jacques, Martin 1989c, 'Opening Speech on Manifesto for New Times', *News and Views*, 41st CPGB Congress Special Edition, 52.

Jacques, Martin 1991, 'The Last Word', *Marxism Today*, 35(12): 28–9.

Jacques, Martin and Francis Mulhern 1981a, 'Editors' Preface', in *The Forward March of Labour Halted?*, edited by M. Jacques and F. Mulhern, London: NLB/Verso with *Marxism Today*.

Jacques, Martin and Francis Mulhern (eds) 1981b, *The Forward March of Labour Halted?* London: NLB/Verso with *Marxism Today*.

Jäggi, Max, Roger Müller and Sil Schmid 1977, *Red Bologna*, London: Writers and Readers Cooperative.

Jameson, Fredric and Stuart Hall 1990, 'Clinging to the Wreckage: A Conversation', *Marxism Today*, 34(9): 28–31.

Jefferys, S. 1981, 'Forward March of Labour Halted?', in *The Forward March of Labour Halted?*, edited by Martin Jacques and Francis Mulhern, London: NLB/Verso with *Marxism Today*.

Jenkins, Peter, Stuart Hall and Sam Aaronovitch 1982, 'Redrawing the Political Map [Roundtable Discussion]', *Marxism Today*, 26(12): 14–20.

Jessop, Bob, Kevin Bonnett, Simon Bromley and Tom Ling 1984, 'Authoritarian Populism, Two Nations and Thatcherism', *New Left Review*, I/147: 32–60.

Jessop, Bob, Kevin Bonnett, Simon Bromley and Tom Ling 1985, 'Thatcherism and the Politics of Hegemony', *New Left Review*, I/153: 87–101.

Jessop, Bob, Kevin Bonnett, Simon Bromley and Tom Ling 1987, 'Popular Capitalism, Flexible Accumulation and Left Strategy', *New Left Review*, I/165: 104–22.

Jessop, Bob, Kevin Bonnett and Simon Bromley 1990, 'Farewell to Thatcherism? Neoliberalism and New Times', *New Left Review*, I/179: 81–102.

Jobson, Richard 2015, 'A New Hope for an Old Britain? Nostalgia and the British Labour Party's Alternative Economic Strategy, 1970–1983', *Journal of Policy History*, 27(4): 670–94.

Johnstone, Monty 1981, 'Is the Marxist Tradition Democratic?', *Marxism Today*, 25(8): 22–6.

Johnstone, Monty 1985a, 'Back in the USSR', *Marxism Today*, 29(3): 12–17.

Johnstone, Monty 1985b, 'History Lessons', *Marxism Today*, 29(9): 51–2.

Jones, Owen 2011, *Chavs*, London: Verso.

Jones, Paul 2004, *Raymond Williams's Sociology of Culture: A Critical Reconstruction*, Basingstoke: Palgrave Macmillan.

Kartun, Derek 1987, 'Naivety', *Marxism Today*, 31(4): 10.

Kauppi, Niilo 1994, *The Making of an Avant-Garde*, Berlin: Mouton de Gruyter.

Kazin, Michael 1988, 'A People Not a Class', in *The Year Left: Volume 3*, edited by M. Davis and M. Sprinker, New York: Verso.

Keeble, Richard 1994, *The Newspapers Handbook*, London: Routledge.

Kelly, John 1984, 'Gambling with the Tory Vote', *Marxism Today*, 28(8): 47.

Kelsey, Nigel 1965, 'Labour, What Next?', *Marxism Today*, 9(4): 123–5.

Kenner, Hugh 1990, 'The Politics of Plain Style', in *Literary Journalism in the Twentieth Century*, edited by N. Sims, New York: Oxford University Press.

Kennett, Jean 1987, 'Pretentious Reviews', *Marxism Today*, 31(12): 11.

Kenny, Michael 1995a, 'Communism and the New Left', in *Opening the Books*, edited by Geoff Andrews, Nina Fishman and Kevin Morgan, London: Pluto.

Kenny, Michael 1995b, *The First New Left*, London: Lawrence & Wishart.
Kessler, Lauren 1981, *The Dissident Press*, Beverly Hills: Sage.
Kettle, Arnold 1960, 'How New is the "New Left"?', *Marxism Today*, 4(10): 302–8.
Kettle, Arnold 1961, 'Culture and Revolution', *Marxism Today*, 5(10): 301–7.
Kettle, Martin 1987, 'The Natural Alliance', *Marxism Today*, 31(5): 18–23.
Khiabany, Gholam 1997, *Red Pepper: A New Model for the Alternative Press?* Unpublished MA Dissertation, University of Westminster.
Khiabany, Gholam 2000, '*Red Pepper*: A New Model for the Alternative Press?', *Media, Culture & Society*, 22(4): 447–63.
King, Emily 2007, 'Time Out Cover Design, 1970–81', in *Design and the Modern Magazine*, edited by J. Aynsley and K. Forde, Manchester: Manchester University Press.
Kinsey, Richard 1986, 'Crime in the City', *Marxism Today*, 30(5): 6–11.
Klugmann, James 1967, 'Dialogue Between Christianity and Marxism', *Marxism Today*, 11(9): 285–90.
Klugmann, James 1969, 'Experiments!', *Marxism Today*, 13(12): 356.
Klugmann, James 1976a, 'Editorial Comments', *Marxism Today*, 20(1): 1–2.
Klugmann, James 1976c, 'Editorial Comments', *Marxism Today*, 20(7): 201–4.
Knifron, J. 1984, 'Jargon', *Marxism Today*, 28(6): 47.
Kostelanetz, Richard 1995, *Crimes of Culture*, New York: Autonomedia.
Kozolanka, Kirsten 2007, *Power of Persuasion*, Montreal: Black Rose Books
Laclau, Ernesto 1987, 'Class War and After', *Marxism Today*, 31(4): 30–3.
Laclau, Ernesto and Chantal Mouffe 1985, *Hegemony and Socialist Strategy*, London: Verso.
Laing, Dave 1978, 'Interpreting Punk Rock', *Marxism Today*, 22(4): 123–30.
Laing, Stuart 1980, 'Presenting "Things as They Are"', in *Class, Culture and Social Change: A New View of the 1930s*, edited by Frank Gloversmith, Brighton: The Harvester Press.
Laing, Stuart 1992, 'The Politics of Culture: Institutional Change', in *Cultural Revolution? The Challenge of the Arts in the 1960s*, edited by Bart Moore-Gilbert and John Seed, London: Routledge.
Lakoff, George 2004, 'Introduction', in *Thinking Points*, Berkeley: The Rockridge Institute.
Lakoff, Robin 1990, *Talking Power*, New York: Basic Books.
Landry, Charles, David Morley, Russell Southwood and Patrick Wright 1985, *What a Way to Run a Railroad*, London: Comedia.
Lane, Tony 1982, 'The Unions: Caught on the Ebb Tide', *Marxism Today*, 26(9): 6–13.
Lanham, Richard 1974, *Style: An Anti-Textbook*, New Haven: Yale University Press.

Lawrence, Jon and Florence Sutcliffe-Braithwaite 2012, 'Margaret Thatcher and the Decline of Class Politics', in *Making Thatcher's Britain*, edited by B. Jackson and R. Saunders, Cambridge: Cambridge University Press.
Leadbeater, Charlie 1989, 'Power to the Person', in *New Times*, edited by Stuart Hall and Martin Jacques, London: Lawrence & Wishart with *Marxism Today*.
Leadbeater, Charlie 1990, 'Pragmatism Rules, OK?', *Marxism Today*, 34(11): 18–19.
Ledbetter, James 2010, 'Introduction', in Karl Marx 2008, *Dispatches for the New York Tribune*, London: Penguin.
Lee, Alison 1988, 'Black Women's Rights', *Marxism Today*, 32(3): 10.
Lee, Ronald 1986, 'The New Populist Campaign for Economic Democracy: A Rhetorical Exploration', *Quarterly Journal of Speech*, 72: 274–89.
Lehtonen, Mikko 2015, '"What's Going On?" in Finland: Employing Stuart Hall for a Conjunctural Analysis', *International Journal of Cultural Studies*, 19(1): 71–84.
LeMahieu, D.L. 1988, *A Culture for Democracy*, Oxford: Clarendon.
Lenin, Vladimir Il'ich 1989 [1902], *What is to be Done?*, translated by Joe Fineberg and George Hanna, New York: Penguin Books.
Leonard, Peter 1979, 'Restructuring the Welfare State', *Marxism Today*, 23(12): 7–13.
Lestor, Joan 1986, 'Out of Touch', *Marxism Today*, 30(9): 47.
Lewis, John 1967a, 'Questions of Ideology and Culture', *Marxism Today*, 11(7): 222–6.
Lewis, John 1967b, 'Dialogue Between Christianity and Marxism', *Marxism Today*, 11(10): 310–18.
Lewis, John 1972a, 'The Althusser Case: Part I', *Marxism Today*, 16(1): 23–7.
Lewis, John 1972b, 'The Althusser Case: Part II', *Marxism Today*, 16(2): 43–7.
Lewis, Justin 1990, *Art, Culture and Enterprise*, London: Routledge.
Lewis, Justin 1999, 'The Opinion Poll as a Cultural Form', *International Journal of Cultural Studies*, 2(2): 199–221.
Lewis, Justin 2001, *Constructing Public Opinion: How Political Elites Do What They Like and Why We Seem to Go Along With It*, New York: Columbia University Press.
Leys, Colin 1990, 'Still a Question of Hegemony', *New Left Review*, I/181: 119–28.
Lih, Lars T. 2005, *Lenin Rediscovered: What is to be Done? in Context*, Leiden: Brill.
Lindop, Fred 1971, 'Why Did It Happen?', *Marxism Today*, 15(5): 154.
Lindsay, Jack 1958, 'Politics and the Poet', *Marxism Today*, 2(2): 49–54.
Livingstone, Ken 1984, 'Renaissance Labour Style', *Marxism Today*, 28(12): 19–22.
Livingstone, Ken 1985, 'Rate-capping and Realignment', *Marxism Today*, 29(5): 7–13.
Lorimer, Rowland 1993, 'The Socioeconomy of Scholarly and Cultural Book Publishing', *Media, Culture & Society*, 15(2): 203–16.

Lucas, Norman 1975, 'A Cry for Clarity', *Marxism Today*, 19(6): 192.
Luntz, Frank 2007, *Words That Work*, New York: Hyperion Books.
Mahon, John 1968, 'The Record of the Labour Government', *Marxism Today*, 12(8): 231–44.
Mallet, Serge 1975, *Essays on the New Working Class*, St. Louis: Telos Press.
Mandelson, Peter 1987, 'Flowering Image [C5 Interview by Brian Hipkin]', *Marxism Today*, 31(6): 39–40.
Mandelson, Peter 1989, 'Party Presence [Eye-to-Eye Interview by Beatrix Campbell]', *Marxism Today*, 33(10): 6–7.
Marx, Karl and Friedrich Engels 1970 [1845–46], *The German Ideology*, New York: International Publishers.
Marx, Karl and Friedrich Engels 2008 [1848], *The Communist Manifesto*, London: Verso.
Marx-Scouras, Danielle 1996, *The Cultural Politics of Tel Quel*, College Park: Pennsylvania State University Press.
Marxism Today 1957a, 'Soviet Economists Discuss Political Economy Textbook [Part 1]', *Marxism Today*, 1(1): 29–32.
Marxism Today 1957b, 'Soviet Economists Discuss Political Economy Textbook [Part 2]', *Marxism Today*, 1(2): 61–4.
Marxism Today 1960, 'Editorial Comments', *Marxism Today*, 4(7): 193–6.
Marxism Today 1962a, 'Editorial Comments', *Marxism Today*, 6(5): 129–34.
Marxism Today 1962b, 'Editorial Comments', *Marxism Today*, 6(8): 225–9.
Marxism Today 1963, 'Editorial Comments', *Marxism Today*, 7(2): 33–7.
Marxism Today 1983, 'Contents', *Marxism Today*, 27(2): 1.
Marxism Today 1988d, 'Contents', *Marxism Today*, 32(9).
Marxism Today 1991, 'The *Marxism Today* Story', *Marxism Today*, 35(12): 13–22.
Matheson, Donald 2000, 'The Birth of News Discourse: Changes in News Language in British Newspapers, 1880–1930', *Media, Culture & Society*, 22(5): 557–73.
Matheson, Donald 2003, '"Scowling at their Notebooks": How British Journalists Understand their Writing', *Journalism*, 4(2): 165–83.
Mattelart, Armand and Seth Siegelaub (eds) 1979, *Communication and Class Struggle: Volume 1*, New York: IMMRC/International General.
Mattelart, Armand and Seth Siegelaub (eds) 1983, *Communication and Class Struggle: Volume 2*, New York: IMMRC/International General.
McCracken, Ellen 1993, *Decoding Women's Magazines*, Basingstoke: Macmillan.
McGee, Michael 1980, 'The "Ideograph": The Link Between Rhetoric and Ideology', *Quarterly Journal of Speech*, 66.
McGerr, Michael 1986, *The Decline of Popular Politics: The American North, 1865–1928*, New York: Oxford University Press.
McGuigan, Jim 1992, *Cultural Populism*, London: Routledge.
McGuigan, Jim 1997, 'Cultural Populism Revisited', in *Cultural Studies in Question*, edited by Marjorie Ferguson and Peter Golding, Thousand Oaks: Sage.

McGuigan, Jim 2015, 'Introduction', in *Raymond Williams: A Short Counter Revolution: Towards 2000, Revisited*, edited by Jim McGuigan and with additional materials, London: Sage.

McIlroy, John 1999, 'Notes on the Communist Party and Industrial Politics', in *British Trade Unions and Industrial Politics: Volume 2: The High Tide of Trade Unionism, 1964–79*, edited by John McIlroy et al., Aldershot: Ashgate.

McIlroy, John 2006, 'The Establishment of Intellectual Orthodoxy and the Stalinization of British Communism, 1928–1933', *Past and Present*, 192 (August): 187–230.

McIlroy, John, Nina Fishman and Alan Campbell (eds) 1999, *British Trade Unions and Industrial Politics: Volume 2: The High Tide of Trade Unionism, 1964–79*, Aldershot: Ashgate.

McIlroy, John and Sallie Westwood (eds) 1993, *Border Country: Raymond Williams in Adult Education*, Leicester: National Institute of Adult Continuing Education.

McKay, Ian 1982, 'Membership: Renewing the Force', *Comment*, 20(11).

McKnight, David 2009, '*The Sunday Times* and Andrew Neil: The Cultivation of Market Populism', *Journalism Studies*, 10(6): 754–68.

McLennan, Gordon 1983, 'The General Election', *Communist Focus*, 14.

McLennan, Gregor 1984, 'Class Conundrum', *Marxism Today*, 28(5): 29–33.

McRobbie, Angela 1987, 'Parent Power at the Chalkface', *Marxism Today*, 31(5): 24–7.

McRobbie, Angela 1991, 'New Times in Cultural Studies', *New Formations*, 13: 1–17.

McRobbie, Angela 1996, 'Looking Back at New Times and Its Critics', in *Stuart Hall: Critical Dialogues in Cultural Studies*, edited by David Morley and Kuan-Hsing Chen, London: Routledge.

Medhurst, John 2014, *That Option No Longer Exists: Britain 1974–76*, London: Zerobooks.

Medvedev, Roy 1982, 'USSR After Brezhnev', *Marxism Today*, 26(9): 18–25.

Medvedev, Roy 1988, 'Moscow in Motion [Interview]', *Marxism Today*, 32(8): 14–17.

Meredith, Stephen 2007, 'Factionalism on the Parliamentary Right of the British Labour Party in the 1970s: A Reassessment', *Contemporary British History*, 21(1): 55–85.

Meredith, Stephen 2008, *Labours Old and New: The Parliamentary Right of the British Labour Party 1970–79 and the Roots of New Labour*, Manchester: Manchester University Press.

Miliband, Ralph 1985, 'The New Revisionism in Britain', *New Left Review*, I/150: 5–26.

Miliband, Ralph, Leo Panitch and John Saville (eds) 1990, *Socialist Register*, London: Merlin.

Miller, Arthur 1989, 'A Miller's Tale [Interview]', *Marxism Today*, 33(1): 40–3.

Miller, David 1993, 'Official Sources and "Primary Definitions": The Case of Northern Ireland', *Media, Culture & Society*, 15(3): 385–406.

Miller, David 2002, 'Media Power and Class Power: Overplaying Ideology', *Socialist Register*, edited by Leo Panitch and John Saville, London: Merlin.

Mills, Ivor 1974, 'Trends in Youth Culture', *Marxism Today*, 18(12): 379–80.

Milne, Seumas 2010, *The Enemy Within: The Miners' Strike*, second edition, London: Verso.

Milner, Andrew 1993, *Cultural Materialism*, Carlton, Australia: Melbourne University Press.

Milner, Andrew 2002, *Re-Imagining Cultural Studies: The Promise of Cultural Materialism*, London: Sage.

Mirowski, Philip 2013, *Never Let a Serious Crisis Go to Waste: How Neoliberalism Survived the Financial Meltdown*, London and New York: Verso.

Mitchell, Alex 1984, *Behind the Crisis of British Stalinism*, London: New Park.

Morgan, Kevin 1995, 'The Communist Party and the *Daily Worker* 1930–56', in *Opening the Books*, edited by Geoff Andrews, Nina Fishman and Kevin Morgan, London: Pluto.

Morrish, John 1996, *Magazine Editing*, London: Routledge.

Mort, Frank 1989, 'The Politics of Consumption', in *New Times*, edited by Stuart Hall and Martin Jacques, London: Lawrence & Wishart with *Marxism Today*.

Mort, Frank and Nicholas Green 1988, 'You've Never Had It So Good – Again!', *Marxism Today*, 32(5): 30–3.

Mosco, Vincent 1996, *The Political Economy of Communication*, Thousand Oaks: Sage.

Mount, Ferdinand 1985, 'First Principles: A View from the Right', *Marxism Today*, 29(7): 22–4.

Mulgan, Geoff 1989, 'The Power of the Weak', in *New Times*, edited by Stuart Hall and Martin Jacques, London: Lawrence & Wishart with *Marxism Today*.

Mulgan, Geoff 1990, 'The Buck Stops Here', *Marxism Today*, 34(9): 22–7.

Mulhern, Francis 1979, *The 'Moment' of Scrutiny*, London: New Left Books.

Mulholland, Marc 2010, '"Its Patrimony, its Unique Wealth!" Labour-Power, Working Class Consciousness and Crises: An Outline Consideration', *Critique*, 38(3): 375–417.

Murray, Robin 1985, 'Benetton Britain', *Marxism Today*, 29(11): 28–32.

Neil, Andrew 1997, *Full Disclosure*, London: Macmillan.

Neverson, Yvonne 1985, 'Minority Television', *Marxism Today*, 29(4): 44–6.

Nicolson, Jock 1986, 'Political Unionism', *Marxism Today*, 30(10): 11.

Niven, Barbara 1965, 'New Explorations in Russian Painting', *Marxism Today*, 9(2): 44–52.

Offer, Avner 2008, 'British Manual Workers: From Producers to Consumers, c. 1950–2000', *Contemporary British History*, 22(4): 537–71.

Ortu, Claudia 2008, 'The Denial of Class Struggle by British Governments in Their Anti-Union Discourse (1978–2007)', *Critical Discourse Studies*, 5(4): 289–301.

Orwell, George 1984 [1938], *Homage To Catalonia*, Harmondsworth: Penguin in association with Secker and Warburg.

Orwell, George 1987 [1937], *The Road to Wigan Pier*, Harmondsworth: Penguin.
Orwell, George 2004a [1946], 'Why I Write', in *Why I Write*, London: Penguin Books.
Orwell, George 2004b [1946], 'Politics and the English Language', in *Why I Write*, London: Penguin Books.
Osborn, Michael 1986, 'Rhetorical Depiction', in *Form, Genre, and the Study of Political Discourse*, edited by Herbert W. Simons and Aram A. Aghazarian, Columbia, SC: University of South Carolina Press.
Ostertag, Bob 2006, *People's Movements, People's Press: The Journalism of Social Justice Movements*, Boston: Beacon Press.
O'Sullivan, Tim, John Hartley, Danny Saunders and John Fiske 1983, *Media Studies Dictionary*, London: Routledge and Kegan Paul.
Owen, William 1991, *Magazine Design*, New York and London: Phaidon.
Palmer, Michael 1986, '[Viewpoint] The Party Political Agenda', *Marxism Today*, 30(9): 46–7.
Panitch, Leo 2002, 'Rethinking the Labour Party's Transition from Socialism to Capitalism', in *Critical Political Studies*, edited by Abigail B. Bakan and Eleanor MacDonald, Montreal and Kingston: McGill-Queen's University Press.
Panitch, Leo and Colin Leys 1997, *The End of Parliamentary Socialism*, London: Verso.
Parker, Lawrence 2014, 'Opposition in Slow Motion: The CPGB's "Anti-Revisionists" in the 1960s and 1970s', in *Against the Grain*, edited by Evan Smith and Matt Worley, Manchester: Manchester University Press.
Parker, Lawrence 2017, 'Understanding the Formation of the Communist Party of Britain', in *Waiting for the Revolution*, edited by Evan Smith and Matt Worley, Manchester: Manchester University Press.
Payling, Daisy 2017, '"You Have to Start Where You're At": Politics and Reputation in 1980s Sheffield', in *Waiting for the Revolution: The British Far Left From 1956*, edited by Evan Smith and Matthew Worley, Manchester: Manchester University Press.
Pearce, Bert 1971, 'The Strategy of Socialist Revolution in Britain', *Marxism Today*, 15(1): 6–18.
Pearce, Bert 1973, 'The Strategy of Socialist Revolution in Britain: A Reply to Discussion', *Marxism Today*, 17(5).
Pearmain, Andy 2011, *The Politics of New Labour*, London: Lawrence & Wishart.
Pearmain, Andy 2014, 'Dissent from Dissent: The "Smith/Party" Group in the 1970s CPGB', in *Against the Grain*, edited by Evan Smith and Matt Worley, Manchester: Manchester University Press.
Peck, Janice 2001, 'Itinerary of a Thought: Stuart Hall, Cultural Studies, and the Unresolved Problem of the Relation of Culture to "Not Culture"', *Cultural Critique*, 48: 200–49.
Peck, Janice 2006, 'Why We Shouldn't be Bored with the Political Economy versus Cultural Studies Debate', *Cultural Critique*, 64: 92–126.

Perlin, Ross 2011, *Intern Nation*, London: Verso.

Perryman, Mark 1988, 'The Mandela Moment', *Marxism Today*, 32(9): 28–31.

Perryman, Mark 2012, 'The Revolution is Just a T-shirt Away', in *After the Party*, edited by Andy Croft, London: Lawrence & Wishart.

Peters, John Durham 2004, 'The "Marketplace of Ideas": History of the Concept', in *Toward a Political Economy of Culture*, edited by A. Calabrese and C. Sparks, Lanham, MD: Rowman and Littlefield.

Phillips, Louise 1996, 'Rhetoric and the Spread of the Discourse of Thatcherism', *Discourse & Society*, 7(2): 209–41.

Phillips, Louise 1998, 'Hegemony and Political Discourse: The Lasting Impact of Thatcherism', *Sociology*, 32(4): 847–67.

Philo, Greg 1993, 'Political Advertising, Popular Belief and the 1992 British General Election', *Media, Culture & Society*, 15: 407–18.

Philo, Greg 2008, 'Active Audiences and the Construction of Public Knowledge', *Journalism Studies*, 9(4): 535–44.

van der Pijl, Kees 2005, 'Gramsci and Left Managerialism', *Critical Review of International Social and Political Thought*, 8(4): 499–511.

Pillai, Poonam 1992, 'Rereading Stuart Hall's Encoding/Decoding Model', *Communication Theory*, 2(3): 221–33.

Pimlott, Ben 1987, 'Labour's Big Idea', *Marxism Today*, 31(11).

Pimlott, H.F. 2000a, *'Mainstreaming the Margins': A Case Study of the Transformation of Marxism Today*, Unpublished PhD Dissertation, Goldsmiths College, University of London.

Pimlott, H.F. 2000b, '"Mainstreaming the Margins": A Case Study of *Marxism Today*', in *Media Organisations in Society*, edited by James Curran, London: Arnold.

Pimlott, H.F. 2004, '"From the Margins to the Mainstream": The Promotion and Distribution of *Marxism Today*', *Journalism*, 5(2): 203–26.

Pimlott, H.F. 2005a, 'From "Old Left" to "New Labour": Eric Hobsbawm and the Rhetoric of "Realistic Marxism"', *Labour/Le Travail*, 56: 175–97.

Pimlott, H.F. 2005b, 'Politics by Other Means? On the Once and Future State of Cultural Studies', *Topia: A Canadian Journal of Cultural Studies*, 12: 116–23.

Pimlott, H.F. 2006a, '"Write Out of the Margins": Accessibility, Editorship and House Style in *Marxism Today*, 1957–91', *Journalism Studies*, 7(5): 782–806.

Pimlott, H.F. 2006b, 'Marxism's "Communicative Crisis"? Mapping Debates over Leninist Print-Media Practices in the 20th Century', *Socialist Studies*, 2(2): 57–77.

Pimlott, H.F. 2011, '"Eternal Ephemera" or The Durability of "Disposable Literature"', *Media, Culture & Society*, 33(4): 515–41.

Pimlott, H.F. 2013, '"The Radical Type"? G. Allen Hutt, the Communist Party and the Politics of Journalistic Practice', *Journalism Practice*, 7(1): 81–95.

Pimlott, H.F. 2014a, '"Militant Entertainment"? (Sub)Cultural Production of Music,

Ephemera and Style as Politics in the Emergent "Structure of Feeling", 1976–83', for *Fight Back: Punk, Politics and Resistance*, edited by The Subcultures Network, Manchester: Manchester University Press.

Pimlott, H.F. 2014b, '"A Working-Class Intellectual is Something to Be"? Theorizing the Incorporation (and Resistance) of Working-Class Academics as a (Counter-) Hegemonic Process', *Rhizomes*, 27, URL: http://www.rhizomes.net/issue27/pimlott.html

Pimlott, H.F. 2015, 'Vanguard Media: The Promise of Strategic Communication?', in *The Routledge Companion to Alternative and Community Media*, edited by Chris Atton, Abingdon: Routledge.

Pinder, Brian 1961, 'Trade Unions and Coloured Workers', *Marxism Today*, 5(9): 282.

Pitcairn, Lee 1985, 'Crisis in British Communism', *New Left Review*, I/153: 102–20.

Prawer, Siegbert Salomon 1976, *Marx and World Literature*, Oxford: Clarendon Press.

Prior, Mike and Dave Purdy 1979, *Out of the Ghetto*, Nottingham: Spokesman.

Priscott, Dave 1979, 'The British Road to Socialism and the Communist Party', *Marxism Today*, 23(2): 60–3.

Priscott, Dave 1983, 'The Popular Front Revisited', *Marxism Today*, 27(10): 24–30.

Protz, Roger 1979, 'Their Papers and Ours', in *Media, Politics and Culture: A Socialist View*, edited by Carl Gardner, Basingstoke: Macmillan.

Purdy, Dave 1974, 'Some Thoughts on the Party's Policy Towards Prices, Wages and Incomes', *Marxism Today*, 18(8).

Purdy, Dave 1976, 'British Capitalism Since the War: Part 2', *Marxism Today*, 19(10).

Purvis, Trevor and Alan Hunt 1993, 'Discourse, Ideology, Discourse, Ideology, Discourse, Ideology ...', *British Journal of Sociology*, 44(3): 473–99.

Pykett, Lynn 1990, 'Reading the Periodical Press: Text and Context', in *Investigating Victorian Journalism*, edited by L. Brake, A. Jones and L. Madden, Basingstoke: Macmillan.

Rampton, Sheldon and John Stauber 2003, *Weapons of Mass Deception*, New York: Jeremy P. Tarcher/Penguin.

Rehmann, Jan 2014, *Theories of Ideology*, Chicago: Haymarket.

Rehmann, Jan 2015, 'Ideology-Critique with the Conceptual Hinterland of the Theory of the Ideological', *Critical Sociology*, 41(3): 433–48.

Renton, David 2006, *When We Touched the Sky*, Cheltenham: New Clarion.

Richards, Huw 1997, *The Bloody Circus: The Daily Herald and the Left*, London: Pluto Press.

Riddell, John 2013, 'Party Democracy in Lenin's Comintern-and Now', 20 February, URL: http://johnriddell.wordpress.com/2013/02/20/party-democracy-in-lenins-comintern-and-now/ (accessed 22 July 2013).

Roberts, John 1990, *Postmodernism, Politics and Art*, Manchester: Manchester University Press.

Robinson, Andrew 2005, 'Towards an Intellectual Reformation: The Critique of Common Sense and the Forgotten Revolutionary Project of Gramscian Theory', *Critical Review of International Social and Political Philosophy*, 8(4): 469–81.

Ross, Andrew 2014, 'You Are Not A Loan: A Debtors Movement', *Culture Unbound*, 6: 179–88.

Rowbotham, Sheila, Lynne Segal and Hilary Wainwright 2013 [1979], *Beyond the Fragments*, Merlin Press.

Rowthorn, Bob 1982a, 'Britain and Western Europe', *Marxism Today*, 26(5): 25–31.

Ruff, Allen 1997, *'We Called Each Other Comrade': Charles H. Kerr & Company, Radical Publishers*, Chicago: University of Illinois Press.

Rusbridger, Alan 1986, 'Closeup on: John Smith', *Marxism Today*, 30(4): 52.

Rustin, Michael 1986, 'Hung Parliament', *Marxism Today*, 30(2): 15–18.

Rustin, Michael 1989, 'The Trouble with "New Times"', in *New Times*, edited by Stuart Hall and Martin Jacques, London: Lawrence & Wishart with *Marxism Today*.

Rustin, Michael 1994, 'Unfinished Business', in *Altered States*, edited by Mark Perryman, London: Lawrence & Wishart.

Rutherford, Jonathan 1987, 'Moral Panic', *Marxism Today*, 31(9): 10.

Rutherford, Malcolm 1983, 'Review of *The Politics of Thatcherism*', *Marxism Today*, 27(7): 43–4.

Samuel, Raphael 1985, 'The Lost World of British Communism', *New Left Review*, I/154: 3–53.

Samuel, Raphael 1986a, 'Staying Power', *New Left Review*, I/156: 63–113.

Samuel, Raphael 1986b, 'Reopening Old Wounds', *Marxism Today*, 30(10): 60–1.

Samuel, Raphael 1987, 'Class Politics', *New Left Review*, I, 165: 52–91.

Samuels, Stuart 1966, 'The Left Book Club', *Journal of Contemporary History*, 1(2): 65–86.

Savage, Wendy, Jo Richardson, Teresa Gorman, and Jane Woddis 1988, 'Whose Right to Life? [Roundtable chaired by Maria Duggan]', *Marxism Today*, 32(1): 14–19.

Saville, John 1990, '*Marxism Today*: An Anatomy', in *The Socialist Register*, edited by Ralph Miliband et al., London: Merlin Press.

Scammell, Margaret 1995, *Designer Politics: How Elections Are Won*, Basingstoke: Macmillan Press.

Schofield, Camilla 2012, 'A Nation or No Nation? Enoch Powell and Thatcherism', in *Making Thatcher's Britain*, edited by B. Jackson and R. Saunders, Cambridge: Cambridge University Press.

Schwarz, Brian and Colin Mercer 1981, 'Popular Politics and Marxist Theory in Britain', in *Silver Linings*, edited by G. Bridges and R. Brunt, London: Lawrence & Wishart.

Segal, Lynne 1985, 'A New Morality', *Marxism Today*, 29(4): 52–3.

Seifert, Roger and Tom Sibley 2010, 'Communists and the Trade Union Left Revisited: The Case of the UK 1964–79', *World Review of Political Economy*, 1(1): 112–26.

Shelby, A. 1992, 'The Readability Formula: One More Time', *Management Communication Quarterly*, 5(4): 485–95.

Shore, Cris 1990, *Italian Communism*, London: Pluto.

Shore, Elliott 1988, *Talkin' Socialism: J.A. Wayland and the Radical Press*, Lawrence: University Press of Kansas.

Simon, Brian 1968, 'Questions of Ideology and Culture: A Reply to Discussion', *Marxism Today*, 12(5): 155–8.

Simon, Brian 1977, 'Tribute to James Klugmann', *Marxism Today*, 21(11): 322–3.

Simon, Roger 1982, *Gramsci's Political Thought: An Introduction*, London: Lawrence & Wishart.

Simons, Herbert W. 1970, 'Requirements, Problems, and Strategies: A Theory of Persuasion for Social Movements', *Quarterly Journal of Speech*, 56.

Sivanandan, Ambalavaner 1989, 'All That Melts Into Air is Solid: The Hokum of New Times', *Race & Class*, 31(3): 1–30.

Smith, Adam 1976 [1793], *An Inquiry into the Nature and Cause of the Wealth of Nations*, edited by R.H. Campbell and A.S. Skinner, Oxford: Clarendon Press.

Smith, Adrian 1996, *The 'New Statesman': Portrait of a Political Weekly, 1913–31*, London: Frank Cass.

Smith, Evan 2011, '"Are the Kids United?" The Communist Party of the Great Britain, Rock Against Racism, and the Politics of Youth Culture', *Journal for the Study of Radicalism*, 5(2): 85–118.

Smith, Evan and Matt Worley 2014, 'Introduction: The Far Left in Britain from 1956', in *Against the Grain*, edited by Evan Smith and Matt Worley, Manchester: Manchester University Press.

Smith, Evan and Matt Worley 2017, *Waiting for the Revolution: The British Far Left From 1956*, Manchester: Manchester University Press.

Smith, Herbert 1962, 'Marxism and Literature Today', *Marxism Today*, 6(12): 370–3.

Smythe, Dallas 1977, 'Communications: Blindspot of Western Marxism', *Canadian Journal of Political and Society Theory*, 1(3): 1–28.

Socialist Review 1983, 'After the Landslide', *Socialist Review*, 55.

Solomon, Martha 1988, 'Ideology as Rhetorical Constraint', *Quarterly Journal of Speech*, 74: 184–200.

Sparks, Colin 1985, 'The Working-Class Press: Radical and Revolutionary Alternatives', *Media, Culture & Society*, 7(2): 133–46.

Sparks, Colin 1988, 'The Popular Press and Political Democracy', *Media, Culture & Society*, 10(2): 209–23.

Sparks, Colin 1996, 'Stuart Hall, Cultural Studies and Marxism', in *Stuart Hall: Critical Dialogues in Cultural Studies*, edited by David Morley and Kuan-Hsing Chen, London: Routledge.

Spours, Ken 1977, 'Students, Education and the State', *Marxism Today*, 21(11): 339–47.

Steel, Mark 2001, *Reasons to be Cheerful*, London: Scribner.

Steele, Tom 1999, 'Hey Jimmy! The Legacy of Gramsci in British Cultural Politics', in *New

Left, New Right and Beyond, edited by Geoff Andrews, Richard Cockett, Alan Hooper and Michael Williams, Basingstoke: Macmillan.

Steward, Fred 1989, 'Green Times', in *New Times*, edited by Stuart Hall and Martin Jacques, London: Lawrence & Wishart with *Marxism Today*.

Stewart, David 2008, 'The British Labour Party, "Parliamentary Socialism" and Thatcherism, 1979–1990: A Visual Perspective', *Visual Resources*, 24(2): 173–87.

Stoltzfus, Duane C.S. 2007, *Freedom from Advertising: E.W. Scripps's Chicago Experiment*, Urbana: University of Illinois Press.

Swartz, Omar 1999, *Socialism and Communication: Reflections on Language and Left Politics*, Aldershot: Ashgate Publishing.

Szanto, Andras (ed.) 2005, *What Orwell Didn't Know: Propaganda and the New Face of American Politics*, New York: Public Affairs/Perseus Books.

Taylor, G. 1980, 'The Marxist Inertia and the Labour Movement', *Politics and Power*, 1.

Taylor, G. 1987, 'The Other Potsdam Agreement', *News and Views*.

Taylor-Gooby, Peter 1995, 'Comfortable, Marginal and Excluded: Who Should Pay Higher Taxes for a Better Welfare State?', in *British Social Attitudes*, Aldershot: Dartmouth, pp. 1–18.

Therborn, Goran 1984, 'Britain Left Out', in *The Future of the Left*, edited by James Curran, Cambridge: Polity Press and *New Socialist*.

Thomas, James 1998, 'Labour, the Tabloids, and the 1992 General Election', *Contemporary British History*, 12(2): 80–104.

Thomas, James 2005, *Popular Newspapers, the Labour Party and British Politics*, London: Routledge.

Thomas, James 2007, '"Bound in by History": The "Winter of Discontent" in British Politics, 1979–2004', *Media, Culture & Society*, 29(2): 263–83.

Thomas, Peter D. 2009, *The Gramscian Moment*, Leiden: Brill.

Thompson, Duncan 2007, *Pessimism of the Intellect? A History of the New Left Review*, London: Merlin Press.

Thompson, E.P. 1957, 'Socialism and the Intellectuals', *Universities and Left Review*, 1: 31–6.

Thompson, E.P. 1963, *The Making of the English Working Class*, Harmondsworth: Penguin.

Thompson, Willie 1992, *The Good Old Cause: British Communism, 1920–1991*, London: Pluto.

Thomson, George 1957, 'Gramsci: The First Italian Marxist', *Marxism Today*, 1(2): 61–2.

Townsend, Sally and Paul Webster 1983, 'What Does Marx Mean To You?', *Marxism Today*, 27(3): 27–33.

Trickey, Graham 1981, 'Reproducing Royalty', *Marxism Today*, 25(7): 22–4.

Triesman, David 1980, 'Politics, Sport and the Olympics', *Marxism Today*, 24(6): 12–17.

Triesman, David 1981, 'Football in Decline', *Marxism Today*, 25(3): 12–16.

Triesman, David 1983, 'They're Off ...', *Marxism Today*, 27(3): 13–16.
Tunstall, Jeremy 1996, *Newspaper Power*, Oxford: Oxford University Press.
Vaughan, Tom 1958, 'The Theatre in Britain Today', *Marxism Today*, 2(1): 20–4.
Volosinov, Valentin N. 1971, *Marxism and the Philosophy of Language*, Cambridge, MA: Harvard University Press.
Wainwright, Hilary 1988, 'Defence of the Faith?', *Marxism Today*, 32(1): 58.
Waite, Mike 1995, 'Sex 'n' Drugs 'n' Rock 'n' Roll (and Communism)', in *Opening the Books*, edited by Geoff Andrews, Nina Fishman and Kevin Morgan, London: Pluto.
Walesa, Lech 1981, 'Interview with Lech Walesa' [by Monty Johnstone], *Marxism Today*, 25(10): 14–17.
Walker, M. 1988, 'What is to be Done?', *Marxism Today*, 32(6): 12–15.
Walker, Pat (ed.) 1979, *Between Labour and Capital*, Brighton: Harvester Press.
Waltz, Mitzi 2005, *Alternative and Activist Media*, Edinburgh: Edinburgh University Press.
Watkinson, R. 1975, 'A Study of George Grosz', *Marxism Today*, 19(2).
Webster, Paul 1980, 'Notes: *Marxism Today* on the Increase', *Marxism Today*, 24(10): 36.
Webster, Paul 1981, 'Notes: *Marxism Today*', *Marxism Today*, 25(10): 48.
Webster, Paul 1983, '*Marxism Today*: Going For Growth', *Communist Focus*, 10.
West, Pauline 1982, 'Letter', *Marxism Today*, 26(4): 47.
Whitaker, Brian 1981, *News Limited*, London: Minority Press Group.
Widgery, David 1976, *The Left in Britain, 1956–68*, Harmondsworth: Penguin.
Widgery, David 1981, 'The Rise of Radical Rock', *New Socialist*, 2: 34–7.
Widgery, David 1986, *'Beating Time': Riot 'n' Race 'n' Rock 'n' Roll*, London: Chatto and Windus.
Widgery, David 1987, 'Beating Time', *International Socialism*, 2(35).
Wilkie, Richard W. 1976, 'Karl Marx on Rhetoric', *Philosophy & Rhetoric*, 9(3): 232–46.
Williams, Michael 1999, 'The Long Sixties in the Short Twentieth Century', in *New Left, New Right*, edited by Geoff Andrews, Richard Cockett, Alan Hooper and Michael Williams, Basingstoke: Macmillan.
Williams, Raymond 1958, *Culture and Society*, Harmondsworth: Penguin.
Williams, Raymond 1961, *The Long Revolution*, Harmondsworth: Penguin.
Williams, Raymond 1971, *Orwell*, London: Fontana/Collins.
Williams, Raymond 1977a, *Marxism and Literature*, Oxford: Oxford University Press.
Williams, Raymond 1978, 'The Press We Don't Deserve', in *The British Press: A Manifesto*, edited by James Curran, Basingstoke: Macmillan.
Williams, Raymond 1979a, *Politics and Letters: Interviews with New Left Review*, London: New Left Books.
Williams, Raymond 1979b, 'Afterword', in *Modern Tragedy*, London: Verso.

Williams, Raymond 1980a [1978], 'Means of Communication as Means of Production', in *Problems in Materialism and Culture*, London: NLB/Verso.

Williams, Raymond 1980b, 'The Bloomsbury Fraction', in *Problems in Materialism and Culture*, London: NLB/Verso.

Williams, Raymond 1980c [1960], 'Advertising: The Magic System', in *Problems in Materialism and Culture*, London: NLB/Verso.

Williams, Raymond 1980d [1973], 'Base and Superstructure in Marxist Cultural Theory', in *Problems in Materialism and Culture*, London: NLB/Verso.

Williams, Raymond 1981, *Culture*, London: Fontana.

Williams, Raymond 1982, 'Parliament and Democracy', *Marxism Today*, 26(6): 14–21.

Williams, Raymond 1983a, *Towards 2000*, London: Chatto and Windus/Hogarth.

Williams, Raymond 1983b [1976], *Keywords: A Vocabulary of Culture & Society*, London: Flamingo/Fontana Press. Second revised edition.

Williams, Raymond 1983c [1981], 'Crisis in English Studies', in *Writing in Society*, London: Verso.

Williams, Raymond 1986, 'The Uses of Cultural Theory', *New Left Review*, I/158: 19–31.

Williams, Raymond 1989a, *The Politics of Modernism: Against the New Conformists*, London: Verso.

Williams, Raymond 1989b, *The Resources of Hope: Culture, Democracy, Socialism*, edited by Robin Gable and with an introduction by Robin Blackburn, London: Verso.

Williams, Raymond 1989c [1984], 'Socialists and Coalitionists', reprinted in *The Resources of Hope*, London: Verso.

Williams, Raymond 1989d [1980], 'Isn't the News Terrible', reprinted in *What I Came to Say?*, London: Hutchinson.

Williams, Raymond 1989e [1981], 'The Forward March of Labour Halted?', in *The Forward March of Labour Halted?*, edited by M. Jacques and F. Mulhern, London: NLB/Verso with *Marxism Today*, reprinted in R. Williams 1989b, *The Resources of Hope*, London: Verso.

Williams, Raymond 1989f [1985], 'Mining the Meaning', reprinted in *The Resources of Hope*, London: Verso.

Williams, Raymond 1989g [1983], 'Problems of the Coming Period', reprinted in *The Resources of Hope*, London: Verso.

Williams, Raymond 2015, *Raymond Williams: A Short Counter Revolution: Towards 2000, Revisited*, edited by Jim McGuigan and with additional materials, London: Sage.

Williamson, Judith 1986, 'The Problems of Being Popular', *New Socialist*, 42: 14–15.

Williamson, O. 2002, *Contemporary American Orthodox Marxist Rhetoric*. Unpublished PhD Dissertation, available online: http://utminers.utep.edu/omwilliamson/thesis thesis.doc (Accessed 21 January 2004).

Willis, Paul 1977, *Learning to Labour*, Farnborough: Saxon House.

Winship, Janice 1987, *Inside Women's Magazines*, London: Pandora.

Witt, Matt 2005, 'Bad Connections: How Labor Fails to Communicate', *New Labor Forum*, 14(1): 113–20.

Wood, Brennon 1998, 'Stuart Hall's Cultural Studies and the Problem of Hegemony', *British Journal of Sociology*, 49(3): 399–414.

Workers' Life 1979 [1928], 'The Worker Correspondent', in *Communication and Class Struggle: Volume 1*, edited by Armand Mattelart and Seth Siegelaub, New York: IMMRC/International General.

Worley, Matthew 2012, 'Shot by Both Sides: Punk, Politics and the End of "Consenus"', *Contemporary British History*, 26(3): 333–54.

Worley, Matthew 2016, 'Marx-Lenin-Rotten-Strummer: British Marxism and Youth Culture in the 1970s', *Contemporary British History*, 30(4): 505–21.

Worth, Owen 2014, 'Stuart Hall, Marxism Without Guarantees, and "The Hard Road to Renewal"', *Capital and Class*, 38(3): 480–7.

Wright, Anita 1988, 'Alton's Tactic', *Marxism Today*, 32(3): 10.

Wright, Bob 1978, 'Interview with Bob Wright' [Conducted by Pete Coughlin and Dave Wynn], *Marxism Today*, 22(9): 271–8.

Wright, Carl 1986, 'Labour Aid', *Marxism Today*, 30(9): 47.

Wright, Tony 1996, *Socialisms*, London: Routledge.

Yip, David 1983, 'The Chinese Detective: Interview with David Yip' [Interview by Alan Clarke], *Marxism Today*, 27(10): 19–23.

Young, Lewis 2016, 'Internal Party Bulletin or Paper of the Working Class Movement? The Communist Party of Great Britain and the Role of the Daily Worker, 1930–1949', *Media History*, 22(1): 123–34.

Zervigón, Andrés Mario 2010, 'Perusading with the Unseen? *Die Arbeiter-Illustrierte-Zeitung*, Photography, and German Communism's Iconophobia', *Visual Resources*, 26(2): 147–64.

Index

Ablitt, Keith   269, 275, 278n83
abortion activism   276
academic realism   425
accessibility   19, 35, 268, 285, 368–70, 439
　See also 'FOG Index' analysis method
active editorships   199–210
　See also Jacques, Martin
activist/academic divide   339
Adam Smith Institute   164
　See also Smith, Adam
advertising
　about   230–33
　costs   221
　ideological aspects of   230
　importance of   282
　inserts   283
　Marxism Today and   231–33, 278–79, 282, 283, 307–8, 324
　in periodicals   257
　radical left/working class publications and   230–32
affluent workers/*embourgeoisiement* thesis   49
African National Congress   283
agency   10
agitation   23, 26
agitprop (term)   23n28, 326
Alce, Julie   382
Ali, Tariq   435
Alternative Economic Strategy   60, 122
alternative/oppositional media   145, 155, 199, 445–46
　See also socialist/radical left publications
Althusser, Louis   154
Andrews, Geoff   73, 85n298, 246, 342n104
Anglo-Marxist humanism   379
ANL (Anti-Nazi League)   192
Anti-Clause 28 Campaign   173
Arena (cultural journal)   33, 46, 210
argumentation (rhetoric term)   19
Ascherson, Neal   333
Ash, William   381
audiences   222–23, 269, 299, 306, 431, 457
Aune, James   364–65, 405

authoritarian populism   116–18, 129–30, 133, 144–45, 180
autonomy (term)   173

Baker, Alan   309
Barthes, Roland   423n208
base/superstructure model   441
Bateman, Paul   280
Battle of Orgreave   181
BDA (Broad Democratic Alliance)
　Marxism Today and   185, 291, 336, 389
　membership of   179n337
　popular politics and   178–79, 183
　in publications   291
　traditionalists and   63
　working-class institutions and   184
Beardsley, Sally   243
Bellamy, Ron   388
Benn, Tony   121, 122, 272–73, 277, 345, 355
Bennett, Mick   34
Benton, Sarah   30, 61–62, 70, 208–9
Bernal, J.D.   46, 211
Blair, Tony   134, 182
Bloomfield, Jon   61, 336
Bollinger, Stefan   154
Bolshevism   20, 23–24, 193, 229, 313
Bolton, George   309
Bonnett, Kevin   126
book publishing   256, 335–37
Brennan, Irene   63n196, 86, 204, 211, 214, 286
The British Press: A Manifesto   156
British Road to Socialism (manifesto)   38, 56, 57, 62, 92, 205
British Survey of Attitudes   132
Bromley, Simon   126
Brown, Jan   247, 276, 278n82, 278n84, 280, 281
Brunt, Ros   96, 216
bureaucratic statism   119
Burns, Emile   34, 36, 38, 211
Burt, Les   47

Callaghan, James   107, 410
Callaghan, Jim   164
Callaghan, John   51
Callinicos, Alex   443n4

INDEX   519

Campbell, Beatrix   57, 77, 244, 299, 306, 341
Campbell, J.R.   51
Canada   15–16
Capstick, Ken   309
caricatures   280, 430–31
Carritt, Gabriel   213
Central Books   218, 228, 231, 240, 308, 313
Central Committee Outfitters   229
Centre for Contemporary Cultural Studies   417
The Centre for Policy Studies   164
Chadwick, Jon   244
Challenge (magazine)   30
Channel Five section   191, 244, 291, 295–96, 303–4
Charter 88 campaign   173
Chater, Tony   56, 71, 72, 388
Chater group   81, 82
Chater-Costello attack   75–76
Chinese distribution   315n11
choice (term)   173
Christian Democratic Party   61
Christian-Marxist dialogue   53, 434
    See also Marxism
Chun, Linn   453–55
CIPD report   40, 41, 42–43, 64, 68–70
circulation   49–50, 81, 199, 313–14, 316, 321
cities   174n317
City Limits (listings weekly)   244
civil society   141–44, 168, 176
Clarke, John   136
Clarke, Kenneth   348
class consciousness   114
class politics   59, 82, 116
Class Politics: An Answer to Its Critics (book)   86
Clause IV   49
climate change   174n320
Cloud, Dana C.   364–65
Cogito (*theoretical journal*)   30
Cohen, Gerry   237
Cohen, Jack   54n154, 211–12, 380
Cohen, Margaret   376
Collet's (bookshop)   231
Collins, Henry   46
Comedia model   11, 258, 313, 325, 363, 442
Comment (party review)   30, 37n70, 67, 69–70
    See also Benton, Sarah

common sense
    overview   134–40
    communist journalism and   368
    critique of   126–30
    etymology of   137–38
    false consciousness and   144n181
    Gramsci on   137
    Hall on   142–43, 147, 151
    Thatcherism and   142–43, 146, 151
    unity/division on the left and   430–31
    various thinkers on   146
    Williams on   181
communicative crisis   18
communism   364, 414
The Communist (party paper)   26
Communist Design Group   30
Communist International   18
Communist journalism   367–68
Communist parties   18, 203
Communist Party of Great Britain (CPGB)
    audiences and   344
    Central Books and   313
    culture and   189
    design aspects   318–19
    editors and   200
    education tradition within   339–40
    Executive Committee   21–22
    factions   57
    Gorbachev and   94
    jargon/specialised vocabularies   387
    managerialism of   57
    Marxism within   38, 58
    membership growth   50–51, 79
    The Morning Star and   85
    National Party Congress (1965)   51
    organisational practice and political projects   21–22, 25, 205, 443
    party-press relationship   90
    readership and   85, 323
    revision of the *British Road to Socialism*   50
    roles of each   344, 443
    separation of   454
    specialist committees   338
    traditionalist/reformist tendencies within   57–58
    views within   435
    workplace politics and   59

Young Communist League 30
  See also British Road to Socialism (manifesto); Farleigh Press; Johnstone, Monty; New Communist Party
Communist Party of Great Britain, print media
  audiences and circulation of 26–27, 28, 33
  financing of 218
  as organisational base 313
  overview of publications printed 25–26
  party paper 25–26
  relationship with *Marxist Quarterly* 43
  rhetoric/writing styles of 364
  The Star and 84
  theoretical journal 26
  See also *Marxist Quarterly* (journal)
Communist populism 188, 190
Communist Review (periodical) 33, 34, 36, 39
Communist rhetoric 366–68, 373–75
Communist University of London 54, 231, 340, 418
community policing 275
compensation 206, 225, 243–44
Congress Truth (bulletin) 82
Connor, Dan 213
consent 117–18, 129, 134, 137, 145, 151
constitutional authoritarianism 129, 197
consumer magazines 281n97
content analysis 359
contradictions 116–17, 120
contributors 331–35
Cook, Dave 61, 62–63, 70, 187, 306, 316
Corbyn, Jeremy 109n31, 130n127, 457
Cornforth, Maurice 38, 46, 47, 211
correctness (in style) 378, 395, 397, 426
Costello, Mick 73, 81
counter hegemony 154n223, 455
cover design 249–50, 264, 265, 270–78, 306–7
coverage 46, 49, 50, 80, 182–83, 348–60
CPHG (Communist Party Historians' Group, CPGB) 178, 188
CPJ (Commission on Party Journals, CPGB) 34, 35, 37–38, 43
  See also Palme Dutt, Rajani
Crawford, Joan 281
crisis music 192

Crowley, David 274
cultural Marxism 188
cultural materialism 7, 8–9, 15, 146–47, 365, 446–47
cultural politics 192, 193, 417, 458
cultural populism 139, 172, 175, 188, 197–98, 446
cultural production 155
cultural studies
  base/superstructure 125
  common sense 134
  critiques of 136, 157n230
  false consciousness in 145
  Hall's role in 150
  popular politics and 177
  reception of Gramsci 140
  research in 1980s 196
  See also academic realism
culture 176, 189, 190
Curran, James 283n100
Currie, David 62
Czechoslovakia 52

Daily Express (newspaper) 118
The Daily Herald (daily paper) 27
Daily Mail (tabloid) 118
The Daily Worker (daily paper) 27–29, 33, 39, 50, 52, 245
  See also *The Morning Star* (daily paper)
Daniel, Iu. 50
Davidson, Alastair 142, 145–46
Davis, Mary 57
Davis, Tricia 306
Davison, Sally 302
Daylight (periodical) 34, 36–37, 46
Debray, Régis 16–17
decentralisation of organisation/production 169
democracy 121, 127, 167–68
democratic centralism 20–22, 24–25, 85, 93, 167
democratic impulse 139
democratisation of media access 164
Desai, Radhika 163
design process *see* production process
designer socialism 193, 258
designers 258
Devine, Pat 60, 62
difference (value) 173

INDEX 521

Dimitrov, Georgi   410
discursive turn   149
Discussion (theoretical journal)   31
discussion groups   337, 342–43
'Discussion' section (of *Marxism Today*)
    296–99
disposable literature   23n24
dissent   24–25
distribution   318
distribution (of *Marxism Today*)   448
Dobb, Maurice   46, 211
Dunman, Jack   381
Dutt, R.P.   34, 51
Dyer, Richard   244

Eagleton, Terry   419
Eastern European revolutions   299
Economic Committee   338
economism   60n183, 123, 124
Eden, Anthony   127
Edgar, David   215, 216, 385
editing process   206
editorial board   44–45, 66, 210–11
editorial content   292
editorial contents   292
editorial sections   284–93
    See also features
editorial working group   242
editors
    assistants   225–26
    Communist Party of Great Britain leadership bodies and   200
    of *Daily Worker*   39
    editorial board of *Marxism Today*   66
    editorial control   40, 55
    letters-to-the-editor   83
    of *Marxism Today*   44
    Marxism Today editorial board and   211
    of print media   29
    roles/styles of   200, 201
    See also Benton, Sarah; Burns, Emile; Chater, Tony; Gollan, John; Jacques, Martin; Lewis, John; Matthews, George; Townsend, Sally; Turner, Julian
editorships   199–210
editorships, passive and active   199–210
education   291
Egelnick, Max   375, 387, 395–98
election data/results   131, 132, 133

elective dictatorship   129
electoral politics   174
electoral responses   148
electoral strategy   148
Electrical Trades Union   51
electronic media   19
embourgeoisiement thesis/affluent workers
    49
encoding/decoding model   135n145, 138, 151
English magazine design   259, 263
environmental movements   174
esoteric Marxist features   285
Esterson, Simon   270, 278n85
Eurocommunism   61–64, 371
Europe   15–16
Euro-Red (journal)   64

Fabian Society   320
The Face (periodical)   258
Facing Up to the Future (document)   95, 97
factional activity   41–42, 57–58
fake news   380n62
Falber, Reuben   54n154, 56, 237, 241, 375
false consciousness   132–33, 144n181, 145, 196
Fares Fair   187
Farleigh Pres   238–39
Farleigh Press   223, 234, 236, 238–39, 253,
    449
fascist/racist organisations   192
features
    esoteric Marxist features   285
    legitimation/apologist features   285
    overview   285–93
    pagination   287
    political-analytical features   285
    topics of   288–90
feminism   57–58, 77n263, 83, 183–85
Feminist Review (periodical)   283
finances   228–29
finances of   217–30, 231
Financial Times (newspaper)   162
financing   217, 218
Fine, Ben   86, 306
first-personal plural mode of address   422–23
'Focus' (news section)   248
'Focus' (news section of *Marxism Today*)
    248
Focus (review)   84

'FOG Index' analysis method 368–70, 395
Fogarasi, Adalbert 18, 366–67
Foot, Michael 277, 297
Ford, Anna 341
Fordism *see* post-Fordism
format/layout/design changes 267
formatting 269–70
'Forward March' debate 297n123
Foster, John 86n303, 214
Francis, Hywel 309
freedom 139–40
French Revolution 16, 22–23
Friedman, Milton 119
Frith, Simon 273
From Trotsky to Tito (book) 45n106
fundraising 309

Gaitskell, Hugh 166
Galas, Alexander 111
Gang of Four 130n127, 420
Gardiner, Jean 213
Gay Times (magazine) 312n2
gendered demographics 326
Gill, Ken 57
Gillick, Victoria 341
Glasgow University Media Group 162
GLC 180, 186–87
GLEB (Greater London Council's Enterprise Board) 170
Goldsmiths' College 128n118
Gollan, John 38, 45, 47, 54, 200–202, 374
good sense *see* common sense
Gorbachev, Mikhail 94, 193, 277
Gott, Richard 344, 357, 359
Grahl, John 62
Gramsci, Antonio
  on civil society 142–43
  common sense 137–40
  cultural circle 212
  Fordism in work of 169
  Hall's use of 108, 144, 377n45
  hegemony 5, 9, 108, 137, 140–41, 153–54, 155, 193, 377
  ideology 144, 154
  influence of 8, 9, 61
  integral state 141n169
  on intellectual/moral leadership 133
  language in 367
  on Leninist war of manoeuvre 144
  Marxism Today and 54, 77
  on newspapers 24n33
  prison notebook 199–200
  reception of 89
  scholarship on 140
graphic design 270
'The Grid' (*Marxism Today*) 67, 297
Grosz, George 265–66
group cohesiveness 377
The Guardian 357–58, 360

Hall, Stuart
  criticism of 151, 155
  cultural studies and 150
  discursive turn 149
  on economism 123
  encoding/decoding model 135n145, 138, 151
  on Gramsci 108, 140–41, 144, 146, 147, 377n45
  on Hobsbawm 110
  ideology 142, 144
  influence of ideas 418–19
  interviews conducted for *Marxism Today* 333
  Jacques and 115–16, 418
  on labour movements 130–31, 194
  on language analysis 419n191
  on left 193, 432
  Marxism Today and 77, 419–21
  on media's role 446
  metaphors in 431, 433, 440
  on neoliberalism 124
  at *New Left Review* 417
  on NSMs 185
  Peck on 124–25
  political economy's criticism of 126
  popularity of 129–30, 446
  as a public intellectual 416–22
  realism of 436–38
  rhetorical analysis of 172, 371n25, 444
  on the State 434
  subjecthood in thinking 125
  on think tanks 163
  on unemployment 123
  Williams contrasted with 135n145
  writing style 385, 422–28, 436, 444

INDEX 523

Hall, Stuart, 'Thatcherism' (thesis for *Marxism Today*)
    about   115–16
    circulation of   121
    common sense and   134
    counter-hegemony in   148
    lines of argumentation in   120, 122, 142, 197–98
    on new social order   118
    various thinkers on   128, 140
    weaknesses in theory of   147–48
Hammarling, Peter   243
hard left
    about   435–36
    caricatures of   434–35
    critiques of the   439–40, 444
    Hall and   423, 426, 431–32, 444
    Hobsbawm and   410, 413
    Marxism and the   430
    use in writing   431–36
    See also traditionalists
Harper, Clifford   280
Harris, David   425, 427
Harris, Laurence   86
Harvey, David   134n144
Hay, Colin   182
Hayek, Friedrich von   119
Heartfield, John   23n28
Heath, Ted   117n64, 295, 333
Hebdige, Dick   191
hegemony
    apparatus   5, 155, 455
    Gramsci's theory of   140–41, 153–54, 377
    Laclau's discussion group and   146
    Marxism Today's use of theory   193
    subaltern classes and   154–55
    Thatcherism and   129–30, 137
    See also electoral strategy; Hall, Stuart, 'Thatcherism' (thesis for *Marxism Today*)
Heinemann, Margot   34
Heseltine, Michael   347
Heywood, Jackie   99
Hill, Chris   317
historiography   9
Hobsbawm, Eric
    critique of   355
    critique of labour movement   104, 106–10, 113, 114–15

    ethos of   406–7
    influence of Popular Front on   109
    influence on popular politics   177–78
    interviews with   352
    on Klugmann   203–4
    on leftist opponents   413–14
    metaphors in   440
    New Left engagement   44
    photo on cover of *Marxism Today*   273
    political interventions through writing   403, 406, 412–13, 443–44
    realistic Marxism   403, 406, 408–10, 414, 439–40
    reception of work   197, 446
    rhetorical strategy   411, 414
    Universities and Left Review and   47–48
    on voting tactically   91, 278
    writing style   385, 411–12, 414
Hoffman, John   213, 214, 215–16, 294
Hoggart, Richard   417
homeownership   127
Horner, John   46
house style   206, 382–83, 401
human agency   10
Hunt, Alan   310
Hutt, G. Allen   29n48

i-D (periodical)   258
idealists/realists division   405–6
ideas   *see* marketplace of ideas (metaphor)
identity   89, 146
identity politics   171
ideology   9, 144, 154, 190, 230, 373
Illiffe, Steve   375, 393–94
illustrations   265
incomes policy   62, 338
individuality   125, 173, 174
industrial militancy   59
inflation   219
Institute for Policy Research   1
Institute for Workers' Control   125
Institute of Economic Affairs   164
internal factions (CPGB)   25
International Marxist Group   156
International Socialism (theoretical journal)   26, 121
International Socialists/Socialist Workers' Party   53

interviews/roundtable discussions 293–95, 333, 345, 347, 348, 355
Iskra (paper) 23
It Ain't Half Racist, Mum (video) 417

Jackson, Ben 164
Jackson, Jesse 333, 421
Jacques, Martin
  appeal to membership of *Comment* (party review) 67
  audiences 205, 316, 319
  on autonomy of *Marxism Today* 96–97
  Benton and 208–9
  British Road to Socialism 62
  CIPD reports 68–69
  on Communist Party of Great Britain's financial control 218
  Hall and 115–16, 418
  on ideology 190
  illness 91n329
  on Klugmann 204n28
  leadership qualities of 246
  on Left's focus on basic provision and access 175
  Marxism Today Editorial Board and 213
  on *Marxism Today*'s connection with Marxism 89–90
  Marxism Today's transformation and 17, 65–70, 79–80
  McLennan and 87, 98–99
  on the media 195
  on People's March for Jobs 179
  presentation to *Marxism Today* Editorial Collective 100
  production process 213n75
  professional life of 207–10
  reading of *Financial Times* (newspaper) 162
  Resolution 72 and 62–63
  responses to Thatcherism 179–80
  talks given by 55
  on terminal crisis of communism 94
  Theory and Ideology Committee 190
  From Trotsky to Tito 203
  youth culture and 191
Jacques, Martin, editorship of
  accessibility under 310–11
  active editorship of 246
  appointment 56, 61
  assistant 232
  audience of *Marxism Today* 299, 319
  book publishing and 335
  book reviews 303
  broadsheet coverage under 349–51
  on centralisation of control 189–90
  challenges to 73–74, 86n302
  changing roles at *Marxism Today* 71, 99, 212, 229–30
  contributors under 331, 333
  development issues under 341
  'Discussion' section 296–97
  distribution of *Marxism Today* 318
  editorial positions 349n125
  editorial working group and 242
  features under 285–87
  finances of 220, 225–26
  freedom 253–54
  ideological aspects of 438–39
  interviews/roundtable discussions under 295
  journalistic project of 256
  journalistic project of *Marxism Today* 205
  Marxism Today's autonomy and 101–2
  on need for change 382–84
  promotional efforts 343–46
  relationship with Communist Party of Great Britain leadership and *Marxism Today* 78, 88–90
  relationship with *Marxism Today* Editorial Board 213–14
  rhetorical strategy 378
  secretaries 243n189
  section editors and 248
  Thatcherism and 205
  threats to resign 240–41
  topics under 290, 291, 385
  transformation period 65–70
  typesetting/printing decisions 234–37, 292
  use of party publications/groups 338–39
  visual communication 249–50, 255–56, 267, 272, 280
  volunteers 247
  word choice/use under 389, 394, 399, 401
  jargon/specialised vocabularies 377, 386–90

INDEX

Jenkins, Peter 356
Jenkins, Roy 130n127
Jessop, Bob 126
Johnstone, Monty
  Communist Party of Great Britain and 47n118
  criticisms by 216
  Klugmann and 286
  New Left engagement 44
  rejections of writing 42, 56, 203
Jones, Jack 51
journalists 334–35
journals 257, 260, 441

Kenny, Michael 167
Kerrigan, Peter 51
Kettle, Arnold 46, 47, 48, 211
Keynesianism 169
Khomeini, Ayatollah 280
Khrushchev, Nikita 314
Kinnock, Neil 275, 277, 349, 355
Kipling, Rudyard 302, 381
Klugmann, James
  advertisements 282
  design changes to *Marxism Today* 203
  Hobsbawm on 203–4
  house style of 380–81
  Jacques on 204n28
  lectures/talks given by 337
  Marxism Today and 45, 46, 49
  Marxism Today Editorial Board and 38, 48, 53, 211
  passive editorship of 263
  trustworthiness of 45n106
Klugmann, James, editorship of
  appointment 56
  arguments under 59
  book reviews 302–3
  Christianity and 434
  compared to Jacques 201–3, 209–10
  contributors under 331
  culture in 303
  design under 271
  features under 285–86
  hierarchy of voices in 374
  Marxism Today Editorial Board and 242
  membership under 315
  production aspects 234
  promotional efforts 343–46

  reactions to 53–54
  solidification process under 377
  topics under 290, 291, 380
  word choice/use under 386, 394, 399, 440
  writing styles, examples of 374–75
Koivisto, Juha 154
Korean War 38

labour 241
Labour government
  electoral wins 182
  internal divisions of 107–10, 122, 130
  language of 181–82
  Marxism Today's criticism of 186
  media/popular culture and 193
  modernisation programme 120
  rhetoric of national interest 120
  rightward shift of national press and 159–61
  unemployed workers and 114
  See also New Left
Labour Left 71
Labour Monthly (periodical) 34, 37
Labour movement
  Communist Party of Great Britain and 345n111
  external pressures 179
  Hall on 110, 194, 429
  Hobsbawm's critique of the 104, 406–7
  Marxism Today on 3
  National Union of Mineworkers and 85, 130
  sectionalism of 113
  See also Labour Monthly (periodical); *New Socialist* (journal)
Labour Party
  about 60
  Marxism Today and 453, 456
  publishing of 320
  relationship with *New Statesman* 321
  views within 435
  See also New Socialist (journal)
Labour Right 109
Labourism 166–67
Lackersteen, Michael 278n85
Laclau, Ernesto 145–46
Lane, Tony 73–74, 78, 214, 227

language/writing style   18, 19n16, 378–91, 394
Lawrence and Wishart   231, 335–36
Lawrie, Alan   244
layout   255
Leadbeater, Charlie   173, 333
leaflets   23n24
the Left
   hard leftists   414–16
   left press   196, 283–84
   Marxism Today and   1, 13, 77
   party paper   16
   yuppie characterisations   433n233
'Left Alive' (*Marxism Today* event)   77, 306, 341, 361
Left Review (periodical)   210
left unity   77
'Left Unlimited' (*Marxism Today* event)   77, 341
legislation and   129
legitimation/apologist features   285
Lenin, V.I.
   on communication   17
   Hobsbawm's references to   410
   on rhetoric   366–67
   'scaffolding' metaphor   17
   What is to be Done? (pamphlet)   17–18, 24
Leninism   144
The Leninist (journal)   73, 84
Leninist party   17–19, 20–21, 22–23, 24–25, 32
Leninist/Bolshevik model   25
Leninist/vanguard model of production   11
Lennon, John   272–73
letters-to-the-editor   83
The Leveller (periodical)   190, 218
Lewis, John   38, 46, 47
Lewis, Justin   135–36
Leys, Colin   127–28
liberalisation   50
Lindsay, Jack   38, 46
Ling, Tom   126
Link (journal)   69–70
lithography/phototypesetting   450
'Live-Aid'-type spectacles   194
Livingstone, Ken   277, 306, 341, 355
Lloyd, John   333
London District Communist Party   69, 84
Luntz, Frank   133

magazines   241–47, 257, 259, 260–61, 281n97, 360–61
Mahon, John   47, 211, 375
managerialism (of Communist Party of Great Britain)   57
The Manifesto for New Times (manifesto)   97, 171, 323, 348
Marchbank, Pearce   270, 299
Marginson, Paul   244
market research   325
market socialism   170
marketplace   172, 198n418, 362, 457
marketplace of ideas (metaphor)   5, 312–13, 380, 458
Marx, Karl   275, 367
Marxism
   academic interest in   202
   British tradition of   71, 79
   as cohesive   372
   within Communist Party of Great Britain   58
   Communist rhetoric and   373–75
   correct understandings of   38
   cultural Marxism   188
   Hall on   423
   historiography and   9
   influence in 1960s/1970s   195–96
   language as difficult to understand   364
   in *Marxism Today*   89–90, 290, 382
   as a moral critic   373
   opposition by Hall et al.   125
   perceptions of   317
   realism   403, 405, 407–10, 414, 430, 439–40
   rhetoric of   367, 374–75
   scholarly work on   6
   showing/persuading duality   396
   structuralist   202
   us Marxist left   106
   See also Christian-Marxist dialogue; cultural Marxism; structuralist Marxism
Marxism Today Editorial Board
   expansion of   211–12
   feminist perspectives on   184–85
   Jacques and   213–15
   Klugmann and   211
   meetings of   213n77
   new iteration   215–17
   production process and   242

INDEX 527

Theory and Ideology Committee and 215
See also Brennan, Irene; Carritt, Gabriel; Cohen, Jack; Connor, Dan; Edgar, David; Gardiner, Jean; Hobsbawm, Eric; Hoffman, John; Matthews, Betty; Murray, Robin; Rowthorn, Bob; Steward, Fred; Thomson, George; Wake, George; Wright, Nick
Marxism Today Editorial Collective   240–41, 244–45, 248
Marxist political organisations   19
Marxist Quarterly (journal)
   about   34–35, 35n61, 36
   audience for   38–39
   editorial board   38, 47
   last issue   44
   relationship with Communist Party of Great Britain   43
   scope of coverage   37–38
Marxist theory   382
mass media   6, 145, 151, 195
material 'base'   441
Matthews, Betty   86n302, 211–12
Matthews, George   62, 70
Mayo, Marjorie   86
McGahey, Mick   85
McGerr, Michael   20
McGuigan, Jim   146
McKay, Ian   84, 98
McLennan, Gordon
   Jacques and   87, 229
   Marxism Today and   95, 227
   Marxism Today Editorial Board and   74, 96, 101
   political life of   51
   replacement/retirement of   98, 99
   speech to 39th Special Party Congress   87
   Woddis and   56
McLennan, Gregor   395–400
McRobbie, Angela   191
M.E. (Myalgic Encephalomyelitis)   242n186
media coverage   77
media of communication   20
Medvedev, Roy   75
meetings culture   250–51
membership growth/decline   88, 315

membership of Communist Party of Great Britain/*Marxism Today*   88
metaphors, use of   431, 433, 440
militancy   110
militant labourism   51, 73, 75, 197
Mills, James   297
Milne, Seumas   112, 130
Milner, Andrew   147
Miners' Strike (1984–85)   180, 306–9
Minnion, John   243, 280
modalisation (in writing)   423–28
Modern Quarterly (journal)   33–36, 39, 46
Mont Pelerin Society   163
moral panic   376
The Morning Star (daily paper)
   break from Communist Party of Great Britain   85
   financing of   218
   loss of   88
   naming   28–29, 50, 52
   promotional efforts   346
   readership of   330
   See also The Daily Worker (daily paper)
Moscow gold   237
Mouffe, Chantal   138–39, 146
Moving Left show   77, 338, 340, 428
Mulgan, Geoff   173
Mulhern, Frances   335
municipal socialism   186
Murdoch, Rupert   130
Murray, Robin   169, 170, 176, 215
music   192

national news coverage (of *Marxism Today*)   348, 450
National Party Congress (1965)   51, 64
national press   156–60
national press coverage (of *Marxism Today*)   348–60, 362
National Union of Journalists   29n48
National Union of Mineworkers (NUM)   85, 112, 180–81, 295, 306
Nazi-Soviet, Non-Aggression Pact of 1939   28
neoliberalism
   changes under   94–95
   influence of ideas   164–65
   New Right projects and   134
   in the public sphere   164–65

rise of 5
think tanks and 163n267
Toryism and 124
See also Thatcherism
New Communist Party 62
New Internationalist (periodical) 231
New Labour Party 134, 148
New Left 44–45, 166, 167–68, 335
New Left journals *see The New Reasoner* (journal); *Universities and Left Review* (journal)
New Left Review (journal) 40, 48, 128, 129, 283, 319–20
The New Reasoner (journal) 40, 261–62
    See also The Reasoner (journal)
New Right 118, 119, 134, 163
New Social Movements (NSM) 67, 76, 80, 177, 183, 185
    See also feminism
New Socialist (Labour Party journal)
    about 451
    advertising and 231
    circulation 321
    counter-hegemonic coalitions and 455
    design in 260
    financing of 218
    Hall's ideas and 121
    origins of 320
    production/distribution 321
    promotional efforts 346
    readership of 330
    visual communication 258, 269
    Williams and 129, 131
New Statesman (political weekly)
    circulation 326
    financial difficulties of 95n347
    formatting 262, 268
    origins of 320
    promotional efforts 346
    readership of 330, 442
    relationship with Labour Party 321
    relationship with *Marxism Today* 319
    separation of culture/politics in 303
New Times (*Marxism Today* event) 77, 165–72, 175
New Times (*Marxism Today* political project) 96–100, 125–6, 136, 165–6, 168–9, 171–6, 281, 349, 372

newspapers 16, 161, 312, 329–30, 355, 446
1957 Commission on Inner-Party Democracy (report) 21

'One Nation' Toryism 116
open politics 294
Open University 417–18
openness (in *Marxism Today*'s house style) 401
operating costs 219
opinion/information distinction 134
opposition 86
organisation/production, decentralisation of 169
origins 10, 100, 210
Orwell, George 366, 391, 437
Our Time (periodical) 210
overview 44–56
Owen, David 130n127
Owen, William 258

pagination 249
Palme Dutt, Rajani 26, 37
pamphlets 16
Partito Comunista Italiano (political party) 61, 186
party economists 60
Party Group (faction) 57
party paper
    about 16, 26, 31–32
    agitation/propaganda and 23
    communicative crisis and 18
    Communist parties and 18
    Communist Party of Great Britain and 25–26
    language/writing style 18
    Leninist practice and 17, 24–25
    scope of coverage 28
    writers for 18
party review 26, 30
passive editorships 199–210
Pearce, Bert 64, 70, 374–5
Pearmain, Andy 148
Peck, Janice 124–25
the people 146, 157
People's Jubilee (Communist Party event) 340
People's March for Jobs 179
periodicals 256–60, 267–68, 322, 372

INDEX 529

periodicity 262
Perryman, Mark 229n127, 278, 339n86
the personal is political 167–68
Philo, Greg 181
phototypesetting/lithography 234–35, 450
plain style 390–402, 404
pluralism/identity conflict 89
policing 275
political economy 126
Political Letter (monthly) 41
political magazines 95n347
political organisations/parties 3, 15, 20, 50
political publications 271
political theology 414
political trajectory 197, 214, 329
political-analytical features 285
political-cultural criticism 190
politics 146, 150, 404
'Politics and the English Language' (essay) 366, 391
politics of identity 171
Pollitt, Harry 50
popular culture 150, 188, 190, 196
Popular Front 109
popular politics 177–83, 184, 197
position pieces 381–82
post-Fordism 125, 169–70, 175
Powell, Enoch 117n63
Powellism 117
practical consciousness (Williams) 19n16
Prague Spring 52, 54
Pravda (paper) 23
primary definer 395n117
print media
 accessibility of 19
 base/superstructure model and 441
 editors of 29
 the Left and 16
 periodicity and 262
 role of 441
 socialism and 8
 See also socialist/radical left publications
printing costs 219–24
printing press 16
printing/typesetting decisions 233
Prior, Mike 113
Priscott, Dave 64, 70–71, 214n82, 309
Private Eye (magazine) 330
production history (of *Marxism Today*) 12

production process 11, 241–47, 248–52
production values 219–20, 247
promotional efforts 343–46, 362
promotional efforts (of *Marxism Today*) 343–46
proofreading 236
proofreading process 236
propaganda 22n22, 23
property-owning democracy 127
public opinion 135, 182
public sector unionism 109
public sphere 313
public transport 187
publicity 347–48
Punch (subscription agency) 241
Purdy, Dave 60, 113

qualification/conditionality (in writing) 424–30
'Questions of Ideology and Culture' (statement) 51–52, 53

racist/fascist organisations 192
radical left/working class publications 6n15, 217, 218, 230–32, 255
radical papers 312
Rainbow Coalition (of ethnic groups and new social movements) 333
Rakowski, Mieczyslaw 274, 319
Ramelson, Bert 51, 92, 202
RAR (Rock Against Racism campaign) 192–93
readership 97, 323–31, 379–80
reading methods 151
Reagan, Ronald 132
realism 403–6, 430, 436–38, 443
realpolitik *see* realism
The Reasoner (journal) 40, 41, 42, 73n243
 See also The New Reasoner (journal)
Red Letters (journal) 64
Red Pepper (periodical) 262, 312
Red scare 376
reformists 78, 85, 92
Rehmann, Jan 144
religion (as target for socialists) 434
Resolution 72, 62
'Rethinking Socialism for the '90s' (seminar) 165, 216
revisionism 57

Revolutionary Communist Party   232
Reynolds' News (paper)   29n48
rhetoric   364, 391
    See also Hobsbawm, Eric: ethos of
rhetorical strategy   411
right-wing press   151, 164
Robinson, Andrew   137–39
Robinson, Lee   307n163
Rodgers, Bill   130n127
roundtable discussions   293, 294, 295
Rowbotham, Sheila   183
Rowthorn, Bob   60, 62, 76, 214
Russian Civil War   20
Russian Social Democratic Party   18

sales   315, 319, 345
sales (of *Marxism Today*)   451
Samuel, Raphael   86, 86n306
Saville, John   40, 42, 303
'scaffolding' metaphor   17, 24
Scanlon, Hugh   51
Scargill, Arthur   295, 356
Schlesinger, Philip   151–52
Screen (film studies journal)   339
sectarianism   82
sectionalism   105, 113
Segal, Lynne   183
Seifert, Michael   214
self-managed model of production   11
'Selsdon Man' policies   117n64
sense   *see* common sense
7 Days (weekly)   243
sexism   57–58
Shadowdean   239
Shah, Eddie   130
Sharma, Vishnu   99
Simon, Roger   54
Sinyavsky, A.D.   50
Smith, Adam   162n266
Smith, Jane   280
Smith, W.H.   442n3
Smythe, Dallas   6n13
social assistance programmes   135
social contract   60
socialism
    accessibility/popularity of   193
    association with militancy   110
    democratic   361
    equation with bureaucratic statism   119

    first New Left on   168
    French Revolution and   16
    new conception of   122
    origins of   16
    print media and   8
    religious connotations of   414
    utopia and   414
    See also designer socialism; market socialism; municipal socialism
socialist individualism   168, 170
Socialist Review (periodical)   190, 259, 262
Socialist Worker (party paper)   26, 29, 346
Socialist Workers Party   26, 29, 77, 232, 340
socialist/radical left publications   15–16, 18
    See also alternative/oppositional media; print media
solidification process (*Marxism Today*)   376–78
South Essex District Communist Party   55
Soviet communism   414
Spare Rib (magazine)   346
specialised vocabularies/jargon   367–8, 377–8
The Spectator (political magazine)   95n347
'Sport Aid' (event)   195
staff members   225, 246
staffing   227–28
staff/volunteers   241, 243–44, 246–47, 248–49
Stalinism   54, 166–67, 202, 203
Stanley, Frank   47
The Star (newspaper)   72, 78, 81, 82, 84, 87
'Statement on Ideology and Culture'   50, 202, 265, 315
Steward, Fred   215
Straight Left (journal)   73, 82, 84, 99
structuralist Marxism   202
style (in writing)   378
subaltern classes   139–40, 143, 154–55
subscriptions   240–41, 267, 317, 448n8
subsidies   83, 95
The Sun (newspaper)   118
swing voters   135

tabloids   158
talks   337
talks (sponsored by *Marxism Today*)   337
Taylor, Jane   91n329, 242–43, 246–47, 252
Temple, Nina   87n309, 91, 98, 99–100

INDEX 531

Thatcher, Margaret   110, 120–21, 272, 277
　See also Thatcherism; TINA (There is no
　　alternative)
Thatcherism
　overview   115–22
　alternatives to   125–26
　anti-statism and   119
　appeal of   194
　attacks of   111–12, 115
　authoritarian populism   180
　common sense and   136–37, 142–43, 151
　critique of hegemony   129–30
　critiques of   444
　disagreements over   435
　electoral triumph of 1983   131–32
　as form of class politics   116
　hegemony and   137, 142
　legislation and   129
　Marxism Today and   2, 10, 80–81, 166
　political economic approach to   126–27
　The Politics of Thatcherism (collection)
　　336
　popular politics and   197
　popularity of   177
　potency of   173
　productive contradictions within   116–
　　17, 120
　responses to   179–80
　rhetoric of   120–21, 146
　scholarship on   117n62, 140n165
　success of   119
　unemployment under   179
　voter support for   145
　See also neoliberalism
The Politics of Thatcherism (collection)   336
theoretical journal   3, 26, 31
Theory and Ideology Committee   190, 215, 338
theory/practice divide   67–68, 80, 383
　See also Marxist theory
*Thesis on the Organisation and Structure of
　Communist Parties* (Communist International)   18
think tanks   163–65, 163n267
Thomas, James   157–58, 160
Thomas, Peter D.   140–41
Thompson, E.P.   40, 42, 309
Thomson, George   47, 211, 212
Time Out (magazine)   46, 346
TINA (There is no alternative)   182

topic suggestions   248–49
topics   288–90
Toryism   116, 119, 123, 124, 129
tower blocks   414
Townsend, Sally   191, 244, 303
traditionalists
　about   73
　groupings within   73
　Marxism Today and   57, 84, 88, 214–16
　on *Marxism Today* Editorial Board   214
　Marxism Today leadership and   82
　New Communist Party   62–63
　opposition to   69, 342, 415
　reformists and   58, 305
　tension with   52
transformation   442, 447, 457
transportation   187
Tribune (magazine)   346
Triesman, David   243, 244
tropes, use of   431
Trotsky, Leon   17, 366–67, 415
Trotskyist Socialist Workers Party   26
Trump, Donald   380n62
Turner, Julian   96, 100, 227, 229, 236
typesetting/printing decisions   233, 234–37,
　240, 265
typography   265

UK Press Gazette   199n1
unemployment   114, 123, 179
Union Carbide   173
unions   105, 106, 111, 156
United States of America   15–16
Universities and Left Review (journal)   40,
　47–48, 261–62
　See also *New Left Review* (journal)
US Politics   132
USSR   52, 72, 75, 194, 203
　See also Gorbachev, Mikhail; Moscow gold
us/them dichotomy   431
utopia   414

vanguard media   455
Vietnam Solidarity Campaign   53
visual communication
　cover design   264, 269
　Jacques and   249–50, 255–56, 267, 272,
　　280
　Marxism Today and   258, 278–84

visual designers   258
vividness   392
volunteer labour   244
volunteers   241, 244–45, 247
volunteers/staff   241
voting   51, 91, 108, 135
   See also election data/results; public opinion

wage demands   112–13
Wainwright, Hilary   183
Wake, George   213
Walesa, Lech   274
war of position
   about   7–8
   of Communist Party of Great Britain   57
   contrasted with war of manoeuvre   150
   Hall and   417
   magazines as part of   260
   Marxism Today and   458
   municipal socialism and   186
   1980s   133–34
   public opinion and   182
War on Want   283
Warren, Bill   57
Warsaw Pact   203
Watt, David   162
Webster, Paul   245, 318
Wedge (periodical)   190
weekend events   77
Weir, Angela   86
welfare   135
W.H. Smith's   317–18
Whannel, Paddy   417
What is to be Done? (Lenin)   17–18, 24
Whitfield, David   81
Williams, Raymond
   on alternatives to social relations of production   124
   constitutional authoritarianism   129, 197
   critique of Hall's Thatcherism   175
   on cross-class support   137
   cultural materialism and   7, 146–47, 365
   on electoral analysis   131
   Hall contrasted with   135n145
   on Hobsbawm   110–11, 112
   ideology   141
   influence of ideas   418–19
   on language   19n16, 419n191
   on Marxists   9
   on newspapers   107
   on NUM strike   181
   opinion/information distinction   134
   processual-cultural aspect   137
   on rightward shift of national press   156–60, 162
   Towards 2000 (book)   176n328
Williams, Shirley   130n127
Wilson, Elizabeth   86
Wilson, Harold   106, 167, 377
Winter of Discontent (1978–79)   60, 106, 162, 180, 182, 358n146
Woddis, Margaret   55–56
'Women Alive' (*Marxism Today* event)   77
Wood, Brennon   147, 149, 151, 423n208
Wood, John   47
word choice/language   386–91, 440
Workers' Weekly (party paper)   26–27
working class   148–49, 190
working environments   59, 173
World News and Views (periodical)   34, 36
Worsley, Peter   40
Wright, Nick   213
writers' compensation   206, 225
writers' pay   206, 225
writing styles
   overview   378–94
   of academics   384
   of Hall   422–28, 436, 444
   of Hobsbawm   411–12
   importance of   364
   See also plain style

Yip, David   191
Young, Hugo   333
Young Communist League (YCL)   30, 52, 189, 382
   See also Challenge (magazine); *Cogito* (*theoretical journal*)
youth culture   191–92
   See also Young Communist League
yuppie flu (M.E.)   242n186
yuppie left   433n233

Printed in the United States
by Baker & Taylor Publisher Services